THE HISTORY OF THE UNITED STATES

VOLUME I: 1600-1876

THE HISTORY OF THE UNITED STATES

VOLUME I: 1600-1876
SOURCE READINGS

WITHDRAWN

Edited by

NEIL HARRIS · DAVID J. ROTHMAN · STEPHAN THERNSTROM

Harvard University   *Columbia University*   *Brandeis University*

Holt, Rinehart and Winston, Inc.

New York   Chicago   San Francisco   Atlanta   Dallas   Montreal   Toronto   London   Sydney

Preface

This collection is an instrument that will aid the user in understanding the history of the United States. It is designed to bring to life the people and events of the past. History should not be a dry chronicle of names and dates; it deals with characters as real as those of whom we read in the daily newspaper. The documents here assembled will bring the reader close to the figures of earlier eras and thus help explain the evolution of the American nation.

It takes an effort of the imagination to understand that the strange costumes of seventeenth- and eighteenth-century portraits clothed living human beings. Through the curious antique lanes of old towns and through the forest clearings of the wilderness, moved men and women whose emotions, ambitions, and ideas were not exactly the same as our own but also not entirely discontinuous with ours. The student of history must try to comprehend these people, different though they were. Fortunately he can do so through the written material they left behind. The collection that follows has arranged such materials so as to illuminate the development of the Americans through their whole history.

The aim of making these records of the past interesting and understandable dictated the standards of selection as well as the organization of this volume. The editors wished each document to speak directly to the students who will read it. Each selection treats an important subject in a way that will attract and hold the attention of twentieth-century young people who are not themselves historians. Furthermore each item drawn into the collection is long enough so that the student, once immersed in it, can learn something not only of the subject concerned, but also of the language and style and therefore of the way of thinking of the era represented.

The collection is unique in the range of materials represented. The selections touch on all the important aspects of the history of the United States, economic, social and intellectual, as well as political. Each document is presented in a form full enough to convey its own flavor; yet each also fits into a coherent pattern which, taken as a whole, provides a vivid introduction to the American past.

V

Historians refer to sources such as are here assembled as primary. By this they mean that the books or manuscripts from which the selections are drawn are first-hand or eyewitness accounts, printed or written at about the same time as the events with which they deal. Such material is always valuable as evidence of something. But these written survivals from the past fall into several categories, which the reader must understand if he is to make effective use of them.

Some primary sources are produced in the course of contemporary transactions. The people who wrote them intended such documents to serve only specific purpose. A bill of sale or a contract, for instance, completed a business deal, and no one considered the possibility that it might some day prove useful to a historian. Such records consequently are reliable; they are just what they say they are, although what they mean must be explained by interpretation. Among other sources of this sort on which historians depend are acts of legislation and decisions of courts, the journals of legislatures and conventions, and petitions to such bodies about important issues of the times.

Even more useful are materials produced without conscious guile in the normal course of some transaction. Farmers' and businessmen keep records for their own use and therefore try to be as accurate as possible. These records are evidence of how such enterprises really operated. By the same token, letters written for a specific purpose reveal the political concerns of the writers or describe military or domestic events.

Still another kind of primary material is that recorded by participants and observers with some conscious purpose. The reasons why each document was written must therefore be understood, for that may have influenced its contents. Yet the account may nonetheless be valuable. Among such records are journals and diaries, set down from direct observation, as well as the narratives of settlers and travelers. Contemporary histories are usually even more interpretive, for their authors generally wish to make some point that will persuade future readers. More often than not, too, there is some purpose behind the writing of an autobiography. As a man looks back over his life, he wishes to set down the facts, but also to justify his past actions or to draw a moral from them; and he may not be able to separate the two aspects of his writing. The same caution applies to newspaper accounts. Reporters have a professional purpose in chronicling the news, yet their views may well color their stories.

Some contemporary documents, of course, are clearly and explicitly cases of argument or pleading. The authors intend to make a case and select and organize the facts accordingly. The value of these materials lies less in the facts they detail than in the ideas they express. American history is rich in tracts of this sort, whether published originally as pamphlets or as articles in periodicals. Whether the argument is presented with restraint or with fanatical zeal, its importance for the student lies in the view it offers of the thinking of its author.

Other forms of persuasion are also common. Newspaper editorials directly express opinions and thus reflect the ideas of their writers and of their readers. Orations and sermons were long the most familiar means of persuasion; they remain important because they often held the close attention of Americans.

In a quite different category are the unconscious expressions of attitudes and ideas that appear in popular and formal literature. A story, a poem, or a play often reveals the underlying beliefs of people, particularly when written without artifice. Satires and campaign songs thus convey a good deal of information about current political practices, for they show what symbols and concepts aroused popular enthusiasm or mockery.

In arranging their selections from the great variety of primary sources in American history, the editors have held in view the needs of the students who will use this collection. They have held to the highest standards of accurate scholarship. But in the interest of clarity and readability they have modernized antique spellings and punctuation, and they have omitted ellipses from certain passages. Without in the least altering the meaning of the originals, they have sought to make these documents completely accessible to the modern student. The result will enrich the understanding of the American past.

Cambridge, Massachusetts   Oscar Handlin
February 1969

Contents

PART THREE
The Revolutionary Era, 1754–1789

PART FOUR
A Young Republic, 1789–1820

Introduction

PART FIVE
The Problems of Expansion, 1820–1876

THE HISTORY
OF THE
UNITED STATES
VOLUME I: 1600-1876

PART ONE

The New World, 1600–1660

The movement of Europeans to North America, which was merely a trickle in the sixteenth century, dramatically increased in the years following 1600. Many motives drove men to abandon their familiar surroundings and challenge an unknown wilderness. Desperation about the old order mingled with hope for the new. Economic dislocation, religious persecution, political uncertainty, and social confusion helped push many Englishmen away from their native country.

It would be wrong to see the great migration as evidence of weakness and instability alone. The men who provided leadership were often vigorous and optimistic entrepreneurs, able to construct dreams of success that dazzled their followers. Some of them claimed to have discovered an earthly paradise in America, where men could grow wealthy and secure with a minimum of hard work. If there was no gold or silver such as the Spanish found in Mexico and Peru, there was at least the promise of raising valuable commodities—silk, tropical fruits, tobacco, hemp—which would add to the wealth and glory of the mother country. Agriculture and commerce seemed destined to thrive.

Other leaders saw the promise not in natural resources but in emptiness, a spatial void that could be filled by religious and social experiments. Fulfillment would not come from material prosperity itself but through creation of a holy community that could carry out the cosmic work of redemption by establishing a model for the entire world to behold and imitate. A sense of urgency, of energetic and enthusiastic faith, pervaded the exhortations of religious independents who helped establish the New England colonies.

Whether it was economic desire or religious mission that inspired the early settlers, they faced taxing physical and social adjustments. No expectation adequately described the new reality. In Virginia the promised prosperity was slow in coming. Dangers of climate, of Indians, and of dissension threatened to destroy the community before it got under way, while constant supplies of new men and more money were necessary to keep life going until a staple crop could be discovered. It became necessary to tinker with old institutions, to attempt novel kinds of regulations, rewards, and punishments before an effective social order could be established. When tobacco appeared to be the path to riches, the population dispersed, seeking more of the apparently unlimited land on which to grow their crop. A system of administration and social differentiation not very unlike England's began to develop, but there were important differences. Virginia's scattered people lacked towns and easy methods of communication. On their borders were hostile Indians who resented the rapid spread of this new empire, and several times massacred the outnumbered settlers. The colony's great men were often new to their wealth and distinction, and had to learn all at once those methods of absorbing deference that English squires had been practicing for generations.

The New Englanders were better prepared to meet hardship. Not only were their migrations larger and better organized than those of the individual travelers who made their way to the Chesapeake area, but their theology helped make explicable the trials they faced. No calamity or disaster was allowed to pass unnoticed, and even the most casual events of daily life bore religious implications. As a result of New England's communal objectives, its population dispersal was different from the Chesapeake diffusion. Because of the need for church congregations to serve as the basis for social organization, New Englanders moved in groups, and received their land as townships, not as individuals. The town's control of land emphasized the power of local institutions in America. New England selectmen (like Virginia justices of the peace) were men of influence, their power resting not on the dignity and strength of colonial government, but on their status among their neighbors.

The success of English colonization contrasted with the attempts of other European states to settle portions of America. For a time groups of Swedes and Dutch gathered at the mouths of rivers along the Middle Atlantic coast. New Amsterdam particularly was an ambitious attempt by a Dutch trading company to establish a permanent outpost on the North American mainland. Because of inadequate support and overactive supervision, New Amsterdam's growth was slow, and the Dutch settlements were absorbed by the more active English.

The failure of the Dutch governing class pointed up the gifts of the English leaders. Survival in the wilderness rested on the ability to solve many kinds of problems quickly and equitably, and maintain, at the same time, the community's social unity. Puritan Massachusetts owed a great deal to its governor, John Winthrop, who faced political jealousies, religious schisms, Indian attacks, economic inflation, and social deviance, among other dilemmas. Winthrop's personal gifts, however, did not produce undue dependence on one man. A number of other colonies also received enlightened leadership in their early years, but everywhere representative institutions were crucial. Under conditions of permanent emergency the English settlers did not yield to the efficiency of dictatorship in order to satisfy immediate wants as did some other European colonists. Local institutions—town meetings, church vestries—and provincial assemblies shared in the exercise of power, and thus involved large portions of the population in major decisions.

To a large extent, major decisions were made, not at the seat of empire, in Westminster, but in the small, scattered seaboard settlements. In the middle of the seventeenth century England was undergoing the agonies of civil war and regicide. Within the space of twenty years a monarch was executed, a commonwealth established, and another king crowned. It was impossible for civil servants and administrators to impose their concepts of order on their countrymen overseas, and what political turmoil helped establish, barriers of time and distance perpetuated. The ocean was wide; travel and communication were infrequent and unpredictable. The settlers were insulated and isolated by geography, and forced upon their own resources. It was not surprising then, that the steady growth of their settlements by midcentury produced some self-confidence in their political skills, and a feeling that God and historical necessity were uniting to make America a future seat of empire. When they compared their own situation with the lot of their countrymen in the Old World, the settlers felt pleased. Puritans beheld in Boston a bustling metropolis with churches, docks, schools, and commerce where three decades earlier had been only wilderness and savages. Virginia boosters did not have to look to the future as did the authors of promotional literature before the 1620s in order to demonstrate the country's bounty. In almost every material item—diet, dress, recreation, health—the common man of America seemed to hold the advantage over the farmers and workers of seventeenth-century England.

This prosperity, moreover, did not seem purchased at the cost of order and tradition. Though in retrospect the English colonies can be seen developing in novel directions, the early settlers still thought in European terms about the structure and safety of their communities. Hierarchy, rank, servitude, deference, obedience to authority, piety, and prayer were not discarded as unnecessary relics. The outposts of empire were not intended to refute or challenge social arrangements at home, but to purify and re-create them. Unhampered by corruption or tyrannical authority, undamaged by destitution and physical poverty, facing the opportunity to convert the heathen natives and increase and multiply according to the Biblical command, the colonists sought to imitate rather than to innovate. In family life, in education, in religion, in morals, their aims were conservative and traditional. That their effectiveness and appropriateness were lessening, went largely unnoticed before 1660. America was a new world, and they had succeeded in making a first, initial conquest. They had developed from company settlements to political societies. This was impressive enough for forty years. The deeper changes would become clear only afterward.

Encouraging News from America

The first need of the new colonies was for settlers. Without labor the riches of the New World would remain hidden from the English, and its one great asset, land, would be worthless, if unimproved. Eager to obtain colonists, the English companies commissioned tracts to spread the good word about the advantages they offered. This promotional literature, painting the future of American settlement in bright colors, was distributed in the thousands and forms one of the earliest sources of information about the infant colonies.

The following tract was commissioned by the Council for Virginia, anxious to silence charges that Virginia was badly governed, hard to live in, and only a graveyard for healthy Englishmen. Naturally its author emphasizes the benefits Virginia's soil and climate offer individual settlers and the entire nation, while he underplays sources of danger. After allowing for exaggeration, it is still possible to see what kinds of images appealed to seventeenth-century Englishmen and why so many thousands would eventually make the perilous ocean trip or at least purchase shares in the company stock.

THE ESTATE OF THE COLONIE IN VIRGINIA

There is a great distance betwixt the vulgar opinion of men and the judicious apprehension of wise men. Opinion is as blind Oedipus, who could see nothing but would hear all things. But judgment is as Solomon on his throne, able by the spirit of wisdom to discern betwixt contesting truth and falsehood, neither depending upon the popular breath of fame, which is ever partial, nor upon the event of good designs, which are ever casual. These two commanders of our affections have divided the universal spirits of our land, whilst (in the honorable enterprise for plantation in Virginia) some are carried away with the tide of vulgar opinion, and others are encouraged by the principles of religion and reason. But because it is for hawks and not for men to build their nests in air, and because the honor and prosperity of this

From *A True Declaration of the Estate of the Colonie in Virginia* (London, 1610), 3–4, 9–27. Reprinted in [Peter Force] *Tracts and Other Papers* (New York, 1844, 1947), III.

so noble an action is eclipsed by the interposition of clamorous and tragical narrations, the compiler of this relation will endeavor to wash away those spots which foul mouths (to justify their own disloyalty) have cast upon so fruitful, so fertile, and so excellent a country.

You shall find that one hundred and forty years after the destruction of Troy the Ionian colony was carried from Greece to Asia: by which that famous city of Ephesus was first builded and inhabited. You shall find the Egyptians planted Babylon, Argos, and Athens. The Phonecians first inhabited Carthage, Utica and Thebes. Timolcon and the city of Corinth at one time repeopled Sicily with ten thousand souls. The Romans deduced fifty-three colonies out of the city of Rome into the womb of Italy.

Which heroical actions have not been undertaken by so mighty states and princes upon trivial and vulgar motives, when by these courses that first blessing (increase and multiply) hath been sanctified. The meaner sort have been provided, the matter of plagues, famine, and sedition hath been exhausted; the fens of a state politic were drained, the enemies of their peace were bridled, the revenues of their treasury were augmented, and the limits of their dominions were enlarged.

These points being thus defined I come to the possibility [settlement of Virginia] against which three main impediments are objected. First, the dangerous passage by sea. Second, the barrenness of the country. Third, the unwholesomeness of the climate. The storm that separated the admiral from the fleet procuring the first, the famine amongst our men importing the second, the sickness of our men arguing the third. All which discouragements do astonish our men with fear.

To dispel the clouds of fear that threaten shipwrecks and sea dangers: We are not to extenuate the sea's tempestuous violence, nor yet therefore to despair of God's assisting providence. For true it is that when Sir Thomas Gates, Sir George Somers, and Captain Newport were in the 24th of July, 1609, there arose such a storm as if Jonah had been flying unto Tarshish. The heavens were obscured and made an Egyptian night of three days' perpetual horror; the women lamented; the hearts of the passengers failed; the experience of the sea captains was amazed; the skill of the mariners was confounded; the ship most violently leaked. But God that heard Jonah crying out of the belly of hell, he pitied the distresses of his servants. For behold, in the last period of necessity Sir George Somers descried land, which was by so much the more joyful by how much their danger was despairful. The islands on which they fell were the Bermudas, a place hardly accessible through the environing rocks and dangers. Notwithstanding they were forced to run their ships on shore, which through God's providence fell betwixt two rocks that caused her to stand firm and not immediately to be broken, God continuing his mercy unto them, that with their long boats they transported to land before night all their company, men, women, and children, to the number of one hundred and fifty. They carried to shore all the provision of unspent and unspoiled victuals, all their furniture and tackle of the ship, leaving nothing but bared ribs as a prey unto the ocean.

Consider all these things together. At the instant of need they descried land; half an hour more had buried their memorial in the sea. If they had fell by night, what expectation of light from an uninhabited desert? They fell betwixt a labyrinth of rocks which they conceived are moulded into the sea by thunder and lightning. If it had not been so near land their company or provision had perished by water. If they had not found hogs and fish, they had perished by famine. If there had not been fuel, they had perished by want of fire. If there had not been timber, they could not have transported themselves to Virginia, but must have been forgotten forever. He is too impiously fearful that will not trust in God so powerful. What is there in all this tragical comedy that should discourage us with impossibility of the enterprise? When of all the fleet one only ship by a secret leak was endangered, and yet, in the gulf of despair, was so graciously preserved.

After nine months' abode in these islands, on the 10th of May, 1610, they embarked themselves in their two new built pinaces, and after some eleven days sail they arrived near Point Comfort upon the coast of Virginia, where they had intelligence of so woeful a misery as if God had only preserved them to communicate a new extremity.

From which calamity the other arguments of impossibility are framed, for if the country be barren or the situation contagious, as famine and sickness destroy our nation, we strive against the stream of reason and make ourselves the subjects of scorn and derision. Therefore, in this main point of consequence, I will propound this plain and simple method: First, to demonstrate that there is and may be in Virginia a sufficient means (in all abundance) to sustain the life of man. Next, that the climate is wholesome and temperate, agreeing with the constitutions of our men. Third, that those extremities proceeded from accidental and not inherent evils. Lastly, I will delineate the state of the colony as Sir Thomas Gates left it under the government of the honorable Lord De La Warr, whereby it shall appear that all difficulties are amended, and that the state of the country is sufficiently managed.

The natural peas of the country return an increase innumerable, our garden fruits, both roots, herbs, and flowers, do spring up speedily, all things committed to the earth do multiply with an incredible usury.

The beasts of the country, as deer, red and fallow, do answer in multitude (people for people considered) to our proportion of oxen, which appeareth by these experiences. First, the people of the country are apparelled in the skins of these beasts. Next, hard by the fort two hundred in one herd have been usually observed. Further, our men have seen 4,000 of these skins piled up in one wardrobe of Powhatan. There are hares and conies and other beasts proper to the country in plentiful manner.

Our transplanted cattle, as horses, kine, hogs, and goats, do thrive most happily. The turkeys of that country are great and fat, and exceeding in plenty. The rivers from August or September till February, are covered with flocks of wild fowls, as swans, geese, duck, mallard, herons, plowers (to use the words of Sir Thomas Gates) in such abundance as are not in all the world to be equalled.

The fruits: as apples, running on the ground, in bigness and shape of a small lemon, in color and taste like to a preserved apricot. Grapes and walnuts innumerable, the vines being as common as brambles, the walnut trees as the elms in England. What should I speak of cucumbers, musk melons, pumpkins, potatoes, parsnips, carrots, turnips which our gardens yielded with little art and labor. God in this place is ever concurring with his gracious influence, if man strangle not his blessings with careless negligence.

For the healthiness and temperateness of the climate, agreeing to our constitutions, much need not be related, since in all the former treatises it is expressly observed. No man ought to judge of any country by the fens and marshes (such as is the place where Jamestown standeth), except we will condemn all England for the wilds and hundreds of Kent and Essex. In our particular we have an infallible proof of the temper of the country: for of one hundred and odd which were seated at the Falls under the government of Captain Francis West, and of one hundred to the seaward on the south side of the river under the charge of Captain John Martin, of all these two hundred there did not so much as one man miscarry, when in Jamestown, at the same time and in the same months, one hundred sickened and half the number died.

The ground of all those miseries was the permissive providence of God, who, in the fore-mentioned violent storm, separated the head from the body, all the vital powers of regiment being exiled with Sir Thomas Gates in those unfortunate (yet fortunate) islands. The broken remainder of those supplies made a greater shipwreck in the continent of Virginia by the tempest of dissension. Every man undervaluing his own worth would be a commander; every man underprising another's value, denied to be commanded. The emulation of Caesar and Pompey watered the plains of Pharsalia with blood and distracted the sinews of the Roman monarchy. The dissensions of the three besieged captains betrayed the city of Jerusalem to Vespasian. How much more easily might ambitious discord tear in pieces an infant colony, where no eminent and respected magistrates had authority to punish presumptuous disobedience.

The next fountain of woes was secure negligence and improvidence, when every man sharked for his present booty but was altogether careless of succeeding penury. Now, I demand whether Sicily or Sardinia (sometimes the barns of Rome), could hope for increase without manuring? A colony is therefore denominated because they should be *coloni,* the tillers of the earth and stewards of fertility. Our mutinous loiterers would not sow with providence and therefore they reaped the fruits of too dear bought repentance. An incredible example of their idleness is the report of Sir Thomas Gates who affirmeth that after his first coming thither, he hath seen some of them eat their fish raw, rather than they would go a stone's cast to fetch wood and dress it. God sells us all things for our labor, when Adam himself might not live in paradise without dressing the garden.

Unto idleness you may join treasons, wrought by those unhallowed creatures that forsook the colony and exposed their desolate brethren to extreme misery. You shall know that twenty-eight or thirty of the company were appointed (in the ship called the *Swallow*), to truck for corn with the Indians, and having obtained a great quantity by trading, the most seditious of them conspired together, persuaded some and enforced others, to this barbarous project. They stole away the ship, they made a league amongst themselves to be professed pirates, with dreams of mountains of gold and happy robberies. Thus at one instant they wronged the hopes and subverted the cares of the colony, who depending upon their return foreslowed to look out for

7

further provision. They created the Indians our implacable enemies by some violence they had offered. They carried away the best ship (which should have been a refuge, in extremities). They weakened our forces by subtraction of their arms and succours. These are that scum of men that, failing in their piracy, that being pinched with famine and penury after their wild roving upon the sea, when all their lawless hopes failed, bound themselves by mutual oath to agree all in one report: to discredit the land, to deplore the famine, and to protest that this their coming away proceeded from desperate necessity. These are they that roared out the tragical history of the man eating his dead wife in Virginia, when the master of this ship willingly confessed before forty witnesses that at their coming away they left three months' victuals and all the cattle living in the fort. Sometimes they reported that they saw this horrible action, sometimes that Captain Davies said so, sometimes that one Beadle, the lieutenant of Captain Davies did relate it, varying this report into diversity of false colors, which hold no likeness and proportion. But to clear all doubts, Sir Thomas Gates thus relateth the tragedy:

"There was one of the company who mortally hated his wife, and therefore secretly killed her, then cut her in pieces and hid her in divers parts of his house. When the woman was missing, the man suspected, his house searched and parts of her mangled body were discovered, to excuse himself he said that his wife died, that he hid her to satisfy his hunger, and that he fed daily upon her. Upon this his house was again searched, where they found quantities of meal, oatmeal, beans, and peas. He thereupon was arraigned, confessed the murder, and was burned for his horrible villainy."

Now shall the scandalous reports of a viperous generation preponderate the testimonies of so worthy leaders? Shall their venomous tongues blast the reputation of an ancient and worthy peer? Shall sworn lies and combined oaths so far privilege treachery and piracy as to rob us of our hopes, and to quall our noble resolutions? God forbid.

Join unto these another evil. There is great store of fish in the river, especially of sturgeon, but our men provided no more of them than for present necessity, not barrelling up any store against that season the sturgeon returned to the sea. And not to dissemble their folly they suffered fourteen nets (which was all they had) to rot and spoil, which by orderly drying and mending might have been preserved, but being lost, all help of fishing perished.

The state of the colony by these accidents began to find a sensible declining which Powhatan (as a greedy vulture) observing, and boiling with desire of revenge, he invited Captain Ratcliffe and about thirty others to trade for corn, and under the color of fairest friendship he brought them within the compass of his ambush, whereupon they were cruelly murdered and massacred. For upon confidence of his fidelity they went one and one into several houses which caused their several destructions, when if but any six had remained together they would have been a bulwark for the general preservation. After this Powhatan, in the night, cut off some of our boats, he drove away all the deer into the farther part of the country, he and his people destroyed our hogs (to the number of about six hundred), he sent none of his Indians to trade with us but laid secret ambushes in the woods, that if one or two dropped out of the fort alone they were endangered.

Cast up this reckoning together: want of government, store of idleness, their expectations frustrated by the traitors, their market spoiled by the mariners, our nets broken, the deer chased, our boats lost, our hogs killed, our trade with the Indians forbidden, some of our men fled, some murdered, and most by drinking of the brackish water of James fort weakened and endangered, famine and sickness by all these means increased. Here at home the monies came in so slowly that the Lord De La Warr could not be dispatched till the colony was worn and spent with difficulties. Above all, having neither ruler nor preacher, they neither feared God nor man, which provoked the wrath of the Lord of Hosts, and pulled down his judgments upon them.

When Sir Thomas Gates arrived in Virginia, the strange and unexpected condition wherein he found the colony, gave him to understand how never was there more need of all the powers of judgment than at this present, it being now his charge both to save such as he found so forlorn and wretched, as to redeem himself and his from falling into the like calamities. All which considered, he entered into consultation with Sir George Somers and Captain Newport, and the gentlemen and council of the former government. They examined first their store, which after two cakes a day to a man would hold out but sixteen days, the corn of the Indians but newly sowed, and not an eye of sturgeon as yet appeared in the river. And therefore at the same consultation it was concluded by a general approbation that they should abandon the country and in the four pinaces (which remained in the river) they should make for the Newfoundland where, it being fishing time, they might meet with many English ships, into which they hoped to disperse the most of the company.

This conclusion taking effect, upon the seventh of June Sir Thomas Gates (having appointed every ship her complement and number, and delivered likewise to each a proportionable weight of provision) caused every man to repair aboard. His company (and of his company himself) remained last on shore, to keep the town from being burned which some of our own company maliciously threatened. About noon they fell down with the tide to the Island of Hogs, and the next morning to the Mulberry Island, at what time they discovered the long boat of the Lord De La Warr which his Lordship (hearing of this resolution by the Captain of the Fort) suddenly dispatched with letters to Sir Thomas Gates, which informed him of his Lordship's arrival. Upon receipt of these letters Sir Thomas Gates bore up the helm, and that night with a favorable wind relanded all our men at the Fort. Before which, the tenth of June (being Sunday) his Lordship came with all his fleet, went ashore in the afternoon, heard a sermon, read his commission, and entered into consultation for the good of the colony.

Never had any people more just cause to cast themselves at the footstool of God and to reverence his mercy than our distressed colony, for if God had not sent Sir Thomas Gates from the Bermudas within four days, they had all been famished; if God had not directed the heart of that worthy knight to save the Fort from fire at their shipping, they had been destitute of a present harbor and succor; if they had abandoned the Fort any longer time and had not so soon returned, questionless the Indians would have destroyed the Fort, which had been the means of our safety among them, and a terror unto them; if they had set sail sooner and had launched into the vast ocean, who could have promised that they should have encountered the fleet of the Lord De La Warr? This was the arm of the Lord of Hosts, who would have his people to pass the Red Sea and Wilderness, and then to possess the land of Canaan.

The noble Lord Governor, after mature deliberation, delivered some few words to the company, laying just blame upon them for their haughty vanities and sluggish idleness, earnestly entreating them to amend those desperate follies, lest he should be compelled to draw the sword of justice and to cut off such delinquents, which he had rather draw (even to the shedding of his vital blood) to protect them from injuries, heartening them with relation of that store he had brought with him; constituting officers of all conditions to rule over them, allotting every man his particular place to watch vigilantly and work plentifully. The oration and direction being received with a general applause, you might shortly behold the idle and restive diseases of a divided multitude, by the unity and authority of this government, to be substantially cured. Those that knew not the way to goodness before, but cherished singularity and faction, can now chalk out the path of all respective duty and service; every man endeavoring to outstrip each other in diligence, the French preparing to plant the vines, the English laboring in the woods and grounds, every man knoweth his charge and dischargeth the same with alacrity. Neither let any man be discouraged by the relation of their daily labor, the settled times of working requiring no more pains than from six of the clock in the morning until ten, and from two of the clock in the afternoon till four, at both which times they are provided of spiritual and corporal relief. First they enter into the church and make their prayers unto God; next they return to their houses and receive their proportion of food. Nor should it be conceived that this business excludeth gentlemen, whose breeding never knew what a day's labor meant. For though they cannot dig, use the square, nor practice the axe and chisel, yet may the steady spirits of any condition find how to employ the force of knowledge, the exercise of counsel, the operation and power of their best breeding and qualities. The houses which are built are warm and defensible against wind and weather, as if they were tiled and slated, being covered above with strong boards and matted round within, according to the fashion of the Indians. Our forces are now such as are able to tame the fury and treachery of the savages; our forts assure the inhabitants and frustrate all assailants.

The fertility of the soil, the temperature of the climate, the form of government, the condition of our people, their daily invocating of the name of God being thus expressed, why should the success (by the rules of mortal judgment) be despaired? Why should not the rich harvest of our hopes be seasonably expected? I dare say that the resolution of Caesar in France, the designs of Alexander in Greece, the discoveries of Hernando Cortez in the West, and of Manual, King of Portugal, in the East, were not encouraged upon so firm grounds of state and possibility.

The Council of Virginia (finding the smallness of that return which they hoped should have defrayed the charge of a new supply) entered into a deep consultation, and propounded amongst themselves whether it were fit to enter a new contribution, or in time to send for home the Lord De La Warr and to abandon the action. They resolved to send for Sir Thomas Gates, who being come they adjured him to deal plainly with them and to make a true relation of those things which were presently to be had, or hereafter to be hoped for, in Virginia. Sir Thomas Gates, with a solemn and sacred oath, replied that all things before reported were true; that the country yieldeth abundance of wood, as oak, wainscot, walnut trees, bay trees, ash, sassafras. He vouched that there are incredible variety of sweet woods, especially of the balsam tree, which distilleth a precious gum; that there are innumerable white mulberry trees, which in so warm a climate may cherish and feed millions of silk worms, and return us in a very short time as great a plenty of silk as is vented into the whole world from all the parts of Italy; that there are divers sorts of minerals, especially of iron ore, lying upon the ground for ten miles circuit; that a kind of hemp or flax and silk grass do grow there naturally, which will afford stuff for all manner of excellent cordage; that the river swarmeth with sturgeon, the land aboundeth with vines, the woods do harbor exceeding store of beavers, foxes and squirrels, the waters do nourish a great increase of otters, all which are covered with precious furs; that there are in present discovered dyes and drugs of sundry qualities; that the oranges which have been planted did prosper in the winter, which is an infallible argument that lemons, sugar cane, almonds, rice, aniseed, and all other commodities which we have from the States [Netherlands] may be supplied to us in our own country and by our own industry; and lastly, that it is one of the goodliest countries under the sun, interveined with fine main rivers, and promising as rich entrails as any kingdom of the earth to whom the sun is so near a neighbor.

What these things will yield the merchant best knoweth, who findeth by experience that many hundreds of thousands of pounds are yearly spent in Christendom in these commodities. The merchant knoweth that caviar from Russia can be brought hither but once in the year, in regard of the ice, and that sturgeon which is brought from the East countries, can come but twice a year, when from Virginia they may be brought to us in four and twenty days, and in all the cold seasons of the year. The merchants know that the commodities of soap and potash are very scant in Prussia, that they are brought three hundred miles by land and three hundred miles by river before they come to the sea; that they pay a custom there and another in Denmark which enhanceth the prices exceedingly. But in Virginia they may have them without carriage by land or custom (because five navigable rivers do lead up five several ways into the bowels of the whole country). As therefore the like rivers are the cause of the riches of Holland, so will these be to us a wondrous cause of saving of expenses. The merchant knoweth that through the troubles in Poland and Muscovy (whose eternal wars are like the antipathy of the dragon and elephants) all their traffic for masts, deal, pitch, tar, flax, hemp, and cordage are every day more and more endangered, and the woods of those countries are almost exhausted. All which are to be had in Virginia with far less charge and far more safety. Lastly the merchant knoweth that for our commodities in the States, as sweet wines, oranges, lemons, aniseed, etc., that we stand at the devotion of politic princes and states, who for their proper utility devise all courses to grind our merchants, all pretenses to con-

11

fiscate their goods, and to draw from us all marrow of gain by the inquisitive inventions. When in Virginia a few years' labor by planting and husbandry will furnish all our defects with honor and security, especially since the Frenchmen (who are with the Lord Governor) do confidently promise that within two years we may expect a plentiful vintage.

Shall we now be dejected? Shall we cast down our heads like bullrushes because one storm at sea hath deferred our joys and comforts? We are too effeminate in our longings and too impatient of delays. It is but a golden slumber that dreameth of any human felicity, which is not sauced with some contingent misery. Grief and pleasure are the cross sails of the world's ever turning windmill. Let no man, therefore, be over wise, to cast beyond the moon and to multiply needless doubts and questions. Hannibal, by too much wisdom, lost opportunity to have sacked Rome. Charles the Eighth of France, by temporizing, lost the kingdom of Naples and the government of Florence. Henry the Seventh, by too much over-wariness, lost the riches of the golden Indies. Some of our neighbors would join in the action if they might be joint inheritors in the plantation, which is an evident proof that Virginia shall no sooner be quitted by us, than it will be reinhabited by them. A dishonor of that nature that will eternally blemish our nation. He is over blind that doth not see what an inundation of people doth overflow this little island. Shall we vent this deluge, by indirect and unchristian policies? Shall we imitate the bloody and heathenish counsel of the Romans, to leave a Carthage standing that may exhaust our people by foreign war? Or shall we nourish domestic faction, that as in the days of Vitellius and Vespasian, the son may imbrue his hands in the blood of the father? Or shall we follow the barbarous footsteps of the state of China, to imprison our people in a little circle of the earth and consume them by pestilence? Or shall we take an inhuman example from the Muscovite, in a time of famine to put ten thousand of the poor under the ice, as the mice and rats of a state politic? If all these be diabolical and hellish projects, what other means remain to us but by settling so excellent a plantation, to disembark some millions of people upon a land that floweth with all manner of plenty?

To wade a little further, who ever saluted the monuments of antiquity and doth not find that Carthage aspired to be Empress of the World by her opportunity of havens and multitude of shipping? What hindereth the great Mohammedan prince from seizing upon all the territories of Europe, but only the want of skillful mariners? What created the rich and free states of Holland but their winged navy? It was a fit emblem that painted death standing upon the shores of France, Germany, and Spain, looking over into England: intimating to us that so long as we are lords of the narrow seas death stands on the other shores and only can look upon us; but if our wooden walls were ruinated, death would soon make a bridge to come over and devour our nation. When, therefore, our mills of iron and excess of building have already turned our greatest woods into pasture and champion within these few years, neither the scattered forests of England nor the diminished groves of Ireland will supply the defect of our navy. When in Virginia there is nothing wanting but only men's labors, to furnish both prince, state, and merchant, without charge or difficulty. Again, whither shall we transport our cloth and how shall we sustain our artisans? Shall we send it into Turkey? Some private and deceitful avarice hath discredited our merchandise. Into Spain? It aboundeth with sheep and wool. Into Poland and Muscovy? The danger doth overbalance the gain in times of contention. Into France and Germany? They are, for the most part, supplied by their own peace. When if our colony were peopled in Virginia, we shall exchange our store of cloth for other merchandise.

And therefore, he that aimeth at the honor and wealth of his native country, he that esteemeth his own repute as dear as his own eyes, he that endeavoureth to enlarge the dominions of his prince and the kingdom of his God, let him remember what he hath already spent, which is all buried; let him consider the consequences of state, which are all vanished into smoke; let him conceive what a scorn we shall be made to the maligners of our state abroad and our ill affected at home; let him meditate the external riches of other kingdoms, able to buy and sell the monarch of the West; let him hear the triumphant boasting of the Beast of Rome, as though God would not suffer our schismatical and heretical religion to be infused into a new converted region. O all ye worthies, follow the ever sounding trumpet of a blessed honor, let religion be the first aim of your hopes, and other things shall be cast unto you, your names shall be registered to posterity with a glorious title: "These are the men whom God raised to augment the state of their country and to propagate the gospel of Jesus Christ." If God hath scattered his blessings upon you as snow, will you return no tributary acknowledgement of his goodness? If you will, can you select a more excellent subject than to cast down the altars of devils, that you may raise up the altar of Christ, to forbid the sacrifice of men, that they may offer up the sacrifice of contrite spirits, to reduce barbarism and infidelity to civil government and Christianity? Doubt ye not but God hath determined and demonstrated (by the wondrous preservation of those principal persons which fell upon the Bermudas) that he will raise our state and build his church in that excellent climate, if the action be seconded with resolution and religion.

2

Daily Life in Massachusetts

John Winthrop (1588–1649) was the major figure among the first generation of New England Puritans. An attorney and country squire in England, Winthrop was elected Governor of the settlement in 1629, while still in England, and for many of the next twenty years he served as the chief executive of Massachusetts Bay. In a few famous speeches he evocatively presented some of the basic hopes and expectations of the founding Puritans, their ideas of order, of rank, of community, and of religious obligation. On board the *Arbella* just before beginning the great experiment, Winthrop sought to sketch his dream of a holy city, testimony to the glory of God, and a lesson to the world of man.

If *A Modell of Christian Charity* reveals something of Puritan theory, Winthrop's careful *Journal* tells us much about Puritan practice and daily experience. Details of religion, government, housing, warfare, criminal justice, and family life are mingled together, a picture of the frustrations and satisfactions yielded by existence in the Bay Colony, and a testament to Winthrop's gifts of mind and character.

A MODELL OF CHRISTIAN CHARITY
John Winthrop

Written on board the Arbella, *on the Atlantic Ocean*
Anno 1630

God almighty in his most holy and wise providence hath so disposed of the condition of mankind, as in all times some must be rich, some poor, some high and eminent in power and dignity, others mean and in subjection.

Reason: First, to hold conformity with the rest of his works, being delighted to show forth the glory of his wisdom in the variety and difference of the creatures and the glory of his power, in ordering all these differences for the preservation and good of the whole. And the glory of his greatness that as it is the glory of princes to have many officers, so this great King will have many stewards counting himself more

From John Winthrop, *A Modell of Christian Charity, Winthrop Papers* (Boston, 1931), II: 282–283, 294–295. Reprinted by permission of the Massachusetts Historical Society.

honored in dispensing his gifts to man by man, than if he did it by his own immediate hand.

Reason: Secondly, that he might have the more occasion to manifest the work of his spirit. First, upon the wicked in moderating and restraining them, so that the rich and mighty should not eat up the poor, nor the poor and despised rise up against their superiors and shake off their yoke. Secondly, in the regenerate in exercising his graces in them, as in the great ones, their love, mercy, gentleness, temperance, etc., in the poor and inferior sort, their faith, patience, obedience, etc.

Reason: Thirdly, that every man might have need of other, and from hence they might be all knit more nearly together in the bond of brotherly affection. From hence it appears plainly that no man is made more honorable than another, or more wealthy, etc., out of any particular and singular respect to himself, but for the glory of his creator and the common good of the creature, man.

Thus stands the cause between God and us. We are entered into covenant with him for this work, we have taken out a commission, the Lord hath given us leave to draw our own articles, we have professed to enterprise these actions upon these and these ends, we have hereupon besought him of favor and blessing. Now if the Lord shall please to hear us, and bring us in peace to the place we desire, then hath he ratified this covenant and sealed our commission, [and] will expect a strict performance of the articles contained in it, but if we shall neglect the observations of these articles which are the ends we have propounded, and dissembling with our God, shall fall to embrace this present world and prosecute our carnal intentions seeking great things for ourselves and our posterity, the Lord will surely break out in wrath against us, be revenged of such a perjured people, and make us know the price of the breach of such a covenant.

Now the only way to avoid this shipwreck and to provide for our posterity is to follow the counsel of Micah, to do justly, to love mercy, to walk humbly with our God. For this end we must be knit together in this work as one man, we must entertain each other in brotherly affection, we must be willing to abridge ourselves of our superfluities for the supply of others' necessities, we must uphold a familiar commerce together in all meekness, gentleness, patience, and liberality, we must delight in each other, make others' conditions our own, rejoice together, mourn together, labor, and suffer together, always having before our eyes our commission and community in the work, our community as members of the same body. So shall we keep the unity of the spirit in the bond of peace. The Lord will be our God and delight to dwell among us as his own people, and will command a blessing upon us in all our ways, so that we shall see much more of his wisdom, power, goodness and truth than formerly we have been acquainted with. We shall find that the God of Israel is among us, when ten of us shall be able to resist a thousand of our enemies, when he shall make us a praise and glory, that men shall say of succeeding plantations, the Lord make it like that of New England. For we must consider that we shall be as a city upon a hill, the eyes of all people are upon us. So that if we shall deal falsely with our God in this work we have undertaken and so cause him to withdraw his present help from us, we shall be made a story and a by-word through the world, we shall open the mouths of enemies to speak evil of the ways of God and all professors for God's sake, we shall shame the faces of many of God's worthy servants, and cause their prayers to be turned into curses upon us till we be consumed out of the good land whither we are going. And to shut up this discourse with that exhortation of Moses, that faithful servant of the Lord in his last farewell to Israel, Deut. 30., Beloved, there is now set before us life and good, death and evil, in that we are commanded this day to love the Lord our God, and to love one another, to walk in his ways and to keep his commandments and his ordinance, and his laws, and the articles of our covenant with him that we may live and be multiplied, and that the Lord our God may bless us in the land whither we go to possess it. But if our hearts shall turn away so that we will not obey, but shall be seduced and worship other Gods, our pleasures, our profits, and serve them, it is propounded unto us this day we shall surely perish out of the good land whither we pass over this vast sea to possess it. Therefore let us choose life, that we, and our seed, may live, and by obeying his voice, and cleaving to him, for he is our life, and our prosperity.

JOURNAL OF JOHN WINTHROP

May 8, 1632

A general court at Boston. Whereas it was (at our first coming) agreed, that the freemen should choose the assistants, and they the governor, the whole court agreed now that the governor and assistants should all be new chosen every year by the general court, the governor to be always chosen out of the assistants. And accordingly, the old governor, John Winthrop, was chosen.

A proposition was made by the people, that every company of trained men might choose their own captain and officers. But the governor giving them reasons to the contrary, they were satisfied without it.

Every town chose two men to be at the next court, to advise with the governor and assistants about the raising of a public stock, so as what they should agree upon should bind all, etc.

July

At Watertown there was (in the view of divers witnesses) a great combat between a mouse and a snake. And, after a long fight, the mouse prevailed and killed the snake. The pastor of Boston, Mr. Wilson, a very sincere, holy man, hearing of it gave this interpretation. That the snake was the devil; the mouse was a poor, contemptible people, which God had brought hither, which should overcome Satan here and dispossess him of his kingdom. Upon the same occasion he told the governor that, before he was resolved to come into this country, he dreamed he was here, and that he saw a church arise out of the earth, which grew up and became a marvelous goodly church.

February 26, 1633

Two little girls of the governor's family were sitting under a great heap of logs, plucking of birds, and the wind driving the feathers into the house, the governors'

Winthrop's Journal, 1630–1649, James K. Hosmer, ed., (New York, 1908), I: 79, 83–84, 99, 103–104, 111–113, 124–125, 132–134, 143–144, 235–238.

wife caused them to remove away. They were no sooner gone but the whole heap of logs fell down in the place, and had crushed them to death if the Lord, in his special providence, had not delivered them.

August 6, 1633

Two men, servants to one Moody, of Roxbury, returning in a boat from the windmill, struck upon the oyster bank. They went out to gather oysters and, not making fast their boat, when the flood came it floated away and they were both drowned, although they might have waded out on either side. But it was an evident judgment of God upon them, for they were wicked persons. One of them, a little before, being reproved for his lewdness and put in mind of hell, answered that if hell were ten times hotter he had rather be there than he would serve his master, etc. The occasion was because he had bound himself for divers years, and saw that if he had been at liberty he might have had greater wages, though otherwise his master used him very well.

October 11, 1633

The scarcity of workmen had caused them to raise their wages to an excessive rate, so as a carpenter would have three shillings the day, a laborer two shillings and sixpence, etc. And accordingly, those who had commodities to sell advanced their prices sometimes double to that they cost in England, so as it grew to a general complaint, which the court, taking knowledge of, as also of some further evils which were springing out of the excessive rates of wages, they made an order that carpenters, masons, etc., should take but two shillings the day, and laborers but eighteen pence, and that no commodity should be sold at above four pence in the shilling more than it cost for ready money in England, oil, wine, and cheese, in regard of the hazard of bringing, excepted. The evils which were springing were: 1. Many spent much time idly, etc., because they could get as much in four days as would keep them a week. 2. They spent much in tobacco and strong waters, etc., which was a great waste to the commonwealth which, by reason of so many foreign commodities expended, could not have subsisted to this time, but that it was supplied by the cattle and corn which were sold to newcomers at very dear rates.

The ministers in the bay and Saugus did meet, once a fortnight, at one of their houses by course, where some question of moment was debated. Mr. Skelton, the pastor of Salem, and Mr. Williams, who was removed from Plymouth thither, took some exception against it, as fearing it might grow in time to a presbytery or superintendency, to the prejudice of the churches' liberties. But this fear was without cause; for they were all clear in that point, that no church or person can have power over another church. Neither did they in their meetings exercise any such jurisdiction, etc.

May 14, 1634

At the general court Mr. Cotton preached, and delivered this doctrine, that a magistrate ought not to be turned into the condition of a private man without just cause, and to be publicly convict, no more than the magistrates may not turn a private man out of his freehold, etc., without like public trial, etc. This falling in question in the court, and the opinion of the rest of the ministers being asked, it was referred to further consideration.

The court chose a new governor, viz., Thomas Dudley, Esq., the former deputy; and Mr. Ludlow was chosen deputy; and John Haines, Esq., as assistant, and all the rest of the assistants chosen again.

At this court it was ordered that four general courts should be kept every year, and that the whole body of the freemen should be present only at the court of election of magistrates, etc., and that, at the other three, every town should send their deputies, who should assist in making laws, disposing lands, etc. Many good things were made this court. It held three days, and all things were carried very peaceably, notwithstanding that some of the assistants were questioned by the freemen for some errors in their government, and some fines imposed, but remitted again before the court brake up. The court was kept in the meeting-house at Boston, and the new governor and the assistants were together entertained at the house of the old governor, as before.

September 4, 1634

The general court began at Newtown, and continued a week, and then was adjourned fourteen days. Many things were there agitated and concluded, as fortifying Castle Island, Dorchester, and Charlestown. Also against tobacco, and costly apparel, and immodest fashions. And committees appointed for setting out the bounds of towns, with divers other matters which do appear upon record. But the main business, which spent the most time and caused the adjourning of the court, was about the removal of Newtown. They had leave, the last general court, to look out some place for enlargement or removal, with promise of having it confirmed to them if it were not prejudicial to any other plantation. And now they moved that they might have leave to remove to Connecticut. The matter was debated divers days, and many reasons alleged pro and con. The principal reasons for their removal were,

1. Their want of accomodation for their cattle, so as they were not able to maintain their ministers, nor could receive any more of their friends to help them. And here it was alleged by Mr. Hooker, as a fundamental error, that towns were set so near each to other.

2. The fruitfulness and commodiousness of Connecticut, and the danger of having it possessed by others, Dutch or English.

3. The strong bent of their spirits to remove thither.

Against these it was said,

1. That in point of conscience, they ought not to depart from us, being knit to us in one body, and bound by oath to seek the welfare of this commonwealth.

2. That in point of state and civil policy, we ought not to give them leave to depart. 1. Being we were now weak and in danger to be assailed. 2. The departure of Mr. Hooker would not only draw many from us, but also divert other friends that would come to us. 3. We should expose them to evident peril, both from the Dutch (who made claim to the same river, and had already built a fort there) and from the Indians, and also from our own state at home, who would not endure they should sit down without a patent in any place which our king lays claim to.

3. They might be accomodated at home by some enlargement which other towns offered.

4. They might remove to Merrimack, or any other place within our patent.

18

5. The removing of a candlestick is a great judgment, which is to be avoided.

Upon these and other arguments the court being divided, it was put to vote, and of the deputies, fifteen were for their departure, and ten against it. The governor and two assistants were against it (except the secretary, who gave not vote); whereupon no record was entered, because there were not six assistants in the vote, as the patent requires. Upon this grew a great difference between the governor and assistants, and the deputies. They would not yield the assistants a negative voice, and the others (considering how dangerous it might be to the commonwealth, if they should not keep that strength to balance the greater number of the deputies) thought it safe to stand upon it. So, when they could proceed no farther, the whole court agreed to keep a day of humiliation to seek the Lord, which accordingly was done in all the congregations, the 18th day of this month. And the 24th, the court met again. Before they began Mr. Cotton preached (being desired by all the court, upon Mr. Hooker's instant excuse of his unfitness for that occasion). He took his text out of Hag. ii, 4, etc., out of which he laid down the nature or strength (as he termed it) of the magistracy, ministry, and people, viz.,—the strength of the magistracy to be their authority; of the people, their liberty; and of the ministry, their purity. And showed how all of these had a negative voice, etc., and that yet the ultimate resolution, etc., ought to be in the whole body of the people, etc., with answer to all objections, and a declaration of the people's duty and right to maintain their true liberties against any unjust violence, etc., which gave great satisfaction to the company. And it pleased the Lord so to assist him, and to bless his own ordinance, that the affairs of the court went on cheerfully. And although all were not satisfied about the negative voice to be left to the magistrates, yet no man moved aught about it, and the congregation of Newtown came and accepted of such enlargement as had formerly been offered them (by Boston and Watertown). And so the fear of their removal to Connecticut was removed.

At this court Mr. Goodwin, a very reverend and godly man, being the elder of the congregation of Newtown, having, in heat of argument, used some unreverend speech to one of the assistants, and being reproved for the same in the open court, did gravely and humbly acknowledge his fault, etc.

Dec. 11, 1634

This day, after the lecture, the inhabitants of Boston met to choose seven men who should divide the town lands among them. They chose by papers [ballots], and in their choice left out Mr. Winthrop, Coddington, and others of the chief men. Only they chose one of the elders and a deacon, and the rest of the inferior sort, and Mr. Winthrop had the greater number before one of them by a voice or two. This they did, as fearing that the richer men would give the poorer sort no great proportions of land, but would rather leave a great part at liberty for newcomers and for common, which Mr. Winthrop had oft persuaded them unto, as best for the town, etc. Mr. Cotton and divers others were offended at this choice, because they declined the magistrates. And Mr. Winthrop refused to be one upon such an election as was carried by a voice or two, telling them, that though, for his part, he did not apprehend any personal injury nor did doubt of their good affection towards him, yet he was much grieved that Boston should be the first who should shake off their magistrates,

19

especially Mr. Coddington, who had been always so forward for their enlargement, adding further reason of declining this choice, to blot out so bad a precedent. Whereupon, at the motion of Mr. Cotton, who showed them that it was the Lord's order among the Israelites to have all such businesses committed to the elders, and that it had been nearer the rule to have chosen some of each sort, etc., they all agreed to go to a new election, which was referred to the next lecture day.

The reason why some were not willing that the people should have more land in the bay than they might be likely to use in some reasonable time, was partly to prevent the neglect of trades, and other more necessary employments, and partly that there might be place to receive such as should come after, seeing it would be very prejudicial to the commonwealth if men should be forced to go far off for land, while others had much and could make no use of it more than to please their eye with it.

September 22, 1637

Two men were hanged at Boston for several murders. The one, John Williams, a ship carpenter who, being lately come into the country and put in prison for theft, brake out of prison with one John Hoddy whom, near the great pond in the way to Ipswich, beyond Salem, he murdered, and took away his clothes and what else he had, and went in them to Ipswich (where he had been sent to prison), and was there again apprehended. And though his clothes were all bloody, yet he would confess nothing, till about a week after that the body of Hoddy was found by the kine, who, smelling the blood, made such a roaring as the cow-keeper, looking about, found the dead body covered with a heap of stones.

The other, William Schooler, was a vintner in London, and had been a common adulterer (as himself did confess), and had wounded a man in a duel, for which he fled in the Low Country, and from thence he fled from his captain and came into this country, leaving his wife (a handsome, neat woman) in England. He lived with another fellow at Merrimack, and there being a poor maid at Newbury, one Mary Sholy, who had desired a guide to go with her to her master, who dwelt at Pascataquack, he inquired her out and agreed, for fifteen shillings, to conduct her thither. But two days after, he returned, and being asked why he returned so soon, he answered that he had carried her within two or three miles of the place, and then she would go no farther. Being examined for this by the magistrates at Ipswich, and no proof founded against him he was let go. But about a year after, being impressed to go against the Pequods, he gave ill speeches, for which the governor sent warrant for him, and being apprehended (and supposed it had been for the death of the maid, some spake what they had heard, which might occasion suspicion), he was again examined, and divers witnesses produced about it. Whereupon he was committed, arraigned, and condemned, by due proceeding. The effect of the evidence was this:—

1. He had lived a vicious life, and now lived like an atheist.

2. He had sought out the maid, and undertook to carry her to a place where he had never been.

3. When he crossed Merrimack, he landed in a place three miles from the usual path, from whence it was scarce possible she should get into the path.

4. He said he went by Winicowett house, which he said stood on the contrary side of the way.

5. Being, as he said, within two or three miles of Swanscote, where he left her, he went not thither to tell them of her, nor stayed by her that night, nor, at his return home, did tell anybody of her, till he was demanded of her.

6. When he came back he had above ten shillings in his purse, and yet he said she would give him but seven shillings, and he carried no money with him.

7. At his return he had some blood upon his hat, and on his skirts before, which he said was with a pigeon which he killed.

8. He had a scratch on the left side of his nose, and being asked by a neighbor how it came, he said it was with a bramble, which could not be, it being of the breadth of a small nail. And being asked after by the magistrate, he said it was with his piece [gun], but that could not be on the left side.

9. The body of the maid was found by an Indian, about half a year after, in the midst of thick swamp, ten miles short of the place he said he left her in, and about three miles from the place where he landed by Merrimack, and (it was after seen, by the English), the flesh being rotted off it, and the clothes laid all on an heap by the body.

10. He said, that soon after he left her, he met with a bear and he thought that bear might kill her, yet he would not go back to save her.

11. He brake prison and fled as far as Powder Horn Hill, and there hid himself out of the way, for fear of pursuit, and after, when he arose to go forward he could not, but (as himself confessed), was forced to return back to prison again.

At his death he confessed he had made many lies to excuse himself, but denied that he had killed or ravished her. He was very loath to die, and had hope he should be reprived. But the court held him worthy of death, in undertaking the charge of a shiftless maid, and leaving her (when he might have done otherwise) in such a place as he knew she must needs perish, if not preserved by means unknown. Yet there were some ministers and others, who thought the evidence not sufficient to take away his life.

3

A History of New England

Edward Johnson, a well-to-do native of Kent, in England, came to America in 1630 along with John Winthrop. He returned to England for a few years, but in 1636 he moved back and spent the rest of his life in Massachusetts. From 1642 until his death thirty years later, Johnson was the leading figure of Woburn, Massachusetts, acting in various important governmental and military capacities. Captain Johnson, as he became known, was a selectman, a representative to the General Court, and surveyor-general of the arms and munitions of Massachusetts. In 1655 he became speaker of the House of Deputies.

But his practical achievements notwithstanding, Johnson's fame rests on his *Wonder-Working Providence,* the first published history of New England. Composed of both prose and verse, filled with rhetorical passages from the Bible, choked with images both vibrant and turgid, Johnson's history was an authentic expression of Puritan sentiment, breathing the enthusiasm, the heroism, the self-confidence, and the missionary objectives of the first settlers. The narrative contains vital information concerning the development of political and religious institutions in New England, but its emotional intensity and cosmic aims are of even greater value in giving us a portrait of the seventeenth-century Puritan. The *Wonder-Working Providence* was first published, in London, in 1654.

WONDER-WORKING PROVIDENCE OF SIONS SAVIOUR IN NEW ENGLAND
Edward Johnson

CHAPTER XII

And now behold the several regiments of these soldiers of Christ, as they are shipped for his service in the western world, part thereof being come to the town and port of Southampton in England, where they were to be shipped, that they might prosecute this design to the full. One ship called the *Eagle* they wholly purchase, and many more they hire, filling them with the seed of man and beast to sow this yet untilled

From *Johnson's Wonder-Working Providence, 1628–1651,* J. Franklin Jameson, ed. (New York, 1910), 50–54, 56–61, 63–66, 198–203, 209–218.

wilderness withal, making sale of such land as they possess, to the great admiration of their friends and acquaintance, who thus expostulate with them: "What, will not the large income of your yearly revenue content you, which in all reason cannot choose but be more advantagious both to you and yours, than all that rocky wilderness whither you are going, to run the hazard of your life? Have you not here your tables filled with great variety of food, your coffers filled with coin, your houses beautifully built and filled with all rich furniture? Have you not such a gainful trade as none the like in the town where you live? Are you not enriched daily? Are not your children very well provided for as they come to years? Nay, may you not here as pithily practice the two chief duties of a Christian (if Christ give strength), namely mortification and sanctification, as in any place of the world? What helps can you have there that you not carry from hence?" With bold resolvedness these stout soldiers of Christ replied. As death, the king of terror, with all his dreadful attendants, inhumane and barbarous tortures, doubled and trebled by all the infernal furies, have appeared but light and momentary to the soldiers of Christ Jesus, so also the pleasures, profits and honours of this world, set forth in their most glorious splendor and magnitude, cannot entice such soldiers of Christ, whose arms are elevated by him many millions above that brave warrior Ulysses.

Now seeing all can be said will but barely set forth the immoveable resolutions that Christ continued in these men, pass on and attend with tears, if thou hast any, the following discourse, while these men, women and children are taking their last farewell of their native country, kindred, friends and acquaintance, while the ships attend them. Many make choice of some solitary place to echo out their bowel-breaking affections in bidding their friends farewell. "Dear friends," says one, "as near as my own soul doth thy love lodge in my breast. With thought of the heart-burning ravishments that thy heavenly speeches have wrought, my melting soul is poured out at present with these words." Both of them had their farther speech strangled from the depth of their inward dolor, with breast-breaking sobs, till leaning their heads on each other's shoulders they let fall the salt-dropping dews of vehement affection, striving to exceed one another, much like the departure of David and Jonathan. Having a little eased their hearts with the still streams of tears, they recovered speech again. "Ah! my much honored friend, hath Christ given thee so great a charge as to be leader of his people into that far remote and vast wilderness, oh, and alas, thou must die there and never shall I see thy face in the flesh again. Wert thou called to so great a task as to pass the precious ocean and hazard thy person in battle against thousands of malignant enemies there, there were hopes of thy return with triumph. But now, after two, three, or four months spent with daily expectation of swallowing waves and cruel pirates, you are to be landed among barbarous Indians, famous for nothing but cruelty, where you are like to spend your days in a famishing condition for a long space." Scarce had he uttered this but presently he locks his friend fast in his arms. Holding each other thus for some space of time, they weep again. But as Paul to his beloved flock, the other replies, "What do you weeping and breaking my heart? I am now pressed for the service of our Lord Christ, to rebuild the most glorious edifice of Mount Sion in a wilderness, and as John Baptist I must cry, Prepare ye the way of the Lord, make his paths strait, for behold he is coming

23

again, he is coming to destroy Antichrist, and give the whore double to drink the very dregs of his wrath. Then my dear friend unfold thy hands, for thou and I have much work to do, ay and all Christian soldiers the world throughout."

Then hand in hand they lead each other to the sandy banks of the brinish ocean, when clenching their hands fast, they unloose not till enforced to wipe their watery eyes, whose constant streams forced a watery path upon their cheeks, which to hide from the eyes of others they shun society for a time. But being called by occasion they thrust in among the throng now ready to take ship, where they beheld the like affections with their own among divers relations. Husbands and wives with mutual consent are now purposed to part for a time nine hundred leagues asunder, since some providence at present will not suffer them to go together. They resolve their tender affections shall not hinder this work of Christ. The new married and betrothed men, exempt by the law of God from war, now will not claim their privilege, but being constrained by the love of Christ, lock up their natural affections for a time, till the Lord shall be pleased to give them a meeting in this western world, sweetly mixing it with spiritual love in the meantime. Many fathers now take their young Samuels and give them to this service of Christ all their lives. Brethren, sisters, uncles, nephews, nieces, together with all kindred of blood that binds the bowels of affection in a true lover's knot, can now take their last farewell, each of other. Among this company, thus disposed, doth many reverend and godly pastors of Christ present themselves, some in a seaman's habit, and their scattered sheep coming as a poor convoy, loftily take their leave of them as followeth: "What doleful days are these, when the best choice our orthodox ministers can make is to take up a perpetual banishment from their native soil, together with their wives and children. We their poor sheep they may not feed but by stealth should they abide here. Lord Christ, here they are at thy command, they go. This is the door thou hast opened upon our earnest request, and we hope it shall never be shut. For England's sake they are going from England to pray without ceasing for England. O England's thou shalt find New England's prayers prevailing with their God for thee, but now woe alas, what great hardship must these our endeared pastors endure for a long season." With these words they lift up their voices and wept, adding many drops of salt liquor to the ebbing ocean. Then shaking hands they bid adieu with much cordial affection to all their brethren and sisters in Christ, yet now the scorn and derision of those times, and for this their great enterprise counted as so many cracked brains. But Christ will make all the earth know the wisdom he hath endowed them with, shall overtop all the human policy in the world, as the sequel we hope will show.

CHAPTER XIV

And now you have had a short survey of the charges of their New England voyages, see their progress. Being safe aboard, weighing anchor and hoisting sail, they betook them to the protection of the Lord on the wide ocean. No sooner were they dispersed by reason of the wilderness of the sea, but the *Arbella* (for so they called the *Eagle,* which the company purchased, in honor of the Lady Arbella, wife of that godly esquire, Isaac Johnson) espied four ships, as they supposed, in pursuit of them, their suspicion being the more augmented by reason of a report of four Dunkirk men of war who were said to lie waiting for their coming forth. At this fight they make preparation, according to their present condition, comforting one another in the sweet mercies of Christ. The weaker sex betook them to the ship's hold, but the men on decks wait in a readiness for the enemy's approach. At whose courage many of the seamen wonder, not knowing under whose command these their passengers were, even he who makes all his soldiers bold as lions. Yet was he not minded to make trial of his people's valiancy in fight at this time, for the ships coming up with them proved to be their own countrymen and friends, at which they greatly rejoiced, seeing the good hand of their God was upon them, and are further strengthened in faith to rely on Christ for the future time, against all leaks, storms, rocks, sands, and all other wants a long sea voyage procures. But now keeping their course so near as the winds will suffer them, the billows begin to grow lofty and raging, and suddenly bringing them into the vale of death, covering them with the formidable floods, and dashing their bodies from side to side, hurling their unfixed goods from place to place. At these unwonted works many of these people, amazed, find such opposition in nature, that her principles grow feeble and cannot digest her food, loathing all manner of meat, so that the vital parts are hindered from cooperating with the soul in spiritual duties, insomuch that both men, women and children are in a helpless condition for present, and now is the time if ever of recounting this service they have and are about to undertake for Christ. But he, who is very sensible of his people's infirmities, rebukes the winds and seas for their sakes, and then the reverend and godly among them begin to exhort them in the name of the Lord. Many of their horses and other cattle are cast overboard by the way, to the great disheartening of some, but Christ knew well how far his people's hearts would be taken off the main work with these things. And therefore, although he be very tender in providing outward necessaries for his, yet rather than this great work (he intends) should be hindered, their tables shall be spread but thinly in this wilderness for a time. After the Lord had exercised them thus several ways, he sent diseases to visit their ships, that the desert land they were now drawing near unto might not be deserted by them at first entrance, which sure it would have been by many, had not the Lord prevented it by a troublesome passage. At forty days' end, or thereabout, they cast to sound the sea's depth, and find them sixty fathoms, by which they deem the banks of Newfoundland are near, where they being provided with cod line and hook hale up some store of fish to their no small refreshing, and within some space of time after they approach the coast of New England, where they are again provided with mackerel, and that which was their great rejoicing, they discover land. At sight thereof they blessed the Lord.

But before the author proceed any further in this discourse, take here a short survey of all the voyages by sea in the transportation of these armies of the great Jehovah for fifteen years' space to the year 1643, about which time England began to endeavor after reformation, and the soldiers of Christ were set at liberty to bide his battles at home, for whose assistance some of the chief worthies of Christ returned back. The number of ships that transported passengers in this space of time, as is supposed, is 298. Men, women and children passing over this wide ocean, as near as at present can be gathered, is also supposed to be 21,200 or thereabout.

CHAPTER XV

And now all you whose affections are taken with wonderful matters, attend, and you that think Christ hath forgotten his poor despised people, behold, and all you that hopefully long for Christ's appearing to confound Antichrist, consider, and rejoice all ye his churches the world throughout, for the Lamb is preparing his Bride, and oh ye the ancient Beloved of Christ, whom he of old led by the hand from Egypt to Canaan, through that great and terrible wilderness, look here, behold him whom you have pierced, preparing to pierce your hearts with his *Wonder-Working Providence*. If he have showed such admirable acts of his providence toward these, what will he do when the whole nation of English shall set upon reformation according to the direct rule of his word? Assured confidence there is also for all nations, from the undoubted promise of Christ himself.

The winter is passed, the rain is changed and gone. Come out of the holes of the secret places, fear not because your number is but small. Gather into churches, and let Christ be your King. Ye Dutch come out of your hodge-podge, the great mingle-mangle of religion among you hath caused the churches of Christ to increase so little with you. Oh, ye French! Fear not the great swarms of locusts nor the croaking frogs in your land, Christ is reaching out the hand to you. Look what he hath done for these English. Ye Germans that have had such a bloody bickering, Christ is now coming to your aid. Then gather into churches and keep them pure, that Christ may delight to dwell among you. Oh Italy! The seat and center of the beast, Christ will not pick out a people from among you for himself, see here what wonders he works in little time. Oh ye Spaniards and Portugals, Christ will show you the abominations of that beastly whore, who hath made your nations drunk with the wine of her fornication. Dread not that cruel murderous inquisition, for Christ is now making inquisition for them, and behold, here, how he hath rewarded them who dealt cruelly with these his people.

Finally, oh all ye nations of the world, behold great is the work the glorious King of heaven and earth hath in hand. Beware of neglecting the call of Christ. For Christ the great King of all the earth is now going forth in his great wrath and terrible indignation to avenge the blood of his saints. Oh dreadful day, when the patience and long suffering of Christ, that hath lasted so many hundreds of years, shall end. What wondrous works are now suddenly to be wrought for the accomplishment of these things! Then judge all you (whom the Lord Christ hath given a discerning spirit) whether these poor New England people be not the forerunners of Christ's army, and the marvelous providences which you shall now hear, be not the very finger of God, and whether the Lord hath not sent this people to preach in this wilderness, and to proclaim to all nations the near approach of the most wonderful works that ever the sons of men saw. Will you not believe that a nation can be born in a day? Here is a work come very near it, but if you will believe you shall see far greater things than these, and that in very little time. And in the meantime look on the following discourse.

CHAPTER XVII

But to go on with the story, the 12th of July or thereabout, 1630, these soldiers of Christ first set foot on this western end of the world, where arriving in safety, both men, women and children, on the north side of Charles river, they landed near a small island, called Noddle's Island, where one Mr. Samuel Maverick then living, a man of a very loving and courteous behavior, very ready to entertain strangers. On this island he had built a small fort with the help of Mr. David Thompson. On the south side of the river, on a small point of land called Blaxton's Point, planted Mr. William Blaxton. To the southeast of him, near an island called Thompson's Island, lived some few planters more. These persons were the first planters of those parts, having some small trading with the Indians for beaver skins, which moved them to make their abode in those parts, whom these first troops of Christ's army found as fit helps to further their work. At their arrival these small number of Christians gathered at Salem, greatly rejoicing, and the more because they saw so many that came chiefly for promoting the great work of Christ in hand. The Lady Arbella and some other godly women abode at Salem, but their husbands continued at Charlestown, both for the settling the civil government, and gathering another church of Christ. The first court was holden aboard the *Arbella* the 23rd of August, when the much honored John Winthrop, Esq., was chosen Governor for the remainder of that year, 1630. Also, the worthy Thomas Dudley, Esq., was chosen Deputy Governor, and Mr. Simon Bradstreet, Secretary. The people after their long voyage were many of them troubled with the scurvy, and some of them died. The first station they took up was at Charlestown, where they pitched some tents of cloth. Others built them small huts, in which they lodged their wives and children. The first beginning of this work seemed very dolorous. First, for the death of that worthy personage Isaac Johnson, Esq., whom the Lord had endowed with many precious gifts, insomuch that he was had in high esteem among all the people of God, and as a chief pillar to support this new erected building. He very much rejoiced at his death that the Lord had been pleased to keep his eyes open so long as to see one church of Christ gathered before his death, at whose departure there was not only many weeping eyes, but some fainting hearts, fearing the fall of the present work.

The grief of this people was further increased by the sore sickness which befell among them, so that almost in every family lamentation, mourning, and woe was heard, and no fresh food to be had to cherish them. It would assuredly have moved the most locked-up affections to tears no doubt, had they passed from one hut to another and beheld the piteous case these people were in. And that which added to their present distress was the want of fresh water, for although the place did afford plenty, yet for present they could find but one spring, and that not to be come at but when the tide was down, which caused many to pass over to the south side of the river, where they afterward erected some other towns. Yet most admirable it was to see with what Christian courage many of these soldiers of Christ carried it amidst all these calamities, and in October, the Governor, Deputy and Assistants held their second court on the south side of the river, where they then began to build, holding correspondency with Charlestown as one and the same.

At this court many of the first planters came, and were made free, yet afterward none were admitted to this fellowship or freedom but such as were first joined in fellowship with some of the churches of Christ, their chiefest aim being bent to promote his work altogether. The number of freemen this year was 110, or thereabout.

CHAPTER XIX

Toward the latter end of this summer (1636) came over the learned, reverend, and judicious Mr. Henry Dunster, before whose coming the Lord was pleased to provide a patron for erecting a college. His provident hand being now no less powerful in pointing out with his unerring finger a president, abundantly fitted this his servant, and sent him over for to manage the work. And as in all the other passages of this history, the Wonder-Working Providence of Sion's Saviour hath appeared, so more in this work, the fountains of learning being in a great measure stopped in our native country at this time.

It being a work (in the apprehension of all whose capacity could reach to the great sums of money the edifice of a mean college would cost) past the reach of a poor pilgrim people, who had expended the greatest part of their estates on a long voyage, not being ignorant also, that many people in this age are out of conceit with learning, and that the greater part of the people wholly devoted to the plough, amidst all these difficulties it was thought meet learning should plead for itself, and plod out a way to live. Hereupon, all those who had tasted the sweet wine of wisdom's drawing and fed on the dainties of knowledge, began to set their wits a work, the end being firmly fixed on a sure foundation, namely, the glory of God and good of his elect people, in vindicating the truths of Christ and promoting his glorious Kingdom. Upon these resolutions to work they go, and with thankful acknowledgement, readily take up all lawful means as they come to hand. For place they fix their eye upon Newtown, which to tell their posterity whence they came is now named Cambridge. And withal to make the whole world understand that spiritual learning was the thing they chiefly desired, to sanctify the other and make the whole lump holy, and that learning being set upon its right object might not contend for error instead of truth, they chose this place, being then under the orthodox and soul-flourishing ministry of Mr. Thomas Shepherd. The situation of this college is very pleasant, at the end of a spacious plain more like a bowling green than a wilderness, near a fair navigable river, environed with many neighboring towns of note. The building thought by some to be too gorgeous for a wilderness, and yet too mean in others' apprehensions for a college, it is at present enlarging by purchase of the neighbor houses. It hath the conveniences of a fair hall, comfortable studies, and a good library. The chief gift towards the founding of this college was by Mr. John Harvard, a reverend minister. The country being very weak in their public treasury, expended about £500 towards it, and for the maintenance thereof gave the yearly revenue of a ferry passage between Boston and Charlestown, the which amounts to about £ 40 or £ 50 per annum. The Commissioners of the four United Colonies also taking into consideration of what common concernment this work would be (not only to the whole plantations in general, but also to all our English nation), they endeavored to stir up all the people in the several colonies to make a yearly contribution toward it, which by some is observed but by the most very much neglected. This college hath brought forth and nursed up very hopeful plants, to the supplying some churches here. The number of students is much increased of late, so that the present year, 1651, on the twelfth of the sixth month, ten of them took the degree of Bachelor of Art. This hath been a place certainly more free from temptations to lewdness than ordinarily England hath been, yet if men shall presume upon this to send their most exorbitant children the justice of God doth sometimes meet with them and the means doth more harden them in their way. For of late, the godly governors of this college have been forced to expel some, for fear of corrupting the fountain.

CHAPTER XXI

Here the reader is desired to take notice of the wonderful providence of the most high God toward these his new-planted churches, such as were never heard of, since that Jacob's sons ceased to be a people. That in ten or twelve years' planting there should be such a wonderful alteration, a nation to be born in a day, a commonwealth orderly brought forth from a few fugitives. All the foreign plantations that are of forty, fifty, or a hundred years standing, cannot really report the like, although they have had the greatest encouragements earth could afford, kings to countenance them, staple commodities to provoke all manner of merchants to resort unto them, silver, gold, precious stones, or whatever might entice the eye or ear to incline the motion of man toward them. This remote, rocky, barren, bushy, wild, woody wilderness, a receptacle for lions, wolves, bears, foxes, racoons, beavers, otters, and all kind of wild creatures, a place that never afforded the natives better than the flesh of a few wild creatures and parched Indian corn inched out with chestnuts and bitter acorns, now through the mercy of Christ become a second England for fertileness, in so short a space that it is indeed the wonder of the world.

First, to begin with the increase of food, you have heard in what extreme penury these people were in at first planting. For want of food, gold, silver, raiment, or whatsoever was precious in their eyes they parted with (when ships came in). But now take notice how the right hand of the most high hath altered all, and now good white and wheaten bread is no dainty. There are not many towns in the country but the poorest person in them hath a house and land of his own, and bread of his own growing, if not some cattle. Beside, flesh is now no rare food, beef, pork, and mutton being frequent in many houses. So that this poor wilderness hath not only equalized England in food, but goes beyond it in some places. Poultry they have plenty, and great rarity, and in their feasts they have not forgotten the English fashion of stirring up their appetites with variety of cooking their food.

Secondly, for raiment our cloth hath not been cut short. The Lord hath been pleased to increase sheep extraordinarily of late. Hemp and flax here is great plenty, hides here are more for the number of persons than in England. Assuredly the plenty of clothing hath caused much excess of late in those persons who have clambered with excess of wages for their work.

Further, the Lord hath been pleased to turn all the wigwams, huts, and hovels the English dwelt in at their first coming, into orderly, fair, and well-built houses, well furnished many of them, together with orchards filled with goodly fruit trees, and gardens with variety of flowers. There are supposed to be in the Massachusetts government at this day, near a thousand acres of land planted for orchards and gardens. Besides, their fields are filled with garden fruit, there being, as is supposed in this colony, about fifteen thousand acres in tillage, and of cattle about twelve thousand neat, and about three thousand sheep. Thus hath the Lord encouraged his people.

CHAPTER XXII

There was a town and church erected called Woburn this present year [1642], but because all the action of this wandering people meet with great variety of censures, the author will in this town and church set down the manner how this people have populated their towns and gathered their churches.

This town, as all others, had its bounds fixed by the General Court, to the contents of four miles square. The grant is to seven men of good and honest report, upon condition that within two years they erect houses for habitation thereon, and so go on to make a town thereof. These seven men have power to give and grant out lands unto any persons who are willing to take up their dwellings within the said precinct, and to be admitted to all common privileges of the said town, giving them such an ample portion, both of meadow and upland, as their present and future stock of cattle and hands were like to improve, with eye had to others that might after come to populate the said town. This they did without any respect of persons, yet such as were exorbitant and of a turbulent spirit, unfit for a civil society, they would reject till they come to mend their matters. Such came not to enjoy any freehold. These seven men ordered and disposed of the streets of the town, as might be best for improvement of the land, and yet civil and religious society maintained. To which end those that had land nearest the place for sabbath assembly, had a lesser quantity at home and more farther off, to improve for corn. They refused not men for their poverty, but according to their ability were helpful to the poorest sort in building their houses, and distributed to them land accordingly. The poorest had six or seven acres of meadow, and twenty-five of upland, or thereabouts. Thus was this town populated, to the number on sixty families, or thereabout, and after this manner are the towns of New England peopled.

Now to declare how this people proceeded in religious matters, and so consequently all the churches of Christ planted in New England. When they came once to hopes of being such a competent number of people as might be able to maintain a minister, they then surely seated themselves and not before, it being as unnatural for a right New England man to live without an able ministry as for a smith to work his iron without a fire. Therefore this people that went about placing down a town, began the foundation stone with earnest seeking of the Lord's assistance, by humbling of their souls before him in days of prayer, and imploring his aid in so weighty a work. Then they address themselves to attend counsel of the most orthodox and ablest Christians, and more especially of such as the Lord had already placed in the ministry, not rashly running together themselves into a church before they had hopes of attaining an officer to preach the word and administer the seals unto them, choosing rather to continue in fellowship with some other church for their Christian watch over them, till the Lord would be pleased to provide. They after some search meet with a young man named Mr. Thomas Carter, then belonging to the church of Christ at Watertown, a reverend, godly man, apt to teach the sound and wholesome truths of Christ. Having attained their desires in hopes of his coming unto them were they once joined in church estate, he exercised his gifts of preaching and prayer among them in the meantime, and more especially in a day of fasting and prayer. Thus these godly people interest their affections one with the other, both minister and people.

After this they make ready for the work, and the 24th of the 6th month, 1642, they assemble together in the morning about eight of the clock. After the Reverend Mr. Syms had continued in preaching and prayer about the space of four or five hours, the persons that were to join in the covenant, openly and professedly before the congregations and messengers of divers neighbor churches, stood forth and first confessed what the Lord had done for their poor souls, by the work of his spirit in the preaching of his word and providences, one by one. And that all might know their faith in Christ was bottomed upon him, as he is revealed in his word, and that from their own knowledge they also declare the same, according to that measure of understanding the Lord had given them, the elders or any other messengers there present questions. Which being done and all satisfied, they, in the name of the churches to which they do belong, hold out the right hand of fellowship unto them, they declaring their covenant, in words expressed in writing to this purpose:

"We that do assemble ourselves this day before God and his people in an unfeigned desire to be accepted of him as a church of the Lord Jesus Christ, according to the rule of the New Testament, do acknowledge ourselves to be the most unworthy of all others, that we should attain such a high grace, and the most unable of ourselves to the performance of anything that is good, abhorring ourselves for all our former defilements in the worship of God, and other ways, and resting only upon the Lord Jesus Christ for atonement, and upon the power of his grace for the guidance of our whole aftercourse, do here in the name of Christ Jesus, as in the presence of the Lord, from the bottom of our hearts agree together through his grace to give up ourselves, first unto the Lord Jesus as our only King, Priest and Prophet, wholly to be subject unto him in all things, and therewith one unto another, as in a church body, to walk together in all the ordinances of the Gospel, and in all such mutual love and offices thereof as toward one another in the Lord. And all this both according to the present light that the Lord hath given us, as also according to all further light which he shall be pleased at any time to reach out unto us out of the word by the goodness of his grace, renouncing also in the same convenant all errors and schisms, and whatsoever byways that are contrary to the blessed rules revealed in the Gospel, and in particular the inordinate love and seeking after the things of the world."

31

Every church hath not the same for words, for they are not for a form of words.

The 22nd of the 9th month following, Mr. Thomas Carter was ordained pastor in presence of the like assembly. After he had exercised in preaching and prayer the greater part of the day, two persons in the name of the church laid their hands upon his head, and said, "We ordain thee, Thomas Carter, to be pastor unto this church of Christ." Then one of the elders present, being desired of the church, continued in prayer unto the Lord for his more especial assistance of this his servant in his work, being a charge of such weighty importance, as is the glory of God and salvation of souls, that the very thought would make a man to tremble in the sense of his own inability to the work. The people having provided a dwelling house, built at the charge of the town in general, welcomed him unto them with joy, that the Lord was pleased to give them such a blessing, that their eyes may see their teachers.

After this there were divers added to the church daily, after this manner: The person desirous to join with the church, cometh to the pastor and makes him acquainted therewith, declaring how the Lord hath been pleased to work his conversion. The pastor, discerning hopes of the person's faith in Christ, although weak, yet if any appear, he is propounded to the church in general for their approbation touching his godly life and conversation, and then by the pastor and some brethren heard again, who make report to the church of their charitable approving of the person. But before they come to join with the church all persons within the town have public notice of it. Then publicly he declares the manner of his conversion and how the Lord hath been pleased by the hearing of his word preached, and the work of his spirit in the inward parts of his soul, to bring him out of that natural darkness which all men are by nature in and under, as also the measure of knowledge the Lord hath been pleased to endow him withal. And because some men cannot speak publicly to edification, through bashfulness, the less is required of such, and women speak not publicly at all. For all that is desired is to prevent the polluting the blessed ordinances of Christ by such as walk scandalously, and that men and women do not eat and drink their own condemnation, in not discerning the Lord's body. After this manner have the churches of Christ had their beginning and progress hitherto. The Lord continue and increase them the world throughout.

4

The Decline of New Netherland

For more than forty years the United Netherlands maintained colonies on the mainland of North America. For much of the first half of the seventeenth century, the Netherlands was a major cultural and commercial center, its bankers, merchants, artists, and scientists attracting the respect and admiration of other Europeans.

The Dutch West India Company, however, owner of the North American grants, was unable to maintain its government, or to get enough settlers for the safety and economic health of its colonies. Despite its magnificent geographical setting, New Netherland lagged far behind the English settlements to the North and South. The following document, signed by eleven opponents of Governor Peter Stuyvesant, reveals some of the reasons why. Angered by a series of grievances, these New Netherlanders sought greater economic freedom, the encouragement of emigration to their province, and a settlement of foreign-boundary disputes. Though the signers, some of whom went to the Netherlands personally to press their case, received a few concessions, no major alterations in the form of government were made; in 1664 the colony fell easily into the hands of the English.

THE REPRESENTATION
OF NEW NETHERLAND

Among all the people in the world, industrious in seeking out foreign lands, navigable waters and trade, those who bear the name of Netherlanders, will very easily hold their place with the first, as is sufficiently known to all those who have in any wise saluted the threshold of history, and as will also be confirmed by the following relation. The country of which we propose to speak, was first discovered in the year of our Lord 1609, by the ship *Half Moon,* of which Hendrik Hudson was master and supercargo—at the expense of the chartered East India Company, though in search of a different object. It was subsequently called New Netherland by our people, and very justly, as it was first discovered and possessed by Netherlanders, and at their cost; so that even at the present day, those natives of the country who

From *The Representation of New Netherland, 1650, Narratives of New Netherland, 1609–1664,* J. Franklin Jameson, ed. (New York 1909), 293–296, 300–306, 319–322, 324, 327, 333–341, 346–347, 352–354.

are so old as to recollect when the Dutch ships first came here, declare that when they saw them, they did not know what to make of them, and could not comprehend whether they came down from Heaven, or were of the Devil. Some among them, when the first one arrived, even imagined it to be a fish, or some monster of the sea, and accordingly a strange report of it spread over the whole land. We have also heard the savages frequently say, that they knew nothing of any other part of the world, or any other people than their own, before the arrival of the Netherlanders. For these reasons, therefore, and on account of the similarity of climate, situation and fertility, this place is rightly called New Netherland.

The land is naturally fruitful, and capable of supporting a large population, if it were judiciously allotted according to location. The air is pleasant here, and more temperate than in the Netherlands. The winds are changeable, and blow from all points, but generally from the southwest and northwest; the former prevailing in summer, and the latter in winter, at times very sharply, but constituting, nevertheless, the greatest blessing to the country as regards the health of the people, for being very strong and pure, it drives far inland or consumes all damps and superfluous moisture.

The land is adapted to the production of all kinds of winter and summer fruits, and with less trouble and tilling than in the Netherlands. It produces different kinds of wood, suitable for building houses and ships, whether large or small, consisting of oaks of various kinds, as post-oak, white smooth bark, white rough bark, gray bark, black bark, and still another kind which they call, from its softness, butter oak, the poorest of all, and not very valuable; the others, if cultivated as in the Netherlands, would be equal to any Flemish or Brabant oaks. It also yields several species of nut wood, such as oil-nuts, large and small; walnut of different sizes, in great abundance, and good for fuel, for which it is much used, and chestnut, the same as in the Netherlands, growing in the woods without order.

The indigenous fruits consist principally of acorns, some of which are very sweet; nuts of different kinds, chestnuts, beechnuts, but not many mulberries, plums, medlars, wild cherries, black currants, gooseberries, hazel nuts in great quantities, small apples, abundant strawberries throughout the country, with many other fruits and roots which the savages use. There is also plenty of bilberries or blueberries, together with ground-nuts and artichokes, which grow under ground. Almost the whole land is full of vines, in the wild woods as well as on the maize lands and flats; but they grow principally near to and upon the banks of the brooks, streams and rivers, which are numerous, and run conveniently and pleasantly everywhere, as if they were planted there. The grapes comprise many varieties, some white, some blue, some very fleshy, and only fit to make raisins of, others on the contrary juicy; some are very large and others small.

The tame cattle are in size and other respects about the same as in the Netherlands, but the English cattle and swine thrive and grow best, appearing to be better suited to the country than those from Holland. They require, too, less trouble, expense and attention; for it is not necessary in winter to look after such as are dry, or the swine, except that in the time of a deep snow they should have some attention. Milch cows also are much less trouble than they are in Holland, as most of the time, if any care be requisite, it is only for the purpose of giving them occasionally a little hay.

The natives are generally well set in their limbs, slender round the waist, broad across the shoulders, and have black hair and dark eyes. They are very nimble and fleet, well adapted to travel on foot and to carry heavy burdens. They are foul and slovenly in their actions, and make little of all kinds of hardships; to which indeed they are by nature and from their youth accustomed. They are like the Brazilians in color, or as yellow as the people who sometimes pass through the Netherlands and are called Gypsies. The men generally have no beard, or very little, which some even pull out. They use very few words, which they first consider well. Naturally they are very modest, simple and inexperienced; though in their actions high-minded enough, vigorous and quick to comprehend or learn, be it right or wrong, whenever they are so inclined. They are not straightforward as soldiers but perfidious, accomplishing all their enterprises by treachery, using many stratagems to deceive their enemies, and usually ordering all their plans, involving any danger, by night. The desire of revenge appears to be born in them. They are very obstinate in defending themselves when they cannot run, which however they do when they can; and they make little of death when it is inevitable, and despise all tortures which can be inflicted upon them while dying, manifesting no sorrow, but usually singing until they are dead. They understand how to cure wounds and hurts, or inveterate sores and injuries, by means of herbs and roots, which grow in the country, and which are known to them. Their clothing, both for men and women, is a piece of duffels or leather in front, with a deer skin or elk's hide over the body. Some have bears' hides of which they make doublets; others have coats made of the skins of raccoons, wild-cats, wolves, dogs, otters, squirrels, beavers and the like, and also of turkey's feathers. At present they use for the most part duffels cloth, which they obtain in barter from the Christians. They make their stockings and shoes of deer skins or elk's hide, and some have shoes made of corn-husks, of which they also make sacks. Their money consists of white and black *zeewant,* which they themselves make. Their measure and valuation is by the hand or by the fathom; but their corn is measured by *denotas,* which are bags they make themselves. Ornamenting themselves consists in cutting their bodies, or painting them with various colors, sometimes even all black, if they are in mourning, yet generally in the face. They hang *zeewant,* both white and black, about their heads, which they otherwise are not wont to cover, but on which they are now beginning to wear hats and caps bought of the Christians. They also put it in their ears, and around their necks and bodies, wherewith after their manner they appear very fine. They have long deer's hair which is dyed red, and of which they make rings for the head, and other fine hair of the same color, to hang from the neck like tresses, of which they are very proud. They frequently smear their skin and hair with different kinds of grease. They can almost all swim. They themselves make the boats they use, which are of two kinds, some of entire trees, which they hollow out with fire, hatchets and adzes, and which the Christians call canoes; others are made of bark, which they manage very skilfully, and which are also called canoes.

Traces of the institution of marriage can just be perceived among them, and nothing more. A man and woman join themselves together without any particular ceremony other than that the man by previous agreement with the woman gives her some *zeewant* or cloth, which on their separation, if it happens soon, he often takes again. Both men and women are utterly unchaste and shamelessly promiscuous in their intercourse, which is the cause of the men so often changing their wives and the women their husbands. Ordinarily they have but one wife, sometimes two or three, but this is generally among the chiefs. They have also among them different conditions of persons, such as noble and ignoble. The men are generally lazy, and do nothing until they become old and unesteemed, when they make spoons, wooden bowls, bags, nets and other similar articles; beyond this the men do nothing except fish, hunt and go to war. The women are compelled to do the rest of the work, such as planting corn, cutting and drawing fire-wood, cooking, taking care of the children and whatever else there is to be done. Their dwellings consist of hickory saplings, placed upright in the ground and bent arch-wise; the tops are covered with barks of trees, which they cut for this purpose in great quantities. Some even have within them rough carvings of faces and images, but these are generally in the houses of the chiefs. In the fishing and hunting seasons, they lie under the open sky or little better. They do not live long in one place, but move about several times in a year, at such times and to such places as it appears best and easiest for them to obtain subsistence.

They are divided into different tribes and languages, each tribe living generally by itself and having one of its number as a chief, though he has not much power or distinction except in their dances or in time of war. Among some there is not the least knowledge of God, and among others very little, though they relate many strange fables concerning Him.

They are in general much afraid of the Devil, who torments them greatly; and some give themselves up to him, and hold the strangest notions about him. But their devils, they say, will have nothing to do with the Dutch. No haunting of spirits and the like are heard of among them. They make offerings to the Devil sometimes, but with few solemnities. They believe in the immortality of the soul. They have some knowledge of the sun, moon and stars, of which they are able to name many, and they judge tolerably well about the weather. There is hardly any law or justice among them, except sometimes in war matters, and then very little. The nearest of blood is the avenger. The youngest are the most courageous, and do for the most part what they please. Their weapons formerly were the bow and arrow, which they employ with wonderful skill, and the cudgel, but they now, that is, those who live near the Christians or have many dealings with them, generally use firelocks and hatchets, which they obtain in trade. They are exceedingly fond of guns, sparing no expense for them; and are so skilful in the use of them that they surpass many Christians. Their food is coarse and simple, drinking water as their only beverage, and eating the flesh of all kinds of animals which the country affords, cooked without being cleansed or dressed. They eat even badgers, dogs, eagles and such like trash, upon which Christians place no value. They use all kinds of fish, which they commonly cook without removing the entrails, and snakes, frogs and the like. They know how to preserve fish and meat until winter, and to cook them with corn-meal. They make their bread of maize, but it is very plain, and cook it either whole or broken in a pestle block.

After Their High Mightinesses, the Lords States General, were pleased, in the year of our Lord 1622, to include this province in their grant to the Honorable West India Company, their Honors deemed it necessary to take into possession so naturally beautiful and noble a province, which was immediately done, as opportunity offered, the same as in all similar beginnings. Since the year of our Lord 1623, four forts have been built there by order of the Lords Directors.

These forts, both to the south and north, are so situated as not only to close and control the said rivers, but also to command the plantations between them, as well as those round about them, and on the other side of the river as far as the ownership by occupation extends. These the Honorable Company declared they owned and would maintain against all foreign or domestic powers who should attempt to seize them against their consent. Yet, especially on the northeast side of New Netherland this has been not at all regarded or observed by the English living to the eastward; for notwithstanding possession was already fully taken by the building and occupation of Fort Good Hope, and there was no neglect from time to time in warning them, in making known our rights, and in protesting against their usurpation and violence, they have disregarded all these things and have seized and possessed, and still hold, the largest and best part of New Netherland, that is, on the east side of the North River, from Cape Cod to within six leagues of the North River, where the English have now a village called Stamford, from whence one could travel in a summer's day to the North River and back again, if one knows the Indian path.

This and similar difficulties these people now wish to lay to our charge, all under the pretence of a very clear conscience, notwithstanding King James, of most glorious memory, chartered the Virginia Companies upon condition that they should remain an hundred miles from each other, according to our reckoning. They are willing to avail themselves of this grant, but by no means to comply with the terms stipulated in it.

In short, it is just this with the English, they are willing to know the Netherlanders, and to use them as a protection in time of need, but when that is past, they no longer regard them, but play the fool with them. This happens so only because we have neglected to populate the land; or, to speak more plainly and truly, because we have, out of regard for our own profit, wished to scrape all the fat into one or more pots, and thus secure the trade and neglect population.

We cannot sufficiently thank the Fountain of all Goodness for His having led us into such a fruitful and healthful land, which we, with our numerous sins, still heaped up here daily, beyond measure, have not deserved. We are also in the highest degree beholden to the Indians, who not only have given up to us this good and fruitful country, and for a trifle yielded us the ownership, but also enrich us with their good and reciprocal trade, so that there is no one in New Netherland or who trades to New Netherland without obligation to them. Great is our disgrace now, and happy should we have been, had we acknowledged these benefits as we ought, and had we striven to impart the Eternal Good to the Indians, as much as was in our power, in return for what they divided with us. It is to be feared that at the Last Day they will stand up against us for this injury. Lord of Hosts forgive us for not having conducted therein more according to our reason; give us also the means and so direct our hearts that we in future may acquit ourselves as we ought for the salvation of our own souls and of theirs, and for the magnifying of thy Holy Name, for the sake of Christ. Amen.

As we shall speak of the reasons and causes which have brought New Netherland into the ruinous condition in which it is now found to be, we deem it necessary to state first the difficulties. We represent it as we see and find it, in our daily experience. To describe it in one word, (and none better presents itself,) it is *bad government,* with its attendants and consequences, that is, to the best of our knowledge, the true and only foundation stone of the decay and ruin of New Netherland. This government from which so much abuse proceeds, is twofold, that is; in the Fatherland by the Managers, and in this country. We shall first briefly point out some orders and mistakes issuing from the Fatherland, and afterwards proceed to show how abuses have grown up and obtained strength here.

The Managers of the Company adopted a wrong course at first, and as we think had more regard for their own interest than for the welfare of the country, trusting rather to flattering than true counsels. This is proven by the unnecessary expenses incurred from time to time, the heavy accounts of New Netherland, the registering of colonies—in which business most of the Managers themselves engaged, and in reference to which they have regulated the trade—and finally the not peopling the country. It seems as if from the first, the Company have sought to stock this land with their own employees, which was a great mistake, for when their time was out they returned home, taking nothing with them, except a little in their purses and a bad name for the country, in regard to its lack of sustenance and in other respects. In the meantime there was no profit, but on the contrary heavy monthly salaries, as the accounts of New Netherland will show.

Had the Honorable West India Company, in the beginning, sought population instead of running to great expense for unnecessary things, which under more favorable circumstances might have been suitable and very proper, the account of New Netherland would not have been so large as it now is, caused by building the ship *New Netherland* at an excessive outlay, by erecting three expensive mills, by brickmaking, by tar-burning, by ash-burning, by salt-making and like operations, which through bad management and calculation have all gone to nought, or come to little; but which nevertheless have cost much. Had the same money been used in bringing people and importing cattle, the country would now have been of great value.

The land itself is much better and it is more conveniently situated than that which the English possess, and if there were not constant seeking of individual gain and private trade, there would be no danger that misfortunes would press us as far as they do.

It is impossible for us to rehearse and to state in detail wherein and how often the Company have acted injuriously to this country. They have not approved of our own countrymen settling the land, as is shown in the case of Jacob Walingen and his people at the Fresh River, and quite recently in the cases at the South River; while foreigners were permitted to take land there without other opposition than orders and protests. It could hardly be otherwise, for the garrisons are not kept complete conformably to the Exemptions, and thus the cause of New Netherland's bad condition lurks as well in the Netherlands as here. Yea, the seeds of war, according to the declaration of Director Kieft, were first sown by the Fatherland; for he said he had express orders to exact the contribution from the Indians; which would have been very well if the land had been peopled, but as it was, it was premature.

Trade, without which, when it is legitimate, no country is prosperous, is by their acts so decayed, that it amounts to nothing. It is more suited for slaves than freemen, in consequence of the restrictions upon it and the annoyances which accompany the exercise of the right of inspection. We approve of inspection, however, so far as relates to contraband.

The Directors here, though far from their masters, were close by their profit. They have always known how to manage their own matters very properly and with little loss, yet under pretext of the public business. They have also conducted themselves just as if they were the sovereigns of the country. As they desired to have it, so it always had to be; and as they willed so was it done. "The Managers," they say, "are masters in Fatherland, but we are masters in this land." As they understand it it will go, there is no appeal. And it has not been difficult for them hitherto to maintain this doctrine in practice; for the people were few and for the most part very simple and uninformed, and besides, they needed the Directors every day. And if perchance there were some intelligent men among them, who could go upon their own feet, them it was sought to oblige.

The bowl has been going round a long time for the purpose of erecting a common school and it has been built with words, but as yet the first stone is not laid. Some materials only are provided. The money nevertheless, given for the purpose, has already found its way out and is mostly spent; or may even fall short, and for this purpose also no fund invested in real estate has ever been built up.

The poor fund, though the largest, contains nothing except the alms collected among the people, and some fines and donations of the inhabitants. A considerable portion of this money is in the possession of the Company, who have borrowed it from time to time, and kept it. They have promised, for years, to pay interest. But in spite of all endeavor neither principal nor interest can be obtained from them.

Flying reports about asylums for orphans, for the sick and aged, and the like have occasionally been heard, but as yet we can not see that any attempt, order or direction has been made in relation to them. From all these facts, then, it sufficiently appears that scarcely any proper care or diligence has been used by the Company or its officers for any ecclesiastical property whatever—at least, nothing as far as is known—from the beginning to this time.

The Administration of Director Stuyvesant in Particular

We wish much we were already through with this administration, for it has grieved us, and we know ourselves powerless; nevertheless we will begin, and as we have already spoken of the public property, ecclesiastical and civil, we will consider how it is in regard to the administration of justice, and giving decisions between man and man. And first, to point as with a finger at the manners of the Director and council. As regards the Director, from his first arrival to this time, his manner in court has been to treat with violence, dispute with or harass one of the two parties, not as becomes a judge, but as a zealous advocate, which has given great discontent to every one, and with some it has gone so far and has effected so much, that many of them dare bring no matter before the court, if they do not stand well or tolerably so with the Director. For whoever has him opposed, has as much as the sun and moon against him. Though he has himself appointed many of the councillors, and placed them under obligation to him, and some pretend that he can overpower the rest by plurality of votes, he frequently puts his opinion in writing, and that so fully that it covers several pages, and then he adds verbally, "Monsieur, this is my advice, if any one has aught to say against it, let him speak." If then any one rises to make objection, which is not easily done, though it be well grounded, His Honor bursts out immediately in fury and makes such gestures, that it is frightful; yea, he rails out frequently at the councillors for this thing and the other, with ugly words which would better suit the fish-market than the council chamber; and if this be all endured, His Honor will not rest yet unless he has his will. To demonstrate this by examples and proof, though easily done, would nevertheless detain us too long; but we all say and affirm that this has been his common practice from the first and still daily continues. And this is the condition and nature of things in the council on the part of the Director, who is its head and president. Let us now briefly speak of the councillors individually. The Vice Director, Lubbert van Dincklagen, has for a long time on various occasions shown great dissatisfaction about many different matters, and has protested against the Director and his appointed councillors, but only lately, and after some others made resistance. He was, before this, so influenced by fear, that he durst venture to take no chances against the Director, but had to let many things pass by and to submit to them. He declared afterwards that he had great objections to them, because they were not just, but he saw no other way to have peace. This man then is overruled. Let us proceed farther. Monsieur la Montagne had been in the council in Kieft's time, and was then very much suspected by many. He had no commission from the Fatherland, was driven by the war from his farm, is also very much indebted to the Company, and therefore is compelled to dissemble. But it is sufficiently known from himself that he is not pleased, and is opposed to the administration. Brian Newton, lieutenant of the soldiers, is the next. This man is afraid of the Director, and regards him as his benefactor. Besides being very simple and inexperienced in law, he does not understand our Dutch language, so that he is scarcely capable of refuting the long written opinions, but must and will say *yes*. Sometimes the commissary, Adrian Keyser, is admitted into the council, who came here as secretary. This man has not forgotten much law, but says that he *lets God's water run over God's field*. He cannot and dares not say anything, for so much can be said against him that it is best that he should be silent. The captains of the ships, when they are ashore, have a vote in the Council; as Ielmer Thomassen, and Paulus Lenaertson, who was made equipment-master upon his first arrival, and who has always had a seat in the council, but is still a free man. What knowledge these people, who all their lives sail on the sea, and are brought up to ship-work, have of law matters and of farmers' disputes any intelligent man can imagine. Besides, the

Director himself considers them so guilty that they dare not accuse others, as will appear from this passage at Curacao, before the Director ever saw New Netherland. As they were discoursing about the price of carracks, the Director said to the minister and others, "Domine Johannes, I thought that I had brought honest ship-masters with me, but I find that I have brought a set of thieves"; and this was repeated to these councillors, especially to the equipment-master, for Captain Ielmer was most of the time at sea. They have let it pass unnoticed—a proof that they were guilty. But they have not fared badly; for though Paulus Lenaertssen has small wages, he has built a better dwellinghouse here then anybody else. How this has happened is mysterious to us; for though the Director has knowledge of these matters, he nevertheless keeps quiet when Paulus Lenaertssen begins to make objections, which he does not easily do for any one else, which causes suspicion in the minds of many. There remains to complete this court-bench, the secretary and the *fiscaal,* Hendrick van Dyck, who had previously been an ensign-bearer. Director Stuyvesant has kept him twenty-nine months out of the meetings of the council, for the reason among others which His Honor assigned, that he cannot keep secret but will make public, what is there resolved. He also frequently declared that he was a villain, a scoundrel, a thief and the like. All this is well known to the *fiscaal,* who dares not against him take the right course, and in our judgment it is not advisable for him to do so; for the Director is utterly insufferable in word and deed. What shall we say of a man whose head is troubled, and has a screw loose, especially when, as often happens, he has been drinking. To conclude, there is the secretary, Cornelius van Tienhoven. Of this man very much could be said, and more than we are able, but we shall select here and there a little for the sake of brevity. He is cautious, subtle, intelligent and sharp-witted—good gifts when they are well used. He is one of those who have been longest in the country, and every circumstance is well known to him, in regard both to the Christians and the Indians. With the Indians, moreover, he has run about the same as an Indian, with a little covering and a small patch in front, from lust after the prostitutes to whom he has always been mightily inclined, and with whom he has had so much to do that no punishment or threats of the Director can drive him from them. He is extremely expert in dissimulation. He pretends himself that he bites when asleep, and that he shows externally the most friendship towards those whom he most hates. He gives every one who has any business with him—which scarcely any one can avoid—good answers and promises of assistance, yet rarely helps anybody but his friends; but twists continually and shuffles from one side to the other. In his words and conduct he is shrewd, false, deceitful and given to lying, promising every one, and when it comes to perform, at home to no one.

Great distrust has also been created among the inhabitants on account of Heer Stuyvesant being so ready to confiscate. There scarcely comes a ship in or near here, which, if it do not belong to friends, is not regarded as a prize by him. Though little comes of it, great claims are made to come from these matters, about which we will not dispute; but confiscating has come to such repute in New Netherland, that nobody anywise conspicuous considers his property to be really safe. It were well if the report of this thing were confined to this country; but it has spread among the neighboring English—north and south—and in the West Indies and Caribbee Islands. Everywhere there, the report is so bad, that not a ship dare come hither from those places; and good credible people who come from thence, by the way of Boston, and others here trading at Boston, assure us that more than twenty-five ships would come here from those islands every year if the owners were not fearful of confiscation. It is true of these places only and the report of it flies everywhere, and produces like fear, so that this vulture is destroying the prosperity of New Netherland, diverting its trade, and making the people discouraged, for other places not so well situated as this, have more shipping. All the permanent inhabitants, the merchant, the burgher and peasant, the planter, the laboring man, and also the man in service, suffer great injury in consequence; for if the shipping were abundant, everything would be sold cheaper, and necessaries be more easily obtained then they are now, whether they be such as the people themselves, by God's blessing, get out of the earth, or those they otherwise procure, and be sold better and with more profit; and people and freedom would bring trade. New England is a clear example that this policy succeeds well, and so especially is Virginia.

Besides this, the country of the Company is so taxed, and is burdened and kept down in such a manner, that the inhabitants are not able to appear beside their neighbors of Virginia or New England, or to undertake any enterprise. It seems—and so far as is known by us all the inhabitants of New Netherland declare—that the Managers have scarce any care or regard for New Netherland, except when there is something to receive, for which reason, however, they receive less.

Although we are well assured and know, in regard to the mode of redress of the country, we are only children, and Their High Mightinesses are entirely competent, we nevertheless pray that they overlook our presumption and pardon us if we make some suggestions according to our slight understanding thereof, in addition to what we have considered necessary in our petition to Their High Mightinesses.

In our opinion this country will never flourish under the government of the Honorable Company, but will pass away and come to an end of itself without benefiting thereby the Honorable Company, so that it would be better and more profitable for them, and better for the country, that they should divest themselves of it and transfer their interests.

To speak specifically. Provision ought to be made for public buildings, as well ecclesiastical as civil, which, in beginnings, can be ill dispensed with. It is doubtful whether divine worship will not have to cease altogether in consequence of the departure of the minister, and the inability of the Company. There should be a public school, provided with at least two good masters, so that first of all in so wild a country, where there are many loose people, the youth be well taught and brought up, not only in reading and writing, but also in the knowledge and fear of the Lord. As it is now, the school is kept very irregularly, one and another keeping it according to his pleasure and as long as he thinks proper. There ought also to be an almshouse and an orphan asylum, and other similar institutions.

The country must also be provided with godly, honorable and intelligent rulers who are not too indigent, or indeed are not too covetous. A covetous chief makes poor subjects. The manner the country is now governed falls severely upon it, and is intolerable, for nobody is unmolested or secure in his property longer than the Director pleases, who is generally strongly inclined to confiscating; and although one does well, and gives the Heer what is due to him, one must still study always to please him if he would have quiet. A large population would be the consequence of a good government, as we have shown according to our knowledge in our petition; and although to give free passage and equip ships, if it be necessary, would be expensive at first, yet if the result be considered, it would be an exceedingly wise measure, if by that means farmers and laborers together with other needy people were brought into the country, with the little property which they have; as also the Fatherland has enough of such people to spare. We hope it would then prosper, especially as good privileges and exemptions, which we regard as the mother of population, would encourage the inhabitants to carry on commerce and lawful trade. Every one would be allured hither by the pleasantness, situation, salubrity and fruitfulness of the country, if protection were secured within the already established boundaries. It would all, with God's assistance, then, according to human judgment, go well, and New Netherland would in a few years be a worthy place and be able to do service to the Netherland nation, to repay richly the cost, and to thank its benefactors.

5

The Good Life
in the Chesapeake

Little is known about the author of the following pamphlet. Hammond claimed to have spent more than twenty years in America participating in the disorders that occurred in Maryland in 1652. He supported the positions of Governor Stone and the Proprietor, Lord Baltimore. For this, he was placed under sentence of death by parliamentary commissioners sent out from England, but he managed to escape.

Much of Hammond's analysis is reminiscent of the promotional literature published some forty years earlier. Like the writers commissioned by the Virginia Company, he insists on the benevolence of the climate, the fertility of the soil, and the possibilities for personal advancement. But emphases have changed somewhat during the four decades of Virginia's history, and Hammond's discussion was meant to appeal to settlers whose values, backgrounds, and purposes varied from the hopes of the early founders.

THE TWO FRUITFULL SISTERS
VIRGINIA AND MARY-LAND
John Hammond

It is the glory of every nation to enlarge themselves, to encourage their own foreign attempts, and to be able to have of their own, within their own territories, as many several commodities as they can attain to, that so others may rather be beholding to them, then they to others; and to this purpose have encouragements, privileges and immunities been given to any discoveries or adventurers into remote colonies, by all politic commonwealths in the world.

But alas, we Englishmen (in all things else famous, and to other countries terrible) do not only fail in this, but villify, scandalize and cry down such parts of the unknown world, as have been found out, settled and made flourishing, by the charge, hazard and diligence of their own brethren, as if because removed from us, we either account them people of another world or enemies.

This is too truly made good in the odiums and cruel slanders cast on those two famous countries of Virginia and Maryland, whereby those countries, not only are many times at a stand, but are in danger to molder away, and come in time to

From John Hammond, *Leah and Rachel, or the Two Fruitfull Sisters Virginia and Mary-Land, Narratives of Early Maryland, 1633–1684*, Clayton C. Hall, ed. (New York, 1910), 283–300.

nothing; nor is there anything but the fertility and natural gratefulness of them left a remedy to prevent it.

To let our own nation (whose common good I covet, and whose commonwealth's servant I am, as born to no other use) be made sensible of these injuries, I have undertaken in this book to give the true state of those places, according to the condition they are now in; and to declare either to distressed or discontented, that they need not doubt because of any rumor detracting from their goodness, to remove and cast themselves and fortunes upon those countries.

In respect these two sister countries (though distinct governments) are much of one nature, both for produce and manner of living; I shall only at present treat of the elder sister Virginia, and in speaking of that include both.

The country is reported to be an unhealthy place, a nest of rogues, whores, dissolute and rooking persons; a place of intolerable labor, bad usage and hard diet, etc.

To answer these several calumnies, I shall first show what it was. Next, what it is.

At the first settling and many years after it deserved most of those aspersions (nor were they then aspersions but truths). It was not settled at the public charge, but when found out, challenged and maintained by adventurers, whose avarice and inhumanity brought in these inconveniences, which to this day brands Virginia.

Then were jails emptied, youth seduced, infamous women drilled in, the provisions all brought out of England, and that embezzled by the trustees (for they durst neither hunt, fowl, nor fish, for fear of the Indian, which they stood in awe of), their labor was almost perpetual, their allowance of victuals small, few or no cattle, no use of horses nor oxen to draw or carry (which labors men supplied themselves), all which caused a mortality; no civil courts of justice but under a martial law, no redress of grievances, complaints were repaid with stripes, moneys with scoffs, tortures made delights, and in a word all and the worst that tyranny could inflict or act. Which when complained of in England (but so were they kept under that it was long ere they would suffer complaints to come home), the bondage was taken off, the people set free, and had lands assigned to each of them to live of themselves and enjoy the benefit of their own industry. Men then began to call what they labored for their own, they fell to making themselves convenient housing to dwell in, to plant corn for their food, to range the woods for flesh, the rivers for fowl and fish, to find out somewhat staple for supply of clothing, to continue a commerce, to purchase and breed cattle, etc. But the bud of this growing happiness was again nipped by a cruel massacre committed by the natives, which again pulled them back and kept them under, enforcing them to get into forts (such as the infancy of those times afforded). They were taken off from planting, their provisions destroyed, their cattle, hogs, horses, etc., killed up, and brought to such want and penury, that diseases grew rife, mortality exceeded. But receiving a supply of men, ammunition and victuals out of England, they again gathered heart, pursued their enemies, and so often worsted them, that the Indians were glad to sue for peace, and they, desirous of a cessation, consented to it.

They again began to bud forth, to spread further, to gather wealth, which they rather profusely spent (as gotten with ease) than providently husbanded or aimed at any public good, or to make a country for posterity. But from hand to mouth, neglecting discoveries, planting of orchards, providing for the winter preservation of their stocks, or thinking of anything staple or firm. And while tobacco, the only commodity they had to subsist on, bore a price, they wholly and eagerly followed that, neglecting their very planting of corn, and much relied on England for the chiefest part of their provisions; so that being not always amply supplied, they were often in such want, that their case and condition being related in England, it hindered and kept off many from going thither, who rather cast their eyes on the barren and freezing soil of New England, than to join with such an indigent and sottish people as were reported to be in Virginia.

Yet was not Virginia all this while without divers honest and virtuous inhabitants, who observing the general neglect and licentiousness there, caused assemblies to be called and laws to be made tending to the glory of God, the severe suppression of vices, and the compelling them not to neglect (upon strict punishments) planting and tending such quantities of corn, as would not only serve themselves, their cattle and hogs plentifully, but to be enabled to supply New England (then in want) with such proportions, as were extreme reliefs to them in their necessities.

From this industry of theirs and great plenty of corn (the main staff of life), proceeded that great plenty of cattle and hogs (now innumerable) and out of which not only New England hath been stocked and relieved, but all other parts of the Indies inhabited by Englishmen.

The inhabitants now finding the benefit of their industries, began to look with delight on their increasing stocks (as nothing more pleasurable than profit), to take pride in their plentifully furnished tables, to grow not only civil but great observers of the Sabbath, to stand upon their reputations, and to be ashamed of that notorious manner of life they had formerly lived and wallowed in.

They then began to provide and send home for gospel ministers, and largely contributed for their maintenance; but Virginia savoring not handsomely in England, very few of good conversation would adventure thither, (as thinking it a place wherein surely the fear of God was not), yet many came, such as wore black coats, and could babble in a pulpit, roar in a tavern, exact from their parishioners, and rather by their dissoluteness destroy than feed their flocks.

Loath was the country to be wholly without teachers, and therefore rather retain these than to be destitute; yet still endeavors for better in their places, which were obtained, and these wolves in sheep's clothing, by their assemblies questioned, silenced, and some forced to depart the country.

Then began the gospel to flourish; civil, honorable, and men of great estates flocked in; famous buildings went forward, orchards innumerable were planted and preserved; tradesmen set on work and encouraged, staple commodities, as silk, flax, potash, etc. of which I shall speak further hereafter, attempted on, and with good success brought to perfection; so that this country which had a mean beginning, many back friends, two ruinous and bloody massacres, hath by God's grace outgrown all, and is become a place of pleasure and plenty.

And having briefly laid down the former state of Virginia, in its infancy, and filth, and the occasion of its scandalous aspersions, I come to my main subject, its present condition and happiness (if anything can be justly called happy in this transitory life otherwise than as blessings which in the well using whereof, a future happiness may be expected).

I affirm the country to be wholesome, healthy, and fruitful; and a model on which industry may as much improve itself in, as in any habitable part of the world; yet not such a lubberland as the fiction of the land of ease is reported to be.

In the country's minority, and before they had well cleared the ground to let in air (which now is otherwise), many imputed the stifling of the woods to be cause of such sickness, but I rather think the contrary. For divers new rivers lately settled, were at their first coming upon them as woody as James River, the first place they settled in, and yet those rivers are as healthy as any former settled place in Virginia or England itself. I believe (and that not without reason) it was only want of such diet, good drinks, and wholesome lodgings as best agreed with our English natures, which were the cause of so much sickness as were formerly frequent, which we have now amended and therefore enjoy better health. To which I add, and that by experience since my coming into England (and many if not all Virginians can do the like), that change of air does much alter the state of our bodies, by which many travelers thither may expect some sickness, yet little danger of mortality.

If any are minded to repair thither, if they are not in a capacity to defray their own charges let them not be seduced by those mercenary spirits that know little of the place, nor aim at any good of theirs, but only by foisting and flattering them to gain a reward of those they procure them for. Beware them.

Let such as are so minded not rashly throw themselves upon the voyage, but observe the nature, and enquire the qualities of the persons with whom they engage to transport themselves, or if (as not acquainted with such as inhabit there, but go with merchants and mariners, who transport them to others), let their convenant be such, that after their arrival they have a fortnight's time assigned them to enquire of their master, and make choice of such as they intend to expire their time with, nor let that brand of selling of servants be any discouragement to deter any from going, for if a time must be served, it is all one with whom it be served, provided they be people of honest repute, with which the country is well replenished.

And be sure to have your contract in writing and under hand and seal, for if you go over upon promise made to do this or that, or to be free or your own men, it signifies nothing, for by a law of the country (waiving all promises) any one coming in, and not paying their own passages, must serve if men or women four years, if younger according to their years, but where an indenture is, that is binding and observing.

The usual allowance for servants is (besides their charge of passage defrayed) at their expiration, a year's provision of corn, double apparel, tools necessary, and land according to the custom of the country, which is an old delusion, for there is no land customary due to the servant, but to the master, and therefore that servant is unwise that will not dash out that custom in his covenant, and make that due land absolutely his own, which although at the present not of so great consequence, yet will be of much worth, as I shall hereafter make manifest.

47

When you go aboard, expect the ship somewhat troubled and in a hurliburly, until you clear the land's end, and that the ship is rummaged, and things put to rights, which many times discourages the passengers, and makes them wish the voyage unattempted; but this is but for a short season, and washes off when at sea, where the time is pleasantly passed away, though not with such choice plenty as the shore affords.

But when you arrive and are settled, you will find a strange alteration, an abused country giving the lie in your own approbations to those that have calumniated it. And these infallible arguments may convince all incredible and obstinate opinions, concerning the goodness and delightfulness of the country: that never any servants of late times have gone thither, but in their letters to their friends commend and approve of the place, and rather invite than dissuade their acquaintance from coming thither. Another is this, that seldom (if ever) any that hath continued in Virginia any time, will or do desire to live in England, but post back with what expedition they can; although many are landed men in England, and have good estates here, and divers ways of preferments propounded to them, to entice and persuade their continuance.

The labor servants are put to is not so hard nor of such continuance as husbandmen nor handicraftmen are kept at in England. As I said, little or nothing is done in winter time, none ever work before sun rising nor after sun set. In the summer they rest, sleep, or exercise themselves five hours in the heat of the day. Saturday afternoon is always their own, the old holidays are observed and the Sabbath spent in good exercise.

The women are not (as is reported) put into the ground to work, but occupy such domestic employments and housewifery as in England, that is dressing victuals, righting up the house, milking, employed about dairies, washing, sewing, etc., and both men and women have times of recreation, as much or more than in any part of the world besides. Yet some wenches that are nasty, beastly and not fit to be so employed are put into the ground, for reason tells us, they must not at charge be transported and then maintained for nothing, but those that prove so awkward are rather burdensome than servants desirable or useful.

The country is fruitful, apt for all and more than England can or does produce. The usual diet is such as in England, for the rivers afford innumerable sorts of choice fish (if they will take the pains to make wires or hire the natives, who for a small matter will undertake it), winter and summer, and that in many places sufficient to serve the use of man, and to fatten hogs. Water-fowl of all sorts are (with admiration to be spoken of) plentiful and easy to be killed, yet by many degrees more plentiful in some places than in othersome. Deer all over the country, and in many places so many that venison is accounted a tiresome meat; wild turkeys are frequent, and so large that I have seen some weigh near threescore pounds; other beasts there are whose flesh is wholesome and savory, such are unknown to us; and therefore I will not stuff my book with superfluous relation of their names; huge oysters and plenty of them in all parts where the salt water comes.

The country is exceedingly replenished with neat cattle, hogs, goats and tame fowl, but not many sheep; so that mutton is somewhat scarce, but that defect is supplied with store of venison, other flesh and fowl. The country is full of gallant orchards, and the fruit generally more luscious and delightful than here, witness the peach and quince. The latter may be eaten raw savorily, the former differs and as much exceeds ours as the best relished apple we have doth the crab, and of both most excellent and comfortable drinks are made. Grapes in infinite manners grow wild, so do walnuts, chestnuts, and abundance of excellent fruits, plums and berries, not growing or known in England; grain we have, both English and Indian for bread and beer, and peas besides English of ten several sorts, all exceeding ours in England; the gallant root of potatoes are common, and so are all sorts of roots, herbs and garden stuff.

It must needs follow then that diet cannot be scarce, since both rivers and woods afford it, and that such plenty of cattle and hogs are everywhere, which yield beef, veal, milk, butter, cheese and other made dishes, pork, bacon, and pigs, and that as sweet and savory meat as the world affords; these with the help of orchards and gardens, oysters, fish, fowl and venison, certainly cannot but be sufficient for a good diet and wholesome accomodation, considering how plentifully they are, and how easy with industry to be had.

Those servants that will be industrious may in their time of service gain a competent estate before their freedoms, which is usually done by many, and they gain esteem and assistance that appear so industrious. There is no master almost but will allow his servant a parcel of clear ground to plant some tobacco in for himself, which he may husband at those many idle times he hath allowed him and not prejudice but rejoice his master to see it, which in time of shipping he may lay out for commodities, and in summer sell them again with advantage, and get a sow-pig or two, which anybody almost will give him, and his master suffer him to keep them with his own. By that time he is for himself, he may have cattle, hogs and tobacco of his own, and come to live gallantly; but this must be gained (as I said) by industry and affability, not by sloth nor churlish behavior.

And whereas it is rumored that servants have no lodging other than on boards, by the fireside, it is contrary to reason to believe it: first, as we are Christians; next as people living under a law, which compels as well the master as the servant to perform his duty; nor can true labor be either expected or exacted without sufficient clothing, diet, and lodging; all which both their indentures (which must inviolably be observed) and the justice of the country requires.

But if any go thither, not in a condition of a servant, but pay his or her passage, which is some six pounds, let them not doubt but it is money well laid out; yet however let them not fail, although they carry little else, to take a bed along with them, and then few houses but will give them entertainment, either out of courtesy, or on reasonable terms; and I think it better for any that goes over free, and but in a mean condition, to hire himself for reasonable wages of tobacco and provision the first year, provided he happen in an honest house, and where the mistress is noted for a good housewife, of which there are very many (notwithstanding the cry to the contrary) for by that means he will live free of disbursement, have something to help him the next year, and be carefully looked to in his sickness (if he chance to fall sick). And let him so covenant that exceptions may be made, that he work not much in the hot weather, a course we always take with our new hands (as they call them) the first year they come in.

If they are women that go after this manner, that is paying their own passages, I advise them to sojourn in a house of honest repute, for by their good carriage they may advance themselves in marriage, by their ill, overthrow their fortunes. And although loose persons seldom live long unmarried if free, yet they match with as dissolute as themselves, and never live handsomely or are ever respected.

Now for those that carry over families and estates with a determination to inhabit, my advice is that they neither sojourn, for that will be chargeable; nor on the sudden purchase, for that may prove unfortunate; but that they for the first year hire a house (for seats are always to be hired), and by that means they will not only find content and live at a cheap rate, but be acquainted in the country and learn the worth and goodness of the plantation they mean to purchase; and so not rashly entangle themselves in an ill bargain, or find where a convenient parcel of land is for their turns to be taken up.

Yet are the inhabitants generally affable, courteous and very assistant to strangers (for what but plenty makes hospitality and good neighborhood) and no sooner are they settled, but they will be visiting, presenting and advising the stranger how to improve what they have, how to better their way of livelihood.

Justice is there duly and daily administered; hardly can any travel two miles together, but they will find a justice which hath power of himself to hear and determine mean differences, to secure and bind over notorious offenders, of which very few are in the country.

In every county are courts kept, every two months, and oftener if occasion require, in which courts all things are determined without exceptions; and if any dislike the proceedings of those courts, they have liberty to appeal to the Quarter Court, which is four times a year; and from thence to the Assembly, which is once or oftener every year; so that I am confident, more speedy justice and with smaller charge is not in any place to be found.

Theft is seldom punished, as being seldom or never committed; for as the proverb is, where there are no receivers, there are no thieves; and although doors are nightly left open (especially in the summer time), hedges hanging full of clothes, plate frequently used amongst all comers and goers (and there is good store of plate in many houses), yet I never heard of any loss ever received either in plate, linen, or anything else out of their houses all the time I inhabited there.

Indeed I have known some suffer for stealing of hogs, (but not since they have been plentiful) and whereas hogstealing was once punished with death, it is now made penal, and restitution given very amply to the owner thereof.

Cases of murder are punished as in England, and juries allowed, as well in criminal causes, as in all other differences between party and party, if they desire it.

Servants' complaints are freely harkened to, and (if not causelessly made), their masters are compelled either speedily to amend, or they are removed upon second complaint to another service; and oftentimes not only set free (if the abuse merit it), but ordered to give reparation and damage to their servant.

The country is very full of sober, modest persons, both men and women, and many that truly fear God and follow that perfect rule of our blessed Savior, to do as they would be done by; and of such a happy inclination is the country, that many who in England have been lewd and idle, there in emulation or imitation (for example moves more than precept) of the industry of those they find there, not only grow ashamed of their former courses, but abhor to hear of them, and in small time wipe off those stains they have formerly been tainted with. Yet I cannot but confess, there are people wicked enough (as what country is free) for we know some natures will never be reformed, but these must follow the Friar's Rule, *Si non caste, tamen caute* [If not chastely, then at any rate, cautiously]. For if any be known, either to profane the Lord's day, or his name, be found drunk, commit whoredom, scandalize or disturb his neighbor, or give offense to the world by living suspiciously in any bad courses, there are for each of these, severe and wholesome laws and remedies made, provided and duly put in execution. I can confidently affirm, that since my being in England, which is not yet four months, I have been an eye and ear witness of more deceits and villainies (and such as modesty forbids me to utter) than I either ever saw or heard mention made of in Virginia, in my one and twenty years abroad in those parts.

And therefore those that shall blemish Virginia any more, do but like the dog bark against the moon, until they be blind and weary; and Virginia is now in that secure growing condition, that like the moon so barked at, she will pass on her course, maugre [in spite of] all detractors, and a few years will bring it to that glorious happiness, that many of her calumniators will intercede to procure admittance thither, when it will be hard to be attained to. For in small time, little land will be to be taken up; and after a while none at all; and as the mulberry trees grow up, which are by everyone planted, tobacco will be laid by, and we shall wholly fall to making of silk (a sample of 400 lb. hath already been sent for England, and approved of) which will require little labor; and therefore shall have little use of servants. Besides children increase and thrive so well there, that they themselves will sufficiently supply the defect of servants, and in small time become a nation of themselves sufficient to people the country. And few there are but are able to give some portions with their daughters, more or less, according to their abilities; so that many coming out of England have raised themselves good fortunes there merely by matching with maidens born in the country.

And therefore I cannot but admire, and indeed much pity the dull stupidity of people necessitated in England, who rather than they will remove themselves, live here a base, slavish, penurious life; as if there were a necessity to live and to live so, choosing rather than they will forsake England to stuff Newgate, Bridewell and other jails with their carcasses, nay cleave to Tyburn itself, and so bring confusion to their souls, horror and infamy to their kindred or posterity. Others itch out their wearisome lives in reliance of other men's charities, an uncertain and unmanly expectation; some more abhorring such courses betake themselves to almost perpetual and restless toil and drudgeries out of which (while their strength lasts) they (observing hard diets, early and late hours) make hard shift to subsist from hand to mouth, until age or sickness takes them off from labor and directs them the way to beggery, and such indeed are to be pitied, relieved, and provided for.

51

The country is not only plentiful but pleasant and profitable, pleasant in regard of the brightness of the weather, the many delightful rivers on which the inhabitants are settled (every man almost living in sight of a lovely river), the abundance of game, the extraordinary good neighborhood and loving conversation they have one with the other.

Pleasant in their buildings, which although for most part they are but one story besides the loft, and built of wood, yet contrived so delightful, that your ordinary houses in England are not so handsome, for usually the rooms are large, daubed and whitelimed, glazed and flowered, and if not glazed windows, shutters which are made very pretty and convenient.

Pleasant in observing their stocks and flocks of cattle, hogs, and poultry, grazing, whisking and skipping in their sights, pleasant in having all things of their own, growing or breeding without drawing the penny to send for this and that, without which in England they cannot be supplied.

The manner living and trading there is thus: each man almost lives a freeholder, nothing but the value of 12 d. a year to be paid as rent, for every 50 acres of land; firing cost nothing; every man plants his own corn and need take no care for bread; if anything be bought, it is for convenience, exchanged presently, or for a day; payment is usually made but once a year.

In summer when fresh meat will not keep, seeing every man kills of his own, and quantities are inconvenient, they lend from one to another such portions of flesh as they can spare, which is repaid again when the borrower kills his.

If any fall sick, and cannot compass to follow his crop, which if not followed, will soon be lost, the adjoining neighbors will either voluntarily or upon a request join together, and work in it by spells, until the owner recovers, and that gratis, so that no man by sickness lose any part of his year's work.

Let any travel, it is without charge, and at every house is entertainment as in a hostery, and with it hearty welcome are strangers entertained.

In a word, Virginia wants no good victuals, wants not good dispositions, and as God hath freely bestowed it, they as freely impart with it, yet are there as well bad natures as good.

The profit of the country is either by their labor, their stock, or their trade.

By their labors is produced corn and tobacco, and all other growing provisions, and this tobacco however now low-rated, yet a good maintenance may be had out of it (for they have nothing of necessity but clothing to purchase), or can this mean price of tobacco long hold, for these reasons: first that in England it is prohibited, next that they have attained of late those sorts equal with the best Spanish, thirdly that the sickness in Holland is decreasing, which hath been a great obstruction to the sale of tobacco.

And lastly, that as the mulberry tree grows up, tobacco will be neglected and silk, flax, two staple commodities generally fallen upon.

Of the increase of cattle and hogs, which advantage is made, by selling beef, pork, and bacon, and butter etc. either to shipping, or to send to the Barbados, and other islands, and he is a very poor man that hath not sometimes provision to put off.

By trading with Indians for skins, beaver, furs, and other commodities, oftentimes good profits are raised. The Indians are in absolute subjection to the English, so that they both pay tribute to them and receive all their several kings from them, and as one dies they repair to the English for a successor, so that none need doubt it a place of security.

Several ways of advancement there are and employments both for the learned and laborer, recreation for the gentry, traffic for the adventurer, congregations for the ministry (and oh that God would stir up the hearts of more to go over, such as would teach good doctrine, and not paddle in faction, or state matters; they could not want maintenance, they would find an assisting, an embracing, a conforming people).

It is known (such preferment hath this country rewarded the industrious with) that some from being wool-hoppers and of as mean and meaner employment in England have there grown great merchants, and attained to the most eminent advancements the country afforded. If men cannot gain by diligence states in those parts (I speak not only mine own opinion, but divers others, and something by experience) it will hardly be done, unless by mere luck as gamesters thrive, and other accidentals.

Now having briefly set down the present state of Virginia not in fiction, but in reality, I wish the judicious reader to consider what dislike can be had to the country, or upon what grounds it is so infamously injured. I only therein covet to stop those blackmouthed babblers, that not only have and do abuse so noble a plantation, but abuse God's great blessing in adding to England so flourishing a branch, in persuading many souls rather to follow desperate and miserable courses in England, than to engage in so honorable an undertaking as to travel and inhabit there. To those I shall (if admonition will not work on their recreant spirits) only say, "Let him that is filthy be filthy still."

PART TWO

Provincial America, 1660–1754

By 1660 it was clear that the European colonists had made a permanent imprint on the North American continent. The English already possessed thriving settlements in New England and on the Chesapeake, and the next few years would see their conquest of New York, and settlement of Pennsylvania, New Jersey, and the Carolinas as well.

Over the next century something approaching a distinctive life style began to appear in America. There was no easy unity to this pattern, for the colonies differed dramatically among themselves, and even within themselves. New England was becoming famous for its commerce and shipbuilding, its enterprising merchants seizing every opportunity to exploit new routes of trade, but concentrating particularly on the West Indies with their great sugar exports, and on Africa, whose human cargoes of Negro slaves were brought to work the Caribbean and Southern plantations. Cities like Newport and Boston began to acquire the urbane character of cosmopolitan life, although the bulk of New England's population was engaged in agriculture, living in small towns and villages.

To the south of New England lay the middle colonies of New York, New Jersey, and Pennsylvania whose ethnic and religious heritage was quite different. Dutch influences survived in New York long after the weakened West Indies Company was forced to succumb to English expansion. New York City, still lagging in population growth, had nonetheless begun to exploit its superb harbor and its river passage to upper New York and the settlement at Albany. Its merchants, farmers, and fur traders were beginning to give the New Englanders lively competition.

In Pennsylvania, where trade and farming had at least equal opportunities, attention centered on the religious and political innovations of Quakerism. William Penn's colony was certainly the most benevolent proprietorship in North America, its founder insisting on standards of religious tolerance and compassion for the Indians, which were unprecedented in the New World. The city of Philadelphia, with its grid pattern lying between the waters of the Schuylkill and the Delaware, would develop into the most famous city in British North America, and one of the largest in the British Empire, by 1750. Its greatest figure, Benjamin Franklin, pioneered in the establishment of municipal conveniences like fire fighting and care for the sick, and his program of cooperative benevolence would attract interest and support from many other parts of the colonies.

Virginia, the Carolinas, and Georgia, which was founded by James Oglethorpe and his associates as a refuge for imprisoned debtors, possessed fewer towns of importance than their northern neighbors. Their populations had become divided into two distinct and contrasting portions: slave and free. Although many Southerners were suspicious about the legitimacy and future effects of Negro slavery, and some even tried to prohibit the institution by law, the economic advantages of involuntary labor on the growing tobacco, rice, and sugar plantations proved too attractive. The indentured servants, who at one time found the Chesapeake area hospitable to small farming and increasing incomes, were forced to compete with this new labor force, and many of the small farmers went northward to Pennsylvania.

America had begun to attract travelers. Roads were still very poor and communication difficult, but a network of transportation and information exchanges was developing. Wealth in planting or commerce allowed the construction of comfortable and fashionable houses in some parts of the colonies, while cities like Charleston, Boston, and Newport were centers of varied social entertainments. Travelers noted the differences among the various provinces, in religion, language, occupation, and politics, but they could have noted similarities as well.

Provincial Americans shared many experiences, not the least of which was their dependent status upon the British Government. With the Glorious Revolution of 1688, the Protestant succession ended the dangers of Catholic monarchy, and the government at home acquired new direction and vigor. But the instabilities and disorders of the 1670s and 1680s in England were matched by the series of conflicts and insurrections in America. New York, Massachusetts, and Virginia were plagued by the most memorable disorders. Although the issues were frequently confused and local, they all bore on the problem of administering political order while the real source of power was thousands of miles away. In the eighteenth century royal governors found their task increasingly difficult, as colonial assemblies gained assurance and political skill, and demanded more important roles for themselves. The colonies also began to discover special interests, particularly in trading and currency regulations, which put them in opposition to the needs of the home government. Administrators, even the most talented, were hard pressed to satisfy both British officials and powerful local magnates whose antagonism to government could paralyze the programs and shrink the patronage of the British ministers.

A more constructive bond of union was religion. Although the colonies contained a number of religious minorities, including some Catholics and Jews, the vast bulk of the population was Protestant, and often aggressively so. In the late seventeenth century vestiges of the faith in their religious destiny, which had inspired the first Pilgrims and Puritans, lingered on in New England. Theology still provided a filter through which experience could be drawn, and the Salem witch trials of 1691 were a revelation of just how deep and persistent were older ways of viewing reality.

But the witch trials were a late expression, perhaps even a final one, of the old world view. Several prominent Puritans involved repudiated their actions and made public confessions to atone for their guilt. More and more, in the early eighteenth century, the colonists turned their attention to economic matters. The growth of towns, the increase of shipping, and the development of small manufacturing presented fertile fields to imaginative speculators who could overcome religious scruples in pursuing economic goals, even to the point of practicing deceit. In the first years of the eighteenth century many bemoaned the lack of religious fervor in America as an indication of degeneration since the heroic days of the founders.

The religious impulse was far from dead, however; its focus merely shifted. Where once men had followed deferentially the teachings of their ministers and religious leaders, they now demanded more intense personal experiences. Instead of a highly intellectualized theological preaching, they began to respond to more emotional and even theatrical sermons, searching for salvation in an aggressive, occasionally violent, fashion. The revivals, which attracted some attention in the 1720s, spread gradually, until by the 1740s with the visit of the noted British evangelist, George Whitefield, they were surging through all the colonies. The issues of the Great Awakening—itinerant preaching, lay participation, emotional conversions—divided the older churches into battling sects and splintered established denominations into separate and antagonistic groups. By moving over so large an area, however, and involving so many groups of people, the Awakening established new and less tangible bonds of union among the Protestants scattered along the seaboard and helped prepare them for the democratic nationalism just thirty years away.

Another factor emphasizing religious unity was the presence of French power, to the north and west of the English colonies. Until their defeat in the Seven Years' War, the French posed a threat to the physical and spiritual security of the colonists. Since the end of the seventeenth century a staple of colonial literature had been the captivity narrative, detailed and sometimes horrifying descriptions of life spent among the heathen Indians or the Papist French. The Indians practiced physical torture; the French inflicted religious torment. The presence of these perceived dangers made the colonists more aware of the power of British arms, and sustained their loyalties to the distant crown. But when the danger was diminished, after midcentury, there would come more severe tests of their loyalty.

A final bond of union was less physical or religious than intellectual. In communication with the European intellectual world, Americans had begun, by the middle of the eighteenth century, to receive some of the invigorating ideas which were part of the intellectual excitement known as the Enlightenment. Combining foreign inspiration with a native heritage, civic philosophers like Benjamin Franklin utilized the new newspapers and the growing printing industry to disseminate plans of benevolence throughout the distant colonies. With the immediate physical tasks apparently accomplished, there was time to consider the demands of mind and manners. Having conquered the wilderness, Americans were now searching for ways to express their position in the world. Aggressive merchants, ambitious lawyers and administrators, enterprising artisans, and industrious scholars were beginning to yearn for a larger theatre of action. By 1750, these outposts of empire had acquired distinctive economic goals and were beginning to discover the meaning of their colonizing experience. The era of the Revolution lay just ahead.

6

Travels
through New Netherland

Jasper Danckaerts was born at Flushing, in the Netherlands, in 1639. He was a member of a Protestant sect known as the Labadists, and came to America in 1679 to seek a site for his coreligionists. He found a suitable location in Maryland and helped settle a Labadist colony there in 1683. The pietist community never attracted many people and ceased to exist as a separate entity early in the eighteenth century. Danckaerts was naturalized in Maryland in 1684, but he returned to the Netherlands and died there, at Middelburg, between 1702 and 1704.

While engaged on his search for land, Danckaerts kept a journal of his experiences and observations. He traveled up and down the Eastern seaboard, and his interest in even the most trivial and ordinary occurrences of daily life provides a valuable record of the contrasts among the North American settlements and their relations both with the Indians and among each other.

JOURNAL OF JASPER DANCKAERTS

Having then fortunately arrived, by the blessing of the Lord, before the city of New York, on Saturday, the 23d day of September, we stepped ashore about four o'clock in the afternoon, in company with Gerrit, our fellow passenger, who would conduct us in this strange place. He had lived here a long time and had married his wife here, although she and his children were living at present at Zwolle. We went along with him, but as he met many of his old acquaintances on the way, we were constantly stopped. He first took us to the house of one of his friends, who welcomed him and us, and offered us some of the fruit of the country, very fine peaches and full grown apples, which filled our hearts with thankfulness to God. This fruit was exceedingly fair and good, and pleasant to the taste; much better than that in Holland or elsewhere, though I believe our long fasting and craving food made it so agreeable. After taking a glass of Madeira, we proceeded on to Gerrit's father-in-law's, a very old man, half lame, and unable either to walk or stand, who fell upon the neck of his son-in-law, welcoming him with tears of joy. After we had been here

Reprinted with permission from *Journal of Jasper Danckaerts, 1670–1680*, Bartlett B. James and J. Franklin Jameson, eds. (New York, 1913), 43–45, 65–67, 76–80, 131–137, 266–268, 273–275.

a little while, we left our travelling bag, and went out to take a walk in the fields. It was strange to us to feel such stability under us, although it seemed as if the earth itself moved under our feet as the ship had done for three months past, and our body also still swayed after the manner of the rolling of the sea; but this sensation gradually passed off in the course of a few days. As we walked along we saw in different gardens trees full of apples of various kinds, and so laden with peaches and other fruit that one might doubt whether there were more leaves or fruit on them. I have never seen in Europe, in the best seasons, such an overflowing abundance. When we had finished our tour and given our guide several letters to deliver, we returned to his father-in-law's, who regaled us in the evening with milk, which refreshed us much. We had so many peaches set before us that we were timid about eating them, though we experienced no ill effects from them. We remained there to sleep, which was the first time in nine or ten weeks that we had lain down upon a bed undressed, and able to yield ourselves to sleep without apprehension of danger.

September 24th, Sunday

We rested well through the night. I was surprised on waking up to find my comrade had already dressed himself and breakfasted upon peaches. We walked out awhile in the fine, pure morning air, along the margin of the clear running water of the sea, which is driven up this river at every tide. As it was Sunday, in order to avoid scandal and for other reasons, we did not wish to absent ourselves from church. We therefore went, and found there truly a wild worldly world. I say wild, not only because the people are wild, as they call it in Europe, but because almost all the people who go there to live, or who are born there, partake somewhat of the nature of the country, that is, peculiar to the land where they live. We heard a minister preach, who had come from the up-river country, from Fort Orange, where his residence is, an old man, named Domine Schaets, of Amsterdam.

This Schaets, then, preached. He had a defect in the left eye, and used such strange gestures and language that I think I never in all my life have heard any thing more miserable; indeed, I can compare him with no one better than with one D. van Ecke, lately the minister at Armuyden, in Zeeland, more in life, conversation and gestures than in person. As it is not strange in these countries to have men as ministers who drink, we could imagine nothing else than that he had been drinking a little this morning. His text was, "Come unto me all ye," etc., but he was so rough that even the roughest and most godless of our sailors were astonished.

October, 1679

We went from the city, following the Broadway. Upon both sides of this way were many habitations of negroes, mulattoes and whites. These negroes were formerly the proper slaves of the (West India) Company, but, in consequence of the frequent changes and conquests of the country, they have obtained their freedom and settled themselves down where they have thought proper, and thus on this road, where they have ground enough to live on with their families. We left the village called the Bowery lying on the right hand, and went through the woods to New Harlem, a tolerably large village situated on the south side of the island, directly opposite the place where the northeast creek and the East River come together, situated about three hours' journey from New Amsterdam, as old Harlem, in Europe, is situated about three hours' distance from old Amsterdam. As our guide, Gerrit, had some business here, and found many acquaintances, we remained overnight at the house of one Resolved Waldron, schout (sheriff or constable), of the place, who had formerly lived in Brazil, and whose heart was still full of it. This house was constantly filled with people, all the time drinking, for the most part, that execrable rum. He had also the best cider we have tasted.

October 16th, Monday

I was occupied today in copying my journal. In the morning there came an Indian to our house, a man about eighty years of age, whom our people called Jasper, who lived at Hackensack. Concerning this Indian, our old people related that when they lived on Long Island, it was once a very dear time, no provisions could be obtained, and they suffered great want, so that they were reduced to the last extremity; that God the Lord then raised up this Indian, who went out fishing daily in order to bring fish to them every day. If, when he came to the house he found it alone and they were out working in the fields, he did not fail but opened the door, laid the fish on the floor, and proceeded on his way. For this reason these people possess great affection for him, and have given him the name of Jasper, and also my *nitap,* that is, my great friend. He never comes to Manhattan without visiting them and eating with them, as he now did, as among his old friends. We asked him why he had done so much kindness to these people. "I have always been inclined," he answered, "from my youth up to do good, especially to good people known to me. I took the fish to them because Maneto [Indian spirit] said to me, you must take fish to these people, whispering ever in my ear, 'You must take fish to them.' I had to do it or Maneto would have killed me." Our old woman telling us he sometimes got drunk, we said to him he should not do so any more, that the Great Sakemacker [sachem, lord] who is above, was offended at such conduct and would kill him. "No," said he, laughing as if that were a mistake of ours, "it is Maneto who kills those who do evil, and leaves those who do good at peace." "That is only," we replied, "because Maneto is the slave and executioner of the Great Sakemacker above;" and we then asked him if he believed there was such a great and good *sakemacker* there? "Undoubtedly," he said, "but he remains above, and does not trouble himself with the earth or earthly things, because he does nothing except what is good; but Maneto, who also is a *sakemacker,* is here below, and governs all, and punishes and torments those men who do evil and drink themselves drunk." Hereupon we inquired of him why he did so then. "Yes," he said, "I had rather not, but my heart is so inclined that it causes me to do it, although I know it is wrong. The Christians taught it to us, and give us or sell us the drink, and drink themselves drunk." We said to him: "Listen! if we came to live near you, you would never see us drunk, nor would we give or sell you or your people any rum." "That," he replied, "would be good." We told him he must not make such a difference between himself and a Christian, because one was white and the other red, and one wore clothes and the other went almost naked, or one was called a Christian and the other an Indian, that this great and good Sakemacker was the father of us all, and had made us all, and that all who did not do good would be killed by Maneto whether they were called Christians or Indians; but that all who should do good would go to this good *sakemacker* above. "Yes," said he, "we do not know or speak to this *sakemacker,* but Maneto we know and speak to, but you people, who can read and write, know and converse with this *sakemacker.*"

We asked him, where he believed he came from? He answered from his father. "And where did your father come from?" we said, "and your grandfather and great-grandfather, and so on to the first of the race?" He was silent for a little while, either as if unable to climb up at once so high with his thoughts, or to express them without help, and then took a piece of coal out of the fire where he sat, and began to write upon the floor. He first drew a circle, a little oval, to which he made four paws or feet, a head and a tail. "This," said he, "is a tortoise, lying in the water around it," and he moved his hand round the figure, continuing, "This was or is all water, and so at first was the world or the earth, when the tortoise gradually raised its round back up high, and the water ran off of it, and thus the earth became dry." He then took a little straw and placed it on end in the middle of the figure, and proceeded, "The earth was now dry, and there grew a tree in the middle of the earth, and the root of this tree sent forth a sprout beside it and there grew upon it a man, who was the first male. This man was then alone, and would have remained alone; but the tree bent over until its top touched the earth, and there shot therein another root, from which came forth another sprout, and there grew upon it the woman, and from these two are all men produced." We gave him four fish-hooks with which he was much pleased, and immediately calculated how much in money he had obtained. After eating something, he departed.

But at noon he returned with a young Indian, both of them so drunk they could not speak, and having a calabash of liquor with them. We chided him, but to no purpose, for he could neither use his reason nor speak so as to be understood. The young Indian with him was a *sackemaker*'s son, and was bold. He wanted to have a piece of meat that was on the table, and on which we all had to make our dinner, when we told him it was not for him. "Yes," said he, "I see it is so;" nevertheless, and although we offered him something else to eat, he was evilly disposed and dissatisfied, and would take nothing except the piece of meat alone; but that was not given to him. Whereupon Jasper told him he must be quiet, that the old people and we were all his *nitaps*, and by degrees quieted him, they setting together by the fire and drinking their rum. They left afterwards for Long Island.

I must here remark, in passing, that the people in this city, who are almost all traders in small articles, whenever they see an Indian enter the house, who they know has any money, they immediately set about getting hold of him, giving him rum to drink, whereby he is soon caught and becomes half a fool. If he should then buy any thing, he is doubly cheated, in the wares, and in the price. He is then urged to buy more drink, which they now make half water, and if he cannot drink it, they drink it themselves. They do not rest until they have cajoled him out of all his money, or most of it; and if that cannot be done in one day, they keep him, and let him lodge and sleep there, but in some out of the way place, down on the ground, guarding their merchandise and other property in the meantime, and always managing it so that the poor creature does not go away before he has given them all they want. And these miserable Christians are so much the more eager in this respect, because no money circulates among themselves, and they pay each other in wares, in which they are constantly cheating and defrauding each other. Although it is forbidden to sell the drink to the Indians, yet every one does it, and so much the more earnestly, and with so much greater and burning avarice, that it is done in secret. To this extent and further, reaches the damnable and insatiable covetousness of most of those who here call themselves Christians. Truly, our hearts grieved when we heard of these things, which call so grievously upon the Supreme Judge for vengeance. He will not always let His name be so profaned and exposed to reproach and execration.

December 15th, Friday

It was flood tide early this morning, and our servant slept a little too long, for it was not far from high water when he appeared. We hurried, however, into the boat and pushed on as hard as we could, but the flood stopped running, when we were about half way. We continued on rowing, and as the day advanced we caught a favorable wind from the west and spread the sail. The wind gradually increasing brought us to Newcastle about eight o'clock among our kind friends again, where we were welcome anew. We were hardly ashore before the wind, changing from the west to the northwest, brought with it such a storm and rain that, if we had still been on the water, we should have been in great peril. We here again so clearly perceived the providence of the Lord over us, that our hearts were constrained to ascend to Him, and praise Him for what He is and does, especially towards His children. As we have confined ourselves quite strictly to the account of our journey, we deem it serviceable to make some observations upon some general matters concerning Maryland, in addition to what we have before remarked.

As regards its first discoverer and possessor, that was one Lord Baltimore, an English nobleman, in the time of Queen Maria. Having come from Newfoundland along the coast of North America, he arrived in the great bay of Virginia, up which he sailed to its uppermost parts, and found this fine country which he named Maryland after his queen. Returning to England he obtained a charter of the northerly parts of America, inexclusively, although the Hollanders had discovered and began to settle New Netherland. With this he came back to America and took possession of his Maryland, where at present his son, as governor, resides.

As to the present government of Maryland, it remains firm upon the old footing, and is confined within the limits before mentioned. All of Maryland that we have seen, is high land, with few or no meadows, but possessing such a rich and fertile soil, as persons living there assured me that they had raised tobacco off the same piece of land for thirty consecutive years. The inhabitants, who are generally English, are mostly engaged in this production. It is their chief staple, and the money with which they must purchase every thing they require, which is brought to them from other English possessions in Europe, Africa and America. There is, nevertheless, sometimes a great want of these necessaries, owing to the tobacco market being low, or the shipments being prevented by some change of affairs in some quarter, particularly in Europe, or indeed to both causes, as was the case at this time, whereby there sometimes arises a great scarcity of such articles as are

63

most necessary, as we saw when there. So large a quantity of tobacco is raised in Maryland and Virginia, that it is one of the greatest sources of revenue to the crown by reason of the taxes which it yields. Servants and negroes are chiefly employed in the culture of tobacco, who are brought from other places to be sold to the highest bidders, the servants for a term of years only, but the negroes forever, and may be sold by their masters to other planters as many times as their masters choose, that is, the servants until their term is fulfilled, and the negroes for life. These men, one with another, each make, after they are able to work, from 2,500 pounds to 3,000 pounds and even 3,500 pounds of tobacco a year, and some of the masters and their wives who pass their lives here in wretchedness, do the same. The servants and negroes after they have worn themselves down the whole day, and come home to rest, have yet to grind and pound the grain, which is generally maize, for their masters and all their families as well as themselves, and all the negroes, to eat. Tobacco is the only production in which the planters employ themselves, as if there were nothing else in the world to plant but that, and while the land is capable of yielding all the productions that can be raised anywhere, so far as the climate of the place allows. As to articles of food, the only bread they have is that made of Turkish wheat or maize, and that is miserable. They plant this grain for that purpose everywhere.

A few vegetables are planted, but they are of the coarsest kinds and are cultivated in the coarsest manner, without knowledge or care, and they are, therefore, not properly raised, and do not amount to much as regards the production, and still less as to their use. Some have begun to plant orchards, which all bear very well, but are not properly cultivated. The fruit is for the greater part pressed, and makes good cider, of which the largest portion becomes soured and spoiled through their ignorance or negligence, either from not putting it into good casks, or from not taking proper care of the liquor afterwards. Sheep they have none, although they have what is requisite for them if they chose. It is matter of conjecture whether you will find any milk or butter even in summer; we have not found any there at this season of the year. They bestow all their time and care in producing tobacco; each cask or hogshead, as they call it, of which pays two English shillings on exportation, and on its arrival in England, two pence a pound, besides the fees for weighing and other expenses here, and freight and other charges beyond sea. When, therefore, tobacco only brings four or five pence, there is little or nothing left for the owner.

The lives of the planters in Maryland and Virginia are very godless and profane. They listen neither to God nor His commandments, and have neither church nor cloister. Sometimes there is some one who is called a minister, who does not as elsewhere, serve in one place, for in all Virginia and Maryland there is not a city or a village—but travels for profit, and for that purpose visits the plantations through the country, and there addresses the people; but I know of no public assemblages being held in these places; you hear often that these ministers are worse than anybody else, yea, are an abomination.

When the ships arrive with goods, and especially with liquors, such as wine and brandy, they attract everybody, that is, masters, to them, who then indulge so abominably together, that they keep nothing for the rest of the year, yea, do not go away as long as there is any left, or bring anything home with them which might be useful to them in their subsequent necessities. It must therefore go hard with the household, and it is a wonder if there be a single drop left for the future. They squander so much in this way, that they keep no tobacco to buy a shoe or a stocking for their children, which sometimes causes great misery. While they take so little care for provisions, and are otherwise so reckless, the Lord sometimes punishes them with insects, flies, and worms, or with intemperate seasons, causing great famine, as happened a few years ago in the time of the last Dutch war with the English, when the Lord sent so many weevils that all their grain was eaten up as well as almost all the other productions of the field, by reason of which such a great famine was caused that many persons died of starvation, and a mother killed her own child and ate it, and then went to her neighbors, calling upon them to come and see what she had done, and showing them the remains of her child, whereupon she was arrested and condemned to be hung. When she sat or stood on the scaffold, she cried out to the people, in the presence of the governor, that she was now going to God, where she would render an account, and would declare before Him that what she had done she did in the mere delirium of hunger, for which the governor alone should bear the guilt; inasmuch as this famine was caused by the weevils, a visitation from God, because he, the governor, undertook in the preceding summer an expedition against the Dutch residing on the South River, who maintained themselves in such a good posture of defense, that he could accomplish but little; when he went to the Hoere-kill on the west side of that river, not far from the sea, where also he was not able to do much; but as the people subsisted there only by cultivating wheat, and had at this time a fine and abundant harvest in the fields—and from such harvests the people of Maryland generally, and under such circumstances as these particularly, were fed—he set fire to it, and all their other fruits, whether of the trees or the field; whereby he committed two great sins at the same time, namely, against God and His goodness, and against his neighbors, the Dutch, who lost it, and the English who needed it; and had caused more misery to the English in his own country, than to the Dutch in the enemy's country. This wretched woman protesting these words substantially against the governor, before Heaven and in the hearing of every one, was then swung up.

In addition to what the tobacco itself pays on exportation, which produces a very large sum, every hundred acres of land, whether cultivated or not, has to pay one hundred pounds of tobacco a year, and every person between sixteen and sixty years of age must pay three shillings a year. All animals are free of taxation, and so are all productions except tobacco.

It remains to be mentioned that those persons who profess the Roman Catholic religion have great, indeed, all freedom in Maryland, because the governor makes profession of that faith, and consequently there are priests and other ecclesiastics who travel and disperse themselves everywhere, and neglect nothing which serves for their profit and purpose. The priests of Canada take care of this region, and hold correspondence with those here, as is supposed, as well as with those who reside among the Indians. It is said there is not an Indian fort between Canada and

Maryland, where there is not a Jesuit who teaches and advises the Indians, who begin to listen to them too much; so much so, that some people in Virginia and Maryland as well as in New Netherland, have been apprehensive lest there might be an outbreak, hearing what has happened in Europe, as well as among their neighbors at Boston; but they hope the result of the troubles there will determine many things elsewhere. The Lord grant a happy issue there and here, as well as in other parts of the world, for the help of His own elect, and the glory of His name.

July 9th, Tuesday

We started out to go to Cambridge, lying to the northeast of Boston, in order to see their college and printing office. We left about six o'clock in the morning, and were set across the river at Charlestown. We followed a road which we supposed was the right one, but went full half an hour out of the way, and would have gone still further, had not a negro who met us, and of whom we inquired, disabused us of our mistake. We went back to the right road, which is a very pleasant one. We reached Cambridge about eight o'clock. It is not a large village, and the houses stand very much apart. The college building is the most conspicuous among them. We went to it, expecting to see something unusual, as it is the only college, or would-be academy of the Protestants in all America, but we found ourselves mistaken. In approaching the house we neither heard nor saw anything mentionable; but, going to the other side of the building, we heard noise enough in an upper room to lead my comrade to say, "I believe they are engaged in disputation." We entered and went up stairs, when a person met us, and requested us to walk in, which we did. We found there eight or ten young fellows, sitting around, smoking tobacco, with the smoke of which the room was so full, that you could hardly see; and the whole house smelt so strong of it that when I was going up stairs I said, "It certainly must be also a tavern." We excused ourselves, that we could speak English only a little, but understood Dutch or French well, which they did not. However, we spoke as well as we could. We inquired how many professors there were, and they replied not one, that there was not enough money to support one. We asked how many students there were. They said at first, thirty, and then came down to twenty; I afterwards understood there are probably not ten. They knew hardly a word of Latin, not one of them, so that my comrade could not converse with them. They took us to the library where there was nothing particular. We looked over it a little. They presented us with a glass of wine. This is all we ascertained there. The minister of the place goes there morning and evening to make prayer, and has charge over them; besides him, the students are under tutors or masters. Our visit was soon over, and we left them to go and look at the land about there. We found the place beautifully situated on a large plain, more than eight miles square, with a fine stream in the middle of it, capable of bearing heavily laden vessels. As regards the fertility of the soil, we consider the poorest in New York superior to the best here. As we were tired, we took a mouthful to eat, and left. We passed by the printing office, but there was nobody in it; the paper sash, however, being broken, we looked in, and saw two presses with six or eight cases of type. There is not much work done there. Our printing office is well worth two of it, and even more.

July 23d, Tuesday

When New Netherland was first discovered by the Hollanders, the evidence is that New England was not known; because the Dutch East India Company then sought a passage by the west, through which to sail to Japan and China; and if New England had been then discovered, they would not have sought a passage there, knowing it to be the main land; just as when New Netherland and New England did become known, such a passage was sought no longer through them, but farther to the north through Davis and Hudson straits. New England is now described as extending from the Fresh River to Cape Cod and thence to Kennebec, comprising three provinces or colonies: Fresh River or Connecticut, Rhode Island and the other islands to Cape Cod, and Boston, which stretches from thence north. They are subject to no one, but acknowledge the king of England for their lord, and therefore no ships enter unless they have English passports or commissions. They have free trade with all countries; but the return cargoes from there to Europe go to England, except those which go secretly to Holland. There is no toll or duty paid upon merchandise exported or imported, nor is there any impost or tax paid upon land. Each province chooses its own governor from the magistracy, and the magistrates are chosen from the principal inhabitants, merchants or planters. They are all Independents in matters of religion, if it can be called religion; many of them perhaps more for the purposes of enjoying the benefit of its privileges than for any regard to truth and godliness. I observed that while the English flag or color has a red ground with a small white field in the uppermost corner, where there is a red cross, they have here dispensed with this cross in their colors, and preserved the rest. They baptize no children except those of the members of the congregation. All their religion consists in observing Sunday, by not working or going into the taverns on that day; but the houses are worse than the taverns. No stranger or traveller can therefore be entertained on a Sunday, which begins at sunset on Saturday, and continues until the same time on Sunday. At these two hours you see all their countenances change. Saturday evening the constable goes around into all the taverns of the city for the purpose of stopping all noise and debauchery, which frequently causes him to stop his search, before his search causes the debauchery to stop. There is a penalty for cursing and swearing, such as they please to impose, the witnesses thereof being at liberty to insist upon it. Nevertheless you discover little difference between this and other places. Drinking and fighting occur there not less than elsewhere; and as to truth and true godliness, you must not expect more of them than of others. When we were there, four ministers' sons were learning the silversmith's trade.

The soil is not as fertile as in the west. Many persons leave there to go to the Delaware and New Jersey. They manure their lands with heads of fish. They gain their living mostly or very much by fish, which they salt and dry for selling; and by raising horses, oxen, and cows, as well as hogs and sheep, which they sell alive, or slaughtered and salted, in the Caribbean Islands and other places. They are not as good farmers as the Hollanders about New York.

As to Boston particularly, it lies in latitude 42° 20′ on a very fine bay. The city is quite large, constituting about twelve companies. It has three churches, or meeting houses, as they call them. All the houses are made of thin, small cedar shingles, nailed against frames, and then filled in with brick and other stuff; and so are their churches. For this reason these towns are so liable to fires, as have already happened several times; and the wonder to me is, that the whole city has not been burnt down, so light and dry are the materials.

7

Leisler's Rebellion

The 1680s was a turbulent decade for many of the American colonies. The indifferent and easygoing attitude of the home government toward the settlements had vanished, as more rigorous navigation acts were put into effect to protect the English interests. With the accession of the Roman Catholic, James II, in 1685, the Americans feared political restrictions as well. As in England, property rights, charter protections, representative institutions, and Protestantism seemed threatened by the new King's aggressiveness.

The news of James's flight to France and the accession of William and Mary was therefore welcomed in America, but poor communications and confusion concerning the source of legitimate authority plunged many colonies into disorder. Leisler's Rebellion in New York was one such insurrection. Though many of the issues were local and peculiar to New York, the struggle followed a pattern that can be detected in Massachusetts, Maryland, and Virginia as well.

For some New Yorkers, Leisler was a hero, bent on protecting the Protestant religion and the liberties of Englishmen; for others, he was a greedy and brutal villain. The two versions that follow, the first by an opponent, the second by a follower of Leisler, mirror this disagreement and indicate the bitterness of the struggle.

A LETTER FROM A GENTLEMAN OF THE CITY OF NEW YORK

Sir:

I cannot but admire to hear that some gentlemen still have a good opinion of the late disorders committed by Capt. Jacob Leisler and his accomplices in New York, as if they had been for his Majesty's service and the security of that province. And that such monstrous falsehoods do find credit, that the persons before in

Reprinted with permission from "A Letter from a Gentleman of the City of New York (1689)" and from "Loyalty Vindicated from the Reflections of a Virulent Pamphlet called A Letter from a Gentleman of New York (1698)" in *Narratives of the Insurrections, 1675–1690*, Charles M. Andrews, ed. (New York, 1915, 1952), 360–370, 375–377, 393–394.

commission who did labor to oppose and prevent these disorders were Jacobites, or persons ill affected to the happy revolution in England. But it has been often the calamity of all ages to palliate vice with false glosses, and to criminate the best actions of the most virtuous and most pious men. So that truth and innocency, without some defence, has not proved at all times a sufficient bulwark against malicious falsehoods and calumnies. Wherefore I shall endeavor to give you a true and brief account of that matter, as I myself have been a personal witness to most of them.

It was about the beginning of April, 1689, when the first reports arrived at New York that the Prince of Orange, now his present Majesty, was arrived in England with considerable forces, and that the late King James was fled into France, and that it was expected war would be soon proclaimed between England and France.

The Lieut. Governor, Francis Nicholson, and the Council, being Protestants, resolved thereupon to suspend all Roman Catholics from command and places of trust in the government, and accordingly suspended Major Baxter from being a member of Council and captain of a company at Albany, and Bartholomew Russell from being ensign in the fort at New York, they both being Papists who forthwith left their command and departed the province.

And because but three members of the Council were residing in New York, viz., Mr. Frederick Phillips, Col. Stephanus Cortlandt, and Col. Nicholas Bayard, all of Dutch birth, all members, and the two last for the space of near thirty years past, elders and deacons of the Dutch Protestant Church in New York, and most affectionate to the Royal House of Orange, it was resolved by the said Lieut. Governor and Council, to call and convene to their assistance all the justices of the peace and other civil magistrates, and the commission officers in the province, to consult and advise with them what might be proper for the preservation of the peace and the safety of said province, till orders should arrive from England.

Whereupon the said justices, magistrates and officers were accordingly convened and styled by the name of The General Convention for the Province of New York. And all matters of government were carried on and managed by the major vote of that Convention.

And in the first place it was by them agreed and ordered forthwith to fortify the city of New York.

And that for the better security of the fort (since the garrison was weak, and to prevent all manner of doubts and jealousies) a competent number of the city militia should keep guard in said fort, and Nicholas Bayard, colonel of said militia, recommended to give suitable orders accordingly.

And that the revenue should be continued and received by some gentlemen appointed by that Convention, for repairing the fort and fortifying of the city. But against this order Capt. Leisler (who as a captain was a member of that Convention) did enter his dissent, with some few others.

About the middle of May the ship *Beaver* being ready to sail for England, the Lieut. Governor and Council sent in her letters to the Earl (now Duke) of Shrewsbury, then Principal Secretary of State, and to the Lords of the Committee for Trade and Plantations, wherein they signified their rejoicing at the news of his

Royal Highness the Prince of Orange, now his present Majesty's, arrival in England, in order to redress the grievances of the nation.

But against expectation it soon happened that on the last day of said month of May Captain Leisler, having a vessel with some wines in the road [harbor], for which he refused to pay the duty, did in a seditious manner stir up the meanest sort of the inhabitants (affirming that King James being fled the Kingdom, all manner of government was fallen in this province) to rise in arms and forcibly possess themselves of the fort and stores, which accordingly was effected whilst the Lieut. Governor and Council, with the Convention, were met at the City Hall to consult what might be proper for the common good and safety. Where a party of armed men came from the fort and forced the Lieut. Governor to deliver them the keys, and seized also in his chamber a chest with £773, 12 shillings, in money of the government. And though Col. Bayard, with some others appointed by the Convention, used all endeavors to prevent these disorders, all proved vain. For most of those that appeared in arms were drunk, and cried out they disowned all manner of Government. Whereupon, by Capt. Leisler's persuasion, they proclaimed him to be their commander, there being then no other commission officer amongst them.

Capt. Leisler being in this manner possessed of the fort, took some persons to his assistance which he called the Committee of Safety. And the Lieut. Governor, Francis Nicholson, being in this manner forced out of his command, for the safety of his person, which was daily threatened, withdrew out of the province.

About a week after, reports came from Boston that their Royal Highnesses, the Prince and Princess of Orange, were proclaimed King and Queen of England. Whereupon the Council and Convention were very desirous to get that proclamation, and not only wrote for it but some of them hearing that two gentlemen were coming from Connecticut with a copy of said proclamation, went out two days to meet them, in expectation of having the happiness to proclaim it. But Major Gold and Mr. Fitz, missing them, having put the proclamation in Capt. Leisler's hands, he, without taking any notice of the Council or Convention, did proclaim the same, though very disorderly, after which he went with his accomplices to the fort, and the gentlemen of the Council, and magistrates, and most of the principal inhabitants and merchants, went to Col. Bayard's house and drank the health and prosperity of King William and Queen Mary with great expressions of joy.

Two days after, a printed proclamation was procured by some of the Council, dated the 14th of February, 1688, whereby their Majesties confirmed all sheriffs, justices of the peace, collectors and receivers of the revenues, etc., being Protestants, which was forthwith published at the City Hall by the Mayor and Aldermen, accompanied with the Council and most of the chief citizens and merchants. And pursuant thereunto the collector, Matthew Plowman, being a Papist, was forthwith suspended by the Convention, and Col. Bayard, Alderman Paul Richards, Capt. Thomas Winham, and Lieut. John Haynes, merchants, were by them commissionated and appointed to collect the revenue until orders should arrive from England.

But as soon as those gentlemen entered upon the office, Capt. Leisler, with a

71

party of his men in arms and drink, fell upon them at the Custom House, and with naked swords beat them thence, endeavoring to massacre some of them, which were rescued by providence. Whereupon said Leisler beat an alarm, crying about the city, "Treason, Treason," and made a strict search to seize Col. Bayard, who made his escape and departed for Albany, where he stayed all summer in hopes that orders might arrive from England to settle those disorders.

The said Capt. Leisler, finding almost every man of sense, reputation, or estate in the place to oppose and discourage his irregularities, caused frequent false alarms to be made, and sent several parties of his armed men out of the fort, dragged into nasty jails within said fort several of the principal magistrates, officers and gentlemen, and others that would not own his power to be lawful, which he kept in close prison during will and pleasure, without any process or allowing them to bail. And he further published several times, by beat of drums, that all those who would not come into the fort and sign their hands and so thereby to own his power to be lawful, should be deemed and esteemed as enemies to his Majesty and the country, and be by him treated accordingly. By which means many of the inhabitants, though they abhorred his actions, only to escape a nasty jail and to secure their estates, were by fear and compulsion drove to comply, submit and sign to whatever he commanded.

On the 20th of January following, Col. Bayard and Mr. Nicolls had the ill fortune to fall into his hands, and were in a barbarous manner by a party in arms, dragged into the fort and there put into a nasty place, without any manner of process or being allowed to bail, though the same was offered for said Col. Bayard by some of the ablest and richest inhabitants, to the sum of £20,000, either for his appearance to answer, or depart the province, or to go for England. But without any cause given or reasons assigned, laid Col. Bayard in irons, and kept him and Mr. Nicolls close prisoners for the space of fourteen months, where they, with several others that had been long detained prisoners, were set at liberty by Governor Sloughter.

And whilst he kept those gentlemen in prison, he quartered his armed men in their houses, where they committed all manner of outrages. And to give one instance of many others, a party of twelve men were quartered at the house of Col. Bayard with directions to pillage and plunder at discretion, which was bought off with money and plentiful entertainment. But the same day, when that party had received their money, another party came in with naked swords, opened several chambers and chests in said house, and did rob and carry away what money and other goods they found.

It is hardly to be expressed what cruelties Capt. Leisler and his accomplices imposed upon the said prisoners, and all others that would not own his power to be lawful. Neither could the Protestant ministers in the province escape their malice and cruelty, for Mr. Selyns, minister of New York, was most grossly abused by Leisler himself in the church at the time of divine service, and threatened to be silenced, etc.

None in the province but those of his faction had any safety in their estates. For said Capt. Leisler, at will and pleasure, sent to those who disapproved of his actions to furnish him with money, provisions, and what else he wanted, and upon denial sent armed men out of the fort, and forcibly broke open several houses, shops, cellars, vessels, and other places where they expected to be supplied, and without any the least payment or satisfaction, carried their plunder to the fort. All which was extremely approved of by those poor fellows which he had about him, and was forced to feed and maintain. And so he styled those his robberies with the gilded name and pretense, that it was for their Majesties King William and Queen Mary's special service, though it was after found out that whole cargoes of those stolen goods were sold to his friends in the city, and shipped off for the West Indies and elsewhere.

In this manner he, the said Leisler, with his accomplices, did force, pillage, rob and steal from their Majesties' good subjects within this province, almost to their utter ruin, vast sums of money, and other effects, the estimation of the damages done only within this city of New York amounting, as by account may appear, to the sum of £13,959, besides the rapines, spoils and violences done in several parts of the province.

And thus you may see how he used and exercised an exorbitant, arbitrary and unlawful power over the persons and estates of his Majesty's good subjects here, against the known and fundamental laws of the land, and in subversion of the same, to the great oppression of his Majesty's subjects, and to the apparent decay of trade and commerce.

In this calamity, misery and confusion was this province by those disorders enthralled near the space of two years, until the arrival of his Majesty's forces under the command of Major Ingoldsby, who, with several gentlemen of the Council, arrived about the last day of January, 1690–1, which said gentlemen of the Council, for the preservation of the peace, sent and offered to said Leisler, that he might stay and continue his command in the fort, only desiring for themselves and the King's forces quietly to quarter and refresh themselves in the city, till Governor Sloughter should arrive. But the said Leisler, instead of complying, asked Mr. Brooke, one of his Majesty's Council, who were appointed of the Council in this province, and Mr. Brooke, having named Mr. Phillips, Col. Cortland and Col. Bayard, he fell into a passion and cried, "What! Those Papist dogs, rogues! Sacrament! If the King should send three thousand such I would cut them all off." And without any cause given, he proclaimed open war against them. Whereupon they, for self-preservation, protection of the King's forces and stores, and the safety of the city, were necessitated to persuade to their assistance several of their Majesties' good subjects then in opposition against the said Leisler, with no other intent, as they signified to him by several letters and messages, but only for self-security and defense. Yet notwithstanding, the said Leisler proceeded to make war against them and the King's forces, and fired a vast number of great and small shot in the city, whereby several of his Majesty's subjects were killed and wounded as they passed in the streets upon their lawful occasions, though no opposition was made on the other side.

At this height of extremity was it when Governor Sloughter arrived on the 19th of March, 1691, who having published his commission from the City Hall with great signs of joy, by firing all the artillery within and round the city, sent thrice to demand the surrender of the fort from Capt. Leisler and his accomplices, which was thrice denied, but upon great threatenings, the following day surrendered to Governor Sloughter, who forthwith caused the said Capt. Leisler, with some of the chief malefactors, to be bound over to answer their crimes at the next Supreme Court of Judicature, where the said Leisler and his pretended secretary Milborne did appear, but refused to plead to the indictment of the grand jury, or to own the jurisdiction of that court. And so after several hearings, as mutes, were found guilty of high treason and murder, and executed accordingly.

Sir, all what is here set down is true, and can be proved and justified by the men of greatest probity and best figure amongst us. If I were to give a particular narrative of all the cruelties and robberies perpetrated upon their majesties' most affectionate subjects in this province, they would fill a volume. There was no need of any revolution here. There were not ten Jacobites in the whole. They were all well known, and the strictest Protestants, and men of best figure, reputation and estates were at the helm, it may plainly be perceived by the several steps and measures were followed at that time.

Many worthy Protestants in England, and other parts of the world, being sincerely devoted to his Majesty's interest, have yet notwithstanding (unacquainted with our circumstances and not duly apprised of the truth) being more easily induced to give credit to the false glosses and calumnies of bypassed and disaffected persons from this province. But in my observation, most gentlemen that have come hither so prepossessed, after some time spent here have been thoroughly convinced of their mistake, and that those men who suffered death did not from pure zeal for their Majesties' interest and the Protestant religion, but being of desperate fortune, thrust themselves into power of purpose to make up their wants by the ruin and plunder of his Majesty's loyal subjects, and were so far engaged in their repeated crimes, that they were driven to that height of desperation, had not the providence of almighty God prevented it, the whole province had been ruined and destroyed.

LOYALTY VINDICATED

It was with great dread known that the late King James was bound in conscience to endeavor to damn the English nation to Popery and slavery, and therefore no wonder (since he made such large steps towards it in his Kingdoms) that he took a particular care of this province, of which he was proprietor, and at one jump leapt over all the bounds and laws of English right and government, and appointed a governor of this Province of New York [Thomas Dongan] who (although he was a person of large endowments of mind) yet gave active obedience to his prince without reserve, and accepted of a commission giving him power with consent of any seven of his Council to make laws and to raise taxes (as the French King doth) without consent of the people, for the Council are nobody but whom he pleases to name. Hereby the will of the prince became the law, and the estates of the subjects became the King's property. And this Governor and Council were the tools to enslave their country.

These things premised do make way for the answer to the bold assertions of the libeller, who had the author printed the letter ten years before, viz., the time of the Revolution, he would have come under the penalty of spreading false news.

In the third page which is the first of the Letter, he declares that Jacob Leisler and his accomplices committed great disorders in the Revolution. And was ever revolution made without them? What, must the noxious humors of the body natural be loosened and put afloat, and very often with pangs and gripes, before the medicament can officiate the discharge? And must not the body politic suffer a convulsion to pluck up spiritual and temporal tyranny that was taking root in it? But I pray explain yourself, was not the Revolution itself the greatest disorder that could be given to you and the Jacobite party? And therefore you need not admire nor wonder that all those that have a good opinion of the Revolution, have so likewise of Jacob Leisler, and other early instruments of it in this province. Nor is it a wonder that it should be credited, that the persons then in commission in New York were Jacobites, and persons ill affected to the Revolution, for their very commissions from King James were expressly contrary to law.

So that this is the full and true account of this tragedy: New York lay under the curse of an absolute government by King James's commission to Sir Edmund Andros. The people took courage on the first news of the Revolution in England, and shook off the oppressors, and declared for the Prince of Orange. The Lieutenant Governor, the Council, and justices of the peace, which met and called themselves a Convention (being officers constituted by King James) would not declare for the Prince of Orange. Wherefore the people did not think themselves safe in their hands, but seized upon the fort and chose Capt. Leisler commander of the fort until circular letters had procured a return of representatives of the freeholders of the several counties of the province, who on their meeting, making a declaration for his present Majesty, did under their hands and seals constitute Capt. Leisler Commander in Chief until the King's pleasure should be known, and likewise appointed him a Council by the name of a Commission of Safety. And in these persons the government was lodged, who proceeded to support themselves by the most moderate methods could be devised.

The Lieutenant Governor hereupon withdraws out of the province, Major Ingoldsby arrives with authority over none but his foot company, and yet demands the fort, which Capt. Leisler durst not deliver to him without betraying his trust both to the King and people. Major Ingoldsby usurps the title Commander in Chief, he issues orders and warrants to the people to rise in arms to assist him to wrest the fort out of Capt. Leisler's hands, and provokes Capt. Leisler's men in the fort to acts of hostility, by which means one or two men were accidentally killed. Col. Sloughter arrives, demands the fort, which was surrendered to him immediately. The persons of Capt. Leisler and Mr. Milborne are seized and soon after brought to trial. Their plea to the jurisdiction of the Court (which could not by law try them for maladministration in government) violently overruled, and they condemned as mutes, for high treason and murder. They were reprieved until his Majesty's pleasure should be known, and notwithstanding the reprieve, the warrant of execution signed, and they executed.

8

The Presence of Witches

Cotton Mather (1663–1728) was one of the most prolific and illustrious ornaments of the Puritan ministry, the son of another famous minister and a president of Harvard College, Increase Mather. The author of innumerable sermons, tracts, histories, and collections of interesting data, Cotton Mather assiduously gathered material to demonstrate the constant interventions of the devil in the affairs of mankind, particularly in New England, which was founded as a holy commonwealth, and therefore, a natural target for evil spirits.

In his zeal to expose the forces of darkness, Mather, like many of his contemporaries, believed implicitly in the existence of witches, men and women who were in the power of the devil and given the ability to torment their fellow human beings. *The Wonders of the Invisible World* was published in Boston in 1692 to defend this belief and the proceedings that had recently occurred in Salem. Although a number of New Englanders later pronounced the witchcraft trials a delusion and repudiated their roles in them, Cotton Mather believed in their justice to the end of his life. He never gave up his belief in witches or in the special providence of the New England settlements.

THE WONDERS
OF THE INVISIBLE WORLD
Cotton Mather

It was as long ago as the year 1637, that a faithful minister of the Church of England whose name was Mr. Edward Symons, did in a sermon afterwards printed, thus express himself: "At New England now the sun of comfort begins to appear, and the glorious day-star to show itself. There will come times in after ages, when the clouds will over-shadow and darken the sky there. Many now promise to themselves nothing but successive happiness there, which for a time through God's mercy they may enjoy, and I pray God, they may a long time, but in this world there is no happiness perpetual." An observation, or I had almost said, an inspiration, very dismally now verified upon us! It has been affirmed by some who best know New England, that the world will do New England a great piece of injustice, if it acknowledge not a measure of religion, loyalty, honesty, and industry,

From Cotton Mather, *The Wonders of the Invisible World* (London, 1862), 9–17, 120–129.

in the people there, beyond what is to be found with any other people for the number of them. We are still so happy, that I suppose there is no land in the universe more free from the debauching and debasing vices of ungodliness. The body of the people are hitherto so disposed, that swearing, Sabbath-breaking, whoring, drunkenness, and the like, do not make a gentleman but a monster, or a goblin, in the vulgar estimation. All this notwithstanding, we must humbly confess to our God that we are miserably degenerated from the first love of our predecessors. The first planters of these colonies were a chosen generation of men, who were first so pure, as to disrelish many things which they thought wanted reformation elsewhere; and yet withal so peaceable, that they embraced a voluntary exile in a squalid, horrid, American desert, rather than to live in contentions with their brethren. Those good men imagined that they would leave their posterity in a place where they should never see the inroads of profanity or superstition. And a famous person returning hence, could in a sermon before the Parliament, profess, "I have now been seven years in a country, where I never saw one man drunk, or heard one oath sworn, or beheld one beggar in the streets all the while." New England was a true Utopia. But in short, those interests of the Gospel, which were the errand of our fathers into these ends of the earth, have been too much neglected and postponed, and the attainments of a handsome education have been too much undervalued, by multitudes that have not fallen into exorbitances of wickedness; and some, especially of our young ones, when they have got abroad from under the restraints here laid upon them, have become extravagantly and abominably vicious. Hence 'tis, that the happiness of New England has been but for a time, as it was foretold, and not for a long time, as has been desired for us. A variety of calamity has long followed this plantation; and we have all the reason imaginable to ascribe it unto the rebuke of heaven upon us for our manifold apostasies; we make no right use of our disasters. If we do not, "Remember whence we are fallen, and repent, and do the first works." But yet our afflictions may come under a further consideration with us. There is a further cause of our afflictions, whose due must be given him.

The New Englanders are a people of God settled in those which were once the devil's territories; and it may easily be supposed that the devil was exceedingly disturbed, when he perceived such a people here accomplishing the promise of old made unto our blessed Jesus, "That he should have the utmost parts of the earth for his possession." I believe that never were more satanical devices used for the unsettling of any people under the sun, than what have been employed for the extirpation of the vine which God has here planted. But, all those attempts of hell have hitherto been abortive. Wherefore the devil is now making one attempt more upon us, an attempt more difficult, more surprising, more snarled with unintelligible circumstances than any that we have hitherto encountered. We have been advised by some credible Christians yet alive, that a malefactor accused of witchcraft as well as murder, and executed in this place more than forty years ago, did then give notice of a horrible plot against the country by witchcraft and a foundation of witchcraft then laid, which if it were not seasonably discovered, would probably blow up and pull down all the churches in the country. And we have now with horror seen the discovery of such a witchcraft! An army of devils is horribly broke in upon the place which is the center, and after a sort, the first-born of our English settlements. And the houses of the good people there are filled with the doleful shrieks of their children and servants, tormented by invisible hands with tortures altogether preternatural. After the mischiefs there endeavored, and since in part conquered, the terrible plague of evil angels hath made its progress into some other places, where other persons have been in like manner diabolically handled. These our poor afflicted neighbors, quickly after they became infected and infested with these demons, arrive to a capacity of discerning those which they conceive the shapes of their troublers; and notwithstanding the great and just suspicion that the demons might impose the shapes of innocent persons in their spectral exhibitions upon the sufferers (which may perhaps prove no small part of the witch-plot in the issue), yet many of the persons thus represented, being examined, several of them have been convicted of a very damnable witchcraft. Yea, more than one twenty have confessed, that they have signed unto a book which the devil showed them, and engaged in his hellish design of bewitching and ruining our land. We know not, at least I know not, how far the delusions of Satan may be interwoven into some circumstances of the confessions; but one would think all the rules of understanding human affairs are at an end, if after so many most voluntary harmonious confessions, made by intelligent persons of all ages, in sundry towns, at several times, we must not believe the main strokes wherein those confessions all agree; especially when we have a thousand preternatural things every day before our eyes, wherein the confessors do acknowledge their concernment, and give demonstration of their being so concerned. If the devils now can strike the minds of men with any poisons of so fine a composition and operation, that scores of innocent people shall unite, in confessions of a crime which we see actually committed, it is a thing prodigious, beyond the wonders of the former ages, and it threatens no less than a sort of a dissolution upon the world.

Doubtless, the thoughts of many will receive great scandal against New England from the number of persons that have been accused, or suspected, for witchcraft, in this country. But it were easy to offer many things that may answer and abate the scandal. The kingdoms of Sweden, Denmark, Scotland, yea and England itself, as well as the province of New England, have had their storms of witchcraft breaking upon them, which have made most lamentable devastations, which also, I wish, may be the last. And it is not uneasy to be imagined, that God has not brought out all the witchcraft in many other lands with such a speedy, dreadful, destroying jealousy, as burns forth upon such high treasons, committed here in a land of uprightness. Transgressors may more quickly here than elsewhere become a prey to the vengeance of Him "Who has eyes like a flame of fire, and, who walks in the midst of the golden candlesticks." Moreover, there are many parts of the world, who if they do upon this occasion insult over this people of God, need only to be told the story of what happened at Loim, in the Duchy of Gulic, where a popish curate having ineffectually tried many charms to eject the devil out of a damsel there possessed, he passionately bid the devil come out of her into himself; but the devil answered, "What need I meddle with one whom I am sure to have, and hold at the last day as my own for ever!"

The Trial of G.B. at a Court of Oyer and Terminer Held in Salem, 1692

Glad should I have been, if I had never known the name of this man, or never had this occasion to mention so much as the first letters of his name. But the government requiring some account of his trial to be inserted in this book, it becomes me with all obedience to submit unto the order.

This G. B. was indicted for witchcraft, and in the prosecution of the charge against him, he was accused by five or six of the bewitched, as the author of their miseries; he was accused by eight of the confession witches as being a head actor at some of their hellish rendezvouzes, and one who had the promise of being a king in Satan's kingdom, now going to be erected. He was accused by nine persons for extraordinary lifting, and such feats of strength, as could not be done without a diabolical assistance. And for other such things he was accused, until about thirty testimonies were brought in against him; nor were these judged the half of what might have been considered for his conviction. However they were enough to fix the character of a witch upon him according to the rules of reasoning by the judicious Gaule in that case directed.

The court being sensible that the testimonies of the parties bewitched used to have a room among the suspicions or presumptions brought in against one indicted for witchcraft, there were now heard the testimonies of several persons who were most notoriously bewitched and every day tortured by invisible hands, and these now all charged the spectres of G. B. to have a share in their torments. At the examination of this G. B. the bewitched people were grievously harassed with preternatural mischiefs, which could not possibly be dissembled; and they still ascribed it unto the endeavors of G. B. to kill them. And now upon the trial of one of the bewitched persons, testified, that in her agonies, a little black haired man came to her, saying his name was B. and bidding her set her hand to a book which he showed unto her; and bragging that he was a conjurer, above the ordinary rank of witches, that he often persecuted her with the offer of that book, saying, "She should be well, and need fear nobody, if she would but sign it." But he inflicted cruel pains and hurts upon her, because of her denying so to do. The testimonies of the other sufferers concurred with these. And it was remarkable, that whereas biting was one of the ways which the witches used for the vexing of the sufferers, when they cried out of G. B. biting them, the print of the teeth would be seen on the flesh of the complainers, and just such a set of teeth as G. B.'s would then appear upon them, which could be distinguished from those of some other men. Others of them testified, that in their torments, G. B. tempted them to go unto a sacrament, unto which they perceived him with a sound of trumpet, summoning of other witches, who quickly after the sound, would come from all quarters unto the rendezvouz. One of them falling into a kind of trance, affirmed, that G. B. had carried her away into a very high mountain, where he showed her mighty and glorious kingdoms, and said, "he would give them all to her, if she would write in his book," but she told him, "They were none of his to give," and refused the motions, enduring of much misery for the refusal.

It cost the court a wonderful deal of trouble, to hear the testimonies of the sufferers; for when they were going to give in their depositions, they would for a long time be taken with fits, that made them uncapable of saying anything. The Chief Judge asked the prisoner who he thought hindered these witnesses from giving their testimonial. And he answered, "He supposed it was the devil." That honorable person replied, "How comes the devil then to be so loath to have any testimony born against you?" Which cast him into very great confusion.

It has been a frequent thing for the bewitched people to be entertained with apparitions of ghosts of murdered people, at the same time that the spectres of the witches trouble them. These ghosts do always afright the beholders more than all the other spectral representations; and when they exhibit themselves, they cry out of being murdered by the witchcrafts or other violences of the persons who are then in spectre present. It is further considered, that once or twice these apparitions have been seen by others, at the very same time they have shown themselves to the bewitched; and seldom have there been these apparitions, but when something unusual or suspected have attended the death of the party thus appearing. Some that have been accused by these apparitions accosting of the bewitched people, who had never heard a word of any such persons ever being in the world, have upon a fair examination, freely and fully confessed the murders of those very persons, although these also did not know how the apparitions had complained of them. Accordingly several of the bewitched had given in their testimony, that they had been troubled with the apparitions of two women, who said, that they were G. B.'s two wives, and that he had been the death of them; and that the magistrates must be told of it, before whom if B. upon his trial denied it, they did not know but that they should appear again in court. Now, G. B. had been infamous for the barbarous usage of his two late wives, all the country over. Moreover, it was testified, the spectre of G. B. threatening of the sufferers, told them, he had killed (besides others) Mrs. Lawson and her daughter, Ann. And it was noted, that these were the virtuous wife and daughter of one at whom this G. B. might have a prejudice for his being serviceable at Salem village, from whence himself had in ill terms removed some years before. And that when they died, which was long since, there were some odd circumstances about them, which made some of the attendants there suspect something of witchcraft, tho none imagined from what quarter it should come.

Well, G. B. being now upon his trial, one of the bewitched persons was cast into horror at the ghost of B.'s two deceased wives then appearing before him, and crying for vengeance against him. Hereupon several of the bewitched persons were successively called in, who all not knowing what the former had seen and said, concurred in their horror of the apparition, which they affirmed that he had before him. But he, tho much appalled, utterly denied that he discerned anything of it; nor was it any part of his conviction.

Judicious writers have assigned it a great place in the conviction of witches, when persons are impeached by other notorious witches to be as ill as themselves, especially if the persons have been much noted for neglecting the worship of God. Now, as there might have been testimonies enough of G. B.'s antipathy to prayer, and the other ordinances of God, tho by his profession singularly obliged thereunto; so, there now came in against the prisoner, the testimonies of several persons who confessed their own having been horrible witches, and ever since their confessions, had been themselves terribly tortured by the devils and other witches, even like the other sufferers; and therein undergone the pains of many deaths for their confessions.

These now testified that G. B. had been at witch-meetings with them; and that he was the person who had seduced and compelled them into the snares of witchcraft. That he promised them fine clothes for doing it; that he brought poppets to them, and thorns to stick into these poppets, for the afflicting of other people; and that he exhorted them with the rest of the crew, to bewitch all Salem Village, but be sure to do it gradually if they would prevail in what they did.

When the Lancashire witches were condemned I don't remember that there was any considerable further evidence, than that of the bewitched, and than that of some that confessed. We see so much already against G. B. But this being indeed not enough, there were other things to render what had been already produced credible.

A famous divine recites this among the convictions of a witch, "The testimony of the party bewitched, whether pining or dying; together with the joint oaths of sufficient persons that have seen certain prodigious pranks or feats wrought by the party accused." Now, God had been pleased so to leave this G. B. that he had ensnared himself by several instances which he had formerly given for a preternatural strength, and which were now produced against him. He was a very puny man, yet he had often done things beyond the strength of a giant. A gun of about seven foot barrel, and so heavy that strong men could not steadily hold it out with both hands; there were several testimonies, given in by persons of credit and honor, that he made nothing of taking up such a gun behind the lock, with but one hand, and holding it like a pistol, at arms-end. G. B. in his vindication, was so foolish as to say, that an Indian "was there, and held it out at the same time." Whereas none of the spectators ever saw any such Indian; but they supposed, the Black Man (as the witches call the devil; and they generally say he resembles an Indian), might give him that assistance. There was evidence likewise brought in, that he made nothing of taking up whole barrels filled with molasses or cider, in very disadvantageous postures, and carrying of them through the difficultest places out of a canoe to the shore.

Yea, there were two testimonies that G. B. with only putting a forefinger of his right hand into the muzzle of an heavy gun, a fowling-piece of about six or seven foot barrel, did lift up the gun and hold it out at arms-end, a gun which the deponents thought strong men could not with both hands lift up, and hold out at the butt end as usual. Indeed, one of these witnesses was over-persuaded by some

81

persons, to be out of the way upon G. B.'s trial; but he came afterwards with sorrow for his withdrawal, and gave in his testimony. Nor were either of these witnesses made use of as evidences in the trial.

There came in several testimonies relating to the domestic affairs of G. B. which had a very hard aspect upon him; and not only proved him a very ill man, but also confirmed the belief of the character which had been already fastened on him.

'Twas testified, that keeping his two successive wives in a strange kind of slavery, he would when he came home from abroad, pretend to tell the talk which any had with them; that he has brought them to the point of death by his harsh dealings with his wives, and then made the people about him to promise that in case death should happen, they would say nothing of it; that his wives had privately complained unto the neighbors about frightful apparitions of evil spirits with which their house was sometimes infested; and that many such things have been whispered among the neighborhood. There were also some other testimonies relating to the death of people whereby the consciences of an impartial jury were convinced that G. B. had bewitched the persons mentioned in the complaints. But I am forced to omit several passages, in this, as well as in all the succeeding trials, because the scribes who took notice of them, have not supplied me.

One Mr. Ruck, brother-in-law to this G. B. testified, that G. B. and himself, and his sister, who was G. B.'s wife, going out for two or three miles to gather strawberries, Ruck and his sister, the wife of G. B., rode home very softly with G. B. on foot in their company. G. B. stepped aside a little into the bushes, whereupon they halted and helloed for him. He not answering, they went away homewards with a quickened pace, without expectation of seeing him in a considerable while. And yet when they were got near home, to their astonishment they found him on foot with them, having a basket of strawberries. G. B. immediately then fell to chiding his wife, on the account of what she had been speaking to her brother, of him, on the road; which when they wondered at, he said, "He knew their thoughts." Ruck being startled at that, made some reply, intimating, that the devil himself did not know so far; but G. B. answered, "My God makes known your thoughts unto me." The prisoner now at the bar had nothing to answer unto what was thus witnessed against him that was worth considering. Only he said, "Ruck and his wife left a man with him, when they left him." Which Ruck now affirmed to be false; and when the court asked G. B. "What the man's name was?" his countenance was much altered; nor could he say, who 'twas. But the court began to think, that he then stepped aside, only that by the assistance of the Black Man he might put on his invisibility, and in that fascinating mist, gratify his own jealous humor, to hear what they said of him. Which trick of rendering themselves invisible, our witches do in their confessions pretend, that they sometimes are masters of; and it is the more credible because there is demonstration that they often render many other things utterly invisible.

Faltering, faulty, unconstant, and contrary answers upon judicial and deliberate examination, are counted some unlucky symptoms of guilt in all crimes, especially in witchcraft. Now there never was a prisoner more eminent for them than G. B., both at his examination and on his trial. His tergiversations, contradictions, and falsehoods, were very sensible; he had little to say, but that he had heard some things that he could not prove, reflecting upon the reputation of some of the witnesses. Only he gave in a paper to the jury, wherein, altho he had many times before granted, not only that there are witches, but also, that the present sufferings of the country are the effects of horrible witchcraft, yet he now goes to evince it, "that there neither are, nor ever were witches, that having made a compact with the devil, can send a devil to torment other people at a distance." This paper was transcribed out of Ady; which the court presently knew, as soon as they heard it. But he said, he had taken none of it out of any book; for which, his evasion afterwards, was, that a gentleman gave him the discourse in a manuscript, from whence he transcribed it.

The jury brought him in guilty; but when he came to die, he utterly denied the fact, whereof he had been thus convicted.

9

The Pious in Captivity

In the late seventeenth and early eighteenth centuries the inland portions of the British colonies remained sparsely populated and subject to all the dangers of the frontier. Connecticut river towns were particularly vulnerable to marauding Indians and a number of towns, like Deerfield, were burned and sacked.

The Reverend John Williams (1664–1729) was a minister in Deerfield when the Indians attacked in the winter of 1703/4; he was taken prisoner along with many others. Colonists who survived such experiences often wrote them up in the form of captivity narratives, and Williams was no exception. This genre frightened and thrilled most Americans, none of whom lived very far from the threat of Indian or French enemies. Despite the torture of their captors, the hardships of forced marches, and the poison of forced conversions, redeemed captives like Williams indulged in little public bitterness or recrimination. For the devout such experiences were tests of faith, and their eventual release evidence of divine mercy. Williams himself was returned to Boston in 1706, and the following year produced his masterful narrative. He remarried in 1707, fathered five more children, and spent his last years preaching to a rebuilt Deerfield.

THE REDEEMED CAPTIVE RETURNING TO ZION
Reverend John Williams

On Tuesday, the 29th of February, 1703/4, not long before break of day, the enemy came in like a flood upon us; our watch being unfaithful;—an evil, the awful effects of which, in the surprisal of our fort, should bespeak all watchmen to avoid, as they would not bring the charge of blood upon themselves. They came to my house in the beginning of the onset, and by their violent endeavors to break open doors and windows, with axes and hatchets, awaked me out of sleep; on which I leaped out of bed, and, running towards the door, perceived the enemy making their entrance into the house. I called to awaken two soldiers in the chamber, and returning toward my bedside for my arms, the enemy immediately broke into the

From John Williams, *The Redeemed Captive Returning to Zion* (Northampton, 1835), 10–21, 29–32.

room, I judge to the number of twenty, with painted faces, and hideous acclamations. I reached up my hands to the bed-tester for my pistol, uttering a short petition to God, for everlasting mercies for me and mine, on account of the merits of our glorified Redeemer; expecting a present passage through the valley of the shadow of death; saying in myself, as Isa. xxxviii. 10, 11, "I said, in the cutting off of my days, I shall go to the gates of the grave: I am deprived of the residue of my years. I said, I shall not see the Lord, even the Lord, in the land of the living: I shall behold man no more with the inhabitants of the world." Taking down my pistol, I cocked it, and put it to the breast of the first Indian that came up; but my pistol missing fire, I was seized by three Indians, who disarmed me, and bound me naked, as I was in my shirt, and so I stood for near the space of an hour. Binding me, they told me they would carry me to Quebec. My pistol missing fire was an occasion of my life's being preserved; since which I have also found it profitable to be crossed in my own will. The judgment of God did not long slumber against one of the three which took me, who was a captain, for by sunrising he received a mortal shot from my next neighbor's house; who opposed so great a number of French and Indians as three hundred, and yet were no more than seven men in an ungarrisoned house.

I cannot relate the distressing care I had for my dear wife, who had lain in but a few weeks before; and for my poor children, family, and Christian neighbors. The enemy fell to rifling the house, and entered in great numbers into every room. I begged to God to remember mercy in the midst of judgment; that he would so far restrain their wrath, as to prevent their murdering of us; that we might have grace to glorify his name, whether in life or death; and, as I was able, committed our state to God. The enemies who entered the house, were all of them Indians and Macquas, insulted over me awhile, holding up hatchets over my head, threatening to burn all I had; but yet God, beyond expectation, made us in a great measure to be pitied; for though some were so cruel and barbarous as to take and carry to the door two of my children and murder them, as also a negro woman; yet they gave me liberty to put on my clothes, keeping me bound with a cord on one arm, till I put on my clothes to the other; and then changing my cord, they let me dress myself, and then pinioned me again. Gave liberty to my dear wife to dress herself and our remaining children. About sun an hour high, we were all carried out of the house, for a march, and saw many of the houses of my neighbors in flames, perceiving the whole fort, one house excepted, to be taken. Who can tell what sorrows pierced our souls, when we saw ourselves carried away from God's sanctuary, to go into a strange land, exposed to so many trials; the journey being at least three hundred miles we were to travel; the snow up to the knees, and we never inured to such hardships and fatigues; the place we were to be carried to, a Popish country. Upon my parting from the town, they fired my house and barn. We were carried over the river, to the foot of the mountain, about a mile from my house, where we found a great number of our Christian neighbors, men, women, and children, to the number of an hundred, nineteen of which were afterward murdered by the way, and two starved to death, near Cowass, in a time of great scarcity, or famine, the savages underwent there. When we came to the foot of the mountain, they took away our shoes, and gave us in the room of them Indian shoes, to prepare us for our travel.

After this, we went up the mountain, and saw the smoke of the fires in the town, and beheld the awful desolations of Deerfield. And before we marched any farther, they killed a sucking child belonging to one of the English. There were slain by the enemy of the inhabitants of Deerfield, to the number of thirty-eight, besides nine of the neighboring towns. We travelled not far the first day; God made the heathen so to pity our children, that though they had several wounded persons of their own to carry upon their shoulders, for thirty miles, before they came to the river, yet they carried our children, incapable of travelling, in their arms, and upon their shoulders. When we came to our lodging place, the first night, they dug away the snow, and made some wigwams, cut down some small branches of the spruce-tree to lie down on, and gave the prisoners somewhat to eat; but we had but little appetite. I was pinioned and bound down that night, and so I was every night whilst I was with the army. Some of the enemy who brought drink with them from the town fell to drinking, and in their drunken fit they killed my negro man, the only dead person I either saw at the town, or in the way.

In the night an Englishman made his escape; in the morning (March 1), I was called for, and ordered by the general to tell the English, that if any more made their escape, they would burn the rest of the prisoners. He that took me was unwilling to let me speak with any of the prisoners, as we marched; but on the morning of the second day, he being appointed to guard the rear, I was put into the hands of my other master, who permitted me to speak to my wife, when I overtook her, and to walk with her to help her in her journey. On the way, we discoursed of the happiness of those who had a right to an house not made with hands, eternal in the heavens; and God for a father and friend; as also, that it was our reasonable duty quietly to submit to the will of God, and to say, "The will of the Lord be done." My wife told me her strength of body began to fail, and that I must expect to part with her; saying, she hoped God would preserve my life, and the life of some, if not of all our children with us; and commended to me, under God, the care of them. She never spake any discontented word as to what had befallen us, but with suitable expressions justified God in what had happened. We soon made a halt, in which time my chief surviving master came up, upon which I was put upon marching with the foremost, and so made my last farewell of my dear wife, the desire of my eyes, and companion in many mercies and afflictions. Upon our separation from each other, we asked for each other grace sufficient for what God should call us to. After our being parted from one another, she spent the few remaining minutes of her stay in reading the Holy Scriptures; which she was wont personally every day to delight her soul in reading, praying, meditating on, by herself, in her closet, over and above what she heard out of them in our family worship. I was made to wade over a small river, and so were all the English, the water above knee deep, the stream very swift; and after that to travel up a small mountain; my strength was almost spent, before I came to the top of it. No sooner had I overcome the difficulty of that ascent, but I was permitted to sit down, and be unburdened of my pack. I sat pitying those who were behind, and entreated my master to let me go down and help my wife; but he refused, and would not let me stir from him. I asked each of the prisoners (as they passed by me) after her, and heard that, passing through the above-said river, she fell down, and was plunged over head and ears in the water; after which she travelled not far, for at the foot of that mountain, the cruel and bloodthirsty savage who took her slew her with his hatchet at one stroke, the tidings of which were very awful. And yet such was the hard-heartedness of the adversary, that my tears were reckoned to me as a reproach. My loss and the loss of my children was great; our hearts were so filled with sorrow, that nothing but the comfortable hopes of her being taken away, in mercy to herself, from the evils we were to see, feel, and suffer under (and joined to the assembly of the spirits of just men made perfect, to rest in peace, and joy unspeakable and full of glory, and the good pleasure of God thus to exercise us), could have kept us from sinking under, at that time. That Scripture, Job 1.21, "Naked came I out of my mother's womb, and naked shall I return thither: the Lord gave, and the Lord hath taken away; blessed be the name of the Lord,"—was brought to my mind, and from it, that an afflicting God was to be glorified; with some other places of Scripture, to persuade to a patient bearing my afflictions.

We were again called upon to march, with a far heavier burden on my spirits than on my back. I begged of God to overrule, in his providence, that the corpse of one so dear to me, and of one whose spirit he had taken to dwell with him in glory, might meet with a Christian burial, and not be left for meat to the fowls of the air and beasts of the earth; a mercy that God graciously vouchsafed to grant. For God put it into the hearts of my neighbors, to come out as far as she lay, to take up her corpse, carry it to the town, and decently to bury it soon after. In our march they killed a sucking infant of one of my neighbors; and before night a girl of about eleven years of age. I was made to mourn, at the consideration of my flock being, so far, a flock of slaughter, many being slain in the town, and so many murdered in so few miles from the town; and from fears what we must yet expect, from such who delightfully imbrued their hands in the blood of so many of His people. When we came to our lodging place, an Indian captain from the eastward spake to my master about killing me, and taking off my scalp. I lifted up my heart to God, to implore his grace and mercy in such a time of need; and afterwards I told my master, if he intended to kill me, I desired he would let me know of it; assuring him that my death, after a promise of quarter, would bring the guilt of blood upon him. He told me he would not kill me. We laid down and slept, for God sustained and kept us.

On the Sabbath day (March 5), we rested, and I was permitted to pray, and preach to the captives. When we arrived at New France, we were forbidden praying one with another, or joining together in the service of God.

Tuesday, March 7, in the morning, before we travelled, one Mary Brooks, a pious young woman, came to the wigwam where I was, and told me she desired to bless God, who had inclined the heart of her master to let her come and take her farewell of me. Said she, "By my falls on the ice yesterday, I injured myself, causing a miscarriage this night, so that I am not able to travel far; I know they will kill me today; but," says she, "God has (praised be his name!) by his spirit, with his word, strengthened me to my last encounter with death;" and so mentioned to me some places of Scripture seasonably sent in for her support. "And," says she, "I am not afraid of death; I can, through the grace of God, cheerfully submit to his will. Pray for me," said she, at parting, "that God would take me to himself." Accordingly, she was killed that day. I mention it, to the end I may stir up all, in their young days, to improve the death of Christ by faith, to a giving them an holy boldness in the day of death.

The next day (Wednesday, March 8), we were made to scatter one from another into smaller companies; and one of my children was carried away with Indians belonging to the eastern parts. At night my master came to me, with my pistol in his hand, and put it to my breast, and said, "Now I will kill you, for," he said, "you would have killed me with it if you could." But by the grace of God, I was not much daunted, and whatever his intention might be, God prevented my death.

The next day (Thursday, March 9), I was again permitted to pray with that company of captives with me, and we were allowed to sing a psalm together. After which, I was taken from all the company of the English, excepting two children of my neighbors, one of which, a girl of four years of age, was killed by her Macqua master the next morning (Friday, March 10); the snow being so deep when we left the river, that he could not carry the child and his pack too.

[At Shamblee] The next morning the bell rang for mass. My master bid me go to church; I refused; he threatened me, and went away in a rage. At noon the Jesuits sent for me to dine with them, for I ate at their table all the time I was at the fort; and after dinner they told me the Indians would not allow of any of their captives staying in their wigwams whilst they were at church, and were resolved by force and violence to bring us all to church if we would not go without. I told them it was highly unreasonable so to impose upon those who were of a contrary religion, and to force us to be present at such a service as we abhorred, was nothing becoming Christianity. They replied, they were savages, and would not hearken to reason, but would have their wills. Said also, if they were in New England themselves, they would go into their churches and see their ways of worship. I answered, the case was far different, for there was nothing (themselves being judges) as to matter or manner of worship but what was according to the word of God in our churches, and therefore it could not be an offence to any man's conscience. But among them there were idolatrous superstitions in worship. They said, "Come and see, and offer us conviction of what is superstitious in worship." To which I answered, that I was not to do evil that good might come of it, and that forcing in matters of religion was hateful. They answered, "The Indians are resolved to have it so, and they could not pacify them without my coming; and they would engage they should offer no force or violence to cause any compliance with their ceremonies." The next mass, my master bid me go to church. I objected; he rose and forcibly pulled me by my head and shoulders out of the wigwam to the church, which was nigh the door. So I went in and sat down behind the door: and there saw a great confusion, instead of any Gospel order; for one of the Jesuits was at the altar saying mass in a tongue unknown to the savages, and the other, between the altar and the door, saying and singing prayers among the Indians at the same time; and many others were at the same time saying over their Pater-nosters and Ave Mary by tale from their chapelit, or beads on a string. At our going out we smiled at their devotion so managed, which was offensive to them, for they said we made a derision of their worship. When I was here a certain savagess died. One of the Jesuits told me she was a very holy woman, who had not committed one sin in twelve years. After a day or two the Jesuits asked me what I thought of their way now I saw it. I told them I thought Christ said of it, as Mark vii. 7, 8, 9, "Howbeit, in vain do they worship me, teaching for doctrines the commandments of men. For laying aside the commandment of God, ye hold the tradition of men, as the washing of pots and cups; and many other such like things ye do. And he said unto them, Full well ye reject the commandment of God, that ye may keep your own tradition." They told me they were not the commandments of men, but apostolical traditions, of equal authority with the Holy Scriptures; and that after my death I would bewail my not praying to the Virgin Mary, and that I should find the want of her intercession for me with her Son; judging me to hell for asserting the Scriptures to be a perfect rule of faith; and said I abounded in my own sense, entertaining explications contrary to the sense of the Pope, regularly sitting with a General Council, explaining Scripture and making articles of faith. I told them it was my comfort that Christ was to be my judge, and not they, at the great day; and as for their censuring and judging me, I was not moved with it.

One day a certain savagess taken prisoner in Philip's war, who had lived at Mr. Bulkley's at Weathersfield, called Ruth, who could speak English very well and who had been often at my house, being now proselyted to the Romish faith, came into the wigwam, and with her an English maid who was taken in the last war. She was dressed in Indian apparel, and was unable to speak one word of English. She could neither tell her own name nor the name of the place from whence she was taken. These two talked in the Indian dialect with my master a long time; after which my master bade me cross myself; I told him I would not; he commanded me several times, and I as often refused. Ruth said, "Mr. Williams, you know the Scripture, and therefore act against your own light; for you know the Scripture saith, 'Servants, obey your masters'; he is your master and you his servant." I told her she was ignorant and knew not the meaning of the Scripture; telling her I was not to disobey the great God to obey my master, and that I was ready to die and suffer for God if called thereto. On which she talked with my master: I suppose she interpreted what I said. My master took hold of my hand to force me to cross myself, but I struggled with him, and would not suffer him to guide my hand. Upon this he pulled off a crucifix from off his own neck, and bade me kiss it; but I refused once and again. He told me he would dash out my brains with his hatchet if I refused. I told him I should sooner choose death than to sin against God. Then he ran and took up his hatchet and acted as though he would have dashed out my brains. Seeing I was not moved, he threw down his hatchet, saying he would bite off

89

all my nails if I still refused. I gave him my hand and told him I was ready to suffer: he set his teeth in my thumb-nail and gave a gripe, and then said, "No good minister, no love God, as bad as the Devil," and so left off. I have reason to bless God, who strengthened me to withstand. By this he was so discouraged, as never more to meddle with me about my religion. I asked leave of the Jesuits to pray with those English of our town that were with me; but they absolutely refused to give us any permission to pray one with another, and did what they could to prevent our having any discourse together.

10

Political Ambition

Jonathan Belcher (1681/2–1757) was the son of a prosperous Massachusetts merchant. Graduating from Harvard in 1699, Belcher traveled in Europe for several years and then returned home to become a successful merchant himself. After service on the Massachusetts Council, Belcher was appointed Governor of Massachusetts and New Hampshire in 1729/30. He remained in office until political changes in England aided his opponents, who brought about his dismissal in the spring of 1741.

The following letters, to his son, to his agent and brother-in-law, Richard Partridge, and to various important personages in England, illustrate some of the pressures burdening a colonial Governor at a time when the Americans were growing more aggressive about their economic interests, and the British government was becoming more insistent on its own imperial requirements. Like most of his fellow chief executives, Belcher was not very successful in maintaining his power among the colonists, while his influence at Westminster diminished steadily.

THE BELCHER PAPERS

To Richard Partridge

Boston, Nov. 1, 1731

I take a very particular notice of every clause of all your letters, and am fully convinced how much and how sincerely you are attached to my interest and service, nor have I ever had the experience of any one more vigilant and more diligent. I observe also that you say Mr. Wilks has been very hearty and ready to serve me. I see you have interest with Lords Islay and Harrington, and had used it in my favour, and that you had engaged Sir Joseph Jekyll and that you carried Jonathan with you to Mr. H. Walpole, and were kindly received and talked over the affair of the salary to my advantage. You well observe that a Governor can't have too many friends at Court. The Assembly sits here again this week, and you may depend on everything in my power for the relief of the Quakers, and I think I shall be able to

From "The Belcher Papers," Part I, *Collections of the Massachusetts Historical Society*, 6th ser., VI (1893), 36–38, 41, 49–54, 68–71, 216–217, 240–242, 307–309, 381–384, 405, 408–409; "The Belcher Papers," Part II, *Collections*, 6th ser., VII (1894), 19–20, 37–38, 69–70, 243–244, 351, 386–389, 402–403.

get a bill passed that will be pleasing. The Quakers are very sensible of my readiness and sincerity to serve them. As you observe I must walk very circumspectly lest the King's ministers should imagine I am not zealous enough for the honor of the Crown, and lest the House of Commons should think I bear too hard upon the privileges of the people. I'll endeavor to steer as nicely as I can between both. I take notice you have great freedom with the Duke of Newcastle and that his Grace is very friendly to me. We must all take care to pay him great duty and respect and not offend him. Lord Harrington also treated you very kindly, and I am under great obligations to his Lordship for his favorable promise in my behalf. I shall always very thankfully pay what you spend (according to your own prudence) in my affairs, and I desire you to write me what you think reasonable for your own time and troubles besides. What would I give that you were able to get Col. Henry Sherburne my Lieutenant Governor in the room of Dunbar. Try, all of you, what you can do with Duke of Newcastle, Lord Wilmington, Mr. Speaker, Mr. H. Walpole, etc. I should be mighty easy in the government there if this could be done.

To Jonathan Belcher, Jr.

Boston, Nov. 11, 1731

I see you had the great honor of dining with the greatest commoner in Great Britain (the Rt. Hon. Speaker Onslow) who received you with his wonted condescension and civility and would recommend you to a good acquaintance for your better proficiency in the law.

I see you received since your arrival £155. You may depend on my constant care of a seasonable supply that your mind may be easy in its devotion to study. I am hitherto well pleased with all you write and all you have done. I had almost forgot to say that I would have you render me a yearly account of your expense pretty particularly, putting your pocket expense in one gross sum. I never made a voyage to London, but at night one of the last things I did I put down the expense of the day in the most iotical manner (if you'll let me coin a word). Such a method tends to many good purposes, as a thrifty expense, to remind you of what places you have been at, what company you have been in, etc. I am glad you have paid your duty to my Lord Bishop of London, and had received the advantage of his pious counsels. I am pleased you begin to find satisfaction in your new studies, and I have no doubt but it will grow with your diligence and industry in them. I am sensible your French tongue will be of good service to you in the study of the law, and so will be your shorthand at Westminster Hall, where you must constantly attend the several courts. If you are minded to have a degree of Master of Arts, I believe Oxford is esteemed the most ancient and famous university, and will consequently reflect the most honor. Among other things you must endeavor to make and keep up a good city acquaintance. Besides being a good lawyer, I am fond of your being a fine gentleman. Delight then in the study of humanity, that humility, condescension and affability may become perfectly easy and natural to you.

In my several voyages to London I have many times observed a gentleman starting out of a court with a coach and six, fine liveries, etc., and upon enquiry, Who's that? Why, 'tis such a one who has with great industry acquired a fine estate and hitherto lived obscurely, but now is able to make the figure you see. Thus you must content yourself with living pretty much a recluse, for the advantage of study, and having laid a good foundation great will be the advantage to the superstructure, which you will be the better able to embellish and adorn from time to time until the best judges shall say the building is complete. Yet I again charge you to intersperse your tasks and labors with proper recreations; walking, riding, bowling, and billiards are wholesome exercises. Therefore use them for your better health; and to these I would add fencing. I shall be pleased to hear you have put yourself under a good master of this gentlemanly science, and that you endeavor to be a fine dancer. I am glad to hear you so much confine yourself to that best of liquors which the God of Nature has so plentifully furnished for the common benefit of all his creatures. I will by no means have you think of cutting off your hair without my special leave, although it should cost you as much the yearly dressing as to furnish yourself with good wigs. I think nothing a finer ornament to a young gentleman than a good head of hair well ordered and set forth. Don't forget writing to your uncle Oliver, Doctor Coleman and Sewall, though I would not have you run into a numerous correspondence here, lest it should rob you of too much time from your studies and recreations.

To the Bishop of Lincoln

Boston, Nov. 18, 1731

I give your Lordship joy in your son's safe return to us; and your Lordship may rest assured that nothing will be wanting in my power for his service and interest, agreeable whereto I have promised him the Naval Office of New Hampshire (worth about £70 a year) and will help out his pocket money. I assure you, my Lord, I shall with great pleasure advise and assist this young gentleman. Your Lordship, I doubt not, has read the history of this country, and is well knowing with what principles, in what manner, and with what sort of people it was first settled, not with the necessitous refuse and gleanings of mankind (as most of the other plantations), but with men of religion, good knowledge, and substance, and they took care (as well as they could) to hand them down to their posterity. Yet to the shame of my country I must complain, as God of his covenant people of old, I had planted thee a noble vine, wholly a right seed, how then art thou turned into the degenerate plant of a strange vine? New England, my Lord, is become among the King's provinces a mart of nations. The traffic and commerce is great, and I am afraid vice and wickedness grow with it. This is too common as countries become populous and plentiful; but what a vile and ungrateful return is this, my Lord, to the great author of our beings.

I have, my Lord, at one time and another spent about six years in Europe,—twice in Hanover, once at Berlin, in Denmark, in several principalities of Germany, three times at Holland, and once I made a progress through the Kingdom of Great Britain (500 miles in length), and I have, my Lord, the satisfaction to think that no country (I have seen) maintains a greater awe and sense of God and religion than New England does even at this day. And as it has pleased the King to appoint me his vicegerent here, it shall be my care (by the help of God) that my example may give life and energy to my commands for the support and encouragement of good religion and virtue and for bearing down all sorts of vice and impiety. This I am sure will be acceptable to God and the King.

To the Lords of Trade

Boston, Dec. 4, 1731

My Lords, in September last I received two letters from Mr. Secretary Popple respecting an address from the House of Commons as to the state of his Majesty's colonies in America, with respect to laws made, manufacturers set up, and trade carried on, which may affect the trade, navigation and manufactures of Great Britain. As to the Massachusetts province, I find no laws in force for encouraging the produce or manufactures of the country, excepting two—one to encourage the raising of hemp, which gives a bounty; the other to encourage the raising of flax. Besides the above mentioned acts, there are also two resolves for allowing a bounty for every piece of duck or canvas. There are some other manufactures carried on here, as the making brown holland for women's ware, and makes the importation of all calicos and some other India goods so much the less. There are also small quantities of cloth made of linen and cotton for ordinary shirting and sheeting. About three years ago a paper mill was set up, which makes about £200 sterling a year of that commodity. There are several forges for making bar iron, and some furnaces for cast iron, and one slitting mill, the undertaker of which carries on the manufacture of nails. As to the woolen manufacture, there is no law here to encourage it, and the country people who used formerly to make most of their clothing out of their own wool don't now make a third part of what they wear, but are mostly clothed with British manufactures.

As to the province of New Hampshire, the only laws that I find affecting the trade, navigation, or manufactures of Great Britain are an act (passed many years ago) imposing a duty, for the supply of his Majesty's Fort William and Mary with powder, on all shipping trading to and from the said province, and not owned within the same. Another act entitled An Act for Encouraging Iron Works in the Province, which prohibits the exportation of iron ore. The woolen manufacture in the province is much less than formerly, the common lands on which the sheep used to feed being now divided into particular proprieties. The number of them is much reduced, and the people almost wholly clothed with woolen from Great Britain. The manufacturing of flax into linen daily increases, by the great resort of people from Ireland into this province, who are well skilled in that business. The chief trade of the province continues (as for many years past) in the exportation of masts, yards, bowsprits, boards, staves and rafters for England, but principally to Spain and Portugal, and some to the Charrible Islands, with lumber and refuse fish, and the better sort of fish to Spain, Portugal, Italy, etc. Some sloops and small vessels go in the winter (with English and West India goods) to Virginia, Maryland and Carolina, and return with corn and flesh. None of the laws mentioned have been made in either province since my arrival to the governments, and I shall take care not to give my assent to any law that may interfere with his Majesty's royal instructions.

To the Duke of Newcastle

Boston, Nov. 21, 1732

Your Grace has herewith the Journals of the House of Representatives to this time; and although there has not been a shilling in the treasury of this province for eighteen months past, yet I am afraid the Representatives will still be so obstinate against his Majesty's instruction as to run the risk of losing the province, rather than supply the treasury as his Majesty has directed. But of this I shall have the honour to write your Grace more at large in a little time. I have now only to beg of your Grace to give some little attention to my speech to the Assembly of this province, now sitting, respecting the raising of naval stores, as masts, deals, ship timber, pitch, tar, turpentine, hemp, flax and bar iron, which things are originally from the east country and Spain. I say, my Lord Duke, this climate and soil is well adapted for raising these things, and I wish the Assembly would give a larger bounty for raising them; but lest they should not do it sufficiently, might it not be worthy to be laid before the Parliament of Great Britain for their giving a good bounty to encourage the raising of these stores in the British colonies, which perhaps might prevent a vast yearly sum of English money's going to the North Crowns, and instead thereof his Majesty be supplied with naval stores from his own plantations, and in return for the manufactures of Great Britain? I humbly conceive nothing would make these plantations more serviceable to the mother kingdom, nor so naturally divert them from interfering with her manufactures. This is indeed what I have been aiming at ever since my arrival to the government, and have pressed it once and again upon the Assemblies. Some people will object that the stores from America are not so good as what come from the Baltic. Allow it, my Lord Duke, yet a good encouragement would soon make the stores here better. Had not Great Britain better content herself with what she can have by her own labor and industry than part with the nutriment of her body politic, and those strong sinews of power and government, I mean her coin, to foreigners? And the navigation employed in such a trade would be a fine nursery of sailors to the British Crown; and would it not also render Great Britain less subject to the caprice of the Northern Crowns?

To the Lords of Trade

Boston, Jan. 5, 1732/3

After the Assembly's sitting here upwards of nine weeks I dismissed them yesterday by their own request, and now cover to your Lordships the remaining Journals of their House; upon which I think your Lordships will easily observe that the House of Representatives of this Province are continually running wild, nor are their attempts for assuming (in a manner) the whole legislative, as well as the executive part, of the government into their own hands to be endured with honor to his Majesty. They made a vote yesterday fully empowering a committee of their own House to write the agent from time to time on the address and memorial of both Houses. This, most certainly, is assuming a power they have no right to. Had they sat a few days longer I should have expected they would have voted his Majesty's Council a useless part of the legislature.

I have, my Lords, been representing to your Lordships for eighteen months past, the great difficulty under which this province labors through the perverseness and obstinacy of the House of Representatives (or rather of a few designing men of influence among them), and really, my Lords, matters seem now to be hastening to a crisis, that I cannot apprehend the King's government can subsist any longer without his Majesty's immediate care. The officers and soldiers will certainly desert all the forts and garrisons, being naked and unable to do their duty for want of their just pay. The forts on the frontier are all dropping down, and Castle William wants a large repair. I must beg your Lordships to be no longer silent. For really, my Lords, if things thus continue (or still grow worse) this government and province is in a fair way to fall into all confusion and be lost. I humbly beg your Lordships to lay the state of this government before his Majesty, according to your wonted justice and wisdom.

To the Lords of Trade

Boston, June 30, 1733

Since I last wrote your Lordships I have met the new Assembly of this province, and I humbly refer your Lordships to their Journal herewith for their proceedings, by which your Lordships will see they seem resolved to supply no money in support of the King's government, or for paying their just debts, until there comes a conclusive answer to their Address to the King and of their memorial to the House of Commons. I must therefore again beseech your Lordships that these affairs may have dispatch. I have faithfully done all in my power in obedience to the King's royal orders, and what remains must be from his Majesty. I now beg leave to report to your Lordships the great distress and extremity the people of this province are brought to for want of a good medium to carry on their trade and commerce, and think it would be a good service to his Majesty's subjects that your Lordships would send me the King's leave to sign a bill of the nature of that I sent your Lordships in January last, which would make an emission of the best sort of credit bills that were ever yet put forth in this province. For really, my Lords, it is impossible for the traffic to be carried on without something of this kind, nor does the restriction the King has laid me under fully answer the end of preventing a multiplication of paper currency of the low, mean value it constantly is, since Connecticut and Rhode Island issue out what of it they please, without control. Let me therefore again entreat your Lordships that the King's good people under my care may be supported in their trade and business by the benefit of such a bill as I have mentioned.

Your Lordships will observe by the votes of the Massachusetts Assembly that there arose a difficulty about their voting my support, and some men of great influence were entirely against my having any, unless I would break the King's instructions, and sign the bill for supply of the treasury in the way they are contending for, and contrary to the Charter. Thus your Lordships see the difficulty I labor with for paying a strict duty and obedience to his Majesty, and it shall be my care, my Lords, that this people shall never have any other complaint against me; and notwithstanding the opposition made to it, yet I now enclose your Lordships a bill passed by the House of Representatives and by his Majesty's Council for £3000 for my support, and I again pray your Lordships' favor that I may have the royal leave for giving my assent to this bill; and I must freely repeat to your Lordships that there is not the least prospect of a Governor ever being supported by an Assembly here in any other manner, and I believe your Lordships will allow that it is a great hardship on a Governor to spend his salary a year before he gets it, as has been my case hitherto; and as I have often said to your Lordships should my mortality happen while soliciting for leave, the Assembly seems to me to have so little justice or honor as that I don't expect the grant would ever be revived, and the hard fate of Governor Burnet's family must convince the world of what I say in this matter. I therefore entreat your Lordships that the royal leave may have as much dispatch as possible, for by the delay of it the last year it arrived but five days before the then Assembly must have expired, according to the royal Charter, when that grant would have been lost.

To the Duke of Chandos

Boston, Oct. 4, 1733

I will at your command transmit the best account I possibly can of the true value of the New York Oblong. I observe your Grace (with your partners) are inclined to bring forward settlements on these lands, and that your Grace desires to know what method may be necessary (or usual) to strike into for the best accomplishing your design.

As I have been and am concerned in settling wild lands in this country, I take the freedom to enclose to your Grace a copy of one of my leases.

I observe what your Grace says of the estates purchased not long since in Ireland. Your Grace will please to pardon me while I say there is a vast difference between the lands of that kingdom and this country. There they have been inhabited some thousands of years, and have been long since subdued and cultivated to the height; but they are not so in this infant plantation, nor have we a tenth part people enough for the Massachusetts province. Whoever informed your Grace of our numbers was grossly mistaken, because according to the best accounts I have been able to get since my being in the government we have not in the Massachusetts province 120,000 souls, nor 25,000 fit to bear arms. The lands of this province are generally good in their nature; I believe equal to those of Great Britain (if not superior), and in many parts of the province finely accomodated with harbors and rivers, more especially what we call the eastern parts of the province; and if your Grace and partners are inclined to lay out money in lands in these parts, I think it may be done there at this time to considerable profit. This province increases fast, and will in time be undoubtedly the mistress of all the King's provinces in America. Although the islands and southern continent may give productions of a more valuable nature than ours; yet, my Lord Duke, I think they can never become countries like this, which is capable of every thing necessary to the being and comfort of mankind. We suck in and blow out a most healthy air, in a good climate, and the people are generally of brave, athletic constitutions. But from New York southward and all the West Indian Islands, they are situated in latitudes forbidding the general and lasting health which the inhabitants of North America are blessed with. I have, may it please your Grace, seen almost every county of Great Britain, all Holland, great part of France, Germany, some parts of Sweden and Denmark, and of all the countries I have seen New England is the nearest match to its mother country. Your Grace will please to forgive this long detail, and perhaps a native may be too fond of the land he is sprung out of.

To Richard Partridge

Boston, Nov. 5, 1733

I have with a great deal of patience, and with all the reason and rhetoric I am master of, at last persuaded this Assembly to be dutiful to his Majesty in supplying the treasury, agreeable to the Charter and comfortable to the King's royal orders. This has been a long smart battle, and to his Majesty's honor in the end, though his Governor has had a hard task of it, and often threatened to be starved because he wouldn't break the King's orders. I am heartily glad it is over, and I hope this province will live in more peace for the future. I have also obtained £3000 for Governor Burnet's children, on which head I had a special order from the King when I came over. These things I hope will be well accepted, and give the Governor a good reputation with the King and his ministers. If there should at any time attempts be made to my prejudice, you must stir up all the force you can to baffle them. To send over a new Governor hither would give the ministry a vast deal of trouble and vexation; and it would be highly dishonorable and the most cruel injustice to me that could be acted, but I don't suppose they can possibly entertain such thoughts. Yet it will be well to be often at the offices, and to be prudently learning what passes. I am very uneasy about Benjamin Pemberton's getting the Naval Office from me, and must in proper time endeavor to have it restored.

To the Duke of Newcastle

Boston, Nov. 13, 1733

I have, my Lord Duke, had an inconceivable deal of trouble from my arrival in the government to this time by the violent opposition (I may say obstinacy) of the several Assemblies to his Majesty's just and reasonable orders, and have been often threatened by some leading men that I should not have any support, unless I would sign a bill for supplying the treasury contrary to the King's royal instruction. And I have been obliged ever since my being here to live sometimes twelve, sometimes eighteen months on my own fortune to support myself in the defense of the King's honor, and I am glad after all that I have been able to accomplish the several articles I have mentioned, because it does honor to his Majesty, and I am also satisfied they are things that will greatly contribute to the service and interest of the people. The great dispute respecting the supply of the treasury being got over in the manner it is will very much strengthen the King's government here, and make this province more dependent (as it ought to be) on its mother country. For while the House of Representatives had the power of forbidding the payment of half a crown until they had in a formal manner examined and passed upon the account, it gave them an unequal balance in all matters of government. But at present the Assembly seems to be growing more dutiful to the King and inclined that the affairs of the government should run in their proper channels, and I hope they will more and more fall into this reasonable way of thinking, since they constantly find they are not able to move me from a strict obedience and adherence to his Majesty's royal orders.

To the Lords of Trade

Boston, Feb. 18, 1733/4

I had the honor of writing your Lordships 27 November last, since which I have spent a month at New Hampshire, and held a General Assembly there, and now cover to your Lordships what passed in that Assembly and in his Majesty's Council. Your Lordships will find I have done everything in my power to bring that Assembly to a sense of their duty to his Majesty in the repair of the only fort of the province, and to do justice to those whom the province is indebted, and after my expostulating and waiting upon them the length of an unusual session, they would supply no money to the treasury, which has been empty now near three years. The fort is therefore dropping down, and the people naked and defenseless, and those to whom the public is indebted under great oppression; nor do I see it can be otherwise while Col. Dunbar is Lieutenant Governor of that province, and sets himself at the head of a party who are constantly opposing every thing that is proposed for the King's service, and for the good of the province; and Messrs. Wentworth and Atkinson assist all in their power to embroil the affairs of the province.

Your Lordships will find that I sent for Mr. Wentworth and Mr. Atkinson and offered to admit them into his Majesty's Council at New Hampshire, but they would not accept, being set upon doing all the mischief they possibly could in the House of Representatives. Finding, my Lords, the Assembly would do nothing I dissolved them, after which Mr. Atkinson offered to take his oath, but I thought it absolutely inconsistent with the King's honor and authority for him to trifle and make game with his Majesty's royal orders, and therefore refused to admit him. If the insolence of such men must be suffered, it will of course destroy the King's authority and subvert all rule and order. So the Council there consists at present of only ten, and wants two to complete it, and I shall endeavor to find those who will come nearest the character given in his Majesty's instructions to me for Councilors, and I shall then recommend them to your Lordships, and in the mean time I hope your Lordships will not think of recommending any persons whereby to bring me still under greater difficulties in my administration in that province; and since I am sure it is not for his Majesty's service, nor any benefit to the people, or to Colonel Dunbar himself to be in the Lieutenancy in New Hampshire, and since it is impossible for the Governor and him ever to coincide, I must pray your Lordships to acquiesce in his removal, and in the appointment of another. This would give me ease and pleasure in that government. Has it been possible, my Lords, for any gentleman to do more than I have in support of his Majesty's authority and honor? Why must I then be punished by having such a troublesome man tacked to me? I hope your Lordships will justly weigh this matter, and give me relief from him; and I am sure the province (nine in ten) will think themselves happy also.

To Richard Partridge

Boston, April 20, 1734

I come now to what you mention about Colonel Dunbar and Mr. Cook. All the plague and trouble I have ever had in New Hampshire is entirely owing to the former, and the same to the latter in Massachusetts, and the breaches are now so wide, and their malice so rancorous, that it's not possible to think of a reconciliation. No. I must defend myself as well as I can, and while I am a good Governor for the King and to the people, I hope the rage and revenge of two such persons won't hurt me. I suppose at this day nineteen in twenty are well satisfied in the Governor.

If there be any complaint or affidavits against me for maladministration in the government, doubtless I must be served with copies if they are worthy so much notice. As to giving Dunbar a third of my salary, it is unreasonable for him to expect it, since it is settled by law upon me in obedience to the King's instruction, which says they shall settle £600 a year on the King's Governor; but if there must be an allowance of £200 a year out of it to the Lieutenant Governor, then it would be but £400 a year to the King's Governor, and not agreeable to the King's orders. Besides, brother, I make two journeys a year to New Hampshire, each of which constantly costs me £100, so that as the matter now stands I really have not £400 a year, say about £100 sterling a year for a Governor, a poor business, which I hope the King's ministers will not begrudge me. Nor can I be persuaded to do any such thing as to give a man bread out of my own mouth who is constantly trying to destroy me. I now allow him to be captain of the fort, and to have the perquisites of marriages, registers, certificates, and passes, all which I suppose may be worth about £200 a year, though I begrudge him every farthing, considering his vile, insolent treatment, a late instance whereof I shall send from hence in a little time, and were I to give him my whole salary it would signify little, nor would anything satisfy him but to ruin me, were it in his power,—out of which I hope

Almighty God will always preserve me. I am glad to find his character is pretty well known, nor do I believe there is a viler, falser fellow upon the face of the earth. So you and my son, with all your friends, must take care to defend me against his wicked insinuations.

To James E. Oglethorpe

Boston, May 25, 1734

I wish the new colony of Georgia may thrive and flourish and soon become a fine addition to the British empire in America. But if you will allow me, Sir, I will just mention what I fear may discourage inhabitants in the first beginnings of such a settlement, which is, that I have heard one condition of the tenure of their lands is, in case there be no male heir in a family the daughters are all excluded on the death of the father, and the lands to revert to the Trustees or to the Crown. If it be so, the condition is hard. We have here a fine country, capable of naval stores, grain, swine and black cattle, has lead, iron and copper mines, and perhaps the best fishery in the world; and I think I signed grants the last year for sixteen or eighteen towns of six miles square apiece, which is near 400,000 acres of land, and the grant is an absolute estate in fee simple to the several grantees to do with just as they will, except the obligation of building a small hovel for themselves and another for their cattle, and bringing to a few acres of land to English grass in some reasonable time. They pay no quitrent or acknowledgment whatever to the Crown or to the government. But when a father (with his numerous sons and daughters) has spent his (and their) lives in subduing a wilderness at Georgia, that the younger sons and daughters should enjoy no part of the fruit of their labors, but upon the death of their father it must appear they have only been slaves to the eldest heir male, and must become vagabonds and beggars, and in case of no heir male the daughters to be still so by the estate's reverting to the Trustees or to the Crown;—if this be the case, I think it must greatly check the growth of that new colony, by the inhabitants strolling to other parts of America to get lands on the much better terms aforementioned. It's true most of the estates in England are held in such a manner, but it must be considered they have been in cultivation some thousands of years, are become gardens, and capable of raising fortunes for younger children; but it must be centuries before wildernesses will be in such a capacity and situation. You will, Sir, pardon the freedom I have taken, which I think I have done as a true friend to the new colony.

To Lord Egmont

Boston, Nov. 13, 1739

I congratulate your Lordship, with the rest of the Trustees of Georgia, and still more the people there who are spending their lives and little substances to bring forward the settlement of that new colony, that the Trustees are at last resolved to alter the tenure of their grants of land in favor of female succession. I read with a great deal of pleasure the particular account your Lordship gives me of the good reasoning and wise resolutions of your Trustees, and of the generality of the settlers of Georgia, against the introduction of negro (or other) slaves. Indeed, I was always in that way of thinking, that no part of mankind was made to be slaves to their fellow creatures. We have but few in these parts, and I wish there were less. From every white we may hope for a good man to add to the commonwealth. But there is such a natural and general aversion in whites to blacks, that they will never mix or sodder. Nor do even Christians treat them much better than they do their horses and other cattle. I doubt not, my Lord, but these resolutions will prove happy articles for promoting your new plantation.

To Sir Robert Walpole

Boston, Nov. 18, 1740

By some of the last ships from England my friends acquaint me that my unreasonable enemies are implacable, and their malice not to be satiated unless they can accomplish my ruin. While I am, Sir, pursuing my duty to his Majesty in the strictest observance of his royal orders, and doing everything here in my power for the King's honor and interest, and for the welfare of his people, and they at the same time not giving me as much as defrays my annual expense, altho' my whole time is engrossed in the affairs of the government, hard, I think, is my fate to be thus pursued by groundless complaints from my restless enemies. And I cannot but think it unmannerly and rude to a degree that they should continue so to tease and interrupt his Majesty's ministers. Let me then beg of your Honor, as a singular favor, that I may be delivered from such a malicious persecution by your frowning upon my enemies, and that my hands may be strengthened in the government, and my heart encouraged, by your Honor's assurance to my friends of your favor and protection. I have a large family, and laid aside all other ways of life at the time I received the honor of his Majesty's commissions for the two provinces now under my care. And it would be a great severity on me and on my children to be removed only to gratify my enemies and such as may be trying to supplant me, and gaping to feed their needy, hungry, circumstances in my destruction. As I am sure your Honor can make this thing perfectly easy with a word, let me, Sir, humbly hope it from you.

To Thomas Hutchinson

Boston, May 11, 1741

I don't wonder you find such prejudices among the King's ministers against this province when I consider what pains have been taken here for 25 years past to treat the Crown with all possible rudeness and ill manners. Many people take great pains in natural life to destroy their constitutions by whoring, drinking, etc., and finally do the business; and in political life, communities, with other sorts of vices, as pride, obstinacy, wanton use of liberty, and of more than belongs to them, often break up their constitutions. God grant this mayn't be too soon the unhappy case of Massachusetts.

The affairs of Europe I find by your letters and many others are in a most unsettled posture, and we must still wait for the result. A war with France would be the most fatal thing could happen to this miserable province, even beyond the present curse of the land bank, on which you say it would be much better if some other way than by application to Parliament would be found out to suppress it. I assure you the concerned openly declare they defy any act of Parliament to be able to do it. They are grown so brassy and hardy as to be now combining in a body to raise a rebellion, and the day set for their coming to this town is at the election, and their treasurer, I am told, is in the bottom of the design, and I doubt it not. I have this day sent the sheriff and his officers to apprehend some of the heads of the conspirators, so you see we are becoming ripe for a smarter sort of government. What the act of Parliament will be respecting this vile, wicked projection, I can't tell, but if it be no better than the bill I have seen, it will by no means answer the end. The common people here are taught by their advisers to believe they are pretty much out of the reach of the government at home. Nay, our Assembly are sometimes made to think by their leaders that they are as big as the Parliament of Great Britain, but surely as occasions require, I can't help thinking we shall always to our loss and cost find otherwise. The Parliament's rising without doing anything in the paper currencies of the plantations will keep them all in great confusion, and this more especially.

I expect no supply of the treasury this year, no debts to be paid, no government to be supported or defended. In short, Sir, the land bank does so far affect every affair in the Assembly, and throughout the province, that it will be the ruin of government and people, if it be not speedily and effectually crushed.

To Richard Partridge

Boston, July 3, 1741

The 23rd of last month arrived from Bristol, with your kind letter of 30th April, bringing me the melancholy tidings of the King's dismissing me from both my governments, Massachusetts being given to Mr. Shirley, and New Hampshire to Mr. Wentworth. Most certainly, as you say, there is no confidence in man, whose "heart is deceitful above all things and desperately wicked; who can know it?" The great, great man [Sir Robert Walpole], with other great men that you and my other friends have so long attended, and from whom you received from time to time such solemn and sacred assurances of friendship and of my continuances, is a new and flagrant instance of the falsehood, hypocrisy and treachery of mankind.

I must needs own, it gives me a terrible shock, and the more so, when I consider how faithful I have been to the King. And after all to be turned out without fault or complaint I think must be a great discouragement to all faithful servants. But I plainly see truth and justice must never stand in the way of the ease and conveniency of great men. As to what you mention about the land bank, I lay no stress at all upon it. That's but a sham pretense. No! they were resolved to do the thing, *per fas aut nefas* [through right or wrong]. It must be plain to the whole world what an honest and steady part I have acted for destroying that wicked projection, and my letters to you on that head must convince all mankind that I never concerted any thing with you in favor of it.

Upon the whole I desire not too much to look at the wicked instruments that have been used to bring about this extraordinary event of Divine Providence, but I would carry my thoughts higher, and eye the hand of God, fall down and adore and say, "I have sinned, what shall I do unto Thee, O Thou Preserver of men?" I would be dumb and not open my mouth. God is just, and He is still reserving to me many mercies by which and by afflictions may I be led into a stricter obedience to all His holy and righteous laws, and be made happy in a closer communion with Him. Amen.

11

Religion and the Profit Motive

In the early years of the eighteenth century provincial economies grew more complex, and enterprising Americans became more venturesome. Shrewd minds could detect great profits in commerce and even in manufacturing, and some of them were not averse to using sharp and unethical business practices, if these would aid their quest for money.

For some businessmen, however, brought up holding rigorous religious values, their commercial dealings produced guilt feelings along with the profits. Josiah Quinby, the author of the following pamphlet, which was published by John Peter Zenger in 1740, was one of them. Imprisoned for debt after a long and checkered commercial career, Quinby reveals some of the conflicts that afflicted his generation of traders, and along with them some of the opportunities that lay open to a clever New Yorker.

A SHORT HISTORY
OF A LONG JOURNEY
Josiah Quinby

I was born at Westchester in the year 1693, of honest parents and good livers, according to the custom of that place. I being my father's eldest son, he wanted my help on his farm, and so brought me up to husbandry. I had very little schooling. I could read pretty well but was but a poor writer. As my father and mother were of those called Quakers, so they endeavored to bring me up in that way of religion. But I proved rude and very unlucky or mischievous amongst my companions, tho' at some times I was sober and religious.

When I was about 17 years old I grew more sober and religious, and before I was 19 was accounted a member of that church, and had so good an impression of virtue and religion on my mind, that those of that Society received me as such, and the eyes of many were on me for good, hoping that I would prove a good, religious, self-denying man.

I was very sincere and tender in those days, and really intended, through the help of grace that then seemed to rest in me, to have given up my mind to live answerable thereto. But yet at times I grew careless, and after that fell upon several projects and schemes of business.

From *A Short History of a Long Journey; It being some Account of the Life of Josiah Quinby, until he came to enter into the 48th Year of his Age* (New York, 1740), 11–36, 49–54, 56–61.

Some of my business was such that it did not become neither me nor any of that Society to which I belonged, nor indeed any religious Christian. And for these my proceedings, several members and elders of the Meeting that I belonged to, came to me and let me know they were concerned to forward me of the ill consequences of my following such a course of business as I had done. For by this time I had bought and sold many uncertainties, and got into the law, which I had no reason to have done. I was so forward an adventurer that not only many of this county sought to me, and I to them, but also several others from several parts of this government, and some from other adjacent governments, came to me to truck, traffic, buy and sell, in very uncertain affairs and business, some of which went hard on my side, I losing large sums of money. Yet for the most part I got the better of those with whom I ventured.

I got money by large sums, for my dealings were not much in trifles, but in houses, lands, mills, and chiefly things of great consequence. Tho' I also bought some tracts of land fairly, and, dividing them, sold them fairly and gained considerable money by such fair dealings, and I gained money by several projects and contrivances. I had a way to get money yet I had not a faculty to keep it. I got large sums from rich men that were more wise and honest than myself, and fools sometimes got it from me again. I sometimes thought there was a just judgment upon me for this business I followed, for tho' I got large sums of money and great bargains and had money very plenty at times, yet sometimes I wanted money very much, so that I hired 12 or 15 hundred pounds, and for several years I gained above 500 pounds a year, and one year I gained upwards of 900 pounds.

This my going on grieved many of my religious friends, who saw that I was grown more careless concerning religion and virtue than I had been. Whereupon several of the elders again dealt with me, by censoring me for my uncommon proceedings and running of ventures in hazards not much better than gaming. They read to me the advice and counsel of the yearly Meeting of London, and others of Friends' orders and discipline, wherein it is set forth and declared, "That those in unity with that church may not cheat the King by running of goods, nor act deceivably with any of his subjects." And they knowing I was got into a strange sort of juggling business, too much like that of the South Sea Stock, some of them were for denying me, except I would adhere to their counsel. Others advised to the contrary, for though some of my business was wrong, yet they said, "That I was a good commonwealth man, for I had bought and sold a great deal very fairly, and employed many men, whom I generally paid very punctually, so that my word would pass for hundreds of pounds at ready money." They therefore advised me to desist some part of my business, such as they thought unfair, and endeavored to enforce their arguments against me. I answered them with my reasons, and went on still with my notions and business according to my own humor. I undertook and employed many hands in building and rebuilding several stocks of mills, and for my projecting had several sums of money.

As I had made many uncertain bargains of many other kinds, so I have some uncertain bargains concerning mills, one of which I will relate something of in particular, by which you may partly judge of others. The case was this.

I met with some merchants at New York, solid, honest men, and they understanding I was reckoned somewhat acute or famous for projecting or building of mills, and knowing I had a stream which might serve to set a stock of mills on, they viewed the place, and found that at best it would afford but a low head of water. They wanted mills, and as there had been a mill built on the place before by a noted millwright, which mill could never grind so much as 5 bushels an hour of good meal, these merchants thought it impossible for me to build mills there to grind above 6 bushels an hour of good bolting meal, 6 hours in one tide. Yet I proposed to build mills on the said place to great perfection and performance. In the conclusion we agreed, and made the price according to what they should grind for 6 hours together, in an hour, for that was to be the trial. But tho' these men knew and did their common business well, yet they did not know nor believe that I was capable of making any great performance with mills in that place, but I knew it, and therefore I was the more guilty of overreaching them. However, we agreed and went on. I was to build the mills and they were to have them at a price according to the wheat they could grind in 6 hours, in one tide. I had a great mind to have got their consent to have made the said trial with the great pair of stones which was 5 feet broad, and the lesser but 4 feet and 7 inches, for after the mills were finished and both pairs of stones proved by grinding, I offered to drop 164 pounds the price of the mills if they would consent that the trial should be made with the great pair of stones, but they refused that. Now this trial was difficult because in this province of New York wheat and flour are supposed to be the greatest articles of produce we have, and mills being exceeding plenty and wanting custom a great deal of their time, so the millers or owners of mills have been very nice and careful to grind for the bolters in the exactest manner the very best of bolting meal to gain custom.

We then got ready for said trial, and after the stones had ground a little while and seemed to be well settled in their motion, and came to make good bolting meal to the unanimous satisfaction of said judges, then I began to grind measured wheat and went on the trial. The first hour I ground upwards of 16 bushels of wheat, and after that I ground near 18 bushels an hour, and so on until the mills were shut down, grinding as fast and well to the end as at any time at all. Indeed I had a mind to have brought the said little pair of stones to have ground 20 bushels an hour on the trial, but the judges persuaded me that I ground fast enough.

I would not have been so particular in relating this matter, but that several persons, some of whom saw this trial performed and are now living, have urged me to publish the said trial to the world as an advertisement to excite those that are concerned in mills, to endeavor to come to a greater perfection in grinding than is usually performed.

Yet they came to an unreasonable price, nigh two thousand pounds more than they were really worth. I was guilty of this imposition on these men, because I knew most concerning these affairs. For it was not under their notice what a performance I could make. I believe they wanted mills and were willing to give a good honest price for them, but I wanted an advantage. This I do declare to my own shame, and have sincerely thought that I have found as much guilt and condemnation within myself for this thing as ever I found for any deed that ever I did in the course of all my life and business, because this was done with a premeditated design.

However these merchants, after they saw themselves caught, made a vigorous defense against paying so much money, and their lawyers found fault with our bonds and articles of agreement. I sued them, and tho' I seemed too hard for them in the law, yet they found means to avoid the payment of the money, until partly by arbitrations and partly by consent of parties, a great part or all of the extravagant price was dropped, and they finally paid me 975 pounds and court charges. As for their opposition and defense against my unreasonable demands, I think they were to be commended.

Now sometimes men have come to me with a design to overreach me in bargains, knowing that I was very bold and apt to venture, and if such should happen to be bit, as we call it, I did not pity them so much. Many such I have met with, some of which went away with loss, and others with gain and triumph, and thus I have stood many chances. But when I found I had overdone honest men it hath made me heartily sorry for them, and in such cases I have given back many hundreds of pounds.

I often had occasion to travel to New England, and by inquiring there amongst their traders I found by their invoices and bills of parcels made at Boston, that many sorts of goods, especially land goods, were considerably cheaper at New York than they were at Boston. I also observed that barreled pork, wheat and flax seed were much cheaper in Connecticut government than at New York, considering the difference of the moneys. And observing that some of the traders in New England sold many things to the inhabitants extreme dear, I thought some of them used great extortion in dealing so with the people, and that I could use them much better, and perhaps mend thereby my decaying circumstances. So I ventured to trade from New York to New England. I took some hundred pounds worth of goods in New York, and sold them in New England for advance, and I likewise got good returns for New York. I advanced on pork twelve shillings per barrel, on wheat, thirteen pence, and on flax seed, sixteen pence per bushel. And tho' then I sold goods cheap, the returns made out profit enough, and this success encouraged me to go largely the second year. Now the natural courage and boldness of my temper commonly used to lead me to extremes, and now I wanted money, so I ventured to set up several stores in New England, and when it came to be generally known in New York that I kept stores in New England, the merchants in New York were very fond of my custom. One would call me into this store and another into another, so that I have been called into 4 or 5 in going about 40 or 50 rods. Then they would show me their good pennyworths, some again would take me by the hand, others by the coat, some claiming old acquaintance and offering me credit, both Jews and Gentiles. And by such means I was prevailed on to take great quantities of goods where I intended to have taken less. There were several likewise in New England who encouraged me, telling me that they could by trading turn several thousand pounds worth of goods into profitable returns for New York in a year.

Now as I said, being got out of business and into debt, and being both ambitious and loath to break of business, and considering that several times by bold and uncommon enterprises (which I thought more unlikely to hit than this) and yet some of them had taken wonderful turns in my favor, to the amending my circumstances, I now concluded to go on with great business of this kind, and therefore set up stores in several places in New England, giving orders to my storekeepers to sell cheap, considerably cheaper than other traders did. Tho' to the best of my understanding, I ordered everything we sold to be sold for more than what they cost me. And I hoped to make some profit by returns to New York, and by my underselling others I thought to have drawn a vast custom in the several parts in which I traded. I was of opinion that very small gains in a large trade would have made all answer. For as I employed several factors in different towns and places, so I thought every one had his business in selling the goods and taking in suitable returns for New York. And I likewise concluded if a man could get profit by trading in one place or town, so I might get more profit by many factors in several towns.

But as I was much in debt before I entered into this precarious business of so large trading, several of those I owed money to began to think I was got into a more dangerous strain by trading in New England than the business I was in before. Some of them therefore pressed hard on me for their moneys, wherefore I was forced to pay moneys to some and to secure others. Yet still I encouraged myself I should do great matters by trading in very great quantities of goods, and by making profitable returns to New York. But in this I was deceived, for tho' some of my factors were careful, yet others got confused in their accounts and made great mistakes. I myself was but a poor writer, and did not understand such affairs. Neither was I so careful as I should have been, but trusted too much to others.

Towards the latter end of February, 1737/8, I being at New Haven, selling goods and taking in effects for New York, I was taken sick with a sort of a pleurisy, the news of which quickly got to New York amongst my creditors, and was as quickly followed by the news of my death.

The merchants, hearing I was dead, got into a great stir and care how they should get their money. And making inquiry one among another, they found my debts large and many. And altho' they were informed by my letters to them that I had been sick but was recovering, and intended to come home in a little time, yet they were got into such a stir and strife who should get their moneys first, that at my coming home I heard that several of them had ordered writs out against me, thinking (I suppose) I might lay down money or secure the first that arrested me. This I heard was their contrivance, tho' it was for money not then due by several months.

As I had been a man of much business, and had business with great numbers of people, so I had many hearty friends, and some back door friends (as we call them) for I have heard that some of them at that time went to my creditors and informed them that I had a large sea sloop right fitted for the sea, and that in all probability I would take my wife, child, goods, and money, and go off to some foreign part of the world. Some of my creditors were afraid that these reports were likely to be true. By this time I was come home to my house at Mamaroneck from New England, and then heard more of these tumults and discontents amongst the merchants, my creditors at New York, and that some of them had taken out writs against me for the monies as aforesaid. I therefore shut my doors and dispatched a messenger directly to my creditors, and thereby acquainted them that I had heard of their uneasiness concerning the goods I had had of them, and that I understood there were some writs out against me, that I had shut my doors against such writs, and could not stand such a storm as was risen against me. But since it had happened thus, I knew that I could not go on with business. If therefore they would choose a committee, I would deliver all I had into their hands for the use or security of my creditors in general, on a settlement, for that I intended to do them all the justice that was in my power.

We had much discourse and drinking tea together, they seemed very friendly, and in conclusion told me this: That what I offered them was all that my creditors could now expect of me. Tho' they were sorry that my lands were claimed by others and my circumstances so mean, but however they concluded to go to New York and inform my creditors of the state of things, and get power from them to make a settlement if they consented, as they doubted not but they would. And accordingly they went for New York to return within a few days, and accordingly returned. But they brought writs and took me prisoner about the beginning of April, Anno 1738. Others likewise by their orders brought more writs against me, until I was arrested for about eight thousand pounds New York currency. So they brought me to Westchester and delivered me to the high sheriff Isaac Willet, who, as some thought, would have me committed to close jail. I being now in his care, it may not be amiss to mention the usage that prisoners now have, and heretofore have had under the several preceding high sheriffs of this county, which hath been thus. When they have arrested such prisoners that could not get bail because of the largeness of their debts, yet if they were such as the sheriff dare to confide in, he let them have the liberty of the county, until the debt or debts have been ripened to execution. And then such trusty prisoners have come and delivered themselves to jail, and such have had the best of the rooms within the verge and court of the prison house, which is sufficiently commodious and comfortable for debtors, when at the same time those that cannot be trusted, are shut up in a close room, or rooms with bolts, bars and locks. But notwithstanding my debts were so very large and many, yet providence so ordered it that I have had the same favors with the said officer, as hath been usually granted to the most trusty prisoners.

The time passed until about the last of October, Anno 1738, and then I had an execution served on me, in consequence of which I came to this place, and so have continued under this roof from that time until this day, it being the 30th of April, Anno 1740, and I am now 47 years and one month old. As to my living here I have no reason to complain. As to my diet, I live temperately, eat sparingly. And since I have been here, and for many years before, have chiefly drank water, and at some times small beer. As to rum I want none, and as to wine I don't drink a pint in three months. I now generally work part of every day, following some small timber business, by which I earn some money, more than any ever earned here before. The other part of the day I can read, converse with my friends, and recollect the past times. Generally, ever since I came here, I have taken something of the care of the close prisoners, both of the debtors, criminals and condemned. As to those debtors that are kept close, I generally find them some work or employment whereby they can earn their provisions and live tolerable comfortable, without being chargeable either to me or the public. Whereas they used to live by begging, and sometimes almost starved, they now wish and pray that I may continue long here for their said help and comfort. But I wish I could do better for my creditors than I am able to do. I have let that company, viz. my creditors, have considerable money and effects since they have confined me, that I could have kept from them, for which some people blame me, because I have always stood ready and have offered my creditors to deliver all I had to them in the best manner I could, if they would have accepted of it on a settlement. But they have not accepted, and I am now ready to do the same, without the least deceit or evasion if they would, and more I cannot do. I have no blame to lay to their charge. I believe they proceeded against me as they did, believing that it would have proved most to their profit and safety, yet I conceive their so proceeding has made things abundantly more dark and difficult than they would have been, and it is not in my power now to mend it.

For my own part, I do not much regard all that hath or is like to fall on me, for I am fully persuaded that I never have received any wrong by any man, nor by any creature whatsoever, and am satisfied that that affliction, contradiction and punishments which I have met with, are all of them not only just, but more abundantly I have deserved.

And now, if any would inquire further how I can account for these miscarriages and miscomputations which I have made, and being brought up but a ploughman, how I came to run into such a multiplicity of business and inventions that did not properly belong to me, it being beyond my proper sphere, I answer and say, "It was of covetousness in a great measure that thus led me out of the way. For that I had a mind to get money, and then let my mind out to seek after many inventions to satisfy this my inordinate desire, some of which was commendable, and others not good. And so I entered into many undertakings, which in the end hath not only been a hurt to me, but to my said creditors also."

And now coming toward conclusion, I believe that there be many of my friends and acquaintance that would be glad to inquire of me whether I can be content in these times of my confinement. To which I answer, "there is several sorts of content. There is a content proper to beasts and birds, but that is a low and mean sort of content." For altho' they of them that are strong glory in their strength and delight to tear and devour the prey, yet the bear and lion may be bereaved of their whelps, and also miss of their desired prey, and meet with sickness and anguish. And then all their content is turned into bitter torments and strong pains. So also there is some sorts of contents amongst men of all ranks and stations, high and low, which is too much like that of the beasts, soon rushed into the utmost confusion. And so all content that is amongst mankind is low, mean, and to be despised as not

111

fit to be rested in, except it be only which proceeds from a resigned mind to the will of divine providence, and so far the minds of men are reconciled and united to whatever the great wise order of providence brings about. So far mankind may rest, in an undisturbed mind, and say from a true principle of obedience, "Thy will be done, thy Kingdom come."

But now I have been greatly affected and troubled that I should become an instrument to hurt others, either in their minds or estates. I have often most sincerely thought that I could and would willingly suffer the pains of many deaths, if it was possible thereby to take away the damages and offenses from those with whom I have been concerned. But I find that what I cannot possibly bring back must rest as it is.

But sure I am that I cannot rest nor be content in any other temper of mind, than that I stand ready in singleness of heart to do the best for them all for the future, that possible I can. And now I stand open and free to receive counsel from them, and from all others, that can advise me. And in this resolution and disposition of mind I find that content that will not be easily taken away.

But concerning true content and religious influences, I would in modesty and meekness have shut my mouth and held my pen, because of the folly that I have been guilty of. But it is thought a little of the power of resigned mind and warmth of love that makes me bold to declare what is truth. And whosoever he be that knows the power of a full resigned mind, well knows that it makes the spirit of a man bolder than a lion and stronger than the unicorn. The weights of the rocks and hills cannot bear it down, the flames of fire cannot consume it, nor the seas drown it. Its strength is only in the cross of Jesus, and in being resigned, it is found in the deep valley of humility. So this is a light in opposition to that darkness, and it never was nor can be rightly known, only but by being felt, and it is to be felt only in the inmost part. And whoever do so feel as to find it will see it to be that grace and truth that came by Jesus.

And it will float us above the troubles of this unquiet world, where there is felicity and an undisturbed content, and then if the sea should roar and tumults arise in the world, yet there remains a sanctuary to those of a resigned mind. May we all so resign our own wills to his will, who rules in wisdom now and ever more, is that which is heartily desired by,

Your Friend and Well Wisher,
Josiah Quinby

12

The Great Awakening

The series of religious revivals of the 1730s and 1740s, known collectively as the Great Awakening, was a bitterly divisive experience for eighteenth-century Americans. While many found the sudden conversions and energetic preaching of itinerant ministers to be an obvious work of God, others feared the excesses and enthusiasm, and doubted that the conversions were permanent. Schisms and disputes developed in Protestant churches as a result, and the religious unity of many communities was permanently shattered.

Thomas Prince (1687–1758), a Boston minister, supported the cause of the revivals and published his account of them in the 1740s. His was but one of many pamphlets debating the character and piety of evangelicals like George Whitefield and Gilbert Tennent, but Prince's prestige and learning added strength to the cause of the revivalists.

AN ACCOUNT OF THE REVIVAL OF RELIGION IN BOSTON
Thomas Prince

It is, I hope, for the glory of God and the public good, that I have drawn up the following narrative of the late revival of religion here, according to the best of my remembrance.

And that the grace and power of God may appear the more illustrious, it seems fit to give a brief and previous history of the general state of religion here, even from my returning hither in 1717, after above eight years travelling abroad, to the time of this revival at the end of 1740.

On my said return, there were five Congregational churches settled with pastors in this town; though now they are increased to five more. And this town and country were in great tranquility both civil and religious. But though there were many bright examples of piety in every seat and order, yet there was a general complaint among the pious and elderly persons, of the great decay of godliness in the lives and conversations of people both in the town and land, from what they had seen in the days of their fathers. There was scarce a prayer made in public by

From Thomas Prince, *An Account of the Revival of Religion in Boston, in the Years 1740, 1, 2, 3* (Boston, 1823), 3–10, 12–18.

the elder ministers without some heavy lamentation of this decay: in their sermons also they frequently mourned it: and the younger ministers commonly followed their example therein.

Soon after my arrival I was called to preach to the South Church: and in 1718, ordained their co-pastor.

In the spring of 1721, the eight ministers who carried on the public Lecture, taking into consideration the lamentable defect of piety among our young people, agreed to preach a Course of Sermons at the Lecture to them. The audiences were considerably crowded: and while the word of God was loudly sounding, He lifted up His awful rod, by sending the small-pox into the town, which began to spread to our general consternation: scarce a quarter of the people being thought to have had it; and none of the numerous youth under eighteen years of age; it being so many years since that fatal pestilence had prevailed among us. The sermons were quickly printed, with another added by the venerable Dr. Increase Mather, for further benefit. Many of the younger people especially were then greatly awakened: and many hundreds of them quickly after swept into eternity.

In the spring of 1722, the distemper left us: but so little reformed were the surviving youth, that at the end of the summer, the pastors agreed to move their churches to keep in each successively "a day of prayer and fasting, to ask of God the effusion of his Holy Spirit, particularly on the rising generation." And the churches readily received the motion.

But though a solemnity appeared on many, yet it pleased the holy God to humble us and sparingly to give the blessing.

And though in the spring of 1726, in an awakening view of the deplorable decay of family religion, as a principal source of all other decays, the pastors went into a course of Public Lectures on that important subject; yet they had the further sorrow to see those Lectures too thinly attended to expect much benefit from them.

But after all our endeavors, both our security and degeneracy seemed in general to grow, until the night after the Lord's Day, October 29, 1727, when the glorious God arose and fearfully shook the earth through all these countries. By terrible things in righteousness He began to answer us, as the God of our salvation.

On the next morning a very full assembly met at the North Church, for the proper exercises on so extraordinary an occasion. At five in the evening a crowded concourse assembled at the Old Church: and multitudes unable to get in, immediately flowed to the South, and in a few minutes filled that also.

The ministers endeavored to set in with this extraordinary and awakening work of God in nature, and to preach His word in the most awakening manner; to show the people the vast difference between conviction and conversion, between a forced reformation either in acts of piety, justice, charity, or sobriety, by the mere power of fear, and a genuine change of the very frame and relish of the heart by the supernatural efficacy of the Holy Spirit; to lead them on to true conversion and unfeigned faith in Christ, and to guard them against deceiving themselves.

In all our congregations, many seemed to be awakened and reformed: and professing repentance of their sins and faith in Christ, entered into solemn covenant with God, and came into full communion with our several churches. In ours, within eight months after, were about eighty added to our communicants. But then comparatively few of these applied to me to discourse about their souls until they came to offer themselves to the Communion, or afterwards: the most of those who came to me seemed to have passed through their convictions before their coming to converse with me about approaching to the Lord's Table: though I doubt not but considerable numbers were at that time savingly converted.

However the goodness of many seemed as the morning cloud and early dew which quickly passes away. A spiritual slumber seemed soon to seize the generality; even the wise as well as foolish virgins. And though in 1729, the small pox came into town and prevailed again; yet in a few months left us, both unawakened, ungrateful, unreformed. The Holy Spirit awfully withheld his influence in convincing and converting sinners, and enlivening others. In three or four years we rather grew to a greater declension than ever: and so alarmed were the pastors of the town with the dismal view, that in the summer of 1734, they agreed to propose another Course of Days of Prayer and Fasting among our several congregations: "To humble ourselves before God for our unfruitfulness under the means of grace, and to ask the effusion of his Spirit to revive the power of godliness among us," which our people readily complied with and observed.

And though the sovereign God was pleased to give us now and then a sprinkling, for which His name be praised; yet the parching drought continued, and He made us wait for a larger effusion.

In this year the terrible throat-distemper broke out and spread among the youth in the easterly parts of this country, and destroyed multitudes. In some towns it cut off almost all the children. The next year it came into Boston, and began to destroy and strike us with a general awe: but gently treated us, and the next year left us; to melt our hearts into a grateful repentance. And yet we generally seemed to grow more stupid and hard then ever.

About this time indeed, viz. 1735, there was a most remarkable revival of religion in the westerly parts of the country: not only at Northampton, but also in about twelve other congregations in the county of Hampshire, and in about fourteen others in the neighboring colony of Connecticut. And the solemn rumor of that surprising work of God resounding through the country, was a special means of exciting great thoughtfulness of heart in many irreligious people; and great joy in others, both in the view of what the mighty power and grace of God had wrought, and in the hopeful prospect that this blessed work begun would go on and spread throughout the land. And as this excited the extraordinary prayers of many, so it seemed to prepare the way in divers places for that more extensive revival of religion which in five years after followed. But, in the mean while, the general decay of piety seemed to increase among us in Boston. And for the congregation I preach to, though for several years some few offered themselves to our Communion, yet but few came to me in concern about their souls before. And so I perceive it was in others: and I remember some of the ministers were wont to express themselves as greatly discouraged with the growing declension both in principle and practice, especially among the rising generation. From the year 1738, we had received accounts of the Rev. Mr. Whitefield, as a very pious young minister of the

Church of England, rising up in the spirit of the Reformers, and preaching their doctrines first in England and then in America, with surprising power and success: which raised desires in great numbers among us to see and hear him. And having received invitations to come hither, he, from Georgia and South-Carolina, arrived at Rhode-Island, on Lord's Day, Sept. 14, 1740, and the Thursday evening after came to Boston.

He began with a short and fervent prayer: and after singing, took his text from John xvii, 2. Gave us a plain, weighty, regular discourse: representing that all our learning and morality will never save us; and without an experimental knowledge of God in Christ, we must perish in hell for ever. He spake as became the oracles of God in demonstration of the Spirit and of power. And especially when he came to his application, he addressed himself to the audience in such a tender, earnest and moving manner, exciting us to come and be acquainted with the dear Redeemer, as melted the assembly into tears.

Next morning, at Dr. Sewall's and my desire, he preached at the South Church, to further acceptance.

He spake with a mighty sense of God, eternity, the immortality and preciousness of the souls of his hearers, of their original corruption, and of the extreme danger the unregenerate are in; with the nature and absolute necessity of regeneration by the Holy Ghost; and of believing in Christ, in order to our pardon, justification, yielding an acceptable obedience, and obtaining salvation from hell, and an entrance into heaven. His doctrine was plainly that of the Reformers: declaring against putting our good works or morality in the room of Christ's righteousness, or their having any hand in our justification, or being indeed pleasing to God while we are totally unsanctified, acting from corrupt principles, and unreconciled enemies to him: which occasioned some to mistake him as if he opposed morality. But he insisted on it, that the tree of the heart is by original sin exceedingly corrupted, and must be made good by regeneration, that so the fruits proceeding from it may be good likewise: that where the heart is renewed, it ought and will be careful to maintain good works; that if any be not habitually so careful, who think themselves renewed, they deceive their own souls: and even the most improved in holiness, as well as others, must entirely depend on the righteousness of Christ for the acceptance of their persons and services. And though now and then he dropped some expressions that were not so accurate and guarded as we should expect from aged and long studied ministers; yet I had the satisfaction to observe his readiness with great modesty and thankfulness to receive correction as soon as offered.

In short, he was a most importunate wooer of souls to come to Christ for the enjoyment of him, and all his benefits. He distinctly applied his exhortations to the elderly people, the middle aged, the young, the Indians and negroes; and had a most winning way of addressing them. He affectionately prayed for our magistrates, ministers, colleges, candidates for the ministry, and churches, as well as people in general: and before he left us, he in a public and moving manner observed to the people, how sorry he was to hear that the religious assemblies, especially on lectures, had been so thin, exhorted them earnestly to a more general attendance on our public ministrations for the time to come, and told them how glad he should be to hear of the same.

Multitudes were greatly affected and many awakened with his lively ministry. Though he preached every day, the houses were exceedingly crowded: but when he preached in the common, a vaster number attended: and almost every evening the house where he lodged was thronged, to hear his prayers and counsels.

Upon invitation he also preached in several neighboring towns; travelled and preached as far as York, above seventy miles northeast of Boston; returned hither; gave us his farewell affectionate sermon, Lord's Day evening, October 12. Next morning left us; travelled westward to Northampton; thence through Connecticut, New York and New Jersey, to Philadelphia, and thence sailed to South Carolina. And as far as I could then see or learn, he parted in the general esteem and love both of ministers and people: and this seemed to continue until the Journal of his Travels in New England came abroad, wherein some passages offended many, and occasioned their reflections on him.

But upon Mr. Whitefield's leaving us, great numbers in this town were so happily concerned about their souls, as we had never seen any thing like it before, except at the time of the general earthquake: and their desires excited to hear their ministers more than ever: so that our assemblies both on Lectures and Sabbaths were surprisingly increased, and now the people wanted to hear us oftener. In consideration of which, a public Lecture was proposed to be set up at Dr. Colman's church, near the midst of the town, on every Tuesday evening.

Upon the Rev. Mr. Gilbert Tennent's coming and preaching here, the people appeared to be yet much more awakened about their souls than before. He came, I think, on Saturday, December 13, this year: preached at the New North on both the parts of the following day; as also on Monday in the afternoon, when I first heard him, and there was a great assembly.

He did not indeed at first come up to my expectation; but afterwards exceeded it. In private converse with him, I found him to be a man of considerable parts and learning; free, gentle, condescending: and from his own various experience, reading the most noted writers on experimental divinity, as well as the Scriptures, and conversing with many who had been awakened by his ministry in New Jersey, where he then lived; he seemed to have as deep an acquaintance with the experimental part of religion as any I have conversed with; and his preaching was as searching and rousing as ever I heard.

He seemed to have no regard to please the eyes of his hearers with agreeable gesture, nor their ears with delivery, nor their fancy with language; but to aim directly at their hearts and consciences, to lay open their ruinous delusions, show them their numerous, secret, hypocritical shifts in religion, and drive them out of every deceitful refuge wherein they made themselves easy, with the form of godliness without the power. And many who were pleased in a good conceit of themselves before, now found, to their great distress, they were only self-deceived hypocrites. And though while the discovery was making, some at first raged, as they

117

have owned to me and others; yet in the progress of the discovery many were forced to submit; and then the power of God so broke and humbled them, that they wanted a further and even a thorough discovery; they went to hear him, that the secret corruptions and delusions of their hearts might be more discovered; and the more searching the sermon, the more acceptable it was to their anxious minds.

From the terrible and deep convictions he had passed through in his own soul, he seemed to have such a lively view of the divine Majesty, the spirituality, purity, extensiveness, and strictness of his law; with his glorious holiness, and displeasure at sin, his justice, truth, and power in punishing the damned; that the very terrors of God seemed to rise in his mind afresh, when he displayed and brandished them in the eyes of unreconciled sinners. And though some could not bear the representation, and avoided his preaching; yet the arrows of conviction, by his ministry, seemed so deeply to pierce the hearts of others, and even some of the most stubborn sinners, as to make them fall down at the feet of Christ, and yield a lowly submission to him.

And here I cannot but observe, that those who call these convictions by the name of religious frights or fears, and then ascribe them to the mere natural or mechanical influence of terrible words, sounds and gestures, moving tones, or boisterous ways of speaking, appear to me to be not sufficiently acquainted with the subjects of this work, as carried on in the town in general, or with the nature of their convictions; or at least as carried on among the people I have conversed with. For I have had awakened people of every assembly of the Congregational and Presbyterian way in town, in considerable numbers repairing to me from time to time; and from their various and repeated narratives shall show the difference.

I don't remember any crying out, or falling down, or fainting, either under Mr. Whitefield's or Mr. Tennent's ministry all the while they were here; though many, both women and men, both those who had been vicious, and those who had been moral, yea, some religious and learned, as well as as unlearned, were in great concern of soul. But as Dr. Colman well expressed it in his Letter of November 23, 1741, "We have seen little of those extremes or supposed blemishes of this work in Boston, but much of the blessed fruits of it have fallen to our share. God has spoken to us in a more soft and calm wind; and we have neither had those outcries and faintings in our assemblies, which have disturbed the worship in many places; nor yet those manifestations of joy inexpressible, which now fill some of our eastern parts."

As to Mr. Whitefield's preaching—it was, in the manner, moving, earnest, winning, melting: but the mechanical influence of this, according to the usual operations of mechanical powers, in two or three days expired; with many, in two or three hours; and I believe with the most, as soon as the sound was over, or they got out of the house, or in the first conversation they fell into. But with the manner of his preaching, wherein he appeared to be in earnest, he delivered those vital truths which animated all our martyrs, made them triumph in flames; and led his hearers into the view of that vital, inward, active piety, which is the mere effect of the mighty and supernatural operation of a divine Power on the souls of men;

118

which only will support and carry through the sharpest trials, and make meet for the inheritance of the saints in light. His chief and earnest desires and labors appeared to be the same with the apostle Paul for the visible saints at Ephesus; viz. that they might know (i.e. by experience) what is the exceeding greatness of his power (i.e. the power of God) to us-ward who believe, according to the working of his mighty power which he wrought in Christ when he raised him from the dead.—Eph. 1. And they were these things, and this sort of preaching with surprising fervency, that the Holy Spirit was pleased to use as means to make many sensible they knew nothing of these mighty operations, nor of these vital principles within them; but that with Simon Magus, who was a visible believer and professor of Christ and his religion, they were in "the gall of bitterness and in the bonds of iniquity;" i.e. in the state, pollution, guilt and power of sin, which is inexpressibly more disagreeable to the holy God than the most bitter gall to men, and will be bitterness to them, without a mighty change, in the latter end.

It was by such means as these, that the Holy Spirit seized and awakened the consciences of many; and when the mechanical influence on the animal passions ceased, still continued these convictions, not only for many days, but weeks and months after the sound was over; yea, to this very day with some; while they excited others to an earnest and persevering application to Jesus for his Spirit to quicken them, till they came to an hopeful perception of his quickening influence in them; and while in others the sovereign and offended Spirit leaving off to strive, these convictions in their consciences, the effects thereof, have either sooner or later died away.

As to Mr. Tennent's preaching—It was frequently both terrible and searching. It was often for matter justly terrible, as he, according to the inspired oracles, exhibited the dreadful holiness, justice, law, threatenings, truth, power, majesty of God; and His anger with rebellious, impenitent, unbelieving and Christless sinners; the awful danger they were every moment in of being struck down to hell, and being damned for ever; with the amazing miseries of that place of torment. But his exhibitions, both for matter and manner, fell inconceivably below the reality: and though this terrible preaching may strongly work on the natural passions and frighten the hearers, rouse the soul, and prepare the way for terrible convictions; yet those mere natural terrors, and these convictions are quite different things.

Nothing is more obvious than for people to be greatly terrified with the apprehensions of God, enternity and hell, and yet have no convictions.

In Old England and New, where I have been a constant preacher and an observer of the religious state of those who heard me, for above thirty years, many have passed under scores of most dreadful tempests of thunder and lightning.

Yea, even since the Revival, viz. on Friday night, July 30, 1742, at the lecture in the South Church, near nine o'clock being very dark, there came on a very terrible storm of thunder and lightning: and just as the blessing was given, an amazing clap broke over the church with piercing repetitions, which set many a shrieking, and the whole assembly into great consternation for near two hours together. And yet in all these displays of the majesty of God, and terrifying ap-

119

prehensions of danger of sudden destruction; neither in this surprising night, nor in all the course of thirty years have I scarce known any, by these kinds of terrors brought under genuine convictions. And what minister has a voice like God, and who can thunder like Him?

So on Lord's Day, June 3d last, in our time of public worship in the forenoon, when we had been about a quarter of an hour in prayer, the mighty power of God came on with a surprising roar and earthquake; which made the house with all the galleries to rock and tremble, with such a grating noise as if the bricks were moving out of their places to come down and bury us: which exceedingly disturbed the congregation, excited the shrieks of many, put many on flying out, and the generality in motion. But though many were greatly terrified, yet in a day or two their terrors seemed to vanish, and I know of but two or three seized by convictions on this awful occasion.

No! conviction is quite another sort of thing. It is the work of the Spirit of God, a sovereign, free and Almighty agent; wherein He gives the sinful soul such a clear and lively view of the glory of the Divine Sovereignty, omnipresence, holiness, justice, truth and power, the extensiveness, spirituality and strictness of His law; the binding nature, efficacy and dreadfulness of His curses; the multitude and heinousness of its sins both of commission and omission; the horrible vileness, wickedness, perverseness and hypocrisy of the heart, with its utter impotence either rightly to repent, or believe in Christ, or change itself: so that it sees itself in a lost, undone and perishing state; without the least degree of worthiness to recommend it to the holy and righteous God, and the least degree of strength to help itself out of this condition.

Such were the convictions wrought in many hundreds in this town by Mr. Tennent's searching ministry: and such was the case of those many scores of several other congregations as well as mine, who came to me and others for direction under them. And indeed by all their converse I found, it was not so much the terror, as the searching nature of his ministry, that was the principal means of their conviction. It was not merely, nor so much his laying open the terrors of the law and wrath of God, or damnation of hell (for this they could pretty well bear, as long as they hoped these belonged not to them, or they could easily avoid them); as his laying open their many vain and secret shifts and refuges, counterfeit resemblances of grace, delusive and damning hopes, their utter impotence, and impending danger of destruction: whereby they found all their hopes and refuges of lies to fail them, and themselves exposed to eternal ruin, unable to help themselves, and in a lost condition. This searching preaching was both the suitable and principal means of the conviction: though it is most evident, the most proper means are utterly insufficient; and wholly depend on the sovereign will of God, to put forth His power and apply them by this or that instrument, on this or that person, at this or that season, in this or that way or manner; with these or those permitted circumstances, infirmities, corruptions, errors, agencies, oppositions; and to what degree, duration and event He pleases.

A remarkable instance of conviction also, has been sometimes under the ministry of the Rev. Mr. Edwards of Northampton: a preacher of a low and moderate voice, a natural way of delivery; and without any agitation of body, or any thing else in the manner to excite attention; except his habitual and great solemnity, looking and speaking as in the presence of God, and with a weighty sense of the matter delivered. And on the other hand, I have known several very worthy ministers of loud and rousing voices; and yet to their great sorrow the generality of their people, for a long course of years asleep in deep security. It is just as the Holy Spirit pleases, to hide occasions of pride from man: and if Mr. Tennent was to come here again and preach more rousingly than ever, it may be, not one soul would come under conviction by him.

13

Proposals for Living

Benjamin Franklin (1706–1790) was perhaps the most extraordinary and versatile American of his century—printer, author, inventor, philanthropist, philosopher, diplomat, and statesman; any list of his accomplishments would take up immense space. Shortly after moving from Boston to Philadelphia in 1723, Franklin purchased *The Pennsylvania Gazette*, and was soon publishing his famous almanacs as well. His interest in civic improvement, ranging from philosophical societies and hospitals to fire prevention and insurance, reflected the benevolence of the man and the character of the American Enlightenment. Paralleling in time the proposals for human improvement being submitted in contemporary Europe, Franklin's plans were distinguished by their practicality, their simplicity, and, quite frequently, their wry sense of humor. The following selections merely hint at the range of Franklin's thought, and reveal how more secular and profit-oriented was the intellectual life of mid-century America. The "Rules" were drawn up in 1728 and helped form the basis for The Junto, a club of Franklin's acquaintances. *The Way to Wealth* was an assembly of many of the maxims Franklin had popularized in *Poor Richard's Almanac* between 1732, the year of his first Almanac, and 1757, when this compilation first appeared.

RULES FOR A CLUB
FOR MUTUAL IMPROVEMENT
Benjamin Franklin

**Previous Question, To Be Answered
at Every Meeting**

Have you read over these queries this morning, in order to consider what you might have to offer the Junto touching any one of them? viz.

1. Have you met with any thing in the author you last read, remarkable, or suitable to be communicated to the Junto? particularly in history, morality, poetry, physic, travels, mechanic arts, or other parts of knowledge.

From "Rules for a Club Established for Mutual Improvement," "The Way to Wealth," and "Self-denial Not the Essence of Virtue" in *The Works of Benjamin Franklin*, Jared Sparks, ed. (Boston, 1836), II: 9–12, 63–66, 94–103.

2. What new story have you lately heard agreeable for telling in conversation?

3. Hath any citizen in your knowledge failed in his business lately, and what have you heard of the cause?

4. Have you lately heard of any citizen's thriving well, and by what means?

5. Have you lately heard how any present rich man, here or elsewhere, got his estate?

6. Do you know of a fellow citizen, who has lately done a worthy action, deserving praise and imitation; or who has lately committed an error, proper for us to be warned against and avoid?

7. What unhappy effects of intemperance have you lately observed or heard; of imprudence, of passion, or of any other vice or folly?

8. What happy effects of temperance, of prudence, of moderation, or of any other virtue?

9. Have you or any of your acquaintance been lately sick or wounded? If so, what remedies were used, and what were their effects?

10. Whom do you know that are shortly going voyages or journeys, if one should have occasion to send by them?

11. Do you think of any thing at present, in which the Junto may be service-able to *mankind,* to their country, to their friends, or to themselves?

12. Hath any deserving stranger arrived in town since last meeting, that you have heard of? And what have you heard or observed of his character or merits? And whether, think you, it lies in the power of the Junto to oblige him, or encourage him as he deserves?

13. Do you know of any deserving young beginner lately set up, whom it lies in the power of the Junto any way to encourage?

14. Have you lately observed any defect in the laws of your *country,* of which it would be proper to move the legislature for an amendment? Or do you know of any beneficial law that is wanting?

15. Have you lately observed any encroachment on the just liberties of the people?

16. Hath any body attacked your reputation lately? And what can the Junto do towards securing it?

17. Is there any man whose friendship you want, and which the Junto, or any of them, can procure for you?

18. Have you lately heard any member's character attacked, and how have you defended it?

19. Hath any man injured you, from whom it is in the power of the Junto to procure redress?

20. In what manner can the Junto, or any of them, assist you in any of your honorable designs?

21. Have you any weighty affair on hand, in which you think the advice of the Junto may be of service?

22. What benefits have you lately received from any man not present?

23. Is there any difficulty in matters of opinion, of justice, and injustice, which you would gladly have discussed at this time?

24. Do you see any thing amiss in the present customs or proceedings of the Junto, which might be amended?

Any person to be qualified [as a member of the JUNTO], to stand up, and lay his hand upon his breast, and be asked these questions, viz.

1. Have you any particular disrespect to any present members? *Answer.* I have not.

2. Do you sincerely declare, that you love mankind in general, of what profession or religion soever? *Answer.* I do.

3. Do you think any person ought to be harmed in his body, name, or goods, for mere speculative opinions, or his external way of worship? *Answer.* No.

4. Do you love truth for truth's sake, and will you endeavour impartially to find and receive it yourself, and communicate it to others? *Answer.* Yes.

SELF-DENIAL NOT
THE ESSENCE OF VIRTUE

It is commonly asserted, that without self-denial there is no virtue, and that the greater the self-denial the greater the virtue.

If it were said, that he who cannot deny himself any thing he inclines to, though he knows it will be to his hurt, has not the virtue of resolution or fortitude, it would be intelligible enough; but, as it stands, it seems obscure or erroneous.

Let us consider some of the virtues singly.

If a man has no inclination to wrong people in his dealings, if he feels no temptation to it, and therefore never does it, can it be said that he is not a just man? If he is a just man, has he not the virtue of justice?

If to a certain man idle diversions have nothing in them that is tempting, and therefore he never relaxes his application to business for their sake, is he not an industrious man? Or has he not the virtue of industry?

I might in like manner instance in all the rest of the virtues; but, to make the thing short, as it is certain that the more we strive against the temptations to any vice, and practise the contrary virtue, the weaker will that temptation be, and the stronger will be that habit, till at length the temptation has no force, or entirely vanishes; does it follow from thence, that in our endeavours to overcome vice we grow continually less and less virtuous, till at length we have no virtue at all?

If self-denial be the essence of virtue, then it follows that the man, who is naturally temperate, just, &c., is not virtuous; but that in order to be virtuous, he must, in spite of his natural inclination, wrong his neighbours, and eat, and drink, &c., to excess.

But perhaps it may be said, that by the word *virtue* in the above assertion, is meant merit; and so it should stand thus; Without self-denial there is no merit, and the greater the self-denial the greater the merit.

The self-denial here meant, must be when our inclinations are towards vice, or else it would still be nonsense.

By merit is understood desert; and, when we say a man merits, we mean that he deserves praise or reward.

We do not pretend to merit any thing of God, for he is above our services; and the benefits he confers on us are the effects of his goodness and bounty.

All our merit, then, is with regard to one another, and from one to another.

Taking, then, the assertion as it last stands,

If a man does me a service from a natural benevolent inclination, does he deserve less of me than another, who does me the like kindness against his inclination?

If I have two journeymen, one naturally industrious, the other idle, but both perform a day's work equally good, ought I to give the latter the most wages?

Indeed lazy workmen are commonly observed to be more extravagant in their demands than the industrious; for, if they have not more for their work, they cannot live as well. But though it be true to a proverb, that lazy folks take the most pains, does it follow that they deserve the most money?

If you were to employ servants in affairs of trust, would you not bid more for one you knew was naturally honest, than for one naturally roguish, but who has lately acted honestly? For currents whose natural channel is dammed up, till the new course is by time worn sufficiently deep, and become natural, are apt to break their banks. If one servant is more valuable than another, has he not more merit than the other? and yet this is not on account of superior self-denial.

Is a patriot not praiseworthy, if public spirit is natural to him?

Is a pacing-horse less valuable for being a natural pacer?

Nor, in my opinion, has any man less merit for having in general natural virtuous inclinations.

The truth is, that temperance, justice, charity, etc. are virtues, whether practised with, or against our inclinations, and the man, who practises them, merits our love and esteem; and self-denial is neither good nor bad, but as it is applied. He that denies a vicious inclination, is virtuous in proportion to his resolution; but the most perfect virtue is above all temptation; such as the virtue of the saints in heaven; and he, who does a foolish, indecent, or wicked thing, merely because it is contrary to his inclination (like some mad enthusiasts I have read of, who ran about naked, under the notion of taking up the cross), is not practising the reasonable science of virtue, but is a lunatic.

THE WAY TO WEALTH

Courteous Reader

I have heard, that nothing gives an author so great pleasure as to find his works respectfully quoted by others. Judge, then, how much I must have been gratified by an incident I am going to relate to you. I stopped my horse lately, where a great number of people were collected at an auction of merchants' goods. The hour of the sale not being come, they were conversing on the badness of the times; and one of the company called to a plain, clean, old man, with white locks, "Pray, Father Abraham, what think you of the times? Will not these heavy taxes quite ruin the country? How shall we ever be able to pay them? What would you advise us to?" Father Abraham stood up, and replied, "If you would have my advice, I will give it you in short; for *A word to the wise is enough,* as Poor Richard says." They joined in desiring him to speak his mind, and gathering round him, he proceeded as follows.

"Friends," said he, "the taxes are indeed very heavy, and, if those laid on by the government were the only ones we had to pay, we might more easily discharge them; but we have many others, and much more grievous to some of us. We are taxed twice as much by our idleness, three times as much by our pride, and four times as much by our folly; and from these taxes the commissioners cannot ease or deliver us, by allowing an abatement. However, let us hearken to good advice, and something may be done for us; *God helps them that help themselves,* as Poor Richard says.

"It would be thought a hard government, that should tax its people one-tenth part of their time, to be employed in its service; but idleness taxes many of us much more; sloth, by bringing on diseases, absolutely shortens life. *Sloth, like rust, consumes faster than labor wears; while the used key is always bright,* as Poor Richard says. *But dost thou love life, then do not squander time, for that is the stuff life is made of,* as Poor Richard says. How much more than is necessary do we spend in sleep, forgetting, that *The sleeping fox catches no poultry,* and that *There will be sleeping enough in the grave,* as Poor Richard says.

"*If time be of all things the most precious, wasting time must be,* as Poor Richard says, *the greatest prodigality;* since, as he elsewhere tells us, *Lost time is never found again; and what we call time enough, always proves little enough.* Let us then up and be doing, and doing to the purpose; so by diligence shall we do more with less perplexity. *Sloth makes all things difficult, but industry all easy;* and *He that riseth late must trot all day, and shall scarce overtake his business at night;* while *Laziness travels so slowly, that Poverty soon overtakes him. Drive thy business, let not that drive thee;* and *Early to bed, and early to rise, makes a man healthy, wealthy, and wise,* as Poor Richard says.

"So what signifies wishing and hoping for better times? We may make these times better, if we bestir ourselves. *Industry need not wish, and he that lives upon hopes will die fasting. There are no gains without pains; then help, hands, for I have no lands;* or, if I have, they are smartly taxed. *He that hath a trade hath an estate; and he that hath a calling, hath an office of profit and honor,* as Poor Richard says; but then the trade must be worked at, and the calling followed, or neither the estate nor the office will enable us to pay our taxes. If we are industrious, we shall never starve; for, *At the working man's house hunger looks in, but dares not enter.* Nor will the bailiff or the constable enter, for *Industry pays debts, while despair increaseth them.* What though you have found no treasure, nor has any rich relation left you a legacy, *Diligence is the mother of good luck, and God gives all things to industry. Then plough deep while sluggards sleep, and you shall have corn to sell and to keep.* Work while it is called to-day, for you know not how much you may be hindered to-morrow. *One to-day is worth two to-morrows,* as Poor Richard says; and further, *Never leave that till to-morrow, which you can do to-day.* If you were a servant, would you not be ashamed that a good master should catch you idle? Are you then your own master? Be ashamed to catch yourself idle, when there is so much to be done for yourself, your family, your country, and your king. Handle your tools without mittens; remember, that *The cat in gloves catches no mice,* as Poor Richard says. It is true there is much to be done, and perhaps you are weak-handed; but stick to it steadily, and you will see great effects; for *Constant dropping wears away stones;* and *By diligence and patience the mouse ate in two the cable; and Little strokes fell great oaks.*

"Methinks I hear some of you say, 'Must a man afford himself no leisure?' I will tell thee, my friend, what Poor Richard says, *Employ thy time well, if thou meanest to gain leisure; and, since thou art not sure of a minute, throw not away an hour.* Leisure is time for doing something useful; this leisure the diligent man will obtain, but the lazy man never; for *A life of leisure and a life of laziness are two things. Many, without labor, would live by their wits only, but they break for want of stock;* whereas industry gives comfort, and plenty, and respect. *Fly pleasures, and they will follow you. The diligent spinner has a large shift; and now I have a sheep and a cow, everybody bids me good morrow.*

"But with our industry we must likewise be steady, settled, and careful, and oversee our own affairs with our own eyes, and not trust too much to others; for, as Poor Richard says,

I never saw an oft-removed tree,
Nor yet an oft-removed family,
That throve so well as those that settled be.

And again, *Three removes are as bad as a fire;* and again, *Keep thy shop, and thy shop will keep thee;* and again, *If you would have your business done, go; if not, send.* And again,

He that by the plough would thrive,
Himself must either hold or drive.

And again, *The eye of a master will do more work than both his hands;* and again, *Want of care does us more damage than want of knowledge;* and again, *Not to oversee workmen, is to leave them your purse open.* Trusting too much to others' care is the ruin of many; for *In the affairs of this world men are saved, not by faith, but by the want of it;* but a man's own care is profitable; for, *If you would have a faithful servant, and one that you like, serve yourself. A little neglect may breed great mischief; for want of a nail the shoe was lost; for want of a shoe the horse was lost; and for want of a horse the rider was lost, being overtaken and slain by the enemy; all for want of a little care about a horse-shoe nail.*

"So much for industry, my friends, and attention to one's own business; but to these we must add frugality, if we would make our industry more certainly successful. A man may, if he knows not how to save as he gets, keep his nose all his life to the grindstone, and die not worth a groat at last. *A fat kitchen makes a lean will;* and

Many estates are spent in the getting,
Since women for tea forsook spinning and knitting,
And men for punch forsook hewing and splitting.

If you would be wealthy, think of saving as well as of getting. The Indies have not made Spain rich, because her outgoes are greater than her incomes.

"Away then with your expensive follies, and you will not then have so much cause to complain of hard times, heavy taxes, and chargeable families; for

Women and wine, game and deceit,
Make the wealth small and the want great.

And further, *"What maintains one vice would bring up two children.* You may think, perhaps, that a little tea, or a little punch now and then, diet a little more costly, clothes a little finer, and a little entertainment now and then, can be no great matter; but remember, *Many a little makes a mickle.* Beware of little expenses; *A small leak will sink a great ship,* as Poor Richard says; and again, *Who dainties love, shall beggars prove;* and moreover, *Fools make feasts, and wise men eat them.*

"Here you are all got together at this sale of fineries and knick-knacks. You call them *goods;* but, if you do not take care, they will prove *evils* to some of you. You expect they will be sold cheap, and perhaps they may for less then they cost; but, if you have no occasion for them, they must be dear to you. Remember what Poor Richard says; *Buy what thou hast no need of, and ere long thou shalt sell thy necessaries.* And again, *At a great pennyworth pause a while.* He means, that perhaps the cheapness is apparent only, and not real; or the bargain, by straitening thee in thy business, may do thee more harm than good. For in another place he says, *Many have been ruined by buying good pennyworths.* Again, *It is foolish to lay out money in a purchase of repentance;* and yet this folly is practised every day at auctions, for want of minding the Almanac. Many a one, for the sake of finery on the back, have gone with a hungry belly and half-starved their families. *Silks and satins, scarlet and velvets, put out the kitchen fire,* as Poor Richard says.

"These are not the necessaries of life; they can scarcely be called the conveniences; and yet, only because they look pretty, how many want to have them! By these, and other extravagances, the genteel are reduced to poverty, and forced to borrow of those whom they formerly despised, but who, through industry and frugality, have maintained their standing; in which case it appears plainly, that *A ploughman on his legs is higher than a gentleman on his knees,* as Poor Richard says. Perhaps they have had a small estate left them, which they knew not the getting of; they think, *It is day, and will never be night;* that a little to be spent out of so much is not worth minding; but *Always taking out of the meal-tub, and never putting in, soon comes to the bottom,* as Poor Richard says; and then, *When the well is dry, they know the worth of water.* But this they might have known before, if they had taken his advice. *If you would know the value of money, go and try to borrow some; for he that goes a borrowing goes a sorrowing,* as Poor Richard says; and indeed so does he that lends to such people, when he goes to get it in again. Poor Dick further advises, and says,

Fond pride of dress is sure a very curse;
Ere fancy you consult, consult your purse.

And again, *Pride is as loud a beggar as Want, and a great deal more saucy.* When you have bought one fine thing, you must buy ten more, that your appearance may be all of a piece; but Poor Dick says, *It is easier to suppress the first desire, than to satisfy all that follow it.* And it is as truly folly for the poor to ape the rich, as for the frog to swell in order to equal the ox.

Vessels large may venture more,
But little boats should keep near shore.

It is, however, a folly soon punished; for, as Poor Richard says, *Pride that dines on vanity, sups on contempt. Pride breakfasted with Plenty, dined with Poverty, and supped with Infamy.* And, after all, of what use is this pride of appearance, for which so much is risked, so much is suffered? It cannot promote health, nor ease pain; it makes no increase of merit in the person; it creates envy; it hastens misfortune.

"But what madness must it be to *run in debt* for these superfluities? We are offered by the terms of this sale, six months' credit; and that, perhaps, has induced some of us to attend it, because we cannot spare the ready money, and hope now to be fine without it. But, ah! think what you do when you run in debt; you give to another power over your liberty. If you cannot pay at the time, you will be ashamed to see your creditor; you will be in fear when you speak to him; you will make poor, pitiful, sneaking excuses, and, by degrees, come to lose your veracity, and sink into base, downright lying; for *The second vice is lying, the first is running in debt,* as Poor Richard says; and again, to the same purpose, *Lying rides upon Debt's back;* whereas a free-born Englishman ought not to be ashamed nor afraid to see or speak to any man living. But poverty often deprives a man of all spirit and virtue. *It is hard for an empty bag to stand upright.*

"What would you think of that prince, or of that government, who should issue an edict forbidding you to dress like a gentleman or gentlewoman, on pain of imprisonment or servitude? Would you not say that you were free, have a right to dress as you please, and that such an edict would be a breach of your privileges, and such a government tyrannical? And yet you are about to put yourself under such tyranny, when you run in debt for such dress! Your creditor has authority, at his pleasure, to deprive you of your liberty, by confining you in gaol till you shall be able to pay him. When you have got your bargain, you may, perhaps, think little of payment; but, as Poor Richard says, *Creditors have better memories than debtors; creditors are a superstitious sect, great observers of set days and times.* The day comes round before you are aware, and the demand is made before you are prepared to satisfy it; or, if you bear your debt in mind, the term, which at first seemed so long, will, as it lessens, appear extremely short. Time will seem to have added wings to his heels as well as his shoulders. *Those have a short Lent, who owe money to be paid at Easter.* At present, perhaps, you may think yourselves in thriving circumstances, and that you can bear a little extravagance without injury; but

For age and want save while you may:
No morning sun lasts a whole day.

Gain may be temporary and uncertain, but ever, while you live, expense is constant and certain; and *It is easier to build two chimneys, than to keep one in fuel,* as Poor Richard says; so, *Rather go to bed supperless, than rise in debt.*

Get what you can, and what you get hold;
'Tis the stone that will turn all your lead into gold.

And, when you have got the Philosopher's stone, sure you will no longer complain of bad times, or the difficulty of paying taxes.

129

"This doctrine, my friends, is reason and wisdom; but, after all, do not depend too much upon your own industry, and frugality, and prudence, though excellent things; for they may all be blasted, without the blessing of Heaven; and, therefore, ask that blessing humbly, and be not uncharitable to those that at present seem to want it, but comfort and help them. Remember, Job suffered, and was afterwards prosperous.

"And now, to conclude, *Experience keeps a dear school, but fools will learn in no other,* as Poor Richard says, and scarce in that; for, it is true, *We may give advice, but we cannot give conduct.* However, remember this, *They that will not be counselled, cannot be helped;* and further, that, *If you will not hear Reason, she will surely rap your knuckles,* as Poor Richard says."

Thus the old gentleman ended his harangue. The people heard it, and approved the doctrine; and immediately practised the contrary, just as if it had been a common sermon; for the auction opened, and they began to buy extravagantly. I found the good man had thoroughly studied my Almanacs, and digested all I had dropped on these topics during the course of twenty-five years. The frequent mention he made of me must have tired any one else; but my vanity was wonderfully delighted with it, though I was conscious that not a tenth part of the wisdom was my own, which he ascribed to me, but rather the gleanings that I had made of the sense of all ages and nations. However, I resolved to be the better for the echo of it; and, though I had at first determined to buy stuff for a new coat, I went away resolved to wear my old one a little longer. Reader, if thos wilt do the same, thy profit will be as great as mine. I am, as ever, thine to serve thee,

Richard Saunders

PART THREE

The Revolutionary Era, 1754–1789

To American colonists in the eighteenth century, revolution was a most dangerous act. It threatened, they believed, terrible consequences, upheaval, chaos, and bloodshed. They considered war to be far less dangerous; in an era of mercenaries when battles rarely occurred in towns or well-populated villages, armed conflict and even national defeat did not usually touch the day-to-day lives of the people. Revolution, by contrast, affected everybody. Men were forced to examine their most basic loyalties and often brother opposed brother. Uncertainty and confusion held sway, for when the pot boiled anything might come to the top. The colonists knew that, in 1688, England had undergone a bloodless revolution. But how could one be sure that this remarkable achievement would be repeated? Given the perils, one did not begin a revolution for light or transient causes.

And yet, in 1776, Americans chose to revolt. Only a few years before, the colonists had been not only at peace with the mother country but enthusiastic about their ties. In 1763, the Treaty of Paris ended the French and Indian War and the colonists appeared to appreciate, more keenly than ever, the advantages of imperial relations. After all, through English assistance the French had been driven from North America so that peaceful borders and untroubled expansion seemed to be ahead. Even the conduct of the war had brought benefits, as English gold flowed to America in unprecedented amounts to arm, feed, and clothe the troops. Content with the diplomatic settlement and basking in the glow of economic well-being, the colonists' loyalty appeared firm. Few anticipated that within thirteen years the Americans would be in revolt.

Between 1763 and 1776 the colonists came to believe that revolution was imperative and could be conducted without unduly upsetting the social order. During these years they became conscious of their own history and the unusual quality of their political and social life. Their understanding of their past development and present conditions fostered their conviction that revolution was imperative.

British legislation first prompted this introspection. In the aftermath of the French and Indian War, England was caught between heavy expenses and narrowing sources of revenue. It had chosen to take Canada rather than the small but rich Sugar Islands from the French, thereby increasing administrative costs without any prospect of immediate returns. Since it had to defend what it had won in conflict, the mother country turned to the colonies for financial assistance. From Parliament's perspective, the step was logical and appropriate. While England groaned under heavy land taxes, the colonists were practically free of such burdens. Yet the fruits of the war had gone to the Americans; British troops were to protect colonial welfare. Surely, Parliament thought it was right to call upon the colonies to contribute to the benefit of the realm. In 1764 it passed a Revenue Act, then a Stamp Act; upon the latter's repeal it enacted the Townsend Duties and, soon, a Tea Act. To enforce these regulations and collect the duties, Parliament created in America new administrative posts, sent over officials, and established courts. It was determined to compel the colonists to contribute to the costs of empire.

But the colonists did not share Parliament's attitude. The legislation came at a bad time economically, for the flow of funds and the expenditures of the army had stopped after the war and a severe recession set in. The Americans were also angry and insulted for not having been consulted in the making of these decisions. Parliament had acted brusquely and imprudently, without even meaningfully soliciting colonial opinion. Why had not the colonists been allowed to raise the necessary sums by their own methods? Why instead were they saddled with a stamp tax? But most important of all, the colonists believed that Parliament was guilty of more than poor timing and of a lack of political finesse and sensitivity. They saw in English actions nothing less than a basic threat to their way of life. Their lives and liberties were at stake in the confrontation with Parliament on the issue of taxation.

As the colonists read European history, surveyed contemporary governments, and considered their own brief past, they concluded that liberty—the opportunity to live free from arbitrary power—was a phenomena at once rare and temporary. The lesson was apparent in Roman history—a subject they read incessantly—and could be found repeated everywhere from Scandinavia to the Mediterranean: republics all too often degenerated into despotism. Those who did not diligently protect their liberties soon came under the yoke of unlimited power. The colonists believed that England itself was beginning to experience this transformation. Were there not men in England—John Wilkes undoubtedly the most prominent—who had good cause to claim from their imprisonment that Parliament was more intent on protecting its own prerogatives than defending the liberties of the people? Did a similar fate await the colonists? Americans now began to appreciate the self-government that had long been familiar to them. They were living in liberty. Through the power to control taxation, the assemblies, representing the people, had learned to keep the Royal Governor, appointed by the crown, well in check. By supervising his appropriations and controlling his salary, they had used control over the purse to keep power within limits. But did Parliament's intrusion into taxation signal a decline in colonial liberties?

The fears of 1764 became the confirmed beliefs of 1776. Over the course of these years Parliament paid little attention to colonial protests. Its official pronouncements were mostly concerned with reaffirming the supreme and sovereign powers of Parliament—a stance that gave little comfort to the Americans. At the same time, colonial attitudes became more refined and fixed as pamphlet followed pamphlet and the principles of government became a familiar subject of discussion. With logical arguments and vivid language, writers from Pennsylvania's John Dickinson to newcomer Thomas Paine alerted, coaxed, persuaded, and convinced their countrymen of the dangers they faced. Finally, successive British actions corroborated every colonial fear. The Americans watched Parliament continue to tax, to establish courts in the colonies without provision for trial by jury, and to send and quarter troops in peacetime against the inhabitants' will. As expected, the results were such crimes against them as the Boston Massacre of 1770. Surely the time had arrived for the colonists to act with vigilance, to protect their liberties by revolution.

But would the cure be worse than the disease? Would revolution promote more chaos, disorder, and arbitrary rule than even the acts of a stubborn and irresponsible Parliament? By 1776 the colonists confidently answered "no." The imperial crisis prompted them to examine their society as well as their polity, making them aware of their unusual attributes. They began to understand that the American society was not simply a transplanted European community in a different setting. Old World guidelines were not necessarily applicable to New World conditions. There was in America a cohesiveness and stability that was as vital as it was unique. Harmony, and not dissension, characterized the social order, making it unlikely for external conflict with the mother country to spark internal conflict at home. The most dramatic manifestation of this perspective came in the cooperation of all classes in the riots protesting British legislation. Riots were dangerous political weapons. They could begin with one goal and end with another; those who led the mob might find themselves its victim. Yet, wealthy merchants joined, and in fact often headed artisans and laborers in violent protest against various imperial policies, from the Stamp Act to the Tea Act. And their confidence, with only few exceptions, was usually justified. The mob turned on British officials not on the rich, on would-be stamp collectors not on leading citizens. Thus Americans could dare a revolution certain that their liberties would be safer in their own hands than in those of Parliament.

During the course and aftermath of the Revolution, the new nation struggled to fulfill its grandiose goals. Its confidence in the stability of American society was on the whole demonstrated by the events of these years; and through resourceful and

133

imaginative innovations, new meanings and defenses enveloped and expanded traditional practices. The conduct of the war itself was an exceptionally demanding test, not only of courage and military skill but of the strength of the republican ideal. There was some treachery and greed and a good deal of inefficiency in the war effort; but most important, the military brought victory and support to the republican government. The virtue and integrity of George Washington was the outstanding example of a popular commitment. Soldiers and their leaders, for all the loss of pay and the hardships they had suffered, disbanded and went home at the close of hostilities; a few disgruntled officers vaguely considered political action but Washington forthrightly and without exceptional difficulty kept them in bounds. The republic weathered its first crisis handsomely—a battlefield victory by a loyal army.

Moreover, citizens at home also attempted to fulfill republican ideals. At a time when all traditional authority collapsed, when the Royal Governor fled the province and colonial assemblies were without legality, Americans quickly devised new rules and institutions for government. Townspeople gathered to elect representatives to constitutional conventions, which would offer proposals and pass on suggestions. Rather than flounder before the specter of anarchy, they created constitutions and state governments. Their work, in fact, showed surprisingly few signs of tension or haste. The constitutions were carefully composed and often remarkably long-lived, drawing on the colonial experience for lessons in protecting liberty. Thus, they typically weakened the office of Governor by not giving him a final veto on legislation or the exclusive right to make political appointments; they put the bulk of authority in the legislatures, but then created bicameral bodies to check abuses and called for frequent elections to insure responsibility. They banned plural officeholding so that no individual or clique could monopolize authority for its own account. To be sure, the constitutions did not escape older prejudices completely. There were still property requirements for voting and office-holding, and there was scant effort, insofar as slavery was concerned, to implement the idea that all men were created equal. Still the new documents established order and delegated power while protecting individual liberty.

Americans had more difficulty establishing a national government. Long familiar with the operations of local and provincial bodies, they were at once removed from and suspicious of national political institutions. They created, through the Articles of Confederation, a central government that presented no danger to state prerogatives but at the same time was too weak and ill-equipped to protect and promote the general welfare. To its credit, the Confederation government oversaw the military and diplomatic effort and made important starts in settling the question of distributing the western lands, paying the war debt, and regulating the currency; but it was helpless to operate without the goodwill and cheerful compliance of the states. It lacked coercive power—the ability to collect taxes, to enforce treaties, to smooth internal and external relations, to amend its articles without the unanimous approval of the states. These defects were soon apparent and in the summer of 1787 representatives from most of the states gathered at Philadelphia to design a more powerful central government.

The architects of the Constitution were not insensitive to the privileges of the states or the liberties of the citizens. Recognizing that a national government needed more power, they nevertheless tried to hedge and limit its exercise. Their unusual solutions are now familiar, most of them still in effect almost two hundred years later. They ranged from a federal system—with national and state governments each operating in its own sphere—to a bicameral Congress, where the House of Representatives and the Senate watched and checked each other, from an independent Supreme Court, appointed by the President with the approval of the Senate, to an executive who must ratify Congressional legislation but whose veto could be overridden. Would these schemes establish a government of sufficient power that would not trample the liberties of the people? In ratifying conventions, in newspapers, and in pamphlets, Americans debated the issue. Some found the safeguards inadequate; others believed they were more than equal to the task. Everyone recognized that the balance between power and liberty was exceptionally difficult to achieve, that nothing less than the future of republican government in the United States was at stake. One by one the states decided to accept the new Constitution; and in 1790 under the Presidency of George Washington, Americans began their experiment to see whether government power and individual liberty could coexist.

The Making
of a Colonial Legislator

Few colonial documents better express the quality of political life in the eighteenth century than Robert Munford's satire, *The Candidates*. Munford, a member of a wealthy Virginia planter family, knew his materials first-hand. He held various local offices beginning in 1755, at about the age of thirty-five, and from 1765 to 1775, he sat as a representative in the colony's House of Burgesses. A Whig, Munford supported revolution and served as a Major during the Revolutionary War.

Munford wrote *The Candidates* in his spare time, completing the manuscript in 1770. The play was never actually produced and its literary merits are few. Its value rests on its considerable insight into the style and dynamics of political affairs. As the play aptly illustrates, colonial politics were certainly not democratic in conduct. The social standing of men counted most at election time; there were no serious programs or platforms or debates for the electorate. Yet, the system was not aristocratic either. Notice the relationship between even the most gentlemanly of candidates and his constituents. Drink, entertainment, appearances, and speeches were all necessary activities for the would-be office-holder, no matter what his pretentions or sentiments. Eighteenth-century politics was a curious mixture, with touches of aristocratic deference as well as democratic involvement. How the pieces fit together is nicely revealed in the satire that follows.

THE CANDIDATES
Robert Munford

PROLOGUE
By a Friend
Ladies and gentlemen, to-night you'll see
A bard delighting in satiric glee;
In merry scenes his biting tale unfold,

From "The Candidates," as reprinted in Jay B. Hubbell and Douglas Adair, eds., *William and Mary Quarterly*, 5 (1948), 229–245, 252–257.

And high to Folly's eye the mirror hold:
Here eager candidates shall call for votes,
And bawling voters louder stretch their throats:
Here may you view, in groups diverting, join'd
The poor and wealthy rabble of mankind;
All who deserve the lash, the lash will find.
Here characters, whose names are now unknown,
Shall shine again, as in their spheres they shone;
While some may make malicious explanation,
And know them all still living in the nation.
If any present, say, fie, shameless bard!
Hast thou for decency no more regard
Than at thy betters, thus to make a stand,
And boldly point out meanness, contraband,
Depreciating the wisdom of the land?
Tho' such, the wond'rous sympathy of wits,
That every fool will wear the cap that fits,
I boldly answer, how could he mean you,
Who, when he wrote, about you nothing knew?
The state of things was such, in former times,
'Ere wicked kings were punish'd for their crimes:
When strove the candidates to gain their seats
Most heartily, with drinking bouts, and treats;
The meanest vices all the people stain'd,
And drunkenness, and monarchy both reign'd,
With such strong cause his anger to engage,
How could our Bard restrain satiric rage?
But, God forbid, its edge shou'd now apply,
Or on our race-field, when you cast an eye
You there a home-election—should espy.
Science and virtue, now are wider spread,
And crown with dignity, fair Freedom's head.
We only pray this satire ne'er be just,
Save when apply'd to other times, and trust
Its keenness only, a rememb'rancer,
And guard from future evils, may appear.

Act I. Scene I.

Mr. Wou'dbe's house.
Enter Wou'dbe with a newspaper in his hand.

Wou'dbe.   I am very sorry our good old governor Botetourt has left us. He well deserved our friendship, when alive, and that we should for years to come, with gratitude, remember his mild and affable deportment. Well, our little world will soon be up, and very busy towards our next election. Must I again be subject to the

137

humours of a fickle croud? Must I again resign my reason, and be nought but what each voter pleases? Must I cajole, fawn, and wheedle, for a place that brings so little profit?

Enter Ralpho (his Servant).

Ralpho. Sir John Toddy is below, and if your honour is at leisure, would beg to speak to you.

Wou'dbe. My compliments to Sir John, and tell him, I shall be glad of his company. So—Sir John, some time ago, heard me say I was willing to resign my seat in the house to an abler person, and he comes modestly to accept of it.

Enter Sir John Toddy (a Candidate for Office).

Sir John. Mr. Wou'dbe, your most obedient servant, sir; I am proud to find you well. I hope you are in good health, sir?

Wou'dbe. Very well, I am obliged to you, Sir John. Why, Sir John, you surely are practising the grimace and compliments you intend to make use of among the freeholders in the next election, and have introduced yourself to me with the self-same common-place expressions that we candidates adopt when we intend to wheedle a fellow out of his vote—I hope you have no scheme upon me, Sir John?

Sir John. No, sir, upon my honour, sir, it was punctually to know how your lady and family did, sir, 'pon honour, sir, it was.

Wou'dbe. You had better be more sparing of your honour at present, Sir John; for, if you are a candiate, whenever you make promises to the people that you can't comply with, you must say upon honour, otherwise they won't believe you.

Sir John. Upon honour, sir, I have no thought to set up for a candidate, unless you say the word.

Wou'dbe. Such condescension from you, Sir John, I have no reason to expect: you have my hearty consent to do as you please, and if the people choose you their Representative, I must accept of you as a colleague.

Sir John. As a colleague, Mr. Wou'dbe! I was thinking you did not intend to stand a poll, and my business, sir, was to get the favour of you to speak a good word for me among the people.

Wou'dbe. I hope you have no occasion for a trumpeter, Sir John? If you have, I'll speak a good word to you, and advise you to decline.

Sir John. Why, Mr. Wou'dbe, after you declin'd, I thought I was the next *fittenest* man in the country, and Mr. Wou'dbe, if you would be ungenerous, tho' you are a laughing man, you would tell me so.

Wou'dbe. It would be ungenerous indeed, Sir John, to tell you what the people could never be induced to believe. But I'll be ingenuous enough to tell you, Sir John, if you expect any assistance from me, you'll be disappointed, for I can't think you the *fittenest* man I know.

Sir John. Pray, sir, who do you know besides? Perhaps I may be thought as fit as your honour. But, sir, if you are for that, the hardest fend off: damn me, if I care a farthing for you; and so, your servant, sir.

[*Exit Sir John.*

Wou'dbe. So, I have got the old knight, and his friend Guzzle, I suppose, against me, by speaking so freely; but their interest, I believe, has not weight enough among the people, for me to lose any thing, by making them my enemies.

Indeed, the being intimate with such a fool as Sir John, might tend more to my discredit with them, for the people of Virginia have too much sense not to perceive how weak the head must be that is always filled with liquor. Ralpho!—

Enter Ralpho.

Ralpho. Sir, what does your honour desire?

Wou'dbe. I'm going into my library, and if any gentleman calls, you may introduce him to me there.

Ralpho. Yes, sir. But, master, as election-times are coming, I wish you would remember a poor servant, a little.

Wou'dbe. What do you want?

Ralpho. Why, the last suit of clothes your honour gave me is quite worn out. Look here, (*shewing his elbows*) the insigns, (as I have heard your honour say, in one of your fine speeches) the insigns of faithful service. Now, methinks, as they that set up for burgesses, cut a dash, and have rare sport, why might not their servants have a little decreation?

Wou'dbe. I understand you, Ralpho, you wish to amuse yourself, and make a figure among the girls this Election, and since such a desire is natural to the young, and innocent if not carried to excess, I am willing to satisfy you; you may therefore, have the suit I pulled off yesterday, and accept this present as an evidence that I am pleased with your diligence and fidelity, and am ever ready to reward it.

[*Exit Wou'dbe.*

Ralpho. God bless your honour! what a good master! who would not do every thing to give such a one pleasure? But, e'gad, it's time to think of my new clothes: I'll go and try them on. Gadso! this figure of mine is not reconsiderable in its delurements, and when I'm dressed out like a gentleman, the girls, I'm a thinking, will find desistible.

[*Exit.*

Scene II.

A porch of a tavern: a Court-house on one side, and an high road behind.

Captain Paunch, Ned, and several freeholders discovered.

Ned. Well, gentlemen, I suppose we are all going to the barbecue together.

Capt. Paunch. Indeed, sir, I can assure you, I have no such intention.

Ned. Not go to your friend Wou'dbe's treat! He's such a pretty fellow, and you like him so well, I wonder you won't go to drink his liquor.

Capt. P. Aye, aye, very strange: but your friends Strutabout and Smallhopes, I like so little as never to take a glass from them, because I shall never pay the price which is always expected for it, by voting against my conscience: I therefore don't go, to avoid being asked for what I won't give.

Ned. A very distress motive, truly, but for the matter of that, you've not so much to boast of your friend Wou'dbe, if what I have been told of him is true; for I have heard say, he and the fine beast of a gentleman, Sir John Toddy, have joined interess. Mr. Wou'dbe, I was creditly 'formed, was known for to say, he wouldn't serve for a burgess, unless Sir John was elected with him.

139

1st Freeholder. What's that you say, neighbor? has Mr. Wou'dbe and Sir John joined interest?

Ned. Yes, they have; and ant there a clever fellow for ye? a rare burgess you will have, when a fellow gets in, who will go drunk, and be a sleeping in the house! I wish people wouldn't pretend for to hold up their heads so high, who have such friends and associates. There's poor Mr. Smallhopes, who isn't as much attended to, is a very proper gentleman, and is no drunkard, and has no drunken companions.

1st Freeholder. I don't believe it. Mr. Wou'dbe's a cleverer man than that, and people ought to be ashamed to vent such slanders.

2d Freeholder. So I say: and as we are of one mind, let's go strait, and let Mr. Wou'dbe know it.

[*Exeunt two Freeholders.*

3d Freeholder. If Mr. Wou'dbe did say it, I won't vote for him, that's sartain.

4th Freeholder. Are you sure of it, neighbour?

(To Ned.)

Ned. Yes, I am sure of it: d'ye think I'd speak such a thing without having good authority?

4th Freeholder. I'm sorry for't; come neighbour, (*to the 3d Freeholder*) this is the worst news that I've heard for a long time.

[*Exeunt 3rd & 4th Freeholder.*

5th Freeholder. I'm glad to hear it. Sir John Toddy is a clever openhearted gentleman as I ever knew, one that wont turn his back upon a poor man, but will take a chearful cup with one as well as another, and it does honour to Mr. Wou'dbe to prefer such a one, to any of your whifflers who han't the heart to be generous, and yet despise poor folks. Huzza! for Mr. Wou'dbe and for Sir John Toddy.

6th Freeholder. I think so too, neighbour. Mr. Wou'dbe, I always thought, was a man of sense, and had larning, as they call it, but he did not love diversion enough, I like him the better for't. Huzza for Mr. Wou'dbe and Sir John Toddy.

Both. Huzza for Mr. Wou'dbe and Sir John Toddy. Wou'dbe and Toddy, for ever, boys!

[*Exeunt.*

Scene III.

Wou'dbe's house.

Enter Wou'dbe, looking at a letter.

Wou'dbe. This note gives me information, that the people are much displeased with me for declaring in favour of Sir John Toddy. Who could propagate this report, I know not, but was not this abroad, something else would be reported, as prejudicial to my interest; I must take an opportunity of justifying myself in public.

Enter Ralpho.

Ralpho. Mr. Strutabout waits upon your honour.

Wou'dbe. Desire him to walk in.

Enter Mr. Strutabout (another Candidate).

Strutabout. Mr. Wou'dbe, your servant. Considering the business now in hand I think you confine yourself too much at home. There are several little reports circulating to your disadvantage, and as a friend, I would advice you to shew yourself to the people, and endeavour to confute them.

Wou'dbe. I believe, sir, I am indebted to my brother candidates, for most of the reports that are propagated to my disadvantage, but I hope, Mr. Strutabout is a man of too much honour, to say anything in my absence, that he cannot make appear.

Strutabout. That you may depend on, sir. But there are some who are so intent upon taking your place, that they will stick at nothing to obtain their ends.

Wou'dbe. Are you in the secret, sir?

Strutabout. So far, sir, that I have had overtures from Mr. Smallhopes and his friends, to join my interest with their's, against you. This, I rejected with disdain, being conscious that you were the properest person to serve the county; but when Smallhopes told me, he intended to prejudice your interest by scatering a few stories among the people to your disadvantage, it raised my blood to such a pitch, that had he not promised me to be silent, I believe I should have chastised him for you myself.

Wou'dbe. If, sir, you were so far my friend, I am obliged to you: though whatever report he is the author of, will, I am certain, gain little credit with the people.

Strutabout. I believe so; and therefore, if you are willing, we'll join our interests together, and soon convince the fellow, that by attacking you he has injured himself.

Wou'dbe. So far from joining with you, or any body else, or endeavouring to procure a vote for you, I am determined never to ask a vote for myself, or receive one that is unduly obtained.

Enter Ralpho.

Ral. Master, rare news, here's our neighbour Guzzle, as drunk as ever Chief Justice Cornelius was upon the bench.

Wou'dbe. That's no news, Ralpho: but do you call it rare news, that a creature in the shape of man; and endued with the faculties of reason, should so far debase the workmanship of heaven, by making his carcase a receptacle for such pollution?

Ralpho. Master, you are hard upon neighbour Guzzle: our Justices gets drunk and why not poor Guzzle? But sir, he wants to see you.

Wou'dbe. Tell him to come in. (*exit Ralpho*). All must be made welcome now.

Re-enter Ralpho and Guzzle, with an empty bottle.

Guzzle. Ha! Mr. Wou'dbe, how is it?

Wou'dbe. I'm something more in my senses than you, John, tho' not so sensible as you would have me, I suppose.

Guzzle. If I can make you sensible how much I want my bottle filled, and how much I shall love the contents, it's all the senses I desire you to have.

Ralpho. If I may be allowed to speak, neighbour Guzzle, you are wrong; his honour sits up for a burgess, and should have five senses at least.

Guzzle. Five senses! how, what five?

Ralpho. Why, neighbour, you know, eating, drinking, and sleeping are three; t'other two are best known to myself.

141

Wou'dbe. I'm sorry Mr. Guzzle, you are so ignorant of the necessary qualifications of a member of the house of burgesses.

Guzzle. Why, you old dog, I knew before Ralpho told me. To convince you, eating, drinking, and sleeping, are three; fighting and lying are t'others.

Wou'dbe. Why fighting and lying?

Guzzle. Why, because you are not fit for a burgess, unless you'll fight; suppose a man that values himself upon boxing, should stand in the lobby, ready cock'd and prim'd, and knock you down, and bung up both your eyes for a fortnight, you'd be ashamed to shew your face in the house, and be living at our expence all the time.

Wou'dbe. Why lying?

Guzzle. Because, when you have been at Williamsburg, for six or seven weeks, under pretence of serving your county, and come back, says I to you, what news? none at all, says you; what have you been about? says I,—says you—and so out must tell some damned lie, sooner than say you have been doing nothing.

Wou'dbe. No, Guzzle, I'll make it a point of duty to dispatch the business, and my study to promote the good of my county.

Guzzle. Yes, damn it, you all promise mighty fair, but the devil a bit do you perform; there's Strutabout, now, he'll promise to move mountains. He'll make the rivers navigable, and bring the tide over the tops of the hills, for a vote.

Strutabout. You may depend, Mr. Guzzle, I'll perform whatever I promise.

Guzzle. I don't believe it, damn me if I like you.

[*looking angry.*

Wou'dbe. Don't be angry, John, let our actions hereafter be the test of our inclinations to serve you.

[*Exit Strutabout.*

Guzzle. Agreed, Mr. Wou'dbe, but that fellow that slunk off just now, I've no opinion of.

Wou'dbe. (*Looking about*) what, is Mr. Strutabout gone? why, surely, Guzzle, you did not put him to flight?

Guzzle. I suppose I did, but no matter, (*holding up his bottle, and looking at it,*) my bottle never was so long a filling in this house, before; surely, there's a leak in the bottom, (*looks at it again*).

Wou'dbe. What have you got in your bottle, John, a lizard?

Guzzle. Yes, a very uncommon one, and I want a little rum put to it, to preserve it.

Wou'dbe. Hav'n't you one in your belly, John?

Guzzle. A dozen, I believe, by their twisting, when I mentioned the rum.

Wou'dbe. Would you have rum to preserve them, too?

Guzzle. Yes, yes, Mr. Wou'dbe, by all means; but, why so much talk about it, if you intend to do it, do it at once, man, for I am in a damnable hurry.

Wou'dbe. Do what? Who are to be burgesses, John?

Guzzle. Who are to be what? (*looking angry*).

Wou'dbe. Burgesses, who are you for?

Guzzle. For the first man that fills my bottle: so Mr. Wou'dbe, your servant.

[*Exit Guzzle.*

Wou'dbe. Ralpho, go after him, and fill his bottle.

Ralpho. Master, we ought to be careful of the rum, else 'twill not hold out, (*aside*) it's always a feast or a famine with us; master has just got a little Jamaica for his own use, and now he must spill it, and spare it till there's not a drop left.
[*Exit.*

Wou'dbe. (*pulling out his watch.*) 'Tis now the time a friend of mine has appointed for me to meet the freeholders at a barbecue; well, I find, in order to secure a seat in our august senate, 'tis necessary a man should either be a slave or a fool; a slave to the people, for the privilege of serving them, and a fool himself, for thus begging a troublesome and expensive employment.

To sigh, while toddy-toping sots rejoice,
To see you paying for their empty voice,
From morn to night your humble head decline,
To gain an honour that is justly thine,
Intreat a fool, who's your's at this day's treat,
And next another's, if another's meat,
Is all the bliss a candidate acquires,
In all his wishes, or his vain desires.
[*Exit.*
End of the First Act.

Act II. Scene I.

A race-field, a bullock, and several hogs barbecued.
Enter Guzzle, and several freeholders.

Guzzle. Your servant, gentlemen, (*shakes hands all round*) we have got fine weather, thank God: how are crops with you? we are very dry in our parts.

Twist. We are very dry here; Mr. Guzzle, where's your friend Sir John, and Mr. Wou'dbe? they are to treat to-day, I hear.

Guzzle. I wish I could see it, but there are more treats besides their's; where's your friend Mr. Strutabout? I heard we were to have a treat from Smallhopes and him to-day.

Twist. Fine times, boys. Some of them had better keep their money; I'll vote for no man but to my liking.

Guzzle. If I may be so bold, pray, which way is your liking?

Twist. Not as your's is, I believe; but nobody shall know my mind till the day.

Guzzle. Very good, Mr. Twist; nobody, I hope, will put themselves to the trouble to ask.

Twist. You have taken the trouble already.

Guzzle. No harm, I hope, sir.

Twist. None at all, sir: Yonder comes Sir John, and quite sober, as I live.
Enter Sir John Toddy.

Sir John. Gentlemen and ladies, your servant, hah! my old friend Prize, how goes it? how does your wife and children do?

Sarah. At your service, sir. (*making a low courtsey.*)

143

Prize. How the devil come he to know me so well, and never spoke to me before in his life? (*aside.*)

Guzzle. (*whispering Sir John*) Dick Stern.

Sir John. Hah! Mr. Stern, I'm proud to see you; I hope your family are well; how many children? does the good woman keep to the old stroke?

Catharine. Yes, an't please your honour, I hope my lady's well, with your honour.

Sir John. At your service, madam.

Guzzle. (*whispering Sir John*) Roger Twist.

Sir John. Hah! Mr. Roger Twist! your servant, sir. I hope your wife and children are well.

Twist. There's my wife. I have no children, at your service.

Sir John. A pretty girl: why, Roger, it you don't do better, you must call an old fellow to your assistance.

Twist. I have enough to assist me, without applying to you, sir.

Sir John. No offence, I hope, sir; excuse my freedom.

Twist. None at all, sir; Mr. Wou'dbe is ready to befriend me in that way at any time.

Sir John. Not in earnest, I hope, sir; tho' he's a damn'd fellow, I believe.

Guzzle. A truce, a truce—here comes Mr. Wou'dbe.

Enter Mr. Wou'dbe.

Wou'dbe. Gentlemen, your servant. Why, Sir John, you have entered the list, it seems; and are determined to whip over the ground, if you are treated with a distance.

Sir John. I'm not to be distanc'd by you, or a dozen such.

Wou'dbe. There's nothing like courage upon these occasions; but you were out when you chose me to ride for you, Sir John.

Sir John. Let's have no more of your algebra, nor proverbs, here.

Guzzle. Come, gentlemen, you are both friends, I hope.

Wou'dbe. While Sir John confined himself to his bottle and dogs, and moved only in his little circle of pot-companions, I could be with him; but since his folly has induced him to offer himself a candidate for a place, for which he is not fit, I must say, I despise him. The people are of opinion, that I favour this undertaking of his; but I now declare, he is not the man I wish the people to elect.

Guzzle. Pray, sir, who gave you a right to choose for us?

Wou'dbe. I have no right to choose for you; but I have a right to give my opinion: especially when I am the supposed author of Sir John's folly.

Guzzle. Perhaps he's no greater fool than some others.

Wou'dbe. It would be ungrateful in you, Mr. Guzzle, not to speak in favour of Sir John; for you have stored away many gallons of his liquor in that belly of you's.

Guzzle. And he's the cleverer gentleman for it; is not he, neighbours?

1st Freeholder. For sartin; it's no disparagement to drink with a poor fellow.

2d Freeholder. No more it is, tho' some of the quality are mighty proud that way.

3d Freeholder. Mr. Wou'dbe shou'd'n't speak so freely against that.

Twist. Mr. Wou'dbe.

Wou'dbe. Sir.

Twist. We have heard a sartin report, that you and Sir John have joined interest.

Wou'dbe. Well; do you believe it?

Twist. Why, it don't look much like it now, Mr. Wou'dbe; but, mayhap, it's only a copy of your countenance.

Wou'dbe. You may put what construction you please upon my behaviour, gentlemen; but I assure you, it never was my intention to join with Sir John, or any one else.

Twist. Moreover, I've heard a 'sponsible man say, he could prove you were the cause of these new taxes.

Wou'dbe. Do you believe that too? or can you believe that it's in the power of any individual member to make a law himself? If a law is enacted that is displeasing to the people, it has the concurrence of the whole legislative body, and my vote for, or against it, is of little consequence.

Guzzle. And what the devil good do you do then?

Wou'dbe. As much as I have abilities to do.

Guzzle. Suppose, Mr. Wou'dbe, we were to want you to get the price of rum lower'd—wou'd you do it?

Wou'dbe. I cou'd not.

Guzzle. Huzza for Sir John! he has promised to do it, huzza for Sir John!

Twist. Suppose, Mr. Wou'dbe, we should want this tax taken off—cou'd you do it?

Wou'dbe. I could not.

Twist. Huzza for Mr. Strutabout! he's damn'd, if he don't. Huzza for Mr. Strutabout!

Stern. Suppose, Mr. Wou'dbe, we that live over the river, should want to come to church on this side, is it not very hard we should pay ferryage; when we pay as much to the church as you do?

Wou'dbe. Very hard.

Stern. Suppose we were to petition the assembly could you get us clear of that expence?

Wou'dbe. I believe it to be just; and make no doubt but it would pass into a law.

Stern. Will you do it?

Wou'dbe. I will endeavour to do it.

Stern. Huzza for Mr. Wou'dbe! Wou'dbe forever!

[*Exeunt severally; some huzzaing for Mr. Wou'dbe—some for Sir John—some for Mr. Strutabout.*

Scene II.

Another part of the field.

Mr. Strutabout, Mr. Smallhopes, and a number of freeholders round them.

145

1st Freeholder.   Huzza for Mr. Strutabout!

2dFreeholder.   Huzza for Mr. Smallhopes!

3d Freeholder.   Huzza for Mr. Smallhopes and Mr. Strutabout!

4th Freeholder.   Huzza for Mr. Strutabout and Mr. Smallhopes!

Strutabout.   Gentlemen—I'm much obliged to you for your good intentions; I make no doubt but (with the assistance of my friend Mr. Smallhopes) I shall be able to do every thing you have requested. Your grievances shall be redress'd; and all your petitions heard.

Freeholders.   Huzza for Mr. Strutabout and Mr. Smallhopes!

[*Exeunt, huzzaing.*

Act III. Scene I.

Wou'dbe's house.

Enter Wou'dbe and Worthy.

Wou'dbe.   Nothing could have afforded me more pleasure than your letter; I read it to the people, and can with pleasure assure you, it gave them infinite satisfaction.

Worthy.   My sole motive in declaring myself was to serve you, and if I am the means of your gaining your election with honour, I shall be satisfied.

Wou'dbe.   You have always been extremely kind, sir, but I could not enjoy the success I promised myself, without your participation.

Worthy.   I have little inclination to the service; you know my aversion to public life, Wou'dbe, and how little I have ever courted the people for the troublesome office they have hitherto imposed upon me.

Wou'dbe.   I believe you enjoy as much domestic happiness as any person, and that your aversion to a public life proceeds from the pleasure you find at home. But, sir, it surely is the duty of every man who has abilities to serve his country, to take up the burden, and bear it with patience.

Worthy.   I know it is needless to argue with you upon this head: you are determined I shall serve with you, I find.

Wou'dbe.   I am; and therefore let's take the properest methods to insure success.

Worthy.   What would you propose?

Wou'dbe.   Nothing more than for you to shew yourself to the people.

Worthy.   I'll attend you where ever you please.

Wou'dbe.   To-morrow being the day of election, I have invited most of the principal freeholders to breakfast with me, in their way to the courthouse, I hope you'll favour us with your company.

Worthy.   I will; till then, adieu.

[*Exit Worthy.*

Wou'dbe.   I shall expect you. It would give me great pleasure if Worthy would be more anxious than he appears to be upon this occasion; conscious of his abilities and worth, he scorns to ask a vote for any person but me; well, I must turn the tables on him, and solicit as strongly in his favour.

[*Exit Wou'dbe.*

Scene II.

Mr. Julip's House.

Enter Captain Paunch and Mr. Julip (two Gentlemen).

Capt. Well, neighbour, I have come to see you on purpose to know how votes went at the treat yesterday.

Julip. I was not there; but I've seen neighbour Guzzle this morning, and he says, Sir John gives the matter up to Mr. Worthy and Mr. Wou'dbe.

Capt. Mr. Worthy! does he declare, huzza, my boys! well, I'm proud our county may choose two without being obliged to have one of those jackanapes at the head of it, faith: Who are you for now, neighbour?

Julip. I believe I shall vote for the two old ones, and tho' I said I was for Sir John, it was because I lik'd neither of the others; but since Mr. Worthy will serve us, why, to be sartin its our duty to send Wou'dbe and him.

Capt. Hah, faith, now you speak like a man; you are a man after my own heart: give me your hand.

Julip. Here it is, Wou'dbe and Worthy, I say.

Capt. Done, but who comes yonder? surely, it's not Mr. Worthy! 'Tis, I declare.

Enter Mr. Worthy.

Worthy. Gentlemen, your servant, I hope your families are well.

Capt. At your service, sir.

Worthy. I need not, I suppose, gentlemen, inform you that I have entered the list with my old competitors, and have determined to stand a poll at the next election. If you were in the croud yesterday, my friend Wou'dbe, I doubt not, made a declaration of my intentions to the people.

Capt. We know it, thank heaven, Mr. Worthy, tho' neither of us were there: as I did not like some of the candidates I did not choose to be persecuted for a vote that I was resolved never to bestow upon them.

Julip. My rule is never to taste of a man's liquor unless I'm his friend, and therefore, I stay'd at home.

Worthy. Well, my honest friend, I am proud to find that you still preserve your usual independence. Is it possible Captain, that the people can be so misled, as to reject Wou'dbe, and elect Strutabout in his room?

Capt. You know, Mr. Worthy, how it is, as long as the liquor is running, so long they'll be Mr. Strutabout's friends, but when the day comes, I'm thinking it will be another case.

Worthy. I'm sorry, my countymen, for the sake of a little toddy, can be induced to behave in a manner so contradictory to the candour and integrity which always should prevail among mankind.

Capt. It's so, sir, you may depend upon it.

Julip. I'm thinking it is.

Worthy. Well, gentlemen, will you give me leave to ask you, how far you think my declaring will be of service to Mr. Wou'dbe?

Capt. Your declaring has already silenced Sir John Toddy; and I doubt not, but Strutabout and Smallhopes will lose many votes by it.

Worthy. Has Sir John declined? poor Sir John is a weak man, but he has more virtues to recommend him than either of the others.

Julip. So I think, Mr. Worthy, and I'll be so bold as to tell you that, had you not set up, Mr. Wou'dbe and Sir John should have had my vote.

Worthy. Was I a constituent, instead of a candidate, I should do the same.

Julip. Well, captain, you see I was not so much to blame.

Capt. Sir John may be honest, but he is no fitter for that place than myself.

Julip. Suppose he was not, if he was the best that offered to serve us, should not we choose him?

Worthy. Yes, surely: Well, my friends, I'm now on my way, to breakfast at Mr. Wou'dbe's, but I hope to meet you at the court-house today.

Both. Aye, aye, depend upon us.

[*Exit Worthy.*

Capt. Well, neighbour, I hope things now go on better; I like the present appearance.

Julip. So do I.

Capt. Do all you can, old fellow.

Julip. I will.

Capt. I hope you will, neighbour. I wish you well.

Julip. You the same.

[*shake hands, and exeunt.*

Scene III.

Wou'dbe's house, a long breakfast table set out.

Wou'dbe, Worthy, Capt. Paunch, Mr. Julip, Twist, Stern, Prize, and other freeholders; several negroes go backwards and forwards, bringing in the breakfast.

1st Freeholder. Give us your hand, neighbour Worthy, I'm extremely glad to see thee with all my heart: So my heart of oak, you are willing to give your time and trouble once more to the service of your country.

Worthy. Your kindness does me honour, and if my labours be productive of good to my country, I shall deem myself fortunate.

2d Freeholder. Still the same sensible man I always thought him. Damn it, now if every county cou'd but send such a burgess, what a noble house we should have?

3d Freeholder. We shall have no polling now, but all will be for the same, I believe. Here's neighbour Twist, who was resolute for Strutabout, I don't doubt, will vote for Mr. Worthy and Mr. Wou'dbe.

Twist. Yes, that I will: what could I do better?

All. Aye, so will we all.

Wou'dbe. Gentlemen, for your forwardness in favour of my good friend Worthy, my sincere thanks are but a poor expression in the pleasure I feel. For my part, your esteem I shall always attribute more to his than my own desert. But come, let us sit down to breakfast, all is ready I believe; and you're heartily welcome to batchelors quarters. (*they all sit down to the table, he asks each of the*

148

company which they prefer, coffee, tea, or chocolate, and each chooses to his liking; he pours out, and the servants carry it around.)

Worthy. Gentlemen, will any of you have a part of this fine salt shad? (*they answer, yes, if you please; and he helps them.*)

Capt. P. This warm toast and butter is very fine, and the shad gives it an excellent flavour.

Mr. Julip. Boy, give me the spirit. This chocolate, me thinks, wants a little lacing to make it admirable. (*the servants bring it.*)

Prize. Mr. Wou'dbe, do your fishing places succeed well this year?

Wou'dbe. Better than they've been known for some seasons.

Stern. I'm very glad of it: for then I can get my supply from you.

Mr. Julip. Neighbour Stalk, how do crops stand with you?

1st Freeholder. Indifferently well, I thank you; how are you?

Mr. Julip. Oh, very well! we crop it gloriously.

Wou'dbe. You have not breakfasted yet, neighbour, give me leave to help you to another dish.

2d Freeholder. Thank ye, sir, but enough's as good as a feast.

Capt. P. (*looking at his watch.*) I'm afraid we shall be late, they ought to have begun before now.

Wou'dbe. Our horses are at the gate, and we have not far to go.

Freeholders all. Very well, we've all breakfasted. (*they rise from table and the servants take away.*)

1st Freeholder. Come along, my friends, I long to see your triumph. Huzza for Wou'dbe and Worthy!

[*Exit huzzaing.*

Scene V.

The Court-house yard.

The door open, and a number of freeholders seen crowding within.

1st Freeholder. (*to a freeholder coming out of the house*) How do votes go, neighbour? for Wou'dbe and Worthy?

2d Freeholder. Aye, aye, they're just come, and sit upon the bench, and yet all the votes are for them. 'Tis quite a hollow thing. The poll will be soon over. The People croud so much, and vote so fast, you can hardly turn around.

1st Freeholder. How do Strutabout and Smallhopes look? very doleful, I reckon.

2d Freeholder. Like a thief under the gallows.

3d Freeholder. There you must be mistaken, neighbour; for two can't be like one.

1st & 2d Freeholders. Ha, ha, ha,—a good joke, a good joke.

3d Freeholder. Not so good neither, when the subject made it so easy.

1st & 2d Freeholders. Better and better, ha, ha, ha. Huzza for Worthy and Wou'dbe! and confusion to Strutabout and Smallhopes.

The Sheriff comes to the door, and says,

149

Gentleman freeholders, come into court, and give your votes, or the poll will be closed.

Freeholders. We've all voted.

Sheriff. The poll's closed. Mr. Wou'dbe and Mr. Worthy are elected.

Freeholders without and within. Huzza—huzza! Wou'dbe and Worthy for ever boys, bring 'em on, bring 'em on, Wou'dbe and Worthy for ever!

Enter Wou'dbe and Worthy, in two chairs, raised aloft by the freeholders.

Freeholders all. Huzza, for Wou'dbe and Worthy—Huzza for Wou'dbe and Worthy—huzza, for Wou'dbe and Worthy!—(*they traverse the stage, and then set them down.*)

Worthy. Gentlemen, I'm much obliged to you for the signal proof you have given me to-day of your regard. You may depend upon it, that I shall endeavour faithfully to discharge the trust you have reposed in me.

Wou'dbe. I have not only, gentlemen, to return you my hearty thanks for the favours you have conferred upon me, but I beg leave also to thank you for shewing such regard to the merit of my friend. You have in that, shewn your judgment, and a spirit of independence becoming Virginians.

Capt. P. So we have Mr. Wou'dbe, we have done as we ought, we have elected the ablest, according to the writ.

Henceforth, let those who pray for wholesome laws,
And all well-wishers to their country's cause,
Like us refuse a coxcomb—choose a man—
Then let our senate blunder if it can.

[*Exit omnes.*

End of the Candidates.

15

The Contest for Empire

The French and Indian War (1756–1763) was not the first time that the American colonies joined with British Regulars to fight a European conflict on New World soil. Still, the French and Indian War was different for the first and major engagements of the war took place here, and the colonists had an unprecedented interest in its outcome. Victory meant the expulsion of the French as a serious threat from North America, and a basic change in the relationship between the mother country and her colony.

No one, of course, thought of independence in 1755, and the Treaty of Paris (1763) seemed a high point in Anglo-American relations. Yet, from this war, the colonists gained invaluable experience in wilderness fighting. The accounts (1–5 of this selection) of this engagement as drawn from the letters of the Royal Governor of Massachusetts, William Shirley, and his subordinates in the field, such as Robert Orme, and his superiors in London, such as Secretary of State Thomas Robinson, had an obvious importance. Moreover, a very close observer of the war years might have detected critical strains between the mother country and the colonists. Often there was a keen jealousy between the British troops and the provincial American soldiers. The letters (6 and 7) also point to one such incident with a pertinence to an understanding of the events after 1763.

CORRESPONDENCE OF WILLIAM SHIRLEY

William Shirley to Sir Thomas Robinson

Boston, New England, June 20, 1755
Sir,

I had the honour to acquaint you in my last that Major General Braddock had inform'd me by letter from Williamsburg soon after his arrival in America, of the plan of operations he propos'd this year, the attack of the French Forts upon the Ohio with the two British regiments, two of the New York Independent Companies and the Provincial troops of Virginia, Maryland and North Carolina, amounting all

From *Correspondence of William Shirley, Governor of Massachusetts*, Charles H. Lincoln, ed. (New York, 1912), II: 195–203, 207–209, 211–213, 311–313, 315–323, 492–498.

of them to about 2400 men, under his own command; and the reduction of the French Forts at the Strait of Niagara with the two American new rais'd regiments, which service he purposed to put under my command.

The attempt of the reduction of the French Forts at Niagara with mine and Sir William Pepperrell's regiments (as His Excellency had propos'd in his letter) was at the same time determin'd upon by him, and in order to secure the important pass there in the most effectual manner, it was agreed to have some vessells forthwith built to command the navigation of the Lake Ontario; the care of doing which the Commodore hath committed to me.

According to this plan, the French will be attack'd almost at the same time in all their incroachments in North America; and if it should be successfully executed in every part, it seems highly probable that all points in dispute there with them may be adjusted this year, and in case of a sudden rupture between the two Crowns the way pav'd for the reduction of Canada, whenever it shall be His Majesty's pleasure to order it.

The attempt to remove the French from their incroachments in Nova Scotia and at Crown Point were, upon my communicating the propos'd schemes for effecting them, to the General, both intirely approv'd of by him.

A few days ago I had a letter from the General dated 20th of May from Fort Cumberland at Wills Creek in which he complains that the inexpressible disap-pointmts he hath met with, hath retarded his march a month beyond the time he at first intended; but by the advices I have since received from Govr. Morris and Govr. Dinwiddie, I hear he hath surmounted his difficulties, and it was judg'd would proceed the beginning of this month from Fort Cumberland for the French Fort called Fort Du Quesne upon the Ohio, which is computed to be from 90 to 110 miles distance from Wills's Creek, where very possibly he may be arriv'd by this time and begun his attack, in which I have little or no doubt in my own opinion of his succeeding, tho' it is pretty certain the French have sent a reinforce-ment of 900 men (100 of them regular troops) and stores, very lately either to the Ohio or Niagara, and many of their battoes have pass'd by in sight of Oswego.

Your most Humble and most obedient Servant
W. Shirley

2   Robert Orme to William Shirley

Fort Cumberland, July 18, 1755
Dear Sir,

As so much Business of great Importance was transacted between you and the General [Braddock], I thought it my Duty to give you the most early Intelligence of his Death, and the Occasion of it.

On the 8th Instant we encamp'd about ten Miles from the French Fort, and upon calling all the Guides, the General, from the Intelligence he could collect, determin'd to pass the Monongahela twice in order to avoid a very bad and dangerous defile call'd the Narrows. To secure our Passage, Lieut. Col. Gage was order'd, about an hour before Daybreak, to march with a Detachment of 300 Men to make the two Crossings, and to take Post upon Advantageous Ground after the last Crossing.

Sir John St. Clair with a working Party follow'd at Day Break, and the whole march'd at six o'clock. Lt. Col. Gage and Sir John St. Clair's Detachments having made the two Passages, the General pass'd with the Column of Artillery, Ammunition, Provision and Baggage, and the main Body of the Troops about one o'clock. When the whole had march'd about half a mile, the advanc'd Party found some French and Indians posted on a very advantageous Heighth, some of whom fir'd upon one of their flank Parties, which immediately alarm'd the whole, and brought on a very severe Firing without any Order or Execution.

The General immediately sent forward his van guard under the Command of Lieut. Col. Burton to sustain the two Detachments, and instantly form'd the Column in such a manner as to secure it, and to be able to bring more men to Act in case of Necessity.

The two Advanc'd Parties gave way, and fell back upon our Van, which very much disconcerted the Men, and that, added to a manner of fighting they were quite unacquainted with, struck such a Pannick that all the Intreaties, Perswasions, and Examples of the General and Officers could avail nothing, nor could order be ever regain'd; after firing away all their Ammunition they gave ground and left the Artillery, Baggage, etc. in the hands of the Enemy.

The General was with great Difficulty brought out of the Field, he had five Horses Shot under him, and was at last mortally wounded, of which he died the 13th Instant.

I should be extremely happy to have your Directions as soon as possible in relation to the papers of the General, which should go with the Command. As Col. Dunbar seems to think that he has an Independent Command, and as it was always imagin'd that in case of any Accident the whole Command on the Continent devolv'd to you, I shall not part with any Papers 'till I receive your Instructions; I heartily wish you Success, and am with the greatest Sincerity.

Dear Sir,

Your most Obedient, and most Humble Servant

Robt. Orme

I am extremely ill in Bed with the Wound I have receiv'd, and Capt. Morris likewise wounded that I have been oblig'd to beg the favour of Capt. Dobson to write this Letter; I propose to remove to Philadelphia as soon as I'm able; from thence to Boston, where, if you should be anyways near, will do myself the pleasure to wait upon you. Col. Dunbar is returning to this Place with the remainder of the Troops and Convoy. As the whole Baggage fell into the Enemy's hands, the Papers the General had with him are all lost.

3 Governor Robert Dinwiddie of Virginia to William Shirley

Williamsburg, Virginia, July 29th, 1775

Sir,

I doubt not before this you have heard of the unexpected Defeat of our Forces on the Banks of Monongahela under the Command of General Braddock, of his death and many more brave Officers etc. This News gave me a most sensible Concern as I never doubted of the Success of our Arms on the Ohio, as I think we were more numerous than the Enemy, besides having so large a Train of Artillery. But the Battle we may observe is not to the strong, nor the Race to the Swift.

On this misfortune I considered we had four Months of the best Weather in the Year to retrieve our Loss (we have very little Winter here before Xmas) I therefore wrote my thoughts and Opinion to Col. Dunbar; Copy thereof you have here inclosed; on the Death of the General the supreme Command devolves upon you, I therefore thought it necessary to send you a Copy of that Letter, believing Col. Dunbar would do nothing without your Orders. Our Assembly meets next Tuesday when I have no doubt of their qualifying me to reinforce him with 4 or 500 Men if you approve of my Plan.

It's very probable that the French will sit down easy and expect no further Attempts this Year, and it's likely that many of them will go to Canada, if so, I hope the Vessels on Lake Ontario will give a good Account of them. If you should not approve of my Proposal, I hope you will Order Col. Dunbar and the Forces to remain on our Frontiers to defend His Majesty's Colonies from the Insults and Devastation of the Enemy; for if he should leave our Frontiers, it's more than probable they will come over the mountains and rob and murder our People. There has already been many flying Parties of French and Indians, that have murdered forty of our People, rob'd them of what they had and burn'd their Houses; I immediately Ordered three Companies of Rangers to go on our Frontiers to resist their Insults, with Orders to kill all the French Indians they met with.

I do not doubt but you will be of Opinion with me, that Something should be immediately done, and that the Forces remaining are not to sit down quietly after the Loss we have sustained but if the Panic that seized the private Soldiers should be removed, after a Month's Refreshment and recovery of their Spirits they may be able to retrieve our Loss, but this I leave to Your superior Judgment.

I think if we remain easy under this Loss it will give great Spirits to the Enemy, and therefore am of Opinion that something should be done while they remain in Security thinking no more will be attempted this Year, they may be the sooner vanquish'd. I send this Express on purpose for your Orders and Instructions on this emergent Occasion and hope you will give him quick dispatch and no doubt your Orders will be complyed with.

I hope this will find you in possession of the Fort at Niagara and shall be glad to hear General Johnson prevailed with the Six Nations to take up the Hatchet against the French, and that he is on his march to Crown Point. We cannot expect to be fortunate in all our Plans of Operations, but the Success of his Majesties Arms in Nova Scotia gives us great pleasure and in some measure eleviates [sic] the great loss at Monongahela.

The loss of our Artillery is monstrous, as no doubt the Enemy will turn them against us, I know not how much of them are lost but I think if Col. Dunbar had made a Stand at the Meadows, the Enemy wou'd not have attack'd us in an open Field; But I hear he destroyed every thing that was there, Provisions and all, and marched into Fort Cumberland. As he is esteemed a good Officer, no doubt he had good reasons for so doing; but I am fully convinced, they would not have attacked him there. The People in this Dominion are greatly alarmed and I have good reason to think they will do every thing in their power to forward a second Attempt against the Enemy.

I shall wait with great Impatience for the return of this Express, as the future designation of the Forces is entirely with You, I therefore hope you will give the Messenger all possible dispatch.

Wishing you Health and Success in all Your Operations, I remain with great Esteem, and due Respect.

Your Excellency's Most Obedt. humble Servt
Robt. Dinwiddie

4   Thomas Dunbar and Thomas Gage
to William Shirley

Albany, [October] 21, 1755

By Order of His Excellency Major General Shirley Commander in Chief of his Majesty's Forces in North America,—

The different Officers of the late Sir Peter Hallket's and Coll Dunbar's Regiment and Others, who were in the Late Action under Major General Braddock on the Monongahela on the 9th of July 1755, being Called to enquire into the Causes and Circumstances of the bad Behaviour of the King's Troops in the said Action,—

It Appears that the Troops were on their March when the first Alarm was given by a Fire on the Van Guard, Commanded by Coll Gage; That an Order was then given to the Main Body to advance; that they Accordingly Marched forward in good Order and with great Alacrity, but when they had Advanced to a particular place, they were ordered to halt with a design of forming into a Line of Battle, But when that was Attempted, it Proved ineffectual, the Whole falling into Confusion, and all the endeavours of the Officers could not get them into any Regular Form, and being by this time within Reach of the Enemy's Fire, they Appeared Struck with a panick, and though some seemed Willing to Obey, when Ordered to form, Others Crowded upon them, Broke their order, and Prevented it; and in this Irregular Manner they Expended a great part of their Ammunition. Notwithstanding this Confusion, there were several Parties advanced from the Main Body in order to Recover the cannon, but were fired upon, from the Rear by our own people, by which Many were killed, and a great Many of them Discharged their pieces even in the Air; This confusion having now Continued upwards of three hours, an Order was given to beat a Retreat to bring the Men to Cover the Waggons, and Carry off as Much as Could be, they stood about the Waggons for some Little time Without any fire, and then a Smart fire Coming from the Front and Left Flank, the Whole took to Flight; Several Attempts were made to halt the Men, in Order to Make a Regular Retreat, but to no purpose, they went off as fast as they Could, until they got about three Miles from the field of Action, where there were about a hundred Men, halted with much Difficulty untill several Small Bodies Join'd them from the Rear, and then Continued the Retreat.

The Question being Asked, if any of the Men Could be Named, who had behaved Remarkably ill, Answer was made they Could Not Name any in particular and that the Bad behaviour was general; however, that Courts Martial were held on the Armys Arrival at Fort Cumberland, and the men, who had come off unwounded without Arms or Accoutrements were punished.

The Bad behaviour of the Men is in some Measures Attributed to the following Reasons.

1st: They were greatly Harrass'd by dutys unequal to their Numbers, Dispirited by Want of Sufficient Provisions, and not being allowed time to dress the little they had, with nothing to Drink but Water, and that Often Scarce and Bad.

2d: The frequent Conversations of the Provincial Troops and Country people was, that if they engaged the Indians in their European Manner of fighting, they would be Beat, and this some of their Officers Declared as their Opinion, and one of them to Coll Dunbar on the Retreat, for which he Severely Reprimanded him.

3d: The Want of Indians or other irregulars to give timely Notice of the Enemy's Approach, having only three or four guides for out Scouts.

Lastly the Novelty of an invisible enemy and the Nature of the Country, which was entirely a Forest.

Thos. Dunbar Colo.

Thos. Gage Lieut. Colo.

5   William Shirley to Sir Thomas Robinson

Albany, November 5, 1755

Sir,

Yesterday I had the Honour to receive a Letter from You dated the 28th of August, acquainting me that their Excellencies the Lords Justices were pleased to order me to take, for the present and until His Majesty's Pleasure shall be further signified, the Command in Chief of all his Majesty's Forces in North America, in the same manner and with the same powers, as the late General Braddock had it; and by the same conveyance I had the Honour to receive their Commission for that purpose.

I am likewise to acknowledge the receipt of copies of the several Orders, Letters and Instructions, which had been given at different times to the late General for his Guidance and Direction in the King's Service, as also of his letters to you.

You had before, Sir, in your letter of the 31st of July acquainted me the Earl of Holderness had made particular mention in a Letter to you from Hanover, of the high Honour his Majesty had been pleased to do me in Expressing his approbation of my Conduct and Behaviour in his Service; which Mark of his Royal Favour, I have the deepest Sense of, and shall Exert my best Endeavours for promoting his Service upon this Continent in Execution of the great Trust, which I have the Honour to have reposed in me.

In your beforementioned Letter of the 28th August, you likewise signified, Sir, the Directions of the Lords Justices to me, "to make all possible Enquiry into the Causes and Circumstances of the late bad Behaviour of the King's Troops upon the

Monongahela, and to make as many Examples of the most notorious Delinquents, as should be found requisite and expedient to restore the Discipline of his Majesty's Forces in America." In Obedience to these Orders I directed the Commanding Officer of each of the Regiments concerned in that Action to enquire in the most particular and effectual manner into the Causes and Circumstances of the late bad Behaviour of those Troops, and to Report their Opinion to me, as also to let me know whether any and what Courts Martial had been held upon, and Examples made of the most notorious Delinquents among them; and inclos'd is the Report of those Officers, to which I beg leave to referr you [Letter 4 above].

From this Report, as well as other Inquiries, I have made, it appears to me that the bad Behaviour of the Troops was so General, that there seems no room to distinguish any particular Delinquents to make Examples of, more than what the Report informs me hath been already done.

As to the Causes and Circumstances of this ill Behaviour, the Account of which, as given in the Report, doth not seem so distinct and clear as might be; they appear to me, Sir, from the best Inquiries, I have been able to make as follows.

I begin with the Marches, the General made with about 1400 picked troops for twenty days successively before the Action, because the first reason assigned in the latter end of the Report for their bad Behaviour alludes in a great Measure to those Marches, whereby they are supposed to have been harrass'd and dispirited.

In order to set this Article in a just Light, it is proper to acquaint you, Sir, that these Marches were occasioned by Intelligence the General had received of the Garrison of Fort Duquesne's expecting to be very suddenly Strengthned with a Considerable Reinforcement; which the General endeavoured to prevent by investing the Fort before their arrival there; and the Effect of those Marches seems to have been so far from dispiriting the Troops, or laying them under any disadvantages that by this means they passed the most dangerous defiles before they met the Enemy; and the Soldiers thereupon expressed a General Satisfaction, and advanced to meet them with great alacrity, as is taken notice of in the Report itself, the Officers on their part Congratulated the General upon it, as a most fortunate Event; and it seems clear from the disposition of the Kings Troops, and that of the Enemy, at the time of the latter's being discovered, that they were then in one Compact Body, and not possessed themselves of the Eminence, from whence it is observed in the Plan, they did the greatest Execution on the Kings Troops, but that the advanced Party under Lieut. Col. Gage and the working Party under Sir John St. Clair had both pass'd the Hill before they received the Enemy's first Fire, which was made upon them in Front.

I would further observe, Sir, that the General Disposition of the Troops, he took with him, as it appears in the said Plan, seems to have been extremely well formed for the March he was upon, and to prevent Surprize: And though it is said in the Report that the first Alarm of the Enemy was given by a Fire on the Van Guard, Commanded by Colonel Gage, yet it appears that the Scouts and Guides, which preceded the Troops, had given them a few Minutes notice of the Enemy's approach before the Van Guard received that Fire.

As to the Confusion, which the whole Body of Troops was thrown into soon after, the Account given of it in the Report is "That the main body being, upon the first News of the beforementioned Alarm, ordered to advance, they accordingly march'd in good Order and with great Alacrity; but when they had advanced to a particular place, they were ordered to halt with a design of forming into a Line of Battle, but when that was attempted it proved ineffectual the *whole* falling into Confusion."

The Place, at which the main Body halted, is not here mentioned, nor how it happened that the attempt made to form those Troops into a Line of Battle proved ineffectual, and that the whole thereupon fell into Confusion; but an Inspection into the disposition of the Troops when they were engaged with the Enemy, and the Account given me by some Officers, who were Eye Witnesses, and good Judges, may serve to shew the latter circumstances. By the plan it appears that the Van Guard and Working Party had left the two Advanced Cannon and Artillery Stores with the Enemy, and Retreated about 400 Yards: and I have been well informed that those Parties falling back upon the main body, which, it is said, was too close upon their Rear, whilst it was forming, put it into Disorder, and that threw the whole into Confusion, which was increased by their finding themselves surrounded and fir'd upon on all sides by the Enemy, who had by this time possessed themselves of that Eminence. The Effect of this Confusion was, the Men could not be brought to form, nor the whole Body to advance; but they continued about two Hours and a half without either advancing or Retreating, and spent their Ammunition without doing Execution except upon a few Parties of their own, which made some Attempt to recover the advanced Cannon from the Enemy, and to gain the Hill.

The Enemy in the meantime made no use of the advanced Artillery and Stores, which were abandoned to them, except to Fire with their small Arms from behind the Waggons and Carriages. This State of Confusion lasted until Orders were given to Retreat; soon after which the whole Body took to flight (as is set forth in the Report) without any pursuit from the Enemy, and could not be brought to halt before they had fled three Miles.

It seems morally certain, that if the Eminence mark'd out in the Plans had been occupied in time by part of the General's troops, which it is agreed might have been done, he must have with ease defeated the Enemy. Some attempts were made to take possession of it, but it was then too late.

It seems agreed however, that notwithstanding these disadvantages, if the whole Body of the Troops could have been prevailed on to have march'd forward, the Enemy would have been defeated, and that whilst the few Parties, which did advance, continued in Motion it was observed that the Enemy's Fire ceased; but it was in the Power of the Officers, who behaved with the greatest Gallantry and Bravery upon this occasion, particularly the General, to rouse the Men out of that Consternation and Stupidity, which their Confus'd Order, and the Novelty of an Attack made upon them by an Invisible Enemy in a Wilderness Country had thrown them into.

The Baron de Dieskau (the French General who was taken Prisoner at Lake George) in speaking of General Braddock's defeat, said that none of their (the

French) Officers were in the least Surprized at it, as it was a Maxim with them never to Expose Regulars in the Woods, without a sufficient Number of Indians and Irregulars for any Attack that might be Expected.

The inclosed Extract of a Paper dated at Montreal July 25th taken among others of the Baron de Dieskau's intitled "Orders and Instructions pour le Battailon," which was sent four days after to Fort Frontenac on the Lake Ontario, for the Regulation of them in their March thither, will further shew, Sir, what use the French make of Irregulars when join'd with Regulars in Marching through the Woods; Vizt for Scouts, Ranging Parties and Outguards upon their Flanks to prevent Ambuscade or Surprize, which Services, the French call "la petite Guerre." The proportion of Irregulars to the Regular Troops in those Orders is one third of the former to two of the latter; four Cannadeans and Eight Soldiers of the Regulars are there ordered to Embark on board each Battoe.

The System of the French for making this use of Irregulars, when join'd in Service with their Regulars, is doubtless right, but it is as clear that his Majesty must now depend upon Disciplined Regular Troops for the preservation of his American Rights and Territories against the French, who have of late, and it seems to be expected, will continue to pour into North America as many Regular Troops from France, as they can find Opportunities of doing.

The second reason assigned in the Report for the bad behaviour of the Troops, Vizt. "The frequent Conversation of the Provincial Troops, and Country People, that if they engaged the Indians in their European manner of fighting, they would be beat," seems a slight one. It is plain from the Report itself, that it made little or no Impression upon the Soldiers; it is there observed that upon receiving orders to advance to meet the Enemy, "they march'd forward in good Order and *great Alacrity*."

As to the Consequences of the General's Defeat, after his Troops who were concerned in that Action, had join'd the Division, which was left under the Command of Col. Dunbar, I find that *now* the immediate Destruction of great Quantities of the Artillery Stores and Provisions is Condemned by some of the Field Officers. The Copy of an Order from the late General, signed by Capt. Dobson his fourth Aid de Camp hath been produced to me by Col. Dunbar in his own Justification, yet it seems difficult to say how that Order, which was given out from the General at a time, when the Colonel looked upon him, as he says, as a dying Man, and consequently incapable of Command, came to be so readily Complied with, as it seems to have been, and without any Attempt to prevent it, by Application to the General, if that was the Colonels opinion when the Stores were destroyed. I am told by Lieutt. Col. Gage, that upon a Message being sent from Colonel Dunbar to the General, he immediately resigned the Command to him. I won't take upon me to say, Sir, what the Effect of the Panic, to which so much is imputed, might be in the Soldiers after they were all join'd at Colonel Dunbars Camp in Numbers treble to those of the Enemy; but there seems to have been no reason to dread a pursuit from them at that distance.

The reason, which Colonel Dunbar gives for marching the Troops so suddenly to Philadelphia, with design of going into Winter Quarters there in August, is because he says General Braddock designed to go into Winter Quarters there himself. If that was ever his design, I have abundant reason to think he had altered it; For in his Secretary's last Letter to me a few days before the Action at Monongahela he acquainted me that if the Business at Fort Du Quesne should not take up too much time, the General would endeavour, if that was practicable, to join me at Niagara; In which Case I am Confident he would not have Winter'd his Troops near so far to the Westward as Philadelphia; and from my knowledge of the General, it is very difficult for me to Conceive that he would have entertained a thought of going into Winter Quarters in the Month of August, when so great a part of this Continent was entering upon Action.

I have the Honor to be with the highest respect.

Sir

Your most Humble and most Obedient Servant

W. Shirley

6 Governor William Shirley to Major General John Winslow

New York, July 26, 1756

Yesterday the Earl of Loudoun acquainted me that he had been informed, that you and other Officers of the [American Colonial] Provincial Troops have declared that should you be joined by [British] Regular Troops in your March to Ticonderoga for the Reduction of that Fort and Crown point, you would withdraw your Troops and return home, or to that Effect. I don't think it possible for yourself, or any Officer that has the least Sense of Honour and his Duty to make so mutinous a Declaration as this, or even to entertain so criminal a thought: I found this Representation had gained more Credit with his Lordship, than I could wish and I can assure you, it hath given me great Concern, both for the sakes of yourselves and the Governments which have raised the Troops; and I think it behooves you highly to lose no time for clearing up to Lord Loudoun this Imputation upon your Honour and Loyalty to the King: I must desire you will let me hear from you upon it by the return of the Express, which will deliver this to you; and I hope your answer will be such as to give me the satisfaction of being convinc'd that this Charge upon you and the other Provincial Officers is ill grounded.

7 John Winslow to William Shirley

Sir,

Your Excellency's favour from New York of 26th July last I received the last Evening with an Account of the Information given Lord Loudoun in these words. "That you and other Officers of the Provincial Troops under your Command, have declared that in case you should be Joined by the Regular Troops in your March to Ticonderoga for the Reduction of Crown point you would withdraw your

Troops and return home or to that Effect;" and your Excellencys great surprize at so Mutinous a declaration and concern that it had gained Credit with his Lordship.

These facts were they true would have been Exceeding bad, but as all the affairs that I have been concern'd in since I have seen your Excellency have been reduced to writing and nothing done on my part or I hope by the Gentlemen Concerned but what has been look'd on by General Abercromby, Sir Willm Johnson, Colonel Webb, and the Principal Officers of the Army so far from being Mutinous that it has met with their Approbation; and with them I parted and from them receiv'd all tokens of Friendship when I left Albany on the 17th July, and have since pursued those plans that was then Agreed on without the least deviation. I am not sensible of any thing Criminal either in Debate or Otherwise but what Interpretation may be Maliciously made by far fetch'd Inferences of any thing urg'd in Argument before those Gentlemen by designing Persons I dont know; but rest assured it is Impossible that thinking People can believe that they would Countenance any thing like Mutiny.

Your Excellency may remember that the day you left Albany when there was a Convention of Officers and I had the Honour to be present, the Plan was settled that the whole of the Provincials were to proceed forward and Endeavour the Removal of the Incroachments made by the French on his Majesty's Territories and that the Regulars should possess the Posts which we then Occup'd and have a Force at Fort William Henry to assist or sustain us as occasion should require which was then agreable to all concern'd; and in the Situation we remain'd till the 14th. when we made our Grand March from [Fort] Half Moon, and being on my March I receiv'd a verbal order from General Abercromby desiring my return to Albany which I immediately Obey'd and left Army on the March with our Train. When I arriv'd at that place was Informed by the General that it was agreed that one of the Regiments of the Regulars was to go on to Oswego and that Colonel Webb's was to take Possession of the Post at Half Moon, Still Water and Saratoga and also of Fort Edward and that the Provincials must Garrison Fort William Henry, and that while we remain'd at the Forts we were to Supply what Workmen the Engineers had Occasion; for which I made no Objection too although I much better lik'd the first Plan. After which the Inclosed Question was put me which after debating made the Answer to it Annex'd and found no one dissatisfied with it took my leave.

JOHN WINSLOW'S ANSWER TO A QUESTION
OF GENERAL ABERCROMBY,
IN A COUNCIL OF WAR, JULY, 1756

General Abercromby, would be pleas'd to desire General Winslow would inform him what Effect the Junction of his Majesty's Forces would have with the Provincials, if order'd to join them on their intended Expedition.

The above question being ask'd General Winslow said that he would be extremely well pleas'd such a Junction could be made; and that he look'd on himself to be under the Command of the Commander in Chief; But that he apprehended, that if his Majesty's Troops were order'd to join the Provincials, it would almost occasion an universal Desertion, because the Men were rais'd to serve solely under the Command of their own Officers, whose Commissions in the Massachusetts are worded in the following Manner; to be Colonel or Captain etc. in a Regiment or Company, to be employ'd on an Expedition against Crown point, whereof John Winslow Esqr. is Commander in Chief.

General Winslow further informs the Council, that he apprehended the four Provinces would not raise any More Men for any future Service, if his Majesty's Forces were to join the Provincials, and that as soon as he arrives in his Camp he will call a Council of his principal Officers, to know their opinion on the above mention'd Question.

I set out for the Army on the 19th. Overtook them at Saratoga and on the next day pursued our March for Fort Edward and on that day arriv'd at the Fort. On the 21st. Encamped, On the 22nd. Call'd all the Field Officers of that place together and according to my Promise made to Genl. Abercromby laid before them the Question mention'd which they had under debate and Consideration 'till the 24th. and on the 25th: reported to a part of which a Number Protested. The whole Transactions as soon as ended I forwarded to the General and other Governors concern'd in the Expedition. The Generals answer thereto I have not yet receiv'd. *The grand Debate with the Officers in regard to the Junction arises from the General and Field Officers losing their Rank and Command which they were Universally of Opinion they could not give up as the Army was a proper Organiz'd Body* and that they by the Several Governments from whom these Troops were rais'd were *Executors in Trust which was not in their power to resign, and, even should they do it, it would End in a* DISSOLUTION OF THE ARMY as the Privates Universally hold it as one part of the *Terms on which they Enlisted that they were to be Commanded by their own Officers* and this is a Principle so strongly Imbib'd that it is not in the *Power of Man to remove it.*

Your Excellency is full acquainted with the difficulty of Governing new rais'd Troops which on my hands is doubled by their Consisting of several different Governments and put under different Regulations by the Governments that rais'd them and must necessarily conclude my task is no easy one and you may be Assured that I have nothing at heart but the King's Service and the good of my Country which I certainly prefer to any private Advantage to myself or Applause and could the Business be carried on I should not look upon myself Disparag'd to serve under Men of more knowledge but on the other hand should I not freely open the difficulties which are so Obvious and plain to his Majesty's General I should look upon myself as deserving the Gallows as the fate of this Expensive Expedition depends on these matters and must be carried on by Numbers.

Thus have I endeavour'd to set the Fact in the true light and as no Aspersion that I know of lays on me by thos Gentlemen before resited before whom I have been heard and Concern'd with I hope your Excellency will be so far from blaming my Conduct in these Intricate Affairs that they will meet with your Approbation and I obtain the same favourable Opinion from your Excellency this Year as I have hitherto had.

16

The Revolutionary Mobs

Violence was a constant component of the political events that culminated in the outbreak of the American Revolution. From the riots that accompanied the introduction of the Stamp Act in the colonies in 1765, to the Boston Massacre in 1770, to the Boston Tea Party in 1773, Americans had frequent recourse to mob action. British officials and sympathizers found these outbursts brazen, malicious, and symptomatic of the most serious breakdown of the social order. But a surprising number of colonists themselves viewed these incidents with greater enthusiasm and satisfaction. The Boston Massacre—an incident considered by the British to be one in which no more than a handful of hoodlums received their due—was for the colonists an occasion for patriotic discourse by ministers and political leaders, a custom that they continued annually.

The colonial mob was of a very special sort. It is no easy matter to put together a list of people who joined it, or reconstruct with any precision its activities. But there are several valuable contemporary accounts of mob activity that help clarify its character. Three such narratives follow below. The first, written by New York's Lieutenant-Governor, Cadwallader Colden, describes the Stamp Act riot in New York City. The second is an account of the Boston Massacre. The third is a report to a former Governor of Massachusetts, Sir Francis Bernard, of the Boston Tea Party.

ACCOUNT
OF THE STAMP ACT RIOT
Cadwallader Colden

The People of New York are properly Distinguished into different Ranks.

1st The Proprietors of the large Tracts of Land, who include within their claims from 100,000 acres to above one Million of acres under one Grant. Some of these remain in one single Family. Others are, by Devises & Purchases claim'd in common by considerable numbers of Persons.

From "The Account of the Lieutenant-Governor of New York, Cadwallader Colden, of the Stamp Act Riot, Sent to the Secretary of State and the Board of Trade in England" in *The Colden Letter Books*, New York Historical Society, *Collections for the Year 1877* (New York, 1878), II: 68–71, 74–77.

2nd The Gentlemen of the Law make the second class in which properly are included both the Bench & the Bar. Both of them act on the same Principles, & are of the most distinguished Rank in the Policy of the Province.

3rd The Merchants make the third class. Many of them have rose suddenly from the lowest Rank of the People to considerable Fortunes, & chiefly by illicit Trade in the last War. They abhor every limitation of Trade and Duty on it, & therefore gladly go into every Measure whereby they hope to have Trade free.

4^{thly}—In the last Rank may be placed the Farmers and Mechanics. Tho' the Farmers hold their Lands in fee simple, they are as to condition of Life in no way superior to the common Farmers in England; and the Mechanics such only as are necessary in Domestic Life. This last Rank comprehends the bulk of the People, & in them consists the strength of the Province. They are the most usefull and the most Morall, but allwise made the Dupes of the former; and often are ignorantly made their Tools for the worst purposes.

The Gentlemen of the Law, both the Judges & principal Practitioners at the Bar, are either Owners Heirs or strongly connected in family Interest with the Proprietors. In general all the Lawyers unite in promoting Contention, prolonging Suits & encreasing the Expence of obtaining Justice. Every artifice & chicanery in the Law has been so much connived at, or rather encouraged that honest Men who are not of affluent fortunes are deterr'd from defending their Rights or seeking Justice.

People in general Complain of these Things & lament the state of Justice, but yet the power of the Lawyers is such that every Man is afraid of offending them and is deterr'd from makeing any public opposition to their power & the daily increase of it. The Lieut. Governor sensible that he could not do his Majesty or the People committed to his care more eminent piece of service than by reforming the abuses of the Law & the dangerous power of the Lawyers took every opportunity during his administration to promote a Work as necessary as Salutary—this drew upon him the most virulent & malicious Resentment of the Lawyers which they have pursued in a manner that shews they intend, that by the ruin of the only Man who has ventured publicly to oppose them, all others shall be deterred.

The Gentlemen of the Law some years since entered into an association with intention among other things to assume the direction of Government by the influence they had in the Assembly, gained by their family connections and by the profession of the Law, whereby they are unavoidably in the secrets of many Families—many Court their Friendship, & all dread their hatred. By these means, tho' few of them are Members, they rule the House of Assembly in all Matters of Importance. The greatest number of the Assembly being Common Farmers who know little either of Men or Things are easily deluded & seduced.

By this association, united in interest & family Connections with the proprietors of the great Tracts of Land, a Domination of Lawyers was formed in this Province, which for some years past has been too strong for the Executive powers of Government.—A Domination founded on the same Principles and carried on by the same wicked artifices that the Domination of Priests formerly was in the times of ignorance in the papeish Countries. Every Man's character who dares to discover his Sentiments in opposition to theirs is loaded with infamy by every falsehood which malice can invent, and thereby exposed to the brutal Rage of the Mob. Nothing is too wicked for them to attempt which serves their purposes—the Press is to them what the Pulpit was in times of Popery. No man who Reads the Papers publish'd in New York for some time past, & what has happen'd there in consequence of them, can doubt of what is now said, however improbable on first sight it may appear to be.

When the King's [Stamp Act] Order in his Privy Council, of the 26th of July arived in September last it revived all the Rage of the Profession of the Law, & they takeing the advantage of the Spirit of Sedition which was raised in all the Colonies against the act of Parliament for laying a stamp Duty in the Colonies, they turn'd the Rage of the Mob against the Person of the Lieut Governor, after all other methods which their Malice had invented for that purpose had failed. The Malice of the Faction against the Lieut. Governor is so evident that their inclination to expose every failing in his administration cannot be doubted, & when they have nothing to charge him with besides his supporting the Right of the Subject to Appeal to the King, it gives the strongest presumption in his favour that they cannot otherwise blame any part of his administration.

In the night of the 1st of November a great Mob came up to the Fort Gate with two Immages carried on a Scaffold: one representing their gray haired Governor, the other the Devil whispering him in the Ear. After Continuing thus at the Gate, with all the insulting Ribaldry that Malice could invent, they broke open the Lieut. Governor's Coach House which was without the walls of the Fort, carried his chariot round the streets of the Town in triumph with the Immages—returned a second time to the Fort Gate, and in an open place near the Fort, finished their Insult with all the Indignities that the Malice of their Leaders could invent. Their view certainly was to provoke the Garrison, then placed on the Ramparts, to some act which might be called a Commencement of Hostilities, in which case it cannot be said what was farther intended. Being disappointed in this the Mob expended their Rage by destroying everything they found in the House of Major James of the Royal Artillery, for which no reason can be assigned other than his putting the Fort in a proper state of Defence as his Duty in his Department required of him.

While the Lieut Governor was in the Country as usual during the heats of summer he received a Letter from General Gage informing him that the public Papers were crammed with Treason. The Minds of the People disturbed excited & encouraged to Revolt against the Government, to subvert the Constitution & trample on the Laws. That every falsehood that Malice can invent is propagated as Truth to sow dissention & create animosities between Great Britain & the Colonies concluding an offer of such military assistance as the Lieut Governor should think requisite in support of the Civil Authority. The Lieut. Governor immediately answered this Letter with his Opinion that one Battalion would be requisite with the Garrison of the Fort, but that he would immediately return to Town and take the advice of the Council on the subject of his Letter.

Tho' this advice was contrary to the Lieut Governor's private Sentiments he thought it most prudent to submit the matter to the General. The argument made use of by the Council that it would be more safe to shew confidence in the people than to discover a distrust of them by calling in any assistance to the civil power, in the Lt Governor's Opinion goes too far, as it discouraged every precaution. The event has shewn that it was not well judged, for it is most probable that had a Battalion of Regulars been brought to New York, all the Riots and Insults on Government had been prevented. The acting with vigour seemed the more necessary as the eyes of all the other Colonies were on New York where the King had a Fort allwise garrisoned with Regular Troops. The General kept his head Quarters there, and two Friggates and a sloop of War were in the Port. When the Lieut. Governor came to Town he found the General had ordered Major James to carry in such Artillery & Military Stores as he thought necessary for the Defence of the Fort; and two Companies of artillery having opportunely arrived at that time from England they had likewise been ordered into the Fort to strengthen the Garrison. Mr James is certainly a Benevolent Humane Man, & had distinguished himself on several occasions in the late War. No objection could be made to him, but his daring to put the King's Fort in a state of Defence, against the Sovereign Lords the People as they stiled themselves, for which offence they Resolved to make him an example of their Displeasure.

Before these additional Defences were made, & while the Garrison consisted only of 44 Privates & two subaltern officers, the Fort could not have been defended against 100 resolute Men, in which case the Govr must have submitted to every shamefull condition which the insolence of the Leaders of the Mob should think proper to impose upon him. They certainly had this in view while the Fort remained in its defenceless State. But after it was put in that state of offence as well as Defence, in which it was put after the 1st of November by the Engineers of the Army, the stile of the Leaders of the Mob was changed from Threatening to Deprecating, & they only wanted some Colour for desisting from their Designs to save their Credit with the deluded People. It became evident that the Fort could not be carried by assault, & that in the attempt the town would be exposed to Desolation. In the state the Fort then was, it was the Opinion of the Gentlemen of the army, that one Regiment in the city would have been sufficient to have subdued the Seditious Spirit which then prevailed.

The Authors of the Sedition place their Security in the number of offenders, and that no Jury in the Colonies will convict any of them. Were it possible that these men could succeed in their hope of Independency on a British Parliament, many judicious Persons think (tho' they dare not declare what they think) we shall become a most unhappy People. The obligation of Oaths daringly profaned—& every Bond of Society dissolved. The Liberty & Property of Individuals will become subject to the avarice & ambition of wicked Men who have art enough to keep the Colony in perpetual Factions, by deluding an ignorant Mob: and the Colonies must become thereby useless to Great Britain.

THE HORRID MASSACRE
IN BOSTON

Perpetrated in the evening of the fifth day of March, 1770, by soldiers of the Twenty-ninth Regiment, which with the Fourteenth Regiment were then quartered there; with some observations on the state of things prior to that catastrophe. Gathered and printed by the Town of Boston, 1770.

It may be a proper introduction to this narrative, briefly to represent the state of things for some time previous to the said Massacre; and this seems necessary in order to the forming a just idea of the causes of it.

At the end of the late war, in which this province bore so distinguished a part, a happy union subsisted between Great Britain and the colonies. This was unfortunately interrupted by the Stamp Act; but it was in some measure restored by the repeal of it. It was again interrupted by other acts of parliament for taxing America; and by the appointment of a Board of Commissioners, in pursuance of an act, which by the face of it was made for the relief and encouragement of commerce, but which in its operation, it was apprehended, would have, and it has in fact had, a contrary effect. By the said act the said Commissioners were "to be resident in some convenient part of his Majesty's dominions in America." This must be understood to be in some part convenient for the whole. But it does not appear that, in fixing the place of their residence, the convenience of the whole was at all consulted, for Boston, being very far from the centre of the colonies, could not be the place most convenient for the whole. Judging by the act, it may seem this town was intended to be favored, by the Commissioners being appointed to reside here; and that the consequence of that residence would be the relief and encouragement of commerce; but the reverse has been the constant and uniform effect of it; so that the commerce of the town, from the embarrassments in which it has been lately involved, is greatly reduced. For the particulars on this head, see the state of the trade not long since drawn up and transmitted to England by a committee of the merchants of Boston.

The residence of the Commissioners here has been detrimental, not only to the commerce, but to the political interests of the town and province; and not only so, but we can trace from it the causes of the late horrid massacre. Soon after their arrival here in November, 1767, instead of confining themselves to the proper business of their office, they became partizans of Governor Bernard in his political schemes; and had the weakness and temerity to infringe upon one of the most essential rights of the house of commons of this province—that of giving their votes with freedom, and not being accountable therefor but to their constituents. One of the members of that house, Capt. Timothy Folgier, having voted in some affair contrary to the mind of the said Commissioners, was for so doing dismissed from the office he held under them.

These proceedings of theirs, the difficulty of access to them on office-business, and a supercilious behavior, rendered them disgustful to people in general, who in

From *A Short Narrative of the Horrid Massacre in Boston* (Boston, 1770; reprinted, New York, 1849), 13–19, 21–22, 28–30.

consequence thereof treated them with neglect. This probably stimulated them to resent it; and to make their resentment felt, they and their coadjutor, Governor Bernard, made such representations to his Majesty's ministers as they thought best calculated to bring the displeasure of the nation upon the town and province; and in order that those representations might have the more weight, they are said to have contrived and executed plans for exciting disturbances and tumults, which otherwise would probably never have existed; and, when excited, to have transmitted to the ministry the most exaggerated accounts of them.

Unfortunately for us, they have been too successful in their said representations, which, in conjunction with Governor Bernard's, have occasioned his Majesty's faithful subjects of this town and province to be treated as enemies and rebels, by an invasion of the town by sea and land. While the town was surrounded by a considerable number of his Majesty's ships of war, two regiments landed and took possession of it; and to support these, two other regiments arrived some time after from Ireland; one of which landed at Castle Island, and the other in the town.

Thus were we, in aggravation of our other embarrassments, embarrassed with troops, forced upon us contrary to our inclination—contrary to the spirit of Magna Charta—contrary to the very letter of the Bill of Rights, in which it is declared, that the raising or keeping a standing army within the kingdom in time of peace, unless it be with the consent of parliament, is against law, and without the desire of the civil magistrates, to aid whom was the pretence for sending the troops hither; who were quartered in the town in direct violation of an act of parliament for quartering troops in America.

As they were the procuring cause of troops being sent hither, they must therefore be the remote and a blameable cause of all the disturbances and bloodshed that have taken place in consequence of that measure.

We shall next attend to the conduct of the troops, and to some circumstances relative to them.

The challenging the inhabitants by sentinels posted in all parts of the town before the lodgings of officers, which (for about six months, while it lasted), occasioned many quarrels and uneasiness.

Capt. Wilson, of the 59th, exciting the negroes of the town to take away their masters' lives and property, and repair to the army for protection, which was fully proved against him. The attack of a party of soldiers on some of the magistrates of the town—the repeated rescues of soldiers from peace officers—the firing of a loaded musket in a public street, to the endangering a great number of peaceable inhabitants—the frequent wounding of persons by their bayonets and cutlasses, and the numerous instances of bad behavior in the soldiery, made us early sensible that the troops were not sent here for any benefit to the town or province, and that we had no good to expect from such conservators of the peace.

It was not expected, however, that such an outrage and massacre, as happened here on the evening of the fifth instant, would have been perpetrated. There were then killed and wounded, by a discharge of musketry, eleven of his Majesty's subjects, viz.:

Mr. Samuel Gray, killed on the spot by a ball entering his head.

Crispus Attucks, a mulatto, killed on the spot, two balls entering his breast.

Mr. James Caldwell, killed on the spot, by two balls entering his back.

Mr. Samuel Maverick, a youth of seventeen years of age, mortally wounded; he died the next morning.

Mr. Patrick Carr mortally wounded; he died the 14th instant.

Christopher Monk and John Clark, youths about seventeen years of age, dangerously wounded. It is apprehended they will die.

Mr. Edward Payne, merchant, standing at his door; wounded.

Messrs. John Green, Robert Patterson, and David Parker; all dangerously wounded.

The actors in this dreadful tragedy were a party of soldiers commanded by Capt. Preston of the 29th regiment. This party, including the Captain, consisted of eight, who are all committed to jail.

What gave occasion to the melancholy event of that evening seems to have been this. A difference having happened near Mr. Gray's ropewalk, between a soldier and a man belonging to it, the soldier challenged the ropemakers to a boxing match. The challenge was accepted by one of them, and the soldier worsted. He ran to the barrack in the neighborhood, and returned with several of his companions. The fray was renewed, and the soldiers were driven off. They soon returned with recruits and were again worsted. This happened several times till at length a considerable body of soldiers was collected, and they also were driven off, the ropemakers having been joined by their brethren of the contiguous ropewalks. By this time Mr. Gray being alarmed interposed, and with the assistance of some gentlemen prevented any further disturbance. To satisfy the soldiers and punish the man who had been the occasion of the first difference, and as an example to the rest, he turned him out of his service; and waited on Col. Dalrymple, the commanding officer of the troops, and with him concerted measures for preventing further mischief. Though this affair ended thus, it made a strong impression on the minds of the soldiers in general, who thought the honor of the regiment concerned to revenge those repeated repulses. For this purpose they seem to have formed a combination to commit some outrage upon the inhabitants of the town indiscriminately; and this was to be done on the evening of the 5th instant or soon after.

Samuel Drowne [a witness] declares that, about nine o'clock of the evening of the fifth of March current, standing at his own door in Cornhill, he saw about fourteen or fifteen soldiers of the 29th regiment, who came from Murray's barracks, armed with naked cutlasses, swords, &c., and came upon the inhabitants of the town, then standing or walking in Cornhill, and abused some, and violently assaulted others as they met them; most of whom were without so much as a stick in their hand to defend themselves, as he very clearly could discern, it being moonlight, and himself being one of the assaulted persons. All or most of the said soldiers he saw go into King street (some of them through Royal Exchange lane), and there followed them, and soon discovered them to be quarrelling and fighting with the people whom they saw there, which he thinks were not more than a dozen, when the soldiers came first, armed as aforesaid. Of those dozen people, the most of them were gentlemen, standing together a little below the Town House, upon the Exchange. At the appearance of those soldiers so armed, the most of the twelve persons went off, some of them being first assaulted.

The violent proceedings of this party, and their going into King street, "quarrelling and fighting with the people whom they saw there" (mentioned in Mr. Drowne's deposition), was immediately introductory to the grand catastrophe.

These assailants, who issued from Murray's barracks (so called), after attacking and wounding divers persons in Cornhill, as above-mentioned, being armed, proceeded (most of them) up the Royal Exchange lane into King street; where, making a short stop, and after assaulting and driving away the few they met there, they brandished their arms and cried out, "Where are the boogers! where are the cowards!" At this time there were very few persons in the street beside themselves. This party in proceeding from Exchange lane into King street, must pass the sentry posted at the westerly corner of the Custom House, which butts on that lane and fronts on that street. This is needful to be mentioned, as near that spot and in that street the bloody tragedy was acted, and the street actors in it were stationed: their station being but a few feet from the front side of the said Custom House. The outrageous behavior and the threats of the said party occasioned the ringing of the meeting-house bell near the head of King street, which bell ringing quick, as for fire, it presently brought out a number of the inhabitants, who being soon sensible of the occasion of it, were naturally led to King street, where the said party had made a stop but a little while before, and where their stopping had drawn together a number of boys, round the sentry at the Custom House. Whether the boys mistook the sentry for one of the said party, and thence took occasion to differ with him, or whether he first affronted them, which is affirmed in several depositions,—however that may be, there was much foul language between them, and some of them, in consequence of his pushing at them with his bayonet, threw snowballs at him, which occasioned him to knock hastily at the door of the Custom House. From hence two persons thereupon proceeded immediately to the main-guard, which was posted opposite to the State House, at a small distance, near the head of the said street. The officer on guard was Capt. Preston, who with seven or eight soldiers, with fire-arms and charged bayonets, issued from the guardhouse, and in great haste posted himself and his soldiers in front of the Custom House, near the corner aforesaid. In passing to this station the soldiers pushed several persons with their bayonets, driving through the people in so rough a manner that it appeared they intended to create a disturbance. This occasioned some snowballs to be thrown at them, which seems to have been the only provocation that was given. Mr. Knox (between whom and Capt. Preston there was some conversation on the spot) declares, that while he was talking with Capt. Preston, the soldiers of his detachment had attacked the people with their bayonets; and that there was not the least provocation given to Capt. Preston or his party; the backs of the people being toward them when the people were attacked. He also declares, that Capt. Preston seemed to be in great haste and much agitated, and that, according to his opinion, there were not then present in King street above seventy or eighty persons at the extent.

The said party was formed into a half circle; and within a short time after they had been posted at the Custom House, began to fire upon the people.

Captain Preston is said to have ordered them to fire, and to have repeated that order. One gun was fired first; then others in succession, and with deliberation, till ten or a dozen guns were fired; or till that number of discharges were made from the guns that were fired. By which means eleven persons were killed and wounded, as above represented.

A NARRATIVE
OF THE TEA ACT MOB

The Advices received from Boston, in Letters from Gov. Hutchinson, Admiral Montagu, and the Commandant of the Kings Troops at Castle William, and the Information taken here of Capt Scott, lately arrived from thence, contain the following Facts—

That, in the night between the 1st & 2^d of November, anonymous Letters were delivered at the Houses of the Persons Commissioned by the East India Company, for the Sale of Teas sent on their own Account to Boston, requiring them to appear next day at noon at Liberty Tree to make a Public Resignation of their Commission, and Printed notices were posted up in several parts of the Town of Boston desiring the Freemen to meet at Liberty Tree in order to receive such Resignation, and to oblige said Agents to swear they would reship any such Tea to London.

That on the 2^d of November, the *Select Men of Boston, the Town Clerk and three or four Members of the House* of Representatives,—accompanied by a number of Inhabitants, assembled at Liberty Tree for the purposes aforementioned, and that soon after Mr *Molineux*, attended by a number of other persons, calling themselves a Committee of the said Meeting, consisting among others of Mr Denny, Dr Warren, Dr Church, and Mr Johanat, repaired to the House of Mr Clark, one of the said Agents and being asked by Mr Clark what they expected of him, Mr Molineux read a paper, in which, among other things, it was demanded that the persons, to whom it was expected the Tea would be consigned, would engage not to receive it, but that it should be sent back to England, and that one of the Bills of Lading should be delivered to them that they might send it to their Agent in London.

That upon Mr Clarke and the other Agents who were present declaring they would not comply with this Demand, Mr Molineux declared that they either were or would be voted Enemies to their Country and must expect to be treated as such.

That after this the Committee with the Mob that attended them retired, and soon after returned, assaulted Mr Clarke's House, the Doors of which were Shut

From "The Papers of the Former Governor of Massachusetts, Sir Francis Bernard (1773)," *The Barrington-Bernard Correspondence, 1760–1770*, Edward Channing and Archibald Coolidge, eds. (Cambridge, Mass., 1912), 294–302.

from an apprehension of Violence, and having forced open the Doors attempted to make their way up Stairs, but meeting with Resistance they desisted.

That during the proceedings a Mr Hatch a Gentleman in the Commission of the Peace, required the Mob to disperse; but they hooted at him, and one of them having Struck him a blow, he retired.

That on the 5th of Novr a Town Metting was held at Faneuil Hall, at which it was voted that the Honble John Hancock Esqre, Mr John Pitt, Mr Samuel Adams, Mr Samuel Abbot, Dr Joseph Warren, Mr William Powell, and Mr Nathaniel Appleton, should be a Committee to wait on the Agents of the East India Company, and to request them from a regard to their own Character, and the Peace & good Order of the Town and Province, immediately to resign their Appointment, with this request the Agents refused to comply and signified their refusal in Letters to the Honble John Hancock who was Moderator of the Town Meeting.

That on the 12th of Novr Information was given to Mr Oliver the Lieut^t Governor, that an Attack would be made that Evening upon some of the Agents; Intimation of this being given to them they left their Houses, but no such attack was made.

That on the 17th in the Evening a Mob of between one and two hundred people, beset the House of Mr Hutchinson one of the said Agents, but finding that he was not at home, they went to the House of Mr Clarke, another of the said Agents, which they Attacked, and endeavoured to break open the Door, but meeting with resistance they contented themselves with breaking the Glass and Frame of the Window, and then dispersed.

That in consequence of the disturbance before mentioned, the Governor Assembled his Council, and laid before them the necessity of some Measures being taken for preserving the Peace, and supporting the Authority of Government.

That during their deliberations a Petition was delivered from the Agents stating the Insults they had received, and the danger to which they were exposed; and praying that they might be at liberty to resign themselves, and the Property committed to their care, to the Governor and Council, as the Guardians and Protectors of the People, but the Council broke up without coming to any Resolution.

That on the 23^d of Novr the Council met again without doing any thing but referring the Business to a further consideration on the 29th when they took into consideration a Report made by a Committee in which it is stated that the proceedings of Parliament had given just ground of discontent to the People, and those proceedings are assigned as the cause of the present Disturbances.—The Agents are referred to the Justices of the Peace for the protection they desire, and it is declared that the Council had no Authority to take charge of the Tea, and *that should they direct or advise any measure for Landing it, they would of course advise to a Measure for procuring Payment of the Duty, which being inconsistent with the declared Sentiments* of both Houses in the last Winter Sessions of the General Court, they apprehend to be altogether inexpedient and improper.—That with regard to the disturbances the Authors of them ought to be prosecuted, and they advise that the Governor should renew his Orders to the Justices, Sheriff and other Peace Officers, to exert them selves to the utmost for the Security of the Kings Subjects the preservation of Peace & good Order, and for preventing all Offences against the Laws.

That this Report was accordingly agreed to, whereupon the Governor demanded of the Council, whether they would not give him any Advice upon the Disorders then prevailing in the Town of Boston, and it was answered in general, That the Advice already given was intended for that purpose.

That on, or about the 26th of November the Ship Dartmouth [of] Captn Hall, arrived at Boston, having on board a Cargo of Tea consigned by the East India Company to their Agents there; in consequence of which Notifications were posted up, desiring the Inhabitants of the Town and Country to Assemble on the 29th—

That on the 29th the Inhabitants of the said Town & Country in number about five Thousand were accordingly Assembled; whereupon the Governor, (the Council having declined advising to any Measure respecting that unlawful Assembly in particular) Ordered the Sheriff to repair to the said Meeting with a Proclamation, Warning, Exhorting, and Requiring them forthwith to disperse, and to cease all further unlawful Proceedings.

That the Sheriff having been permitted to read this Proclamation, a Question was moved and put, Whether the Assembly should be dispersed in Consequence thereof; and it was unanimously Resolved that they should not.

That Jonathan Williams Esqre was chosen Moderator at this Meeting, and that the said Meeting came to the following Resolutions; amongst others Vizt That they were absolutely determined that the Tea arrived in Captn Hall, should be returned to the place from whence it came at all Events, in the same Ship.—That no Duty should be paid upon it, and that the Owner of the Ship be directed not to Enter the Tea at his Peril. That the Master of the Ship be informed, that he is not at his peril to suffer any of the Tea to be Landed. That a Military Watch should be Appointed for the Security of the Ship and Cargo, of which watch Mr Proctor was appointed Captain, and a List made of the names of the Persons who offered themselves as Volunteers for that purpose.

That the Conduct of the Governor in requiring the Justices of the Peace to meet, in order to suppress any Riot was a reflection on that Assembly and solely calculated to serve the Views of Administration.

That on Tuesday the 30 of November the Inhabitants were again Assembled, when a Letter from the Agents was read, declaring their Willingness to give satisfaction to the Town but as that could only be effected by sending back the Tea, they declared that it was not in their power so to do but that they were willing to Store the Tea until they could write to their Constituents and receive further Orders.

That upon reading this Letter it was moved whether if any of the Agents could be prevailed upon to come to the Meeting their persons might be safe until their Return to the place from whence they should come?—which question having been put it was carried in the Affirmative unanimously and that two Hours should be allowed them, whereupon the Meeting adjourned to the Afternoon.

That upon their Meeting in the Afternoon Report was made that the Agents thinking that nothing would be satisfactory, short of returning the Tea, which was out of their power, they thought it best not to appear, which Report having been voted to be in no degree satisfactory, an Order was made that the Owner & Master of the Ship Dartmouth should attend & it was again unanimously resolved that it should be required of them, that the Tea should be returned to England in the Bottom in which it came, and Capt. Hall was forbid to Assist in Unloading the Tea at his peril, and ordered that if he continued Master of the Vessel, he should carry the same back to London.

That after taking Measures for a Continuance of the Military Watch resolved to be Established on the preceding day, & directing that if they were insulted they should give alarm to the Inhabitants by ringing or tolling the Bells as the case should happen, it was resolved that if any person or persons shall here after Import Tea from Great Britain or if any Master or Masters of any Vessel or Vessels in Great Britain shall take the same on board to be Imported to this place until the unrighteous Act of Parliament laying a Duty upon it should be repealed, he or they should be deemed by this Body an Enemy to his Country and they would prevent the Landing and Sale of the same, and the payment of the Duty thereon and would effect the Return thereof to the place from whence they should come.

That it was further resolved at this Meeting that the foregoing Vote should be printed and sent to England, and all the Sea ports of the Province.

That Mr Saml Adams, the Honble John Hancock Esqre, Willm Philips Esqre John Rowe Esq, Jonathan Williams Esqre be a Committee to transmit fair Copies of the whole proceedings of the Meeting to New York and Philadelphia.

That it is the Determination of the Body to carry their Votes and Resolutions into Execution at the risk of their Lives and Fortunes.

That the Persons who principally proposed the questions on which the above Resolutions and proceedings were founded, were, Mr Adam's, Mr Molineux, Doctor Young & Doctor Warren, & that they used many Arguments to induce the People to concur in these Resolutions.

That after the Dissolution of this unlawful Assembly the Persons called the *Committee of Correspondence;* met from time to time called in the Committee's of other Towns to join with them, kept up a Military Watch on Guard, to prevent the Landing of the Tea, who were Armed with Muskets and Bayonets, and every half hour during the night, regularly passed the Word—*all is well,* like Centinels in a Garrison.

That Mr Hancock the Gov^{rs} Captn of his Cadet Company was one of the Guard on Board the Ships.

That the said Committee appeared to be the Executioners of the Resolves & Orders passed at the aforesaid Assembly.

That this Committee repeatedly sent for the Owner of the Ship Dartmouth requiring him to comply with the request of the Town and send his Ship with the Tea back to England—In excuse for his Refusal he said that he could not obtain a Clearance from the Custom House, wereupon Notifications were again posted upon the 14th of Decem^r for another Meeting of the Inhabitants which was accordingly held in the Afternoon.

That at this Meeting it was determined that the Owner of the Ship Dartmouth should demand at the Custom House a Clearance of the Teas for England, which was accordingly done in the presence of twelve Persons appointed to see it done.

That upon the Refusal of the Custom House to grant such Clearance the Meeting was adjourned to the next day, in order to consider what was to be done, when the said Owner was required to demand a Permit from the Naval Officer to pass the Castle, which being also refused, he was ordered to apply to the Governor in person for such Permit; which being also refused he returned and made his Report to the Meeting; whereupon numbers of the people cried out a Mob, a Mob, & left the House, and immediately a body of Men disguised like Indians, & encouraged by Mr John Hancock, Saml Adams and others repaired to the Wharf, where three Vessels having Tea on board, lay aground, and took possession of the said Vessels, and in two hours the whole of the Tea was consumed.

The Rhetoric of Revolution

One of the most important effects of the new British imperial policy was in prompting many Americans to think for the first time about the most basic constitutional questions. The years after 1763 witnessed an incredible outpouring of pamphlets exploring the premises governing a tie between a mother country and her colony, the dangers of unlimited power, and the requirements for liberty. The Stamp Act, for example, provoked not only riots but the most strenuous efforts to define the proper limits of government in general, and its rights of taxation in particular; and since items of British legislation followed each other in rapid succession, the debate never let up.

All sorts of ingenious distinctions on the rights of Parliamentary taxation emerged from the pamphlet literature. Perhaps the vital result of these discussions was in elevating questions of politics to matters of principle. The pamphlets moved quickly from considerations of internal versus external taxes to the need for the colonists to protect their most vital heritage, liberty. John Dickinson, a leading Philadelphia lawyer, and member of the Pennsylvania legislature, was only one among many Americans who cautioned his countrymen to keep alert and to be prepared to defend their liberties. As the selection from Dickinson's *Letters from a Farmer in Pennsylvania* (1767) well illustrates, once the American-British debate became tied to principle, it would not be easily compromised by ordinary political adjustments.

LETTERS FROM A FARMER IN PENNSYLVANIA
John Dickinson

My dear Countrymen,

Some states have lost their liberty by *particular accidents:* But this calamity is generally owing to the *decay of virtue.* A *people* is travelling fast to destruction, when *individuals* consider *their* interests as distinct from *those of the public.* Such notions are fatal to their country, and to themselves. Yet how many are there, so

From *Letters from a Farmer in Pennsylvania* (reprinted, New York, 1903), Letter XII, 132–146.

weak and *sordid* as to *think* they perform *all the offices of life,* if they earnestly endeavor to increase their own *wealth, power,* and *credit,* without the least regard for the society, under the protection of which they live; who, if they can make an *immediate profit to themselves,* by lending their assistance to those, whose projects plainly tend to the injury of their country, rejoice in their *dexterity,* and believe themselves entitled to the character of *able politicians.* Miserable men! Of whom it is hard to say, whether they ought to be most the objects of *pity* or *contempt:* But whose opinions are certainly as *detestable,* as their practices are *destructive.*

Though I always reflect, with a high pleasure, on the integrity and understanding of my countrymen, which, joined with a pure and humble devotion to the great and gracious author of every blessing they enjoy, will, I hope, ensure to them, and their posterity, all temporal and eternal happiness; yet when I consider, that in every age and country there have been bad men, my heart, at this threatening period, is so full of apprehension, as not to permit me to believe, but that there may be some on this continent, *against whom you ought to be upon your guard* —Men, who either hold, or expect to hold certain advantages, by setting examples of servility to their countrymen.—Men, who trained to the employment, or self taught by a natural versatility of genius, serve as decoys for drawing the innocent and unwary into snares. It is not to be doubted but that such men will diligently bestir themselves on this and every like occasion, to spread the infection of their meanness as far as they can. On the plans *they* have adopted, this is *their* course. *This* is the method to recommend themselves to their *patrons.*

It is not intended, by these words, to throw any reflection upon gentlemen, because they are possessed of offices: For many of them are certainly men of virtue, and lovers of their country. But supposed obligations of *gratitude,* and *honor,* may induce them to be silent. Whether these obligations *ought to be* regarded or not, is not so much to be considered by others, in the judgment they form of these gentlemen, as whether they *think they* ought to be regarded. Perhaps, therefore, we shall act in the properest manner towards them, if we neither *reproach* nor *imitate* them. The persons meant in this letter, are the *base spirited wretches,* who may endeavor to *distinguish themselves,* by their sordid zeal in defending and promoting measures, which *they know, beyond all question,* to be *destructive* to the *just rights* and *true interests* of their country. It is scarcely possible to speak of *these men* with any degree of *patience*—It is scarcely possible to speak of them with any degree of *propriety*—For no words can truly describe their *guilt* and *meanness*—

From *them* we shall learn, how *pleasant* and *profitable* a thing it is, to be for our SUBMISSIVE behavior *well spoken of* at *St. James's,* or *St. Stephen's;* at *Guildhall,* or the *Royal Exchange.* Specious fallacies will be dressed up with all the arts of delusion, to persuade one colony to *distinguish herself from another,* by unbecoming condescensions, *which will serve the ambitious purposes of great men at home,* and therefore will be thought by them *to entitle their assistants in obtaining them* to considerable rewards.

Our fears will be excited. Our homes will be awakened. It will be insinuated to us, with a plausible affectation of *wisdom* and *concern,* how *prudent* it is to please the *powerful*—how *dangerous* to provoke them—and then comes in the perpetual incantation that freezes up every generous purpose of the soul in cold, inactive expectation—"that if there is any request to be made, compliance will obtain a favorable attention."

Our *vigilance* and our *union* are *success* and *safety.* Our *negligence* and our *division* are *distress* and *death.* They are *worse*—They are *shame* and *slavery.* Let us equally shun the benumbing stillness of *overweening sloth,* and the feverish activity of that *ill informed zeal,* which busies itself in maintaining *little, mean* and *narrow* opinions. Let us, with a truly wise *generosity* and *charity,* banish and discourage all *illiberal distinctions,* which may arise from differences in *situation,* forms of *government,* or modes of *religion.* Let us consider ourselves as MEN—FREEMEN—CHRISTIAN FREEMEN—*separated from the rest of the world, and firmly bound together by the same rights, interests* and *dangers.* Let *these* keep our attention inflexibly fixed on the GREAT OBJECTS, which we must CONTINUALLY REGARD, in order to *preserve those rights, to promote those interests,* and to *avert those dangers.*

Let these *truths* be indelibly impressed on our minds—*that* we *cannot be* HAPPY, *without being* FREE—that we cannot be free, *without being secure in our property*—that *we* cannot be secure in our property, *if, without our consent, others may, as by right, take it away*—that *taxes imposed on us by parliament,* do thus take it away—that *duties laid for the sole purpose of raising money,* are taxes—that *attempts* to lay such duties *should be instantly and firmly opposed*—that this opposition can never be effectual, *unless it is the united effort of these provinces*—that therefore BENEVOLENCE *of temper towards each other,* and UNANIMITY *of counsels,* are essential to the welfare of the whole—and lastly, that for this reason, every man among us, who in any manner would encourage either *dissension, dissidence,* or *indifference,* between these colonies, is an enemy to *himself,* and *to his country.*

The belief of these truths, I verily think, my countrymen, is indispensably necessary to your happiness. I beseech you, therefore, "teach them diligently unto your children, and talk of them when you sit in your houses, and when you walk by the way, and when you lie down, and when you rise up." [Deuteronomy 6:7.]

What have these colonies to *ask,* while they continue free? Or what have they to *dread,* but insidious attempts to subvert their freedom? *Their prosperity* does not depend on *ministerial favors doled* out to *particular* provinces. *They* form *one* political body, of which *each colony is a member. Their happiness* is founded on *their constitution;* and is to be promoted, by preserving that constitution in unabated vigor, *throughout every part.* A spot, a speck of decay, however small the limb on which it appears, and however remote it may seem from the vitals, should be alarming. We have *all the rights* requisite for our prosperity. The legal authority of *Great Britain* may indeed lay hard restrictions upon us; but, like the spear of *Telephus,* it will cure as well as wound. Her unkindness will instruct and compel us, after some time, to discover, in our *industry* and *frugality,* surprising remedies—*if our rights continue unviolated:* For as long as the *products of* our *labor,* and the *rewards* of our *care, can properly* be called *our own,* so long it will be worth our while to be *industrious* and *frugal.* But if when we plow—

sow—reap—gather—and thresh—we find, that we plow—sow—reap—gather—and thresh *for others,* whose PLEASURE is to be the SOLE LIMITATION *how much* they shall *take,* and *how much* they shall *leave,* WHY should we repeat the unprofitable toil? *Horses* and *oxen* are content with *that portion of the fruits of their work,* which their *owners* assign them, in order to keep them strong enough to raise successive crops; but even *these beasts* will not submit to draw for their *masters,* until they are *subdued* by *whips* and *goads.*

Let us take care of our *rights,* and we *therein* take care of *our prosperity.* "SLAVERY IS EVER PRECEDED BY SLEEP." *Individuals* may be *dependent* on ministers, if they please. STATES SHOULD SCORN IT;—and if *you* are not wanting *to yourselves,* you will have a *proper regard* paid *you* by *those,* to whom if you are not *respectable,* you will be *contemptible.* But—if *we have already forgot* the *reasons* that urged us with unexpanded unanimity, to exert ourselves two years ago—if *our zeal* for the public good is *worn out* before the *homespun cloths,* which it caused us to have made—if *our resolutions* are *so faint,* as by our present conduct to *condemn* our own late *successful* example—if *we are not affected* by any reverence for the memory of our ancestors, who transmitted to us that freedom in which they had been blessed—if *we are not animated* by any regard for posterity, to whom, by the most sacred obligations, we are bound to deliver down the invaluable inheritance—THEN, indeed, any *minister*—or any *tool* of a minister—or any *creature* of a tool of a minister—or any *lower instrument of administration,* if lower there be, is a *personage* whom it may be dangerous to offend.

If any person shall imagine that he discovers, in these letters, the least dislike of the dependence of these colonies on *Great Britain,* I beg that such person will not form any judgment on *particular expressions,* but will consider the *tenor of all the letters taken together.* In that case, I flatter myself, that every unprejudiced reader will be *convinced,* that the true interests of *Great Britain* are as dear to me, as they ought to be to every good subject.

If I am a *Enthusiast* in any thing, it is in my zeal for the *perpetual dependence* of these colonies on their mother country.—A dependence founded on *mutual benefits,* the continuance of which can be secured only by *mutual affections.* Therefore it is, that with extreme apprehension I view the smallest seeds of discontent, which are unwarily scattered abroad. *Fifty* or *Sixty* years will make astonishing alterations in these colonies; and this consideration should render it the business of *Great Britain* more and more to cultivate our good dispositions towards her: But the misfortune is, that those *great men,* who wrestling for power at home, think themselves very slightly interested in the prosperity of their country *Fifty or Sixty* years hence, but are deeply concerned in blowing up a popular clamor for supposed *immediate advantages.*

For my part, I regard *Great Britain* as a Bulwark, happily fixed between these colonies and the powerful nations of *Europe.* That kingdom remaining safe, we, under its protection, enjoying peace, may dissuse the blessings of religion, science, and liberty, through remote wilderness. It is therefore incontestably our *duty,* and our interest, to support the strength of *Great Britain.* When confiding in that strength, she begins to forget from whence it arose, it will be an easy thing to show the source. She may readily be reminded of the loud alarm spread among her merchants and tradesmen, by the universal association of these colonies, at the time of the *Stamp Act,* not to import any of her MANUFACTURES.

I shall be extremely sorry, if any man mistakes my meaning in any thing I have said. Officers employed by the crown, are, while according to the laws they conduct themselves, entitled to legal obedience, and sincere respect. These it is a duty to render them; and these no good or prudent person will withhold. But when these officers, through rashness or design, desire to enlarge their authority beyond its due limits, and expect improper concessions to be made to them, from regard for the employments they bear, their attempts should be considered as equal injuries to the crown and people, and should be courageously and constantly opposed. To suffer our ideas to be confounded by *names* on such occasions, would certainly be an *inexcusable weakness,* and probably an *irremediable error.*

We have reason to believe, that several of his Majesty's present ministers are good men, and friends to our country; and it seems not unlikely, that by a particular concurrence of events, we have been treated a little more severely than they wished we should be. *They* might not think it prudent to stem a torrent. But what is the difference to *us,* whether arbitrary acts take their rise from ministers, or are permitted by them? Ought any point to be allowed to a good minister, that should be denied to a bad one? The mortality of ministers, is a very frail mortality. A ———— may succeed a *Shelburne*———A ———— may succeed a *Conway.*

We find a new kind of minister lately spoken of at home—"THE MINISTER OF THE HOUSE OF COMMONS." The term seems to have peculiar propriety when referred to these colonies, *with a different meaning annexed* to it, from that in which it is taken there. By the word "minister" we may understand not only a *servant of the crown,* but a *man of influence* among the commons, who regard themselves as having a share in the *sovereignty* over us. The "minister of the house" may, in a point respecting the colonies, be so strong, that the minister of the crown *in* the house, if he is a distinct person, may not choose, even where his sentiments are favorable to us, to come to a pitched battle upon our account. For tho' I have the highest opinion of the deference of the house for the King's minister, yet he may be so good natured, as not to put it to the test, except it be for the mere and immediate profit of his master or himself.

But whatever kind of *minister* he is, that attempts to innovate *a single* iota in the privileges of these colonies, him I hope you will *undauntedly oppose;* and that you will never suffer yourselves to be either *cheated* or *frightened* into any *unworthy obsequiousness.* On such emergencies you may surely, without presumption, believe, that ALMIGHTY GOD himself will look down upon your righteous contest with gracious approbation. You will be a *"band of brothers,"* cemented by the dearest ties—and strengthened with inconceivable supplies of force and constancy, by that sympathetic ardor, which animates good men, confederated in a good cause. Your *honor* and *welfare* will be, as they now are, most intimately concerned; and besides—*you are assigned by divine providence,* in the appointed order of things, the *protectors of unborn ages,* whose *fate* depends upon your *virtue.* Whether *they* shall arise the *generous* and *indisputable heirs* of the noblest patrimonies, or the *dastardly and hereditary drudges* of imperious task-masters, YOU MUST DETERMINE.

To discharge this double duty to *yourselves,* and to your *posterity,* you have nothing to do, but to call forth into use the *good sense* and *spirit* of which you are possessed. You have nothing to do, but to conduct your affairs *peaceably— prudently—firmly—jointly.* By *these means* you will support the character of *freemen,* without losing that of *faithful subjects*—a good character in any government—one of the best under a *British* government.—You will *prove,* that *Americans* have that true *magnanimity* of soul, that can resent injuries, without falling into rage; and that tho' your devotion to *Great Britain* is the most affectionate, yet you can make PROPER DISTINCTIONS, and know what you owe to *yourselves,* as well as *to her*—You will, at the same time that you advance your *interests,* advance your *reputation*—You will convince the world of the *justice of your demands,* and the *purity of your intentions.*—While all mankind must, with unceasing applauses, confess, that YOU indeed DESERVE liberty, who so *well understand* it, so *passionately love* it, so *temperately enjoy* it, and so *wisely, bravely,* and *virtuously assert, maintain,* and *defend* it.

"*Certe ego libertatem, quae mihi a parente meo tradita est, experiar: Verum id frustra an ob rem faciam, in vestra manu situm est, quirites.*"

For my part, I am resolved to contend for the liberty delivered down to me by my ancestors, but whether I shall do it effectually or not, depends on you, my countrymen. "How littlesoever one is able to write, yet when the liberties of one's country are threatened, it is still more difficult to be silent."

A Farmer

18

Common Sense
and Imperial Relations

Perhaps the most famous and widely read pamphlet to emerge from the Revolutionary crisis was Thomas Paine's, *Common Sense,* published in 1776. Paine was born in England in 1737 of a modest family, received a mediocre education, and came to the colonies in 1774. Upon introduction to some important colonial leaders, especially Benjamin Franklin, Paine immediately threw himself into the political events. By 1783, especially on the basis of *Common Sense,* he enjoyed a world-wide reputation as an American radical. Paine, true to his own notion of "brotherhood with every Christian European," did not limit his political activities to the United States. In 1789, while in England, he published an equally famous tract, *Rights of Man,* inspired by the French Revolution. Eventually Paine moved to Paris, was imprisoned when his faction lost power, and was freed through American intervention. His last years were spent in the United States in quiet obscurity.

Common Sense, written after the outbreak of hostilites in April 1775, at Lexington, is a masterpiece of political rhetoric, and justly famous as an extraordinarily moving and effective tract. Paine appealed both logically and passionately to the colonists to break the last cord tying them to the mother country and to strike out for independence. The modern reader of *Common Sense* gains insight into the arts of political persuasion and into the minds of the colonists as they wondered whether or not to take the irrevocable step.

THOUGHTS ON THE PRESENT STATE
OF AMERICAN AFFAIRS
Thomas Paine

In the following pages I offer nothing more than simple facts, plain arguments, and common sense; and have no other preliminaries to settle with the reader than that he will divest himself of prejudice and prepossession, and suffer his reason and his feelings to determine for themselves; that he will put on, or rather that he will not

From *Common Sense* (Philadelphia, 1776; reprinted, Indianapolis, 1953), 18–34.

put off, the true character of a man, and generously enlarge his views beyond the present day.

Volumes have been written on the subject of the struggle between England and America. Men of all ranks have embarked in the controversy, from different motives and with various designs; but all have been ineffectual, and the period of debate is closed. Arms as the last resource decide the contest; the appeal was the choice of the king, and the continent has accepted the challenge.

It has been reported of the late Mr. Pelham (who, though an able minister, was not without his faults) that, on his being attacked in the House of Commons on the score that his measures were only of a temporary kind, replied, "they will last my time." Should a thought so fatal and unmanly possess the colonies in the present contest, the name of ancestors will be remembered by future generations with detestation.

The sun never shined on a cause of greater worth. 'Tis not the affair of a city, a county, a province, or a kingdom, but of a continent—of at least one-eighth part of the habitable globe. 'Tis not the concern of a day, a year, or an age; posterity are virtually involved in the contest, and will be more or less affected even to the end of time by the proceedings now. Now is the seedtime of continental union, faith, and honor. The least fracture now will be like a name engraved with the point of a pin on the tender rind of a young oak; the wound would enlarge with the tree, and posterity read it in full-grown characters.

By referring the matter from argument to arms, a new era for politics is struck—a new method of thinking has arisen. All plans, proposals, etc., prior to the nineteenth of April, i.e., to the commencement of hostilities, [at Lexington] are like the almanacs of the last year, which, though proper then, are superseded and useless now. Whatever was advanced by the advocates on either side of the question then terminated in one and the same point, viz., a union with Great Britain; the only difference between the parties was the method of effecting it—the one proposing force, the other friendship; but it has so far happened that the first has failed, and the second has withdrawn her influence.

As much has been said of the advantages of reconciliation, which, like an agreeable dream, has passed away and left us as we were, it is but right that we should examine the contrary side of the argument and inquire into some of the many material injuries which these colonies sustain, and always will sustain, by being connected with and dependent on Great Britain. To examine that connection and dependence on the principles of nature and common sense; to see what we have to trust to, if separated, and what we are to expect, if dependent.

I have heard it asserted by some that, as America has flourished under her former connection with Great Britain, the same connection is necessary toward her future happiness and will always have the same effect. Nothing can be more fallacious than this kind of argument. We may as well assert that because a child has thrived upon milk that it is never to have meat, or that the first twenty years of our lives is to become a precedent for the next twenty. But even this is admitting more than is true; for I answer roundly that America would have flourished as much, and probably much more, had no European power had anything to do with her. The commerce by which she has enriched herself are the necessaries of life and will always have a market while eating is the custom of Europe.

But she has protected us, say some. That she has engrossed us is true, and defended the continent at our expense as well as her own is admitted; and she would have defended Turkey from the same motive, viz., for the sake of trade and dominion.

Alas! we have been long led away by ancient prejudices and made large sacrifices to superstition. We have boasted the protection of Great Britain without considering that her motive was *interest,* not *attachment;* and that she did not protect us from *our enemies* on *our account* but from *her enemies* on *her own account,* from those who had no quarrel with us on any *other account* and who will always be our enemies on the *same account.* Let Britain waive her pretensions to the continent or the continent throw off the dependence, and we should be at peace with France and Spain, were they at war with Britain.

It has lately been asserted in Parliament that the colonies have no relation to each other but through the parent country, i.e., that Pennsylvania and the Jerseys, and so on for the rest, are sister colonies by the way of England; this is certainly a very roundabout way of proving relationship, but it is the nearest and only true way of proving enemyship, if I may so call it. France and Spain never were, nor perhaps ever will be, our enemies as *Americans,* but as our being the *subjects of Great Britain.*

But Britain is the parent country, say some. Then the more shame upon her conduct. Even brutes do not devour their young nor savages make war upon their families; wherefore the assertion, if true, turns to her reproach; but it happens not to be true, or only partly so, and the phrase "parent" or "mother country" has been jesuitically adopted by the king and his parasites with a low papistical design of gaining an unfair bias on the credulous weakness of our minds. Europe, and not England, is the parent country of America. This New World has been the asylum for the persecuted lovers of civil and religious liberty from *every part* of Europe. Hither have they fled, not from the tender embraces of the mother, but from the cruelty of the monster; and it is so far true of England that the same tyranny which drove the first emigrants from home pursues their descendants still.

In this extensive quarter of the globe, we forget the narrow limits of three hundred and sixty miles (the extent of England) and carry our friendship on a larger scale; we claim brotherhood with every European Christian, and triumph in the generosity of the sentiment.

It is pleasant to observe by what regular gradations we surmount the force of local prejudices as we enlarge our acquaintance with the world. A man born in any town in England divided into parishes will naturally associate most with his fellow parishioners (because their interests in many cases will be common) and distinguish him by the name of "neighbor"; if he meet him but a few miles from home, he drops the narrow idea of a street and salutes him by the name of "townsman"; if he travel out of the county and meet him in any other, he forgets the minor divisions of street and town, and calls him "countryman," i.e., "countyman"; but if in their foreign excursions they should associate in France, or any other part of *Europe,* their local remembrance would be enlarged into that of "Englishmen." And by a just parity of reasoning, all Europeans meeting in America, or any other quarter of the globe, are "countrymen"; for England, Holland, Germany, or Sweden, when compared with the whole, stand in the same places on the larger scale which the divisions of street, town, and county do on the smaller ones—distinctions too limited for continental minds. Not one third of the inhabitants, even of this province [Pennsylvania], are of English descent. Wherefore I reprobate the phrase of parent or mother country applied to England only as being false, selfish, narrow, and ungenerous.

But, admitting that we were all of English descent, what does it amount to? Nothing. Britain, being now an open enemy, extinguishes every other name and title; and to say that reconciliation is our duty is truly farcical. The first king of England of the present line (William the Conqueror) was a Frenchman, and half the peers of England are descendants from the same country; wherefore, by the same method of reasoning, England ought to be governed by France.

Much has been said of the united strength of Britain and the colonies, that in conjunction they might bid defiance to the world. But this is mere presumption; the fate of war is uncertain, neither do the expressions mean anything; for this continent would never suffer itself to be drained of inhabitants to support the British arms in either Asia, Africa, or Europe.

Besides, what have we to do with setting the world at defiance? Our plan is commerce, and that, well attended to, will secure us the peace and friendship of all Europe; because it is the interest of all Europe to have America a free port. Her trade will always be a protection, and her barrenness of gold and silver secure her from invaders.

I challenge the warmest advocate for reconciliation to show a single advantage that this continent can reap by being connected with Great Britain. I repeat the challenge; not a single advantage is derived. Our corn will fetch its price in any market in Europe, and our imported goods must be paid for, buy them where we will.

But the injuries and disadvantages we sustain by that connection are without number, and our duty to mankind at large, as well as to ourselves, instruct us to renounce the alliance; because any submission to or dependence on Great Britain tends directly to involve this continent in European wars and quarrels and sets us at variance with nations who would otherwise seek our friendship and against whom we have neither anger nor complaint. As Europe is our market for trade, we ought to form no partial connection with any part of it. It is the true interest of America to steer clear of European contentions, which she never can do while, by her dependence on Britain, she is made the makeweight in the scale of British politics.

Europe is too thickly planted with kingdoms to be long at peace; and whenever a war breaks out between England and any foreign power, the trade of America goes to ruin *because of her connection with Britain.* The next war may not turn out like the last; and should it not, the advocates for reconciliation now will be wishing for separation then, because neutrality in that case would be a safer convoy than a man-of-war. Everything that is right or natural pleads for separation. The blood of

185

the slain, the weeping voice of nature cries, " *'Tis time to part.*" Even the distance at which the Almighty has placed England and America is a strong and natural proof that the authority of the one over the other was never the design of heaven. The time likewise at which the continent was discovered adds weight to the argument, and the manner in which it was peopled increases the force of it. The Reformation was preceded by the discovery of America—as if the Almighty graciously meant to open a sanctuary to the persecuted in future years, when home should afford neither friendship nor safety.

The authority of Great Britain over this continent is a form of government which sooner or later must have an end. And a serious mind can draw no true pleasure by looking forward, under the painful and positive conviction that what he calls "the present constitution" is merely temporary. As parents, we can have no joy, knowing that this government is not sufficiently lasting to insure anything which we may bequeath to posterity. And by a plain method of argument, as we are running the next generation into debt, we ought to do the work of it; otherwise we use them meanly and pitifully. In order to discover the line of our duty rightly, we should take our children in our hand and fix our station a few years farther into life; that eminence will present a prospect which a few present fears and prejudices conceal from our sight.

Though I would carefully avoid giving unnecessary offense, yet I am inclined to believe that all those who espouse the doctrine of reconciliation may be included within the following descriptions. Interested men, who are not to be trusted, weak men who *cannot* see, prejudiced men who *will not* see, and a certain set of moderate men who think better of the European world than it deserves; and this last class, by an ill-judged deliberation, will be the cause of more calamities to this continent than all the other three.

It is the good fortune of many to live distant from the scene of sorrow; the evil is not sufficiently brought to *their* doors to make *them* feel the precariousness with which all American property is possessed. But let our imaginations transport us a few moments to Boston; that seat of wretchedness will teach us wisdom and instruct us forever to renounce a power in whom we can have no trust. The inhabitants of that unfortunate city who, but a few months ago, were in ease and affluence have now no other alternative than to stay and starve or turn out to beg. Endangered by the fire of their friends if they continue within the city, and plundered by the soldiery if they leave it. In their present condition they are prisoners without the hope of redemption; and in a general attack for their relief they would be exposed to the fury of both armies.

Men of passive tempers look somewhat lightly over the offenses of Great Britain and, still hoping for the best, are apt to call out, "Come, come, we shall be friends again for all this." But examine the passions and feelings of mankind, bring the doctrine of reconciliation to the touchstone of nature, and then tell me whether you can hereafter love, honor, and faithfully serve the power that has carried fire and sword into your land? If you cannot do all these, then are you only deceiving yourselves, and by your delay bringing ruin upon posterity. Your future connection with Britain, whom you can neither love nor honor, will be forced and unnatural, and being formed only on the plan of present convenience will, in a little time, fall into a relapse more wretched than the first. But if you say you still can pass the violations over, then I ask, has your house been burned? Has your property been destroyed before your face? Are your wife and children destitute of a bed to lie on or bread to live on? Have you lost a parent or a child by their hands, and yourself the ruined and wretched survivor? If you have not, then are you not a judge of those who have. But if you have and can still shake hands with the murderers, then are you unworthy the name of husband, father, friend, or lover; and whatever may be your rank or title in life, you have the heart of a coward and the spirit of a sycophant.

This is not inflaming or exaggerating matters, but trying them by those feelings and affections which nature justifies and without which we should be incapable of discharging the social duties of life or enjoying the felicities of it. I mean not to exhibit horror for the purpose of provoking revenge, but to awaken us from fatal and unmanly slumbers, that we may pursue determinately some fixed object. It is not in the power of Britain or Europe to conquer America, if she do not conquer herself by delay and timidity. The present winter is worth an age if rightly employed, but if lost or neglected the whole continent will partake of the misfortune; and there is no punishment which that man will not deserve, be he who or what or where he will, that may be the means of sacrificing a season so precious and useful.

It is repugnant to reason, to the universal order of things, to all examples from former ages, to suppose that this continent can longer remain subject to any external power. The most sanguine in Britain does not think so. The utmost stretch of human wisdom cannot, at this time, compass a plan, short of separation, which can promise the continent even a year's security. Reconciliation is *now* a fallacious dream. Nature has deserted the connection, and art cannot supply her place. For, as Milton wisely expresses, "never can true reconcilement grow where wounds of deadly hate have pierced so deep."

Every quiet method for peace has been ineffectual. Our prayers have been rejected with disdain, and only tended to convince us that nothing flatters vanity or confirms obstinacy in kings more than repeated petitioning—and nothing has contributed more than that very measure to make the kings of Europe absolute. Witness Denmark and Sweden. Wherefore, since nothing but blows will do, for God's sake let us come to a final separation, and not leave the next generation to be cutting throats under the violated unmeaning names of parent and child.

To say they will never attempt it again is idle and visionary; we thought so at the repeal of the Stamp Act, yet a year or two undeceived us; as well may we suppose that nations which have been once defeated will never renew the quarrel.

As to government matters, it is not in the power of Britain to do this continent justice. The business of it will soon be too weighty and intricate to be managed with any tolerable degree of convenience by a power so distant from us and so very ignorant of us; for if they cannot conquer us, they cannot govern us. To be always running three or four thousand miles with a tale or a petition, waiting four or five months for an answer, which, when obtained, requires five or six more to explain it in, will in a few years be looked upon as folly and childishness. There was a time when it was proper, and there is a proper time for it to cease.

Small islands not capable of protecting themselves are the proper objects for kingdoms to take under their care, but there is something very absurd in supposing a continent to be perpetually governed by an island. In no instance has nature made the satellite larger than its primary planet; and as England and America, with respect to each other, reverse the common order of nature, it is evident they belong to different systems—England to Europe, America to itself.

I am not induced by motives of pride, party, or resentment to espouse the doctrine of separation and independence; I am clearly, positively, and conscientiously persuaded that it is the true interest of this continent to be so; that everything short of *that* is mere patchwork, that it can afford no lasting felicity— that it is leaving the sword to our children, and shrinking back at a time when a little more, a little further, would have rendered this continent the glory of the earth.

As Britain has not manifested the least inclination toward a compromise, we may be assured that no terms can be obtained worthy the acceptance of the continent, or any ways equal to the expense of blood and treasure we have been already put to.

The object contended for ought always to bear some just proportion to the expense. The removal of [Lord] North, or the whole detestable junto, is a matter unworthy the millions we have expended. A temporary stoppage of trade was an inconvenience which would have sufficiently balanced the repeal of all the acts complained of, had such repeals been obtained; but if the whole continent must take up arms, if every man must be a soldier, it is scarcely worth our while to fight against a contemptible ministry only. Dearly, dearly do we pay for the repeal of the acts, if that is all we fight for; in a just estimation it is as great a folly to pay a Bunker Hill price for law as for land. As I have always considered the independence of this continent as an event which sooner or later must arrive, so from the late rapid progress of the continent to maturity, the event cannot be far off. Wherefore, on the breaking out of hostilities, it was not worth the while to have disputed a matter which time would have finally redressed, unless we meant to be in earnest; otherwise it is like wasting an estate on a suit at law to regulate the trespasses of a tenant whose lease is just expiring. No man was a warmer wisher for a reconciliation than myself before the fatal nineteenth of April 1775, but the moment the event of that day was made known I rejected the hardened, sullen-tempered Pharaoh of England forever and disdain the wretch that, with the pretended title of father of his people, can unfeelingly hear of their slaughter and composedly sleep with their blood upon his soul.

But admitting that matters were now made up, what would be the event? I answer, the ruin of the continent. And that for several reasons:

First. The powers of governing still remaining in the hands of the king, he will have a negative over the whole legislation of this continent. And as he has shown himself such an inveterate enemy to liberty and discovered such a thirst for arbitrary power, is he or is he not a proper man to say to these colonies, "You shall make no laws but what I please!"? And is there any inhabitant of America so

ignorant as not to know that, according to what is called the "present Constitution,"
that this continent can make no laws but what the king gives leave to; and is there
any man so unwise as not to see that (considering what has happened) he will
suffer no law to be made here but such as suits *his* purpose? We may be as
effectually enslaved by the want of laws in America as by submitting to laws made
for us in England. After matters are made up (as it is called), can there be any
doubt but the whole power of the crown will be exerted to keep this continent as
low and humble as possible? Instead of going forward we shall go backward, or be
perpetually quarrelling, or ridiculously petitioning. We are already greater than the
king wishes us to be, and will he not hereafter endeavor to make us less? To bring
the matter to one point, is the power who is jealous of our prosperity a proper
power to govern us? Whoever says "No" to this question is an independent, for
independence means no more than whether we shall make our own laws or whether
the king, the greatest enemy this continent has or can have, shall tell us "there shall
be no laws but such as I like."

But the king, you will say, has a negative in England; the people there can
make no laws without his consent. In point of right and good order, there is
something very ridiculous that a youth of twenty-one (which has often happened)
shall say to several millions of people older and wiser than himself, "I forbid this
or that act of yours to be law." But in this place I decline this sort of reply, though
I will never cease to expose the absurdity of it, and only answer that England being
the king's residence, and America not so, makes quite another case. The king's
negative *here* is ten times more dangerous and fatal than it can be in England; for
there he will scarcely refuse his consent to a bill for putting England into as strong
a state of defense as possible, and in America he would never suffer such a bill to
be passed.

America is only a secondary object in the system of British politics. England
consults the good of *this* country no farther than it answers her *own* purpose.
Wherefore her own interest leads her to suppress the growth of *ours* in every case
which does not promote her advantage or in the least interferes with it. A pretty
state we should soon be in under such a secondhand government, considering what
has happened! Men do not change from enemies to friends by the alteration of a
name. And in order to show that reconciliation now is a dangerous doctrine, I
affirm *that it would be policy in the king at this time to repeal the acts, for the sake
of reinstating himself in the government of the provinces,* in order that *he may
accomplish by craft and subtlety in the long run what he cannot do by force and
violence in the short one*. Reconciliation and ruin are nearly related.

Secondly. That as even the best terms which we can expect to obtain can
amount to no more than a temporary expedient, or a kind of government by
guardianship, which can last no longer than till the colonies come of age, so the
general face and state of things in the interim will be unsettled and unpromising.
Emigrants of property will not choose to come to a country whose form of
government hangs but by a thread, and who is every day tottering on the brink of
commotion and disturbance; and numbers of the present inhabitants would lay hold
of the interval to dispose of their effects and quit the continent.

But the most powerful of all arguments is that nothing but independence, i.e., a continental form of government, can keep the peace of the continent and preserve it inviolate from civil wars. I dread the event of a reconciliation with Britain now, as it is more than probable that it will be followed by a revolt somewhere or other, the consequences of which may be far more fatal than all the malice of Britain.

Thousands are already ruined by British barbarity (thousands more will probably suffer the same fate). Those men have other feelings than us who have nothing suffered. All they now possess is liberty; what they before enjoyed is sacrificed to its service, and having nothing more to lose they disdain submission. Besides, the general temper of the colonies toward a British government will be like that of a youth who is nearly out of his time; they will care very little about her. And a government which cannot preserve the peace is no government at all, and in that case we pay our money for nothing; and pray what is it that Britain can do, whose power will be wholly on paper, should a civil tumult break out the very day after reconciliation? I have heard some men say, many of whom I believe spoke without thinking, that they dreaded an independence, fearing that it would produce civil war. It is but seldom that our first thoughts are truly correct, and that is the case here; for there are ten times more to dread from a patched-up connection than from independence. I make the sufferer's case my own, and I protest that, were I driven from house and home, my property destroyed, and my circumstances ruined, that as a man, sensible of injuries, I could never relish the doctrine of reconciliation or consider myself bound thereby.

The colonies have manifested such a spirit of good order and obedience to continental government as is sufficient to make every reasonable person easy and happy on that head. No man can assign the least pretense for his fears on any other grounds than such as are truly childish and ridiculous, viz., that one colony will be striving for superiority over another.

Where there are no distinctions, there can be no superiority; perfect equality affords no temptation. The republics of Europe are all (and we may say always) in peace. Holland and Switzerland are without wars, foreign or domestic. Monarchical governments, it is true, are never long at rest; the crown itself is a temptation to enterprising ruffians at home; and that degree of pride and insolence ever attendant on regal authority swells into a rupture with foreign powers in instances where a republican government, by being formed on more natural principles, would negotiate the mistake.

If there is any true cause of fear respecting independence, it is because no plan is yet laid down. Men do not see their way out. Wherefore, as an opening into that business, I offer the following hints, at the same time modestly affirming that I have no other opinion of them myself than that they may be the means of giving rise to something better. Could the straggling thoughts of individuals be collected, they would frequently form materials for wise and able men to improve into useful matter.

Let the assemblies be annual, with a president only. The representation more equal, their business wholly domestic, and subject to the authority of a Continental Congress.

Let each colony be divided into six, eight, or ten convenient districts, each district to send a proper number of delegates to Congress, so that each colony send at least thirty. The whole number in Congress will be at least 390. Each Congress to sit and to choose a president by the following method: When the delegates are met, let a colony be taken from the whole thirteen colonies by lot, after which let the whole Congress choose (by ballot) a president from out of the delegates of *that* province. In the next Congress, let a colony be taken by lot from twelve only, omitting that colony from which the president was taken in the former Congress, and so proceeding on till the whole thirteen shall have had their proper rotation. And in order that nothing may pass into a law but what is satisfactorily just, not less than three fifths of the Congress to be called a majority. He that will promote discord under a government so equally formed as this would have joined Lucifer in his revolt.

But where, says some, is the king of America? I'll tell you, friend, he reigns above, and does not make havoc of mankind like the royal brute of Britain. Yet that we may not appear to be defective even in earthly honors, let a day be solemnly set apart for proclaiming the charter; let it be brought forth placed on the divine law, the word of God; let a crown be placed thereon, by which the world may know that, so far as we approve of monarchy, that in America *the law is king*. For as in absolute governments the king is law, so in free countries the law *ought* to be king; and there ought to be no other. But lest any ill use should afterward arise, let the crown at the conclusion of the ceremony be demolished and scattered among the people, whose right it is.

A government of our own is our natural right; and when a man seriously reflects on the precariousness of human affairs, he will become convinced that it is infinitely wiser and safer to form a Constitution of our own in a cool, deliberate manner while we have it in our power than to trust such an interesting event to time and chance. If we omit it now, some Massanello [an adventurer] may hereafter arise who, laying hold of popular disquietudes, may collect together the desperate and the discontented, and by assuming to themselves the powers of government may sweep away the liberties of the continent like a deluge. Should the government of America return again into the hands of Britain, the tottering situation of things will be a temptation for some desperate adventurer to try his fortune, and in such a case what relief can Britain give? Ere she could hear the news, the fatal business might be done, and ourselves suffering like the wretched Britons under the oppression of the conqueror. Ye that oppose independence now, ye know not what ye do; ye are opening a door to eternal tyranny by keeping vacant the seat of government. There are thousands and tens of thousands who would think it glorious to expel from the continent that barbarous and hellish power which has stirred up the Indians and the Negroes to destroy us; the cruelty has a double guilt: it is dealing brutally by us and treacherously by them.

To talk of friendship with those in whom our reason forbids us to have faith and our affections, wounded through a thousand pores, instruct us to detest is madness and folly. Every day wears out the little remains of kindred between us and them; and can there be any reason to hope that, as the relationship expires, the affection will increase, or that we shall agree better when we have ten times more and greater concerns to quarrel over than ever?

Ye that tell us of harmony and reconciliation, can ye restore to us the time that is past? Can ye give to prostitution its former innocence? Neither can ye reconcile Britain and America. The last cord now is broken, the people of England are presenting addresses against us. There are injuries which nature cannot forgive; she would cease to be nature if she did. As well can the lover forgive the ravisher of his mistress as the continent forgive the murders of Britain. The Almighty has implanted in us these unextinguishable feelings for good and wise purposes. They are the guardians of his image in our hearts. They distinguish us from the herd of common animals. The social compact would dissolve and justice be extirpated [from] the earth, or have only a casual existence, were we callous to the touches of affection. The robber and the murderer would often escape unpunished did not the injuries which our tempers sustain provoke us into justice.

O ye that love mankind! Ye that dare oppose not only the tyranny but the tyrant, stand forth! Every spot of the Old World is overrun with oppression. Freedom has been hunted round the globe. Asia and Africa have long expelled her. Europe regards her like a stranger, and England has given her warning to depart. O! receive the fugitive, and prepare in time an asylum for mankind.

19

Declaring for Independence

The weeks that preceded the Declaration of Independence were busy ones for John Adams. As delegate from Massachusetts to the Second Continental Congress in Philadelphia, he helped to govern the nation in its first and most trying days. As diary-keeper by habit and a practiced letter-writer, he found the time to write often to his wife Abigail, who was at home in the Boston suburb of Braintree. His correspondence with her offers the student of the Revolution a rare glimpse behind these momentous events.

John Adams was no mere participant in history, but a leader. He graduated from Harvard in 1755 and was admitted to the bar. He took an active interest in town politics and played a key role in composing Massachusetts' reply to the Stamp Act. His energy was used to defend patriots, although his sense of justice led him also to serve as counsel to British soldiers accused of murdering colonists at the Boston Massacre. Adams was elected to the First Continental Congress, and then to the Second. During the Revolution he held several key diplomatic posts and eventually served as Washington's Vice-President and, in 1797, as his successor. Whatever his reputation for aloofness, his letters reveal an extremely sensitive man. His passionate involvement in the cause of American liberty is extraordinarily clear in the letters of 1776.

THE ADAMS PAPERS

John Adams to Abigail Adams

February 18, 1776

My dearest Friend

I sent you from New York a Pamphlet intitled Common Sense, written in Vindication of Doctrines which there is Reason to expect that the further Encroachments of Tyranny and Depredations of Oppression, will soon make the common Faith: unless the cunning Ministry, by proposing Negociations and Terms of Reconciliation, should divert the present Current from its Channell.

Reprinted by permission of the publishers from L. H. Butterfield, editor, *Adams Family Correspondence*, Volumes I & II. Cambridge, Mass.: The Belknap Press of Harvard University Press, Copyright, 1963, by the Massachusetts Historical Society. I: 348–349, 352–353, 362–363, 369–370, 381–382, 388, 391–392, 410–411; II: 27–31.

Reconciliation if practicable and Peace if attainable, you very well know would be as agreable to my Inclinations and as advantageous to my Interest, as to any Man's. But I see no Prospect, no Probability, no Possibility. And I cannot but despise the Understanding, which sincerely expects an honourable Peace, for its Credulity, and detest the hypocritical Heart, which pretends to expect it, when in Truth it does not. The News Papers here are full of free Speculations, the Tendency of which you will easily discover. The Writers reason from Topicks which have been long in Contemplation, and fully understood by the People at large in New England, but have been attended to in the southern Colonies only by Gentlemen of free Spirits and liberal Minds, who are very few. I shall endeavour to inclose to you as many of the Papers and Pamphlets as I can, as long as I stay here.

The Events of War are uncertain: We cannot insure Success, but We can deserve it.

Write me as often as you can—tell me all the News. Desire the Children to write to me, and believe me to be theirs and yours.

Abigail Adams to John Adams

Saturday Evening March 2 [1776]

I was greatly rejoiced at the return of your servant to find you had safely arrived, and that you were well. I had never heard a word from you after you left New York, and a most ridiciolous story had been industerously propagated in this and the neighbouring Towns to injure the cause and blast your Reputation, viz. that you and your President had gone on board a Man of War from N–y and saild for England. I should not mention so idle a report, but that it had given uneasiness to some of your Friends, not that they in the least credited the report, but because the Gaping vulgar swallowed the story. One man had deserted them and proved a traitor, an other might &c. I assure you such high Disputes took place in the publick house of this parish, that some men were collerd and draged out of the shop, with great Threats for reporting such scandelous lies, and an unkle of ours offerd his life as a forfeit for you if the report proved true.

However it has been a nine days marvel and will now cease. I heartily wish every Tory was Extirpated [from] America, they are continually by secret means undermineing and injuring our cause.

I am charmed with the Sentiments of Common Sense; and wonder how an honest Heart, one who wishes the welfare of their country, and the happiness of posterity can hesitate one moment at adopting them; I want to know how those Sentiments are received in Congress? I dare say their would be no difficulty in procuring a vote and instructions from all the Assemblies in New England for independancy. I most sincerely wish that now in the Lucky Minuet it might be done.

I have been kept in a continual state of anxiety and expectation ever since you left me. It has been said to morrow and to morrow for this month, but when the dreadfull to morrow will be I know not—but hark! the House this instant shakes with the roar of Cannon.—I have been to the door and find tis a cannonade from our Army, orders I find are come for all the remaining Militia to repair to the Lines a monday night by twelve o clock. No Sleep for me to Night; and if I cannot who have no guilt upon my Soul with regard to this Cause, how shall the misirible wretches who have been the procurers of this Dreadfull Scene and those who are to be the actors, lie down with the load of Guilt upon their Souls.

Sunday Eve March 3

I went to Bed after 12 but got no rest, the Cannon continued firing and my Heart Beat pace with them all night. We have had a pretty quite day, but what to morrow will bring forth God only knows.

Monday Evening

Tolerable quiet to day. The Militia have all musterd with 3 days provision and are all marched by 8 o clock this afternoon tho their notice was no longer than 8 o clock Saturday, and now we have scarcly a Man but our regular guards either in W[eymouth,] H[ingham] or B[raintree] or M[ilton] and the Militia from the more remote towns are call'd in as Sea coast Guards. Can you form to yourself an Idea of our Sensations.

I have just returned from P[enn']s Hill where I have been sitting to hear the amazing roar of cannon and from whence I could see every shell which was thrown. The sound I think is one of the Grandest in Nature and is of the true Species of the Sublime. Tis now an incessant Roar. But O the fatal Ideas which are connected with the sound. How many of our dear country men must fall?

Tuesday morning

I went to bed about 12 and rose again a little after one. I could no more sleep than if I had been in the ingagement. The ratling of the windows, the jar of the house and the continual roar of 24 pounders, the Bursting of shells give us such Ideas, and realize a scene to us of which we could scarcly form any conception. About Six this morning, there was quiet; I rejoiced in a few hours calm. I hear we got possession of Dorchester Hill Last Night. 4000 thousand men upon it to day—lost but one Man. The Ships are all drawn round the Town.

Sunday Eve March 10

I had scarcly finished these lines when my Ears were again assaulted with the roar of Cannon. I could not write any further. My Hand and heart will tremble, at this domestick fury, and firce civil Strife, which cumber all our parts. Tho,

Blood and destruction are so much in use
And Dreadfull objects so familiar,

Yet is not pitty chok'd, nor my Heart grown Callous. I feel for the unhappy wretches who know not where to fly for safety. I feel still more for my Bleading Country men who are hazarding their lives and their Limbs.—A most Terible and incessant Cannonade from half after 8 till Six this morning. I hear we lost four men kill'd and some wounded in attempting to take the Hill nearest the Town call'd Nook Hill. We did some work, but the fire from [the ships] Beat [off our] Men so that they did not [secure] it but retired to the fort upon the other Hill.

I have not got all the perticuliars I wish I had but, as I have an opportunity of sending this I shall endeavour to be more perticuliar in my next.

All our Little ones send duty. Tommy has been very sick with what is call'd the Scarlet or purple fever, but has got about again.

If we have [no] Reinforcements here, I believe we shall be driven from the sea coast, but in what so ever state I am I will endeavour to be therewith content.

195

Man wants but Little here below
Nor wants that Little long.

You will excuse this very incorrect Letter. You see in what purtubation it has been written and how many times I have left of. Adieu pray write me every opportunity. Yours.

John Adams to Abigail Adams

March 19, 1776

Yesterday I had the long expected and much wish'd Pleasure of a Letter from you, of various Dates from the 2d. to the 10 March.

This is the first Line I have received since I left you. Since my arrival here, I have written to you as often as I could. I am much pleased with your Caution, in your Letter, in avoiding Names both of Persons and Places, or any other Circumstances, which might designate to Strangers, the Writer, or the Person written to, or the Persons mentioned. Characters and Descriptions will do as well.

The Lye, which you say occasioned such Disputes at the Tavern, was curious enough.—Who could make and spread it? Am much obliged to an Unkle, for his Friendship: my worthy fellow Citizens may be easy about me. I never can forsake what I take to be their Interests. My own have never been considered by me, in Competition with theirs. My Ease, my domestic Happiness, my rural Pleasures, my Little Property, my personal Liberty, my Reputation, my Life, have little Weight and ever had, in my own Estimation, in Comparison of the great Object of my Country. I can say of it with great Sincerity, as Horace says of Virtue—to America only and her Friends a Friend.

You ask, what is thought of Common sense. Sensible Men think there are some Whims, some Sophisms, some artfull Addresses to superstitious Notions, some keen attempts upon the Passions, in this Pamphlet. But all agree there is a great deal of good sense, delivered in a clear, simple, concise and nervous Style.

His Sentiments of the Abilities of America, and of the Difficulty of a Reconciliation with G.B. are generally approved. But his Notions, and Plans of Continental Government are not much applauded. Indeed this Writer has a better Hand at pulling down than building.

It has been very generally propagated through the Continent that I wrote this Pamphlet. But altho I could not have written any Thing in so manly and striking a style, I flatter myself I should have made a more respectable Figure as an Architect, if I had undertaken such a Work. This Writer seems to have very inadequate Ideas of what is proper and necessary to be done, in order to form Constitutions for single Colonies, as well as a great Model of Union for the whole.

Your Distresses which you have painted in such lively Colours, I feel in every Line as I read. I dare not write all that I think upon this Occasion.

My Love, Duty, Respects, and Compliments, wherever they belong.

Abigail Adams to John Adams

Braintree, March 31, 1776

I wish you would ever write me a Letter half as long as I write you; and tell me if you may where your Fleet are gone? What sort of Defence Virginia can make against our common Enemy? Whether it is so situated as to make an able Defence? Are not the Gentery Lords and the common people vassals, are they not like the uncivilized Natives Brittain represents us to be? I hope their Riffel Men who have shewen themselves very savage and even Blood thirsty; are not a specimen of the Generality of the people.

I am willing to allow the Colony great merit for having produced a Washington but they have been shamefully duped by a Dunmore. I have sometimes been ready to think that the passion for Liberty cannot be Eaquelly Strong in the Breasts of those who have been accustomed to deprive their fellow Creatures of theirs. Of this I am certain that it is not founded upon that generous and christian principal of doing to others as we would that others should do unto us.

Do not you want to see Boston; I am fearfull of the small pox, or I should have been in before this time. I got Mr. Crane to go to our House and see what state it was in. I find it has been occupied by one of the Doctors of a Regiment, very dirty, but no other damage has been done to it. The few things which were left in it are all gone.

The Town in General is left in a better state than we expected, more oweing to a percipitate flight than any Regard to the inhabitants, tho some individuals discovered a sense of honour and justice and have left the rent of the Houses in which they were, for the owners and the furniture unhurt, or if damaged sufficient to make it good.

I feel very differently at the approach of spring to what I did a month ago. We knew not then whether we could plant or sow with safety, whether when we had toild we could reap the fruits of our own industery, whether we could rest in our own Cottages, or whether we should not be driven from the sea coasts to seek shelter in the wilderness, but now we feel as if we might sit under our own vine and eat the good of the land.

Tho we felicitate ourselves, we sympathize with those who are trembling least the Lot of Boston should be theirs. But they cannot be in similar circumstances unless pusilanimity and cowardise should take possession of them. They have time and warning given them to see the Evil and shun it.—I long to hear that you have declared an independancy—and by the way in the new Code of Laws which I suppose it will be necessary for you to make I desire you would Remember the Ladies, and be more generous and favourable to them than your ancestors. Do not put such unlimited power into the hands of the Husbands. Remember all Men would be tyrants if they could. If perticuliar care and attention is not paid to the Laidies we are determined to foment a Rebelion, and will not hold ourselves bound by any Laws in which we have no voice, or Representation.

That your Sex are Naturally Tyrannical is a Truth so thoroughly established as to admit of no dispute, but such of you as wish to be happy willingly give up the harsh title of Master for the more tender and endearing one of Friend. Why then, not put it out of the power of the vicious and the Lawless to use us with cruelty and indignity with impunity. Men of Sense in all Ages abhor those customs which treat us only as the vassals of your Sex. Regard us then as Beings placed by providence under your protection and in immitation of the Supreem Being make use of that power only for our happiness.

Your ever faithful friend.

197

John Adams to Abigail Adams

April 14, 1776

You justly complain of my short Letters, but the critical State of Things and the Multiplicity of Avocations must plead my Excuse.—ask what Sort of Defence Virginia can make. I believe they will make an able Defence. Their Militia and minute Men have been some time employed in training them selves, and they have Nine Battallions of regulars as they call them, maintained among them, under good Officers, at the Continental Expence. They have set up a Number of Manufactories of Fire Arms, which are busily employed. They are tolerably supplied with Powder, and are successfull and assiduous, in making Salt Petre. Their neighbouring Sister or rather Daughter Colony of North Carolina, which is a warlike Colony, and has several Battallions at the Continental Expence, as well as a pretty good Militia, are ready to assist them, and they are in very good Spirits, and seem determined to make a brave Resistance.—The Gentry are very rich, and the common People very poor. This Inequality of Property, gives an Aristocratical Turn to all their Proceedings, and occasions a strong Aversion in their Patricians, to Common Sense. But the Spirit of these Barons, is coming down, and it must submit.

As to Declarations of Independency, be patient. Read our Privateering Laws, and our Commercial Laws. What signifies a Word.

As to your extraordinary Code of Laws, I cannot but laugh. We have been told that our Struggle has loosened the bands of Government every where. That Children and Apprentices were disobedient—that schools and Colledges were grown turbulent—that Indians slighted their Guardians and Negroes grew insolent to their Masters. But your Letter was the first Intimation that another Tribe more numerous and powerfull than all the rest were grown discontented.—This is rather too coarse a Compliment but you are so saucy, I wont blot it out.

Depend upon it, We know better than to repeal our Masculine systems. Altho they are in full Force, you know they are little more than Theory. We dare not exert our Power in its full Latitude. We are obliged to go fair, and softly, and in Practice you know We are the subjects. We have only the Name of Masters, and rather than give up this, which would compleatly subject Us to the Despotism of the Peticoat, I hope General Washington, and all our brave Heroes would fight. I am sure every good Politician would plot, as long as he would against Despotism, Empire, Monarchy, Aristocracy, Oligarchy, or Ochlocracy.—A fine Story indeed. I begin to think the Ministry as deep as they are wicked. After stirring up Tories, Landjobbers, Trimmers, Bigots, Canadians, Indians, Negroes, Hanoverians, Hessians, Russians, Irish Roman Catholicks, Scotch Renegadoes, at last they have stimulated the ladies to demand new Priviledges and threaten to rebell.

John Adams to John Quincy Adams

Philadelphia, April 18, 1776

My dear Son

I thank you for your agreable Letter of the Twenty fourth of March.

I rejoice with you that our Friends are once more in Possession of the Town of Boston, and am glad to hear that so little damage is done to our House.

I hope you and your Sister and Brothers will take proper Notice of these great Events, and remember under whose wise and kind Providence they are all conducted. Not a Sparrow falls, nor a Hair is lost, but by the Direction of infinite Wisdom. Much less are Cities conquered and evacuated. I hope that you will all remember, how many Losses, Dangers, and Inconveniences, have been borne by your Parents, and the Inhabitants of Boston in general for the Sake of preserving Freedom for you, and yours—and I hope you will all follow the virtuous Example if, in any future Time, your Countrys Liberties should be in Danger, and suffer every human Evil, rather than Give them up.—My Love to your Mamma, your Sister and Brothers, and all the Family. I am your affectionate Father,
John Adams

John Adams to Abigail Adams

April 23d, 1776

This is St. Georges Day, a Festival celebrated by the English, as Saint Patricks is by the Irish, St. Davids by the Welch, and St. Andrews by the Scotch. The Natives of old England in this City heretofore formed a Society, which they called Saint Georges Clubb, or Saint Georges Society. Upon the Twenty third of April annually, they had a great Feast. But The Times and Politicks have made a schism in the society so that one Part of them are to meet and dine at the City Tavern, and the other att the Bunch of Grapes, Israel Jacob's, and a third Party go out of Town.

One sett are staunch Americans, another staunch Britons I suppose, and a Third half Way Men, Neutral Beings, moderate Men, prudent Folks—for such is the Division among Men upon all Occasions and every Question. This is the Account, which I have from my Barber, who is one of the Society and zealous on the side of America, and one of the Philadelphia Associators.

Burne has prepared a String of Toasts for the Clubb to drink to day at Israels.
The Thirteen united Colonies.
The free and independent States of America.
The Congress for the Time being.
The American Army and Navy.
The Governor and Council of South Carolina, &c. &c. &c.
An happy Election for the Whiggs on the first of May &c.

John Adams to Abigail Adams

May 17, 1776

I have this Morning heard Mr. Duffil [preach] upon the Signs of the Times. He run a Parrallell between the Case of Israel and that of America, and between the Conduct of Pharaoh and that of George.

Jealousy that the Israelites would throw off the Government of Egypt made him issue his Edict that the Midwives should cast the Children into the River, and the other Edict that the Men should make a large Revenue of Brick without Straw. He concluded that the Course of Events, indicated strongly the Design of Providence that We should be separated from G. Britain, &c.

Is it not a Saying of Moses, who am I, that I should go in and out before this great People? When I consider the great Events which are passed, and those greater which are rapidly advancing, and that I may have been instrumental of touching some Springs, and turning some small Wheels, which have had and will have such Effects, I feel an Awe upon my Mind, which is not easily described.

G[reat] B[ritain] has at last driven America, to the last Step, a compleat Seperation from her, a total absolute Independence, not only of her Parliament but of her Crown, for such is the Amount of the Resolve of the 15th.

Confederation among ourselves, or Alliances with foreign Nations are not necessary, to a perfect Seperation from Britain. That is effected by extinguishing all Authority, under the Crown, Parliament and Nation as the Resolution for instituting Governments, has done, to all Intents and Purposes. Confederation will be necessary for our internal Concord, and Alliances may be so for our external Defense.

I have Reasons to believe that no Colony, which shall assume a Government under the People, will give it up. There is something very unnatural and odious in a Government 1000 Leagues off. An whole Government of our own Choice, managed by Persons whom We love, revere, and can confide in, has charms in it for which Men will fight. Two young Gentlemen from South Carolina, now in this City, who were in Charlestown when their new Constitution was promulgated, and when their new Governor and Council and Assembly walked out in Procession, attended by the Guards, Company of Cadetts, Light Horse &c., told me, that they were beheld by the People with Transports and Tears of Joy. The People gazed at them, with a Kind of Rapture. They both told me, that the Reflection that these were Gentlemen whom they all loved, esteemed and revered, Gentlemen of their own Choice, whom they could trust, and whom they could displace if any of them should behave amiss, affected them so that they could not help crying.

They say their People will never give up this Government.

In one or two of your Letters you remind me to think of you as I ought. Be assured there is not an Hour in the Day, in which I do not think of you as I ought, that is with every Sentiment of Tenderness, Esteem, and Admiration.

John Adams to Abigail Adams

Philadelphia July 3, 1776

Your Favour of June 17. dated at Plymouth, was handed me, by Yesterdays Post. I was much pleased to find that you had taken a Journey to Plymouth, to see your Friends in the long Absence of one whom you may wish to see. The Excursion will be an Amusement, and will serve your Health. How happy would it have made me to have taken this Journey with you?

The Information you give me of our Friends refusing his [government] Appointment, has given me much Pain, Grief and Anxiety. I believe I shall be obliged to follow his example. I have not Fortune enough to support my family, and what is of more Importance, to support the Dignity of that exalted Station. It is too high and lifted up, for me; who delight in nothing so much as Retreat, Solitude,

Silence, and Obscurity. In private Life, no one has a Right to censure me for following my own Inclinations, in Retirement, Simplicity, and Frugality: in public Life, every Man has a Right to remark as he pleases, at least he thinks so.

Yesterday the greatest Question was decided, which ever was debated in America, and a greater perhaps, never was or will be decided among Men. A Resolution was passed without one dissenting Colony "that these united Colonies, are, and of right ought to be free and independent States, and as such, they have, and of Right ought to have full Power to make War, conclude Peace, establish Commerce, and to do all the other Acts and Things, which other States may rightfully do." You will see in a few days a Declaration setting forth the Causes, which have impell'd Us to this mighty Revolution, and the Reasons which will justify it, in the Sight of God and Man. A Plan of Confederation will be taken up in a few days.

When I look back to the Year 1761, and recollect the Argument concerning Writs of Assistance, in the Superiour Court which I have hitherto considered as the Commencement of the Controversy, between Great Britain and America, and run through the whole Period from that Time to this, and recollect the series of political Events, the Chain of Causes and Effects, I am surprized at the Suddenness, as well as Greatness of this Revolution. Britain has been fill'd with Folly, and America with Wisdom, at least this is my Judgment.—Time must determine. It is the Will of Heaven, that the two Countries should be sundered forever. It may be the Will of Heaven that America shall suffer Calamities still more wasting and Distresses yet more dreadfull. If this is to be the Case, it will have this good Effect, at least: it will inspire Us with many Virtues, which We have not, and correct many Errors, Follies, and Vices, which threaten to disturb, dishonour, and destroy Us. The furnace of Affliction produces Refinement, in States as well as Individuals. And the new Governments we are assuming, in every Part, will require a Purification from our Vices, and an Augmentation of our Virtues or they will be no Blessings. The People will have unbounded Power. And the People are extreamly addicted to Corruption and Venality, as well as the Great.—I am not without Apprehensions from this Quarter. But I must submit all my Hopes and Fears, to an overruling Providence, in which, unfashionable as the Faith may be, I firmly believe.

John Adams to Abigail Adams

Philadelphia, July 3d, 1776

Had a Declaration of Independency been made seven Months ago, it would have been attended with many great and glorious Effects. . . . We might before this Hour, have formed Alliances with foreign States. We should have mastered Quebec and been in Possession of Canada. . . . You will perhaps wonder, how such a Declaration would have influenced our Affairs, in Canada, but if I could write with Freedom I could easily convince you, that it would, and explain to you the manner how.—Many Gentlemen in high Stations and of great Influence have been duped, by the ministerial Bubble of Commissioners to treat. . . . And in real, sincere Expectation of this Event, which they so fondly wished, they have been slow and languid, in promoting Measures for the Reduction of that Province. Others there are in the Colonies who really wished that our Enterprise in Canada would be defeated, that the Colonies might be brought into Danger and Distress between two Fires, and be thus induced to submit. Others really wished to defeat the Expedition to Canada, lest the Conquest of it, should elevate the Minds of the People too much to hearken to those Terms of Reconciliation which they believed would be offered Us. These jarring Views, Wishes and Designs, occasioned an opposition to many salutary Measures, which were proposed for the Support of that Expedition, and caused Obstructions, Embarrassments and studied Delays, which have finally, lost Us the Province.

All these Causes however in Conjunction would not have disappointed Us, if it had not been for a Misfortune, which could not be foreseen, and perhaps could not have been prevented, I mean the Prevalence of the small Pox among our Troops. . . . This fatal Pestilence compleated our Destruction. It is a Frown of Providence upon Us, which We ought to lay to heart.

But on the other Hand, the Delay of this Declaration to this Time, has many great Advantages attending it.—The Hopes of Reconciliation, which were fondly entertained by Multitudes of honest and well meaning tho weak and mistaken People, have been gradually and at last totally extinguished.Time has been given for the whole People, maturely to consider the great Question of Independence and to ripen their Judgments, dissipate their Fears, and allure their Hopes, by discussing it in News Papers and Pamphletts, by debating it, in Assemblies, Conventions, Committees of Safety and Inspection, in Town and County Meetings, as well as in private Conversations, so that the whole People in every Colony of the 13, have now adopted it, as their own Act.—This will cement the Union, and avoid those Heats and perhaps Convulsions which might have been occasioned, by such a Declaration Six Months ago.

But the Day is past. The Second Day of July 1776, will be the most memorable Epocha, in the History of America.—I am apt to believe that it will be celebrated, by succeeding Generations, as the great anniversary Festival. It ought to be commemorated, as the Day of Deliverance by solemn Acts of Devotion to God Almighty. It ought to be solemnized with Pomp and Parade, with Shews, Games, Sports, Guns, Bells, Bonfires and Illuminations from one End of this Continent to the other from this Time forward forever more.

You will think me transported with Enthusiasm but I am not.—I am well aware of the Toil and Blood and Treasure, that it will cost Us to maintain this Declaration, and support and defend these States.—Yet through all the Gloom I can see the Rays of ravishing Light and Glory. I can see that the End is more than worth all the Means. And that Posterity will tryumph in that Days Transaction, even altho We should rue it, which I trust in God We shall not.

20

The States at War

The legend of George Washington is such a common-place to students of American history that there is a real danger in his grandeur overcoming his very significant contributions to the new nation. Washington's first major public role was Commander-in-Chief of the Continental Army, but his service in the French and Indian War as General Braddock's aide, his efforts in 1755 at the age of twenty-three to organize Virginia's defenses, and his fifteen years of service in the House of Burgesses, all prepared him well for this position.

His letters, which were written during the War, reveal time and again that it was no easy matter to forge an army out of the raw American farmer. Moreover, even during this great crisis, there was a surprising amount of debate and discussion over the place of the military in a republican government: Should the army be professional? What ought to be the position of the political arm of the government (here the Continental Congress) toward the military? Could an army be clothed and equipped without far greater coercion than the several states seemed prepared to accept? Would an army once victorious accept dissolution, or might it vie for control of the government? If ultimately, the new republic and its army reached a *modus vivendi* and managed to conduct a successful war against the British, much of the credit belongs to Washington.

THE WRITINGS
OF GEORGE WASHINGTON

1   To the President of Congress

Camp at Cambridge July 10, 1775
Sir,

I arrived safe at this Place on the 3d inst., after a Journey attended with a good deal of Fatigue, and retarded by necessary Attentions to the successive Civilities which accompanied me in my whole Rout. Upon my arrival, I immediately visited the several Posts occupied by our Troops, and as soon as the Weather permitted,

From *The Writings of George Washington*, Worthington C. Ford, ed. (New York, 1891), III: 8–18; IV: 438–451; VI: 257–265; IX: 102–109; XI: 330–334.

reconnoitred those of the Enemy. I found the latter strongly entrench'd on Bunker's Hill about a Mile from Charlestown, and advanced about half a Mile from the Place of the last Action. The Bulk of their Army commanded by Genl. Howe, lays on Bunker's Hill, and the Remainder on Roxbury Neck, except the Light Horse, and a few Men in the Town of Boston. On our side we have thrown up Intrenchments on Winter and Prospect Hills, the Enemies camp in full View at the Distance of little more than a Mile. The Troops in this Town are intirely of the Massachusetts: The Remainder of the Rhode Island Men, are at Sewall's Farm: Two Regiments of Connecticut and 9 of the Massachusetts are at Roxbury. The Residue of the Army, to the Number of about 700, are posted in several small Towns along the Coast, to prevent the Depredations of the Enemy: Upon the whole, I think myself authorized to say, that considering the great Extent of Line, and the nature of the Ground we are as well secured as could be expected in so short a Time and under the Disadvantages we labour. These consist in a Want of Engineers to construct proper Works and direct the men, a Want of Tools, and a sufficient Number of Men to man the Works in Case of an attack.

It is our unanimous Opinion to hold and defend these Works as long as possible. The Discouragement it would give the Men and its contrary Effects on the ministerial Troops, thus to abandon our Incampment in their Face, form'd with so much Labor, added to the certain Destruction of a considerable and valuable Extent of Country, and our Uncertainty of finding a Place in all Respects so capable of making a stand, are leading Reasons for this Determination: at the same Time we are very sensible of the Difficulties which attend the Defence of Lines of so great extent, and the Dangers which may ensue from such a Division of the Army.

My earnest Wishes to comply with the Instructions of the Congress in making an early and complete Return of the State of the Army, has led into an involuntary Delay in addressing you, which has given me much Concern. Having given orders for this Purpose immediately on my Arrival, I was led from Day to Day to expect they would come in, and therefore detained the Messenger. They are not now so complete as I could wish, but much Allowance is to be made for Inexperience in Forms, and a Liberty which has been taken (not given) on this subject. These Reasons I flatter myself will no longer exist, and of Consequence more Regularity and exactness in future prevail.

We labor under great Disadvantages for Want of Tents, for tho' they have been help'd out by a Collection of now useless sails from the Sea Port Towns, the Number is yet far short of our Necessities. The Colleges and Houses of this Town are necessarily occupied by the Troops which affords another Reason for keeping our present Situation: But I most sincerely wish the whole Army was properly provided to take the Field, as I am well assured, that besides greater Expedition and Activity in case of Alarm, it would highly conduce to Health and discipline. As Materials are not to be had here, I would beg leave to recommend the procuring a farther supply from Philadelphia as soon as possible.

I should be extremely deficient in Gratitude, as well as Justice, if I did not take the first opportuny to acknowledge the Readiness and Attention which the provincial Congress and different Committees have shewn to make every Thing as convenient and agreeable as possible: but there is a vital and inherent Principle of Delay incompatible with military service in transacting Business thro' such numerous and different Channels. I esteem it therefore my Duty to represent the Inconvenience that must unavoidably ensue from a dependence on a Number of Persons for supplies, and submit it to the Consideration of the Congress whether the publick Service will not be best promoted by appointing a Commissary General for these purposes.

I find myself already much embarrassed for Want of a Military Chest; these embarrassments will increase every day: I must therefore request that Money may be forwarded as soon as Possible. The want of this most necessary Article, will I fear produce great Inconveniences if not prevented by an early Attention. I find the Army in general, and the Troops raised in Massachusetts in particular, very deficient in necessary Cloathing. Upon Inquiry there appears no Probability of obtaining any supplies in this Quarter. And the best Consideration of this Matter I am able to form, I am of Opinion that a Number of hunting Shirts not less than 10,000, would in a great Degree remove this Difficulty in the cheapest and quickest manner. I know nothing in a speculative View more trivial, yet if put in Practice would have a happier Tendency to unite the Men, and abolish those Provincial Distinctions which lead to Jealousy and Dissatisfaction. In a former part of this Letter I mentioned the want of Engineers; I can hardly express the Disappointment I have experienced on this Subject. The Skill of those we have, being very imperfect and confined to the mere manual Exercise of Cannon: Whereas—the War in which we are engaged requires a Knowledge comprehending the Duties of the Field and Fortifications. If any Persons thus qualified are to be found in the Southern Colonies, it would be of great publick Service to forward them with all expedition. Upon the Article of Ammunition I must re-echo the former Complaints on this Subject: We are so exceedingly destitute, that our Artillery will be of little Use without a supply both large and seasonable: What we have must be reserved for the small Arms, and that managed with the utmost Frugality.

2   To the President of Congress

On the Heights of Haerlem, 24 September, 1776
Sir,

From the hours allotted to sleep, I will borrow a few moments to convey my thoughts on sundry important matters to Congress. I shall offer them with the sincerity, which ought to characterize a man of candor, and with the freedom, which may be used in giving useful information without incurring the imputation of presumption.

We are now, as it were, upon the eve of another dissolution of our army. The remembrance of the difficulties, which happened upon that occasion last year, and the consequences, which might have followed the change if proper advantages had been taken by the enemy, added to a knowledge of the present temper and situation of the troops, reflect but a very gloomy prospect in the appearances of things now, and satisfy me beyond the possibility of doubt, that, unless some speedy and effectual measures are adopted by Congress, our cause will be lost. It is in vain to expect, that any more than a trifling part of this army will again engage in the service on the encourgement offered by Congress. When men find that their townsmen and companions are receiving twenty, thirty, and more dollars for a few months' service, which is truly the case, it cannot be expected, without using compulsion; and to force them into the service would answer no valuable purpose. When men are irritated, and their passions inflamed, they fly hastily and cheerfully to arms; but, after the first emotions are over, to expect among such people as compose the bulk of an army, that they are influenced by any other principles than those of interest, is to look for what never did, and I fear never will happen; the Congress will deceive themselves, therefore, if they expect it. A soldier, reasoned with upon the goodness of the cause he is engaged in, and the inestimable rights he is contending for, hears you with patience, and acknowledges the truth of your observations, but adds that it is of no more importance to him than to others. The officer makes you the same reply, with this further remark, that his pay will not support him, and he cannot ruin himself and family to serve his country, when every member of the community is equally interested, and benefitted by his labors. The few, therefore, who act upon principles of disinterestedness, comparatively speaking, are no more than a drop in the ocean.

It becomes evident to me than, that, as this contest is not likely to be the work of a day, as the war must be carried on systematically, and to do it you must have good officers, there are in my judgment no other possible means to obtain them but by establishing your army upon a permanent footing, and giving your officers good pay. This will induce gentlemen and men of character to engage; and, till the bulk of your officers is composed of such persons as are actuated by principles of honor and a spirit of enterprise, you have little to expect from them. They ought to have such allowances, as will enable them to live like and support the character of gentlemen, and not be driven by a scanty pittance to the low and dirty arts, which many of them practise, to filch from the public more than the difference of pay would amount to, upon an ample allowance. Besides, something is due to the man, who puts his life in your hands, hazards his health, and forsakes the sweets of domestic enjoyment. Why a captain in the Continental service should receive no more than five shillings currency per day for performing the same duties, that an officer of the same rank in the British service receives ten shillings for, I never could conceive; especially when the latter is provided with every necessary he requires upon the best terms, and the former can scarce procure them at any rate. There is nothing that gives a man consequence and renders him fit for command, like a support that renders him independent of every body but the state he serves.

With respect to the men, nothing but a good bounty can obtain them upon a permanent establishment; and for no shorter time, than the continuance of the war, ought they to be engaged; as facts incontestably prove, that the difficuly and cost of enlistments increase with time. When the army was first raised at Cambridge, I am persuaded the men might have been got, without a bounty, for the war. After this, they began to see that the contest was not likely to end so speedily as was imagined, and to feel their consequence by remarking, that, to get in their militia in the course of the last year, many towns were induced to give them a bounty.

If the present opportunity is slipped, I am persuaded that twelve months more will increase our difficulties fourfold. I shall therefore take the freedom of giving it as my opinion, that a good bounty should be immediately offered, aided by the proffer of at least a hundred or a hundred and fifty acres of land, and a suit of clothes and blanket to each non-comissioned officer and soldier; as I have good authority for saying, that, however high the men's pay may appear, it is barely sufficient, in the present scarcity and dearness of all kinds of goods, to keep them in clothes, much less afford support to their families.

If this encouragement then is given to the men, and such pay allowed the officers as will induce gentlemen of character and liberal sentiments to engage, and proper care and precaution are used in the nomination, (having more regard to the characters of persons, than to the number of men they can enlist,) we should in a little time have an army able to cope with any that can be opposed to it, as there are excellent materials to form one out of. But while the only merit an officer possesses is his ability to raise men, while those men consider and treat him as an equal, and, in the character of an officer, regard him no more than a broomstick, being mixed together as one common herd, no order nor discipline can prevail; nor will the officer ever meet with that respect, which is essentially necessaary to due subordination.

To place any dependence upon militia is assuredly resting upon a broken staff. Men just dragged from the tender scenes of domestic life, unaccustomed to the din of arms, totally unacquainted with every kind of military skill, (which being followed by want of confidence in themselves, when opposed to troops regularly trained, disciplined, and appointed, superior in knowledge and superior in arms,) makes them timid and ready to fly from their own shadows. Besides the sudden change in their manner of living, (particularly in the lodging,) brings on sickness in many, impatience in all, and such an unconquerable desire of returing to their respective homes, that it not only produces shameful and scandalous desertions among themselves, but infuses the like spirit in others. Again, men accustomed to unbounded freedom and no control cannot brooke the restraint, which is indispensably necessary to the good order and government of an army; without which, licentiousness and every kind of disorder triumphantly reign. To bring men to a proper degree of subordination is not the work of a day, a month, or even a year; and, unhappily for us and the cause we are engaged in, the little discipline I have been laboring to establish in the army under my immediate command is in a manner done away, by having such a mixture of troops, as have been called together within these few months.

The jealousy of a standing army, and the evils to be apprehended from one, are remote, and, in my judgment, situated and circumstanced as we are, not at all to be dreaded; but the consequence of wanting one, according to my ideas formed from the present view of things, is certain and inevitable ruin. Another matter highly worthy of attention is, that other rules and regulations may be adopted for the government of the army, than those now in existence; otherwise the army, but for the name, might as well be disbanded. For the most atrocious offences, one or two instances only excepted, a man receives no more than thirty-nine lashes; and these, perhaps, through the collusion of the officer, who is to see it inflicted, are given in such a manner as to become rather a matter of sport than punishment.

It is evident that this punishment is inadequate to many crimes it is assigned to. As a proof of it, thirty or forty soldiers will desert at a time, and of late a practice prevails (as you will see by my letter of the 22d) of the most alarming nature and which will, if it cannot be checked, prove fatal both to the country and army; I mean the infamous practice of plundering. For, under the idea of Tory property, or property that may fall into the hands of the enemy, no man is secure in his effects, and scarcely in his person. In order to get at them, we have several instances of people being frightened out of their houses, under pretence of those houses being ordered to be burnt, and this is done with a view of seizing the goods; nay, in order that the villany may be more effectually concealed, some houses have actually been burnt, to cover the theft. I have, with some others, used my utmost endeavors to stop this horrid practice; but under the present lust after plunder, and want of laws to punish offenders, I might almost as well attempt to remove Mount Atlas.

An army formed of good officers moves like clockwork; but there is no situation upon earth less enviable, nor more distressing, than that person's, who is at the head of troops which are regardless of order and discipline, and who are unprovided with almost every necessary. In a word, the difficulties, which have for ever surrounded me since I have been in the service, and kept my mind constantly upon the stretch, the wounds, which my feelings as an officer have received by a thousand things, which have happened contrary to my expectation and wishes; the effect of my own conduct, and present appearance of things, so little pleasing to myself, as to render it a matter of no surprise to me if I should stand capitally censured by Congress; added to a consciousness of my inability to govern an army composed of such discordant parts, and under such a variety of intricate and perplexing circumstances;—induces not only a belief, but a thorough conviction in my mind, that it will be impossible, unless there is a thorough change in our military system, for me to conduct matters in such a manner as to give satisfaction to the public, which is all the recompense I aim at, or ever wished for.

3   To the President of Congress

Valley Forge, 23 December, 1777
Sir,

Full as I was in my representation of the matters in the commissary's department yesterday, fresh and more powerful reasons oblige me to add, that I am now convinced beyond a doubt, that, unless some great and capital change suddenly takes in that line, this army must inevitably be reduced to one or other of these three things; starve, dissolve, or disperse in order to obtain subsistence in the best manner they can. Rest assured, Sir, this is not an exaggerated picture, and that I have abundant reason to suppose what I say.

Yesterday afternoon, receiving information that the enemy in force had left the city, and were advancing towards Derby with the apparent design to forage, and draw subsistence from that part of the country, I ordered the troops to be in readiness, that I might give every opposition in my power; when behold, to my great mortification, I was not only informed, but convinced, that the men were unable to stir on account of provision, and that a dangerous mutiny, begun the night before, and which with difficulty was suppressed by the spirited exertions of some officers, was still much to be apprehended for want of this article. This brought forth the only commissary in the purchasing line in this camp; and, with him, this melancholy and alarming truth, that he had not a single hoof of any kind to slaughter, and not more than twenty-five barrels of flour! From hence form an opinion of our situation when I add, that he could not tell when to expect any.

All I could do under these circumstances, was to send out a few light parties to watch and harass the enemy, whilst other parties were instantly detached different ways to collect, if possible, as much provision as would satisfy the present pressing wants of the soldiery. But will this answer? No, Sir; three or four days of bad weather would prove our destruction. What then is to become of the army this winter? And if we are so often without provisions now, what is to become of us in the spring, when our force will be collected, with the aid perhaps of militia to take advantage of an early campaign, before the enemy can be reinforced? These are considerations of great magnitude, meriting the closest attention; finding that the inactivity of the army, whether for want of provisions, clothes, or other essentials, is charged to my account, not only by the common vulgar but by those in power, it is time to speak plain in exculpation of myself. With truth, then, I can declare, that no man in my opinion ever had his measures more impeded than I have, by every department of the army.

Since the month of July we have had no assistance from the quartermaster-general, and to want of assistance from this department the commissary-general charges great part of his deficiency.

The soap vinegar, and other articles allowed by Congress, we see none of, nor have we seen them, I believe, since the battle of Brandywine. The first, indeed, we have now little occasion for; few men having more than one shirt, many only the moiety of one, and some none at all. In addition as a further proof of the inability of an army, under the circumstances of this, to perform the common duties of soldiers, (besides a number of men confined to hospitals for want of shoes, and others in farmers' houses on the same account,) we have, by a field-return this day made, no less than two thousand eight hundred and ninety-eight men now in camp unfit for duty, because they are barefoot and otherwise naked. By the same return it appears, that our whole strength in Continental troops, including the eastern brigades, which have joined us since the surrender of General Burgoyne, exclusive of the Maryland troops sent to Wilmington, amounts to no more than eight thousand two hundred in camp fit for duty; notwithstanding which, and that since the 4th instant, our numbers fit for duty, from the hardships and exposures they have undergone, particularly on account of blankets (numbers having been obliged, and still are, to sit up all night by fires, instead of taking comfortable rest in a natural and common way), have decreased near two thousand men.

209

We find gentlemen, without knowing whether the army was really going into winter-quarters or not I can assure those gentlemen, that it is a much easier and less distressing thing to draw remonstrances in a comfortable room by a good fireside, than to occupy a cold, bleak hill, and sleep under frost and snow, without clothes or blankets. However, although they seem to have little feeling for the naked and distressed soldiers, I feel superabundantly for them, and, from my soul, I pity those miseries, which it is neither in my power to relieve or prevent.

It is for these reasons, therefore, that I have dwelt upon the subject; and it adds not a little to my other difficulties and distress to find, that much more is expected of me than is possible to be performed, and that upon the ground of safety and policy I am obliged to conceal the true state of the army from public view, and thereby expose myself to detraction and calumny. The honorable committee of Congress went from camp fully possessed of my sentiments respecting the establishment of this army, the necessity of auditors of accounts, the appointment of officers, and new arrangements. I have no need, therefore, to be prolix upon these subjects, but I refer to the committee. I shall add a word or two to show, first, the necessity of some better provision for binding the officers by the tie of interest to the service, as no day nor scarce an hour passes without the offer of a resigned commission (otherwise I much doubt the practicability of holding the army together much longer, and in this I shall probably be thought the more sincere, when I freely declare, that I do not myself expect to derive the smallest benefit from any establishment that Congress may adopt, otherwise than as a member of the community at large in the good, which I am persuaded will result from the measure, by making better officers and better troops); and, secondly, to point out the necessity of making the appointments and arrangements without loss of time. We have not more than three months, in which to prepare a great deal of business. If we let these slip or waste, we shall be laboring under the same difficulties all next campaign, as we have been this, to rectify mistakes and bring things to order.

In short, there is as much to be done in preparing for a campaign, as in the active part of it. Every thing depends upon the preparation that is made in the several departments, and the success or misfortunes of the next campaign will more than probably originate with our activity or supineness during this winter.

4 To Lieutenant-Colonel John Laurens
About to Sail for France to Confer with This Ally

New Windsor, 15 January, 1781
Dear Sir,

In compliance with your request I shall commit to writing the result of our conferences on the present state of American affairs, in which I have given you my ideas with that freedom and explicitness, which the objects of your commission, my entire confidence in you, and the exigency demand. To me it appears evident:

That, considering the diffused population of these States, the consequent difficulty of drawing together its resources, the composition and temper of *a part* of the inhabitants, the want of a sufficient stock of national wealth as a foundation for revenue, and the almost total extinction of commerce, the efforts we have been compelled to make for carrying on the war have exceeded the natural abilities of this country, and by degrees brought it to a crisis, which renders immediate and efficacious succors from abroad indispensable to its safety.

That the patience of the army, from an almost uninterrupted series of complicated distress, is now nearly exhausted, and their discontents matured to an extremity, which has recently had very disagreeable consequences, and which demonstrates the absolute necessity of speedy relief, a relief not within the compass of our means. You are too well acquainted with all their sufferings for want of clothing, for want of provisions, for want of pay.

That, the people being dissatisfied with the mode of supporting the war, there is cause to apprehend, that evils actually felt in the prosecution may weaken those sentiments which began it, founded, not on immediate sufferings, but on a speculative apprehension of future sufferings from the loss of their liberties. There is danger, that a commercial and free people, little accustomed to heavy burthens, pressed by impositions of a new and odious kind, may not make a proper allowance for the necessity of the conjuncture, and may imagine they have only exchanged one tyranny for another.

That, from all the foregoing considerations result, 1st, absolute necessity of an immediate, ample, and efficacious succor in money, large enough to be a foundation for substantial arrangements of finance, to revive public credit, and give vigor to future operations; 2dly, the vast importance of a decided effort of the allied arms on this continent, the ensuing campaign, to effectuate once for all the great objects of the alliance, the liberty and independence of these States. Without the first we may make a feeble and expiring effort the next campaign, in all probability the period to our opposition. With it, we should be in a condition to continue the war, as long as the obstinacy of the enemy might require. The first is essential to the latter; both combined would bring the contest to a glorious issue, crown the obligations, which America already feels to the magnanimity and generosity of her ally, and perpetuate the union by all the ties of gratitude and affection, as well as mutual advantage, which alone can render it solid and indissoluble.

That, next to a loan of money, a constant naval superiority on these coasts is the object most interesting. This would instantly reduce the enemy to a difficult defensive, and, by removing all prospect of extending their acquisitions, would take away the motives for prosecuting the war. Indeed, it is not to be conceived how they could subsist a large force in this country, if we had the command of the seas, to interrupt the regular transmission of supplies from Europe. This superiority, (with an aid in money,) would enable us to convert the war into a vigorous offensive. I say nothing of the advantages to the trade of both nations, nor how infinitely it would facilitate our supplies. With respect to us, it seems to be one of *two* deciding points; and it appears, too, to be the interest of our allies, abstracted from the immediate benefits to this country, to transfer the naval war to America. The number of ports friendly to them, hostile to the British, the materials for repairing their disabled ships, the extensive supplies towards the subsistence of their fleet, are circumstances which would give them a palpable advantage in the contest of these seas.

211

That no nation will have it more in its power to repay what it borrows than this. Our debts are hitherto small. The vast and valuable tracts of unlocated lands, the variety and fertility of climates and soils, the advantages of every kind which we possess for commerce, insure to this country a rapid advancement in population and prosperity, and a certainty, its independence being established, of redeeming in a short term of years the comparatively inconsiderable debts it may have occasion to contract.

That, notwithstanding the difficulties under which we labor, and the inquietudes prevailing among the people, there is still a fund of inclination and resource in the country, equal to great and continued exertions, provided we have it in our power to stop the progess of disgust, by changing the present system, and adopting another more consonant with the spirit of the nation, and more capable of activity and energy in public measures; of which a powerful succor of money must be the basis. The people are discontented; but it is with the feeble and oppressive mode of conducting the war, not with the war itself. They are not unwilling to contribute to its support, but they are unwilling to do it in a way that renders private property precarious; a necessary consequence of the fluctuation of the national currency, and of the inability of government to perform its engagements oftentimes coercively made. A large majority are still firmly attached to the independence of these States, abhor a reunion with Great Britain, and are affectionate to the alliance with France; but this disposition cannot supply the place of means customary and essential in war, nor can we rely on its duration amidst the perplexities, oppressions, and misfortunes, that attend the want of them.

If the foregoing observations are of any use to you, I shall be happy. I wish you a safe and pleasant voyage, the full accomplishment of your mission, and a speedy return; being, with sentiments of perfect friendship, regard, and affection, dear Sir, &c.

5 Farewell Orders to the Armies of the United States

Rocky Hill, near Princeton, [Sunday] 2 November 1783

The United States in Congress assembled, after giving the most honorable testimony to the merits of the federal armies, and presenting them with the thanks of their country for their long, eminent and faithful services, having thought proper, by their proclamation bearing date the 18th day of October last, to discharge such part of the troops as were engaged for the war, and to permit the officers on furlough to retire from service from and after to-morrow; which proclamation having been communicated in the public papers for the information and government of all concerned, it only remains for the Commander-in-chief to address himself once more, and that for the last time, to the armies of the United States (however widely dispersed the individuals who compose them may be), and to bid them an affectionate, a long farewell.

But before the Commander-in-chief takes his final leave of those he holds most dear, he wishes to indulge himself a few moments in calling to mind a slight review of the past. He will then take the liberty of exploring with his military friends their future prospects, of advising the general line of conduct, which, in his opinion, ought to be pursued; and he will conclude the address by expressing the obligations he feels himself under for the spirited and able assistance he has experienced from them, in the performance of an arduous office.

A contemplation of the complete attainment (at a period earlier than could have been expected) of the object, for which we contended against so formidable a power, cannot but inspire us with astonishment and gratitude. The disadvantageous circumstances on our part, under which the war was undertaken, can never be forgotten. The singular interpositions of Providence in our feeble condition were such, as could scarcely escape the attention of the most unobserving; while the unparalleled perseverance of the armies of the United States, through almost every possible suffering and discouragement for the space of eight long years, was little short of a standing miracle.

It is not the meaning nor within the compass of this address, to detail the hardships peculiarly incident to our service, or to describe the distresses, which in several instances have resulted from the extremes of hunger and nakedness, combined with the rigors of an inclement season; nor is it necessary to dwell on the dark side of our past affairs. Every American officer and soldier must now console himself for any unpleasant circumstances, which may have occurred, by a recollection of the uncommon scenes in which he has been called to act no inglorious part, and the astonishing events of which he has been a witness; events which have seldom, if ever before, taken place on the stage of human action; nor can they probably ever happen again. For who has before seen a disciplined army formed at once from such raw materials? Who, that was not a witness, could imagine, that the most violent local prejudices would cease so soon; and that men, who came from the different parts of the continent, strongly disposed by the habits of education to despise and quarrel with each other, would instantly become but one patriotic band of brothers? Or who, that was not on the spot, can trace the steps by which such a wonderful revolution has been effected, and such a glorious period put to all our warlike toils?

It is universally acknowledged, that the enlarged prospects of happiness, opened by the confirmation of our independence and sovereignty, almost exceeds the power of description. And shall not the brave men, who have contributed so essentially to these inestimable acquisitions, retiring victorious from the field of war to the field of agriculture, participate in all the blessings, which have been obtained? In such a republic, who will exclude them from the rights of citizens, and the fruits of their labors? In such a country, so happily circumstanced, the pursuits of commerce and the cultivation of the soil will unfold to industry the certain road to competence. To those hardy soldiers, who are actuated by the spirit of adventure, the fisheries will afford ample and profitable employment; and the extensive and fertile regions of the West will yield a most happy asylum to those, who, fond of domestic enjoyment, are seeking for personal independence. Nor is it possible to conceive, that any one of the United States will prefer a national bankruptcy, and a dissolution of the Union, to a compliance with the requisitions of Congress, and the payment of its just debts; so that the officers and soldiers may expect considerable assistance, in recommencing their civil occupations, from the sums due to them from the public, which must and will most inevitably be paid.

In order to effect this desirable purpose, and to remove the prejudices, which may have taken posession of the minds of any of the good people of the States, it is earnestly recommended to all the troops, that, with strong attachments to the Union, they should carry with them into civil society the most conciliating dispositions, and that they should prove themselves not less virtuous and useful as citizens, than they have been persevering and victorious as soldiers. What though there should be some envious individuals, who are unwilling to pay the debt the public has contracted, or to yield the tribute due to merit; yet let such unworthy treatment produce no invective, or any instance of intemperate conduct. Let it be remembered, that the unbiassed voice of the free citizens of the United States has promised the just reward and given the merited applause. Let it be known and remembered, that the reputation of the federal armies is established beyond the reach of malevolence; and let a consciousness of their achievements and fame still incite the men, who composed them, to honorable actions; under the persuasion that the private virtues of economy, prudence, and industry, will not be less amiable in civil life, than the more splendid qualities of valor, perseverance, and enterprise were in the field. Every one may rest assured, that much, very much, of the future happiness of the officers and men, will depend upon the wise and manly conduct, which shall be adopted by them when they are mingled with the great body of the community. And, although the General has so frequently given it as his opinion in the most public and explicit manner, that, unless the principles of the Federal Government were properly supported, and the powers of the Union increased, the honor, dignity, and justice of the nation would be lost forever; yet he cannot help repeating, on this occasion, so interesting a sentiment, and leaving it as his last injunction to every officer and every soldier, who may view the subject in the same serious point of light, to add his best endeavors to those of his worthy fellow citizens towards effecting these great and valuable purposes, on which our very existence as a nation so materially depends.

The Commander-in-chief conceives little is now wanting, to enable the soldier, to change the military character into that of the citizen, but that steady and decent tenor of behavior, which has generally distinguished, not only the army under his immediate command, but the different detachments and separate armies, through the course of the war. From their good sense and prudence he anticipates the happiest consequences; and, while he congratulates them on the glorious occasion, which renders their services in the field no longer necessary, he wishes to express the strong obligations he feels himself under for the assistance he has received from every class and in every instance. He presents his thanks in the most serious and affectionate manner to the general officers, as well for their counsel on many interesting occasions, as for their ardor in promoting the success of the plans he had adopted; to the commandants of regiments and corps, and to the other officers, for their great zeal and attention in carrying his orders promptly into execution; to the staff, for their alacrity and exactness in performing the duties of their several departments; and to the non-commissioned officers and private soldiers, for their extraordinary patience and suffering, as well as their invincible fortitude in action. To the various branches of the army, the General takes this last and solemn opportunity of professing his inviolable attachment and friendship. He wishes more than bare professions were in his power; that he were really able to be useful to them all in future life. He flatters himself, however, they will do him the justice to believe, that whatever could with propriety be attempted by him has been done.

And being now to conclude these his last public orders, to take his ultimate leave in a short time of the military character, and to bid a final adieu to the armies he has so long had the honor to command, he can only again offer in their behalf his recommendations to their grateful country, and his prayers to the God of armies. May ample justice be done them here, and may the choicest of Heaven's favors, both here and hereafter, attend those, who, under the Divine auspices, have secured innumerable blessings for others. With these wishes and this benediction, the Commander-in-chief is about to retire from service. The curtain of separation will soon be drawn, and the military scene to him will be closed for ever.

Ratifying the Constitution

Although the men who gathered in Philadelphia during the summer of 1787 were united on the need for a stronger government to replace the Confederation of the States, many of their countrymen vehemently disagreed. When the work of the Convention went before the states for ratification—at least nine would have to approve it for the new government to go into effect—its basic goals were often hotly debated. Some states, particularly weak ones like Georgia or Delaware, immediately ratified the document. But in others, New York and Virginia, for example, there were closely fought contests over the fate of the new government.

It is no easy matter to know what divided the Federalists—those who favored the new Constitution—from the Anti-Federalists. The following selections from the debate in the Virginia State Ratifying Convention offer some interesting clues. Was one camp more democratic than the other? Read the arguments of Anti-Federalist, George Mason. Was the other camp more interested in paying the war debt in full value for personal as well as public reasons? Look at the arguments of Federalists like Edmund Randolph and James Madison. But one must also be attentive to other issues: Were some participants more certain than others that the new government would not trample the liberties of the people? If so, what gave one group but not the other this confidence? These questions are a starting point for understanding why some men became Federalists, and others, Anti-Federalists.

THE VIRGINIA DEBATES

Mr. George Mason. Mr. Chairman, whether the Constitution be good or bad, the present clause clearly discovers that it is a national government, and no longer a Confederation. I mean that clause which gives the first hint of the general government laying direct taxes. The assumption of this power of laying direct taxes does, of itself, entirely change the confederation of the states into one consolidated government. This power, being at discretion, unconfined, and without any kind of control, must carry every thing before it. The very idea of converting what was

From *The Debates in the Several Conventions on the Adoption of the Federal Constitution*, Jonathan Elliot, ed. (Washington, D.C., 1836), III: 30–38, 80–84.

formerly a confederation to a consolidated government, is totally subversive of every principle which has hitherto governed us. This power is calculated to annihilate totally the state governments. Will the people of this great community submit to be individually taxed by two different and distinct powers? Will they suffer themselves to be doubly harassed? These two concurrent powers cannot exist long together; the one will destroy the other: the general government being paramount to, and in every respect more powerful than the state governments, the latter must give way to the former. Is it to be supposed that one national government will suit so extensive a country, embracing so many climates, and containing inhabitants so very different in manners, habits, and customs? It is ascertained, by history, that there never was a government over a very extensive country without destroying the liberties of the people: history also, supported by the opinions of the best writers, shows us that monarchy may suit a large territory, and despotic governments ever so extensive a country, but that popular governments can only exist in small territories. Is there a single example, on the face of the earth, to support a contrary opinion? Where is there one exception to this general rule? Was there ever an instance of a general national government extending over so extensive a country, abounding in such a variety of climates, &c., where the people retained their liberty? I solemnly declare that no man is a greater friend to a firm union of the American states than I am; but, sir, if this great end can be obtained without hazarding the rights of the people, why should we recur to such dangerous principles? Requisitions have been often refused, sometimes from an impossibility of complying with them; often from that great variety of circumstances which retards the collection of moneys; and perhaps sometimes from a wilful design of procrastinating. But why shall we give up to the national government this power, so dangerous in its nature, and for which its members will not have sufficient information? Is it not well known that what would be a proper tax in one state would be grievous in another? The gentleman who hath favored us with a eulogium in favor of this system, must, after all the encomiums he has been pleased to bestow upon it, acknowledge that our federal representatives must be unacquainted with the situation of their constituents. Sixty-five members cannot possibly know the situation and circumstances of all the inhabitants of this immense continent. When a certain sum comes to be taxed, and the mode of levying to be fixed, they will lay the tax on that article which will be most productive and easiest in the collection, without consulting the real circumstances or convenience of a country, with which, in fact, they cannot be sufficiently acquainted.

The mode of levying taxes is of the utmost consequence; and yet here it is to be determined by those who have neither knowledge of our situation, nor a common interest with us, nor a fellow-feeling for us.

Why should we give up this dangerous power of individual taxation? Why leave the manner of laying taxes to those who, in the nature of things, cannot be acquainted with the situation of those on whom they are to impose them, when it can be done by those who are well acquainted with it?

I candidly acknowledge the inefficacy of the Confederation; but requisitions have been made which were impossible to be complied with—requisitions for more gold and silver than were in the United States. If we give the general government the power of demanding their quotas of the states, with an alternative of laying direct taxes in case of non-compliance, then the mischief would be avoided; and the certainty of this conditional power would, in all human probability, prevent the application, and the sums necessary for the Union would be then laid by the states, by those who know how it can best be raised, by those who have a fellow-feeling for us. Give me leave to say, that the sum raised one way with convenience and ease, would be very oppressive another way. Why, then, not leave this power to be exercised by those who know the mode most convenient for the inhabitants, and not by those who must necessarily apportion it in such manner as shall be oppressive?

With respect to the representation so much applauded, I cannot think it such a full and free one as it is represented; but I must candidly acknowledge that this defect results from the very nature of the government. It would be impossible to have a full and adequate representation in the general government; it would be too expensive and too unwieldy. We are, then, under the necessity of having this a very inadequate representation. Is this general representation to be compared with the real, actual, substantial representation of the state legislatures? It cannot bear a comparison. To make representation real and actual, the number of representatives ought to be adequate; they ought to mix with the people, think as they think, feel as they feel,—ought to be perfectly amenable to them, and thoroughly acquainted with their interest and condition. Now, these great ingredients are either not at all, or in a small degree, to be found in our federal representatives; so that we have no real, actual, substantial representation: but I acknowledge it results from the nature of the government. The necessity of this inconvenience may appear a sufficient reason not to argue against it; but, sir, it clearly shows that we ought to give power with a sparing hand to a government thus imperfectly constructed. To a government which, in the nature of things, cannot but be defective, no powers ought to be given but such as are absolutely necessary. There is one thing in it which I conceive to be extremely dangerous. Gentlemen may talk of public virtue and confidence; we shall be told that the House of Representatives will consist of the most virtuous men on the continent, and that in their hands we may trust our dearest rights. This, like all other assemblies, will be composed of some bad and some good men; and, considering the natural lust of power so inherent in man, I fear the thirst of power will prevail to oppress the people.

But my principal objection is, that the Confederation is converted to one general consolidated government, which, from my best judgment of it, (and which perhaps will be shown, in the course of this discussion, to be really well founded,) is one of the worst curses that can possibly befall a nation. Does any man suppose that one general national government can exist in so extensive a country as this? I hope that a government may be framed which may suit us, by drawing a line between the general and state governments, and prevent that dangerous clashing of interest and power, which must, as it now stands, terminate in the destruction of one or the other. When we come to the judiciary, we shall be more convinced that this government will terminate in the annihilation of the state governments: the question then will be, whether a consolidated government can preserve the freedom and secure the rights of the people.

If such amendments be introduced as shall exclude danger, I shall most gladly put my hand to it. When such amendments as shall, from the best information, secure the great essential rights of the people, shall be agreed to by gentlemen, I shall most heartily make the greatest concessions, and concur in any reasonable measure to obtain the desirable end of conciliation and unanimity. An indispensable amendment in this case is, that Congress shall not exercise the power of raising direct taxes till the states shall have refused to comply with the requisitions of Congress. On this condition it may be granted; but I see no reason to grant it unconditionally, as the states can raise the taxes with more ease, and lay them on the inhabitants with more propriety, than it is possible for the general government to do. If Congress hath this power without control, the taxes will be laid by those who have no fellow-feeling or acquaintance with the people. This is my objection to the article now under consideration. It is a very great and important one. I therefore beg gentlemen to consider it. Should this power be restrained, I shall withdraw my objections to this part of the Constitution; but as it stands, it is an objection so strong in my mind, that its amendment is with me a *sine qua non* of its adoption. I wish for such amendments, and such only, as are necessary to secure the dearest rights of the people.

Mr. Pendleton. Mr. Chairman, my worthy friend has expressed great uneasiness in his mind, and informed us that a great many of our citizens are also extremely uneasy, at the proposal of changing our government; but that, a year ago, before this fatal system was thought of, the public mind was at perfect repose. It is necessary to inquire whether the public mind was at ease on the subject, and if it be since disturbed, what was the cause. What was the situation of this country before the meeting of the federal Convention? Our general government was totally inadequate to the purpose of its institution; our commerce decayed; our finances deranged; public and private credit destroyed: these and many other national evils rendered necessary the meeting of that Convention. If the public mind was then at ease, it did not result from a conviction of being in a happy and easy situation: it must have been an inactive, unaccountable stupor. The federal Convention devised the paper on your table as a remedy to remove our political diseases. What has created the public uneasiness since? Not public reports, which are not to be depended upon; but mistaken apprehensions of danger, drawn from observations on government which do not apply to us. When we come to inquire into the origin of most governments of the world, we shall find that they are generally dictated by a conqueror, at the point of the sword, or are the offspring of confusion, when a great popular leader, taking advantage of circumstances, if not producing them, restores order at the expense of liberty, and becomes the tyrant over the people. It may well be supposed that, in forming a government of this sort, it will not be favorable to liberty: the conqueror will take care of his own emoluments, and have little concern for the interest of the people. In either case, the interest and ambition of a despot, and not the good of the people, have given the tone to the government. A government thus formed must necessarily create a continual war between the governors and governed.

Writers consider the two parties (the people and tyrants) as in a state of perpetual warfare, and sound the alarm to the people. But what is our case? We are

219

perfectly free from sedition and war: we are not yet in confusion: we are left to consider our real happiness and security: we want to secure these objects: we know they cannot be attained without government. Is there a single man, in this committee, of a contrary opinion? What was it that brought us from a state of nature to society, but to secure happiness? And can society be formed without government? Personify government: apply to it as a friend to assist you, and it will grant your request. This is the only government founded in real compact. There is no quarrel between government and liberty; the former is the shield and protector of the latter. The war is between government and licentiousness, faction, turbulence, and other violations of the rules of society, to preserve liberty. Where is the cause of alarm? We, the people, possessing all power, form a government, such as we think will secure happiness: and suppose, in adopting this plan, we should be mistaken in the end; where is the cause of alarm on that quarter? In the same plan we point out an easy and quiet method of reforming what may be found amiss. No, but, say gentlemen, we have put the introduction of that method in the hands of our servants, who will interrupt it from motives of self-interest. What then? We will resist, did my friend say? conveying an idea of force. Who shall dare to resist the people? No, we will assemble in Convention; wholly recall our delegated powers, or reform them so as to prevent such abuse; and punish those servants who have perverted powers, designed for our happiness, to their own emolument. Here, then, sir, there is no cause of alarm on this side; but on the other side, rejecting of government, and dissolving of the Union, produce confusion and despotism.

But an objection is made to the form: the expression, We, the people, is thought improper. Permit me to ask the gentlemen who made this objection, who but the people can delegate powers? Who but the people have a right to form government? The expression is a common one, and a favorite one with me. The representatives of the people, by their authority, is a mode wholly inessential. If the objection be, that the Union ought to be not of the people, but of the state governments, then I think the choice of the former very happy and proper. What have the state governments to do with it? Were they to determine, the people would not, in that case, be the judges upon what terms it was adopted.

But the power of the Convention is doubted. What is the power? To propose, not to determine. This power of proposing was very broad; it extended to remove all defects in government: the members of that Convention, who were to consider all the defects in our general government, were not confined to any particular plan. Were they deceived? This is the proper question here. Then the question must be between this government and the Confederation. The latter is no government at all. It has been said that it has carried us, through a dangerous war, to a happy issue. Not that Confederation, but common danger, and the spirit of America, were bonds of our union: union and unanimity, and not that insignificant paper, carried us through that dangerous war. "United, we stand; divided, we fall!" echoed and reëchoed through America—from Congress to the drunken carpenter—was effectual, and procured the end of our wishes, though now forgotten by gentlemen, if such there be, who incline to let go this stronghold, to catch at feathers; for such all substituted projects may prove.

This spirit had nearly reached the end of its power when relieved by peace. It was the spirit of America, and not the Confederation, that carried us through the war: thus I prove it. The moment of peace showed the imbecility of the federal government: Congress was empowered to make war and peace; a peace they made, giving us the great object, independence, and yielding us a territory that exceeded my most sanguine expectations. Unfortunately, a single disagreeable clause, not the object of the war, has retarded the performance of the treaty on our part. Congress could only recommend its performance, not enforce it; our last Assembly (to their honor be it said) put this on its proper grounds—on honorable grounds; it was as much as they ought to have done. This single instance shows the imbecility of the Confederation; the debts contracted by the war were unpaid; demands were made on Congress; all that Congress was able to do was to make an estimate of the debt, and proportion it among the several states; they sent on the requisitions, from time to time, to the states, for their respective quotas. These were either complied with partially, or not at all. Repeated demands on Congress distressed that honorable body; but they were unable to fulfill those engagements, as they so earnestly wished. What was the idea of other nations respecting America? What was the idea entertained of us by those nations to whom we were so much indebted? The inefficacy of the general government warranted an idea that we had no government at all. Improvements were proposed, and agreed to by twelve states; but were interrupted, because the little state of Rhode Island refused to accede to them. This was a further proof of the imbecility of that government. Need I multiply instances to show that it is wholly ineffectual for the purposes of its institution? Its whole progress since the peace proves it.

Shall we then, sir, continue under such a government, or shall we introduce that kind of government which shall produce the real happiness and security of the people? When gentlemen say that we ought not to introduce this new government, but strengthen the hands of Congress, they ought to be explicit. In what manner shall this be done? If the union of the states be necessary, government must be equally so; for without the latter, the former cannot be effected. Government must then have its complete powers, or be ineffectual; a legislature to fix rules, impose sanctions, and point out the punishment of the transgressors of these rules; an executive to watch over officers, and bring them to punishment; a judiciary, to guard the innocent, and fix the guilty, by a fair trial. Without an executive, offenders would not be brought to punishment; without a judiciary, any man might be taken up, convicted, and punished without a trial. Hence the necessity of having these three branches. Would any gentleman in this committee agree to vest these three powers in one body—Congress? No. Hence the necessity of a new organization and distribution of those powers. If there be any feature in this government which is not republican, it would be exceptionable. From all the public servants responsibility is secured, by their being representatives, mediate or immediate, for short terms, and their powers defined. It is, on the whole complexion of it, a government of laws, not of men.

But it is represented to be a consolidated government, annihilating that of the states—a consolidated government, which so extensive a territory as the United

States cannot admit of, without terminating in despotism. If this be such a government, I will confess, with my worthy friend, that it is inadmissible over such a territory as this country. Let us consider whether it be such a government or not. I should understand a consolidated government to be that which should have the sole and exclusive power, legislative, executive, and judicial, without any limitation. Is this such a government? Or can it be changed to such a one? It only extends to the general purposes of the Union. It does not intermeddle with the local, particular affairs of the states. Can Congress legislate for the state of Virginia? Can they make a law altering the form of transferring property, or the rule of descents, in Virginia? In one word, can they make a single law for the individual, exclusive purpose of any one state? It is the interest of the federal to preserve the state governments; upon the latter the existence of the former depends: the Senate derives its existence immediately from the state legislatures; and the representatives and President are elected under their direction and control; they also preserve order among the citizens of their respective states, and without order and peace no society can possibly exist. Unless, therefore, there be state legislatures to continue the existence of Congress, and preserve order and peace among the inhabitants, this general government, which gentlemen suppose will annihilate the state governments, must itself be destroyed. When, therefore, the federal government is, in so many respects, so absolutely dependent on the state governments, I wonder how any gentleman, reflecting on the subject, could have conceived an idea of a possibility of the former destroying the latter.

Mr. Madison then arose.— I shall not attempt to make impressions by any ardent professions of zeal for the public welfare. We know the principles of every man will, and ought to be, judged, not by his professions and declarations, but by his conduct; by that criterion, I mean, in common with every other member, to be judged; and, should it prove unfavorable to my reputation, yet it is a criterion from which I will by no means depart. Comparisons have been made between the friends of this Constitution and those who oppose it: although I disapprove of such comparisons, I trust that, in point of truth, honor, candor, and rectitude of motives, the friends of this system, here and in other states, are not inferior to its opponents. But professions of attachment to the public good, and comparisons of parties, ought not to govern or influence us now. We ought, sir, to examine the Constitution on its own merits solely: we are to inquire whether it will promote the public happiness: its aptitude to produce this desirable object ought to be the exclusive subject of our present researches. In this pursuit, we ought not to address our arguments to the feelings and passions, but to those understandings and judgments which were selected by the people of this country, to decide this great question by a calm and rational investigation.

Before I proceed to make some additions to the reasons which have been adduced by my honorable friend over the way, I must take the liberty to make some observations on what was said by another gentleman, (Mr. Patrick Henry.) He told us that this Constitution ought to be rejected because it endangered the public liberty, in his opinion, in many instances. Give me leave to make one answer to that observation: Let the dangers which this system is supposed to be replete with be clearly pointed out: if any dangerous and unnecessary powers be given to the general legislature, let them be plainly demonstrated; and let us not rest satisfied with general assertions of danger, without examination. If powers be necessary, apparent danger is not a sufficient reason against conceding them. He has suggested that licentiousness has seldom produced the loss of liberty; but that the tyranny of rulers has almost always effected it. Since the general civilization of mankind, I believe there are more instances of the abridgment of the freedom of the people by gradual and silent encroachments of those in power, than by violent and sudden usurpations; but, on a candid examination of history, we shall find that turbulence, violence, and abuse of power, by the majority trampling on the rights of the minority, have produced factions and commotions, which, in republics, have, more frequently than any other cause, produced despotism. If we go over the whole history of ancient and modern republics, we shall find their destruction to have generally resulted from those causes. If we consider the peculiar situation of the United States, and what are the sources of that diversity of sentiment which pervades its inhabitants, we shall find great danger to fear that the same causes may terminate here in the same fatal effects which they produced in those republics. This danger ought to be wisely guarded against. Perhaps, in the progress of this discussion, it will appear that the only possible remedy for those evils, and means of preserving and protecting the principles of republicanism, will be found in that very system which is now exclaimed against as the parent of oppression.

I must confess I have not been able to find his usual consistency in the gentleman's argument on this occasion. He informs us that the people of the country are at perfect repose—that is, every man enjoys the fruits of his labor peaceably and securely, and that every thing is in perfect tranquillity and safety. I wish sincerely, sir, this were true. If this be their happy situation, why has every state acknowledged the contrary? Why were deputies from all the states sent to the general Convention? Why have complaints of national and individual distresses been echoed and reechoed throughout the continent? Why has our general government been so shamefully disgraced, and our Constitution violated? Where-fore have laws been made to authorize a change, and wherefore are we now assembled here? A federal government is formed for the protection of its individual members. Ours has attacked itself with impunity. Its authority has been disobeyed and despised. I think I perceive a glaring inconsistency in another of his arguments. He complains of this Constitution, because it requires the consent of at least three fourths of the states to introduce amendments which shall be necessary for the happiness of the people. The assent of so many he urges as too great an obstacle to the admission of salutary amendments, which, he strongly insists, ought to be at the will of a bare majority. We hear this argument, at the very moment we are called upon to assign reasons for proposing a constitution which puts it in the power of nine states to abolish the present inadequate, unsafe, and pernicious Confederation! In the first case, he asserts that a majority ought to have the power of altering the government, when found to be inadequate to the security of public happiness. In the last case, he affirms that even three fourths of the community have not a right to alter a government which experience has proved to be subversive of national felicity! nay, that the most necessary and urgent alterations cannot be made without the absolute unanimity of all the states! Does not the thirteenth article of the Confederation expressly require that no alteration shall be made without the unanimous consent of all the states? Could any thing in theory be more perniciously improvident and injudicious than this submission of the will of the majority to the most trifling minority? Have not experience and practice actually manifested this theoretical inconvenience to be extremely impolitic? Let me mention one fact, which I conceive must carry conviction to the mind of any one: the smallest state in the Union has obstructed every attempt to reform the government; that little member has repeatedly disobeyed and counteracted the general authority; nay, has even supplied the enemies of its country with provisions. Twelve states had agreed to certain improvements which were proposed, being thought absolutely necessary to preserve the existence of the general government; but as these improvements, though really indispensable, could not, by the Confederation, be introduced into it without the consent of every state, the refractory dissent of that little state prevented their adoption. The inconveniences resulting from this requisition, of unanimous concurrence in alterations in the Confederation, must be known to every member in this Convention; it is therefore needless to remind them of them. Is it not self-evident that a trifling minority ought not to bind the majority? Would not foreign influence be exerted with facility over a small minority? Would the honorable gentleman agree to continue the most radical defects in the old system, because the petty state of Rhode Island would not agree to remove them?

The honorable member then told us that there was no instance of power once transferred being voluntarily renounced. Not to produce European examples, which may probably be done before the rising of this Convention, have we not seen already, in seven states, (and probably in an eighth state,) legislatures surrendering some of the most important powers they possessed? But, sir, by this government, powers are not given to any particular set of men; they are in the hands of the people; delegated to their representatives chosen for short terms; to representatives responsible to the people, and whose situation is perfectly similar to their own. As long as this is the case we have no danger to apprehend. When the gentleman called our recollection to the usual effects of the concession of powers, and imputed the loss of liberty generally to open tyranny, I wish he had gone on farther. Upon his review of history, he would have found that the loss of liberty very often resulted from factions and divisions; from local considerations, which eternally lead to quarrels; he would have found internal dissensions to have more frequently demolished civil liberty, than a tenacious disposition in rulers to retain any stipulated powers.

22

The New American

One of the most perceptive accounts of the reality and promise of American life after the Revolution was written not by a native, but by a newcomer, St. John de Crevecoeur. Born in Normandy, France, Crevecoeur received his formal education in England and then migrated to French Canada in 1754. He served with General Montcalm in the French and Indian War, and after the French defeat he moved to the British colonies. He lived in New York between 1769 and 1780, working as a farmer.

As Crevecoeur thought about his adopted land, he wondered what held this heterogeneous people together. As an immigrant, he was properly sensitive to the incredible diversity of the inhabitants—they seemed to come from every European nation. And yet, Crevecoeur also recognized that life in the New World transformed the European. The dynamics of this process of change and its implications for the United States were the basic questions that Crevecoeur set out to answer when he made his famous inquiry: What is an American?

LETTERS FROM AN AMERICAN FARMER
St. John de Crevecoeur

WHAT IS AN AMERICAN

I wish I could be acquainted with the feelings and thoughts which must agitate the heart and present themselves to the mind of an enlightened Englishman, when he first lands on this continent. He must greatly rejoice that he lived at a time to see this fair country discovered and settled; he must necessarily feel a share of national pride, when he views the chain of settlements which embellishes these extended shores. When he says to himself, this is the work of my countrymen, who, when convulsed by factions, afflicted by a variety of miseries and wants, restless and impatient, took refuge here. They brought along with them their national genius, to which they principally owe what liberty they enjoy, and what substance they possess. Here he sees the industry of his native country displayed in a new manner, and traces in their works the embryos of all the arts, sciences, and ingenuity which

From *Letters from an American Farmer* (first published 1782; reprinted, New York, 1912), Chapter III.

flourish in Europe. Here he beholds fair cities, substantial villages, extensive fields, an immense country filled with decent houses, good roads, orchards, meadows, and bridges, where a hundred years ago all was wild, woody, and uncultivated! What a train of pleasing ideas this fair spectacle must suggest; it is a prospect which must inspire a good citizen with the most heartfelt pleasure. The difficulty consists in the manner of viewing so extensive a scene. He is arrived on a new continent; a modern society offers itself to his contemplation, different from what he had hitherto seen. It is not composed, as in Europe, of great lords who possess everything, and of a herd of people who have nothing. Here are no aristocratical families, no courts, no kings, no bishops, no ecclesiastical dominion, no invisible power giving to a few a very visible one; no great manufacturers employing thousands, no great refinements of luxury. The rich and the poor are not so far removed from each other as they are in Europe. Some few towns excepted, we are all tillers of the earth, from Nova Scotia to West Florida. We are a people of cultivators, scattered over an immense territory, communicating with each other by means of good roads and navigable rivers, united by the silken bands of mild government, all respecting the laws, without dreading their power, because they are equitable. We are all animated with the spirit of an industry which is unfettered and unrestrained, because each person works for himself. If he travels through our rural districts he views not the hostile castle, and the haughty mansion, contrasted with the clay-built hut and miserable cabin, where cattle and men help to keep each other warm, and dwell in meanness, smoke, and indigence. A pleasing uniformity of decent competence appears throughout our habitations. The meanest of our log-houses is a dry and comfortable habitation. Lawyer or merchant are the fairest titles our towns afford; that of a farmer is the only appellation of the rural inhabitants of our country. It must take some time ere he can reconcile himself to our dictionary, which is but short in words of dignity, and names of honour. There, on a Sunday, he sees a congregation of respectable farmers and their wives, all clad in neat homespun, well mounted, or riding in their own humble waggons. There is not among them an esquire, saving the unlettered magistrate. There he sees a parson as simple as his flock, a farmer who does not riot on the labour of others. We have no princes, for whom we toil, starve, and bleed: we are the most perfect society now existing in the world. Here man is free as he ought to be; nor is this pleasing equality so transitory as many others are. Many ages will not see the shores of our great lakes replenished with inland nations, nor the unknown bounds of North America entirely peopled. Who can tell how far it extends? Who can tell the millions of men whom it will feed and contain? for no European foot has as yet travelled half the extent of this mighty continent!

The next wish of this traveller will be to know whence came all these people? they are a mixture of English, Scotch, Irish, French, Dutch, Germans, and Swedes. From this promiscuous breed, that race now called Americans have arisen. The eastern provinces must indeed be excepted, as being the unmixed descendants of Englishmen. I have heard many wish that they had been more intermixed also: for my part, I am no wisher, and think it much better as it has happened. They exhibit a most conspicuous figure in this great and variegated picture; they too enter for a great share in the pleasing perspective displayed in these thirteen provinces. I know it is fashionable to reflect on them, but I respect them for what they have done; for the accuracy and wisdom with which they have settled their territory; for the decency of their manners; for their early love of letters; their ancient college, the first in this hemisphere; for their industry; which to me who am but a farmer, is the criterion of everything. There never was a people, situated as they are, who with so ungrateful a soil have done more in so short a time. Do you think that the monarchical ingredients which are more prevalent in other governments, have purged them from all foul stains? Their histories assert the contrary.

In this great American asylum, the poor of Europe have by some means met together, and in consequence of various causes; to what purpose should they ask one another what countrymen they are? Alas, two thirds of them had no country. Can a wretch who wanders about, who works and starves, whose life is a continual scene of sore affliction or pinching penury; can that man call England or any other kingdom his country? A country that had no bread for him, whose fields procured him no harvest, who met with nothing but the frowns of the rich, the severity of the laws, with jails and punishments; who owned not a single foot of the extensive surface of this planet? No! urged by a variety of motives, here they came. Every thing has tended to regenerate them; new laws, a new mode of living, a new social system; here they are become men: in Europe they were as so many useless plants, wanting vegetative mould, and refreshing showers; they withered, and were mowed down by want, hunger, and war; but now by the power of transplantation, like all other plants they have taken root and flourished! Formerly they were not numbered in any civil lists of their country, except in those of the poor; here they rank as citizens. By what invisible power has this surprising metamorphosis been performed? By that of the laws and that of their industry. The laws, the indulgent laws, protect them as they arrive, stamping on them the symbol of adoption; they receive ample rewards for their labours; these accumulated rewards procure them lands; those lands confer on them the title of freemen, and to that title every benefit is affixed which men can possibly require. This is the great operation daily performed by our laws. From whence proceed these laws? From our government. Whence the government? It is derived from the original genius and strong desire of the people ratified and confirmed by the crown. This is the great chain which links us all, this is the picture which every province exhibits, Nova Scotia excepted. There the crown has done all; either there were no people who had genius, or it was not much attended to: the consequence is, that the province is very thinly inhabited indeed; the power of the crown in conjunction with the musketos has prevented men from settling there. Yet some parts of it flourished once, and it contained a mild harmless set of people. But for the fault of a few leaders, the whole were banished. The greatest political error the crown ever committed in America, was to cut off men from a country which wanted nothing but men!

What attachment can a poor European emigrant have for a country where he had nothing? The knowledge of the language, the love of a few kindred as poor as himself, were the only cords that tied him: his country is now that which gives him land, bread, protection, and consequence: *Ubi panis ibi patria,* is the motto of all emigrants. What then is the American, this new man? He is either an European, or the descendant of an European, hence that strange mixture of blood, which you will find in no other country. I could point out to you a family whose grandfather was an Englishman, whose wife was Dutch, whose son married a French woman, and whose present four sons have now four wives of different nations. *He* is an American, who, leaving behind him all his ancient prejudices and manners, receives new ones from the new mode of life he has embraced, the new government he obeys, and the new rank he holds. He becomes an American by being received in the broad lap of our great *Alma Mater*. Here individuals of all nations are melted into a new race of men, whose labours and posterity will one day cause great changes in the world. Americans are the western pilgrims, who are carrying along with them that great mass of arts, sciences, vigour, and industry which began long since in the east; they will finish the great circle. The Americans were once scattered all over Europe; here they are incorporated into one of the finest systems of population which has ever appeared, and which will hereafter become distinct by the power of the different climates they inhabit. The American ought therefore to love this country much better than that wherein either he or his forefathers were born. Here the rewards of his industry follow with equal steps the progress of his labour; his labour is founded on the basis of nature, *self-interest;* can it want a stronger allurement? Wives and children, who before in vain demanded of him a morsel of bread, now, fat and frolicsome, gladly help their father to clear those fields whence exuberant crops are to arise to feed and to clothe them all; without any part being claimed, either by a despotic prince, a rich abbot, or a mighty lord. Here religion demands but little of him; a small voluntary salary to the minister, and gratitude to God; can he refuse these? The American is a new man, who acts upon new principles; he must therefore entertain new ideas, and form new opinions. From involuntary idleness, servile dependence, penury, and useless labour, he has passed to toils of a very different nature, rewarded by ample subsistence.—This is an American.

British America is divided into many provinces, forming a large association, scattered along a coast 1500 miles extent and about 200 wide. This society I would fain examine, at least such as it appears in the middle provinces; if it does not afford that variety of tinges and gradations which may be observed in Europe, we have colours peculiar to ourselves. For instance, it is natural to conceive that those who live near the sea, must be very different from those who live in the woods; the intermediate space will afford a separate and distinct class.

Men are like plants; the goodness and flavour of the fruit proceeds from the peculiar soil and exposition in which they grow. We are nothing but what we derive from the air we breathe, the climate we inhabit, the government we obey, the system of religion we profess, and the nature of our employment. Here you will find but few crimes; these have acquired as yet no root among us. I wish I was able to trace all my ideas; if my ignorance prevents me from describing them properly, I hope I shall be able to delineate a few of the outlines, which are all I propose.

Those who live near the sea, feed more on fish than on flesh, and often encounter that boisterous element. This renders them more bold and enterprising;

this leads them to neglect the confined occupations of the land. They see and converse with a variety of people; their intercourse with mankind becomes extensive. The sea inspires them with a love of traffic, a desire of transporting produce from one place to another; and leads them to a variety of resources which supply the place of labour. Those who inhabit the middle settlements, by far the most numerous, must be very different; the simple cultivation of the earth purifies them, but the indulgences of the government, the soft remonstrances of religion, the rank of independent freeholders, must necessarily inspire them with sentiments, very little known in Europe among people of the same class. What do I say? Europe has no such class of men; the early knowledge they acquire, the early bargains they make, give them a great degree of sagacity. As freemen they will be litigious; pride and obstinacy are often the cause of law suits; the nature of our laws and governments may be another. As citizens it is easy to imagine, that they will carefully read the newspapers, enter into every political disquisition, freely blame or censure governors and others. As farmers they will be careful and anxious to get as much as they can, because what they get is their own. As northern men they will love the cheerful cup. As Christians, religion curbs them not in their opinions; the general indulgence leaves every one to think for themselves in spiritual matters; the laws inspect our actions, our thoughts are left to God. Industry, good living, selfishness, litigiousness, country politics, the pride of freemen, religious indifference, are their characteristics. If you recede still farther from the sea, you will come into more modern settlements; they exhibit the same strong lineaments, in a ruder appearance. Religion seems to have still less influence, and their manners are less improved.

Now we arrive near the great woods, near the last inhabited districts; there men seem to be placed still farther beyond the reach of government, which in some measure leaves them to themselves. How can it pervade every corner; as they were driven there by misfortunes, necessity of beginnings, desire of acquiring large tracts of land, idleness, frequent want of economy, ancient debts; the re-union of such people does not afford a very pleasing spectacle. When discord, want of unity and friendship; when either drunkenness or idleness prevail in such remote districts; contention, inactivity, and wretchedness must ensue. There are not the same remedies to these evils as in a long established community. The few magistrates they have, are in general little better than the rest; they are often in a perfect state of war; that of man against man, somtimes decided by blows, sometimes by means of the law; that of man against every wild inhabitant of these venerable woods, of which they are come to dispossess them. There men appear to be no better than carnivorous animals of a superior rank, living on the flesh of wild animals when they can catch them, and when they are not able, they subsist on grain. He who would wish to see America in its proper light, and have a true idea of its feeble beginnings and barbarous rudiments, must visit our extended line of frontiers where the last settlers dwell, and where he may see the first labours of settlement, the mode of clearing the earth, in all their different appearances; where men are wholly left dependent on their native tempers, and on the spur of uncertain industry, which often fails when not sanctified by the efficacy of a few moral rules. There, remote from the power of example and check of shame, many families exhibit the most hideous parts of our society. They are a kind of forlorn hope, preceding by ten or twelve years the most respectable army of veterans which come after them. In that space, prosperity will polish some, vice and the law will drive off the rest, who uniting again with others like themselves will recede still farther; making room for more industrious people, who will finish their improvements, convert the loghouse into a convenient habitation, and rejoicing that the first heavy labours are finished, will change in a few years that hitherto barbarous country into a fine fertile, well regulated district. Such is our progress, such is the march of the Europeans toward the interior parts of this continent. In all societies there are off-casts; this impure part serves as our precursors or pioneers; my father himself was one of that class, but he came upon honest principles, and was therefore one of the few who held fast; by good conduct and temperance, he transmitted to me his fair inheritance, when not above one in fourteen of his contemporaries had the same good fortune.

Forty years ago this smiling country was thus inhabited; it is now purged, a general decency of manners prevails throughout, and such has been the fate of our best countries.

Exclusive of those general characteristics, each province has its own, founded on the government, climate, mode of husbandry, customs, and peculiarity of circumstances. Europeans submit insensibly to these great powers, and become, in the course of a few generations, not only Americans in general, but either Pennsylvanians, Virginians, or provincials under some other name. Whoever traverses the continent must easily observe those strong differences, which will grow more evident in time. The inhabitants of Canada, Massachusetts, the middle provinces, the southern ones will be as different as their climates; their only points of unity will be those of religion and language.

Europe contains hardly any other distinctions but lords and tenants; this fair country alone is settled by freeholders, the possessors of the soil they cultivate, members of the government they obey, and the framers of their own laws, by means of their representatives. This is a thought which you have taught me to cherish; our difference from Europe, far from diminishing, rather adds to our usefulness and consequences as men and subjects. Had our forefathers remained there, they would only have crowded it, and perhaps prolonged those convulsions which had shook it so long. Every industrious European who transports himself here, may be compared to a sprout growing at the foot of a great tree; it enjoys and draws but a little portion of sap; wrench it from the parent roots, transplant it, and it will become a tree bearing fruit also. Colonists are therefore entitled to the consideration due to the most useful subjects; a hundred families barely existing in some parts of Scotland, will here in six years, cause an annual exportation of 10,000 bushels of wheat: 100 bushels being but a common quantity for an industrious family to sell, if they cultivate good land. It is here then that the idle may be employed, the useless become useful, and the poor become rich; but by riches I do not mean gold and silver, we have but little of those metals; I mean a better sort of wealth, cleared lands, cattle, good houses, good clothes, and an increase of people to enjoy them.

There is no wonder that this country has so many charms, and presents to

Europeans so many temptations to remain in it. A traveller in Europe becomes a stranger as soon as he quits his own kingdom; but it is otherwise here. We know, properly speaking, no strangers; this is every person's country; the variety of our soils, situations, climates, governments, and produce, hath something which must please everybody. No sooner does an European arrive, no matter of what condition, than his eyes are opened upon the fair prospect; he hears his language spoke, he retraces many of his own country manners, he perpetually hears the names of families and towns with which he is acquainted; he sees happiness and prosperity in all places disseminated; he meets with hospitality, kindness, and plenty everywhere; he beholds hardly any poor, he seldom hears of punishments and executions; and he wonders at the elegance of our towns, those miracles of industry and freedom. He cannot admire enough our rural districts, our convenient roads, good taverns, and our many accommodations; he involuntarily loves a country where everything is so lovely. When in England, he was a mere Englishman; here he stands on a larger portion of the globe, not less than its fourth part, and may see the productions of the north, in iron and naval stores; the provisions of Ireland, the grain of Egypt, the indigo, the rice of China. He does not find, as in Europe, a crowded society, where every place is over-stocked; he does not feel that perpetual collision of parties, that difficulty of beginning, that contention which oversets so many. There is room for everybody in America; has he any particular talent, or industry? he exerts it in order to procure a livelihood, and it succeeds. Is he a merchant? the avenues of trade are infinite; is he eminent in any respect? he will be employed and respected. Does he love a country life? pleasant farms present themselves; he may purchase what he wants, and thereby become an American farmer. Is he a labourer, sober and industrious? he need not go many miles, nor receive many informations before he will be hired, well fed at the table of his employer, and paid four or five times more than he can get in Europe. Does he want uncultivated lands? thousands of acres present themselves, which he may purchase cheap. Whatever be his talents or inclinations, if they are moderate, he may satisfy them. I do not mean that every one who comes will grow rich in little time; no, but he may procure an easy, decent maintenance, by his industry. Instead of starving he will be fed, instead of being idle he will have employment; and these are riches enough for such men as come over here. The rich stay in Europe, it is only the middling and the poor that emigrate. Would you wish to travel in independent idleness, from north to south, you will find easy access, and the most cheerful reception at every house; society without ostentation, good cheer without pride, and every decent diversion which the country affords, with little expense. It is no wonder that the European who has lived here a few years, is desirous to remain; Europe with all its pomp, is not to be compared to this continent, for men of middle stations, or labourers.

An European, when he first arrives, seems limited in his intentions, as well as in his views; but he very suddenly alters his scale; two hundred miles formerly appeared a very great distance, it is now but a trifle; he no sooner breathes our air than he forms schemes, and embarks in designs he never would have thought of in his own country. There the plenitude of society confines many useful ideas, and

231

often extinguishes the most laudable schemes which here ripen into maturity. Thus Europeans become Americans. This great metamorphosis has a double effect, it extinguishes all his European prejudices, he forgets that mechanism of subordination, that servility of disposition which poverty had taught him; and sometimes he is apt to forget too much, often passing from one extreme to the other. If he is a good man, he forms schemes of future prosperity, he proposes to educate his children better than he has been educated himself; he thinks of future modes of conduct, feels an ardour to labour he never felt before. Pride steps in and leads him to everything that the laws do not forbid: he respects them; with a heart-felt gratitude he looks toward the east, toward that insular government from whose wisdom all his new felicity is derived, and under whose wings and protection he now lives. These reflections constitute him the good man and the good subject. Ye poor Europeans, ye, who sweat, and work for the great—ye, who are obliged to give so many sheaves to the church, so many to your lords, so many to your government, and have hardly any left for yourselves—ye, who are held in less estimation than favourite hunters or useless lap-dogs—ye, who only breathe the air of nature, because it cannot be withheld from you; it is here that ye can conceive the possibility of those feelings I have been describing; it is here the laws of naturalisation invite every one to partake of our great labours and felicity, to till unrented, untaxed lands!

After a foreigner from any part of Europe is arrived, and become a citizen; let him devoutly listen to the voice of our great parent, which says to him, "Welcome to my shores, distressed European; bless the hour in which thou didst see my verdant fields, my fair navigable rivers, and my green mountains!—If thou wilt work, I have bread for thee; if thou wilt be honest, sober, and industrious, I have greater rewards to confer on thee—ease and independence. I will give thee fields to feed and clothe thee; a comfortable fireside to sit by, and tell thy children by what means thou hast prospered; and a decent bed to repose on. I shall endow thee beside with the immunities of a freeman. If thou wilt carefully educate thy children, teach them gratitude to God, and reverence to that government, that philanthropic government, which has collected here so many men and made them happy. I will also provide for thy progeny; and to every good man this ought to be the most holy, the most powerful, the most earnest wish he can possibly form, as well as the most consolatory prospect when he dies. Go thou and work and till; thou shalt prosper, provided thou be just, grateful, and industrious."

PART FOUR

A Young Republic,
1789–1820

With the elections of 1789 and the inaugural of George Washington three months later, the history of the modern American republic began. The adventure of constitutional government was novel and even frightening to many experienced American leaders. Having thrown off a king and the protections of a vast empire, they were about to embark on an unprecedented voyage. The new government rested solely upon the consent of its citizenry; none of the traditional sanctions of divine royalty, hereditary nobility, established church, or habits of obedience existed to guarantee its success. Major economic and political problems remained unsolved. At home, hostile Indians and European occupation loomed across national frontiers. Abroad, old enemies and even new allies competed for the foreign trade that was necessary for economic prosperity. Every major political decision involved perilous consequences, and there were few guiding lines. The history of the world presented many analogies, but few Americans were certain of their applications. No republic of this size had been attempted for almost eighteen hundred years, and history was strewn with the relics of earlier hopes.

In this atmosphere of crisis and self-consciousness, no problem was too small to deserve serious discussion. The simple question of what to entitle the President, and the etiquette of his congressional reception, plunged the Senate into prolonged debate. With few established conventions or the solace of unquestioned traditions, every phrase, gesture, and act of government acquired enormous emotional significance. Even the greatness of Washington and confidence in his personal character were not enough entirely to allay fears that the executive office might ultimately turn into an engine of repression, and return to America those evils which the Revolution was intended to destroy forever.

Washington's Presidency did give vital stability to the new state, however, and his person provided a link with the revered Revolutionary past and even the older days of British administration. To gain still further security, some Americans sought inspiration from the past. The new federal buildings in Washington were based upon designs that Greeks and Romans had employed thousands of years earlier. Some hoped that the columns, domes, and friezes would ally the young government with the cause of beauty, and bestow upon it some of the legitimacy of the classical world. Modifications and adaptations were necessary, of course, but purists viewed them with suspicion and feared that in their rage to make all things new, Americans might end by erecting only monuments to their barbarism and bad taste.

In some areas, tradition seemed less important than innovation. The Revolutionary spirit was not confined to government. No aspect of human society was too trivial for reformers who wished the American state to signal a new era in the affairs of mankind. Schemes of reformation, from penal institutions to systems of spelling, were canvassed and debated. Having escaped some of the constraints of tryanny and superstition, Americans could now use a benevolent rationalism to devise institutions for the improvement of humanity. Moreover, these institutions of education and communication would help give a common identity to a people whose heterogeneous racial and religious origins were re-emphasized by their dispersion over an enormous tract of land.

Rationalism, however, was not the only means of unification. The great men of the Revolutionary era were frequently deists, who had little or no formal religious connections, and who considered themselves children of the Enlightenment in their devotion to general schemes of human improvement. But the alliance between evangelicals and deists against orthodox religious establishments came to an end in the 1790s. In the first decade of the new century a wave of revivalism swept over many of the frontier areas and included older settlements as well. Baptists and Methodists gathered in camp meetings in the territories of Kentucky and Tennessee, seeking an experience of grace and engaging often in violent and ecstatic behavior. Revivalism was seen by some as a means of providing unity in an atmosphere of sectarian dispute and of reawakening Protestant fervor in an age when unchurched citizens far outnumbered members of congregations.

Religious virture could also be promoted by encouraging the study of American history. Although George Washington was reviled by political opponents while in office, he was practically deified by this generation, and his death in 1799 touched off a stream of eulogistic biographies and sermons. A pantheon of heroes was one way of stimulating an attachment to American values, and Washington's disinterestedness, honesty, and strength of will were attractive qualities to celebrate. Some biographers, like Mason Weems, emphasized this hero's religious faith as an instrument to convince younger Americans that true glory and patriotism were impossible without religion.

Washington's death came only months before the momentous elections of 1800, which transferred power to another Revolutionary figure, Thomas Jefferson. Jefferson's election was in many ways a repudiation of the policies of his predecessor, John Adams, who failed to retain a wide support for his leadership. Adams' willingness to accept legislation curtailing civil liberties contributed to his downfall, but the ease of transition from a Federalist to a Democratic-Republican administration, testified to the success of constitutional government. After a decade of trial, the republic was strong enough to withstand a change of party without the destruction or subversion of any of its major political institutions.

Jefferson's Presidency began with high hopes and great enthusiasm. The simplicity of his famous inaugural testified to his commitment to agrarian virtues, and his belief that on the virtue of free, independent, yeomen farmers rested the future of the country. But however popular his domestic policies were, and however experienced and cosmopolitan Jefferson stood in European circles, he was helpless to avoid the effects of the great European war in progress. Believing that involvement in the conflict might cost the United States its independence, Jefferson adopted strenuous and aggressive policies to isolate the country from the din of battle. His embargo, however, increased domestic discord without solving foreign problems, and the cessation of foreign commerce only served to stimulate domestic manufacturing, which Jefferson feared so much.

His fellow Virginian, James Madison, was also unable to steer an independent course, and, by 1812, less than three decades after the Revolution was over, the United States was again at war with Great Britain. The optimism and expansionism with which Americans began the war was tempered by a succession of defeats, including the humiliating disaster of the burning of Washington. Although sea victories and some stalemated land battles indicated that resistance to Britain would be stiff, it was less military skill than the reluctance of the Liverpool government to pursue an American war at a time of domestic trouble, which led to the Peace of Ghent. The treaty was far better than many Americans had expected. Although it settled few of the issues which had led to the war in the first place, it did not penalize the United States, and indicated permanent British acceptance of an independent America, and the possibility of a rapprochement in the years ahead.

After the Treaty of Ghent, the bitter party feuding which had characterized the first administrations ended. James Monroe presided over an era that gave greater energy to economic development and geographical expansion than to political disputes. While the "Good Feelings" frequently disguised harsh political competition, no single issue divided the mass of the population. Beneath the surface, however, forces were building that would eventuate, forty years later, in bitter civil war.

To some, the symbol of these forces was the angry debate over the admission of Missouri in 1820, and the question of the expansion of slavery. To Jefferson the issue tolled like "a firebell in the night," warning of disaster to follow. Sensitive observers had begun to notice that national expansion had split the young republic into great sections, often holding incompatible goals and interests. The middle states and New England, traditionally the centers of international commerce, were nursing the first large-scale domestic industries and seeking a tariff on manufactured goods imported from abroad. The slaveholding South, centering more and more of its capital on the raising of cotton, found the tariff unnecessary and discriminatory to its economic position. And Western farmers, filling up the Mississippi and Ohio river valleys, spreading out into the territory purchased from France in 1807 by Jefferson, were demanding internal improvements to ease their problems of transportation and communication with coastal cities. Still muted as an issue, but on the minds of many, was the dilemma of slavery. In 1820 there were still Southerners ready to attack the institution as a denial of American principles, but they were growing fewer, and the attacks of Northerners were growing more angry. Economic disputes were still the most obvious source of sectional disagreement, but the country was becoming more aware of the paradox of servitude in a nation of free men.

The first thirty years of constitutional government had witnessed remarkable political and economic growth. The number of states in the Union had almost doubled, the population had almost tripled to more than nine and one-half million, and the federal government was sovereign over a territory of more than two million square miles. Great innovations in transport would soon defy the tyranny of distance, and bring Western farmers and Southern planters in close connection with the burgeoning cities of the Northeast. Even more impressive was the obvious and satisfying stability of the Constitution itself. War, economic crisis, even threats of insurrection and secession had not seriously challenged its effectiveness. Still worried about the danger of Old World powers, Americans had accepted a new position of power in the Western Hemisphere, and in the Monroe Doctrine committed themselves to an energetic role in the defense of its independence from foreign colonialism. And artists, writers, and scholars had begun, at least tentatively, to shape the contours of a distinctive national culture. No longer an outpost of the European world, and not quite yet a distinctive and coherent civilization, the United States by 1820 had demonstrated the power of its republican ideology and had channeled the emotional fervor of its Revolutionary era into viable and stable political institutions.

23

A Reformed Mode of Spelling

Noah Webster (1758–1843) was born in Connecticut and graduated from Yale in 1778. He read law and was admitted to the Hartford bar, but he practiced only for a few years. His real interests lay in education and the use of language, and he began the preparation of spelling books in the early 1780s. In a short time he had published a spelling book, a grammar, and a reader, all designed specifically for American school children. In time Webster's spelling books would sell tens of millions of copies, as would his famous *American Dictionary of the English Language* upon which he labored for two decades. In addition, Webster published pamphlets on American political problems and was an ardent nationalist and supporter of the federal Constitution.

Webster's zeal to chart and promote a distinctively American way of spelling was part of a larger climate of reformation that followed the Revolution. Lexicography, no less than slavery, education, women's rights, and legal codes, seemed a legitimate subject for experimentation, all in the interests of patriotism, rationality, and efficiency.

DISSERTATIONS ON THE ENGLISH LANGUAGE
Noah Webster

It has been observed by all writers on the English language, that the orthography or spelling of words is very irregular; the same letters often representing different sounds, and the same sounds often expressed by different letters. For this irregularity, two principal causes may be assigned:

1. The changes to which the pronunciation of a language is liable, from the progress of science and civilization.

2. The mixture of different languages, occasioned by revolutions in England, or by a predilection of the learned, for words of foreign growth and ancient origin.

To the first cause may be ascribed the difference between the spelling and pronunciation of Saxon words. The northern nations of Europe originally spoke much in gutturals. This is evident from the number of aspirates and guttural letters,

From *Dissertations on the English Language* (Boston, 1789), 391–406.

which still remain in the orthography of words derived from those nations; and from the modern pronunciation of the collateral branches of the Teutonic, the Dutch, Scotch and German. Thus *k* before *n* was once pronounced; as in *knave, know;* the *gh* in *might, though, daughter,* and other similar words; the *g* in *reign, feign,* &c.

But as savages proceed in forming languages, they lose the guttural sounds, in some measure, and adopt the use of labials, and the more open vowels. The ease of speaking facilitates this progress, and the pronunciation of words is softened, in proportion to a national refinement of manners. This will account for the difference between the ancient and modern languages of France, Spain and Italy; and for the difference between the soft pronunciation of the present languages of those countries and the more harsh and guttural pronunciation of the northern inhabitants of Europe.

In this progress, the English have lost the sounds of most of the guttural letters. The *k* before *n* in *know,* the *g* in *reign,* and in many other words, are become mute in practice; and the *gh* is softened into the sound of *f,* as in *laugh,* or is silent, as in *brought.*

To this practice of softening the sounds of letters, or wholly suppressing those which are harsh and disagreeable, may be added a popular tendency to abbreviate words of common use. Thus *Southwark,* by a habit of quick pronunciation, is become *Suthark; Worcester* and *Leicester* are become *Wooster* and *Lester; business, bizness; colonel, curnel; cannot, will not, cant, wont.* In this manner the final *e* is not heard in many modern words, in which it formerly made a syllable. The words *clothes, cares,* and most others of the same kind, were formerly pronounced in two syllables.

Of the other cause of irregularity in the spelling of our language, I have treated sufficiently in the first Dissertation. It is here necessary only to remark, that when words have been introduced from a foreign language into the English, they have generally retained the orthography of the original, however ill adapted to express the English pronunciation. Thus *fatigue, marine, chaise,* retain their French dress, while, to represent the true pronunciation in English, they should be spelt *fateeg, mareen, shaze.* Thus thro an ambition to exhibit the etymology of words, the English, in *Philip, physic, character, chorus,* and other Greek derivatives, preserve the representatives of the original ϕ and χ; yet these words are pronounced, and ought ever to have been spelt, *Fillip, fyzzic* or *fizzic, karacter, korus.*

But such is the state of our language. The pronunciation of the words which are strictly *English,* has been gradually changing for ages, and since the revival of science in Europe, the language has received a vast accession of words from other languages, many of which retain an orthography very ill suited to exhibit the true pronunciation.

The question now occurs: ought the Americans to retain these faults which produce innumerable inconveniences in the acquisition and use of the language, or ought they at once to reform these abuses, and introduce order and regularity into the orthography of the AMERICAN TONGUE?

Let us consider this subject with some attention.

Several attempts were formerly made in England to rectify the orthography of the language. But I apprehend their schemes failed of success, rather on account of their intrinsic difficulties than on account of any necessary impracticability of a reform. It was proposed, in most of these schemes, not merely to throw out superfluous and silent letters, but to introduce a number of new characters. Any attempt on such a plan must undoubtedly prove unsuccessful. It is not to be expected that an orthography, perfectly regular and simple, such as would be formed by a "Synod of Grammarians on principles of science," will ever be substituted for that confused mode of spelling which is now established. But it is apprehended that great improvements may be made, and an orthography almost regular, or such as shall obviate most of the present difficulties which occur in learning our language, may be introduced and established with little trouble and opposition.

The principal alterations necessary to render our orthography sufficiently regular and easy, are these:

1. The omission of all superfluous or silent letters; as *a* in *bread*. Thus *bread, head, give, breast, built, meant, realm, friend*, would be spelt *bred, hed, giv, brest built, ment, relm, frend*. Would this alteration produce any inconvenience any embarrassment or expense? By no means. On the other hand, it would lessen the trouble of writing, and much more, of learning the language; it would reduce the true pronunciation to a certainty; and while it would assist foreigners and our own children in acquiring the language, it would render the pronunciation uniform, in different parts of the country, and almost prevent the possibility of changes.

2. A substitution of a character that has a certain definite sound for one that is more vague and indeterminate. Thus by putting *ee* instead of *ea* or *ie*, the words *mean, near, speak, grieve, zeal*, would become *meen, neer, speek, greev, zeel*. This alteration would not occasion a moment's trouble; at the same time it would prevent a doubt respecting the pronunciation; whereas the *ea* and *ie* having different sounds, may give a learner much difficulty. Thus *greef* should be substituted for *grief; kee* for *key; beleev* for *believe; laf* for *laugh; dawter* for *daughter; plow* for *plough; tuf* for *tough; proov* for *prove; blud* for *blood;* and *draft* for *draught*. In this manner *ch* in Greek derivatives should be changed into *k*; for the English *ch* has a soft sound, as in *cherish;* but *k* always a hard sound. Therefore *character, chorus, cholic, architecture*, should be written *karacter, korus, kolic, arkitecture;* and were they thus written, no person could mistake their true pronunciation.

Thus *ch* in French derivatives should be changed into *sh; machine, chaise, chevalier*, should be written *masheen, chaze, shevaleer;* and *pique, tour, oblique*, should be written *peek, toor, obleek*.

3. A trifling alteration in a character or the addition of a point would distinguish different sounds, without the substitution of a new character. Thus a very small stroke across *th* would distinguish its two sounds. A point over a vowel, in this manner, *à*, or *ò*, or *ī*, might answer all the purposes of different letters. And for the dipthong *ow*, let the two letters be united by a small stroke, or both engraven on the same piece of metal, with the left hand line of the *w* united to the *o*.

239

These, with a few other inconsiderable alterations, would answer every purpose, and render the orthography sufficiently correct and regular.

The advantages to be derived from these alterations are numerous, great and permanent.

1. The simplicity of the orthography would facilitate the learning of the language. It is now the work of years for children to learn to spell; and after all, the business is rarely accomplished. A few men, who are bred to some business that requires constant exercise in writing, finally learn to spell most words without hesitation; but most people remain, all their lives, imperfect masters of spelling, and liable to make mistakes, whenever they take up a pen to write a short note. Nay, many people, even of education and fashion, never attempt to write a letter, without frequently consulting a dictionary.

But with the proposed orthography, a child would learn to spell, without trouble, in a very short time, and the orthography being very regular, he would ever afterwards find it difficult to make a mistake. It would, in that case, be as difficult to spell *wrong* as it is now to spell *right*.

Besides this advantage, foreigners would be able to acquire the pronunciation of English, which is now so difficult and embarrassing that they are either wholly discouraged on the first attempt, or obliged, after many years' labor, to rest contented with an imperfect knowledge of the subject.

2. A correct orthography would render the pronunciation of the language as uniform as the spelling in books. A general uniformity thro the United States would be the event of such a reformation as I am here recommending. All persons, of every rank, would speak with some degree of precision and uniformity. Such a uniformity in these states is very desirable; it would remove prejudice, and conciliate mutual affection and respect.

3. Such a reform would diminish the number of letters about one sixteenth or eighteenth. This would save a page in eighteen; and a saving of an eighteenth in the expense of books, is an advantage that should not be overlooked.

4. But a capital advantage of this reform in these states would be, that it would make a difference between the English orthography and the American. This will startle those who have not attended to the subject; but I am confident that such an event is an object of vast political consequence.

The alteration, however small, would encourage the publication of books in our own country. It would render it, in some measure, necessary that all books should be printed in America. The English would never copy our orthography for their own use; and consequently the same impressions of books would not answer for both countries. The inhabitants of the present generation would read the English impressions; but posterity, being taught a different spelling, would prefer the American orthography.

Besides this, a *national language* is a band of *national union*. Every engine should be employed to render the people of this country *national;* to call their attachments home to their own country; and to inspire them with the pride of national character. However they may boast of independence, and the freedom of their government, yet their *opinions* are not sufficiently independent; an astonishing respect for the arts and literature of their parent country, and a blind imitation of its manners, are still prevalent among the Americans. Thus an habitual respect for another country, deserved indeed and once laudable, turns their attention from their own interests, and prevents their respecting themselves.

Objections

1. "This reform of the Alphabet would oblige people to relearn the language, or it could not be introduced."

But the alterations proposed are so few and so simple that an hour's attention would enable any person to read the new orthography with facility; and a week's practice would render it so familiar that a person would write it without hesitation or mistake. Would this small inconvenience prevent its adoption? Would not the numerous national and literary advantages resulting from the change induce Americans to make so inconsiderable a sacrifice of time and attention? I am persuaded they would.

But it would not be necessary that men advanced beyond the middle stage of life should be at the pains to learn the proposed orthography. They would, without inconvenience, continue to use the present. They would read the *new* orthography, without difficulty; but they would write in the *old*. To men thus advanced, and even to the present generation in general, if they should not wish to trouble themselves with a change, the reformation would be almost a matter of indifference. It would be sufficient that children should be taught the new orthography, and that as fast as they come upon the stage they should be furnished with books in the American spelling. The progress of printing would be proportioned to the demand for books among the rising generation. This progressive introduction of the scheme would be extremely easy; children would learn the proposed orthography more easily than they would the old; and the present generation would not be troubled with the change; so that none but the obstinate and capricious could raise objections or make any opposition. The change would be so inconsiderable and made on such simple principles that a column in each newspaper printed in the new spelling, would in six months, familiarize most people to the change, show the advantages of it, and imperceptibly remove their objections. The only steps necessary to insure success in the attempt to introduce this reform would be a resolution of Congress, ordering all their acts to be engrossed in the new orthography, and recommending the plan to the several universities in America; and also a resolution of the universities to encourage and support it. The printers would begin the reformation by publishing short paragraphs and small tracts in the new orthography; school books would first be published in the same; curiosity would excite attention to it, and men would be gradually reconciled to the plan.

2. "This change would render our present books useless."

This objection is in some measure answered under the foregoing head. The truth is, it would not have this effect. The difference of orthography would not render books printed in one illegible to persons acquainted only with the other. The difference would not be so great as between the orthography of Chaucer and of the present age; yet Chaucer's works are still read with ease.

3. "This reformation would injure the language by obscuring etymology."

This objection is unfounded. In general, it is not true that the change would obscure etymology; in a few instances it might; but it would rather restore the etymology of many words; and if it were true that the change would obscure it, this would be no objection to the reformation.

It will perhaps surprise my readers to be told that, in many particular words, the modern spelling is less correct than the ancient. Yet this is a truth that reflects dishonor on our modern refiners of the language. Chaucer, four hundred years ago, wrote *bilder* for *builder; dedly* for *deadly; ernest* for *earnest; erly* for *early; brest* for *breast; hed* for *head;* and certainly his spelling was the most agreeable to the pronunciation. Sidney wrote *bin, examin, sutable,* with perfect propriety. Dr. Middleton wrote *explane, genuin, revele,* which is the most easy and correct orthography of such words; and also *luster, theater,* for *lustre, theatre.* In these and many other instances the modern spelling is a corruption; so that allowing many improvements to have been made in orthography, within a century or two, we must acknowledge also that many corruptions have been introduced.

In answer to the objection, that a change of orthography would obscure etymology, I would remark, that the etymology of most words is already lost, even to the learned; and to the unlearned, etymology is never known. Where is the man that can trace back our English words to the elementary radicals? In a few instances, the student has been able to reach the primitive roots of words; but I presume the radicals of one tenth of the words in our language, have never yet been discovered, even by Junius, Skinner, or any other etymologist. Any man may look into Johnson or Ash and find that *flesh* is derived from the Saxon *floce; child* from *clid; flood* from *flod; lad* from *leode;* and *loaf* from *laf* or *hlaf.* But this discovery will answer no other purpose than to show, that within a few hundred years the spelling of some words has been a little changed. We should still be at a vast distance from the primitive roots.

In many instances indeed etymology will assist the learned in understanding the composition and true sense of a word; and it throws much light upon the progress of language. But the true sense of a complex term is not always, nor generally, to be learnt from the sense of the primitives or elementary words. The current meaning of a word depends on its use in a nation. This true sense is to be obtained by attending to good authors, to dictionaries and to practice, rather than to derivation. The former *must* be *right;* the latter *may* lead us into *error.*

But to prove of how little consequence a knowledge of etymology is to most people, let me mention a few words. The word *sincere* is derived from the Latin, *sine cera,* without wax; and thus it came to denote *purity of mind.* I am confident that not a man in a thousand ever suspected this to be the origin of the word; yet all men, that have any knowledge of our language, use the word in its true sense, and understand its customary meaning, as well as Junius did, or any other etymologist.

Yea or *yes* is derived from the imperative of a verb *avoir* to have, as the word is now spelt. It signifies therefore *have, or possess,* or *take* what you ask. But does this explication assist us in using the word? And does not every countryman who labors in the field, understand and use the word with as much precision as the profoundest philosophers?

The word *temper* is derived from an old root, *tem,* which signified *water.* It was borrowed from the act of *cooling* or moderating heat. Hence the meaning of *temperate, temperance,* and all the ramifications of the original stock. But does this help us to the modern current sense of these words? By no means. It leads us to understand the formation of languages, and in what manner an idea of a visible action gives rise to a correspondent abstract idea; or rather, how a word, from a literal and direct sense, may be applied to express a variety of figurative and collateral ideas. Yet the customary sense of the word is known by practice, and as well understood by an illiterate man of tolerable capacity, as by men of science.

The word *always* is compounded of *all* and *ways;* it had originally no reference to time; and the etymology or composition of the word would only lead us into error. The true meaning of words is that which a nation in general annex to them. Etymology therefore is of no use but to the learned; and for them it will still be preserved so far as it is now understood, in dictionaries and other books that treat of this particular subject.

4. "The distinction between words of different meanings and similar sound would be destroyed."

"That distinction," to answer in the words of the great Franklin, "is already destroyed in pronunciation." Does not every man pronounce *all* and *awl* precisely alike? And does the sameness of sound ever lead a hearer into a mistake? Does not the construction render the distinction easy and intelligible, the moment the words of the sentence are heard? Is the word *knew* ever mistaken *new,* even in the rapidity of pronouncing an animated oration? Was *peace* ever mistaken for *piece; pray* for *prey; flour* for *flower?* Never, I presume, is this similarity of sound the occasion of mistakes.

If therefore an identity of *sound,* even in rapid speaking, produces no inconvenience, how much less would an identity of *spelling,* when the eye would have leisure to survey the construction? But experience, the criterion of truth, which has removed the objection in the first case, will also assist us in forming our opinion in the last.

There are many words in our language which, with the *same orthography,* have *two* or more *distinct meanings.* The word *wind,* whether it signifies *to move round,* or *air in motion,* has the *same spelling;* it exhibits no distinction to the *eye* of a silent reader; and yet its meaning is never mistaken. The construction shows at sight in which sense the word is to be understood. *Hail* is used as an expression of joy or to signify frozen drops of water falling from the clouds. *Rear* is to raise up, or it signifies the hinder part of an army. *Lot* signifies fortune or destiny; a plat of ground; or a certain proportion or share; and yet does this diversity, this contrariety of meanings, ever occasion the least difficulty in the ordinary language of books? It cannot be maintained. This diversity is found in all languages; and altho it may be

243

considered as a defect, and occasion some trouble for foreign learners, yet to natives it produces no sensible inconvenience.

5. "It is idle to conform the orthography of words to the pronunciation, because the latter is continually changing."

This is one of Dr. Johnson's objections, and it is very unworthy of his judgment. So far is this circumstance from being a real objection, that it is alone a sufficient reason for the change of spelling. On his principle of *fixing the orthography,* while the *pronunciation is changing,* any *spoken language* must, in time, lose all relation to the *written language;* that is, the sounds of words would have no affinity with the letters that compose them. In some instances, this is now the case; and no mortal would suspect from the spelling, that *neighbour, wrought,* are pronounced *nabur, rawt.* On this principle, Dr. Johnson ought to have gone back some centuries, and given us, in his dictionary, the primitive Saxon orthography, *wol* for *will; ydilnesse* for *idleness; eyen* for *eyes; eche* for *each,* &c. Nay, he should have gone as far as possible into antiquity, and, regardless of the changes of pronunciation, given us the primitive radical language in its purity. Happily for the language, that doctrine did not prevail till his time; the spelling of words changed with the pronunciation; to these changes we are indebted for numberless improvements; and it is hoped that the progress of them, in conformity with the national practice of speaking, will not be obstructed by the erroneous opinion, even of Dr. Johnson. How much more rational is the opinion of Dr. Franklin, who says, "the orthography of our language began to be fixed too soon." If the pronunciation must vary, from age to age (and some trifling changes of language will always be taking place), common sense would dictate a correspondent change of spelling. Admit Johnson's principles; take his pedantic orthography for the standard; let it be closely adhered to in future; and the slow changes in the pronunciation of our national tongue will in time make as great a difference between our *written* and *spoken* language as there is between the pronunciation of the present English and German. The *spelling* will be no more a guide to the pronunciation than the orthography of the German or Greek. This event is actually taking place, in consequence of the stupid opinion, advanced by Johnson and other writers, and generally embraced by the nation.

All these objections appear to me of very inconsiderable weight, when opposed to the great, substantial and permanent advantages to be derived from a regular national orthography.

Sensible I am how much easier it is to propose improvements than to *introduce* them. Everything *new* starts the idea of difficulty; and yet it is often mere novelty that excites the appearance; for on a slight examination of the proposal, the difficulty vanishes. When we firmly *believe* a scheme to be practicable, the work is *half* accomplished. We are more frequently deterred by fear from making an attack than repulsed in the encounter.

Habit also is opposed to changes; for it renders even our errors dear to us. Having surmounted all difficulties in childhood, we forget the labor, the fatigue, and the perplexity we suffered in the attempt, and imagine the progress of our studies to have been smooth and easy. What seems intrinsically right is so merely thro habit.

Indolence is another obstacle to improvements. The most arduous task a reformer has to execute, is to make people *think;* to rouse them from that lethargy which, like the mantle of sleep, covers them in repose and contentment.

But America is in a situation the most favorable for great reformations; and the present time is, in a singular degree, auspicious. The minds of men in this country have been awakened. New scenes have been, for many years, presenting new occasions for exertion; unexpected distresses have called forth the powers of invention; and the application of new expedients has demanded every possible exercise of wisdom and talents. Attention is roused; the mind expanded; and the intellectual faculties invigorated. Here men are prepared to receive improvements, which would be rejected by nations whose habits have not been shaken by similar events.

Now is the time, and *this* the country, in which we may expect success, in attempting changes favorable to language, science and government. Delay, in the plan here proposed, may be fatal; under a tranquil general government, the minds of men may again sink into indolence; a national acquiescence in error will follow; and posterity be doomed to struggle with difficulties, which time and accident will perpetually multiply.

Let us then seize the present moment, and establish a *national language,* as well as a national government. Let us remember that there is a certain respect due to the opinions of other nations. As an independent people, our reputation abroad demands that in all things we should be federal; be *national;* for if we do not respect *ourselves,* we may be assured that *other nations* will not respect us. In short, let it be impressed upon the mind of every American that to neglect the means of commanding respect abroad is treason against the character and dignity of a brave independent people.

24

The Congress Begins

William Maclay (1743–1804) was a Pennsylvania attorney and landowner who served for some years in the state legislature. In 1789 he was elected a United States Senator for Pennsylvania, but was defeated for re-election in 1791 by a Federalist. Maclay's journal is one of our few sources for the early congressional debates for at this time no official record was being prepared for the public.

As an opponent of Hamilton's financial program, Maclay fought the chartering of the United States Bank and defended the interests of small farmers. Since Jefferson did not arrive in New York until the spring of 1790, almost a year after the new government began operations, Maclay was a leader of the group fearing a revival of monarchical oppression. The depth of his suspicions is a reminder of the experimental and innovative character of republican government in the late eighteenth century and the anxiety of many Americans concerning the future of the Constitution.

THE JOURNAL
OF WILLIAM MACLAY

28th April, 1789

This day I ought to note with some extraordinary mark. I had dressed and was about to set out, when General Washington, the greatest man in the world, paid me a visit. I met him at the foot of the stairs. Mr. Wynkoop just came in. We asked him to take a seat. He excused himself on account of the number of his visits. We accompanied him to the door. He made us complaisant bows—one before he mounted and the other as he went away on horseback.

I may as well minute a remark here as anywhere else, and, indeed, I wish it were otherwise, not for what we have, but for what others want; but we have really more republican plainness and sincere openness of behavior in Pennsylvania than in any other place I have ever been. I was impressed with a different opinion until I have had full opportunity of observing the gentlemen of New England, and sorry indeed am I to say it, but no people in the Union dwell more on trivial distinctions and matters of mere form. They really seem to show a readiness to stand on punctilio and ceremony. A little learning is a dangerous thing ('tis said). May not the same be said of breeding? It is certainly true that people little used with

From *The Journal of William Maclay* (New York, 1890, 1927), 4–12, 22–25, 27–28, 49, 106–114.

company are more apt to take offense, and are less easy, than men much versant in public life. They are an unmixed people in New England, and used only to see neighbors like themselves; and when once an error of behavior has crept in among them, there is small chance of its being cured; for, should they go abroad, being early used to a ceremonious and reserved behavior, and believing that good manners consists entirely in punctilios, they only add a few more stiffened airs to their deportment, excluding good humor, affability of conversation, and accommodation of temper and sentiment as qualities too vulgar for a gentleman.

30 April, Thursday

This is a great, important day. Goddess of etiquette, assist me while I describe it. The Senate met. The Vice-President rose in the most solemn manner. This son of *Adam* seemed impressed with deeper gravity, yet what shall I think of him? He often, in the midst of his most important airs—I believe when he is at loss for expressions (and this he often is, wrapped up, I suppose, in the contemplation of his own importance)—suffers an unmeaning kind of vacant laugh to escape him. This was the case to-day, and really to me bore the air of ridiculing the farce he was acting. "Gentlemen, I wish for the direction of the Senate. The President will, I suppose, address the Congress. How shall I behave? How shall we receive it? Shall it be standing or sitting?"

Here followed a considerable deal of talk from him which I could make nothing of. Mr. Lee began with the House of Commons (as is usual with him), then the House of Lords, then the King, and then back again. The result of his information was, that the Lords sat and the Commons stood on the delivery of the King's speech. Mr. Izard got up and told how often he had been in the Houses of Parliament. He said a great deal of what he had seen there. [He] made, however, this sagacious discovery, that the Commons stood because they had no seats to sit on, being arrived at the bar of the House of Lords. It was discovered after some time that the King sat, too, and had his robes and crown on.

Mr. Adams got up again and said he had been very often indeed at the Parliament on those occasions, but there always was such a crowd, and *ladies along*, that for his part he could not say how it was. Mr. Carrol got up to declare that he thought it of no consequence how it was in Great Britain; they were no rule to us, etc. But all at once the Secretary, who had been out, whispered to the Chair that the Clerk from the Representatives was at the door with a communication. Gentlemen of the Senate, how shall he be received? A silly kind of resolution of the committee on that business had been laid on the table some days ago. The amount of it was that each House should communicate to the other what and how they chose; it concluded, however, something in this way: That everything should be done with all the *propriety* that was *proper*. The question was, Shall this be adopted, that we may know how to receive the Clerk? It was objected [that] this will throw no light on the subject; it will leave you where you are. Mr. Lee brought the House of Commons before us again. He reprobated the rule; declared that the Clerk should not come within the bar of the House; that the proper mode was for the Sergeant-at-Arms, with the mace of his shoulder, to meet the Clerk at the door and receive his communication; we are not, however, provided for this ceremonious

247

way of doing business, having neither mace nor sergeant nor Masters in Chancery, who carry down bills from the English Lords.

Here we sat an hour and ten minutes before the President arrived—this delay was owing to Lee, Izard, and Dalton, who had stayed with us while the Speaker came in, instead of going to attend the President. The President advanced between the Senate and Representatives, bowing to each. He was placed in the chair by the Vice-President; the Senate with their president on the right, the Speaker and the Representatives on his left. The Vice-President rose and addressed a short sentence to him. The import of it was that he should now take the oath of office as President. He seemed to have forgot half what he was to say, for he made a dead pause and stood for some time, to appearance, in a vacant mood. He finished with a formal bow, and the President was conducted out of the middle window into the gallery, and the oath was administered by the Chancellor. Notice that the business done was communicated to the crowd by proclamation, etc., who gave three cheers, and repeated it on the President's bowing to them.

As the company returned into the Senate chamber, the President took the chair and the Senators and Representatives their seats. He rose, and all arose also, and addressed them (see the address). This great man was agitated and embarrassed more than ever he was by the leveled cannon or pointed musket. He trembled, and several times could scarce make out to read, though it must be supposed he had often read it before. He put part of the fingers of his left hand into the side of what I think the tailors call the fall of the breeches changing the paper into his left hand. After some time he then did the same with some of the fingers of his right hand. When he came to the words *all the world,* he made a flourish with his right hand, which left rather an ungainly impression. I sincerely, for my part, wished all set ceremony in the hands of the dancing-masters, and that this first of men had read off his address in the plainest manner, without ever taking his eyes from the paper, for I felt hurt that he was not first in everything. He was dressed in deep brown, with metal buttons, with an eagle on them, white stockings, a bag, and sword.

From the hall there was a grand procession to Saint Paul's Church, where prayers were said by the Bishop. The procession was well conducted and without accident, as far as I have heard. The militia were all under arms, lined the street near the church, made a good figure, and behaved well.

The Senate returned to their chamber after service, formed, and took up the address. Our Vice-President called it *his most gracious speech.* I can not approve of this. A committee was appointed on it—Johnson, Carrol, Patterson. Adjourned. In the evening there were grand fireworks.

May 1st

Attended at the Hall at eleven. The prayers were over and the minutes reading. When we came to the minute of the speech it stood, *His most gracious speech.* I looked all around the Senate. Every countenance seemed to wear a blank. The Secretary was going on: I must speak or nobody would. "Mr. President, we have lately had a hard struggle for our liberty against kingly authority. The minds of men are still heated: everything related to that species of government is odious to the people. The words prefixed to the President's speech are the same that are usually placed before the speech of his Britannic Majesty. I know they will give offense. I consider them as improper. I therefore move that they be struck out, and that it stand simply address or speech, as may be judged most suitable."

Mr. Adams rose in his chair and expressed the greatest surprise that anything should be objected to on account of its being taken from the practice of that Government under which we had lived so long and happily formerly; that he was for a dignified and respectable government, and as far as he knew the sentiments of people they thought as he did; that for his part he was one of the first in the late contest [the Revolution], and, if *he could have thought of this, he never would have drawn his sword.*

Painful as it was, I had to contend with the Chair. I admitted that the people of the colonies (now States) had enjoyed formerly great happiness under that species of government, but the abuses of that Government under which they had smarted had taught them what they had to fear from that kind of government; that there had been a revolution in the sentiments of people respecting government equally great as that which had happened in the Government itself; that even the modes of it were now abhorred; that the enemies of the Constitution had objected to it the facility there would be of transition from it to kingly government and all the trappings and splendor of royalty; that if such a thing as this appeared on our minutes, they would not fail to represent it as the first step of the ladder in the ascent to royalty. The Vice-President rose a second time, and declared that he could not possibly conceive that any person could take offense at it.

Up now rose Mr. Read, and declared for the paragraph. He saw no reason to object to it because the British speeches were styled *most gracious.* If we chose to object to words because they had been used in the same sense in Britain, we should soon be at a loss to do business. I had to reply. "It is time enough to submit to necessity when it exists. At present we are at no loss for words. The words speech or address without any addition will suit us well enough."

The unequivocal declaration that he would never have drawn his sword, etc., has drawn my mind to the following remarks: that the motives of the actors in the late Revolution were various can not be doubted. The abolishing of royalty, the extinguishment of patronage and dependencies attached to that form of government, were the exalted motives of many revolutionists, and these were the improvements meant by them to be made of the war which was forced on us by Britisth aggression—in fine, the amelioration of government and bettering the condition of mankind. These ends and none other were publicly avowed, and all our constitutions and public acts were formed in this spirit. Yet there were not wanting a party whose motives were different. They wished for the loaves and fishes of government, and cared for nothing else but a translation of the diadem and scepter from London to Boston, New York, or Philadelphia; or, in other words, the creation of a new monarchy in America, and to form niches for themselves in the temple of royalty.

This spirit manifested itself strongly among the officers at the close of the war, and I have been afraid the army would not have been disbanded if the common soldiers could have been kept together. This spirit they developed in the Order of Cincinnati, where I trust it will spend itself in a harmless flame and soon become

249

extinguished. That Mr. Adams should, however, so unequivocally avow this motive, at a time when a republican form of government is secure to every State in the Union, appears to me a mark of extreme folly.

Mem., 1790

It is worthy of remark that about this time a spirit of reformation broke out in France which finally abolished all titles and every trace of the feudal system. Strange, indeed, that in that very country [America], where the flame of freedom had been kindled, an attempt should be made to introduce these absurdities and humiliating distinctions which the hand of reason, aided by our example, was prostrating in the heart of Europe. I, however, will endeavor (as I have hitherto done) to use the resentment of the Representatives to defeat Mr. Adams and others on the subject of titles. The pompous and lordly distinctions which the Senate have manifested a disposition to establish between the two Houses have nettled the Representatives, and this business of titles may be considered as part of the same tune. While we are debating on titles I will, through the Speaker, Mr. Muhlenberg, and other friends, get the idea suggested of answering the President's address without any title, in contempt of our deliberations, which still continue on that subject. This once effected, will confound them [the Senators] completely, and establish a precedent they will not dare to violate.

May 8th

Attended a joint committee on the papers of the old Congress. Made progress in the business. Agreed to meet at half-past ten on Monday and report. Senate formed. The Secretary, as usual, had made some mistakes, which were rectified, and now Mr. Elsworth moved for the report of the Joint Committee to be taken up on the subject of titles. It was accordingly done. Mr. Lee led the business. He took his old ground—all the world, civilized and savage, called for titles; that there must be something in human nature that occasioned this general consent; that, therefore, he conceived it was right. Here he began to enumerate many nations who gave titles—such as Venice, Genoa, and others. The Greeks and Romans, it was said, had no titles, "but" (making a profound bow to the Chair) "you were pleased to set us right in this with respect to the Conscript Fathers the other day." Here he repeated the Vice-President's speech of the 23d ultimo [April], almost verbatim all over.

Mr. Elsworth rose. He had a paper in his hat, which he looked constantly at. He repeated almost all that Mr. Lee had said, but got on the subject of kings—declared that the sentence in the primer of *fear God and honor the king* was of great importance; that kings were of divine appointment; that Saul, the head and shoulders taller than the rest of the people, was elected by God and anointed by his appointment.

I sat, after he had done, for a considerable time, to see if anybody would rise. At last I got up and first answered Lee as well as I could with nearly the same arguments, drawn from the Constitution, as I had used on the 23d ult. I mentioned that within the space of twenty years back more light had been thrown on the subject of governments and on human affairs in general than for several generations before; that this light of knowledge had diminished the veneration for titles, and that mankind now considered themselves as little bound to imitate the follies of civilized nations as the brutalities of savages; that the abuse of power and the fear of bloody masters had extorted titles as well as adoration, in some instances from the trembling crowd; that the impression now on the minds of the citizens of these States was that of horror for kingly authority.

Izard got up. He dwelt almost entirely on the antiquity of kingly government. He could not, however, well get further back than Philip of Macedon. He seemed to have forgot both Homer and the Bible. He urged for something equivalent to nobility having been common among the Romans, for they had three names that seemed to answer to honorable, or something like it, before and something behind. He did not say Esquire. Mr. Carrol rose and took my side of the question. He followed nearly the track I had been in, and dwelt much on the information that was now abroad in the world. He spoke against kings. Mr. Lee and Mr. Izard were both up again. Elsworth was up again. Langdon was up several times, but spoke short each time. Patterson was up, but there was no knowing which side he was of. Mr. Lee considered him as against him and answered him, but Patterson finally voted with Lee. The Vice-President repeatedly helped the speakers for titles. Esworth was enumerating how common the appellation of President was. The Vice-President put him in mind that there were presidents of fire companies and of a cricket club. Mr. Lee at another time was saying he believed some of the States authorized title by their Constitutions. The Vice-President, from the chair, told him that Connecticut did it. At sundry other times he interfered in a like manner. I had been frequently up to answer new points during the debate.

I collected myself for a last effort. I read the clause in the Constitution against titles of nobility; showed that the spirit of it was against not only granting titles by Congress, but against the permission of foreign potentates granting *any titles whatever;* that as to kingly government, it was equally out of the question, as a republican government was guaranteed to every State in the Union; that they were both equally forbidden fruit of the Constitution. I called the attention of the House to the consequences that were like to follow; that gentlemen seemed to court a rupture with the other House. The Representatives had adopted the report, and were this day acting on it, or according to the spirit of the report. We were proposing a title. Our conduct would mark us to the world as actuated by the spirit of dissension, and the characters of the Houses would be as aristocratic and democratical.

The report [of the Committee on Titles] was, however, rejected. "Excellency" was moved for as a title by Mr. Izard. It was withdrawn by Mr. Izard, and "highness" with some prefatory word, proposed by Mr. Lee. Now long harangues were made in favor of this title. "Elective" was placed before. It was insisted that such a dignified title would add greatly to the weight and authority of the Government both at home and abroad. I declared myself totally of a different opinion; that at present it was impossible to add to the respect entertained for General Washington; that if you gave him the title of any foreign prince or potentate, a belief would follow that the manners of that prince and his modes of government would be adopted by the President. (Mr. Lee had, just before I got up, read over a list of the titles of all the princes and potentates of the earth, marking

251

where the word "highness" occurred. The Grand Turk had it, all the princes of Germany had [it], sons and daughters of crown heads, etc.) That particularly "elective highness," which sounded nearly like "electoral highness," would have a most ungrateful sound to many thousands of industrious citizens who had fled from German oppression; that "highness" was part of the title of a prince or princes of the blood, and was often given to dukes; that it was degrading our President to place him on a par with any prince of any blood in Europe, nor was there one of them that could enter the list of true glory with him.

But I will minute no more. The debate lasted till half after three o'clock, and it ended in appointing a committee to consider of a title to be given to the President. This whole silly business is the work of Mr. Adams and Mr. Lee; Izard follows Lee, and the New England men, who always herd together, follow Mr. Adams. Mr. Thompson says this used to be the case in the old Congress. I had, to be sure, the greatest share in this debate, and must now have completely sold (no, sold is a bad word, for I have got nothing for it) every particle of court favor, for a court our House seems determined on, and to run into all the fooleries, fopperies, fineries, and pomp of royal etiquette; and all this for Mr. Adams.

May 9th

Attended the Hall at ten o'clock to go on the Judicial Committee. Met many of the members. I know not the motive, but I never was received with more familiarity, nor quite so much, before by the members. Elsworth in particular seemed to show a kind of fondness. The Judicial Committee did no business. Senate formed. It took a long time to correct the minutes. Otis keeps them miserably. At length the committee came in and reported a title—*His Highness the President of the United States of America and Protector of the Rights of the Same.*

I rose. Mr. President, the Constitution of the United States has designated our Chief Magistrate by the appellation of the *President of the United States of America.* This is his title of office, nor can we alter, add to, or diminish it without infringing the Constitution. In like manner persons authorized to transact business with foreign powers are styled *Ambassadors, Public Ministers,* etc. To give them any other appellation would be an equal infringement. As to grades or orders or titles of nobility, nothing of the kind can be established by Congress.

Can, then, the President and Senate do that which is prohibited to the United States at large? Certainly not. Let us read the Constitution: *No title of nobility shall be granted by the United States.* The Constitution goes further. The servants of the public are prohibited from accepting them from any foreign state, king, or prince. So that the appellations and terms given to nobility in the Old World are contraband language in the United States, nor can we apply them to our citizens consistent with the Constitution. As to what the common people, soldiers, and sailors of foreign countries may think of us, I do not think it imports us much. Perhaps the less they think, or have occasion to think of us, the better.

But suppose this a desirable point, how is it to be gained? The English excepted, foreigners do not understand our language. We must use Hohen Mogende to a Dutchman. Beylerbey to a Turk or Algerine, and so of the rest. From the English indeed we may borrow terms that would not be wholly unintelligible to our own citizens. But will they thank us for the compliment? Would not the plagiarism be more likely to be attended with contempt than respect among all of them? It has been admitted that all this is nonsense to the philosopher. I am ready to admit that every high-sounding, pompous appellation, descriptive of qualities which the object does not possess, must appear bombastic nonsense in the eye of every wise man. But I can not admit such an idea with respect to government itself. Philosophers have admitted not the utility but the necessity of it [government], and their labors have been directed to correct the vices and expose the follies which have been ingrafted upon it, and to reduce the practice of it to the principles of common sense, such as we see exemplified by the merchant, the mechanic, and the farmer, whose every act or operation tends to a productive or beneficial effect, and, above all, to illustrate this fact, that government was instituted for the benefit of the people, and that no act of government is justifiable that has not this for its object. Such has been the labor of philosophers with respect to government, and sorry indeed would I be if their labors should be in vain.

May 26th

Attended the Hall early. Was the first. Mr. Morris came next, the Vice-President next. I made an apology to the Vice-President for the absence of our chaplain, Mr. Linn. There had been some conversation yesterday in the Senate about the style of the Bishop. It had been entered on the minutes *right reverend*. The Vice-President revived the discourse; got at me about titles. I really never had opened my mouth on the affair of yesterday. He, however, addressed to me all he said, concluding: "You are against titles. But there are no people in the world so much in favor of titles as the people of America; and the Government never will be properly administered until they are adopted in the fullest manner." "We think differently, indeed, on the same subject. I am convinced that were we to adopt them in the fashion of Europe, we would ruin all. You have told us, sir, that they are idle in a philosophic point of view. Governments have been long at odds with common sense. I hope the conduct of America will reconcile them. Instead of adding respect to government, I consider that they would bring the personages who assume them into contempt and ridicule."

July 14th

The Senate met, and one of the bills for organizing one of the public departments—that of Foreign Affairs—was taken up. After being read, I begged leave of the Chair to submit some general observations, which, though apparently diffuse, I considered as pertinent to the bill before us, the first clause of which was, "There shall be an Executive Department," etc. There are a number of such bills, and may be many more, tending to direct the most minute particle of the President's conduct. If he is to be directed, how he shall do everything, it follows he must do nothing without direction. To what purpose, then, is the executive power lodged with the President, if he can do nothing without a law directing the mode, manner, and, of course, the thing to be done?" May not the two Houses of Congress, on this principle, pass a law depriving him of all powers? You may say it will not get his approbation. But two thirds of both Houses will make it a law without him, and the Constitution is undone at once.

253

Gentlemen may say, How is the Government then to proceed on these points? The simplest in the world. The President communicates to the Senate that he finds such and such officers necessary in the execution of the Government, and nominates the man. If the Senate approve, they will concur in the measure; if not, refuse their consent, etc., when the appointments are made. The President, in like manner, communicates to the House of Representatives that such appointments have taken place, and require adequate salaries. Then the House of Representatives might show their concurrence or disapprobation, by providing for the officer or not. I thought it my duty to mention these things, though I had not the vanity to think that I would make any proselytes in this stage of the business; and, perhaps, the best apology I could make was not to detain them long. I likewise said that, if the Senate were generally of my mind, a conference between the Houses should take place. But the sense of the House would appear on taking the question upon the first clause. The first clause was carried.

Now came the second clause. It was for the appointment of a chief clerk by the Secretary, who, in fact, was to be the principal, *"whenever the said principal officer shall be removed from office by the President of the United States."* There was a blank pause at the end of it. I was not in haste, but rose first: Mr. President, whoever attends strictly to the Constitution of the United States, will readily observe that the part assigned to the Senate was an important one—no less than that of being the great check, the regulator and corrector, or, if I may so speak, the balance of this Government. In their legislative capacity they not only have the concoction of all bills, orders, votes, or resolutions, but may originate any of them, save money bills. In the executive branch they have likewise power to check and regulate the proceedings of the President. Thus treaties, the highest and most important part of the Executive Department, must have a concurrence of two thirds of them. All appointments under the President and Vice-President, must be by their advice and consent, unless they concur in passing a law divesting themselves of this power. By the checks which are intrusted with them upon both the Executive and the other branch of the Legislature, the stability of the Government is evidently placed in their hands.

The approbation of the Senate was certainly meant to guard against the mistakes of the President in his appointments to office. I do not admit the doctrine of holding commissions 'during pleasure' as constitutional, and shall speak to that point presently. But, supposing for a moment, that to be the case, is not the same guard equally necessary to prevent improper steps in removals as in appointments? Certainly, common inference or induction can mean nothing short of this. It is a maxim in legislation as well as reason, and applies well in the present case, that it requires the same power to repeal as to enact. The depriving power should be the same as the appointing power.

But was this a point left at large by the Constitution? Certainly otherwise. Five or six times in our short Constitution is the trial by impeachment mentioned. In one place, the House of Representatives shall have the sole power of impeachment. In another, the Senate shall have the sole power to try impeachments. In a third, judgment shall not extend further than to removal from office, and disqualification to hold or enjoy offices, etc. The President shall not pardon in cases of impeachment. The President, Vice-President, and *all civil officers* of the United States, shall be removed from office on impeachment, etc. No part of the Constitution is so fully guarded as or more clearly expressed than this part of it. And most justly, too, for every good Government guards the reputation of her citizens as well as their life and property. Every turning out of office is attended with reproach, and the person so turned out is stigmatized with infamy. By means of impeachment a fair hearing and trial are secured to the party. Wthout this, what man of independent spirit would accept of such an office? Of what service can his abilities be to the community if afraid of the nod or beck of a superior? He must consult his will in every matter. Abject servility is most apt to mark the line of his conduct, and this on the one hand will not fail to be productive of despotism and tyranny on the other; for I consider mankind composed nearly of the same materials in America as in Asia, in the United States as in the East Indies. The Constitution certainly never contemplated any other mode of removing from office. The case is not omitted here; the most ample provision is made. If gentlemen do not like it, let them obtain an alteration of the Constitution; but this can not be done by law.

If the virtues of the present Chief Magistrate are brought forward as a reason for vesting him with extraordinary powers, no nation ever trod more dangerous ground. His virtues will depart with him, but the powers which you give him will remain, and if not properly guarded will be abused by future Presidents if they are men. This, however, is not the whole of the objection I have to the clause. A chief clerk is to be appointed, and this without any advice or consent of the Senate. This chief clerk, on the removal of the Secretary, will become the principal in the office, and so may remain during the presidency, for the Senate can not force the President into a nomination for a new officer. This is a direct stroke at the power of the Senate. Sir, I consider the clause as exceptional every way, and therefore move you to strike it out.

Langdon jumped up in haste; hoped the whole would not be struck out, but moved that the clause only of the President's removing should be struck out. Up rose Elsworth, and a most elaborate speech indeed did he make, but it was all drawn from writers on the distribution of government. The President was the executive officer. He was interfered with in the appointment, it is true, but not in the removal. The Constitution had taken one, but not the other, from him. Therefore, removal remained to him entire. He carefully avoided the subject of impeachment. He absolutely used the following expressions with regard to the President: *"It is sacrilege to touch a hair of his head, and we may as well lay the President's head on the block and strike it off with one blow."* The way he came to use these words was after having asserted that removing from office was his (the President's) privilege, we might as well do this as to deprive him of it. He [Elsworth] had sore eyes, and had a green silk over them. On pronouncing the last of the two sentences, he paused, put his handkerchief to his face, and either shed tears or affected to do so.

When he sat down both Butler and Izard sprang up. Butler, however, continued up. He began with a declaration that he came into the House in the most perfect state of indifference, and rather disposed to give the power in question to the President. But the arguments of the honorable gentleman from Connecticut [Elsworth], in endeavoring to support the clause, had convinced him, in the clearest manner, that the clause was highly improper, and he would vote against it. Izard now got at it, and spoke very long against the clause. Strong got up for the clause, and a most confused speech he made, indeed. I have notes of it, but think it really not worth answering, unless to show the folly of some things that he said. Dr. Johnson rose and told us twice before he proceeded far that he would not give an opinion on the power of the President. This man's conscience would not let him; he is a thorough-paced courtier, yet he wishes not to lose his interest with the President. However, his whole argument went against the clause, and at last he declared he was against the whole of it. Mr. Lee rose. He spoke long and pointedly against the clause. He repeated many of my arguments, but always was polite enough to acknowledge the mention I had made of them. He spoke from a paper which he held in his hand. He continued until it was past three o'clock, and an adjournment was called for and took place.

In looking over my notes I find I omitted to set down sundry arguments which I used. But no matter; I will not do it now.

July 15th

Senate met. Mr. Carrol showed impatience to be up first. He got up and spoke a considerable length of time. The burden of his discourse seemed to be the want of power in the President, and a desire of increasing it. Great complaints of what is called the *atrocious assumption of power in the States.* Many allusions to the power of the British kings. *The king can do no wrong.* If anything improper is done, it should be the Ministers that should answer. How strangely this man has changed!

The Collection bill was called for and read for the first time. Now Elsworth rose with a most lengthy debate. The first words he said were, "In this case the Constitution is our only rule, for we are sworn to support it." But [he] neither quoted it nor ever named it afterward except as follows. He said by allusion, "I buy a square acre of land. I buy the trees, water, and everything belonging to it. The executive power belongs to the President. The removing of officers is a tree on this acre. The power of removing is, therefore, his. It is in him. It is nowhere else. Thus we are under the necessity of ascertaining by implication where the power is." He called Dr. Johnson Thomas Aquinas by implication, too, and said things rather uncivil to some other of his opponents. Most carefully did he avoid entering on the subject of impeachment. After some time, however, he got fairly on new ground. Lamented the want of power in the President. Asked, Did we *ever quarrel* with the power of the Crown of Great Britain? No, we contended with the power of the Parliament. No one ever thought the power of the Crown too great. [He] said he was growing infirm, should die, and should not see it, but the Government would fail for want of power in the President. He would have power as far as he would be seen in his coach-and-six. "We must extend the executive arm." (Mr. Lee yesterday had said something about the Dutch.) "If we must have examples," said he, "let us draw them from the people whom we used always to imitate; from the nation who have made all others bow before them, and not from the Dutch, who are divided and factious." He said a great deal more, but the above is all I minuted down at the time. Mr. Izard rose and answered. Mr. Butler rose and spoke. It was after three. Mr. Lee rose; said he had much to say, but would now only move an adjournment. As it was late, the House accordingly adjourned.

July 16th

Attended pretty early this morning. Many were, however, there before me. It was all huddling away in small parties. Our Vice-President was very busy indeed; running to every one. He openly attacked Mr. Lee before me on the subject in debate, and they were very loud on the business. I began to suspect that the court party had prevailed. Senate, however, met, and at it they went. Mr. Lee began, but I really believe the altercation, though not a violent one, which he had with the Vice-President had hurt him, for he was languid and much shorter than ever I had heard him on almost any subject. Mr. Patterson got up. For a long time you could not know what he would be at. After, however, he had warmed himself with his own discourse, as the Indians do with their war-songs, he said he was for the clause continuing. He had no sooner said so than he assumed a bolder tone of voice; flew over to England; extolled its Government; wished, in the most unequivocal language, that our President had the same powers; said, let us take a second view of England; repeating nearly the same thing. Let us take a third view of it, said he. And then he abused Parliament for having made themselves first triennial and lastly septennial. Speaking of the Constitution, he said expressly these words, speaking of the removing of officers: "There is not a word of removability in it." His argument was that the Executive held this as a matter of course.

Mr. Wyngate got up and said something for striking out. Mr. Read rose, and was swinging on his legs for an hour. He had to talk a great deal before he could bring himself to declare against the motion. But now a most curious scene opened. Dalton rose and said a number of things in the most hesitating and embarrassed manner. It was his recantation; [he] had just now altered his mind. From what had been said by the honorable gentleman from Jersey, he was now for the clause. Mr. Izard was so provoked that he jumped up; declared nothing had fallen from that gentleman that could possibly convince any man; that men might pretend so, but the thing was impossible.

Mr. Morris' face had reddened for some time. He rose hastily, threw censure on Mr. Izard; declared that the canting man behaved like a man of honor; that Patterson's arguments were good and sufficient to convince any man. The truth, however, was that everybody believed that John Adams was the great converter.

But now recantation was in fashion. Mr. Bassett recanted, too, though he said he had prepared himself on the other side. We now saw how it would go, and I could not help admiring the frugality of the court party in procuring recantations, or votes, which you please. After all the arguments were ended and the question taken the Senate was ten to ten, and the Vice-President with joy cried out, "It is not a vote!" without giving himself time to declare the division of the House and give his vote in order. Every man of our side, in giving his sentiments, spoke with great freedom, and seemed willing to avow his opinion in the openest manner. Not a man

257

of the others who had made any speech to the merits of the matter, but went about it and about it. I called this singing the war-song, and I told Mr. Morris I would give him every one whom I heard sing the war-song; or, in other words, those who could not avow the vote they were fully minded to give until they had raised spirits enough by their own talk to enable them to do it. Grayson made a speech. It was not long, but he had in it this remarkable sentence: "The matter predicted by Mr. Henry is now coming to pass: consolidation is the object of the new Government, and the first attempt will be to destroy the Senate, as they are the representatives of the State Legislatures."

It has long been a maxim with me that no frame of government whatever would secure liberty or equal administration of justice to a people unless virtuous citizens were the legislators and Governors. I live not a day without finding new reason to subscribe to this doctrine. What avowed and repeated attempts have I seen to place the President above the powers stipulated for him by the Constitution!

The vote stood: For striking out—Butler, Izard, Langdon, Johnson, Wyngate, Few, Gunn, Grayson, Lee, Maclay—ten. Against striking out: Read, Bassett, Elsworth, Strong, Dalton, Patterson, Elmer, Morris, Henry, Carrol—ten; and John Adams.

25

The American Hero

Mason L. Weems (1759–1825), born in Maryland, was an Episcopal clergyman and book agent. After his ordination in England, he returned to America to spend most of his life wandering through the country selling books, some of which he wrote himself. Weems's emphasis on good works and religious piety was expressed in a series of biographies and moralizing tracts. Besides Washington, his subjects included Benjamin Franklin, William Penn, and the Revolutionary hero, General Francis Marion.

Of all his works, the most memorable was the study of Washington, which appeared for the first time in 1800, only months after the great man's death. Deliberately seeking to produce a best seller, Weems was remarkably successful; in the next one hundred years more than eighty printings were made, some of his episodes becoming staples of children's literature. Although Weems's inventiveness and imagination far outweighed his commitment to historical accuracy, this semifictional account profoundly influenced all subsequent biographers, positively or negatively. The popularity of his fables shows some of the qualities Americans demanded from their heroes, even though such standards were rarely attainable.

THE LIFE OF WASHINGTON
Mason L. Weems

CHAPTER II

BIRTH AND EDUCATION

To this day numbers of good Christians can hardly find faith to believe that Washington was, bona fide, *a Virginian! What! a buckskin!"* say they with a smile, *"George Washington a buckskin! pshaw! impossible! he was certainly an European: So great a man could never have been born in America."*

So *great a man could never have been born in America!* Why that's the very *prince of reasons* why he should have been born here! Nature, we know, is fond of

Reprinted by permission of the publishers from Marcus Cunliffe, editor, Mason L. Weems, *The Life of Washington.* Cambridge, Mass.: The Belknap Press of Harvard University Press, Copyright, 1962, by the President and Fellows of Harvard College. Pp. 6–12, 162–177, 181–182, 185–186.

harmonies; and *paria paribus,* that is, *great things to great,* is the rule she delights to work by. Where, for example, do we look for the *whale* "the biggest born of nature?" not, I trow, in a *millpond,* but in the main ocean; *"there go the great ships,"* and there are the spoutings of whales amidst their boiling foam.

By the same rule, where shall we look for Washington, the greatest among men, but in *America?* That greatest Continent, which, rising from beneath the frozen pole, stretches far and wide to the south, running almost *"whole the length of this vast terrene,"* and sustaining on her ample sides the roaring shock of half the watery globe. And equal to its size, is the furniture of this vast continent, where the Almighty has reared his cloud-capt mountains, and spread his sea-like lakes, and poured his mighty rivers, and hurled down his thundering cataracts in a style of the *sublime,* so far superior to any thing of the kind in the other continents, that we may fairly conclude that great men and great deeds are designed for America.

This seems to be the verdict of honest analogy; and accordingly we find America the honoured cradle of Washington, who was born on Pope's creek, in Westmoreland county, Virginia, the 22nd of February, 1732. His father, whose name was Augustin Washington, was also a Virginian, but his grandfather (John) was an Englishman, who came over and settled in Virginia in 1657.

His father fully persuaded that a marriage of virtuous love comes nearest to angelic life, early stepped up to the *altar* with glowing cheeks and joy sparkling eyes, while by his side, with soft warm hand, sweetly trembling in his, stood the angel form of the lovely Miss Dandridge.

After several years of great domestic happiness, Mr. Washington was separated by death, from this excellent woman, who left him and two children to lament her early fate.

Fully persuaded still, that *"it is not good for man to be alone,"* he renewed, for the second time, the chaste delights of matrimonial love. His consort was Miss Mary Ball, a young lady of fortune, and descended from one of the best families in Virginia.

. . . . By his first wife, Mr. Washington had two children, both sons— Lawrence and Augustin. By his second wife, he had five children, four sons and a daughter—George, Samuel, John, Charles, and Elizabeth. Those *over delicate* ones, who are ready to faint at thought of a second marriage, might do well to remember, that the greatest man that ever lived was the son of this second marriage! . . .

To assist his son to overcome that selfish spirit which too often leads children to fret and fight about trifles, was a notable care of Mr. Washington. For this purpose, of all the presents, such as cakes, fruit, &c. he received, he was always desired to give a liberal part to his play-mates. To enable him to do this with more alacrity, his father would remind him of the love which he would hereby gain, and the frequent presents which would in return be made *to him;* and also would tell of that great and good God, who delights above all things to see children love one another, and will assuredly reward them for acting so amiable a part. . . .

Never did the wise Ulysses take more pains with his beloved Telemachus, than did Mr. Washington with George, to inspire him with an *early love of truth.* "Truth, George," (said he) "is the loveliest quality of youth. I would ride fifty miles, my son, to see the little boy whose heart is so *honest,* and his lips so *pure,* that we may depend on every word he says! O how lovely does such a child appear in the eyes of every body! His parents doat on him; his relations glory in him; they are constantly praising him to their children, whom they beg to imitate him. They are often sending for him, to visit them; and receive him, when he comes, with as much joy as if he were a little angel, come to set pretty examples to their children.

"But, Oh! how different, George, is the case with the boy who is so given to lying, that nobody can believe a word he says! He is looked at with aversion wherever he goes, and parents dread to see him come among their children. Oh, George! my son! rather than see you come to this pass, dear as you are to my heart, gladly would I assist to nail you up in your little coffin, and follow you to your grave. Hard, indeed, would it be to me to give up my son, whose little feet are always so ready to run about with me, and whose fondly looking eyes and sweet prattle make so large a part of my happiness: but still I would give him up, rather than see him a common liar.

"Pa, (said George very seriously) do I ever tell lies?"

"No, George, I *thank God* you do not, my son; and I rejoice in the hope you never will. At least, you shall never, from me, have cause to be guilty of so shameful a thing. Many parents, indeed, even compel their children to this vile practice, by barbarously beating them for every little fault; hence, on the next offence, the little terrified creature slips out a *lie!* just to escape the rod. But as to yourself, George, you know I have *always* told you, and now tell you again, that, whenever by accident you do any thing wrong, which must often be the case, as you are but a poor little boy yet, without *experience* or *knowledge,* never tell a falsehood to conceal it; but come *bravely* up, my son, like a *little man,* and tell me of it: and instead of beating you, George, I will but the more honour and love you for it, my dear."

This, you'll say, was sowing good seed!—Yes, it was: and the crop, thank God, was, as I believe it ever will be, where a man acts the true parent, that is, the *Guardian Angel,* by his child.

The following anecdote is a *case in point.* It is too valuable to be lost, and too true to be doubted; for it was communicated to me by the same excellent lady to whom I am indebted for the last.

"When George," said she, "was about six years old, he was made the wealthy master of a *hatchet!* of which, like most little boys, he was immoderately fond, and was constantly going about chopping every thing that came in his way. One day, in the garden, where he often amused himself hacking his mother's pea-sticks, he unluckily tried the edge of his hatchet on the body of a beautiful young English cherry-tree, which he barked so terribly, that I don't believe the tree ever got the better of it. The next morning the old gentleman finding out what had befallen his tree, which, by the by, was a great favourite, came into the house, and with much warmth asked for the mischievous author, declaring at the same time, that he would not have taken five guineas for his tree. Nobody could tell him any thing about it. Presently George and his hatchet made their appearance. *George,* said his father, *do you know who killed that beautiful little cherry-tree yonder in the garden?* This was a *tough question;* and George staggered under it for a moment; but quickly recovered himself: and looking at his father, with the sweet face of youth brightened with the inexpressible charm of all-conquering truth, he bravely cried out, *"I can't tell a lie, Pa; you know I can't tell a lie. I did cut it with my hatchet."*— *Run to my arms, you dearest boy,* cried his father in transports, *run to my arms; glad am I, George, that you killed my tree; for you have paid me for it a thousand fold. Such an act of heroism in my son, is more worth than a thousand trees, though blossomed with silver, and their fruits of purest gold.* . . .

CHAPTER XII
THE DEATH OF WASHINGTON

If the prayers of millions could have prevailed, Washington would have been immortal on earth. And if fulness of peace, riches, and honours could have rendered that immortality happy, Washington had been blessed indeed. But this world is not the place of true happiness. Though numberless are the satisfactions, which a prudence and virtue like Washington's may enjoy in this world, yet they fall short, infinite degrees, of that pure, unembittered felicity, which the Almighty parent has prepared in heaven for the spirits of the just.

To prepare for this immensity of bliss, is the real errand on which God sent us into the world. Our preparation consists in acquiring those great virtues, purity and love, which alone can make us *worthy* companions of angels, and fit partakers of their exalted delights. Washington had wisely spent life in acquiring the IMMORTAL VIRTUES. *"He had fought the good fight"* against his own unreasonable affections; *he had glorified God,* by exemplifying the charms of virtue to men; *he had borne the heat and burden of the day*—his *great* day of duty; and the evening (of old age) being come, the servant of God must now go to receive his wages. Happy Washington! If crowns and kingdoms could have purchased such peace as thine, such hopes big with immortality, with what begging earnestness would crowns and kingdoms have been offered by the mighty conquerors of the earth, in their dying moments of *terror* and *despair!*

On the 14th of December, 1799 (when he wanted but 9 weeks and 2 days of being 68 years old), he rode out to his mill, 3 miles distant. The day was raw and rainy. The following night he was attacked with a violent pain and inflammation of the throat. The lancet of one of his domestics was employed, but with no advantage. Early in the morning, Dr. Craik, the friend and physician of his youth and age, was sent for. Alarmed at the least appearance of danger threatening a life so dear to him, Dr. Craik advised to call in, immediately, the consulting assistance of his friends, the ingenious and learned Drs. Dick, of Alexandria, and Brown, of Port Tobacco. They came on the wings of speed. They felt the awfulness of their situation. The greatest of human beings was lying low: a life, of all others the most *revered,* the most *beloved,* was at stake. And if human skill could have saved—if the sword of genius, and the buckler of experience could have turned the stroke of death, Washington had still lived. But his *hour was come.*

It appears, that, from the commencement of the attack, he was favoured with a presentiment, that he was now laid down to rise no more. He took, however, the medicines that were offered him, but it was principally from a sense of *duty*.

It has been said that a man's death, is generally a copy of his life. It was Washington's case exactly. In his last illness he behaved with the firmness of a soldier, and the resignation of a christian.

The inflammation in his throat was attended with great pain, which he bore with the fortitude that became him. He was, once or twice, heard to say that, *had it pleased God, he should have been glad to die a little easier; but that he doubted not that it was for his good*.

Every hour now spread a sadder gloom over the scene. Despair sat on the faces of the physicians; for they saw that their art had failed! The strength of the mighty was departing from him; and death, with his sad harbingers, chills and paleness, was coming on apace.

Mount Vernon, which had long shone the queen of elegant joys, was now about to suffer a sad eclipse! an eclipse, which would soon be mournfully visible, not only through the United States, but throughout the whole world.

Sons and daughters of Columbia, gather yourselves together around the bed of your expiring father—around the last bed of him to whom under God you and your children owe many of the best blessings of this life. When Joseph the prime minister of Egypt heard his *shepherd father* was sick, he hastened up, to see him; and fell on his face and kissed him, and wept a long while. But Joseph had never received such services from Jacob as you have received from Washington. But we call you not to weep for Washington. We ask you not to view those eyes, now sunk and hollow, which formerly darted their lightning flashes against your enemies—nor to feel that heart, now faintly labouring, which so often throbbed with more than mortal joys when he saw his young countrymen charging like lions, upon the foes of liberty. No! we call you not to weep, but to rejoice. Washington, who so often conquered himself, is now about to conquer the last enemy.

Silent and sad, his physicians sat by his bedside, looking on him as he lay panting for breath. They thought on the past, and the tear swelled in their eyes. He marked it, and, stretching out his hand to them, and shaking his head, said, *"O no!—don't! don't!"* then with a delightful smile added, "I am dying, gentlemen: but, thank God, I am not afraid to die."

Feeling that the hour of his departure out of this world was at hand, he desired that every body would quit the room. They all went out, and according to his wish, left him—with his God.

There, by himself, like Moses alone on the top of Pisgah, he seeks the face of God. There, *by himself,* standing as on the awful boundary that divides time from eternity, that separates this world from the next, he cannot quit the long-frequented haunts of the one, nor launch away into the untried regions of the other, until (in humble imitation of the world's great Redeemer) he has poured forth into the bosom of his God those strong sensations which the solemnity of the situation naturally suggested.

With what angel fervour did he adore that *Almighty Love*, which, though inhabiting the heaven of heavens, deigned to wake his sleeping dust—framed him so fearfully in the womb—nursed him on a tender mother's *breast*—watched his helpless infancy—guarded his heedless youth—preserved him from the dominion of his passions—inspired him with the love of virtue—led him safely up to man—and, from such low beginnings, advanced him to such unparalleled usefulness and glory among men! These, and ten thousand other precious gifts heaped on him, unasked, many of them long before he had the knowledge to ask, overwhelmed his soul with gratitude unutterable, exalted to infinite heights his ideas of eternal love, and bade him without fear resign his departing spirit into the arms of his Redeemer God, whose mercies are over all his works.

He is now about to leave the great family of man, in which he has so long sojourned! The yearnings of his soul are over his brethren! How fervently does he adore that *goodness,* which enabled him to be so serviceable to them! That *grace,* which preserved him from injuring them by violence or fraud! How fervently does he pray that the *unsuffering kingdom of God may come,* and that the earth may be filled with the richest fruits of righteousness and peace!

He is now about to leave his *country!* that dear spot which gave him birth!—that dear spot for which he has so long watched and prayed, so long toiled and fought; and whose beloved children he has so often sought to gather, even as a hen gathereth her chickens under her wings. He sees them now spread abroad like flocks in goodly pastures; like favoured Israel in the land of promise. He remembers how God, by a mighty hand, and by an out-stretched arm, brought their fathers into this good land, a land flowing with milk and honey: and blessed them with the blessings of heaven above, and the earth beneath; with the blessings of LIBERTY and of PEACE, of RELIGION and of LAWS, above all other people. He sees that, through the rich mercies of God, they have now the precious opportunity to continue their country the GLORY of the earth, and a refuge for the poor and for the persecuted of all lands! The transporting sight of such a cloud of blessings, trembling close over the heads of his countrymen, together with the distressing uncertainty whether they will put forth their hands and enjoy them, shakes the *parent soul* of Washington with feelings *too strong* for his *dying frame!* The last tear that he is ever to shed now steals into his eye—the last groan that he is ever to heave is about to issue from his faintly labouring heart.

Feeling that the silver chord of life is loosing, and that his spirit is ready to quit her old companion the body, he extends himself on his bed—closes his eyes for the *last* time, with his own hands—folds his arms decently on his breast, then breathing out *"Father of mercies! take me to thyself,"*—he fell asleep.

Swift on angels' wings the brightening saint ascended; while voices more than human were heard (*in Fancy's ear*) warbling through the happy regions, and hymning the great procession towards the gates of heaven. His glorious coming was seen far off, and myriads of mighty angels hastened forth, with golden harps, to welcome the honoured stranger. High in front of the shouting hosts, were seen the beauteous forms of FRANKLIN, WARREN, MERCER, SCAMMEL, and of him who fell at Quebec, with all the virtuous patriots, who, on the side of Columbia, toiled or bled for *liberty* and *truth.* But oh! how changed from what they were, when, in their days of flesh, bathed in sweat and blood, they fell at the parent feet of their weeping country! Not the homeliest infant suddenly springing into a soul-enchanting Hebe—not dreary winter, suddenly brightening into spring, with all her bloom and fragrance, ravishing the senses, could equal such glorious change. Oh! where are now their wrinkles and grey hairs? Where their ghastly wounds and clotted blood? Their forms are of the stature of angels—their robes like morning clouds streaked with gold—the stars of heaven, like crowns glitter on their heads—immortal youth, *celestial rosy red,* sits blooming on their cheeks; while infinite benignity and love beam from their eyes. Such were the forms of thy sons, O Columbia! such the brother band of thy martyred saints, that now poured forth from heaven's wide-opening gates, to meet thy Washington; to meet their beloved chief, who in the days of his mortality, had led their embattled squadrons to the war. At sight of him, even these *blessed spirits* seem to feel new raptures, and to look more dazzling bright. In joyous throngs they pour around him—they devour him with their eyes of love—they embrace him in transports of tenderness unutterable; while from their roseate cheeks, tears of joy, such as angels weep, roll down.

All that followed was too much for the over-dazzled eye of *Imagination.* She was seen to return, with the quick panting bosom and looks entranced of a fond mother, near swooning at sudden sight of a dear loved son, deemed *lost,* but now *found,* and raised to *kingly honours!* She was heard passionately to exclaim, with palms and eyes lifted to heaven, *"O, who can count the stars of Jacob, or number the fourth part of the blessings of Israel!—Let me die the death of Washington, and may my latter end be like his!"*

Let us now return to all that remained of Washington on the earth. He had expressly ordered in his will that he should be buried in a private *manner, and without any parade.* But this was impossible; for who could stay at home when it was said, *"to-day general Washington is to be buried!"* On the morning of the 18th, which was fixed on for his funeral, the people poured in by thousands to pay him the *last respect, and,* as they said, *to take their last look.* And, while they looked on him, nature stirred that at their hearts, which quickly brought the best blood into their cheeks, and rolled down the tears from their eyes. About two o'clock, they bore him to his long home, and buried him in his own family vault, near the banks of the great Potomac. And to this day, often as the ships of war pass that way, they waken up the thunder of their loudest guns, pointed to the spot, as if to tell the sleeping hero that he is not forgotten in his narrow dwelling.

The news of his death soon reached Philadelphia, where congress was then in session. A question of importance being on the carpet that day, the house, as usual, was much interested. But, soon as it was announced—"GENERAL WASHINGTON IS DEAD"—an instant stop was put to all business—the tongue of the orator was struck dumb—and a midnight silence ensued, save when it was interrupted by deepest sighs of the members, as, with drooping foreheads rested on their palms, they sat, each absorbed in mournful cogitation. Presently, as utterly unfit for business, both houses adjourned; and the members retired slow and sad to their lodgings, like men who had suddenly heard of the death of a father.

For several days hardly any thing was done in congress; hardly any thing thought of but to talk of and to praise the departed Washington. In this patriotic work all parties joined with equal alacrity and earnestness. In this all were *federalists,* all were *republicans.* Elegant addresses were exchanged between the two houses of congress and the president, and all of them replete with genius and gratitude.

Then, by unanimous consent, congress came to the following resolutions:

1st. That a grand marble monument should be erected at the city of Washington, under which, with permission of his lady, the body of the general should be deposited.

2d. That there should be a funeral procession from congress hall to the German Lutheran church to hear an oration delivered by one of the members of congress.

3d. That the members of congress should wear full mourning during the session.

4th. That it should be recommended to the people of the United States, to wear crape on the left arm, as mourning, for 30 days.

But, thank God, the people of the United States needed not the hint contained in the last resolution. Though they could not all very elegantly speak, yet their actions showed that they all very deeply *felt* what they owed to Washington. For in every city, village, and hamlet, the people were so struck on hearing of his death, that long before they heard of the resolution of congress, they ran together to ease their troubled minds in talking and hearing talk of Washington, and to devise some public mode of testifying their sorrow for his death. Every where throughout the continent, churches and court houses were hung in black, mourning was put on, processions were made, and sermons preached, while the crowded houses listened with pleasure to the praises of Washington, or sighed and wept when they heard of his toils and battles for his country.

CHAPTER XIII
CHARACTER OF WASHINGTON

When the children of the years to come, hearing his great name re-echoed from every lip, shall say to their fathers, *"what was it that raised Washington to such height of glory?"* let them be told that it was HIS GREAT TALENTS, CONSTANTLY GUIDED AND GUARDED BY RELIGION. For how shall man, *frail man,* prone to inglorious ease and pleasure, ever ascend the arduous steps of virtue, unless animated by the *mighty hopes* of religion? Or what shall stop him in his swift descent to infamy and vice, if unawed by that dread power which proclaims to the guilty that their secret crimes are seen, and shall not go unpunished? Hence the wise, in all ages, have pronounced, that *"there never was a truly great man without religion."*

There have, indeed, been *courageous generals,* and *cunning statesmen,* without religion, but mere courage or cunning, however paramount, never yet made a man great.

No! to be truly great, a man must have not only great talents, but those talents must be constantly exerted on great, i. e. good actions—*and perseveringly* too—for if he should turn aside to vice—farewel to his heroism. . . . But, sensual and grovelling as man is, what can incline and elevate him to those things like religion, that divine power, to whom alone it belongs to present those vast and eternal *goods* and *ills* which best alarm our fears, enrapture our hopes, inflame the worthiest loves, rouse the truest avarice, and in short touch every spring and passion of our souls in favour of virtue and noble actions. . . .

"*There exists,*" says Washington, "*in the economy of nature, an inseparable connexion between duty and advantage.*"—The whole life of this great man bears glorious witness to the truth of this his favourite aphorism. At the giddy age of fourteen, when the spirits of youth are all on tiptoe for freedom and adventures, he felt a strong desire to go to sea; but, very opposite to his wishes, his mother declared that she could not bear to part with him. His trial must have been very severe; for I have been told that a midshipman's commission was actually in his pocket—his trunk of clothes on board the ship—his honour in some sort pledged—his young companions importunate with him to go—and his whole soul panting for the promised pleasures of the voyage; but religion whispered "*honour thy mother, and grieve not the spirit of her who bore thee.*"

Instantly the glorious boy sacrificed inclination to duty—dropt all thoughts of the voyage, and gave tears of joy to his widowed mother, in clasping to her bosom a dear child who could deny himself to make her happy. . . .

"Well," replied she embracing him tenderly, "*God, I hope, will reward my dear boy for this, some day or other.*" Now see here, young reader, and learn that HE who prescribes our duty, is able to reward it. Had George left his fond mother to a broken heart, and gone off to sea, 'tis next to certain that he would never have taken that active part in the French and Indian war, which, by securing to him the hearts of his countrymen, paved the way for all his future greatness.

Now for another instance of the wonderful effect of religion on Washington's fortune. Shortly after returning from the war of Cuba, Lawrence (his *half* brother) was taken with the consumption, which made him so excessively fretful, that his *own* brother, Augustin, would seldom come near him. But George, whose heart was early under the softening and sweetening influences of religion, felt such a tenderness for his poor sick brother, that he not only put up with his peevishness, but seemed, from what I have been told, never so happy as when he was with him. He accompanied him to the island of Bermuda, in quest of health—and, after their return to Mount Vernon, often as his duty to lord Fairfax permitted, he would come down from the back woods to see him. And while with him he was always contriving or doing something to cheer and comfort his brother. Sometimes with his gun he would go out in quest of partridges and snipes, and other fine flavoured game, to tempt his brother's sickly appetite, and gain him strength. At other times he would sit for hours and read to him some entertaining book—and, when his cough came on, he would support his drooping head, and wipe the cold dew from his forehead, or the phlegm from his lips, and give him his medicine, or smooth his pillow; and all with such alacrity and artless tenderness as proved the sweetest cordial to his brother's spirits. For he was often heard to say to the Fairfax family, into which he married, that "*he should think nothing of his sickness, if he could but always have his brother George with him."* Well, what was the consequence? Why, when Lawrence came to die, he left almost the whole of his large estate to George, which served as another noble step to his future greatness. . . .

In the winter of '77, while Washington, with the American army lay encamped at Valley Forge, a certain good old FRIEND, of the respectable family and name of Potts, if I mistake not, had occasion to pass through the woods near head-quarters. Treading his way along the venerable grove, suddenly he heard the sound of a human voice, which as he advanced increased on his ear, and at length became like the voice of one speaking much in earnest. As he approached the spot with a cautious step, whom should he behold, in a dark natural bower of ancient oaks, but the commander in chief of the American armies on his knees at prayer! Motionless with surprise, friend Potts continued on the place till the general, having ended his devotions, arose, and, with a countenance of angel serenity, retired to headquarters: friend Potts then went home, and on entering his parlour called out to his wife, "Sarah, my dear! Sarah! All's well! all's well! George Washington will yet prevail!"

"What's the matter, Isaac?" replied she; "thee seems moved."

"Well, if I seem moved, 'tis no more than what I am. I have this day seen what I never expected. Thee knows that I always thought the sword and the gospel utterly inconsistent; and that no man could be a soldier and a christian at the same time. But George Washington has this day convinced me of my mistake."

He then related what he had seen, and concluded with this prophetical remark—"If George Washington be not a man of God, I am greatly deceived—and still more shall I be deceived if God do not, through him, work out a great salvation for America." . . .

"Of all the dispositions and habits which lead to the prosperity of a nation," says Washington, "religion is the indispensable support. Volumes could not trace all its connexions with private and public happiness. Let it simply be asked, where is the security for property, for reputation, for life itself, if there be no fear of God on the minds of those who give their oaths in courts of justice!"

But some will tell us, that *human laws* are sufficient for the purpose!

Human laws!—Human nonsense! For how often, even where the cries and screams of the wretched called aloud for lightning-speeded vengeance, have we not seen the sword of human law loiter in its coward scabbard, afraid of angry royalty? Did not that vile queen Jezebel, having a mind to compliment her husband with a vineyard belonging to poor Naboth, suborn a couple of villains to take a false oath against him, and then cause him to be dragged out with his little motherless, crying babes, and barbarously stoned to death?

Great God! what bloody tragedies have been acted on the poor ones of the earth, by kings and great men, who were *above* the laws, and had no sense of religion to keep them in awe!—And if men be not above the laws, yet what horrid crimes! what ruinous robberies! what wide-wasting flames! what cruel murders may they not commit in *secret,* if they be not withheld by the sacred arm of religion! "In vain, therefore," says WASHINGTON, "would that man claim the tribute of patriotism, who should do any thing to discountenance religion and morality, those great pillars of human happiness, those firmest props of the duties of men and citizens. The mere politician, equally with the pious man, ought to respect and cherish them."

But others have said, and with a serious face too, that a *sense of honour,* is sufficient to preserve men from base actions! O blasphemy to sense! Do we not daily hear of *men of honour,* by dice and cards, draining their fellow-citizens of the last cent, reducing them to a dung-hill, or driving them to a pistol? Do we not daily hear of *men of honour* corrupting their neighbours' wives and daughters, and then murdering their husbands and brothers in duels? Bind such selfish, such inhuman beings, by a sense of honour!! Why not bind roaring lions with cobwebs? "No," exclaims Washington, "whatever a sense of honour may do on men of refined education, and on minds of a peculiar structure, reason and experience both forbid us to expect that national morality can prevail, in exclusion of religious principles."

And truly Washington had abundant reason, from his own *happy experience,* to recommend religion so heartily to others.

For besides all those inestimable favours which he received from her at the hands of her celestial daughters, the *Virtues;* she threw over him her own magic mantle of *Character.* And it was this that immortalized Washington. By inspiring his countrymen with the profoundest veneration for him as the *best of men,* it naturally smoothed his way to supreme command; so that when War, that monster of hell, came on roaring against America, with all his death's heads and garments rolled in blood, the nation unanimously placed Washington at the head of their armies, from a natural persuasion that so good a man must be the peculiar favourite of Heaven, and the fastest friend of his country. How far this precious instinct in favour of goodness was corrected, or how far Washington's conduct was honourable to religion and glorious to himself and country, bright ages to come, and happy millions yet unborn, will, we hope, declare.

26

Spreading the Gospel

Lorenzo Dow (1777–1834) was one of the most famous, if eccentric, evangelists of his era. Born in Connecticut, he began his Methodist preaching while in his teens, traveling immense distances on horseback to carry the gospel into isolated rural areas of New England. After a trip to Europe he returned to spend some time preaching in the South, where he witnessed and helped inspire some of the violent ecstasies of camp meetings. His later years were spent preparing revised editions of his journals and issuing a series of pamphlets on various subjects. His preachings and writings were characteristically vivid and militant, suggesting the temperament of a man who willingly bore the hardships of itineracy and the hostility of the unconverted to carry his version of religious truth to frontier America.

THE JOURNAL
OF LORENZO DOW

I was born, October 16, 1777, in Coventry, Tolland County, State of Connecticut. My parents were born in the same town and descended from English ancestors. They had a son, and then three daughters, older than myself, and one daughter younger. They were very tender towards their children, and endeavored to educate them well, both in religion and common learning.

When I was two years old, I was taken sick; and my parents having been a long journey and returning homeward, heard of my dangerous illness, and that I was dead, and they expected to meet the people returning from my funeral. But to their joy, I was living; and beyond the expectation of all, I recovered.

When I was between three and four years old, one day, while I was at play with my companion, I suddenly fell into a muse about God and those places called heaven and hell, which I heard people converse about, so that I forgot my play, which my companion observing, desired to know the cause. I asked him if ever he said his prayers, morning or night; to which he replied, "No." Then said I, "You are wicked, and I will not play with you." So I quit his company and went into the house.

My mind, frequently on observing the works of creation, desired to know the cause of things; and I asked my parents many questions which they scarcely knew how to answer.

From *The Life, Travels, Labors, and Writings of Lorenzo Dow* (New York, 1859), 13–18, 20–22, 24, 27, 30–31, 126–127, 132–135, 155–157.

One day I was the means of killing a bird, and upon seeing it gasp, I was struck with horror. And upon seeing any beast struggle in death it made my heart beat hard, as it would cause the thoughts of my death to come into my mind. Death appeared such a terror to me, I sometimes wished that I might be translated as Enoch and Elijah were; and at other times I wished I had never been born.

When past the age of thirteen years, and about the time that JOHN WESLEY died, (1791), it pleased God to awaken my mind by a dream of the night, which was, that an old man came to me at mid-day, having a staff in his hand, and said to me, "Do you ever pray?" I told him, "No." Said he, "You must;" and then went away. He had not been long gone before he returned; and said again, "Do you pray?" I again said, "No." And after his departure I went out of doors, and was taken up by a whirlwind and carried above the skies. At length I discovered, across a gulf, as it were through a mist of darkness, a glorious place, in which was a throne of ivory overlaid with gold, and God sitting upon it, and Jesus Christ at his right hand, and angels and glorified spirits celebrating praise.—Oh! the joyful music! I thought the angel Gabriel came to the edge of heaven, holding a golden trumpet in his right hand, and cried to me with a mighty voice to know if I desired to come there. I told him I did. Said he, "You must go back to yonder world, and if you will be faithful to God, you shall come here in the end."

With reluctance I left the beautiful sight and came back to the earth again. And then I thought the old man came to me the third time and asked me if I had prayed. I told him I had. "Then," said he, "BE FAITHFUL, AND I WILL COME AND LET YOU KNOW AGAIN." I thought that was to be when I should be blest. And when I awakened, behold it was a dream. But it was strongly impressed on my mind, that this singular dream must be from God; and the way that I should know it, I should let my father know of it at such a time and in such a place, viz. as he would be feeding the cattle in the morning, which I accordingly did. No sooner had I done it than keen conviction seized my heart. I knew I was unprepared to die. Tears begun to run down plentifully, and I again resolved to seek the salvation of my soul. I began that day to pray in secret; but how to pray or what to pray for, I scarcely knew.

If now I had had any one to instruct me in the way and plan of salvation, I doubt not but I should have found salvation. But, alas, I felt like one wandering and benighted in an unknown wilderness, who wants both light and a guide. The Bible was like a sealed book; so mysterious I could not understand it. And in order to hear it explained, I applied to this person and that book; but got no satisfactory instruction. I frequently wished I had lived in the days of the prophets or apostles, that I could have had sure guides; for by the misconduct of professors, I thought there were no Bible saints in the land. Thus with sorrow many months heavily rolled away.

But at length, not finding what my soul desired, I began to examine the cause more closely, if possible to find it out: and immediately the doctrine of unconditional *reprobation* and particular *election* was exhibited to my view—that the state of all was unalterably fixed by God's *"eternal decrees."* Here discouragements arose, and I began to slacken my hand by degrees, until I entirely left off

271

secret prayer, and could not bear to read or hear the scriptures, saying, "If God has foreordained whatever comes to pass, then all our labors are vain."

Feeling still condemnation in my breast, I concluded myself reprobated. Despair of mercy arose, hope was fled, and I was resolved to end my wretched life; concluding the longer I live, the more sin I shall commit, and the greater my punishment will be; but the shorter my life, the less sin, and of course the less punishment, and the sooner I shall know that the worst of my case. Accordingly I loaded a gun, and withdrew to a wilderness.

As I was about to put my intention into execution, a sudden solemn thought darted into my mind, "Stop and consider what you are about: if you end your life, you are undone for ever; but if you omit it a few days longer, it may be that something will turn up in your favor." This was attended with a small degree of hope, that if I waited a little while, it should not be altogether in vain. And I thought I felt thankful that God prevented me from sending my soul to everlasting misery.

About this time there was much talk about the people called Methodists, who were lately come into the western part of New England. There were various reports and opinions concerning them. Some said they were the deceivers that were to come in the last times; that such a delusive spirit attended them, that it was dangerous to hear them preach, lest they should lead people out of the good old way which they had been brought up in; and that they would deceive if possible the very elect. Some, on the other hand, said they were a good sort of people.

A certain man invited Hope Hull to come to his own town, who appointed a time when he would endeavor, if possible, to comply with his request. The day arrived, and the people flocked out from every quarter to hear, as they supposed, a new gospel. I went to the door and looked in to see a Methodist; but to my surprise he appeared like other men. I heard him preach from—"This is a faithful saying and worthy of all acception, that Christ Jesus came into the world to save sinners." And I thought he told me all that ever I did.

The next day he preached from these words: "Is there no balm in Gilead? Is there no Physician there? Why then is not the health of the daughter of my people recovered?" Jer. viii. 22.

As he drew the analogy between a person sick of a consumption and a sin-sick soul, he endeavored also to show how the real balm of Gilead would heal the consumption; and to spiritualize it, in the blood of Christ healing the soul; in which he described the way to heaven, and pointed out the way-marks, which I had never heard described so clearly before. I was convinced that this man enjoyed something that I was destitute of, and consequently that he was a servant of God.

He then got upon the application, and pointing his finger towards me, made this expression: "Sinner, there is a frowning Providence above your head, and a burning hell beneath your feet; and nothing but the brittle thread of life prevents your soul from falling into endless perdition. But, says the sinner, What must I do? You must pray. But I can't pray. If you don't pray, then you'll be damned." And as he brought out the last expression he either stamped with his foot on the box on which he stood, or smote with his hand upon the Bible, which both together came home like a dagger to my heart. I had like to have fallen backwards from my seat, but saved myself by catching hold of my cousin who sat by my side, and I durst not stir for some time for fear lest I should tumble into hell. My sins, and the damnable nature of them, were in a moment exhibited to my view; and I was convinced that I was unprepared to die.

After the assembly was dismissed, I went out of doors. All nature seemed to wear a gloomy aspect; and every thing I cast my eyes upon seemed to bend itself against me, and wish me off the face of the earth.

I went to a funeral of one of my acquaintance the same day, but durst not look upon the corpse, for fear of becoming one myself. I durst not go near the grave, fearing lest I should fall in, and the earth come in upon me; for if I then died, I knew I must be undone. So I went home with a heavy heart.

I durst not close my eyes in sleep, until I first attempted to supplicate the throne of grace for preservation through the night. The next morning, as I went out of doors, a woman passing by told me that my cousin the evening before had found the pardoning love of God. This surprised me, that one of my companions was taken and I was left. I instantly came to a resolution to forsake my sins and seek the salvation of my soul. I made it my practice to pray thrice in a day for about the space of a week; when another of my cousins, brother to the former, was brought to cry for mercy in secret retirement in a garden, and his cries were so loud that he was heard upwards of a mile. The same evening he found comfort.

One evening there being, by my desire, a prayer-meeting appointed by the young converts, I set out to go; and on my way, by the side of a wood, I kneeled down and made a solemn promise to God, if he would pardon my sins and give me an evidence of my acceptance, that I would forsake all those things wherein I had formerly thought to have taken my happiness, and lead a religious life devoted to him; and with this promise I went to meeting.

I believe that many present felt the power of God. Saints were happy and sinners were weeping on every side: but I could not shed a tear. Then I thought within myself, if I could weep I would begin to take hope; but, oh! how hard is my heart! I went from one to another to know if there was any mercy for me. The young converts answered, "God is all love; he is all mercy." I replied, "God is just too, and justice will cut me down." I saw no way how God could be *just* and yet show me mercy.

When I got home, I went into my bedroom; and, kneeling down, I strove to look to God for mercy again; but found no comfort. I then lay down to rest, but durst not close my eyes in sleep, for fear I should never awake, until I awaked in endless misery.

I strove to plead with God for mercy, for several hours, as a man would plead for his life; until at length being weary in body, as the night was far spent, I fell into a slumber.

I thought I heard the voice of God's justice saying, "Take the unprofitable servant, and cast him into utter darkness." I put my hands together, and cried in my heart, "The time has been, that I might have had religion, but now it is too late; mercy's gate is shut against me, and my condemnation for ever sealed:—Lord, I

273

give up; I submit; I yield; if there be mercy in heaven for me, let me know it; and if not, let me go down to hell and know the worst of my case." As these words flowed from my heart, I saw the Mediator step in, as it were, between the Father's justice and my soul, and these words were applied to my mind with great power; "Son! thy sins which are many are forgiven thee; thy faith hath saved thee; go in peace."

The burden of sin and guilt and the fear of hell vanished from my mind, as perceptibly as a hundred pounds weight falling from a man's shoulder; my soul flowed out in love to God, to his ways and to his people; yea, and to *all* mankind.

As soon as I obtained deliverance, I said in my heart, I have now found Jesus and his religion, but I will keep it to myself. But instantly my soul was so filled with peace, and love, and joy, that I could no more keep it to myself, seemingly, than a city set on a hill could be hid. At this time daylight dawned into the window. I arose, and went out of doors; and, behold, every thing I cast my eye upon, seemed to be speaking forth the praise and wonders of the Almighty. It appeared more like a new world than any thing else I can compare it to. This happiness is easier felt than described.

CHAPTER II
CALL TO PREACH, ETC.

One day being alone in a solitary place, whilst kneeling before God, these words were suddenly impressed on my mind: "Go ye into all the world, and preach the gospel to every creature." I instantly spoke out, "Lord, I am a child, I cannot go; I cannot preach." These words followed in my mind: "Arise, and go, for I have sent you." I said, "Send by whom thou wilt send, only not by me, for I am an ignorant, illiterate youth, not qualified for the important task." The reply was, "What God hath cleansed, call not thou common." I resisted the impression as a temptation of the devil; and then my Saviour withdrew from me the light of his countenance. I dared not believe that God had called me to preach, for fear of being deceived; and durst not disbelieve it, for fear of grieving the Spirit of God: thus I halted between two opinions.

1794

One day a prayer meeting being appointed in the town, and I feeling it my indispensable duty to go, I sought for my parents' consent in vain. Still, something was crying in my ears, "Go, go;" but fearing that my parents would call me a disobedient child, I resisted what I believe was required of me, and felt conscience to accuse me, and darkness to cover my mind. But at length, finding a spirit of prayer, I had faith to believe that God would bless me, though from the fourteenth of May to the ninth of June, I felt the sharp, keen, fiery darts of the enemy.

Sunday, October fifth, was the first time that I (with a trembling mind) attempted to open my mouth in public vocal prayer in the society.

A little previous to this time, upon considering what I must undergo if I entered upon the public ministry, I began to feel discouraged, and had thoughts of altering the situation of my life to excuse me from the work; but I could get no peace of mind until I gave them entirely up, though my trials in this respect were exceedingly great.

Nov. 19th

My mind has been buffeted and greatly agitated, not tempted in the common sense of the word, so that my sleep departed from me, and caused me to walk and wring my hands for sorrow. Oh, *the corruption of wicked* nature! I feel the plague of a hard heart, and a mind prone to wander from God; something within which has need to be done away, and causes a burden, but no guilt, and from which discouragements frequently arise tending to slacken my hands.

I dreamed that I saw a man in a convulsion fit, and his countenance was expressive of hell. I asked a bystander what made his countenance look so horrible. Said he, "The man was sick and relating his past experience, his calls from time to time, and his promises to serve God; and how he had broke them; and now, said he, I am sealed over to eternal damnation, and instantly the convulsion seized him." This shocked me so much that I instantly awaked, and seemingly the man was before my eyes.

I dropped asleep again, and thought I saw all mankind in the air suspended by a brittle thread over hell, yet in a state of carnal security. I thought it to be my duty to tell them of it, and again awaked; and these words were applied to my mind with power: "There is a dispensation of the gospel committed unto you, and wo unto you if you preach not the gospel." I strove to turn my mind on something else; but it so strongly followed me, that I took it as a warning from God. And in the morning, to behold the beautiful sun to arise and shine into the window, whilst these words followed—"Unto you that fear my name, shall the Sun of Righteousness arise, with healing in his wings"—Oh! how happy I felt! The help of kings and priests is vain without the help of God.

December 31st

The year is now at a close. I see what I have passed through. What is to come the ensuing year, God only knows. But may the God of peace be with me, and grant me strength in proportion to my day, that I may endure to the end, and receive the crown of life. I felt my heart drawn to travel the world at large; but to trust God by faith, like the birds, for my daily bread was difficult, as my strength was small; and I shrunk from it.

CHAPTER III

MY BEGINNING TO TRAVEL

1796

March 30th. This morning early I set out for Rhode Island in quest of J. Lee, who was to attend a quarterly meeting there. As I was coming away, we joined in prayer, taking leave of each other; and as I got on my road, I looked about, and espied my mother looking after me until I got out of sight; this caused me some tender feelings afterwards.

Until this time I have enjoyed the comforts of a kind father's house; and oh! must I now become a wanderer and stranger upon earth until I get to my long-home!

Monday, October 10th

I rode twenty miles to Adams, and thence to Stanford: at these places we had refreshing seasons.

Wednesday, 12th

I rode thirty miles across the Green Mountain, in fifteen of which there was not a sign of a house; and the road being new, it frequently was almost impassable. However, I reached my appointment, and though weary in body, my soul was happy in God.

Leaving the state of Vermont, I crossed Connecticut river, through Northfield to Warwick, Massachusetts, where we had a refreshing season.

Thence I went to Orange, and preached in the Presbyterian meeting house, the clergyman having left the town. Being this day nineteen years old, I addressed myself to the youth. I spent a few days here; and, though meeting with some opposition, we had refreshing seasons.

October 20th

Satan pursues me from place to place. Oh! how can people dispute there being a devil! If they underwent as much as I do with his buffetings, they would dispute it no more. He throwing in his fiery darts, my mind is harassed like punching the body with forks and clubs. Oh that my Saviour would appear and sanctify my soul, and deliver me from all within that is contrary to purity!

23rd

I spoke in Hardwick to about four hundred people, thence went to Petersham and Wenchendon, to Fitchburgh, and likewise to Notown, where God gave me one spiritual child. Thence to Ashburnham, where we had some powerful times.

November 1st

I preached in Ringe, and a powerful work of God broke out shortly after, though some opposition attended it; but it was very solemn.

Some here, I trust, will bless God in the day of eternity that ever they saw my face in this vale of tears.

In my happiest moments I feel something that wants to be done away. Oh! the buffeting of Satan! if I never had any other hell, it would be enough.

Thence proceeded to Marlborough, where our meetings were not in vain.

Whilst I am preaching I feel happy. But as soon as I have done, I feel such horror, without guilt, by the buffetings of Satan, that I am ready to sink like a drowning man, sometimes to that degree that I have to hold my tongue between my teeth to keep from uttering blasphemous expressions; and I can get rid of these horrible feelings only by retirement in earnest prayer and exertion of faith in God.

Part Second

CHAPTER I
CAROLINAS AND TENNESSEE TOUR

October 28th, 1803

After an absence of about seven months, I arrived back in Georgia, having travelled upwards of four thousand miles. When I left this state, I was handsomely equipped for travelling, by some friends whom God had raised me up in time of need, after my trials on my journey from New England. My equipment was as follows: My horse cost forty-five pounds, a decent saddle and cloth, portmanteau and bag, umbrella and lady's shove whip, a double suit of clothes, a blue broadcloth cloak (given me by a gentleman), shoes, stockings, cased hat, a valuable watch, with fifty-three dollars in my pocket for spending-money, &c., &c. But now on my return I had not the same valuable horse, and my watch I parted with for pecuniary aid to bear my expenses. My pantaloons were worn out, and my riding chevals were worn through in several places.

I had no stockings, shoes, nor moccasins, for the last several hundred miles, nor outer garment, having sold my cloak in West Florida. My coat and vest were worn through to my shirt; my hat-case and umbrella were spoiled by prongs of trees, whilst riding in the woods. Thus with decency I was scarcely able to get back to my friends as I would. It is true, I had many pounds and handsome presents offered me in my journey, but I could not feel freedom to receive them, only just what would serve my present necessity, to get along to my appointments, as I was such a stranger in the country, and so many to watch me (as an impostor) for evil, and but few to lift up my hands for good.

As I considered that the success and opening of many years depended on these days, I was not willing to give any occasion for the gospel to be blamed, or any occasion to hedge up my way. For it was with seriousness and consideration that I undertook these journeys, from conviction of duty, that God required it at my hands. And, knowing that impostors are fond of money, I was convinced that Satan would not be found wanting to whisper in the minds of the people, that my motives were sinister or impure.

Major John Oliver came and took me by the hand, calling me father, saying, "When you preached in Petersburgh last, your text was constantly ringing in my ears, for days together, whether I would deal kindly and truly with the Master, &c.; so I had no peace until I set out to seek the Lord: and since, my wife and I have been brought to rejoice in the Almighty."

He gave me a vest, pantaloons, umbrella, stockings, handkerchief, and a watch, &c. Another gave me a pair of shoes and a coat, a third, a cloak, and a few shillings for spending-money from some others. Thus I find that Providence, whose tender care is over all his works, by his kind hand is still preserving me. Oh, may I never betray his great cause committed to my charge!

February 14th

I had heard about a singularity called the *jerks or jerking exercise,* which appeared first near Knoxville in August last, to the great alarm of the people, which reports at first I considered as vague and false. But at length, like the Queen of Sheba, I set out to go and see for myself, and sent over these appointments into this country accordingly.

When I arrived in sight of this town, I saw hundreds of people collected in little bodies, and observing no place appointed for meeting, before I spoke to any, I got on a log and gave out a hymn; which caused them to assemble around, in solemn attentive silence. I observed several involuntary motions in the course of the meeting, which I considered as a specimen of the jerks. I rode seven miles behind a man across streams of water, and held meeting in the evening, being ten miles on my way.

In the night I grew uneasy, being twenty-five miles from my appointment for next morning at eleven o'clock. I prevailed on a young man to attempt carrying me with horses until day, which he thought was impracticable, considering the darkness of the night, and the thickness of the trees. Solitary shrieks were heard in these woods, which he told me were said to be the cries of murdered persons. At day we parted, being still seventeen miles from the spot, and the ground covered with a white frost. I had not proceeded far, before I came to a stream of water, from the springs of the mountain, which made it dreadful cold. In my heated state I had to wade this stream five times in the course of an hour, which I perceived so affected my body, that my strength began to fail. Fears began to arise that I must disappoint the people, till I observed some fresh tracks of horses, which casued me to exert every nerve to overtake them, in hopes of aid or assistance on my journey, and soon I saw them on an eminence. I shouted for them to stop till I came up. They inquired what I wanted? I replied, I had heard there was a meeting at Seversville by a stranger, and was going to it. They replied, that they had heard that a crazy man was to hold forth there, and were going also; and perceiving that I was weary, they invited me to ride: and soon our company was increased to forty or fifty, who fell in with us on the road from different plantations. At length I was interrogated whether I knew any thing about the preacher. I replied, "I have heard a good deal about him, and have heard him preach, but I have no great opinion of him." And thus the conversation continued for some miles before they found me out, which caused some color and smiles in the company. Thus, I got on to meeting; and after taking a cup of tea gratis, I began to speak to a vast audience, and I observed about thirty to have the jerks. Though they strove to keep still as they could, these emotions were involuntary and irresistible, as any unprejudiced eye might discern. Lawyer Porter, who had come a considerable distance, got his heart touched under the word, and being informed how I came to meeting, voluntarily lent me a horse to ride near one hundred miles, and gave me a dollar, though he had never seen me before.

Hence to Marysville, where I spoke to about one thousand five hundred; and many appeared to feel the word, but about fifty felt the jerks. At night I lodged with one of the Nicholites, a kind of Quakers who do not feel free to wear colored clothes. I spoke to a number of people at his house that night. Whilst at tea, I observed his daughter (who sat opposite to me at table) to have the jerks, and dropped the tea-cup from her hand in the violent agitation. I said to her, "Young woman, what is the matter?" She replied, "I have got the jerks." I asked her how long she had it? She observed, "A few days," and that it had been the means of the awakening and conversion of her soul, by stirring her up to serious consideration about her careless state, &c.

Sunday, February 19th, I spoke in Knoxville to hundreds more than could get into the courthouse, the governor being present. About one hundred and fifty appeared to have the jerking exercise, among whom was a circuit preacher (Johnson) who had opposed them a little before, but he now had them powerfully; and I believe he would have fallen over three times had not the auditory been so crowded that he could not unless he fell perpendicularly.

After meeting, I rode eighteen miles to hold a meeting at night. The people of this settlement were mostly Quakers, and they had said (as I was informed) the Methodists and Presbyterians have the *jerks* because they *sing* and *pray* so much; but we are a still, peaceable people, wherefore we do not have them. However, about twenty of them came to the meeting, to hear one, as they said, somewhat in a Quaker line. But their usual stillness and silence was interrupted, for about a dozen of them had the jerks as keen and as powerful as any I had seen, so as to have occasioned a kind of grunt or groan when they would jerk. It appears that many have undervalued the great revival, and attempted to account for it altogether on natural principles; therefore it seems to me (from the best judgment I can form) that God hath seen proper to take this method to convince people, that he will work in a way to show his power, and sent the *jerks* as a sign of the times, partly in judgment for the people's unbelief, and yet as a mercy to convict people of divine realities.

I have seen Presbyterians, Methodists, Quakers, Baptists, Episcopalians, and Independents, exercised with the *jerks*—gentleman and lady, black and white, the aged and the youth, rich and poor, without exception; from which I infer, as it cannot be accounted for on natural principles, and carries such marks of involuntary motion, that it is no trifling matter. I believe that those who are most pious and given up to God, are rarely touched with it, and also those naturalists who wish and try to get it to philosophize upon it, are excepted. But the lukewarm, lazy, half-hearted, indolent professor is subject to it; and many of them I have seen, who, when it came upon them, would be alarmed and stirred up to redouble their diligence with God; and after they would get happy, were thankful it ever came upon them. Again, the wicked are frequently more afraid of it than the small-pox or yellow fever; these are subject to it. But the persecutors are more subject to it than any; and they sometimes have cursed, and swore, and damned it whilst jerking. There is no pain attending the jerks except they resist it, which if they do, it will weary them more in an hour than a day's labor, which shows that it requires the *consent* of the *will* to avoid suffering.

20th

I passed by a meeting-house, where I observed the undergrowth had been cut up for a camp-meeting, and from 50 to 100 saplings left breast-high, which to me appeared so slovenish that I could not but ask my guide the cause, who observed they were topped so high and left for the people to jerk by. This so excited my attention that I went over the ground to view it, and found where the people had laid hold of them and jerked so powerfully that they had kicked up the earth as a horse stamping flies. I observed some emotion both this day and night among the people. A Presbyterian minister (with whom I stayed) observed, "Yesterday whilst I was preaching some had the jerks, and a young man from North Carolina mimicked them out of derision, and was seized with them himself (which was the case with many others). He grew ashamed, and on attempting to mount his horse to go off, his foot jerked about so that he could not put it into the stirrup; some youngsters seeing this assisted him on, but he jerked so that he could not sit alone, and one got up to hold him on, which was done with difficulty. I observing this, went to him and asked him what he thought of it?" Said he, "I believe God sent it on me for my wickedness, and making so light of it in others;" and he requested me to pray for him.

I observed his wife had it; she said she was first attacked with it in bed. Dr. Nelson said he had frequently strove to get it in order to philosophize upon it, but could not, and observed they could not account for it on natural principles.

Friday, 19th

Camp-meeting commenced at Liberty. Here I saw the *jerks;* and some danced: a strange exercise indeed. However, it is involuntary, yet requires the consent of the will: i. e. the people are taken jerking irresistibly; and if they strive to resist it, it worries them much: yet is attended by no bodily pain, and those who are exercised to dance, (which in the pious seems an antidote to the jerks.), if they resist, it brings deadness and barrenness over the mind; but when they yield to it they feel happy, although it is a great cross. There is a heavenly smile and solemnity on the countenance, which carries a great conviction to the minds of beholders. Their eyes when dancing seem to be fixed upwards, as if upon an invisible object, and they lost to all below.

Sunday, 21st

I heard Doctor Tooley, a man of liberal education, who had been a noted deist, preach on the subject of the jerks and the dancing exercise. He brought ten passages of scripture to prove that dancing was once a religious exercise, but corrupted at Aaron's calf, and from thence young people got it for amusement. I believe the congregation and preachers were generally satisfied with his remarks.

Sunday, 25th

I spoke for the last time at Natchez. I visited Seltzertown, Greenville, and Gibson Port. This last place was a wilderness not two years ago, but now contains near thirty houses, with a courthouse and jail. We held a quarterly meeting on Clarke's creek. Some supposed I would get no campers, but at this quarterly meeting I wanted to know if there were any backsliders in the auditory, and if there were and they would come forward, I would pray with them. An old backslider, who had been happy in the old settlement, with tears came forward and fell upon his knees, and several followed his example. A panic seized the congregation, and a solemn awe ensued. We had a cry and shout, and it was a weeping, tender time. The devil was angry, and some without persecuted, saying, "Is God deaf, that they cannot worship him without such a noise?" though they perhaps would make a greater noise when drinking a toast. This prepared the way for the camp-meeting, and about thirty from this neighborhood went thirty miles or upwards, and encamped on the ground. The camp-meeting continued four days. The devil was angry at this also, and though his emissaries contrived various projects to raise a dust, their efforts proved ineffectual. In general there was good decorum, and about fifty were awakened, and five professed justifying faith; so that it may now be said that the country which was a refuge for scape-gallowses a few years since, in Spanish times, is in a hopeful way, and the wilderness begins to bud and blossom as the rose, and the barren land becomes a fruitful field. I crossed the Mississippi into Louisiana, and visited several settlements, holding religious meetings. I believe there is a peculiar providence in such a vast territory falling to the United States, as liberty of conscience may now prevail as the country populates, which before was prohibited by the inquisition.

27

The Transit of Culture

Benjamin Henry Latrobe (1764–1820) was trained as an architect and engineer in Europe. He emigrated to America in 1796, and spent several years in Virginia, planning houses and civil engineering projects. Among his other assignments was the exterior of the Virginia State Capitol, which had been designed by Thomas Jefferson.

Latrobe's most famous work, however, was done in Philadelphia and Washington. He designed the Bank of Pennsylvania, the first major Greek revival building in America, and planned the famous Philadelphia Water-works. In 1803 Jefferson appointed him surveyor of the public buildings in Washington, where he helped complete the Capitol, and he was involved with its reconstruction after the British burned it during the War of 1812. Besides his numerous building and engineering projects, which included work in Baltimore and New Orleans, Latrobe trained a series of influential pupils who helped erect the great monuments of the next generation. An accomplished scholar and linguist, he also wrote some important reports and addresses on the subject of engineering and the fine arts.

THE JOURNAL
OF LATROBE

The President of the United States

Philadelphia, May 21, 1807
Sir:

I am very sensible of the honor you do me in discussing with me the merits of the detail of the public building. I know well that *to you* it is my duty to obey implicitly or to resign my office: to myself it is my duty to maintain myself in a situation in which I can provide for my family by all honorable means. If in any instance my duty to you obliged me to act contrary to my judgment, I might fairly and honorably say with Shakespeare's apothecary: "My poverty, not my will consents." Such excuse, however, I have never wanted, for although in respect to the panel lights I am acting diametrically contrary to my judgment, no mercenary motive whatever has kept me at my post, but considerations very superior to

From Benjamin Henry Latrobe, *The Journal of Latrobe* (New York, 1905), 137–141, 205–209.

money—the attachment arising from gratitude and the highest esteem. At the same time I candidly confess that the question has suggested itself to my mind: What shall I do when the condensed vapor of the hall showers down upon the heads of the members from one hundred skylights, as it now does from the skylights of our anatomical hall, as it did from the six skylights of the Round House, as it does from the lantern of the Pennsylvania Bank, and as it does from that of our university—an event I believe to be as certain as that cold air and cold glass will condense warm vapor? This question I have asked myself for many months past. I shall certainly not cut my throat as the engineer of Staines Bridge did when the battlement failed, and his beautiful bridge fell because the commissioners had ordered him to proceed contrary to his judgment. But I dare not think long enough on the subject to frame an answer to my own mind, but go blindly on, hoping that "*fata viano invenient*" [fate will find a way].

In respect to the general subject of cupolas, I do not think that they are *always,* nor even *often,* ornamental. My *principles* of good taste are rigid in Grecian architecture. I am a bigoted Greek in the condemnation of the Roman architecture of Baalbec, Palmyra, Spaletro, and of all the buildings erected subsequent to Hadrian's reign. The immense size, the bold plan and arrangements of the buildings of the Romans down almost to Constantine's arch, plundered from the triumphal arches of former emperors, I admire, however, with enthusiasm, but think their decorations and details absurd beyond tolerance from the reign of Severus downward. Wherever, therefore, the Grecian style can be copied without impropriety, I love to be a mere, I would say a *slavish,* copyist, but the forms and the distribution of the Roman and Greek buildings which remain are in general inapplicable to the objects and uses of our public buildings. Our religion requires churches wholly different from the temples, our Government, our legislative assemblies, and our courts of justice, buildings of entirely different principles from their basilicas; and our amusements could not possibly be performed in their theaters or amphitheaters. But that which principally demands a variation in our buildings from those of the ancients is the difference of our climate. To adhere to the subject of cupolas, although the want of a belfry, which is an Eastern accession to our religious buildings, rendered them necessary appendages to the church, yet I cannot admit that because the Greeks and Romans did not place elevated cupolas upon their temples, they may not when necessary be rendered also beautiful. The Lanthorne of Demosthenes, than which nothing of the kind can be more beautiful, is mounted upon a magnificent mass of architecture harmonizing with it in character and style. The question would be as to its real or apparent utility in the place in which it appeared, for nothing in the field of good taste, which ought never to be at warfare with good sense, can be beautiful which appears useless or unmeaning.

If our climate were such as to admit of doing legislative business in open air, that is under the light of an open orifice in the crown of a dome, as at the Parthenon, I would never put a cupola on any spherical dome. It is not the *ornament,* it is the *use* that I want.

If you will be pleased to refer to Degodetz, you will see that there is a rim

283

projecting above the arch of the Parthenon at the opening. This rim, in the dome projected for the centerpiece of the Capitol, is raised by me into a low pedestal for the purpose of covering a skylight, which could then be admitted, although I think it inadmissible in a room of business. But I should prefer the hemisphere, I confess. As to the members of Congress, with the utmost respect for the Legislature, I should scarcely *consult*, but rather *dictate* in matters of taste.

I beg pardon for this trespass on your time. You have spoiled me by your former indulgence in hearing my opinions expressed with candor.

Peculiar Customs

March 18, 1819

I went, this morning, with Mr. Planton to see his wife's picture of the Treaty of Ghent. It is an excellent painting in many points of view, and there are parts of it, separate figures and groups, that have very extraordinary merit. But its inherent sin, especially in America, is its being an allegorical picture. When the mythology of antiquity was the substance of its religion, and the character and history of every deity were known to every individual of the nation, allegorical representations were a kind of written description of the subject represented, and might be generally understood. But since Hercules and Minerva and the rest of the deities are in fashion only as decorations of juvenile poetry, and are known by character only to those few who have had classical educations, an allegorical picture stands as much in need of an interpreter as an Indian talk.

Mrs. Planton has painted exceedingly well, but has judged very ill. In another respect, also, her American feeling has betrayed her into error. She has painted a picture of the largest size in oil, of course a picture calculated for duration, and forming an historical record, to represent evanescent feelings, the feelings of unexpected and, of course, riotous and unreasonable triumph. Britannia is represented as laying her flag, her rudder (emblems of naval superiority), her laurels, and other symbols of victory and dominion, at the feet of America, who approaches in a triumphal car. She kneels in the posture of an humble suppliant, while Hercules and Minerva threaten her with the club and the spear: all this is caricature. But the whole of this group, excepting Hercules, is admirably painted. The figure of Britannia is very graceful and well drawn, and the drapery has superior merit. The group on the right is also uncommonly well conceived and executed. The whole picture does, indeed, infinite credit to the artist and to her country, for she is a Philadelphian. The great fault is the choice of the subject, for the signing of negotiation of a treaty, as a matter of fact, can at best be but a collection of expressive likenesses of persons writing or conversing, and has nothing picturesque about it. Strength, fortitude, courage, and some good luck, on our side, were not wanting to "conquer the treaty," in the French fashionable phrase; and admirable talent was displayed in the negotiation. But these are not very well paintable.

As to allegory, generally it is a most difficult branch of the art of the painter and sculptor, and belongs rather to the poetical department. Yet sometimes the sculptor and painter have succeeded in rendering sentiment intelligible by the chisel and pencil; for instance, in the personification of Peace, by Canova, where a pair of doves make their nest in a helmet.

Some years ago Dr. Thornton, of Washington, described, before a large company, the allegorical group which it was his intention, as commissioner of the city of Washington, to place in the center of the Capitol, around the statue of the general.

"I would," said he, "place an immense rock of granite in the center of the dome. On the top of the rock should stand a beautiful female figure, to represent Eternity or Immortality. Around her neck, as a necklace, a serpent—the rattlesnake of our country—should be hung, with its tail in its mouth—the ancient and beautiful symbol of endless duration. At the foot of the rock another female figure, stretching her hands upward in the attitude of distressful entreaty, should appear, ready to climb the steep. Around her a group of children, representing Agriculture, the Arts and Sciences, should appear to join in the supplication of the female. This female is to personify Time, or our present state of existence. Just ascending the rock, the noble figure of General Washington should appear to move upward, invited by Immortality, but also expressing some reluctance in leaving the children of his care.

"There," said he, "Mr. Latrobe, is your requisite in such works of art; it would represent a matter of fact, a truth, for it would be the very picture of the general's sentiments, feelings, and expectations in departing this life—regret at leaving his people, but hoping and longing for an immortality of happiness and of fame. You yourself have not ingenuity sufficient to pervert its meaning, and all posterity would understand it."

The doctor was so full of his subject that I was unwilling to disturb his good humor; but I said that I thought his group might tell a very different story from what he intended. He pressed me so hard that at last I told him that, supposing the name and character of General Washington to be forgotten, or at least that the group had been found in the ruins of the Capitol, and the learned antiquarians of two thousand years hence were assembled to decide its meaning, I thought then that they would thus explain it:

"There is a beautiful woman on the top of a dangerous precipice, to which she invites a man, apparently well enough inclined to follow her. Who is this woman? Certainly not a very good sort of a one, for she has a snake about her neck. The snake indicates, assuredly, her character—cold, cunning, and poisonous. She can represent none but some celebrated courtesan of the day. But there is another woman at the foot of the rock, modest and sorrowful, and surrounded by a family of small children. She is in a posture of entreaty, and the man appears half-inclined to return to her. She can be no other than his wife. What an expressive group! How admirable the art which has thus exposed the dangerous precipice to which the beauty and the cunning of the abandoned would entice the virtuous, even to the desertion of a beautiful wife and the mother of a delightful group of children!"

I was going on, but the laughter of the company and the impatience of the doctor stopped my mouth. I had said enough, and was not easily forgiven.

28

The Cost of Embargo

Henry Adams (1838–1918) was a great-grandson of one President and grandson of another. Although he failed to gain political power or prominence himself, he turned from his anger with the incivilities of the late nineteenth century to immerse himself in the chronicles of earlier, more inspiring eras. He became an accomplished historian, teaching for a number of years at Harvard before moving to Washington. There, he turned to the early national period, producing biographies of Albert Gallatin and John Randolph. In 1889 he published the first two volumes of his *History of the United States*, which covered the first administration of Jefferson. In the next two years he published seven more volumes, which went through 1816 and the last years of James Madison's Presidency.

Adams' portrait of Thomas Jefferson, his great-grandfather's friend and antagonist, was a masterful and ironic glimpse of unsuccessful statesmanship. The image of the great Republican leader, unintentionally destroying the sources of his political power in his desperate search to avoid war, was one of the great aesthetic accomplishments of the *History*. It was also, of course, a vindication and defense of Adams' own distinguished ancestor.

THE SECOND ADMINISTRATION OF THOMAS JEFFERSON
Henry Adams

CHAPTER XII

The embargo was an experiment in politics well worth making. In the scheme of President Jefferson's statesmanship, non-intercourse was the substitute for war,—the weapon of defence and coercion which saved the cost and danger of supporting army or navy, and spared America the brutalities of the Old World. Failure of the embargo meant in his mind not only a recurrence to the practice of war, but to every political and social evil that war had always brought in its train. In such a case the crimes and corruptions of Europe, which had been the object of his

From *History of the United States of America during the Second Administration of Thomas Jefferson* (New York, 1890), II: 272–289.

political fears, must, as he believed, sooner or later teem in the fat soil of America. To avert a disaster so vast, was a proper motive for statesmanship, and justified disregard for smaller interests. Jefferson understood better than his friends the importance of his experiment; and when in pursuing his object he trampled upon personal rights and public principles, he did so, as he avowed in the Louisiana purchase, because he believed that a higher public interest required the sacrifice:—

"My principle is, that the conveniences of our citizens shall yield reasonably, and their taste greatly, to the importance of giving the present experiment so fair a trial that on future occasions our legislators may know with certainty how far they may count on it as an engine for national purposes."

Hence came his repeated entreaties for severity, even to the point of violence and bloodshed:—

"I do consider the severe enforcement of the embargo to be of an importance not to be measured by money, for our future government as well as present objects."

Everywhere, on all occasions, he proclaimed that embargo was the alternative to war. The question next to be decided was brought by this means into the prominence it deserved. Of the two systems of statesmanship, which was the most costly,—which the most efficient?

The dread of war, radical in the Republican theory, sprang not so much from the supposed waste of life or resources as from the retroactive effects which war must exert upon the form of government; but the experience of a few months showed that the embargo as a system was rapidly leading to the same effects. Indeed, the embargo and the Louisiana purchase taken together were more destructive to the theory and practice of a Virginia republic than any foreign war was likely to be. Personal liberties and rights of property were more directly curtailed in the United States by embargo than in Great Britain by centuries of almost continuous foreign war. No one denied that a permanent embargo strained the Constitution to the uttermost tension; and even the Secretary of the Treasury and the President admitted that it required the exercise of the most arbitrary, odious, and dangerous powers. From this point of view the system was quickly seen to have few advantages. If American liberties must perish, they might as well be destroyed by war as be stifled by non-intercourse.

While the constitutional cost of the two systems was not altogether unlike, the economical cost was a point not easily settled. No one could say what might be the financial expense of embargo as compared with war. Yet Jefferson himself in the end admitted that the embargo had no claim to respect as an economical measure. The Boston Federalists estimated that the net American loss of income, exclusive of that on freights, could not be less than ten per cent for interest and profit on the whole export of the country,—or ten million eight hundred thousand dollars on a total export value of one hundred and eight millions. This estimate was extravagant, even if the embargo had been wholly responsible for cutting off American trade; it represented in fact the loss resulting to America from Napoleon's decrees, the British orders, and the embargo taken together. Yet at least the embargo was more destructive than war would have been to the interests of foreign commerce.

287

Even in the worst of foreign wars American commerce could not be wholly stopped,—some outlet for American produce must always remain open, some inward bound ships would always escape the watch of a blockading squadron. Even in 1814, after two years of war, and when the coast was stringently blockaded, the American Treasury collected six million dollars from imports; but in 1808, after the embargo was in full effect, the customs yielded only a few thousand dollars on cargoes that happened to be imported for some special purpose. The difference was loss, to the disadvantage of embargo. To this must be added loss of freight, decay of ships and produce, besides enforced idleness to a corresponding extent; and finally the cost of a war if the embargo system should fail.

In other respects the system was still costly. The citizen was not killed, but he was partially paralyzed. Government did not waste money or life, but prevented both money and labor from having their former value. If long continued, embargo must bankrupt the government almost as certainly as war; if not long continued, the immediate shock to industry was more destructive than war would have been. The expense of war proved, five years afterward, to be about thirty million dollars a year, and of this sum much the larger portion was pure loss; but in 1808, owing to the condition of Europe, the expense need not have exceeded twenty millions, and the means at hand were greater. The effect of the embargo was certainly no greater than the effect of war in stimulating domestic industry. In either case the stimulus was temporary and ineffective; but the embargo cut off the resources of credit and capital, while war gave both an artificial expansion. The result was that while embargo saved perhaps twenty millions of dollars a year and some thousands of lives which war would have consumed, it was still an expensive system, and in some respects more destructive than war itself to national wealth.

The economical was less serious than the moral problem. The strongest objection to war was not its waste of money or even of life; for money and life in political economy were worth no more than they could be made to produce. A worse evil was the lasting harm caused by war to the morals of mankind, which no system of economy could calculate. The reign of brute force and brutal methods corrupted and debauched society, making it blind to its own vices and ambitious only for mischief. Yet even on that ground the embargo had few advantages. The peaceable coercion which Jefferson tried to substitute for war was less brutal, but hardly less mischievous, than the evil it displaced. The embargo opened the sluice-gates of social corruption. Every citizen was tempted to evade or defy the laws. At every point along the coast and frontier the civil, military, and naval services were brought in contact with corruption; while every man in private life was placed under strong motives to corrupt. Every article produced or consumed in the country became an object of speculation; every form of industry became a form of gambling. The rich could alone profit in the end; while the poor must sacrifice at any loss the little they could produce.

If war made men brutal, at least it made them strong; it called out the qualities best fitted to survive in the struggle for existence. To risk life for one's country was no mean act even when done for selfish motives; and to die that others might more happily live was the highest act of self-sacrifice to be reached by man. War, with all its horrors, could purify as well as debase; it dealt with high motives and vast interests; taught courage, discipline, and stern sense of duty. Jefferson must have asked himself in vain what lessons of heroism or duty were taught by his system of peaceable coercion, which turned every citizen into an enemy of the laws,—preaching the fear of war and of self-sacrifice, making many smugglers and traitors, but not a single hero.

If the cost of the embargo was extravagant in it effects on the Constitution, the economy, and the morals of the nation, its political cost to the party in power was ruinous. War could have worked no more violent revolution. The trial was too severe for human nature to endure. At a moment's notice, without avowing his true reasons, President Jefferson bade foreign commerce to cease. As the order was carried along the seacoast, every artisan dropped his tools, every merchant closed his doors, every ship was dismantled. American produce—wheat, timber, cotton, tobacco, rice—dropped in value or became unsalable; every imported article rose in price; wages stopped; swarms of debtors became bankrupt; thousands of sailors hung idle round the wharves trying to find employment on coasters, and escape to the West Indies or Nova Scotia. A reign of idleness began; and the men who were not already ruined felt that their ruin was only a matter of time.

The British traveller, Lambert, who visited New York in 1808, described it as resembling a place ravaged by pestilence:

"The port indeed was full of shipping, but they were dismantled and laid up; their decks were cleared, their hatches fastened down, and scarcely a sailor was to be found on board. Not a box, bale, cask, barrel, or package was to be seen upon the wharves. Many of the counting-houses were shut up, or advertised to be let; and the few solitary merchants, clerks, porters, and laborers that were to be seen were walking about with their hands in their pockets. The coffee-houses were almost empty; the streets, near the water-side, were almost deserted; the grass had begun to grow upon the wharves."

In New England, where the struggle of existence was keenest, the embargo struck like a thunderbolt, and society for a moment thought itself at an end. Foreign commerce and shipping were the life of the people,—the ocean, as Pickering said, was their farm. The outcry of suffering interests became every day more violent, as the public learned that this paralysis was not a matter of weeks, but of months or years. New Englanders as a class were a law-abiding people; but from the earliest moments of their history they had largely qualified their obedience to the law by the violence with which they abused and the ingenuity with which they evaded it. Against the embargo and Jefferson they concentrated the clamor and passion of their keen and earnest nature. Rich and poor, young and old, joined in the chorus; and one lad, barely in his teens, published what he called "The Embargo: a Satire,"—a boyish libel on Jefferson, which the famous poet and Democrat would afterward have given much to recall:—

"And thou, the scorn of every patriot name,
Thy country's ruin, and her councils' shame.

. . . .

289

Go, wretch! Resign the Presidential chair,
Disclose thy secret measures, foul or fair;
Go search with curious eye for hornèd frogs
'Mid the wild waste of Louisiana bogs;
Or where Ohio rolls his turbid stream
Dig for huge bones, thy glory and thy theme."

The belief that Jefferson, sold to France, wished to destroy American commerce and to strike a deadly blow at New and Old England at once, maddened the sensitive temper of the people. Immense losses, sweeping away their savings and spreading bankruptcy through every village, gave ample cause for their complaints. Yet in truth, New England was better able to defy the embargo than she was willing to suppose. She lost nothing except profits which the belligerents had in any case confiscated; her timber would not harm for keeping, and her fish were safe in the ocean. The embargo gave her almost a monopoly of the American market for domestic manufactures; no part of the country was so well situated or so well equipped for smuggling. Above all, she could easily economize. The New Englander knew better than any other American how to cut down his expenses to the uttermost point of parsimony; and even when he became bankrupt he had but to begin anew. His energy, shrewdness, and education were a capital which the embargo could not destroy, but rather helped to improve.

The growers of wheat and live stock in the Middle States were more hardly treated. Their wheat, reduced in value from two dollars to seventy-five cents a bushel, became practically unsalable. Debarred a market for their produce at a moment when every article of common use tended to rise in cost, they were reduced to the necessity of living on the produce of their farms; but the task was not then so difficult as in later times, and the cities still furnished local markets not to be despised. The manufacturers of Pennsylvania could not but feel the stimulus of the new demand; so violent a system of protection was never applied to them before or since. Probably for that reason the embargo was not so unpopular in Pennsylvania as elsewhere, and Jefferson had nothing to fear from political revolution in this calm and plodding community.

The true burden of the embargo fell on the Southern States, but most severely upon the great State of Virginia. Slowly decaying, but still half patriarchal, Virginia society could neither economize nor liquidate. Tobacco was worthless; but four hundred thousand negro slaves must be clothed and fed, great establishments must be kept up, the social scale of living could not be reduced, and even bankruptcy could not clear a large landed estate without creating new encumbrances in a country where land and negroes were the only forms of property on which money could be raised. Stay-laws were tried, but served only to prolong the agony. With astonishing rapidity Virginia succumbed to ruin, while continuing to support the system that was draining her strength. No episode in American history was more touching than the generous devotion with which Virginia clung to the embargo, and drained the poison which her own President held obstinately to her lips. The cotton and rice States had less to lose, and could more easily bear brankruptcy; ruin was to them—except in Charleston—a word of little meaning; but the old society of

Virginia could never be restored. Amid the harsh warnings of John Randolph it saw its agonies approach; and its last representative, heir to all its honors and dignities, President Jefferson himself woke from his long dream of power only to find his own fortunes buried in the ruin he had made.

Except in a state of society verging on primitive civilization, the stoppage of all foreign intercourse could not have been attempted by peaceable means. The attempt to deprive the laborer of sugar, salt, tea, coffee, molasses, and rum; to treble the price of every yard of coarse cottons and woollens; to reduce by one half the wages of labor, and to double its burdens,—this was a trial more severe than war; and even when attempted by the whole continent of Europe, with all the resources of manufactures and wealth which the civilization of a thousand years had supplied, the experiment required the despotic power of Napoleon and the united armies of France, Austria, and Russia to carry it into effect. Even then it failed. Jefferson, Madison, and the Southern Republicans had no idea of the economical difficulties their system created, and were surprised to find American society so complex even in their own Southern States that the failure of two successive crops to find a sale threatened beggary to every rich planter from the Delaware to the Sabine. During the first few months, while ships continued to arrive from abroad and old stores were consumed at home, the full pressure of the embargo was not felt; but as the summer of 1808 passed, the outcry became violent. In the Southern States, almost by common consent debts remained unpaid and few men ventured to oppose a political system which was peculiarly a Southern invention; but in the Northern States, where the bankrupt laws were enforced and the habits of business were comparatively strict, the cost of the embargo was soon shown in the form of political revolution.

The relapse of Massachusetts to Federalism and the overthrow of Senator Adams in the spring of 1808 were the first signs of the political price which President Jefferson must pay for his passion of peace. In New York the prospect was little better. Governor Morgan Lewis, elected in 1804 over Aaron Burr by a combination of Clintons and Livingstons, was turned out of office in 1807 by the Clintons. Governor Daniel D. Tompkins, his successor, was supposed to be a representative of De Witt Clinton and Ambrose Spencer. To De Witt Clinton the State of New York seemed in 1807 a mere appendage,—a political property which he could control at will; and of all American politicians next to Aaron Burr none had shown such indifference to party as he. No one could predict his course, except that it would be shaped according to what seemed to be the interests of his ambition. He began by declaring himself against the embargo, and soon afterward declared himself for it. In truth, he was for or against it as the majority might decide; and in New York a majority could hardly fail to decide against the embargo. At the spring election of 1808, which took place about May 1, the Federalists made large gains in the legislature. The summer greatly increased their strength, until Madison's friends trembled for the result, and their language became despondent beyond reason. Gallatin, who knew best the difficulties created by the embargo, began to despair. June 29 he wrote: "From present appearances the Federalists will turn us out by 4th of March next." Ten days afterward he explained the reason of his fears: "I think that Vermont is lost; New Hampshire is in a bad neighborhood; and Pennsylvania is extremely doubtful." In August he thought the situation so serious that he warned the President:—

"There is almost an equal chance that if propositions from Great Britain, or other events, do not put it in our power to raise the embargo before the 1st of October, we will lose the Presidential election. I think that at this moment the Western States, Virginia, South Carolina, and perhaps Georgia are the only sound States, and that we will have a doubtful contest in every other."

Two causes saved Madison. In the first place, the opposition failed to concentrate its strength. Neither George Clinton nor James Monroe could control the whole body of opponents to the embargo. After waiting till the middle of August for some arrangement to be made, leading Federalists held a conference at New York, where they found themselves obliged, by the conduct of De Witt Clinton, to give up the hope of a coalition. Clinton decided not to risk his fortunes for the sake of his uncle the Vice-President; and this decision obliged the Federalists to put a candidate of their own in the field. They named C. C. Pinckney of South Carolina for President, and Rufus King of New York for Vice-President, as in 1804.

From the moment his opponents divided themselves among three candidates, Madison had nothing to fear; but even without this good fortune he possessed an advantage that weighed decisively in his favor. The State legislatures had been chosen chiefly in the spring or summer, when the embargo was still comparatively popular; and in most cases, but particularly in New York, the legislature still chose Presidential electors. The people expressed no direct opinion on national politics, except in regard to Congressmen. State after State deserted to the Federalists without affecting the general election. Early in September Vermont elected a Federalist governor, but the swarm of rotten boroughs in the State secured a Republican legislature, which immediately chose electors for Madison. The revolution in Vermont surrendered all New England to the Federalists. New Hampshire chose Presidential electors by popular vote; Rhode Island did the same,—and both States, by fair majorities, rejected Madison and voted for Pinckney. In Massachusetts and Connecticut the legislatures chose Federalist electors. Thus all New England declared against the Administration; and had Vermont been counted as she voted in September, the opposition would have received forty-five electoral votes from New England, where in 1804 it had received only nine. In New York the opponents of the embargo were very strong, and the nineteen electoral votes of that State might in a popular election have been taken from Madison. In this case Pennsylvania would have decided the result. Eighty-eight electoral votes were needed for a choice. New England, New York, and Delaware represented sixty-seven. Maryland and North Carolina were so doubtful that if Pennsylvania had deserted Madison, they would probably have followed her, and would have left the Republican party a wreck.

The choice of electors by the legislatures of Vermont and New York defeated all chance of overthrowing Madison; but apart from these accidents of management the result was already decided by the people of Pennsylvania. The wave of

Federalist success and political revolution stopped short in New York, and once more the Democracy of Pennsylvania steadied and saved the Administration. At the October election of 1808,—old Governor McKean having at last retired,—Simon Snyder was chosen governor by a majority of more than twenty thousand votes. The new governor was the candidate of Duane and the extreme Democrats; his triumph stopped the current of Federalist success, and enabled Madison's friends to drive hesitating Republicans back to their party. In Virginia, Monroe was obliged to retire from the contest, and his supporters dwindled in numbers until only two or three thousand went to the polls. In New York, De Witt Clinton contented himself with taking from Madison six of the nineteen electoral votes and giving them to Vice-President Clinton. Thus the result showed comparatively little sign of the true Republican loss; yet in the electoral college where in 1804 Jefferson had received the voices of one hundred and sixty-two electors, Madison in 1808 received only one hundred and twenty-two votes. The Federalist minority rose from fourteen to forty-seven.

In the elections to Congress the same effects were shown. The Federalists doubled their number of Congressmen, but the huge Republican majority could well bear reduction. The true character of the Eleventh Congress could not be foretold by the party vote. Many Nothern Republicans chosen to Congress were as hostile to the embargo as though they had been Federalists. Elected on the issue of embargo or anti-embargo, the Congress which was to last till March 5, 1811, was sure to be factious; but whether factious or united, it could have neither policy nor leader. The election decided its own issue. The true issue thenceforward was that of war; but on this point the people had not been asked to speak, and their representatives would not dare without their encouragement to act.

The Republican party by a supreme effort kept itself in office; but no one could fail to see that if nine months of embargo had so shattered Jefferson's power, another such year would shake the Union itself. The cost of this "engine for national purposes" exceeded all calculation. Financially, it emptied the Treasury, bankrupted the mercantile and agricultural class, and ground the poor beyond endurance. Constitutionally, it overrode every specified limit on arbitrary power and made Congress despotic, while it left no bounds to the authority which might be vested by Congress in the President. Morally, it sapped the nation's vital force, lowering its courage, paralyzing its energy, corrupting its principles, and arraying all the active elements of society in factious opposition to government or in secret paths of treason. Politically, it cost Jefferson the fruits of eight years painful labor for popularity, and brought the Union to the edge of a precipice.

Finally, frightful as the cost of this engine was, as a means of coercion the embargo evidently failed. The President complained of evasion, and declared that if the measure were faithfully executed it would produce the desired effect; but the people knew better. In truth, the law was faithfully executed. The price-lists of Liverpool and London, the published returns from Jamaica and Havana, proved that American produce was no longer to be bought abroad. On the continent of Europe commerce had ceased before the embargo was laid, and its coercive effects were far exceeded by Napoleon's own restrictions; yet not a sign came from Europe to show that Napoleon meant to give way. From England came an answer to the embargo, but not such as promised its success. On all sides evidence accumulated that the embargo, as an engine of coercion, needed a long period of time to produce a decided effect. The law of physics could easily be applied to politics; force could be converted only into its equivalent force. If the embargo—an exertion of force less violent than war—was to do the work of war, it must extend over a longer time the development of an equivalent energy. Wars lasted for many years, and the embargo must be calculated to last much longer than any war; but meanwhile the morals, courage, and political liberties of the American people must be perverted or destroyed; agriculture and shipping must perish; the Union itself could not be preserved.

Under the shock of these discoveries Jefferson's vast popularity vanished, and the labored fabric of his reputation fell in sudden and general ruin. America began slowly to struggle, under the consciousness of pain, toward a conviction that she must bear the common burdens of humanity, and fight with the weapons of other races in the same bloody arena; that she could not much longer delude herself with hopes of evading laws of Nature and instincts of life; and that her new statesmanship which made peace a passion could lead to no better result than had been reached by the barbarous system which made war a duty.

29

Two Presidents Reminisce

Relations between America's second and third Presidents were not always good. Friends in their youth, both struggling in the cause of national independence, their subsequent political careers revealed deep differences in their philosophies of government as they fought each other for office and influence. After Jefferson left the White House in 1809, however, it was possible to effect a reconcilation with Adams. Their ambitions dormant, their greatness achieved, they could reflect on the nature of the society they had formed. Between 1813 and 1826 Adams and Jefferson exchanged a remarkable series of letters, discussing not only the issues of the day but speculating on the future, reminiscing about the past, and trading anecdotes and erudition on an enormous variety of subjects.

The following two letters, written shortly after their reconciliation took place, reveal something of the philosophical differences that had divided them. Opposed in temperament, taste, and theory, the two men shared a vibrant curiosity about the world and a consuming interest in the fate of the Republic. Their deaths, occurring within hours of each other on the fiftieth anniversary of Independence, July 4, 1826, formed one of the most moving coincidences in American history.

THE ADAMS-JEFFERSON LETTERS

Jefferson to Adams

Monticello Oct. 28. 13
Dear Sir

According to the reservation between us, of taking up one of the subjects of our correspondence at a time, I turn to your letters of Aug. 16. and Sep. 2.

I agree with you that there is a natural aristocracy among men. The grounds of this are virtue and talents. Formerly bodily powers gave place among the aristoi. But since the invention of gunpowder has armed the weak as well as the strong with

Reprinted with permission of The University of North Carolina Press from *The Adams-Jefferson Letters*, Lester J. Cappon, ed. (Chapel Hill, N.C., 1959), II: 387–392, 397–402. This book was published for the Institute of Early American History and Culture.

missile death, bodily strength, like beauty, good humor, politeness and other accomplishments, has become but an auxiliary ground of distinction. There is also an artificial aristocracy founded on wealth and birth, without either virtue or talents; for with these it would belong to the first class. The natural aristocracy I consider as the most precious gift of nature for the instruction, the trusts, and government of society. And indeed it would have been inconsistent in creation to have formed man for the social state, and not to have provided virtue and wisdom enough to manage the concerns of the society. May we not even say that that form of government is the best which provides the most effectually for a pure selection of these natural aristoi into the offices of government? The artificial aristocracy is a mischievous ingredient in government, and provision should be made to prevent it's ascendancy. On the question, What is the best provision, you and I differ; but we differ as rational friends using the free exercise of our own reason, and mutually indulging it's errors. *You* think it best to put the Pseudo-aristoi into a separate chamber of legislation where they may be hindered from doing mischief by their coordinate branches, and where also they may be a protection to wealth against the Agrarian and plundering enterprises of the Majority of the people. I think that to give them power in order to prevent them from doing mischief, is arming them for it, and increasing instead of remedying the evil. For if the coordinate branches can arrest their action, so may they that of the coordinates. Mischief may be done negatively as well as positively. Of this a cabal in the Senate of the U.S. has furnished many proofs. Nor do I believe them necessary to protect the wealthy; because enough of these will find their way into every branch of the legislation to protect themselves. From 15. to 20. legislatures of our own, in action for 30. years past, have proved that no fears of an equalisation of property are to be apprehended from them.

I think the best remedy is exactly that provided by all our constitutions, to leave to the citizens the free election and separation of the aristoi from the pseudo-aristoi, of the wheat from the chaff. In general they will elect the real good and wise. In some instances, wealth may corrupt, and birth blind them; but not in sufficient degree to endanger the society.

It is probable that our difference of opinion may in some measure be produced by a difference of character in those among whom we live. From what I have seen of Massachusets and Connecticut myself, and more from what I have heard, and the character given of the former by yourself, who know them so much better, there seems to be in those two states a traditionary reverence for certain families, which has rendered the offices of the government nearly hereditary in those families. I presume that from an early period of your history, members of these families happening to possess virtue and talents, have honestly exercised them for the good of the people, and by their services have endeared their names to them.

But altho' this hereditary succession to office with you may in some degree be founded in real family merit, yet in a much higher degree it has proceeded from your strict alliance of church and state. These families are canonised in the eyes of the people on the common principle 'you tickle me, and I will tickle you.' In Virginia we have nothing of this. Our clergy, before the revolution, having been secured against rivalship by fixed salaries, did not give themselves the trouble of acquiring influence over the people. Of wealth, there were great accumulations in particular families, handed down from generation to generation under the English law of entails. But the only object of ambition for the wealthy was a seat in the king's council. All their court then was paid to the crown and it's creatures; and they Philipised in all collisions between the king and people. Hence they were unpopular; and that unpopularity continues attached to their names. A Randolph, a Carter, or a Burwell must have great personal superiority over a common competitor to be elected by the people, even at this day.

At the first session of our legislature after the Declaration of Independence, we passed a law abolishing entails. And this was followed by one abolishing the privilege of Primogeniture, and dividing the lands of intestates equally among all their children, or other representatives. These laws, drawn by myself, laid the axe to the root of Pseudo-aristocracy. And had another which I prepared been adopted by the legislature, our work would have been compleat. It was a Bill for the more general diffusion of learning. This proposed to divide every county into wards of 5. or 6. miles square, like your townships; to establish in each ward a free school for reading, writing and common arithmetic; to provide for the annual selection of the best subjects from these schools who might receive at the public expence a higher degree of education at a district school; and from these district schools to select a certain number of the most promising subjects to be compleated at an University, where all the useful sciences should be taught. Worth and genius would thus have been sought out from every condition of life, and compleatly prepared by education for defeating the competition of wealth and birth for public trusts.

My proposition had for a further object to impart to these wards those portions of self-government for which they are best qualified, by confiding to them the care of their poor, their roads, police, elections, the nomination of jurors, administration of justice in small cases, elementary exercises of militia, in short, to have made them little republics, with a Warden at the head of each, for all those concerns which, being under their eye, they would better manage than the larger republics of the county or state. A general call of ward-meetings by their Wardens on the same day thro' the state would at any time produce the genuine sense of the people on any required point, and would enable the state to act in mass, as your people have so often done, and with so much effect, by their town meetings. The law for religious freedom, which made a part of this system, having put down the aristocracy of the clergy, and restored to the citizen the freedom of the mind, and those of entails and descents nurturing an equality of condition among them, this on Education would have raised the mass of the people to the high ground of moral respectability necessary to their own safety, and to orderly government; and would have compleated the great object of qualifying them to select the veritable aristoi, for the trusts of government. Altho' this law has not yet been acted on but in a small and inefficient degree, it is still considered as before the legislature, with other bills of the revised code, not yet taken up, and I have great hope that some patriotic spirit will, at a favorable moment, call it up, and make it the key-stone of the arch of our government.

With respect to Aristocracy, we should further consider that, before the establishment of the American states, nothing was known to History but the Man of the old world, crouded within limits either small or overcharged, and steeped in the vices which that situation generates. A government adapted to such men would be one thing; but a very different one that for the Man of these states. Here every one may have land to labor for himself if he chuses; or, preferring the exercise of any other industry, may exact for it such compensation as not only to afford a comfortable subsistence, but wherewith to provide for a cessation from labor in old age. Every one, by his property, or by his satisfactory situation, is interested in the support of law and order. And such men may safely and advantageously reserve to themselves a wholsome controul over their public affairs, and a degree of freedom, which in the hands of the Canaille of the cities of Europe, would be instantly perverted to the demolition and destruction of every thing public and private. The history of the last 25. years of France, and of the last 40. years in America, nay of it's last 200. years, proves the truth of both parts of this observation.

But even in Europe a change has sensibly taken place in the mind of Man. Science had liberated the ideas of those who read and reflect, and the American example had kindled feelings of right in the people. An insurrection has consequently begun, of science, talents and courage against rank and birth, which have fallen into contempt. It has failed in it's first effort, because the mobs of the cities, the instrument used for it's accomplishment, debased by ignorance, poverty and vice, could not be restrained to rational action. But the world will recover from the panic of this first catastrophe. Science is progressive, and talents and enterprize on the alert. Resort may be had to the people of the country, a more governable power from their principles and subordination; and rank, and birth, and tinsel-aristocracy will finally shrink into insignificance, even there. This however we have no right to meddle with. It suffices for us, if the moral and physical condition of our own citizens qualifies them to select the able and good for the direction of their government, with a recurrence of elections at such short periods as will enable them to displace an unfaithful servant before the mischief he meditates may be irremediable.

I have thus stated my opinion on a point on which we differ, not with a view to controversy, for we are both too old to change opinions which are the result of a long life of inquiry and reflection; but on the suggestion of a former letter of yours, that we ought not to die before we have explained ourselves to each other. We acted in perfect harmony thro' a long and perilous contest for our liberty and independance. A constitution has been acquired which, tho neither of us think perfect, yet both consider as competent to render our fellow-citizens the happiest and the securest on whom the sun has ever shone. If we do not think exactly alike as to it's imperfections, it matters little to our counry which, after devoting to it long lives of disinterested labor, we have delivered over to our successors in life, who will be able to take care of it, and of themselves. Ever and affectionately yours,

Th: Jefferson

Adams to Jefferson

Quincy November 15.13
Dear Sir

I cannot appease my melancholly commiseration for our Armies in this furious snow storm in any way so well as by studying your Letter of Oct. 28.

We are now explicitly agreed, in one important point, vizt. That "there is a natural Aristocracy among men; the grounds of which are Virtue and Talents."

You very justly indulge a little merriment upon this solemn subject of Aristocracy. I often laugh at it too, for there is nothing in this laughable world more ridiculous than the management of it by almost all the nations of the Earth. But while We smile, Mankind have reason to say to Us, as the froggs said to the Boys, What is Sport to you is Wounds and death to Us. When I consider the weakness, the folly, the Pride, the Vanity, the Selfishness, the Artifice, the low craft and meaning cunning, the want of Principle, the Avarice the unbounded Ambition, the unfeeling Cruelty of a majority of those (in all Nations) who are allowed an aristocratical influence; and on the other hand, the Stupidity with which the more numerous multitude, not only become their Dupes, but even love to be Taken in by their Tricks: I feel a stronger disposition to weep at their destiny, than to laugh at their Folly.

But tho' We have agreed in one point, in Words, it is not yet certain that We are perfectly agreed in Sense. Fashion has introduced an indeterminate Use of the Word "Talents." Education, Wealth, Strength, Beauty, Stature, Birth, Marriage, graceful Attitudes and Motions, Gait, Air, Complexion, Physiognomy, are Talents, as well as Genius and Science and learning. Any one of these Talents, that in fact commands or influences true Votes in Society, gives to the Man who possesses it, the Character of an Aristocrat, in my Sense of the Word.

Pick up, the first 100 men you meet, and make a Republick. Every Man will have an equal Vote. But when deliberations and discussions are opened it will be found that 25, by their Talents, Virtues being equal, will be able to carry 50 Votes. Every one of these 25, is an Aristocrat, in my Sense of the Word; whether he obtains his one Vote in Addition to his own, by his Birth Fortune, Figure, Eloquence, Science, learning, Craft Cunning, or even his Character for good fellowship and a bon vivant.

What gave Sir William Wallace his amazing Aristocratical Superiority? His Strength. What gave Mrs. Clark, her Aristocratical Influence to create Generals Admirals and Bishops? her Beauty. What gave Pompadour and Du Barry the Power of making Cardinals and Popes? their Beauty. You have seen the Palaces of Pompadour and Du Barry: and I have lived for years in the Hotel de Velentinois, with Franklin who had as many Virtues as any of them. In the investigation of the meaning of the Word "Talents" I could write 630 Pages, as pertinent as John Taylors of Hazelwood. But I will select a single Example: for female Aristocrats are nearly as formidable in Society as male.

A daughter of a green Grocer, walks the Streets in London dayly with a baskett of Cabbage, Sprouts, Dandlions and Spinage on her head. She is observed by the Painters to have a beautiful Face, an elegant figure, a graceful Step and a debonair. They hire her to Sitt. She complies, and is painted by forty Artists in a Circle around her. The scientific Sir William Hamilton outbids the Painters, sends her to Schools for a genteel Education and Marries her. This Lady not only causes the Tryumphs of the Nile of Copinhagen and Trafalgar, but seperates Naples from France and finally banishes the King and Queen from Sicilly. Such is the Aristocracy of the natural Talent of Beauty. Millions of Examples might be quoted from History sacred and profane, from Eve, Hannah, Deborah Susanna Abigail, Judith, Ruth, down to Hellen Madame de Maintenon and Mrs. Fitcherbert. For mercy's sake do not compel me to look to our chaste States and Territories, to find Women, one of whom lett go, would, in the Words of Holopherne's Guards "deceive the whole Earth."

The Proverbs of Theognis, like those of Solomon, are Observations on human nature, ordinary life, and civil Society, with moral reflections on the facts. I quoted him as a Witness of the Fact, that there was as much difference in the races of Men as in the breeds of Sheep; and as a sharp reprover and censurer of the sordid mercenary practice of disgracing Birth by preferring gold to it. Surely no authority can be more expressly in point to prove the existence of Inequalities, not of rights, but of moral intellectual and physical inqualities in Families, descents and Generations. If a descent from, pious, virtuous, wealthy litterary or scientific Ancestors is a letter of recommendation, or introduction in a Mans his favour, and enables him to influence only one vote in Addition to his own, he is an Aristocrat, for a democrat can have but one Vote. Aaron Burr had 100,000 Votes from the single Circumstance of his descent from President Burr and President Edwards.

Your commentary on the Proverbs of Theognis reminded me of two solemn Charactors, the one resembling John Bunyan, the other Scarron. The one John Torrey: the other Ben. Franklin. Torrey a Poet, an Enthusiast, a superstitious Bigot, once very gravely asked my Brother Cranch, "whether it would not be better for Mankind, if Children were always begotten from religious motives only"? Would not religion, in this sad case, have as little efficacy in encouraging procreation, as it has now in discouraging it? I should apprehend a decrease of population even in our Country where it increases so rapidly. In 1775 Franklin made a morning Visit, at Mrs. Yards to Sam. Adams and John. He was unusually loquacious. "Man, a rational Creature"! said Franklin. "Come, Let Us suppose a rational Man. Strip him of all his Appetites, especially of his hunger and thirst. He is in his Chamber, engaged in making Experiments, or in pursuing some Problem. He is highly entertained. At this moment a Servant Knocks, "Sir dinner is on Table." "Dinner! Pox! Pough! But what have you for dinner?" Ham and Chickens. "Ham"! "And must I break the chain of my thoughts, to go down and knaw a morsel of a damn'd Hogs Arse"? "Put aside your Ham." "I will dine tomorrow."

Take away Appetite and the present generation would not live a month and no future generation would ever exist. Thus the exalted dignity of human Nature would be annihilated and lost. And in my opinion, the whole loss would be of no more importance, than putting out a Candle, quenching a Torch, or crushing a Firefly, *if in this world only We have hope.*

Your distinction between natural and artificial Aristocracy does not appear to me well founded. Birth and Wealth are conferred on some Men, as imperiously by Nature, as Genius, Strength or Beauty. The Heir is honours and Riches, and power has often no more merit in procuring these Advantages, than he has in obtaining an handsome face or an elegant figure. When Aristocracies, are established by human Laws and honour Wealth and Power are made hereditary by municipal Laws and political Institutions, then I acknowledge artificial Aristocracy to commence: but this never commences, till Corruption in Elections becomes dominant and uncontroulable. But this artificial Aristocracy can never last. The everlasting Envys, Jealousies, Rivalries and quarrells among them, their cruel rapacities upon the poor ignorant People their followers, compell these to sett up Caesar, a Demagogue to be a Monarch and Master, pour mettre chacun a sa place ["to put each one in his place"]. Here you have the origin of all artificial Aristocracy, which is the origin of all Monarchy. And both artificial Aristocracy, and Monarchy, and civil, military, political and hierarchical Despotism, have all grown out of the natural Aristocracy of "Virtues and Talents." We, to be sure, are far remote from this. Many hundred years must roll away before We shall be corrupted. Our pure, virtuous, public spirited federative Republick will last for ever, govern the Globe and introduce the perfection of Man, his perfectability being already proved by Price Priestly, Condorcet Rousseau Diderot and Godwin.

"Mischief has been done by the Senate of U.S." I have known and felt more of this mischief, than Washington, Jefferson and Madison altoge [the]r. But this has been all caused by the constitutional Power of the Senate in Executive Business, which ought to be immediately, totally and eternally abolished.

Your distinction between the aristoi and pseudo aristoi, will not help the matter. I would trust one as soon as the other with unlimited Power. The Law wisely refuses an Oath as a witness in his own cause to the Saint as well as to the Sinner.

No Romance would be more amusing, than the History of your Virginian and our new England Aristocratical Families. Yet even in Rhode Island, where there has been no Clergy, no Church, and I had almost said, no State, and some People say no religion, there has been a constant respect for certain old Families. 57 or 58 years ago, in company with Col. Counsellor, Judge, John Chandler, whom I have quoted before, a Newspaper was brought in. The old Sage asked me to look for the News from Rhode Island and see how the Elections had gone there. I read the List of Wantons, Watsons, Greens, Whipples, Malbones etc. "I expected as much" said the aged Gentleman, "for I have always been of Opinion, that in the most popular Governments, the Elections will generally go in favour of the most ancient families." To this day when any of these Tribes and We may Add Ellerys, Channings Champlins etc are pleased to fall in with the popular current, they are sure to carry all before them.

You suppose a difference of Opinion between You and me, on the Subject of Aristocracy. I can find none. I dislike and detest hereditary honours, Offices

301

Emoluments established by Law. So do you. I am for ex[c]luding legal hereditary distinctions from the U.S. as long as possible. So are you. I only say that Mankind have not yet discovered any remedy against irresistable Corruption in Elections to Offices of great Power and Profit, but making them hereditary.

But will you say our Elections are pure? Be it so; upon the whole. But do you recollect in history, a more Corrupt Election than that of Aaron Burr to be President, or that of De Witt Clinton last year. By corruption, here I mean a sacrifice of every national Interest and honour, to private and party Objects.

I see the same Spirit in Virginia, that you and I see in Rhode Island and the rest of New England. In New York it is a struggle of Family Feuds. A fewdal Aristocracy. Pensylvania is a contest between German, Irish and old English Families. When Germans and Irish Unite, they give 30,000 majorities. There is virtually a White Rose and a Red Rose a Caesar and a Pompey in every State in this Union and Contests and dissentions will be as lasting. The Rivalry of Bourbons and Noailleses produced the French Revolution, and a similar Competition for Consideration and Influence, exists and prevails in every Village in the World.

Where will terminate the Rabies Agri ["madness for land"]? The Continent will be scattered over with Manors, much larger than Livingstons, Van Ranselaers or Phillips's. Even our Deacon Strong will have a Principality among you Southern Folk. What Inequality of Talents will be produced by these Land Jobbers?

Where tends the Mania for Banks? At my Table in Philadelphia, I once proposed to you to unite in endeavours to obtain an Amendment of the Constitution, prohibiting to the separate States the Power of creating Banks; but giving Congress Authority to establish one Bank, with a branch in each State; the whole limited to Ten Millions of dollars. Whether this Project was wise or unwise, I know not, for I had deliberated little on it then and have never thought it worth thinking much of since. But you spurned the Proposition from you with disdain.

This System of Banks begotten, hatched and brooded by Duer, Robert and Governeur Morris, Hamilton and Washington, I have always considered as a System of national Injustice. A Sacrifice of public and private Interest to a few Aristocratical Friends and Favourites. My scheme could have had no such Effect.

Verres plundered Temples and robbed a few rich Men; but he never made such ravages among private property in general, nor swindled so much out of the pocketts of the poor and the middle Class of People as these Banks have done. No people but this would have borne the Imposition so long. The People of Ireland would not bear Woods half pence. What Inequalities of Talent, have been introduced into this Country by these Aristocratical Banks!

Our Winthrops, Winslows, Bradfords, Saltonstalls, Quincys, Chandlers, Leonards Hutchinsons Olivers, Sewalls etc are precisely in the Situation of your Randolphs, Carters and Burwells, and Harrisons. Some of them unpopular for the part they took in the late revolution, but all respected for their names and connections and whenever they fall in with the popular Sentiments, are preferred, cetoris paribus to all others. When I was young, the Summum Bonum in Massachusetts, was to be worth ten thousand pounds Sterling, ride in a Chariot, be Colonel of a Regiment of Militia and hold a seat in his Majesty's Council. No

Mans Imagination aspired to any thing higher beneath the Skies. But these Plumbs, Chariots, Colonelships and counsellorships are recorded and will never be forgotten. No great Accumulations of Land were made by our early Settlers. Mr. Bausoin a French Refugee, made the first great Purchases and your General Dearborne, born under a fortunate Starr is now enjoying a large Portion of the Aristocratical sweets of them.

As I have no Amanuenses but females, and there is so much about generations in this letter that I dare not ask any one of them to copy it, and I cannot copy it myself I must beg of you to return it to me, your old Friend

John Adams

30

American Diplomacy

John Quincy Adams (1767–1848) had one of the most brilliant and varied political careers in American history. Seeing Europe for the first time as a child when he accompanied his father on a diplomatic mission for the Continental Congress, he returned frequently in later life as minister to various European states. During his father's Presidency he served as Minister to Prussia, and in subsequent years he was, among other things, a United States Senator, Boylston Professor of Rhetoric at Harvard University, and Secretary of State for eight years under James Monroe. In 1825 Adams became President, and, although he was defeated by Andrew Jackson in the next election, he resumed his political career several years later serving as a Congressman between 1831 and his death in 1848, where he achieved new popularity as a leader of the antislavery forces and an eloquent defender of civil liberties.

During all this time Adams kept a diary, which was published in twelve imposing volumes in the 1870s. Pugnacious, stubborn, awesomely conscientious, Adams personified energy and integrity to the day of his death. His aggressiveness and intelligence, complemented by the tact and patience of some of his fellow commissioners at Ghent, were helpful in reaching a treaty more favorable to America's interest than any believed possible a short time earlier. *The Diary of John Quincy Adams* reveals not only some of the issues involved, but the clashing interests and personalities of an enormously gifted diplomatic team.

THE DIARY
OF JOHN QUINCY ADAMS

April 1, 1814

Mr. Nathaniel H. Strong this morning brought me dispatches from the Secretary of State—one addressed to Mr. Bayard and myself, the other to me alone; letters from Mr. Gallatin and Mr. Bayard, at Amsterdam, and one from Mr. Bourne, enclosing one from Mr. Beasley. The dispatch to Mr. Bayard and me, of which Mr. Bayard

From *Memoirs of John Quincy Adams*, Charles Francis Adams, ed. (Philadelphia, 1874), II: 590–602, 656, III: 4–9, 14–20, 24–29, 32, 36–38, 41–42, 51–60, 66–73, 99, 101–102, 119–120, 126, 138–139.

retained the original and enclosed to me a copy, directs us both to repair, immediately upon the receipt of it, to Gottenburg, there to enter upon a negotiation of peace with England, conformably to a proposal made by the British Government and accepted by that of the United States. Mr. Monroe intimates that there will be other American Commissioners; but his letter is dated 8th January, before the nominations were made. Mr. Henry Clay and Mr. Jonathan Russell were the persons ultimately appointed.

April 28

I had finally fixed upon this day for my departure on the journey to Gottenburg, and was employed from the time of my rising until half-past one P.M. in finishing any preparations. I had visits during the morning from Mr. Hurd, Mr. Norman, and Mr. Montréal; the last of whom informed me that a courier had this morning arrived from the Emperor with the news that Napoleon Bonaparte, on having the decree of the French State notified to him, declaring that he was cashiered, had immediately abdicated the throne, and thus that the war is at an end. With this prospect of a general peace in Europe I commenced my journey to contribute, if possible, to the restoration of peace to my own country. The weight of the trust committed, though but in part, to me, the difficulties, to all human appearance insuperable, which forbid the hope of success, the universal gloom of the prospect before me, would depress a mind of more sanguine complexion than mine. On the providence of God alone is my reliance. The prayer for light and vigilance, and presence of mind and fortitude and resignation, in fine, for strength proportioned to my trial, is incessant upon my heart. The welfare of my family and country, with the interests of humanity, are staked upon the event. To Heaven alone it must be committed.

June 30

At eleven o'clock this morning the American Commissioners now here had a meeting at my chamber. Mr. Bayard, Mr. Clay, and Mr. Russell attended it. The conversation was desultory. We proposed to have regular meetings, and to keep a journal of our proceedings, when we shall all be assembled. We received information that Mr. Gallatin had arrived in Paris.

July 8

I dined again at the table-d'hôte at one. The other gentlemen dined together, at four. They sit after dinner and drink bad wine and smoke cigars, which neither suits my habits nor my health, and absorbs time which I cannot spare. I find it impossible, even with the most rigorous economy of time to do half the writing that I ought.

Aug. 8

We had a meeting of the mission at noon, in which we had some deliberation concerning the manner in which it would be proper to proceed with the British Commissioners. At one o'clock we went, accompanied by Mr. Hughes, to the Hôtel des Pays-Bas, and found the British Commissioners already there. They are James, Lord Gambier, Henry Goulburn, Esquire, a member of Parliament and Under-Secretary of State, and William Adams, Esquire, a Doctor of Civil Laws. The Secretary to the Commission is Anthony St. John Baker.

305

Mr. Goulburn, the second British Commissioner, renewed the professions of the sincere desire of the British Government for peace, and added the most explicit declaration that nothing that had occurred since the first proposal for this negotiation would have the slightest effect on the disposition of Great Britain with regard to the terms upon which the pacification might be concluded. These points he was charged by his colleagues to state; with a request to be informed whether they were such as by our instructions we were authorized to discuss: 1. The forcible seizure of mariners on board of American merchant vessels, and, connected with that subject, the claim of the King of Great Britain to the allegiance of all the native-born subjects of Great Britain. 2. The including of the Indian allies of Great Britain; and, for the purpose of obtaining a permanent pacification, the drawing of a boundary line for the Indians; and it was necessary to observe that on both parts of this point Great Britain considered them as a *sine qua non* to the conclusion of a treaty. 3. The partial revision of the boundary line between the United States and the British possessions in North America—upon which, on a question asked by Mr. Bayard, he explained that in such revision Great Britain did not contemplate an acquisition of territory.

Mr. Gallatin said that so far as respected the including of the Indians in the peace, the United States would have neither interest nor wish to continue the war with the Indians when that with Great Britain should be terminated; that Commissioners had already been appointed to treat of peace with the Indians, and very probably the peace might already be made. He said that the policy of the United States towards the Indians was the most liberal of that pursued by any nation; that our laws interdicted the purchase of lands from them by any individual, and that every precaution was used to prevent the frauds upon them which had heretofore been practised by others. He stated that this proposition to give them a distinct boundary, different from the boundary already existing, and by a treaty between the United States and Great Britain, was not only new, it was unexampled. No such treaty had been made by Great Britain, either before or since the American Revolution, and no such treaty had, to his knowledge, ever been made by any other European power.

Mr. Goulburn said that they were certainly treated as in some respects sovereigns, since treaties were made with them both by Great Britain and the United States.

Treaties with them Mr. Gallatin admitted, but treaties between European powers defining their boundaries there were, to his knowledge, none.

Mr. Bayard asked what was understood by Great Britain to be the effect and operation of the boundary line proposed. Was it to restrict the United States from making treaties with them hereafter as heretofore? from purchasing their lands, for instance? Was it to restrict the Indians from selling their lands? Was it to alter the condition of the Indians, such as it has hitherto existed?

Mr. Goulburn answered that it was intended as a barrier between the British possessions and the territories of the United States; that it was not to restrict the Indians from selling their lands, although it would restrict the United States from purchasing them.

Aug. 13

Lord Gambier and Dr. Adams, Mr. Baker and Mr. Gambier, Mr. Shaler and Mr. Meulemeester, dined with us. Lord Gambier told me that he had been in Boston in the year 1770, with his uncle, who then had the naval command there; that he was then a boy of twelve years of age; that in 1778 he was at New York during our contest, and then commanded a frigate. He spoke to me of my father as having known him at that time, and also of the family of Mr. Bowdoin. He mentioned the English Bible Society, of which he said he had the happiness to be one of the vice-presidents, and of a correspondence they had with the Bible Society in Boston, of which I told him I was a member. He expressed great satisfaction at the liberality with which they had sent a sum of money to replace the loss of some Bibles which had been taken by a privateer as they were going to Halifax.

Aug. 19

On taking their seats at the table, Mr. Goulburn had a dispatch from their Government before him, which, he informed us, was the answer to that which they had sent by their messenger. He proceeded to state its contents. As we had requested to be explicitly informed of the views and intentions of Great Britain in proposing this article, we were to know that the Indian territories were to be interposed as a barrier between the British Dominions and the United States, to prevent them from being conterminous to each other, and that neither Great Britain nor the United States should acquire by any purchase any of these Indian lands. For the line Great Britain was willing to take the treaty of Greenville for the basis, with such modifications as might be agreed upon. It was required by Great Britain that the United States would stipulate to have no naval force upon the Lakes, from Ontario to Superior; and neither to build any forts in future, nor to preserve those already built upon their borders. It would also be necessary for Great Britain to obtain a communication between the provinces of New Brunswick and Canada, a mere road from Halifax to Quebec, which would take off a small corner of the province of Maine. These propositions must be considered as proofs of the moderation of Great Britain, since she might have demanded a cession of all the borders of the Lakes to herself. She would also require a continuance of the right of navigating the Mississippi, as secured to her by the former treaties.

Mr. Gallatin asked what was proposed to be done with the inhabitants, citizens of the United States, already settled beyond the line of the Treaty of Greenville—the Territories of Michigan, of Illinois, and part of the State of Ohio, amounting perhaps to one hundred thousand, many of whom had been settled there with their ancestors one hundred years.

Mr. Goulburn said that their case had not been considered by the British Government; that it might be a foundation for the United States to claim a particular modification of the line, and if that should not be agreed to they might remove.

Dr. Adams said that undoubtedly they must shift for themselves.

Mr. Bayard asked whether the proposition respecting the Indian pacification and boundary was still presented as a *sine qua non;* to which they answered that undoubtedly it was.

He asked whether that relating to the Lakes was of the same character.

Dr. Adams answered, "One *sine qua non* at a time is enough. It will be time enough to answer your question when you have disposed of that we have given you."

In my account of our conference with the British Commissioners this morning I omitted to state the following facts. Mr. Gallatin, adverting to the late account in the English newspapers of their having taken possession of Moose Island, in the Bay of Passamaquoddy, enquired whether the statement which had been published was correct, that they meant to keep it.

They said it was; that it was a part of the province of Nova Scotia; that they did not even consider it a subject for discussion.

Mr. Goulburn said he could demonstrate in the most unanswerable manner that it belonged to them, and Dr. Adams said we might as well contest their right to Northamptonshire.

Mr. Gallatin asked whether, in requiring us to keep no naval force on the Lakes and no forts on their shores, they intended to reserve the right of keeping them there themselves. They said they certainly did.

After the conference was finished, Mr. Bayard said to Mr. Goulburn, that if the conferences were suspended he supposed Goulburn would take a trip to England. Goulburn said, "Yes, and I suppose you will take a trip to America."

In general, their tone was more peremptory and their language more overbearing than at former conferences. Their deportment this day was peculiarly offensive to Mr. Bayard. Mr. Clay has an inconceivable idea, that they will finish by receding from the ground they have taken.

Sept. 1

This morning I paid a visit to the British Plenipotentiaries and to Mrs. Goulburn. I did not, however, see her, but only her husband. I told him I hoped his Government would reconsider some parts of their former propositions before they sent their final instructions. He did not think it probable, and I found the more I ,conversed with him the more the violence and bitterness of his passion against the United States disclosed itself. His great point in support of the Indian boundary was its necessity for the security of Canada. He said that the United States had manifested the intention and the determination of conquering Canada; that, "excepting us," he believed it was the astonishment of the whole world that Canada had not been conquered at the very outset of the war; that nothing had saved it but the excellent dispositions and military arrangements of the Governor who commanded there; that in order to guard against the same thing in future, it was necessary to make a barrier against our settlements, upon which neither party should encroach; that the Indians were but a secondary object, but that as being the allies of Great Britain she must include them, as she made peace with other powers, including Portugal as her ally; that the proposition that we should stipulate not to arm upon the Lakes was made with the same purpose—the security of Canada. He could not see that there was anything humiliating in it; that the United States could never be in any danger of invasion from Canada, the disproportion of force was too great. But Canada must always be in the most imminent danger of invasion from the United States, unless she was guarded by some such stipulation as they now demanded; that it could be nothing to the United States, to agree not to arm upon the Lakes, since they never had actually done it before the present war. Why should they object to disarming there, where they had never before had a gun floating?

I answered that the conquest of Canada had never been an object of the war on the part of the United States; that Canada had been invaded by us in consequence of the war, as they themselves had invaded many parts of the United States—it was an effect, and not a cause, of the war; that the American Government never had declared the intention of conquering Canada.

He insisted that the Indians must be considered as independent nations, and that we ourselves made treaties with them and acknowledged boundaries of their territories.

I said that, wherever they would form settlements and cultivate lands, their possessions were undoubtedly to be respected, and always were respected, by the United States; that some of them had become civilized in a considerable degree—the Cherokees, for example, who had permanent habitations, and a state of property like our own. But the greater part of the Indians could never be prevailed upon to adopt this mode of life; their habits and attachments and prejudices were so averse to any settlement, that they could not reconcile themselves to any other condition than that of wandering hunters. It was impossible for such people ever to be said to have possessions. Their only right upon land was a right to use it as hunting-grounds, and when those lands where they hunted became necessary or convenient for the purposes of settlement, the system adopted by the United States was, by amicable arrangement with them, to compensate them for renouncing the right of hunting upon them, and for removing to remoter regions better suited to their purposes and mode of life. This system of the United States was an improvement upon the former practice of all European nations, including the British. The original settlers of New England had set the first example of this liberality towards the Indians, which was afterwards followed by the founder of Pennsylvania. Between it and taking the lands for nothing, or exterminating the Indians who had used them, there was no alternative. To condemn vast regions of territory to perpetual barrenness and solitude that a few hundred savages might find wild beasts to hunt upon it, was a species of game law that a nation descended from Britons would never endure. It was incompatible with the moral as with the physical nature of things. If Great Britain meant to preclude forever the people of the United States from settling and cultivating those territories, she must not think of doing it by a treaty. She must formally undertake, and accomplish, their utter extermination. If the Government of the United States should ever submit to such a stipulation, which I hoped they would not, all its force, and that of Britain combined with it, would not suffice to carry it long into execution. It was opposing a feather to a torrent. The population of the United States in 1810 passed seven millions; at this hour it undoubtedly passed eight. As it continued to increase in such proportions, was it in human experience, or in human power, to check its progress by a bond of paper purporting to exclude posterity from the natural means of subsistence which they would derive from the cultivation of the soil? Such a treaty, instead of closing the old sources of discussion, would only open new ones. A war thus finished would immediately be followed by another, and Great Britain would ultimately find that she must substitute the project of exterminating the whole American people for that of opposing against them her barrier of savages.

"What!" said Mr. Goulburn, "is it, then, in the inevitable nature of things that the United States must conquer Canada?"

"No."

"But what security, then, can Great Britain have for her possession of it?"

"If Great Britain does not think a liberal and amicable course of policy towards America would be the best security, as it certainly would, she must rely upon her general strength, upon the superiority of her power in other parts of her relations with America, upon the power which she has upon another element, to indemnify herself, by sudden impression upon American interests, more defenceless against her superiority, and in their amount far more valuable, than Canada ever was or ever will be."

Sept. 8, III. 45

Just before rising, I heard Mr. Clay's company retiring from his chamber. I had left him with Mr. Russell, Mr. Bentzon, and Mr. Todd at cards. They parted as I was about to rise. I was up nearly half an hour before I had daylight to read or write.

Sept. 20

I was closing my copy of four pages, when the third note from the British Plenipotentiaries was brought to me. The British note is overbearing and insulting in its tone, like the two former ones; but it abandons a great part of the *sine qua non,* adhering at the same time inflexibly to the remainder. The effect of these notes upon us when they first come is to deject us all. We so fondly cling to the vain hope of peace, that every new proof of its impossibility operates upon us as a disappointment. We had a desultory and general conversation upon this note, in which I thought both Mr. Gallatin and Mr. Bayard showed symptoms of despondency. In discussing with them I cannot always restrain the irritability of my temper. Mr. Bayard meets it with more of accommodation than heretofore, and sometimes with more compliance than I expect. Mr. Gallatin, having more pliability of character and more playfulness of disposition, throws off my heat with a joke. Mr. Clay and Mr. Russell are perfectly firm themselves, but sometimes partake of the staggers of the two other gentlemen.

Mr. Gallatin said this day that the *sine qua non* now presented—that the Indians should be positively included in the peace, and placed in the state they were in before the war—would undoubtedly be rejected by our Government if it was now presented to them, but that it was a bad point for us to break off the negotiation upon; that the difficulty of carrying on the war might compel us to admit the principle at last, for now the British had so committed themselves with regard to the Indians that it was impossible for them further to retreat.

Mr. Bayard was of the same opinion, and recurred to the fundamental idea of breaking off upon some point which shall unite our own people in the support of the war.

In this sentiment we all concur. But, as its tendency is to produce compliance with the British claims, it is necessary to guard against its leading us in that career too far. I said it was not more clear to me that the British would not finally abandon their present *sine qua non,* than it had been that they would adhere to their first; that if the point of the Indians was a bad point to break upon, I was very sure we should never find a good one. If that would not unite our people, it was a hopeless pursuit.

Mr. Gallatin repeated, with a very earnest look, that it was a bad point to break upon.

"Then," said I, with a movement of impatience and an angry tone, "it is a good point to admit the British as the sovereigns and protectors of our Indians."

Gallatin's countenance brightened, and he said, in a tone of perfect good humor, "That's a non-sequitur." This turned the edge of the argument into mere jocularity. I laughed, and insisted that it was a sequitur, and the conversation easily changed to another point.

Sept. 25

We met at one o'clock, and sat until past five, debating the new draft of our answer to the British note. I had proposed to leave out a large part of Mr. Gallatin's draft, but he insisted upon retaining most of what he had written, and it was retained. In this debate I had continued evidence of two things. One, that if any one member objects to anything I have written, all the rest support him in it, and I never can get it through. The other, that if I object to anything written by Mr. Gallatin, unless he voluntarily abandons it every other member supports him, and my objection is utterly unavailing.

In repelling an insolent charge of the British Plenipotentiaries against the Government of the United States, of a system of perpetual encroachment upon the Indians under the pretence of purchases, I had taken the ground of the moral and religious duty of a nation to settle, cultivate, and improve their territory—a principle perfectly recognized by the laws of nations, and, in my own opinion, the only solid and unanswerable defence against the charge in the British note. Gallatin saw and admitted the weight of the argument, but was afraid of ridicule. Bayard, too, since he has been reading Vattel, agreed in the argument, and was willing to say it was a duty. But the terms God, and Providence, and Heaven, Mr. Clay thought were canting, and Russell laughed at them. I was obliged to give them up, and with them what I thought the best argument we had.

Oct. 12

I made a draft of an answer to the last note from the British Plenipotentiaries, but had not finished it when the time of our meeting came. At the meeting, Mr. Gallatin produced his draft, and I read parts of mine. They differed much in the tone of the composition. The tone of all the British notes is arrogant, overbearing, and offensive. The tone of ours is neither so bold nor so spirited as I think it should be. It is too much on the defensive, and too excessive in the caution to say nothing irritating. I have seldom been able to prevail upon my colleagues to insert anything in the style of retort upon the harsh and reproachful matter which we receive. And they are now so resolved to make the present note short, that they appeared to reject everything I had written, and even much of Mr. Gallatin's draft. We agree to accept the article offered to us as an ultimatum. Mr. Gallatin's idea is to adopt it, as perfectly conformable to the views we ourselves had previously taken of the subject. Mine is to consider and represent it as a very great concession, made for the sake of securing the peace. But in this opinion I am alone. I also strongly urged the expediency of avowing as the sentiment of our Government that the cession of Canada would be for the interest of Great Britain as well as the United States. I had drawn up a paragraph upon the subject conformable to our instructions. My colleagues would not adopt it.

Oct. 30

I began making a draft for the project of a treaty. Mr. Gallatin was employed in the same manner. At two o'clock we had a meeting of the mission, but Mr. Clay was not present until the meeting was over, and Mr. Russell not at all. We looked over the articles drawn by Mr. Gallatin and myself, which being unfinished, we agreed to meet every day, at two o'clock, until the whole project shall be prepared. Mr. Gallatin proposes to renew the two articles of the Treaty of Peace of 1783, the stipulation for our right to fish, and dry and cure fish, within the waters of the British jurisdiction, and the right of the British to navigate the Mississippi. To this last article, however, Mr. Clay makes strong objections. He is willing to leave the matter of the fisheries as a nest-egg for another war, but to make the peace without saying anything about it; which, after the notice the British have given us, will be in fact an abandonment of our right. Mr. Clay considers this fishery as an object of trifling amount; and that a renewal of the right of the British to navigate the Mississippi would be giving them a privilege far more important than that we should secure in return. And as he finds, as yet, no member of the mission but himself taking this ground, he grows earnest in defence of it.

Nov. 10, VI. 30

A second day belated. On examining the drafts for the note with the amendments of Messrs. Clay, Bayard, and Russell, I found more than three-fourths of what I had written erased. There was only one paragraph to which I attached importance, but that was struck out with the rest. It was the proposal to conclude the peace on the footing of the state before the war, applied to all the subjects of dispute between the two countries, leaving all the rest for the future and pacific negotiation.

I stated in candor that I considered my proposal as going that full length; that I was aware it would be a departure from our instructions as prepared in April, 1813. But the Government, for the purpose of obtaining peace, had revoked our instructions of that date upon a point much more important in its estimation, the very object of the war; and I have no doubt would have revoked them on the other point, had it occurred to them that they would prove an obstacle to the conclusion of peace. I felt so sure that they would now gladly take the state before the war as the general basis of the peace, that I was prepared to take on me the responsibility of trespassing upon their instructions thus far. Not only so, but I would at this moment cheerfully give my life for a peace on this basis. If peace was possible, it would be on no other. I had, indeed, no hope that the proposal would be accepted.

But on the rupture it would make the strongest case possible in our favor, for the world both in Europe and America. It would put the continuance of the war entirely at the door of England, and force out her objects in continuing it.

Mr. Clay finally said that he would agree to the insertion of my proposal in the note, but reserving to himself the right of refusing to sign the treaty if the offer should be accepted and the principle extended beyond his approbation.

Mr. Clay objected to the formal concluding article, and thought it ridiculous, and he recurred again to the paragraph proposing the state before the war as the general basis of the treaty. He said the British Plenipotentiaries would laugh at us for it. They would say, "Ay, ay! pretty fellows you, to think of getting out of the war as well as you got into it!"

I think it very probable this commentary will be made on our proposal; but what would be the commentary on our refusing peace on those terms? Mr. Russell dined with us about five o'clock, and immediately after dinner Mr. Hughes took our note and project to the British Plenipotentiaries.

Nov. 27

About eleven in the morning, Mr. Gallatin came into my chamber, with a note received from the British Plenipotentiaries. They have sent us back with this note the project of a treaty which we had sent them, with marginal notes and alterations proposed by them. They have rejected all the articles we had proposed on impressment, blockade, indemnities, amnesty, and Indians. They have definitively abandoned the Indian boundary, the exclusive military possession of the Lakes, and the uti possidetis; but with a protestation that they will not be bound to adhere to these terms hereafter, if the peace should not be made now. Within an hour after receiving these papers we had a meeting of the mission at my chamber, when the note and the alterations to our project proposed by the British Plenipotentiaries were read, and we had some desultory conversation upon the subject. All the difficulties to the conclusion of a peace appear to be now so nearly removed, that my colleagues all considered it as certain. I think it myself probable.

Nov. 28

At eleven o'clock we met, and continued in session until past four, when we adjourned to meet again at eleven to-morrow morning. Our principal discussion was on an article proposed by the British Government as a substitute for the eighth of our project. And they have added a clause securing to them the navigation of the Mississippi, and access to it with their goods and merchandise through our territories.

To this part of the article Mr. Clay positively objected. Mr. Gallatin proposed to agree to it, proposing an article to secure our right of fishing and curing fish within the British jurisdiction. Mr. Clay lost his temper, as he generally does whenever this right of the British to navigate the Mississippi is discussed. He was utterly averse to admitting it as an equivalent for a stipulation securing the contested part of the fisheries. He said the more he heard of this the more convinced he was that it was of little or no value. He should be glad to get it if he could, but he was sure the British would not ultimately grant it. That the navigation of the Mississippi, on the other hand, was an object of immense importance . . .

313

Mr. Gallatin said that the fisheries were of great importance in the sentiment of the eastern section of the Union; that if we should sign a peace without securing them to the full extent in which they were enjoyed before the war, and especially if we should abandon any part of the territory, it would give a handle to the party there, now pushing for a separation from the Union and for a New England Confederacy, to say that the interests of New England were sacrificed, and to pretend that by a separate confederacy they could obtain what is refused to us.

Mr. Clay said that there was no use in attempting to conciliate people who never would be conciliated; that it was too much the practice of our Government to sacrifice the interests of its best friends for those of its bitterest enemies; that there might be a party for separation at some future day in the Western States, too.

I observed to him that he was now speaking under the impulse of passion, and that on such occasions I would wish not to answer anything; that assuredly the Government would be reproached, and the greatest advantage would be taken by the party opposed to it, if any of the rights of the Eastern States should be sacrificed by the peace; that the loss of any part of the fisheries would be a subject of triumph and exultation, both to the enemy and to those among us who had been opposed to the war; that if I should consent to give up even Moose Island, where there was a town which had been for many years regularly represented in the Legislature of the State of Massachusetts, I should be ashamed to show my face among my countrymen; that as to the British right of navigating the Mississippi, I considered it as nothing, considered as a grant from us. It was secured to them by the Peace of 1783, they had enjoyed it at the commencement of the war, it had never been injurious in the slightest degree to our own people, and it appeared to me that the British claim to it was just and equitable. The boundary fixed by the Peace of 1783 was a line due west from the Lake of the Woods to the Mississippi, and the navigation of the river was stipulated for both nations. It has been since that time discovered that a line due west from the Lake of the Woods will not touch the Mississippi, but goes north of it. The boundary, therefore, is annulled by the fact. Two things were contemplated by both parties in that compact—one, that the line should run west from the Lake of the Woods; the other, that it should touch the Mississippi. In attempting now to supply the defect, we ask for the line due west, and the British ask for the shortest line to the Mississippi. Both demands stand upon the same grounds—the intention of both parties at the Peace of 1783. If we grant the British demand, they touch the river and have a clear right to its navigation. If they grant our demand, they do not touch the river; but in conceding the territory they have a fair and substantial motive for reserving the right of navigating the river. I was not aware of any solid answer to this argument.

Dec. 11

The meeting was in my chamber, and it was near noon before we were all assembled. The questions were resumed.

Mr. Gallatin said it was an extraordinary thing that the question of peace or war now depended solely upon two points, in which the people of the State of Massachusetts alone were interested—Moose Island, and the fisheries within British jurisdiction.

I said that was the very perfidious character of the British propositions. They wished to give us the appearance of having sacrificed the interests of the Eastern section of the Union to those of the Western, to enable the disaffected in Massachusetts to say, the Government of the United States has given up *our* territory and *our* fisheries merely to deprive the British of their right to navigate the Mississippi.

Mr. Russell said it was peculiarly unfortunate that the interests thus contested were those of a disaffected part of the country.

Mr. Clay said that he would do nothing to satisfy disaffection and treason; he would not yield anything for the sake of them.

"But," said I, "you would not give disaffection and treason the right to say to the people that their interests had been sacrificed?"

He said, No. But he was for a war three years longer. He had no doubt but three years more of war would make us a warlike people, and that then we should come out of the war with honor. Whereas at present, even upon the best terms we could possibly obtain, we shall have only a half-formed army, and half retrieve our military reputation. He was for playing *brag* with the British Plenipotentiaries; they had been playing *brag* with us throughout the whole negotiation; he thought it was time for us to begin to play *brag* with them. He asked me if I knew how to play *brag*. I had forgotten how. He said the art of it was to beat your adversary by holding your hand, with a solemn and confident phiz, and outbragging him. He appealed to Mr. Bayard if it was not.

"Ay," said Bayard: "but you may lose the game by bragging until the adversary sees the weakness of your hand." And Bayard added to me, "Mr. Clay is for bragging a million against a cent."

I said the principle was the great thing which we could not concede; it was directly in the face of our instructions. We could not agree to it, and I was for saying so, positively, at once. Mr. Bayard said that there was *nothing* left in dispute but the principle. I did not think so.

"Mr. Clay," said I, "supposing Moose Island belonged to Kentucky and had been for many years represented as a district in your Legislature, would you give it up as nothing? Mr. Bayard, if it belonged to Delaware, would you?" Bayard laughed, and said Delaware could not afford to give up territory.

Mr. Gallatin said it made no difference to what State it belonged, it was to be defended precisely in the same manner, whether to one or to another.

It was agreed positively to object to the British proposals on both points—the first, as inconsistent with the admitted basis of the status ante bellum; and the second, as unnecessary, contrary to our instructions, and a new demand, since we had been told that they had brought forward *all* their demands.

Dec. 22

After returning home, I walked round the Coupure, and, as I was coming back, met in the street Mr. Bayard, who told me that the answer from the British Plenipotentiaries to our last note had been received; that it accepted our proposal to say nothing in the treaty about the fisheries or the navigation of the Mississippi, and, indeed, placed the remaining points of the controversy at our own disposal. As soon as I came into my chamber, Mr. Gallatin brought me the note. It agrees to be silent upon the navigation of the Mississippi and the fisheries, and to strike out the whole of the eighth article, marking the boundary from the Lake of the Woods westward. They also refer again to their declaration of the 8th of August, that Great Britain would not hereafter grant the liberty of fishing, and drying and curing fish, within the exclusive British jurisdiction, without an equivalent. They accepted our proposed paragraph respecting the islands in Passamaquoddy Bay, with the exception of a clause for their restitution if the contested title to them should not be settled within a limited time. Instead of which, they gave a declaration that no unnecessary delay of the settlement should be interposed by Great Britain.

Dec. 24

Mr. Clay was not ready with his copy of the treaty at three o'clock, and Mr. Hughes called upon the British Plenipotentiaries to postpone the meeting until four. At that hour we went to their house, and after settling the protocol of yesterday's conference, Mr. Baker read one of the British copies of the treaty; Mr. Gallatin and myself had the two other copies before us, comparing them as he read. A few mistakes in the copies were rectified, and then the six copies were signed and sealed by the three British and the five American Plenipotentiaries. Lord Gambier delivered to me the three British copies, and I delivered to him the three American copies, of the treaty, which he said he hoped would be permanent; and I told him I hoped it would be the last treaty of peace between Great Britain and the United States. We left them at half-past six o'clock.

Jan. 5, 1815

The banquet today was at the Hôtel de Ville, and was given by subscription by the principal gentlemen of the city. We sat down to table about five o'clock, in the largest hall of the building, fitted up for the occasion with white cotton hangings. The American and British flags were intertwined together under olive-trees, at the head of the hall. Mr. Goulburn and myself were seated between the Intendant and the Mayor, at the centre of the cross-piece of the table. There were about ninety persons seated at the table. As we went into the hall, "Hail Columbia" was performed by the band of music. It was followed by "God save the King," and these two airs were alternately repeated during the dinnertime, until Mr. Goulburn thought they became tiresome. I was of the same opinion. The Intendant and the Mayor alternately toasted "His Britannic Majesty," and "the United States," "the Allied Powers," and "the Sovereign Prince," "the Negotiators," and "the Peace." I then remarked to Mr. Goulburn that he must give the next toast, which he did. It was, "the Intendant and the Mayor; the City of Ghent, its prosperity; and our gratitude for their hospitality and the many acts of kindness that we had received from them." I gave the next and last toast, which was, "Ghent, the city of peace; may the gates of the temple of Janus, here closed, not be opened again for a century!"

31

The Appeal
of the New World

Frances Wright (1795–1852) was born in Scotland
and grew up a precocious and insatiable reader of
history and philosophy. Fascinated by the political and
social novelties of America, Fanny Wright sailed for
the New World in 1818, and spent more than two years
in the United States. Her letters of description back
home were numerous and detailed and, after returning
to England in 1821, she decided to publish some of
them as *Views of Society and Manners in America*. She
returned to the United States with Lafayette in 1824
and founded the experimental community of Nashoba
in Tennessee, where she tried to train and educate
Negro slaves as a means of integrating them into free
society. After many trips to Europe, an increasing involvement with utopian communities, and a career of
lecturing on education, social reform, free thought, and
women's rights, Fanny Wright died in 1852.

Views of Society formed one of the most favorable
pictures of the new republic that a European had drawn
up to that time. Fanny Wright's enthusiasm for American institutions, with the crucial exception of slavery,
led often to distortions and misjudgments but reveal
something of the tremendous inspiration that the American experiment held for European reformers.

VIEWS OF SOCIETY AND MANNERS
IN AMERICA
Frances Wright

Agriculture

It were difficult, perhaps, to conceive man placed in a more enviable position than
he is as a cultivator of the soil in these states. Agriculture here assumes her most
cheerful aspect, and (some Europeans might smile doubtingly, but it is true) all
her ancient classic dignity, as when Rome summoned her consuls from the plough.
I have seen those who have raised their voice in the senate of their country, and

Reprinted by permission of the publishers from Paul R. Baker, editor, Frances Wright, *Views of Society and Manners in America*. Cambridge, Mass.: The Belknap Press of Harvard University Press, Copyright, 1963, by the President and Fellows of Harvard College. Pp. 99–101, 118–119, 194–202, 205–206, 208, 215–218, 267–270.

whose hands have fought her battles, walking beside the team and minutely directing every operation of husbandry, with the soil upon their garments and their countenances bronzed by the meridian sun. And how proudly does such a man tread his paternal fields! his ample domains improving under his hand, his garners full to overflowing, his table replenished with guests, and with a numerous offspring, whose nerves are braced by exercise and their minds invigorated by liberty. It was finely answered by an American citizen to a European who, looking around him, exclaimed, "Yes; this is all well. You have all the vulgar and the substantial, but I look in vain for the *ornamental*. Where are your ruins and your poetry?" "There are our ruins," replied the republican, pointing to a Revolutionary soldier who was turning up the glebe; and then, extending his hand over the plain that stretched before them, smiling with luxuriant farms and little villas, peeping out from beds of trees, "There is our poetry." . . .

The position of this country, its boundless territory, its varied soils and climates, its free institutions, and, favoured by these circumstances, the rapid increase of its population—all combine to generate in this people a spirit of daring enterprise as well as of proud independence. They spurn at little hindrances in narrow room, and prefer great difficulties in a wide horizon. In flying to the wilderness, they fly a thousand constraints which society must always impose, even under the fairest laws. They have here no longer to jostle with the crowd; their war is only with nature; their evils, therefore, are chiefly physical, and the comforts they may forego are amply compensated by the frets and cares from which they may be released. It is curious to consider the effect which this release from moral ills seems to have upon the constitution. Those who safely weather out the first hard seasoning, or who, from choosing their ground more judiciously, escape with but very little, are often found to live to an unusual age. It is a singular fact that the citizens of the new states are often remarkable for uncommon longevity and universally for uncommon stature. This cannot be accounted for by supposing that they are more exposed to air and exercise—the American farmer is this universally —and though universally the average of his stature is above that of Europeans, it were, perhaps, more just to ascribe this varying standard of bodily vigor to the less or greater pressure of mental solicitude. . . .

In the country, especially, service, however, well paid for, is a favour received. Every man is a farmer and a proprietor; few therefore can be procured to work for hire, and these must generally be brought from a distance. Country gentlemen complain much of this difficulty. Most things, however, have their good and their evil. I have remarked that the American gentry are possessed of much more personal activity than is common on other countries. They acquire, as children, the habit of doing for themselves what others require to be done for them, and are, besides, saved from the sin of insolence, which is often so early fixed in the young mind. Some foreigners will tell you that insolence here is with the poor. Each must speak from his own experience. I have never met with any, though I will confess that if I did it would offend me less than the insolence offered by the rich to the poor has done elsewhere. But insolence forms no characteristic of the American, whatever be his condition in life. I verily believe that you might travel from the

Canada frontier to the Gulf of Mexico, or from the Atlantic to the Missouri and never receive from a *native-born citizen* a rude word, it being understood always that you never *give one*.

On arriving at a tavern in this country, you excite no kind of *sensation,* come how you will. The master of the house bids you good day, and you walk in. Breakfast, dinner, and supper are prepared at stated times, to which you must generally contrive to accommodate. There are seldom more hands than enough to dispatch the necessary work. You are not therefore beset by half-a-dozen menials, imagining your wants before you know them yourself; make them known, however, and, if they be rational, they are generally answered with tolerable readiness, and I have invariably found with perfect civility. One thing I must notice, that you are never anywhere charged for attendance. The servant is not yours but the innkeeper's; no demands are made upon you except by the latter. This saves much trouble, and indeed is absolutely necessary in a house where the servant's labour is commonly too valuable to be laid at the mercy of every whimsical traveller. But this arrangement originates in another cause—the republican habits and feelings of the community. I honor the pride which makes a man unwilling to sell his personal service to a fellow creature; to come and go at the beck of another—is it not natural that there should be some unwillingness to do this? It is the last trade to which an American, man or woman, has recourse; still some must be driven to it, particularly of the latter sex, but she always assumes with you the manner of an equal. I have never in this country hired the attendance of any but native Americans, and never have met with an uncivil word, but I could perceive that neither would one have been taken. Honest, trusty, and proud, such is the American in service; there is a character here which all who can appreciate it will respect. . . .

Sectional Interests

Looking to the general plan of the central government, it will be seen with what extreme nicety the different interests of the multitudinous parts of this great confederacy are balanced, or employed as checks one upon the other. In the course of years these interests may be somewhat more distinctly marked than they are at present; some have even thought that they may be more strongly opposed. This appears more than doubtful. But even admitting the supposition, we cannot calculate the probable effects of this without counting for something the gradual strengthening of the national Union by the mixture of the people, the marriages and friendships conracted between the inhabitants of the different states, the tide of emigration, which shifts the population of one to the other, the course of prosperity enjoyed under a government more and more endeared as time more and more tries its widsom and imparts sanctity to its name. The time was when none or but a few of these sacred bonds existed, and still a friendly sympathy was not wanting among the different and uncemented communities scattered along the shores of the Atlantic.

During their colonial existence, the inhabitants of these states had but little intercourse with each other. Vast forests separated often the scanty population of the infant provinces. Varying climate and religion influenced also their customs and character; but still, however parted by trackless wastes, how little connected soever by the ties of private friendship, they had always two things in common—language and a fierce spirit of liberty, which sufficed to bind with a sure though invisible chain all the members of the scattered American family. The strength of this chain has seldom been fully appreciated by the enemies of America. They expected to break it even during the War of the Revolution, and were certain that it would of itself give way when the high-toned sentiment kept alive by a struggle for independence should subside, or when the pressure of common danger being removed, the necessity of cordial co-operation should not be equally apparent. Experience has hitherto happily disproved these calculations. The advantages of a vigorous and the blessings of a beneficent government, directing the energies and presiding over the welfare of the great whole, have been more and more felt and understood, while the influence of just laws, and still more the improved intercourse of the states one with another, have broken down prejudices and, in a great measure, obliterated distinctions of character among the different quarters of the republic.

The portion of the Union that has most generally preserved her ancient moral distinction is New England. The reason may be found in the rigidity of her early religious creed and in the greater separation of her people from the rest of the nation. Strictly moral, well-educated, industrious, and intelligent, but shrewd, cautious, and, as their neighbours say, at least, peculiarly long-sighted to their interests, the citizens of New England are the Scotch of America. Like them, they are inhabitants of a comparatively poor country and send forth legions of hardy adventurers to push their fortunes in richer climes. There is this difference, however, that the Scotchman traverses the world and gathers stores to spend them afterwards in his own barren hills, while the New Englander carries his penates with him and plants a colony on the shores of the Ohio, with no less satisfaction than he would have done on those of the Connecticut.

The nursery of backwoodsmen, New England, sends forth thousands and of course takes in few, so that her citizens are less exposed to the visitation of foreigners, and even to mixture with the people of other states, than is usual with their more southern neighbours. This has, perhaps, its advantages and disadvantages: it preserves to them all the virtues of a simple state of society, but with these also some of its prejudices; it serves to entrench them against luxury, but imparts to them something of a provincial character. Zealously attached to their own institutions, they have sometimes coldly espoused those of the nation. The Federal opposition chiefly proceeded from this quarter of the Union.

The political conduct of New England subsequent to the establishment of the federal government sunk her a little for some years in the esteem of the nation. The narrowness of her policy was charged to some peculiar selfishness of character in her people, but their conduct during the Revolutionary struggle redeems them from this charge and leads us to ascribe their errors to defect of judgment rather than to obliquity of principle. Since the war the liberal party, ever numerous, has gained the ascendant, and consequently the eastern states are resuming that place in the national councils which they originally held. . . . New York and Pennsylvania may perhaps be considered as the most *influential* states of the Union. . . . They are "the key-stones of the federal arch." Their rich and extensive territories seem to comprise all the interests into which the Union is divided. Commerce, agriculture, and manufactures are all powerfully represented by them on the floor of Congress. Their western division has much in common with the Mississippi states, and their eastern with those of the Atlantic. Their population stands conspicuous for national enterprise and enlightened policy, whether as regards the internal arrangement of their own republics or their share in the federal councils. These powerful states return no less than fifty members to Congress, being more than a fourth of the whole body. In proportion as the western states increase, this preponderance will be taken from them; in the meantime, however, it is in no case exerted to the prejudice of the general interests of the Union.

Whether it be from their wealth, or their more central position affording them the advantage of a free intercourse with the citizens of all the states of the Union, as well as foreigners from all parts of the world, the people of Pennsylvania and New York, but more particularly of the latter, have acquired a liberality of sentiment which imparts dignity to their public measures. They raise extensive funds, not only for the general education of their citizens (which is equally the case elsewhere), the founding of libraries, and seminaries of learning, but in the clearing of rivers, making roads and canals, and promoting other works of extensive utility, which might do honor to the richest empires of Europe. The progress of the New York state during the last thirty years is truly astonishing. Within this period, her population has more than quadrupled, and the value of property more than doubled. She has subdued the forest from Hudson to Erie and the Canadian frontier, and is now perfecting the navigation of all her great waters and connecting them with each other. . . .

No state in the Union can point to a longer line of public services than Virginia: she rung the first alarm of the Revolution by the mouth of her Patrick Henry; she led the army of patriots in the person of her Washington; she issued the Declaration of Independence from the pen of her Jefferson; she bound the first link of the federal Union by the hand of her Madison—she has given to the republic four of the purest patriots and wisest statesmen that ever steered the vessel of a state. . . .

The dignified position taken by Virginia in the national councils has placed her at the head of the republics of the South, whose policy, it may be remarked, has uniformly been liberal and patriotic and, on all essential points, in accordance with that of the central and western states. Whatever be the effect of black slavery upon the moral character of the southern population—and that upon *the mass* it must be deadly mischievous there can be no question—it has never been felt in the national Senate. Perhaps the arrangement has been prudent, or at least fortunate, which has somewhat tempered the democracy of American government in the south Atlantic states. By the existing constitution of Virginia and the states south of her, the qualifications required of a representative throw the legislative power into the hands of the more wealthy planters, a race of men no less distinguished for the polish of their manners and education than for liberal sentiments and general

321

philanthropy. They are usually well-travelled in their own country and in Europe, possess enough wealth to be hospitable and seldom sufficient to be luxurious, and are thus, by education and condition, raised above the degrading influence which the possession of arbitrary power has on the human mind and the human heart. To the slight leaven of aristocracy, therefore, thrown into the institutions of Virginia and the Carolinas, we may, perhaps, attribute, in part, their generous and amiable bearing in the national councils. We must not omit, however, the ameliorating effect produced by the spread of education and the effect of liberal institutions on the white population generally. Even before the close of the Revolutionary War, Mr. Jefferson thought "a change already perceptible"; and we have a substantial proof that the change traced by that philosopher in the character of his fellow citizens was not imaginary, the first act of the Virginia legislature being the abolition of the slave trade. May she now set an example to her neighbouring states, as she then did to the world, by combating steadfastly the difficulties which her own fears or selfish interests may throw in the way of emancipation!

But the quarter of the republic to which the eye of a stranger turns with most curiosity is the vast region to the west of the Alleghenies. The character of these republics is necessarily as unique as their position, and their influence is already powerful upon the floor of Congress.

In glancing at their geographical position, the foreigner might hastily be led to consider them as growing rivals rather than friendly supporters of the Atlantic states. It will be found, however, that they are at present powerful cementers of the Union, and that the feelings and interests are such as to draw together the north and south divisions of the confederacy.

The new canals will probably draw off the produce of the western counties of New York to the Atlantic; still, however, a portion will find its way down the western waters, as their navigation shall be perfected from Erie to New Orleans. At all events, this route will continue to be preferred by the western counties of Pennsylvania, shortly destined to be the seat, if they are not so already, of flourishing manufactures. The advance made in this branch of industry during the last war and for some years previously has received some checks since the peace, but appears likely soon to proceed with redoubled energy.

It may be worth observing that there is something in the character of the American population, as well as in the diverse products of the soil, which seems favourable to the growth of manufactures. I do not allude merely to their mechanical ingenuity, which has shown itself in so many important inventions and improvements in shipbuilding, bridges, steamboat-navigation, implements of husbandry and machinery of all kinds, but to that proud feeling of independence, which disinclines them from many species of labour resorted to by Europeans. There are some farther peculiarities in the condition and character of the scattered population of the West, which rendered the birth of manufactures simultaneous with that of agriculture. In planting himself in the bosom of the wilderness, the settler is often entirely dependent upon his own industry for every article of food and raiment. While he wields the axe and turns up the soil, his wife plies the needle and the spinning wheel, and his children draw sugar from the maple and work at the loom. The finely watered state of Ohio affords so easy an egress for its internal produce that could a sure market have been found, it seems little likely that it would have attempted for many years any great establishments of domestic manufactures. But the policy of foreign countries threw so many checks in the way of the agriculturist and so completely suspended commerce that the new stimulus given to human industry was felt in the most remote corners of the Union.

The instantaneous effect produced by the commercial regulations of Europe, it seems almost impossible to credit; cotton mills and fulling mills, distilleries, and manufactories of every description, sprung, as it were, out of the earth, in city, town, village, and even on the forested shores of the western waters. The young Ohio, for instance, which had existed but eight years, in 1811 poured down the western waters woollen, flaxen, and cotton goods, of admirable but coarse texture, spirituous liquors, sugars, &c., to the value of two millions of dollars. . . .

The reviving ascendancy of the manufacturing over the commercial interest creates a strong community of feeling between the northern and western sections of the Union. Pittsburgh, the young Manchester of the United States, must always have the character of a western city, and its maritime port be New Orleans. Corinth was not more truly the eye of Greece than is Pittsburgh of America. Pennsylvania, in which it stands, uniting perfectly the characters of an Atlantic and a western state, is truly the keystone of the federal arch.

But if the new states are thus linked with the North, they have also some feelings in common with the South, and thus, drawing two ways, seem to consolidate that confederacy which Europeans have sometimes prophesied they would break. In the first place, Kentucky and Tennessee, the oldest members of this young family, have not only been peopled from Virginia and the Carolinas, but originally made part of those states. Generously released from their jurisdiction, they still retain a marked affection for their parents, and have, too, a community of evil with them, as well as of origin, in the form of black slavery. It is not unlikely that the mixture of slaveholding and nonslaveholding states to the west of the Alleghenies helps to balance the interests between the northern and southern sections of the Union on the floor of Congress. . . .

It is plain that in the course of a few generations the most populous and powerful division of the American family will be watered by the Mississippi, not the Atlantic. From the character of their infancy we may prophesy that the growing preponderance of the western republics will redound to the national honor and will draw more closely the social league, which binds together the great American family.

Bred up under the eye and fostered by the care of the federal government, they have attached themselves to the national institutions with a devotion of feeling unknown in the older parts of the republic. Their patriotism has all the ardor and their policy all the ingenuousness of youth. I have already had occasion to observe upon the enthusiasm with which they asserted the liberties and honor of their country during the last war. Their spirit throughout that contest was truly chivalrous. The anecdotes recorded not only of the valour, but of the romantic generosity of the western army of volunteers, might grace the noblest page of the

Revolutionary history. Nor have the people of the West shown themselves less generous in the Senate than the field. In the hall of the Representatives, they are invariably on the side of what is most honorable and high-minded. Even should they err, you feel that you would rather err with them than be wise with more long-headed or more cold-hearted politicians.

In considering America generally, one finds a character in her foreign to Europe —something which there would be accounted accounted visionary: a liberality of sentiment and a nationality of feeling, not founded upon the mere accident of birth, but upon the appreciation of that civil liberty to which she owes all her greatness and happiness. It is to be expected, however, that in the democracies of the West, these distinctions will be yet more peculiarly marked.

It seems to be a vulgar belief in Europe that the American wilderness is usually settled by the worst members of the community. The friend I write to is well aware that it is generally by the best. The love of liberty, which the emigrant bears with him from the shores of the Connecticut, the Hudson, or Potomac, is exalted and refined in the calm and seclusion of nature's primeval woods and boundless prairies. Some reckless spirits, spurning all law and social order, must doubtless mingle with the more virtuous crowd, but these rarely settle down as farmers. They start ahead of the advanced guard of civilization, and form a wandering troop of hunters, approximating in life and, sometimes, in character to the Indians, their associates. At other times they assume the occupation of shepherds, driving on their cattle from pasture to pasture, according as fancy leads them on from one fair prairie to another still fairer, or according as the approaching tide of population threatens to encroach upon their solitude and their wild dominion. . . .

I have given but a rude sketch of the great divisions of this republic; a subject of this kind admits not of much precision, or, at any rate, my pencil is not skilled enough to handle it ably. I wish you to observe, however, that the birth of the new states has tended to consolidate the Union, and that their growing importance is likely to be felt in the same manner, contrary to the calculations of long-sighted politicians, who foretold that as the integral parts of this great political structure should strengthen and multiply, the cement which held them together would crumble away, and that as the interests of the extended community should become more various, it would be distracted with more party animosities.

The fact is that every sapient prophecy with regard to America has been disproved. We were forewarned that she was too free, and her liberty has proved her security; too peaceable, and she has been found sufficient for her defence; too large, and her size has ensured her union. These numerous republics, scattered through so wide a range of territory, embracing all the climates and containing all the various products of the earth, seem destined, in the course of years, to form a world within themselves, independent alike of the treasures and the industry of all the other sections of the globe. . . . A people who have bled together for liberty, who equally appreciate and equally enjoy that liberty which their own blood or that of their fathers has purchased, who feel, too, that the liberty which they love has found her last asylum on their shores—such a people are bound together by ties of amity and citizenship far beyond what is usual in national communities. . . .

Education

The education of youth, which may be said to form the basis of American government, is in every state of the Union made a national concern. Upon this subject, therefore, the observations that apply to one may be considered as, more or less, applying to all. The portion of this widespread community that paid the earliest and most anxious attention to the instruction of its citizens was New England. This probably originated in the great democracy of her colonial institutions. Liberty and knowledge ever go hand in hand.

If the national policy of some of the New England states has been occasionally censurable, the internal arrangement of all amply redeems her character. There is not a more truly virtuous community in the world than that found in the democracies of the East. The beauty of their villages, the neatness and cleanliness of their houses, the simplicity of their manners, the sincerity of their religion, despoiled in a great measure of its former Calvinistic austerity, their domestic habits, pure morals, and well-administered laws must command the admiration and respect of every stranger. I was forcibly struck in Connecticut with the appearance of the children, neatly dressed, with their satchels on their arms and their faces blooming with health and cheerfulness, dropping their courtesy to the passenger as they trooped to school. The obeisance thus made is not rendered to station but to age. Like the young Spartans, the youth are taught to salute respectfully their superiors in years, and the artlessness and modesty with which the intelligent young creatures reply to the stranger's queries might give pleasure to Lycurgus himself.

The state of Connecticut has appropriated a fund of a million and a half of dollars to the suport of public schools. In Vermont, a certain portion of land has been laid off in every township, whose proceeds are devoted to the same purpose. In the other states, every township taxes itself to such amount as is necessary to defray the expense of schools, which teach reading, writing, and arithmetic to the whole population. In larger towns these schools teach geography and the rudiments of Latin. These establishments, supported at the common expense, are open to the whole youth, male and female, of the country. Other seminaries of a higher order are also maintained in the more populous districts, half the expense being discharged by appropriated funds and the remainder by a small charge laid on the scholar. The instruction here given fits the youth for the state colleges, of which there is one or more in every state. The university of Cambridge, in Massachusetts, is the oldest and, I believe, the most distinguished establishment of the kind existing in the Union.

Perhaps the number of colleges founded in this widespread family of republics may not, in general, be favourable to the growth of distinguished universities. It best answers, however, the object intended, which is not to raise a few very learned citizens but a well-informed and liberal-minded community. . . .

If we must seek the explanation of national manners in national institutions and early education, all the characteristics of the American admit of an easy explanation. The foreigner is at first surprised to find in the ordinary citizen that intelligence and those sentiments which he had been accustomed to seek in the writings of philosophers and the conversation of the most enlightened. The better half of our education in the Old World consists of unlearning: we have to unlearn when we come from the nursery, to unlearn again when we come from the school, and often to continue unlearning through life, and to quit the scene at last without having rid ourselves of half the false notions which had been implanted in our young minds. All this trouble is saved here. The impressions received in childhood are few and simple, as are all the elements of just knowledge. Whatever ideas may be acquired are learned from the page of truth and embrace principles often unknown to the most finished scholar of Europe. Nor is the *manner* in which education is here conducted without its influence in forming the character. I feel disposed at least to ascribe to it that mild friendliness of demeanor which distinguishes the American. It is violence that begets violence, and gentleness, gentleness. I have frequently heard it stated by West Indians that a slave invariably makes the hardest slave driver. In English schools it is well known that the worst-used *fag* becomes, in his turn, the most cruel tyrant, and in a British ship of war it will often be found that the merciless disciplinarian has learned his harshness in the school of suffering. The American, in his infancy, manhood, or age, never feels the hand of oppression. Violence is positively forbidden in the school, in the prisons, on shipboard, in the army; everywhere, in short, where authority is exercised, it must be exercised without appeal to the argument of a blow.

Not long since a master was dismissed from a public school, in a neighbouring state, for having struck a boy. The little fellow was transformed in a moment from a culprit to an accuser. "Do you dare to strike me? You are my teacher, but not my tyrant." The schoolroom made common cause in a moment, the fact was enquired into, and the master dismissed. No apology for the punishment was sought in the nature of the offence which might have provoked it. As my informer observed, "It was thought that the man who could not master his own passions was unfit to control the passions of others; besides, that he had infringed the rules of the school and forfeited the respect of his scholars." By this early exemption from arbitrary power, the boy acquires feelings and habits which abide with him through life. He feels his own importance as a human and a thinking being, and learns to regard violence as equally degrading to him who exercises it and to him who submits to it. You will perceive how the seeds of pride and gentleness are thus likely to spring up together in the same mind. In the proper union and tempering of these two qualities were, perhaps, found the perfection of national as well as of individual character.

In the education of women, New England seems hitherto to have been peculiarly liberal. The ladies of the eastern states are frequently possessed of the most solid acquirements, the modern and even the dead languages, and a wide scope of reading; the consequence is that their manners have the character of being more composed than those of my gay young friends in this quarter. I have already stated, in one of my earlier letters, that the public attention is now everywhere turned to the improvement of female education. In some states, colleges for girls are established under the eye of the legislature, in which are taught all those important branches of knowledge that your friend Dr. Rush conceived to be so requisite.

In other countries it may seem of little consequence to inculcate upon the female mind "the principles of government, and the obligations of patriotism," but it was wisely forseen by that venerable apostle of liberty that in a country where a mother is charged with the formation of an infant mind that is to be called in future to judge of the laws and support the liberties of a republic, the mother herself should well understand those laws and estimate those liberties. Personal accomplishments and the more ornamental branches of knowledge should certainly in America be made subordinate to solid information. This is perfectly the case with respect to the men; as yet the women have been educated too much after the European manner. French, Italian, dancing, drawing engage the hours of the one sex (and this but too commonly in a lax and careless way), while the more appropriate studies of the other are philosophy, history, political economy, and the exact sciences. It follows, consequently, that after the spirits of youth have somewhat subsided, the two sexes have less in common in their pursuits and turn of thinking than is desirable. A woman of a powerful intellect will of course seize upon the new topics presented to her by the conversation of her husband. The less vigorous or the more thoughtless mind is not easily brought to forego trifling pursuits for those which occupy the stronger reason of its companion.

I must remark that in no particular is the liberal philosophy of the Americans more honorably evinced than in the place which is awarded to women. The prejudices still to be found in Europe, though now indeed somewhat antiquated, which would confine the female library to romances, poetry, and belleslettres, and female conversation to the last new publication, new bonnet, and *pas seul,* are entirely unknown here. The women are assuming their place as thinking beings, not in despite of the men, but chiefly in consequence of their enlarged views and exertions as fathers and legislators. . . .

Slavery

And now, my dear friend, I approach the conclusion of the voluminous correspondence which I have addressed to you from this country. You contrive to persuade me that the information I have collected has often possessed for you the merit of novelty. I have, however, to regret that my personal observation has been confined to a portion of this vast country, the whole of whose surface merits the study of a more discerning traveller than myself. I own that as regards the southern states I have ever felt a secret reluctance to visit their territory. The sight of slavery is revolting everywhere, but to inhale the impure breath of its pestilence in the free winds of America is odious beyond all that the imagination can conceive. I do not mean to indulge in idle declamation either against the injustice of the masters or upon the degradation of the slave. This is a subject upon which it is difficult to reason, because it is so easy to feel. The difficulties that stand in the way of emancipation, I can perceive to be numerous; but should the masters content themselves with idly deploring the evil, instead of "setting their shoulder to the wheel" and actively working out its remedy, neither their courtesy in the drawing room, their virtues in domestic life, nor even their public services in the senate and the field will preserve the southern planters from the reprobation of their northern brethren, and the scorn of mankind. The Virginians are said to pride themselves upon the peculiar tenderness with which they visit the sceptre of authority upon their African vassals. As all those acquainted with the character of the Virginia planters, whether Americans or foreigners, appear to concur in bearing testimony to their humanity, it is probable that they are entitled to the praise which they claim. But in their position, justice should be held superior to humanity; to break the chains would be more generous than to gild them, and, whether we consider the interests of the master or the slave, decidedly more useful. It is true that this neither can nor ought to be done too hastily. To give liberty to a slave before he understands its value is, perhaps, rather to impose a penalty than to bestow a blessing; but it is not clear to me that the southern planters are duly exerting themselves to prepare the way for that change in the condition of their black population which they profess to think not only desirable but inevitable. From the conversation of some distinguished Virginians, I cannot but apprehend that they suffer themselves to be disheartened by the slender success which has hitherto attended the exertions of those philanthropists who have made the character and condition of the negro their study and care. "Look into the cabins of our free negroes," said an eminent individual, a native of Virginia, in conversing with me lately upon this subject; "you will find there little to encourage the idea that to impart the rights of freemen to our black population is to ameliorate their condition, or to elevate their character." It is undoubtedly true that the free negroes of Maryland and Virginia form the most wretched and consequently the most vicious portion of the black population. The most casual observation is sufficient to satisfy a stranger of the truth of this statement. I have not seen a miserable half-clad negro in either state whom I have not found, upon enquiry, to be in possession of liberty. But what argument is to be adduced from this? That to emancipate the African race would be to smite the land with a worse plague than that which defaces it already? The history of the negro in the northern states will save us from so revolting a conclusion. To argue that he constitutes, even there, the least valuable portion of the population, will not affect the question. If his character be there *improving,* a fact which none will deny, we have sufficient data upon which to ground the belief that he may, in time, be rendered a useful member of society, and that the vice and wretchedness which here dwell in the cabins of the emancipated negroes may be traced, in part, to the mixture of freedmen and slaves now observed in the black population. Were the whole race emancipated, their education would necessarily become a national object, the white population would be constrained to hire their service, and they themselves be under the necessity of selling it. At present, when restored by some generous planter to their birthright of liberty, the sons of Africa forfeit the protection of a master without securing the guardianship of the law. To their untutored minds, the gift of freedom is only a release from labour. Poor, ignorant, and lazy, it is impossible that they should not soon be vicious. To exonerate herself from the increasing weight of black pauperism, Virginia has imposed a restriction upon the benevolence of her citizens by a law which exacts of the citizen who emancipates his vassals that he shall remove them without the precincts of the state. . . . Why does not Virginia recur to the plan marked out by herself in the first year of her independence? Has she not virtue to execute what she had wisdom to conceive? She has made so many noble sacrifices to humanity and patriotism, her history records so many acts of heroism and disinterested generosity, that I am willing to persuade myself she is equal to this also. Nor can she be so blind to the future as not to perceive the consequences with which she is threatened, should she not take some active measures to eradicate the Egyptian plague which covers her soil. A servile war is the least of the evils which could befall her; the ruin of her moral character, the decay of her strength, the loss of her political importance, vice, indolence, degradation—these are the evils that will overtake her.

But I shall weary you with my commentaries upon an evil that is so far removed from your sight. Had you studied with me the history and character of the American republic, did you see in her so many seeds of excellence, so bright a dawning of national glory, so fair a promise of a brilliant meridian day, as your friend imagines that she can discern, you would share all that regret, impatience, and anxiety, with which she regards every stain that rests upon her morals, every danger that threatens her peace. An awful responsibility has devolved on the American nation; the liberties of mankind are entrusted to their guardianship; the honor of freedom is identified with the honor of their republic; the agents of tyranny are active in one hemisphere; may the children of liberty be equally active in the other! May they return with fresh ardor to the glorious work which they formerly encountered with so much success—in one word, may they realize the conviction lately expressed to me by their venerable President that "the day is not very far distant when a slave will not be found in America!"

PART FIVE

The Problems
of Expansion, 1820–1876

In the 1820s a new generation matured and came to power in the United States. It had not participated in forging the nation, nor could it remember the debate on the Constitution or the events of 1776. This was, therefore, a time of acute testing for the republic. Were the values and goals of the Founding Fathers relevant or appropriate to their children and grandchildren? When Washington, Jefferson, Adams, and Madison were Presidents, hardly anyone doubted that the spirit of the Revolution was still alive. Citizens shared keen memories of fighting the Redcoats and few feared for the unity of the states; but now without these ties or experiences, a second and third generation might find their inherited traditions inapplicable as they confronted new problems and opportunities.

Moreover, the nation could not simply rely on old formulas or pat applications of tested principles. Pressing issues after 1820 demanded innovative and imaginative solutions. The Founding Fathers had imagined a country of sturdy freemen, tilling their own soil; but what was one to do with the growing number of textile factories in New England towns? They had believed that slavery would gradually disappear; but what was one to do when cotton fastened the institution firmly onto the South? They had imagined a nation of settled farmers; but what was one to do when countrymen refused to sit still and the lines of wagons moving westward swelled daily? They had invoked the general welfare and decried factionalism in politics; but what was one to say of burgeoning political parties and bitterly fought partisan election campaigns? The past was not a specific enough guide to the present problems.

After 1820, the United States began its growth as a major industrial nation, laying the foundation for the tremendous economic development that occurred after the Civil War. In 1830 the production of bituminous coal was barely over 100,000 tons; by 1860 it had climbed to 6,000,000 tons. In 1820 the manufacture of pig iron was only 54,000 tons; by 1860 it stood at 821,000 tons. By the turn of the next century these figures also would be dwarfed, but the first encounter with industrialism, the initial confrontation of the republic and the machine, occurred between 1820 and 1860.

The confrontation was frightening. Americans, surveying the English experience, feared that the factory might bring slums and violent strikes, and divide the nation as it degraded its laborers. Wealth and power might not be worth this cost; but, in fact, the United States avoided these dire results. Entrepreneurs, conscious of the dangers, prudently and paternally supervised the life of their workers. In Lowell, Massachusetts, for example, the textile-mill owners kept close watch over the young girls who tended the machines in company-sponsored boarding houses, and European travelers as well as local officials often testified to the moral integrity of the factory hands. Furthermore, there was long an acute shortage of labor in the first decades of the nineteenth century so that entrepreneurs not only invested in the newest labor-saving machinery but also tried to make working conditions as attractive as possible in order to recruit laborers to the factory. The founders of Lowell, hoping to draw New England farm girls to the mills, assured their families that the experience would be neither demeaning nor humiliating. Private profit and the workers' welfare often fitted together neatly. Finally, after 1840, an influx of immigrants supplied the factory owners' need for labor. The Europeans were docile. Coming from the country where they had faced starvation, the Irish, for instance, found the work hard but not intolerable. Owners became less paternal as immigrants increasingly made up the labor force. But many Americans had already concluded that industrialism would probably not corrupt the country.

The expanding plantation system transformed the South as extensively as the machine affected the North. The declining profits of tobacco cultivation at the end of the eighteenth century had persuaded many observers that slavery would not long survive. But the rise of textile manufacturing in England and New England created a large market for cotton. Factories called for more and more raw materials and the plantation turned to filling the demand.

For some Southerners the plantation style of life held an attraction. They treated their slaves favorably, delighted in social visits with neighbors, in holding local and state political office, and in living leisurely as gentlemen; but the more typical planter ran his establishment like a business, a cotton-growing factory requiring all the oversight and diligence of a capitalistic enterprise. He managed his work force rigorously to obtain the greatest return; he valued slaves for their market price, buying or selling accordingly. To maintain order and control he had recourse to coercion. But planters also bought obedience by keeping the perspectives of the slaves as limited as possible, to prevent them from imagining a life apart from slavery. Bennet Barrow, a wealthy Louisiana planter, advised his colleagues not to educate a slave or to allow him to visit with any frequency on other plantations or in towns. "You must," he also added, "make him as comfortable as possible at home . . . and by that means create in him a habit of perfect dependence on you." By varying combinations of these strategies, masters kept their slaves obediently at work. After 1830, few doubted the viability of the plantation system.

During these years Americans migrated westward in mounting numbers so that by 1860 almost as many people lived in the new states as in the original thirteen colonies. In the decades after 1820 Americans rapidly settled Ohio, Illinois, Indiana, Wisconsin, Michigan, and Missouri. By 1860, the North Central states held almost eight million people, and more than half of them had not been born in the region.

These circumstances might have fragmented the community and even the nation. It was one thing if masters did not know their slaves or owners their workers; but what would become of a community where neighbors did not know each other? Actually, however, migration encouraged rather than weakened community ties. The trip west and the first years of settlement forced men to rely upon each other for basic assistance. Neighbors banded together not only to construct houses but as vigilantes, to keep law and order. Moreover, without very many resources of their own, Western settlers turned frequently to the national government to build roads and supply troops, and generally to promote their welfare. They felt a national allegiance even more keenly than Easterners and Southerners.

The claims of the sections clashed in Washington, and the result was not always generous accommodation. Earlier, the focus of political attention usually had been on the state capitals. But even by the close of Washington's administration, national politics played an important part in the development of the country, and, whether for reasons of personality or ideology, the political scene was frequently stormy. At first, the strength of political organization fluctuated. At times there were bitter battles, at others good feeling prevailed. The accession of Andrew Jackson to the Presidency, however, sparked several lasting changes. First, elections became increasingly party-centered as Whigs and Democrats competed for support. Second, political organizations bcame more permanent and elaborate, feeding on the spoils of victory. Moreover, the two parties competed for power by attempting to capture wide public backing; the Whigs, abandoning all elitist notions in 1840, pursued mass support as keenly as the Jacksonians. As a result, voter participation reached unprecedented levels in Presidential elections. At the same time, national politics began to rival state politics in importance; more and more often, Washington became the appropriate place to seek assistance, to assert interests and ideas.

The outstanding quality of national politics after 1820, however, was sectionalism. Party organization was too new and weak to give members a national outlook. Men voted in Congress by states rather than by parties. They campaigned on election day under a party banner, but when it came time to make up their minds

333

on an issue, they paid most attention to the interests of their state. Southerners tended to live together in Washington, and vote together in Congress; Western and Northern representatives were only slightly less clannish. Party loyalties were not strong enough to weaken sectional allegiance. Membership in a national organization like the Whigs or the Democrats was not vital enough to encourage a national perspective.

If no pressing questions had confronted the nation, sectionalism might have made little difference. But the country urgently needed guidance in settling the slavery problem, and national political institutions did not provide it. They were, of course, not alone in their failure; Protestant churches, for example, split over the issue; but when political parties also divided, civil war followed.

The first abolitional agitation coincided with the growing awareness that the peculiar institution would not die out of its own accord. To the abolitionists, slavery controverted the fundamental precepts of Christian morality as well as the basic ideals of the republic. Reformers convinced of the innate perfectibility of man were eagerly attempting to cure the insane, rehabilitate the criminal, and teach the deaf and dumb. They found it intolerable to accept the perpetuation of slavery in the United States. At first, audiences greeted their messages with little enthusiasm, but when slavery threatened to expand into the Western territories, more and more citizens thought it best to limit the institution. Southerners, for their part, reacted to all criticisms defensively and rigidly, preferring to block out the messages rather than try to reach a solution within a national framework. Convinced that their style of life, economic well-being, and physical safety depended on slavery, they saw themselves as a persecuted and misunderstood minority and retreated intellectually, socially, and politically inward.

The parties were unable to bridge these divisions. As other institutions splintered over the issue of slavery, the political arena became one of the last meeting places for all sections, offering a forum for discussion and a mechanism for effecting adjustments; but as Southerner separated from Northerner, the Democratic party became the party of the South, and the Republicans, successors to the Whigs, became the party of the North. This political reaction was all the more tragic for there was certainly in the North and West and in some parts of the South a vague but genuine sentiment for the union—a feeling that put the perpetuation of the United States above all other considerations. But the parties could not translate this emotion into workable political programs. Each side reiterated its demands; and when, in 1860, the South believed that Lincoln's election as President tipped the balance of power to the North, it took the final step of separation. The Union, rather than let its sisters depart in peace, resorted to arms. Even at the cost of civil war, it would not allow the nation to disintegrate.

Neither North nor South could marshall men and equipment speedily and efficiently, and quick success eluded both sides. Slowly over four years, the greater resources of the Union became increasingly important, and when General Ulysses S. Grant made full use of them, the North finally earned a hard-fought victory. The problems posed by peace were hardly less simple, and the Union did not reveal special skill or sensitivity in confronting them. The Republicans lacked any consistent or carefully considered program. They moved unsteadily from one measure to another, rarely considering the wider significance and implications of their actions. By the time military occupation was over in 1876, there were deep wounds that would take decades or longer to heal. The Union was preserved and the Negro free; but the North liberated the slaves without sustained attention to their welfare. It secured their political rights in law, but paid little attention to realities—political, social, or economic. The South, crushed and bitter, resented the harshness of military reconstruction, and when finally left to its own devices it all too often remained isolated in spirit and temperament. The nation in 1876 was still far from at peace with itself.

32

A Frontier Community

The American frontier was an endless source of wonderment, pride, security, confusion, embarrassment, and humor in the early days of the nineteenth century. No traveler from Europe could resist a look at the rural parts of the country, and Americans themselves read avidly about the customs and manners of their Western countrymen. Observations varied with the traveler; some found the inconveniences as much a trial as the settlers' rudeness; others defended the life as humble and democratic, the heart and mainstay of America. Yet, certain common themes run through most of the accounts—themes that contradict any simple notion of the frontier as the home of individualism.

Descriptions of the journey across the Plains made it clear that few men moved alone. Migrants stayed together not only because of the danger of Indian attacks but because of everyday needs and concerns as well. If wagons were too heavy for one pair of oxen to pull up a hill, the pioneer doubled the teams by first borrowing his neighbor's and then lending his own. So, too, once having located in a new community, settlers did not desert one another.

This account by Caroline S. Kirkland was a typical presentation of life in the West and enjoyed a wide readership when it appeared in 1839. Kirkland's story, *A New Home, Who'll Follow?* reveals clearly her own prejudices; but it also reflects much that was central to frontier existence.

A NEW HOME
Caroline S. Kirkland

When my husband purchased two hundred acres of wild land and drew with a piece of chalk on the bar-room table the plan of a village, I little thought I was destined to make myself famous by handing down to posterity a faithful record of the advancing fortunes of that favoured spot.

"The madness of the people" in those days of golden dreams took more commonly the form of city-building; but there were a few who contented themselves with planning villages, on the banks of streams which certainly never could be

From Caroline S. Kirkland (Mary Clavers, pseud.), *A New Home, Who'll Follow?* (1839), 8–9, 67–69, 82–83, 88–91, 111, 114–115.

expected to bear navies, but which might yet be turned to account in the more homely way of grinding or sawing—operations which must necessarily be performed somewhere for the wellbeing of those very cities. It is of one of these humble attmpts that it is my lot to speak, and I make my confession at the outset, warning any fashionable reader who may have taken up my book, that I intend to be "decidedly low."

'Tis true there are but meagre materials for anything which might be called a story. I have never seen a cougar—nor been bitten by a rattlesnake. The reader who has patience to go with me to the close of my desultory sketches, must expect nothing beyond a meandering recital of common-place occurrences—mere gossip about every-day people, little enhanced in value by any fancy or ingenuity of the writer; in short, a very ordinary pen-drawing; which, deriving no interest from colouring, can be valuable only for its truth.

A home on the outskirts of civilization—habits of society which allow the maid and her mistress to do the honours in complete equality, and to make the social tea visit in loving conjunction—such a distribution of the duties of life as compels all, without distinction, to rise with the sun or before him—to breakfast with the chickens—then,

"Count the slow clock and dine exact at noon"—

to be ready for tea at four, and for bed at eight—may certainly be expected to furnish some curious particulars for the consideration of those whose daily course almost reverses this primitive arrangement—who "call night day and day night," and who are apt occasionally to forget, when speaking of a particular class, that "those creatures" are partakers with themselves of a common nature.

I can only wish, like other modest chroniclers, my respected prototypes, that so fertile a theme had fallen into worthier hands.

It did not require a very long residence in Michigan, to convince me that it is unwise to attempt to stem directly the current of society, even in the wilderness, but I have since learned many ways of *wearing round* which give me the opportunity of living very much after my own fashion, without offending, very seriously, any body's prejudices.

No settlers are so uncomfortable as those who, coming with abundant means as they suppose, to be comfortable, set out with a determination to live as they have been accustomed to live. They soon find that there are places where the "almighty dollar" is almost powerless; or rather, that powerful as it is, it meets with its conqueror in the jealous pride of those whose services must be had in order to live at all.

"Luff when it blows," is a wise and necessary caution. Those who forget it and attempt to carry all sail set and to keep an unvarying course, blow which way it will, always abuse Michigan, and are abused in their turn. Several whom we have known to set out with this capital mistake have absolutely turned about again in despair, revenging themselves by telling very hard stories about us nor'westers. You may say any thing you like of the country or its inhabitants: but beware how you raise a suspicion that you despise the homely habits of those around you. This is never forgiven.

337

It would be in vain to pretend that this state of society can ever be agreeable to those who have been accustomed to the more rational arrangements of the older world. The social character of the meals, in particular, is quite destroyed, by the constant presence of strangers, whose manners, habits of thinking, and social connexions are quite different from your own, and often exceedingly repugnant to your taste. Granting the correctness of the opinion which may be read in their countenances that they are "as good as you are," I must insist, that a greasy cook-maid, or a redolent stable-boy, can never be, to my thinking, an agreeable table companion—putting pride, that most terrific bug-bear of the woods, out of the question.

If the best man now living should honour my humble roof with his presence—if he should happen to have an unfortunate *penchant* for eating out of the dishes, picking his teeth with his fork, or using the fire-place for a pocket handkerchief, I would prefer he should take his dinner *solus* or with those who did as he did.

But, I repeat it; those who find these inconveniences most annoying while all is new and strange to them, will by the exertion of a little patience and ingenuity, discover ways and means of getting aside of what is most unpleasant, in the habits of their neighbours: and the silent influence of example is daily effecting much towards reformation in many particulars. Neatness, propriety, and that delicate forbearance of the least encroachment upon the rights or the enjoyments of others, which is the essence of true elegance of manner, have only to be seen and understood to be admired and imitated; and I would fain persuade those who are groaning under certain inflictions to which I have but alluded, that the true way of overcoming all the evils of which *they* complain is to set forth in their own manners and habits, all that is kind, forbearing, true, lovely, and of good report. They will find ere long that their neighbours have taste enough to love what is so charming, even though they see it exemplified by one who sits *all day* in a carpeted parlor, teaches her own children instead of sending them to the district school, hates "the breath of garlic eaters," and—oh fell climax!—knows nothing at all of soap-making.

Some of my dear theorizing friends in the civilized world had dissuaded me most earnestly from bringing a maid with me.

"She would always be discontented and anxious to return; and you'll find plenty of good farmer's daughters ready to live with you for the sake of earning a little money."

Good souls! how little did they know of Michigan! I have since that day seen the interior of many a wretched dwelling, with almost literally nothing in it but a bed, a chest, and a table; children ragged to the last degree, and potatoes the only fare; but never yet saw I one where the daughter was willing to own herself obliged to live out at service. She would "hire out" long enough to buy some article of dress perhaps, money to pay the doctor, or for some such special reason; but never as a regular calling, or with an acknowledgment of inferior station.

This state of things appalled me at first; but I have learned a better philosophy since. I find no difficulty now in getting such aid as I require, and but little in retaining it as long as I wish, though there is always a desire of making an occasional display of independence. Since living with one for wages is considered by common consent a favour, I take it as a favour; and, this point once conceded, all goes well. Perhaps I have been peculiarly fortunate; but certainly with one or two exceptions, I have little or nothing to complain of on this essential point of domestic comfort.

To be sure, I had one damsel who crammed herself almost to suffocation with sweatmeats and other things which she esteemed very nice; and ate up her own pies and cake, to the exclusion of those for whom they were intended; who would put her head in at a door, with—"*Miss* Clavers, did you hollar? I thought I *heered* a yell."

And another who was highly offended, because room was not made for her at table with guests from the city, and that her company was not requested for tea-visits. And this latter high-born damsel sent in from the kitchen a circumstantial account *in writing,* of the instances wherein she considered herself aggrieved; well written it was too, and expressed with much *naïveté,* and abundant respect. I answered it in the way which "turneth away wrath." Yet it was not long before this fiery spirit was aroused again, and I was forced to part with my country belle.

You discover a thousand requisites that you had never thought of, and it is well if you do not come to the angry conclusion that every body is in league against you and your plans. Perhaps the very next day after you have by extra personal exertion, an offer of extra price, or a bonus in some other form, surmounted some prodigious obstacle, you walk down to survey operations with a comfortable feeling of self-gratulation, and find yourself in complete solitude, every soul having gone off to election or town meeting. No matter at what distance these important affairs are transacted, so fair an excuse for a *ploy* can never pass unimproved; and the virtuous indignation which is called forth by any attempt at dissuading one of the sovereigns from exercising "the noblest privilege of a freeman," to forward your business and his own, is most amusingly provoking.

I once ventured to say, in my feminine capacity merely, and by way of experiment, to a man whose family I knew to be suffering for want of the ordinary comforts:

"I should suppose it must be a great sacrifice for you, Mr. Fenwick, to spend two days in going to election."

The reply was given with the air of Forrest's William Tell, and in a tone which would have rejoiced Miss Martineau's heart—"Yes, to be sure; but ought not a man to do his duty to his country?"

This was unanswerable, of course. I hope it consoled poor Mrs. Fenwick, whose tattered gown would have been handsomely renewed by those two days' wages.

The circumstance of living all summer, in the same apartment with a cooking fire, I had never happened to see alluded to in any of the elegant sketches of western life which had fallen under my notice. It was not until I actually became the inmate of a log dwelling in the wilds, that I realized fully what "living all in one room" meant. The sleeping apparatus for the children and the sociable Angeline, were in the loft; but my own bed, with its cunning fence of curtains; my bureau, with its "Alps on Alps" of boxes and books; my entire cooking array; my centre-table, which bore, sad change! the remains of to-day's dinner, and the preparations for to-morrow, all covered mysteriously under a large cloth, the only refuge from the mice: these and ten thousand other things, which a summer's day would not suffice me to enumerate, cumbered this one single apartment; and to crown the whole was the inextinguishable fire.

I took especial care to be impartial in my own visiting habits, determined at all sacrifice to live down the impression that I felt *above* my neighbours. In fact, however we may justify certain exclusive habits in populous places, they are strikingly and confessedly ridiculous in the wilderness. What can be more absurd than a feeling of proud distinction, where a stray spark of fire, a sudden illness, or a day's contre-temps, may throw you entirely upon the kindness of your humblest neighbour? If I treat Mrs. Timson with neglect to-day can I with any face borrow her broom to-morrow? And what would become of me, if in revenge for my declining her invitation to tea this afternoon, she should decline coming to do my washing on Monday?

"Mother wants your sifter," said Miss Ianthe Howard, a young lady of six years' standing, attired in a tattered calico, thickened with dirt; her unkempt locks straggling from under that hideous substitute for a bonnet, so universal in the western country, a dirty cotton handkerchief, which is used, *ad nauseam,* for all sorts of purposes.

"Mother wants your sifter, and she says she guesses you can let her have some sugar and tea, 'cause you've got plenty."

This excellent reason, "'cause you've got plenty," is conclusive as to sharing with your neighbours. Whoever comes into Michigan with nothing, will be sure to better his condition; but wo to him that brings with him any thing like an appearance of abundance, whether of money or mere household conveniences. To have them, and not be willing to share them in some sort with the whole community, is an unpardonable crime. You must lend your best horse to *qui que ce soit,* to go ten miles over hill and marsh, in the darkest night, for a doctor; or your team to travel twenty after a "gal;" your wheel-barrows, your shovels, your utensils of all sorts, belong, not to yourself, but to the public, who do not think it necessary even to *ask* a loan, but take it for granted. The two saddles and bridles of Montacute spend most of their time travelling from house to house a-manback; and I have actually known a stray martingale to be traced to four dwellings two miles apart, having been lent from one to another, without a word to the original proprietor, who sat waiting, not very patiently, to commence a journey.

Then within doors, an inventory of your plenishing of all sorts, would scarcely more than include the articles which you are solicited to lend. Not only are all kitchen utensils as much your neighbours as your own, but bedsteads, beds, blankets, sheets, travel from house to house, a pleasant and effectual mode of securing the perpetuity of certain efflorescent peculiarities of the skin, for which Michigan is becoming almost as famous as the land "'twixt Maidenkirk and John o' Groat's." Sieves, smoothing irons, and churns run about as if they had legs; one brass kettle is enough for a whole neighbourhood; and I could point to a cradle which has rocked half the babies in Montacute. For my own part, I have lent my broom, my thread, my tape, my spoons, my cat, my thimble, my scissors, my shawl, my shoes; and have been asked for my combs and brushes: and my husband, for his shaving apparatus and his pantaloons.

Many English families reside in our vicinity, some of them well calculated to make their way any where; close, penurious, grasping and indefatigable; denying themselves all but the necessaries of life, in order to add to their lands, and make the most of their crops; and somewhat apt in bargaining to overreach even the wary pumpkin-eaters, their neighbours: others to whom all these things seem so foreign and so unsuitable, that one cannot but wonder that the vagaries of fortune should have sent them into so uncongenial an atmosphere. The class last mentioned, generally live retired, and show little inclination to mingle with their rustic neighbours; and of course, they become at once the objects of suspicion and dislike. The principle of "let-a-be for let-a-be" holds not with us. Whoever exhibits any desire for privacy is set down as "praoud," or something worse; no matter how inoffensive, or even how benevolent he may be; and of all places in the world in which to live on the shady side of public opinion, an American back-woods settlement is the very worst, as many of these unfortunately mistaken emigrants have been made to feel.

The better classes of English settlers seem to have left their own country with high-wrought notions of the unbounded freedom to be enjoyed in this; and it is with feelings of angry surprise that they learn after a short residence here, that this very universal freedom abridges their own liberty to do as they please in their individual capacity; that the absolute democracy which prevails in country places, imposes as heavy restraints upon one's free-will in some particulars, as do the over-bearing pride and haughty distinctions of the old world in others; and after one has changed one's whole plan of life, and crossed the wide ocean to find a Utopia, the waking to reality is attended with feelings of no slight bitterness. In some instances within my knowledge these feelings of disappointment have been so severe as to neutralize all that was good in American life, and to produce a degree of sour discontent which increased every real evil and went far towards alienating the few who were kindly inclined toward the stranger.

33

Morals and the Machine

The introduction of the machine and the factory in America was not without its difficulty, for, judging by the English experience, many observers feared for the moral welfare of the nation. In England they saw harsh working conditions and increasing friction between classes in strikes and labor organizations. Would the factory bring these evils to the new republic?

The founding of Lowell, Massachusetts, in the 1820s by a group of Boston entrepreneurs was a venture in profitmaking through the manufacture of textiles. But it was also an attempt to order industrial organization so as to prevent the noxious effects so prevalent in England. The two goals were not contradictory. The sponsors had to attract a large and reliable labor force, and in a country where small farmers predominated, this was no simple task. They decided to employ the young ladies of New England agricultural families. New England farming was not in so profitable a state that the families would not welcome some extra money. Still, fathers would have to be assured of their daughters' physical and moral welfare—the way the nation would have to be assured of the wholesome effects of industry. By design and good fortune, the Lowell entrepreneurs attracted a labor supply and helped convince the nation that industry could be controlled. The following selection by a Lowell minister, Henry A. Miles, was what the nation in general and fathers in particular wanted to hear.

LOWELL, AS IT WAS AND AS IT IS
Henry A. Miles

Lowell has been highly commended by some, as a model community, for its good order, industry, spirit of intelligence, and general freedom from vice. It has been strongly condemned, by others, as a hotbed of corruption, tainting and polluting the whole land. We all, in New England, have an interest in knowing what are the exact facts of the case. We are destined to be a great manufacturing people. The

From *Lowell, As It Was and As It Is* (Lowell, 1845), 62–63, 67–76, 101–105, 129–135, 140–153, 160–161, 174–179, 214–215.

influences that go forth from Lowell, will go forth from many other manufacturing villages and cities. If these influences are pernicious, we have a great calamity impending over us. Rather than endure it, we should prefer to have every factory destroyed; the character of our sons and daughters being of infinitely more importance than any considerations "wherewithal they shall be clothed." If, on the other hand, a system has been introduced, carefully provided with checks and safeguards, and strong moral and conservative influences, it is our duty to see that this system be faithfully carried out, so as to prevent the disastrous results which have developed themselves in the manufacturing towns of other countries. Hence the topics above named assume the importance of the highest moral questions. They will justify and demand the most careful consideration. The author writes after a nine years' residence in this city, during which he has closely observed the working of the factory system, and has gathered a great amount of statistical facts which have a bearing upon this subject. He believes himself to be unaffected by any partisan views, as he stands wholly aside from the sphere of any interested motives. He enters upon this part of his work, feeling, in the outset, that he has no case, one way or the other, to make out.

A Lowell Boarding-House

Each of the long blocks of boarding-houses is divided into six or eight tenements, and are generally three stories high. These tenements are finished off in a style much above the common farm-houses of the country, and more nearly resemble the abodes of respectable mechanics in rural villages. They are all furnished with an abundant supply of water, and with suitable yards and out-buildings. These are constantly kept clean, the buildings well painted, and the premises thoroughly whitewashed every spring, at the Corporation's expense. The front room is usually the common eating-room of the house, and the kitchen is in the rear. The keeper of the house, (commonly a widow, with her family of children,) has her parlor in some part of the establishment; and in some houses there is a sitting-room for the use of the boarders. The remainder of the apartments are sleeping-rooms. In each of these are lodged two, four, and in some cases six boarders; and the room has an air of neatness and comfort, exceeding what most of the occupants have been accustomed to in their paternal homes. In many cases, these rooms are not sufficiently large for the number who occupy them; and oftentimes that attention is not paid to their ventilation which a due regard to health demands. These are points upon which a reform is called for; and, in the construction of new boarding-houses, this reform should be attempted. At the same time, it should in justice be added, that the evil alluded to is not peculiar to Lowell, and will not probably appear to be a crying one, if the case should be brought into comparison with many of the apartments of milliners and sempstresses in the boarding-houses of our cities.

As one important feature in the management of these houses, it deserves to be named that male operatives and female operatives do not board in the same tenement; and the following Regulations, printed by one of the companies, and given to each keeper of their houses, are here subjoined, as a simple statement of the rules generally observed by all the Corporations.

Regulations to be observed by persons occupying the Boarding-houses belonging to the Merrimack Manufacturing Company.

They must not board any persons not employed by the company, unless by special permission.

No disorderly or improper conduct must be allowed in the houses.

The doors must be closed at 10 o'clock in the evening; and no person admitted after that time, unless a sufficient excuse can be given.

Those who keep the houses, when required, must give an account of the number, names, and employment of their boarders; also with regard to their general conduct, and whether they are in the habit of attending public worship.

The buildings, both inside and out, and the yards about them, must be kept clean, and in good order. If the buildings or fences are injured, they will be repaired and charged to the occupant.

No one will be allowed to keep swine.

The hours of taking meals in these houses are uniform throughout all the Corporations in the city, and are as follows: Dinner—always at half past twelve o'clock. Breakfast—from November 1 to February 28, before going to work, and so early as to begin work as soon as it is light; through March at half past seven o'clock; from April 1 to September 19, at seven o'clock; and from September 20 to October 31, at half past seven o'clock. Supper—always after work at night, that is, after seven o'clock, from March 20 to September 19; after half-past seven o'clock, from September 20 to March 19. The time allowed for each meal is thirty minutes for breakfast, when that meal is taken after beginning work; for dinner, thirty minutes, from September 1 to April 30; and forty-five minutes from May 1 to August 31.

That this time is too short for a due regard to health, must be obvious to all. And yet it is probably as long as most business men allow to themselves; it is probably as long as is spent at the tables of more than half of our public hotels. For the sake of the operatives we wish that the time for meals was lengthened; but we do not see the propriety of calling in this quarter for a reform in those habits of hasty eating which pervade the whole country, and characterize our nation. The food that is furnished in these houses is of a substantial and wholesome kind, is neatly served, and in sufficient abundance. Operatives are under no compulsion to board in one tenement rather than another; it is for the interest of the boarding-house keeper, therefore, to have her bill of fare attractive.

The rents of the company's houses are purposely low, averaging only from one third to one half of what similar houses rent for in the city. There is no intention on the part of the Corporation to make any revenue from these houses. They are a great source of annual expense. But the advantages of supervision are more than an equivalent for this. No tenant is admitted who has not hitherto borne a good character, and who does not continue to sustain it. In many cases the tenant has long been keeper of the house, for six, eight, or twelve years, and is well known to hundreds of her girls as their adviser and friend and second mother.

The influence which this system of boarding-houses has exerted upon the good order and good morals of the place, has been vast and beneficent. By it the care and influence of the superintendent are extended over his operatives, while they are out of the mill, as well as while they are in it. Employing chiefly those who have no permanent residence in Lowell, but are only temporary boarders, upon any embarrassment of affairs they return to their country homes, and do not sink down here a helpless caste, clamouring for work, starving unless employed, and hence ready for a riot, for the destruction of property, and repeating here the scenes enacted in the manufacturing villages of England. To a very great degree the future condition of Lowell is dependent upon a faithful adhesion to this system; and it will deserve the serious consideration of those old towns which are now introducing steam mills, whether, if they do not provide boarding-houses, and employ chiefly other operatives than resident ones, they be not bringing in the seeds of future and alarming evil.

Hours of Labor

The following table shows the average hours per day of running the mills, throughout the year, on all the Corporations in Lowell:

	h.	m.		h.	m.
January	11	24	July	12	45
February	12	00	August	12	45
March	11	52	September	12	23
April	13	31	October	12	10
May	12	45	November	11	56
June	12	45	December	11	24

In addition to the above, it should be stated, that lamps are never lighted on Saturday evening, and that four holidays are allowed in the year, viz. Fast Day, Fourth of July, Thanksgiving Day, and Christmas Day.

No fact connected with the manufacturing business, has been so often, or so strongly objected to as this, which appears from the above table, that the average daily time of running the mills is twelve hours and ten minutes. It is no part of the object of this book to defend any thing which may be shown to be wrong, its sole purpose being a careful presentation of facts. Arguments are not needed to prove that toil, if it be continued for this length of time, each day, month after month, and year after year, is excessive, and too much for the tender frames of young women to bear. No one can more sincerely desire, than the writer of this book, that they had more leisure time for mental improvement and social enjoyment. It must be remembered, however, that their work is comparatively light. All the hard processes, not conducted by men, are performed by machines, the movements of which female operatives are required merely to oversee and adjust. And then as to their long confinement and care, there is a mitigation which, in discussions on this subject, has been almost altogether overlooked, but which is of such vital importance that it merits the most careful attention.

We have given above the hours per day of operating the mills. It must be well understood what this means. These are the hours for running the wheels. It does not follow that all operatives work this number of hours, or are in attendance this number of hours. This is not the case. By a system adjusted to secure this end, by keeping engaged a number of spare hands, by occasional permissions of absence, and by an allowed exchange of work among the girls, the average number of hours in which they are actually employed is not more than ten and a half. They are out to go shopping, to repair their clothes, to take care of themselves in any occasional illness, to see friends visiting the city, to call on sick friends here; nor are reasonable requests of this kind refused. Many of these girls, moreover, in the course of each year, take a vacation of a few weeks, to return to their homes. In these absences the work of the mill is not suspended. The wheels continue their revolutions for the prescribed number of hours. The processes are temporarily superintended by other hands. To suppose that every operative is on duty just as long as the machinery is in motion, is an error of the most deceptive kind. Yet this fallacy has been assumed in almost all the discussions on this subject. The fact has been overlooked of the great number of absences from the mills. These absences reduce the average of work-hours for the girls to the number just stated—ten and a half. This is not a mere assertion. It is a carefully ascertained, and well established fact, in verification of which proof will now be submitted.

Each overseer keeps a record of all the time his hands are employed, in days and quarter of days. These records, in one mill in the city, have been subjected to a thorough analysis. The space of time over which this analysis has been carried is one year. In Boott Mill, No. 1, there are one hundred and six girls who have been employed one year, working by the job. This is the whole number in that mill who are thus employed and have worked that time; and their time record gives the following results: Average number of days per year to each girl, two hundred and sixty and eighty-six one hundredths. Average number of hours per day, to each girl, ten hours and eight minutes.

Moral Police of the Corporations

It has been seen what a large amount of capital is here invested, and what manifold and extensive operations this capital sets in motion. The productiveness of these works depends upon one primary and indispensable condition—the existence of an industrious, sober, orderly, and moral class of operatives. Without this, the mills in Lowell would be worthless. Profits would be absorbed by cases of irregularity, carelessness, and neglect; while the existence of any great moral exposure in Lowell would cut off the supply of help from the virtuous homesteads of the country. Public morals and private interests, identical in all places, are here seen to be linked together in an indissoluble connection. Accordingly, the sagacity of self-interest, as well as more disinterested considerations, has led to the adoption of a strict system of moral police.

Before we proceed to notice the details of this system, there is one consideration bearing upon the character of our operatives, which must all the while be borne in mind. *We have no permanent factory population.* This is the wide gulf which separates the English manufacturing towns from Lowell. Only a very few of our operatives have their homes in this city. The most of them come from the distant interior of the country, as will be proved by statistical facts which will be presented in a subsequent chapter.

To the general fact, here noticed, should be added another, of scarcely less importance to a just comprehension of this subject,—*the female operatives Lowell do not work, on an average, more than four and a half years in the factories.* They then return to their homes, and their places are taken by their sisters, or by other female friends from their neighborhood.

Here, then, we have two important elements of difference between English and American operatives. The former are resident operatives, and are operatives for life, and constitute a permanent, dependent factory caste. The latter come from distant homes, to which in a few years they return, to be the wives of the farmers and mechanics of the country towns and villages. The English visitor to Lowell, when he finds it so hard to understand why American operatives are so superior to those of Leeds and Manchester, will do well to remember what a different class of females we have here to *begin* with—girls well educated in virtuous rural homes; nor must the Lowell manufacturer forget, that we forfeit the distinction, from that moment, when we cease to obtain such girls as the operatives of the city.

To obtain this constant importation of female hands from the country, it is necessary to secure *the moral protection of their characters while they are resident in Lowell.* This, therefore, is the chief object of that moral police referred to, some details of which will now be given.

It should be stated, in the outset, that no persons are employed on the Corporations who are addicted to intemperance, or who are known to be guilty of any immoralities of conduct. As the parent of all other vices, intemperance is most carefully excluded. Absolute freedom from intoxicating liquors is understood, throughout the city, to be a prerequisite to obtaining employment in the mills, and any person known to be addicted to their use is at once dismissed.

A more strictly and universally temperate class of persons cannot be found, than the nine thousand operatives of this city; and the fact is as well known to all others living here, as it is of some honest pride among themselves. In relation to other immoralities, it may be stated, that the suspicion of criminal conduct, association with suspected persons, and general and habitual light behavior and conversation, are regarded as sufficient reasons for dismissions, and for which delinquent operatives are discharged.

In respect to discharged operatives, there is a system observed, of such an effectual and salutary operation, that it deserves to be minutely described.

Any person wishing to leave a mill, is at liberty to do so, at any time, after giving a fortnight's notice. The operative so leaving, if of good character, and having worked a year, is entitled, as a matter of right, to an honorable discharge, made out after a printed form, with which every counting-room is supplied. That form is as follows:

347

Mr. or Miss —— ——, has been employed by the —— Manufacturing Company, in a —— Room, — years — months, and is honorably discharged.

—— ——, *Superintendent.*

LOWELL, —— ——

This discharge is a letter of recommendation to any other mill in the city, and not without its influence in procuring employment in any other mill in New England. A record of all such discharges is made in each counting-room, in a book kept for that purpose.

So much for honorable discharges. Those dishonorable have another treatment. The names of all persons dismissed for bad conduct, or who leave the mill irregularly, are also entered in a book kept for that purpose, and these names are sent to all the counting-rooms of the city, and are there entered on *their* books. *Such persons obtain no more employment throughout the city.* The question is put to each applicant, "Have you worked before in the city, and if so, where is your discharge?" If no discharge be presented, an inquiry of the applicant's name will enable the superintendent to know whether that name stands on his book of dishonorable discharges, and he is thus saved from taking in a corrupt or unworthy hand. This system, which has been in operation in Lowell from the beginning, is of great and important effect in driving unworthy·persons from our city, and in preserving the high character of our operatives.

Any description of the moral care, studied by the Corporations, would be defective if it omitted a reference to the overseers. Every room in every mill has its first and second overseer. The former, or, in his absence, the latter, has the entire care of the room, taking in such operatives as he wants for the work of the room, assigning to them their employment, superintending each process, directing the repairs of disordered machinery, giving answers to questions of advice, and granting permissions of absence. At his small desk, near the door, where he can see all who go out or come in, the overseer may generally be found; and he is held responsible for the good order, propriety of conduct, and attention to business, of the operatives of that room. Hence, this is a post of much importance, and the good management of the mill is almost wholly dependent upon the character of its overseers. It is for this reason that peculiar care is exercised in their appointment. Raw hands, and of unknown characters, are never placed in this office. It is attained only by those who have either served a regular apprenticeship as machinists in the Repair Shop, or have become well known and well tried, as third hands, and assistant overseers. It is a post for which there are always many applicants, the pay being two dollars a day, with a good house, owned by the company, and rented at the reduced charge before notice. The overseers are almost universally married men, with families; and as a body, numbering about one hundred and eighty, in all, are among the most permanent residents, and most trustworthy and valuable citizens of the place. A large number of them are members of our churches, and are often chosen as council men in the city government, and representatives in the State legislature. The guiding and salutary influence which they exert over the operatives, is one of the most essential parts of the moral machinery of the mills.

As closely connected with the foregoing statements, the following note from a superintendent may be here republished, which was sent in reply to questions proposed to him in the Spring of 1841:—

Dear Sir:—

I employ in our mills, and in the various departments connected with them, thirty overseers, and as many second overseers. My overseers are married men, with families, with a single exception, and even he has engaged a tenement, and is to be married soon. Our second overseers are younger men, but upwards of twenty of them are married, and several others are soon to be married. Sixteen of our overseers are members of some regular church, and four of them are deacons. Ten of our second overseers are also members of the church, and one of them is the superintendent of a Sunday School. I have no hesitation in saying that in all the sterling requisites of character, in native intelligence, and practical good sense, in sound morality, and as active, useful, and exemplary citizens, they may, as a class, safely challenge comparison with any class in our community. I know not, among them all, an intemperate man, nor, at this time, even what is called a moderate drinker.

Yours truly,

Lowell, May 10, 1841

Still another source of trust which a Corporation has, for the good character of its operatives, is the moral control which they have over one another. Of course this control would be nothing among a generally corrupt and degraded class. But among virtuous and high-minded young women, who feel that they have the keeping of their characters, and that any stain upon their associates brings reproach upon themselves, the power of opinion becomes an ever-present, and ever-active restraint. A girl, *suspected* of immoralities, or serious improprieties of conduct, at once loses caste. Her fellow-boarders will at once leave the house, if the keeper does not dismiss the offender. In self-protection, therefore, the matron is obliged to put the offender away. Nor will her former companions walk with, or work with her; till at length, finding herself everywhere talked about, and pointed at, and shunned, she is obliged to relieve her fellow-operatives of a presence which they feel brings disgrace. From this power of opinion, there is no appeal; and as long as it is exerted in favor of propriety of behavior and purity of life, it is one of the most active and effectual safeguards of character.

It may not be out of place to present here the regulations, which are observed alike on all the Corporations, which are given to the operatives when they are first employed, and are posted up conspicuously in all the mills. They are as follows:—

Regulations to be Observed by All Persons Employed by the

——Manufacturing Company, in the Factories.

Every overseer is required to be punctual himself, and to see that those employed under him are so.

The overseers may, at their discretion, grant leave of absence to those employed under them, when there are sufficient spare hands in the room to supply their place; but when there are not sufficient spare hands, they are not allowed to grant leave of absence unless in cases of absolute necessity.

All persons are required to observe the regulations of the room in which they are employed. They are not allowed to be absent from their work without the consent of their overseer, except in case of sickness, and then they are required to send him word of the cause of their absence.

349

All persons are required to board in one of the boarding houses belonging to the company, and conform to the regulations of the house in which they board.

All persons are required to be constant in attendance on public worship, at one of the regular places of worship in this place.

Persons who do not comply with the above regulations will not be employed by the company.

Persons entering the employment of the company, are considered as engaging to work one year.

All persons intending to leave the employment of the company, are required to give notice of the same to their overseer, at least two weeks previous to the time of leaving.

Any one who shall take from the mills, or the yard, any yarn, cloth, or other article belonging to the company, will be considered guilty of STEALING—and prosecuted accordingly.

The above regulations are considered part of the contract with all persons entering the employment of the——MANUFACTURING COMPANY. All persons who shall have complied with them, on leaving the employment of the company, shall be entitled to an honorable discharge, which will serve as a recommendation to any of the factories in Lowell. No one who shall not have complied with them will be entitled to such a discharge. —— ——, Agent

Boarding-House Statistics

It has been before stated that in many cases the keepers of the boarding-houses retain their places for eight, ten, or twelve years. Standing in the place of parents to their girls, their future welfare is a matter of deep interest to these matrons, and frequently they have some knowledge of the after fortunes of their boarders, through sisters and neighbors, who have succeeded them in the mills. It, hence, appeared probable, that by extensive and careful inquiries of the matrons, important facts might be collected in respect to the health and character of their girls, while boarders, and of their honorable standing in life, after they had retired from Lowell. For this purpose a series of questions was prepared, copies of which were handed to three or four matrons on each Corporation, and their written replies have been returned to the author, and will here be subjoined. There was no selection of houses from which to seek returns, and there is no selection of returns so as to present only favorable cases.

The questions were as follows:—

1. How long have you kept a boarding-house on this Corporation?
2. How many boarders have you now?
3. How many boarders have you had in all since you kept the house?
4. How many of your girls have, to your knowledge, been married?
5. How many have died?
6. How many have gone home sick?
7. How many of your boarders have been dismissed from the Corporation for bad conduct?
8. Have you ever had much sickness in your house?

9. How many cases do you think, which have lasted a week, and have had the care of a physician?

The replies will be copied exactly as they were returned.

Case 1.   Have kept a boarding-house on the Appleton four and a half years; have now nineteen boarders; have had probably, in all, a hundred and fifty; knows of ten of these that have been married; not one of her girls, while a boarder, has died; three have gone home sick; none of her boarders have been dismissed for bad conduct; have had but little sickness; perhaps eight cases that have lasted a week, and had the care of a physician.

Case 2.   Have kept a boarding-house on the Hamilton nineteen years; have now sixteen boarders; have had twenty-five, upon an average, all the time; know of over two hundred of my girls that have been married, having kept an account of them till within two years past; only one of my boarders has died in my house; fifteen have gone home sick; one of my boarders has been dismissed from the Corporation for bad conduct; never have had much sickness; perhaps ten cases corresponding to the description in Question 9.

Case 3.   Have kept a boarding-house on the Lowell Corporation eleven years; have now twenty-five boarders; have had, perhaps, two hundred in all; know of as many as fifty of them that have been married; not one has died in my house; none have ever been sent home sick; one of my boarders was turned off from the Corporation for bad conduct; have had very little sickness in my house; can remember but eleven cases that have lasted a week and been attended by a physician.

Case 4.   Have kept a boarding-house on the Merrimack for twelve years; have now sixteen boarders; presume I have had four hundred in all; can remember eighty of these that have been married; none have died at my house; have heard of the death of eleven; three have gone home sick; none dismissed from my house for bad conduct; have had but little sickness in my house, perhaps ten or twelve cases that have lasted a week.

Case 5.   Have kept a boarding-house on the Appleton, eight years and seven months; have now sixteen boarders; cannot tell how many I have had in all, perhaps two hundred and seventy-five; know of forty-five of my girls that have been married; eight have died; twelve have gone home sick; none have been dismissed from my house for bad conduct; have had much sickness in my house, should think as many as twenty cases lasting a week.

Case 6.   Have kept a boarding-house on the Hamilton for nineteen years; have now nineteen boarders; probably have had three hundred in all; can recollect only nineteen of my girls that have been married; two have died from my house; twelve have gone home sick; three have been dismissed for bad conduct; never have had much sickness; can remember fourteen cases lasting a week.

Case 7.   Have been matron on the Merrimack nine years; have now sixteen boarders; have had two hundred and fifteen since I kept the house; know of sixty of my girls who have been married; three have died in my house, and have heard of the death of six others; seven have gone home sick; none have been dismissed from my house for bad conduct; never have had much sickness, not more than seven or eight cases lasting a week.

351

34

Life on a
Southern Plantation

No easy generalizations can describe slave life on ante-bellum American plantations. There were important differences between being a slave in the Upper South and the Lower South, between working on a large plantation and a small one, between serving a kind resident planter and a narrow-minded overseer. Yet, the institution of slavery shared more common characteristics than differences. A black on one plantation may have had a few more amenities than his counterpart on another—but both served in bondage and labored for the economic welfare of their masters.

It is difficult to re-create the style of slave life; for obvious reasons slaves left almost no written legacy of servitude. Yet a good many records do survive of plantation life, set down, to be sure, by the owners. This selection is excerpted from the records of Bennet H. Barrow (1811–1854), a cotton planter in Louisiana. Barrow inherited his lands from his father and ran a lucrative plantation. He lived well, indulged in the proper sports, and had some interest in politics but never held an office above the parish level. He seems to have been very much a man of his day, sharing the virtues and vices of his peers. He kept his records well, and, from them, one can piece together some notion of what it was like to be a slave in the pre-Civil War South.

THE DIARY
OF BENNET H. BARROW

1   Rules of Highland Plantation (May 1838)

No negro shall leave the place at any time without my permission, or in my absence that of the Driver the driver in that case being responsible, for the cause of such absence. which ought never to be omitted to be enquired into—

The Driver should never leave the plantation, unless on business of the plantation—

From Edwin Adams Davis, *Plantation Life in the Florida Parishes of Louisiana, 1836–1846, as Reflected in the Diary of Bennet H. Barrow* (New York: Columbia University Press, 1943), 126–136, 392–399, 406–410, 427–437. Copyright 1943 Columbia University Press.

No negro shall be allowed to marry out of the plantation

No negro shall be allowed to sell anything without my express permission   I have ever maintained the doctrine that my negroes have no time Whatever, that they are always liable to my call without questioning for a moment the propriety, of it, I adhere to this on the grounds of expediency and right. The verry security of the plantation requires that a general and uniform control over the people of it should be exercised. Who are to protect the plantation from the intrusions of ill designed persons When evry body is a broad? Who can tell the moment When a plantation might be threatened with destruction from Fire—could the flames be arrested if the negroes are scattered throughout the neighborhood, seeking their amusement. Are these not duties of great importance, and in which evry negro himself is deeply interested to render this part of the rule justly applicable, however, it would be necessary that such a settled arrangement should exist on the plantation as to make it unnecessary for a negro to leave it—or to have a good plea for doing so—You must, therefore make him as comfortable at Home as possible, affording him What is essentially necessary for his happiness—you must provide for him Your self and by that means creat in him a habit of perfect dependence on you—Allow it ounce to be understood by a negro that he is to provide for himself, and you that moment give him an undeniable claim on you for a portion of his time to make this provision, and should you from necessity, or any other cause, encroach upon his time—disappointment and discontent are seriously felt—if I employ a labourer to perform a certain quantum of work per day and I agree to pay him a certain amount for the performance of said work When he has accomplished it I of course have no further claim on him for his time or services—but how different is it with a slave—Who can calculate the exact profit or expence of a slave one year with another, if I furnish my negro with evry necessary of life, without the least care on his part—if I support him in sickness, however long it may be, and pay all his expenses, though he does nothing—if I maintain him in his old age, when he is incapable of rendering either himself or myself any service, am I not entitled to an exclusive right to his time   good feelings, and a sense of propriety would all ways prevent unnecessary employment on the Sabbath, and policy would check any exaction of excessive labor in common—Whatever other privilages I allow the Driver, he is not suffered to send any negro off the plantation, unless he sends him to me or some extraordinary circumstances arises that could make it proper that a message should be sent to a neighbour for as his transactions are confined solely to the plantation there rarely could exist a necessity to communicate with me,   if he sends him for his own purpose, he is answerable for his absence as the negro would be, did he go away without any permission at all—I never give a negro a Pass to go from home without he first states particularly where he wishes to go, and assigns a cause for his desiring to be absent. if he offers a good reason, I never refuse, but otherwise, I never grant him a Pass, and feel satisfied that no practice is more prejudicial to the community, and to the negros themselves, and that of giving them general Pass'es—to go Where they please   I am so opposed to this plan that I never permit any negro to remain on my plantation, whose Pass does not authorize him expressly to come to it—Some think that after a negro has done his work it is an act of oppression to confine him to the plantation, when he might be strolling about the neighborhood for his amusement and recreation—this is certainly a mistaken humanity. Habit is evry thing—The negro who is accustomed to remain constantly at Home, is just as satisfied with the society on the plantation as that which he would find elsewhere, and the verry restrictions laid upon him being equally imposed on others, he does not feel them, for society is kept at Home for them—As the Driver is answerable for the good conduct of the negroes, and the proper application of their time he ought always to be present to attend, otherwise he could never with propriety be charged with neglect, in which case all responsibility would be at an End—No rule that I have stated is of more importance than that relating to negroes marrying out of the plantation it seems to me, from What observations I have made it is utterly impossible to have any method, or regularity When the men and women are permitted to take wives and husbands indiscriminately off the plantation, negroes are verry much desposed to pursue a course of this kind, and without being able to assign any good reason, though the motive can be readily perceived, and is a strong one with them, but one that tends not in the Least to the benefit of the Master, or their ultimate good. the inconveniences that at once strikes one as arising out of such a practice are these—

First—in allowing the men to marry out of the plantation, you give them an uncontrolable right to be frequently absent

2d Wherever their wives live, there they consider their homes, consequently they are indifferent to the interest of the plantation to which they actually belong—

3d—it creates a feeling of independance, from being, of right, out of the control of the masters for a time—

4th—They are repeatedly exposed to temptation from meeting and asociating with negroes from different directions, and with various habits & vices—

5th—Where there are several women on a plantation, they may have husbands from different plantations belonging to different persons. These men posess different habits are acustomed to different treatment, and have different privileges, so your plantation every day becomes a rendeezvous of a medly of characters. Negroes who have the privilege of a monthly Passes to go where they please, and at any hour that they say they have finished their work, to leave their Master's plan'tn come into yours about midday, When your negroes are at work, and the Driver engaged, they either take possession of houses their wives live—and go to sleep or stroll about in perfect idleness—feeling themselves accessible to every thing. What an example to those at work at the time—can any circumstance be more Intrusive of good order and contentment

Sixthly—When a man and his wife belong to different persons, they are liable to be separated from each other, as well as their children, either by caprice of either of the parties, or When there is a sale of property—this keeps up an unsettled state of things, and gives rise to repeated now connections—it might be asked how does this rule answer when there are several men on a plantation and few women—or vice versa, When there several women, & few men—For to adopt rules merely because they are good in themselves and not to pursue a plan Which would make them applicable, would be Fallacious—I prefer giving them money of Christmas to their making any thing, thereby creating an interest with you and yours. &c. I furnish my negroes regularly with their full share of allowance weakly. 4 pound & 5 pound of meat to evry thing that goes in the field—2 pound over 4 years 1½ between 15 months and 4 years old—Clear good meat—I give them cloths twice a year, two suits—one pair shoues for winter evry third year a blanket—"single negro—two." I supply them with tobacco if a negro is suffered to sell any thing he chooses without any inquiry being made, a spirit of trafficing at once is created. to carry this on, both means and time are necessary, neither of which is he of right possessed. A negro would not be content to sell only What he raises or makes or either corn (should he be permitted) or poultry, or the like, but he would sell a part of his allowance allso, and would be tempted to commit robberies to obtain things to sell. Besides, he would never go through his work carefully, particularly When other engagements more interesting and pleasing are constantly passing through his mind, but would be apt to slight his work That the general conduct of master has a verry considerable influence on the character and habits of his slave, will be readily admitted. When a master is uniform in his own habits & conduct, his slaves know his wishes, and What they are to expect if they act in opposition to, or conformity with them, therefore, the more order and contentment Exist.

A plantation might be considered as a piece of machinery, to operate successfully, all of its parts should be uniform and exact, and the impelling force regular and steady; and the master, if he pretended at all to attend to his business, should be their impelling force.

If a master exhibits no extraordinary interest in the proceedings on his plantation, it is hardly to be expected that any other feelings but apathy, and perfect indifference could exist with his negroes, and it would be unreasonable for him, Who as the princaple incitements, And is careless, to expect attention and exaction from those, Who have no other interest than to avoid the displeasure of their master. in the different departments on the plantation as much destinction and separation are kept up as possible with a view to create responsibility—The Driver has a directed charge of every thing, but there are subordinate persons, who take the more immediate care of the different departments. For instance, I make one persons answerable for my stock. Horses cattle hogs &c. another the plantation utensils &c. one the sick—one the poultry. another providing for and taking care of the children whose parents are in the field &c. As good a plan as could be adopted, to establish security and good order on the plantation is that of constituting a watch at night, consisting of two or more men. they are answerable of all trespasses commited during their watch, unless they produce the offender. or give immediate alarm. When the protection of a plantation is left to the negroes generally, you at once perceive the truth of the maxim that what is evry one's business, is no one's business. but when a regular watch is Established, Each in turn performs his tour of duty, so that the most careless is at times, made to be observant and watchful—the verry act of organizing a watch bespeaks a care and attention on the part of a master, Which, has the due influence on the negro—

Most of the above rules "in fact with the exception of the last" I have adopted since 1833. And with success—get your negroes ounce disciplined and planting is a

355

pleasure—A H[ell] without it never have an Overseer—Every negro to come up Sunday after their allowance Clean & head well combed—it gives pride to every one, the fact of master feeling proud of them, When clean &c.

Never allow any man to talk to your negros, nothing more injurious.

2   The Diary (September) 1838

September 1

Clear warm—picking above best picking this year—3 sick gave evry cotton picker a light Whipping for picking trashy cotten

2 Clear wind North—and quit cool—sudden change—hands averged higher yesterday than they have this year—163—upwards of 20 Bales out—Ten Bales behind last year & 30 Bales behind 1836—difference in the season

3 Clear. quite cold. picking cotten Gns place—good picking—started all my Gins—don't like the appearance of my crop. most ragged looking crop I ever had. bent & broke down—2 sick—3 lame &c.

4 Clear wind East—cool. picking home (above) since dinner

5 Cloudy wind East—best picking today I've had this year—went to Ruffins with Family—and went in the swamp Killing Aligators—after dinner went driving started two large Bucks in Wades field—stood on the roade between Roberts and Ruffins—one came through—Sidney Flower took first Shot standing—neither of his *shots* were fatal—ran to me missed first fire second wounded him verry badly—ran short distance & stoped. nearly falling—Ruffin shot at him behind —ran short distance & fell—Hounds still after the other Deer—our shooting turned it Back—went in pursuit of the *1st one* he jumped up some few steps from us—and ran a mile—by this time it was dark 4 dogs came to us and we followed it—jumped it between my field and the lower part Lane place—Came running directly to us—and had Ruffins Horse of stood would have touched him fired as it passed (missed) ran few steps dogs bayed it—found him standing. erect head & tail up ready for battle—gave him another loade. ran short distance dogs caught him—hour after night—verry Large and fat 4 prongs

6 Few clouds. cool mornings—Took jos Bell—Fanny Bell & Grey Luzbourough colts of Lucillas up to train—also Pressure & Dick Haile—a strong string —O. jacob cut the end of his right Fore finger nearly off—two others slightly cut—with Broad ax—avreage 170 pound Cotten yesterday—appearance of rain to night sprinkle

7 Few clouds—wind East—fine picking. avreaged 183 yesterday—cotten 40 Bales out last night—30 Bales behind last year at this time. went down to see john Joor his cotten has suffered verry much for want of rain

8 Cloudy warm—hand generally did not pick as well yesterday as day before—fine picking—highest yesterday & this year 260. Atean small boy Owens the best boy I ever saw

9 Clear pleasant hands picked Finely yesterday aveaged 209

10 Clear verry cool morning—upwards of 50 Bales out 30 odd Gined fine picking

11   Clear cool morning. Four first rate cotten pickers sick hands picked well yesterday   Atean 300. Dave L. 310.   highest this year—sent to Town after my Bagging & rope. waiting for it 3 weaks past—Knocked the blind Teeth out of my Grey Luzbourough Colt. Little Independence.

12   Clear cool mornings—5 sick   picking above—20 Bales out at Gns pressing Home—the best cotten and best picking in upper new corn land cotten I ever saw

13   Clear cool morning—weighd cotten in the field—5 sick   Augue & Fever

14   Cloudy   warm—most of the hands picked well yesterday highest 325 Atean—will have picked off of the new corn land above (50 acres) 25 Bales   at least 50 Bales to pick—averaged yesterday 209—25 Bales pressed last night

15   Cloudy. *sprinkling* of rain—Hands picked higher yesterday than they have done this year—Avreaged 226—Owens boy 13 years old picked 200—best boy I ever saw. verry light sprinkle rain this evening.

16   Stormy looking day. great deal of rain last night and still raining—wind from the East. hands picked well yesterday   highest average this year 234½

17   dark & Cloudy—wind South—women spinning   men & trash gang trashing cotten and raising House—Between 90 & 100 Bales out. 49 Pressed   70 Gind in No

18   Cloudy damp morning—some rain at noon. picking cotten since Breakfast—went driving with james Leak   Dr Desmont and Sidney Flower. started two Fawns in my field, ran some time. dogs quit them.

19   Clear pleasant morning—62 Bales pressed last night—Cotten bend down verry much from wind on Sunday—between 90 & 100 Bales out in No—Went hunting in my field   started 3 Deer. Killed a fine young Buck—Several joined me afterwards—went driving on the swamp—started a Deer   dogs ran off—in coming out of the drive started a Bear. only one dog—he became too much frightened to do any thing

20   Clear   pleasant   picking P. Rice bottom—hands pick well considering the storm—several sick

21   Verry Foggy morning—Com'enced hauling Cotten this morning—1st shipment—Bales will avreage 470 lbs   upwards of 100 out in No   100 & 15 of 400. this time last year had out 125—25 behind last year. owing to the season—cotten more backward in opening—at first picking—never had Cotten picked more trashy than yesterday. And to day by dinner—some few picked badly—5 sick & 2 children

22   Considerable rain before Breakfast, Appearance of a bad day—pressing—4 sick—Caught Darcas with dirt in cotton bag last night. weighed 15 pounds—Tom Beauf picked badly yesterday morning   Whiped him. few Cuts—left the field some time in the evening without his Cotton and have not seen him since—He is in the habit of doing so yearly. except last year   Heavy rains during the day   women spinning—trashing Cotten   men & children—Tom B. showed himself—"sick"—Cotten picked since the storm looks verry badly—Cotten market opened this year at 13 & 13¾ cts—Bagging & *cordage* 20 & 24 and 8½ & 9 cts—Porke from $16 to $24 a Barrel—Never com'ence hauling Cotten that it did'ent

357

rain—worked the ford at Little Creek in the Gns field—Wind blowing cool from the North since 2 oclock—Here I am sitting with the Baby in my lap "Bennet B." Emily criticising the History of Georgia—Caroline and John at all Kinds of mischief

23 Clear verry cool wind from the North—nine degrees colder than yesterday morning—intend most of the hands to dry and trash Cotten to day. Frank Kish Henry & Isreal pressed Bales to day. $1 each—Killed Wild Cow this morning. as Fat as could well be

24 Clear quit cold—P. Dhoertys Gin House *Burnt* down on Friday night Last. light enoughf at my scaffold yard to read names & figures on the sleight —& at least 5 miles—Mr. Tisdale our Trainer came down from K.y yesterday— had my cart Wheels tired yesterday at Ruffins

25 Clear cool—went to Town—hauled 49 Bales to Ratliffs Landing yesterday—12 to Town to day 61 in all—went driving yesterday Killed two Fawns—and one young Buck in my Gns field with the most singular Horns I ever heard of or Saw—verry fat—several sick. most this year

26 Clear pleasant weather. Shiped to day Eighty Bales Cotten. verry fine —6 or 7 Lying up—picked badly for two days past—Cotten Selling 14 cts

27 Clear pleasant—went hunting in the swamp in company of Dr Desmont J. Leake, & Mr Pain from Isle of Madeaira—a large wine importer—verry Large— Killed 3 Deer. lost Mr Pain, stayed untill after dark firing Guns &c. the old gentleman found the brier and Came up to Ruffins well scratched & bloody— he refused to call Leake by his name—having lost a cargo of Wine. Vessel springing a *Leak*

28 Cloudy cool wind from the North—jno Joor sent a hand up to ex-change with me, yesterday, his hands pick verry badly—Dennis and Tom *"Beauf"* ran off on Wednesday—Dennis came in yesterday morning after I went hunting. "Sick"—left the Sick House this morning—if I can see either of them and have a gun at the time will let them have the contents of it—Dennis returned to the Sick House at dinner

29 Foggy morning—warm day A G. Barrow—Dr Walker & Wm Munson stayed with me last night went Hunting to day Munson missed—Emily went to Woodville yesterday—Hands picked better yesterday than they have done. since the storm—avreged 200. Tom B. went to picking Cotten this morning—did'ent bring his Cotten to be weighed—came to me after I went to Bed

3 Slave Births: 1835–1839

Mother	Child	Date of Birth	Comments
L. Lucy	Louisa	October 5, 1835	
Mary		September 15, 1835	
Margaret	Orange	February 1, 1836	
Cealy	Jane Bello	April 22, 1836	
Candis	Issac	August 1, 1836	

Sidney		July 10, 1836	Born dead
Maria	Kitty	July 10, 1836	
Harriet	Ned	November 20, 1836	
Patty		December 19, 1836	Died
Leah	Adeline	March 6, 1837	
Margaret	Edmond	September 21, 1837	Died
Mary	Rose	January 9, 1838	
Sidney	Robert	February 21, 1838	
Edny		June 7, 1838	
Fanny		July 4, 1838	Died
Jane		September 29, 1838	Died
Candis		October 12, 1838	Died
Maria	Horrace	November 30, 1838	
Harriet	Sally	December 2, 1838	
Leah		December 10, 1838	Died
L. Lucey	Anzy	March , 1839	
Luce	Jobe	June 10, 1839	
Patty	Vina	July 20, 1839	
L. Hannah	Mathilda	July 20, 1839	
Mary	Elsa	July 23, 1839	
Luckey		July 26, 1839	Dwindled away

4 Slave Deaths: 1836–1839

Old Rheuben	1836 60 years	
Old Betty	1836 65 years	Found dead. Cripple 5 years.
Billy	1836	Died of worms 6 hours after taken
Nelly	1837 26 years	Died 24 hours after I saw her. Received some injury. In the family way.
Easter	1837 50 years	Died of Pleurisy, drinking, &c. Relapse, died very suddenly. Great loss.
William	1837 3 years	Died suddenly. Worms.
Hanover	1837 6 years	Died of worms, suddenly.
George	1837 30 years	Drowned in attempting to cross L. Creek in Gns field at dark, and in a verry heavy storm, on a mule. Irreparable loss in every respect. September 6.
Edny's child	1838 one week old	Died of Lock jaw, June 13.
Candis' child	1838 one week old	Died of Lock jaw, October 19.
Harriet's Ned	1838	Died suddenly, December 1.
Fanny's child	4 months old	Died from carelessness.
Jane's child		Died from disease of mother.
Leah's child	1838 one week old	December 17.
Sidney's child	1839 2 years old	Sick for 10 or 12 days. Recovering. Caught violent cold and sore throat. Strangled, died in 24 hours after relapse. September 19.

Misconduct and Punishments: 1840–1841

Darcas		Left the field without the consent of the Driver. Pretending to be sick.
Anica		Filthiness, in the milk and butter. Her and Darcas alike. December 10, 1840 improved very much.
Peter		Told me several lies Christmas, Drunkard, etc.
Candis		Saw Dennis while runaway.
Jenney		Saw Dennis while runaway.
Patience		Not trashing cotten well. Leaving yellow locks in it etc.
Julia		Not trashing cotten well.
Bet	X*	Not trashing cotten well.
Creasy		Not trashing cotten well.
F. Jerry		For going to town with very dirty clothes and keeping himself so, "generally."
Patty		Inattention to work and herself.
Lavenia		Inattention to work and herself.
L. Hannah		For taking rails and breaking good ones.
O. Hannah	X	Not trashing cotton enough. Found the gin stopped every time I've been down at the Gns. place.
Bet	X	Not trashing cotton enough.
Harriet		Not trashing cotton enough, and dirty clothes.
F. Jerry	X	Up too late and out of his house.
D. Bartley	X	Up after 10 o'clock.
Wade	X	Up after 10 o'clock.
Wash		Carelessness with his plough, horses, gear, etc.
Ralph	X	Neglect of his horses.
Randall		Up too late, sleeping in chair, etc.
Dave L.		Neglect in hauling cotton repeatedly.
D. Bartley	X	For not picking as well as he can, etc.
F. Jerry	X	For not picking as well as he can, etc.
Wash	X	Behaving very badly this season, so far.
T. Jim	X	Not picking well.
Fanny	X	Not picking well.
Creasy		Bad conduct, impudence to Driver and neglected work.
G. Jerry	X	Neglect in planting peas, and slow.
Jenny	X	Neglect in planting peas, and slow.
Patience	X	Did not go in the field till breakfast "late" and told the Driver "Alfred" she was sick and had been to the house for a dose of oil, and told me the same, found she had not been and she acknowledged the lie, but told Margaret she would give her some cloth if she would get the earache and tell Patty she had been here after oil, etc. And told me a dozen lies while questioning her. Gave her a very severe whipping.
Levi	X	Carelessness with his oxen and talking to the workman. Neglect of business.
Maria		For not reporting herself when sick. Remained in the Quarter 3 days without my knowledge.

Patty		And all the house ones for general bad conduct. Can't let a peach get ripe, etc.
Jane		The meanest negro living. Filth in cooking. Saw me coming to the house at 120. left the kitchen, etc. Of[f] near two days, foiled her having anything to do with anyone, and chained at nights.
O. Fill	X	Not reporting the plough hands for injuring the cotton covering up bottom limbs, etc.
Demps		Sound beating with my stick. Impudence of manner.
Atean	X	Covering up cotton limbs with ploughs.
Luce		Neglect of child. Its foot burnt.
Jim		Inattention to work, moving seed and impudence to Driver.
G. Jerry		Inattention to work.
Lize	X	Inattention to work.
Bet	XX	Careless in dropping seed, disowning it, etc.
Anica		Meaness to the sick, and hiding from me, etc.
Dennis		Severity to his mules.
Patty		For going over to Dr. Walker's during my absence, etc.
Milley	X	For going over to Dr. Walker's during my absence, etc.
Israel	X	Hiding from work. Moving cotton, etc. and not picking.

* X signifies whipping.
** XX signifies unusually severe whipping.

6   Inventory of the Estate of Bennet H. Barrow

Succession of Bennett H. Barrow, deceased
State of Louisiana, Parish of West Feliciana

Be it Remembered, that on this the fourteenth day of June in the year of our Lord One thousand eight hundred and fifty-four, I, Bertrand Haralson, Recorder in and for said Parish. Have attended this day, at the late residence of Bennett H. Barrow, deceased, for making an Inventory and appraisement of all the property, real and personal, belonging to Bennett H. Barrow, deceased.

The following is a true Proces Verbal of the Separate Estate of the deceased;

SLAVES	
Stephen, aged 6 years, valued at two hundred 50 dollars	250.00
Roden, aged 5 years, valued at two hundred dollars	200.00
Jack, aged 51 years, valued at eight hundred dollars	800.00
Eliza, aged 44 years, valued at five hundred dollars	500.00
Bazil, aged 20 years, valued at six hundred dollars	600.00
Little Cato, aged 37 years, valued at six hundred dollars	600.00
Hetty, aged 36 years, valued at five hundred dollars	500.00
Amos, an infant, valued at fifty dollars	50.00
Temps, aged 43 years, valued at fifty dollars	50.00
Lindy, aged 23 years, valued at seven hundred dollars	700.00
Virginia, aged 2 years, valued at One hundred & fifty dollars	150.00
Sidney, aged 39 years, valued at six hundred & fifty dollars	650.00
Aggy, aged 20 years, valued at seven hundred & fifty dollars	750.00

Angelle, an infant, valued at fifty dollars	50.00
Cynthis, aged 13 years, valued at four hundred dollars	400.00
Suckey, aged 9 years, valued at three hundred dollars	300.00
Spencer, aged 7 years, valued at three hundred dollars	300.00
Nelly, aged 5 years, valued at two hundred dollars	200.00
Litty, an infant, valued at fifty dollars	50.00
Rosiese, aged 4 years, valued at two hundred dollars	200.00
Fanny, aged 33 years, valued at Seven hundred dollars	700.00
Little Judy, aged 13 years, valued at five hundred dollars	500.00
Ralph, aged 34 years, valued at four hundred dollars	400.00
Ester Jim, aged 34 years, valued at nine hundred & fifty dollars	950.00
Little Nancy, aged 18 years, valued at seven hundred dollars	700.00
Old Suckey, aged 56 years, valued at One hundred dollars	100.00
Rachael, aged 25 years, valued at Six hundred dollars	600.00
Emeline, aged 4 years, valued at one hundred & fifty dollars	150.00
Essex, an infant, valued at One Hundred dollars	100.00
Mathew, aged 20 years, valued at eight hundred & fifty dollars	850.00
Israel, aged 37 years, valued at eight hundred dollars	800.00
Lucy, aged 71 years, valued at ten dollars	10.00
Lavinia, aged 31 years, valued at Seven hundred & fifty dollars	750.00
Annis, aged 13 years, valued at five hundred dollars	500.00
Polly, aged 8 years, valued at three hundred & fifty dollars	350.00
Caroline, aged 6 years, valued at Two hundred & fifty dollars	250.00
Josephine, aged 4 years, valued at One hundred & fifty dollars	150.00
Angeline, aged 2 years, valued at One hundred dollars	100.00
Dave, aged 46 years, valued at Seven hundred dollars	700.00
Little Jim, aged 24 years, valued at nine hundred dollars	900.00
Maria, aged 19 years, valued at six hundred dollars	600.00
Old Jimmy, aged 59 years, valued at five dollars sic [sick]	005.00
Nat, aged 28 years, valued at Eight hundred & fifty dollars	850.00
Levy, aged 39 years, valued at four hundred & fifty dollars	450.00
Grace, aged 29 years, valued at six hundred dollars	600.00
Little Jack, aged 9 years, valued at three hundred dollars	300.00
Gilson, aged 7 years, valued at two hundred dollars	200.00
Edward, aged 2 years, valued at One Hundred & fifty dollars	150.00
Dennis, aged 44 years, valued at nine hundred & fifty dollars	950.00
Ettienne, aged 37 years, valued at One thousand dollars	1,000.00
Dicy, aged 4 years, valued at two hundred dollars	200.00
Randel, aged 1 years, valued at one hundred dollars	100.00
Jeny, aged 39 years, valued at nine hundred dollars	900.00
Milly, aged 29 years, valued at six hundred dollars	600.00
Kesiah, aged 10 years, valued at three hundred dollars	300.00
Lotty, aged 7 years, valued at two hundred dollars	200.00
Minerva, aged 3 years, valued at one hundred & fifty	150.00
Patience, aged 43 years, valued at five hundred dollars	500.00
Ester Nat, aged 29 years, valued at Seven hundred dollars	700.00
Josh, aged 69 years, valued at One hundred dollars	100.00
Leah, aged 33 years, valued at Seven hundred & fifty dollars	750.00
Littleton, aged 21 years, valued at nine hundred dollars	900.00

35

The Appeal of Jackson

The political supporters of Andrew Jackson were an odd mixture—frontiersmen, small bankers, commercial farmers, businessmen starting out on their careers. Jackson's style may be part of the explanation for this coalition. A military hero, he appeared very much a leader and a man of the people. But there was another important ingredient in Jackson's appeal and that was his conception that the proper government was limited government. He was a strict constructionist of the Constitution. Jackson's nationalism was beyond question but he did not seek to extend the powers of the federal government at the expense of the state. In fact, quite the reverse was true, and in the 1830s this stance had wide support, albeit for very different reasons. Under this principle, for example, the government would stay out of central banking, leaving it to state institutions—a move that would free more funds for circulation and please eager businessmen looking for capital and ambitious farmers wanting to purchase more lands.

The strict constructionist side of Jacksonian politics was especially evident in the President's veto of the Maysville Internal Improvements Act. How was it that the hero of the Westerner denied him federal support for a road? The event is described in full detail by one of Jackson's most important advisers and his successor in the Presidency, Martin Van Buren. The account is obviously by a loyal friend—but a critical reading will illuminate a very important facet of Jacksonian democracy.

THE AUTOBIOGRAPHY
OF MARTIN VAN BUREN

Having for several years made the subject of Internal Improvements by the Federal Government my study, apprehensions of the evils their prosecution, as the Constitution stood, might entail upon the Country had become grave, and sincerely believing that the adverse current which had set in that direction might and could only be arrested thro' the General's extraordinary popularity I early and assidu-

Reprinted with permission from *The Autobiography of Martin Van Buren*, John C. Fitzpatrick, ed., Fourteenth Report of the Historical Manuscripts Commission, American Historical Association, June 14, 1919, 312–328, 337–338.

ously pressed the matter upon his consideration. He embraced my suggestions not only with alacrity but with that lively zeal with which he received every proposition which he thought could be made conducive to the public good. I propose to give a succinct account of the steps that proceeded from our conversations; and I will first briefly notice some of the General's characteristic qualities by which their advancement was essentially promoted. It is however far from my intention to attempt a complete portraiture of individual character. I am conscious that such attempts often, not to say generally, manifest the ambition of the author to shew his skill in depicting a perfectly good or an absolutely bad character instead of a desire to portray his subject as he really was, and that the picture, when finished is thus a reflection of his imagination rather than a reliable representation of real life. I hope to make the world better acquainted with the true character of Andrew Jackson than it was before, but I design to do this chiefly by correct reports of what he said and did on great occasions.

Although firm to the last degree in the execution of his resolution when once formed, I never knew a man more free from conceit, or one to whom it was to a greater extent a pleasure, as well as a recognized duty, to listen patiently to what might be said to him upon any subject under consideration until the time for action had arrived. Akin to his disposition in this regard was his readiness to acknowledge error whenever an occasion to do so was presented and a willingness to give full credit to his co-actors on important occasions without ever pausing to consider how much of the merit he awarded was at the expense of that due to himself. In this spirit he received the aid of those associated with him in the public service in the preparation of the public documents that were issued under his name, wholly indifferent in regard to the extent to which their participation was known, solicitous only that they should be understood by those to whom they were addressed as a true record of his opinions, his resolutions and his acts. That point secured he cared little either as to the form of words in which they were expressed, or as to the agency through which the particular exposition was concocted.

Neither, I need scarcely say, was he in the habit of talking, much less of boasting of his own achievements. Content with the part he had actually taken in the conduct and solution of any important public question and never having reason to complain of the opinions formed and expressed of his acts by a large majority of his Countrymen he had neither a desire nor a motive to parade his own or to shine in borrowed plumes.

I have already spoken of Gen. Jackson's early preference for the self-denying theory and strict-construction doctrines of the old republican school. But the principle of internal improvements by the Federal Government, so far from being acted upon when he was first in Congress, was, disavowed by the great leader of the administration, and a large share of Gen. Jackson's time was spent in the camp whilst the subject was debated by the rising men of the day from 1816 to 1823, when he re-appeared on the floor of Congress. There was besides a peculiarity in his position at the latter period which, tho' it could not—as nothing could—lead him, to do wrong when it became necessary to act, was nevertheless well calculated to lessen somewhat, for the moment at least, his active participation in this particular branch of legislation. To give to that peculiarity the weight to which it was entitled the reader must bear in mind the influence exerted by Pennsylvania in bringing Gen. Jackson forward for the Presidency, an influence which will not I think be over-estimated when it is regarded as having controlled the result; and this consideration deserves to be constantly remembered whilst canvassing the merits of his subsequent course upon several very important points.

Pennsylvania is in every sense of the word a great state and worthy of high respect—great in her material resources and great in the constant industry, the morality and general intelligence of her People. When to the credit she derives from these sources is added that which has naturally accrued from the moderate and sound character of her general course it will be seen how well she has deserved the honor shewn her by her sister States in the title with which they have distinguished her of "the key stone of the arch of the Union."

It is nevertheless true that she has for a long time presented a favorable field for the agitation of political questions which address themselves to special interests in the communities upon which they are pressed. Internal Improvements by the Federal Government, a high protective tariff and a Bank of the United States had, for many years before Gen. Jackson's accession to the Presidency, been regarded as favorite measures with the good people of Pennsylvania. In respect to the first, which is now the subject of our consideration, both of the great Reports of the Committees on Roads and Canals, at the period when it embraced a large share of the attention of Congress, were from Pennsylvanians,—Mr. Wilson and Mr. Hemphill. Yet these measures and the question of the removal of the Indians, which had so strongly excited their misdirected sympathies, were destined to be the principal domestic subjects on which Gen. Jackson's Administration, if he succeeded in the election, was to be employed. With the two last, (the Bank and the Tariff) he had made himself familiar and as to them his course was fixed; and, foreseeing the necessity he would be under upon those points to run counter to the wishes of his Pennsylvania friends at the very threshold of his administration, it was natural that a man of his generous temper, and of whose character fidelity to friendship was the crowning grace, should have been desirous to avoid any addition to the issues between himself and his no less generous supporters, as far as that could be avoided without dereliction of duty.

It was under such circumstances, and never having made the constitutional question in relation to the power of Congress over the matter a subject of critical examination, that he voted in 1823–4 and 5, in favor of the acts "to provide for the necessary surveys for roads and canals", and "authorizing a subscription to the stock of the Chesapeake and Delaware Canal Company" and a few other propositions of similar import, which votes were vehemently urged, by his opponents, against his subsequent course.

None but the men who were active and conspicuous in the service of the Federal Government at that day, and of these now few remain amongst us, can form any adequate opinion of the power and influence which those who had embarked their political fortunes in attempts to commit the General Government irretrievably to the promotion and construction of Internal Improvements, had acquired both in Congress and among the most alert and enterprising portions of the People. The wild spirit of speculation, to whose career our ever growing and ever moving population and our expanded and expanding territory offered the fairest field, became wilder over the prospect before it and the wits of Congressmen were severely tasked in devising and causing to be surveyed and brought forward under captivating disguises the thousand local improvements with which they designed to dazzle and seduce their constituents. It required an extraordinary degree of resolution in a public man to attempt to resist a passion that had become so rampant, but this consideration might stimulate but could not discourage Gen. Jackson so long as he was convinced that the course presented for his consideration was the path of duty. He was unfeignedly grateful to Pennsylvania for what she had done for him, he knew well that upon this question as upon those of the removal of the Indians and of the Bank she had taken a lead in the wrong direction, he was extremely loth to add another to the great points upon which his duty would compel him to throw himself in the way of her gratification, but for all and against all such appeals and motives he promptly opposed the suggestions of right, and the ever present and ever operative sense of an official obligation superior to personal feeling.

He appreciated to their full extent the arguments in support of the inexpediency of the legislation which he was asked to arrest, whilst the Constitution remained unaltered, but preferred to meet the question on constitutional grounds. No Cabinet councils were called: not another member of the Cabinet was consulted before his decision had become irrevocable. It was understood between us that I should keep an eye upon the movements of Congress and bring to his notice the first Bill upon which I might think his interference would be preferable, and that when such a case was presented, we would take up the question of Constitutional power and examine it deliberately and fully.

The Bill authorizing a subscription to the stock of the Maysville, Washington, Paris and Lexington Turnpike-road Company appeared to me to present the looked for occasion. Its local character was incontestably established by the fact that the road commenced and ended in the same State. It had passed the House and could undoubtedly pass the Senate. The road was in Mr. Clay's own State and Mr. Clay was, the General thought—whether rightfully or not is now immaterial,—pressing the measure and the question it involved upon him rather for political effect than for public ends, and it was his preference, in accordance with a sound military axiom to make his enemy's territory the theatre of the war whenever that was practicable.

I brought the subject to the President's notice during one of our daily rides, immediately after the passage of the Bill by the House and proposed to send him on our return the brief of which I have spoken and of which I had before promised him a perusal. I had myself no hesitation in respect to the course that ought to be pursued and spoke of it accordingly. He received my suggestions favorably, appeared sensible of the importance of the proposed step and at parting begged me not to delay sending him the brief—which was done as soon as I got to my house.

Within five days after the passage of the Bill by the House of Representatives I received from him the following note.

(PRIVATE)

May 4th, 1830

My Dear Sir,

I have been engaged to day as long as my head and eyes would permit, poring over the manuscript you handed me; as far as I have been able to decipher it I think it one of the most lucid expositions of the Constitution and historical accounts of the departure by Congress from its true principles that I have ever met with.

It furnishes clear views upon the constitutional powers of Congress. The inability of Congress under the Constitution to apply the funds of the Government to private, not national purposes I never had a doubt of. The Kentucky road bill involves this very power and I think it right boldly to meet it at the threshold. With this object in view I wish to have an interview with you and consult upon this subject that the constitutional points may be arranged to bear upon it with clearness so that the people may fully understand it.

Can I see you this evening or Thursday morning?

Your friend

Andrew Jackson

MR. VAN BUREN

TO THE PRESIDENT

My Dear Sir,

I thank you for your favorable opinion of the notes. This matter has for a few days past borne heavily on my mind, and brought it to the precise conclusion stated in your note. Under this impression I had actually commenced throwing my ideas on paper to be submitted to you when I should get through, to see whether it is not possible to defeat the aim of our adversaries in either respect, viz; whether it be to draw you into the approval of a Bill most emphatically *local*, and thus endeavor to saddle you with the latitudinarian notions upon which the late administration acted, or to compel you to take a stand against internal improvements generally, and thus draw to their aid all those who are interested in the ten thousand schemes which events and the course of the Government for a few past years have engendered. I think I see land, and that it will be in our power to serve the Country and at the same time counteract the machinations of those who mingle their selfish and ambitious views in the matter. We shall have time enough; the Bill has not yet passed the Senate and you have, you know, ten days after that.

Yours truly

M. Van Buren

W. May 4th 1830

I requested him some days after to obtain from the Secretary of the Treasury the financial statement which [later] accompanied the *veto*-Message, and received in reply the following spirited note.

(PRIVATE)

May 15th, 1830

Dear Sir,

Your note is received. I am happy that you have been looking at the proceedings of Congress. The appropriations now exceed the available funds in the Treasury, and the estimates always exceed the real amount available. I have just called upon the

Secretary of the Treasury for the amount of the estimated available balance on the 1st January 1831.

The people expected reform retrenchment and economy in the administration of this Government. This was the cry from Maine to Louisiana, and instead of these the great object of Congress, *it would seem*, is to make mine one of the most extravagant administrations since the commencement of the Government. This must not be; The Federal Constitution must be obeyed, State-rights preserved, our national debt *must be paid, direct taxes and loans avoided* and the Federal union preserved. These are the objects I have in view, and regardless of all consequences, will carry into effect.

Yr. friend

A. J.

Mr. V. B. Sec. of State

Let me see you this evening or in the morning.

Not one out of twenty of the opposition members believed that President Jackson, notwithstanding his proverbial indifference to the assumption of responsibility, in respect to measures he believed to be right, would venture to veto an act for the internal improvement of the Country in the then state of public opinion upon the subject and after the votes he had so recently given in favor of such acts. If they had thought otherwise they would not have presented him a Bill so purely local in its character. Apprehensive that they would, when his designs became known to them, change their course in that respect, and avail themselves of the selfish views and unsettled opinions of a sufficient number of those who had been elected as Jackson men to substitute a Bill for a work more national in its pretensions, I was extremely solicitous that nothing should be said upon the subject until it should be too late for such a step, and pressed that point upon the General. It was the only one, I knew, that required to be pressed and it was, moreover, that which I was persuaded would be the most difficult for him. He was entirely unreserved in his public dealings—the People, he thought, should know every thing and "give it to Blair" (or *Blar* as he pronounced it)—was almost always his prompt direction when ever any information was brought to him which affected or might affect the public interest.

Col. Johnson, of Kentucky, was induced by Western members, who had been alarmed by floating rumors, to sound the President and if he found that there existed danger of such a result to remonstrate with him, in their names and his own, against a *veto*. At the moment of his appearance the President and myself were engaged in an examination of the exposé of the state of the Treasury to which I have referred, and alone. After a delay natural to a man possessed as the Colonel was of much real delicacy of feeling and having an awkward commission in hand, he said that he had called at the instance of many friends to have some conversation with the General upon a very delicate subject and was deterred from entering upon it by an apprehension that he might give offense. He was kindly told to dismiss such fears, and assured that as the President reposed unqualified confidence in his friendship he could say nothing on any public matter that would give offense. He then spoke of the rumors in circulation, of the feelings of the General's Western friends in regard to the subject of them, of his apprehensions of the uses that Mr. Clay would make of a veto, and encouraged by the General's apparent interest, and warmed by his own, he extended his open hand and exclaimed "General! If this hand were an anvil on which the sledge hammer of the smith was descending and a fly were to light upon it in time to receive the blow he would not crush it more effectually than you will crush your friends in Kentucky if you veto that Bill!" Gen. Jackson evidently excited by the bold figure and energetic manner of Col. Johnson, rose from his seat and advanced towards the latter, who also quitted his chair, and the following questions and answers succeeded very rapidly: "Sir, have you looked at the condition of the Treasury—at the amount of money that it contains—at the appropriations already made by Congress—at the amount of other unavoidable claims upon it?"—"No! General, I have not! But there has always been money enough to satisfy appropriations and I do not doubt there will be now!"—"Well, I have, and this is the result," (repeating the substance of the Treasury exhibit,) "and you see there is no money to be expended as my friends desire. Now, I stand committed before the Country to pay off the National Debt, at the earliest practicable moment; this pledge I am determined to redeem, and I cannot do this if I consent to encrease it without necessity. Are you willing—are my friends willing to lay taxes to pay for internal improvements?—for be assured I will not borrow a cent except in cases of absolute necessity!"—"No!" replied the Colonel, "that would be worse than a *veto!*"

These emphatic declarations delivered with unusual earnestness and in that peculiarly impressive manner for which he was remarkable when excited quite overcrowed the Colonel who picked up the green bag which he usually carried during the session and manifested a disposition to retreat. As he was about to leave I remarked to him that he had evidently made up his mind that the General had determined to veto the Bill at all events, but that when he reflected how much of the President's earnestness was occasioned by his own strong speech and how natural it was for a man to become excited when he has two sets of friends, in whom he has equal confidence, urging him in different directions, he would be less confident in his conclusion. Reminded by this observation that he had suffered the guard which he had imposed on himself to be broken down by the Colonel's *sledge-hammer,* the General told him that he was giving the matter a thorough investigation and that their friends might be assured that he would not make up his mind without looking at every side of it,—that he was obliged to him for what he had said and wished all his friends to speak to him as plainly.

The Colonel with his accustomed urbanity deported himself as if reassured and appeared to consider the case not so desperate as he had at first imagined, but his manner was assumed for the purpose of quieting my apprehensions which he perceived and understood. When he returned to the House he replied to the eager enquiries of his Western friends that the General had thanked him and assured him that he would thoroughly examine the subject, but his private opinion decidedly was that nothing less than a voice from Heaven would prevent the old man from vetoing the Bill, and he doubted whether that would!

Still so strong was the impression derived from Gen. Jackson's habit of never concealing his views upon a subject on which his mind was made up, that the

369

incredulity of the members was but slightly removed by the Colonel's report: what he would do in the matter remained an open question to the last. The consequence was that the importunities of his friends were increased, but as the detailed account of Col. Johnson's embassy discouraged direct remonstrances with the President they were addressed to me, and in my efforts to keep both sides quiet by statements of the difficulties with which the subject was environed by reason of the conflicting struggles of the friends of the Administration, I exposed my own course to some suspicion or affected suspicion in the end. The General told me, on my return from England, that one of the charges brought against me by Mr. Calhoun's friends, to justify the rejection of my nomination as Minister, was that I had been opposed to the *veto* and had tried to prevent him from interposing it.

The impression among the General's Western friends, that he would destroy his popularity by a *veto*, was universal and prevailed also extensively among those from the North. The Pennsylvania members generally were rampant in their opposition and most of them voted for the Bill after the *veto* was interposed. Being with him to a very late hour the night before the Message was sent up, he asked me to take an early breakfast with him, as Congress was on the point of breaking up, and would therefore meet at an early hour. On going up stairs to his office, he leaning on my arm on account of his extreme physical weakness, I observed that our friends were frightened. "Yes," he replied,—"but don't mind that! The thing is here" (placing his hand on the breast-pocket of his coat) "and shall be sent up as soon as Congress convenes."

It was sent up that morning and a scene ensued that baffled all our calculations. If there was any sentiment among our opponents which we knew to be universal, before the reading of the *veto*-Message, it was that it would prove the political death warrant of the Administration and we were prepared to hear denunciations against the violence and destructive effects of the measure and the reckless insult offered to the House by the President in sending it. But no such clamor arose, and the first and principal objection that was made against the Message, when the reading was finished, and which was persevered in to the end, was that it was "an *electioneering document*" sent to Congress for political effect!—and that the "*hand of the magician*" was visible in every line of it!

It was indeed received with unbounded satisfaction by the great body of the disinterested and genuine friends of the Administration throughout the Country. Col. Hayne, of South Carolina, at the great Charleston dinner given to inaugurate nullification, and thro' its means to put that Administration to the severest trial that any had ever been exposed to in our Country spoke of the *veto as* "the most auspicious event which had taken place in the history of the Country for years past." I refer but to one other of those acceptable exhibitions of public feeling which pervaded the Union, tho' less imposing in form not less gratifying. Col. [Robert] Ramsay, one of the Representatives from Pennsylvania, an excitable but honest man and true patriot, irritated almost beyond endurance by the *veto*, followed us from the Capitol to the White House, after the close of the session, and, presuming on the strength of his friendship for the General, fairly upbraided him for his course. The latter bore his reproaches, for such they really were altho' intended only as a remonstrance which he thought allowable in a devoted friend, with a degree of mildness that excited my admiration, begging the dissatisfied representative to say no more upon the subject until he had seen his constituents and venturing to prophesy that he would find them pleased with the veto. The worthy Pennsylvanian received the intimation as an additional injury and parted from us in an exceedingly bad humor. A short time afterwards, as I was one day approaching the President he held up to me in an exultant manner, a paper which proved to be a letter from our good friend Ramsay in which he announced the confirmation of the General's prediction and acknowledged that, in that case at least, the latter had known his constituents better than he himself had known them.

And yet this measure was but the entering wedge to the course of action by which that powerful combination known as the Internal Improvement party was broken asunder and finally annihilated. The power which a combined influence of that description, addressing itself to the strongest passion of man's nature and wielded by a triumvirate of active and able young statesmen as a means through which to achieve for themselves the glittering prize of the Presidency, operating in conjunction with minor classes of politicians, looking in the same general direction and backed by a little army of cunning contractors, is capable of exerting in communities so excitable as our own, can easily be imagined. The danger in offending and the difficulty of resisting such an influence were equally apparent. The utmost prudence was required in respect to the ground that should be occupied by the President in the first step that he was to take in the prosecution of the great reform that he had in view. His own past course increased the necessity of great circumspection at the start. His name was, in very deed, a tower of strength, but prudence as well as sound principle dictated that their partiality should not be put to an unreasonable test by the ground he now took, on an occasion of intense interest, in a document which, as we all well knew, would have to pass through the severest scrutiny.

In view of this state of things the *veto*-Message assumed the following positions:—

1st. The construction of Internal Improvements under the authority of the Federal Government was not authorized by the Constitution.

2nd. Altho' the true view of the Constitution in regard to the power of appropriation was probably that taken in Madison's Report concerning the alien and sedition laws, by which it was confined to cases where the particular measure which the appropriation was designed to promote was within the enumerated authorities vested in Congress, yet every Administration of the Government had, in respect to appropriations of money only adopted in practice (several cases of which were mentioned) a more enlarged construction of the power. This course, it was supposed, had been so long and so extensively persisted in as to render it difficult, if not impracticable, to bring the operations of the Government back to the construction first referred to. The Message nowhere admitted that the more enlarged construction which had obtained so strong a foothold, was a true exposition of the Constitution, and it conceded that its restriction against abuse, viz., that the works which might be thus aided should be "of a general, not

371

local—National, not State" character, a disregard of which distinction would of necessity lead to the subversion of the Federal System, was unsafe, arbitrary in its nature and inefficient.

3d. Although he might not feel it to be his duty to interprose the Executive veto against the passage of Bills appropriating money for the construction of such works as were authorized by the States, and were National in their character the President did not wish to be understood as assenting to the expediency of embarking the General Government in a system of that kind at this time; but he could never give his approval to a measure having the character of that under consideration, not being able to regard it in any other light than as a measure of a purely local character; or if it could be considered National no further distinction between the appropriate duties of the General and State Governments need be attempted, for there could be no local interest that might not, under such a construction, be denominated, with equal propriety, National.

His *veto* was placed on that specific ground, and the rest of the Message was principally taken up in discussing the propriety and expediency of deferring all other action upon the subject, even of appropriations for National works until the Public Debt should be paid and amendments of the Constitution adopted by which such appropriation could be protected against the abuses to which they were exposed.

For seven years of General Jackson's administration was the general subject thus banished from the halls of Congress and by my election as his successor that virtual interdict (if it may be so termed) was extended to eleven years. It was in consequence of the steps of which I have spoken that the project of a system of Internal Improvements by the Federal Government was—there is every reason to believe—forever withdrawn from the action of that Government. Not that any such consequence can be attributed to the opinion or action of any man who may for a season be placed at its head, for no one conversant with human nature or with the course of political events will ever expect with confidence such a result from such causes. The opinion I have expressed is founded on more potent considerations. Every effort in the direction referred to was certainly suspended for eleven years and other fields of exertion in behalf of such works were soon found and occupied. To a people as impulsive as ours eleven years of denial and delay are almost equivalent to an eternal veto, and those who maintained that the passion for Internal Improvements, so rampant at the seat of the Federal Government at the commencement of the Jackson administration, would seek other and constitutional directions for its gratification, if that could be perseveringly denied to it there for even a shorter period, stand justified by the event. All of the works of that character which it was ever hoped might prove safe and useful to the Country, have been made by or under the authority of the State Governments. All motive for enlisting the interference of the National Government for generations to come, has thus been superseded. In the cases of wild and unprofitable or speculative projects, losses, to the extent of many millions, which the Treasury would have sustained if these works had been constructed under Federal authority, have fallen with a weight diminished by the vigilance inspired by private interest and by State supervision, upon the shoulders of those who expected to make money by them, instead of emptying the national coffers, to be recruited by taxes collected from the mass of the people who would have derived no exclusive advantages from their success.

We have had two administrations of the Federal Government whose politics were of the Governmental-improvement stamp, but none of the old projects have been brought forward—resolutions in favour of Internal Improvements have been dropped from the partisan platforms of the party that suported those administrations. The theory and the practice—except as to cases not involved in the general question—are both exploded as regards the action of the Federal Government and the signal advantages which the Country has reaped from this result will be elsewhere noticed.

36

The Reform Impulse

America in the 1830s and 1840s witnessed one of the most vigorous outpourings of reform and humanitarian sentiments that ever swept this nation. Citizens gave unprecedented attention to the plight of the poor, the criminal, the deaf, the dumb, and the blind, as well as to the insane; they discovered the injustices of women not sharing equal rights with men and the inhumanity of slaves enjoying almost no rights. As a result of this reform impulse, schools for the handicapped opened, penitentiaries received careful planning, insane asylums were built, a women's rights movement began, and abolitionists undertook their agitation.

What lay behind this outburst of energy? How was a woman like Dorothea Dix able to persuade state legislature after state legislature to make a significant outlay of funds for politically the least important and most handicapped of groups—the insane? Dix, a Boston schoolteacher who left her classroom as an invalid in 1835, at the age of thirty-three, discovered in herself incredible energy to work for the next thirty years for the welfare of the insane. She touched the mind and conscience of the nation. Her appeal to the Pennsylvania Legislature on behalf of the insane is a statement of the formula that worked well time and again. In it may be some answers to the larger issue of the origins of the American reform efforts in the ante-bellum era.

MEMORIAL
Dorothea Dix

To the Honorable, the Senate and the House of Representatives
of the Commonwealth of Pennsylvania:
Gentlemen:

I come to represent to you the condition of a numerous and unhappy class of sufferers, who fill the cells and dungeons of the poor houses, and the prisons of your state. I refer to the pauper and indigent insane, epileptics, and idiots of Pennsylvania. I come to urge their claims upon the commonwealth for protection and support, such protection and support as is only to be found in a well conducted Lunatic Asylum.

From *Memorial to the Honorable, the Senate and the House of Representatives of the Commonwealth of Pennsylvania* (Harrisburg, 1845), 3–10, 53–55.

I do not solicit you to be generous; this is an occasion rather for the dispensation of *justice*. These most unfortunate beings have claims, those *claims* which bitter misery and adversity creates, and which it is your solemn obligation as citizens and legislators to cancel. To this end, as the advocate of those who are disqualified by a terrible malady, from pleading their own cause, I ask you to provide for the immediate establishment of a State Hospital for the Insane.

If this shall appear to some of you an untimely demand on the State Treasury; and a too hastily, too importunately urged suit, I must ask all such to go forth, as I have done, and traversing the state in its length and breadth, examine with patient care the condition of this suffering, dependent multitude, which are gathered to your alms-houses and your *prisons,* and scattered under adverse circumstances in indigent families; *weigh the iron chains, and shackles, and balls, and ring-bolts, and bars, and manacles; breathe the foul atmosphere of those cells and dens, which too slowly poisons the springs of life; examine the furniture of these dreary abodes; some for a bed have the luxury of a truss of straw; and some have the cheaper couch, which the hard, rough plank supplies! Examine their apparel. The air of heaven is their only vesture. Are you disquieted and pained to learn these facts? There are worse realities yet to be revealed under your vigilant investigations. The revolting exposure of men; the infinitely more revolting and shocking exposure of women; with combinations of miseries and horrors that will not bear recital. Do you start and shrink from the grossness of this recital? what then is it to witness the appalling reality?* Do your startled perceptions refuse to admit these truths? They exist still; the proof and *the condition* alike; *neither have passed away*. The idiot mother; the naked women in the packing boxes; but yet for these last, perhaps, the legal measures resorted to for their relief have been availing. Perhaps both judge and jury have interposed for those, some merciful change. This relief may be but temporary, and may disappear with the first indignant excitement which procured it; for the effectual, permanent remedy and alleviation of all these troubles and miseries, this appeal is now made to the Legislature of Pennsylvania; and, gentlemen, you perceive that it is *just, not generous action,* I ask at your hands.

It cannot be forgotten that, successively in the years of 1838 and 1840, earnest efforts were made by benevolent citizens of the state, to procure for the pauper and indigent insane, the benefits of curative treatment and hospital protection.

The result was, an appropriation by the Legislature, and the appointment of commissioners to carry forward and complete the establishment of a state institution. The work was shortly interdicted through the influence of circumstances which it is unnecessary to explain here.

Meanwhile, the evil for which the wise and benevolent sought a remedy, has gone on to increase. Sufferings have been multiplied with additional cases of the malady. Many who might have been restored by timely treatment, have become, either through the violence of disease, or unavoidable mismanagement, hopelessly insane. Many others are fast verging to the same pitiable condition; and new cases of almost daily occurrence, remind the beholder that a similar destiny awaits these, if no asylum opens its friendly shelter, and renders remedial care in season to avert the impending calamity.

You are not solicited to commence a work of doubtful value, capable of producing uncertain benefits. The age of experiment has passed by: the experience of those of your sister states, who have preceeded you in this enterprise of mercy, assures you that thousands, through the skillful care received in hospitals for the insane, have been restored to society and to usefulness, to reason and to happiness.

Beside recent and curable cases, there is yet another class, the very extremity and certainty of whose condition appeals most strongly and affectingly to your humane sensibilities. I mean those from whom, in all probability, the light of reason is forever veiled: dependent, irresponsible, often much suffering beings, they seem from the very entireness and certain duration of their dependence, to demand a peculiar consideration. Abandon not these of your fellow-citizens to any miseries which you can cause to be relieved or mitigated.

This subject comes home to all, to every one: on this ground all alike may suffer; the rich and the poor, the learned and the uneducated, the young, the mature, and the aged; from this malady none are sure of exemption; and the often reverses of fortune teach, that none are so prosperous that they may not need to share the asylum which is solicited now to shelter others.

Through the bond of our common humanity, we may become as they now are. Let imagination for a moment place you in their stead, or rather let it so place those you love, those you cherish, those who are dearer to you than is your own life, and then declare, if you could abandon them to the horrid noisome cell; and to ignorant pauper attendants; uninterested, unpaid, and reluctant nurses; or could you yield them to the strong holds of the jails and prisons, there to be companions of the felon, and the thief, and the abased vicious drunkard: there to be abandoned to their caprices, and subject to their daily taunts, and heartless jeers. I am not suggesting unreal, impossible conditions; you can witness these scenes as I have done, and learn too; corroboration of these hardships and sufferings from the unwilling keepers of these unfortunate men and women, who, dangerous to the community, through property-destroying or homicidal propensities, must endure this bondage till a state asylum open its doors to receive them. There are some, but the number is not large, who, bound down to low views of the mutual obligations of man to man, and to imperfect perceptions of the sublime truths of the moral law, will argue, that many, very many of those who are found in wretched circumstances in alms-houses and in prisons, have, by their own follies and vices brought on themselves the calamity, which henceforth casts them out from the accustomed walks of life. No doubt this is true; but why should society visit upon the transgressor who becomes insane, a so much harsher retribution, than upon the transgressor who retains his senses? It is very well known, that by far the largest portion of those who become wholly dependent on public charity, have been brought to that condition either by their own indiscretion or misdemeanors; yet these find the sympathy they seek, and the aid they solicit; for them an appropriate home is often provided, and their necessities are bountifully administered to. There is yet another view of this subject.

Suppose the insane in many cases to have wrought their own ruin, shall man be more just than God? Does not he send his sun to shine upon the evil and unthankful, as upon the obedient and the good? Again, is it not to the habits, the customs, the temptations of civilized life and society, that we owe most of these calamities? Should not society, then, make the compensation which alone can be made for these disastrous fruits of its social organization? Concede this, and I do not known how it is to be evaded; and your course of action is made plain by a duty not to be mistaken. Economy, justice, humanity, and mercy, that attribute of the Deity, combine to direct your deliberations, and determine your judgment.

Of the *fifty-eight* counties in this State, *twenty-one* contain poor-house establishments; and the remaining *thirty-seven* sustain their paupers by annual distribution in families, who receive them at "the lowest rate for which they are bidden." I think it may be conceded, that in the majority of cases, defective as is the poorhouse supervision for the insane, they are more comfortable, or rather, often less borne down by the accumulation of their sufferings in these institutions, than in private families, where every arrangement is interfered with, and from which all quiet is banished. Few have skill to control the furious, or to manage the refractory; and not many have that patient endurance which is tested to the utmost in the care of excied insane persons.

Next after private families and poor-houses, the insane will be found in the jails and penitentiaries. Passing from the prisons, &c., we perceive that in the state, are at present two established hospitals or asylums for the insane—not including that populous department of the Philadelphia Alms-house, which is called the Alms-house Hospital for the Insane. The asylum at Frankford, about six miles north of the city, and established by the Society of Friends, in May 1817, and which can receive about fifty patients, and the Pennsylvania Hospital for the Insane, west of the Schuylkill, nearly two miles from the city, have been severally established by the humanity and munificence of private individuals, chiefly citizens of Philadelphia. These two institutions are almost constantly filled to their utmost capacity; or when vacancies occur by the recovery and removal of patients, they are shortly filled by others, whose distressed friends seek for them the benefits which these institutions are so well calculated to secure. The latter asylum, which is under the superintendence of Dr. Kirkbride, can receive but about two hundred patients with their attendants, so that we find a very large number whose recent attack or the violence of the malady, make peculiarly the subjects of judicious hospital treatment, altogether without the means of relief. The only provision, therefore, and this made by individual benefactions, for the insane of the large state of Pennsylvania, is found in the immediate vicinity of the commercial capital. Far and wide, over an extent of hundreds of miles, from east to west, and north to south, are large numbers of your citizens *declining into irrecoverable insanity* through the want of an institution, which it now depends upon the Legislature of Pennsylvania to establish on a broad and secure foundation.

It is not expected, it is not asked, that at this time you should make ample provision for all the insane of the state. If at this period you build a hospital to receive *recent cases,* and such as may still be judged capable of restoration; if you will take from your prisons such as are there most unrighteously imprisoned, you will accomplish an amount of good, which exceeds computation; a good that will

377

reach to and bless, succeeding generations; and at some more prosperous period in your financial concerns, you may be able to complete, what now you commence upon a moderate and limited plan, that is to say, you may establish as many institutions as the wants of a populous country, and the consequent dependence and maladies of a portion of the community require and will demand.

The *importance of timely remedial treatment* is obvious. The opinion of all the intelligent medical men in Pennsylvania, and throughout the Union, supports this view. It may be gratifying to read several brief extracts from the annual reports of several of the hospitals for the insane in the United States.

Dr. Butler, of the Hartford Retreat for the Insane, writes in his report for 1844, "The results of the early commitment of the cases of insanity to the curative appliances of this and similar institutions, present a most convincing evidence of its good policy as well as of its humanity. They justify us in expecting, that of cases where the duration of disease *has been less than one year,* from eighty to ninety per cent. will recover; where it has existed from one to five years, from twenty to thirty per cent.; from five to ten years, about twelve per cent.; and when of longer duration, not more than five per cent. *Delay* in applying the appropriate treatment, rapidly diminishes the chances of recovery."

Dr. Kirkbride, of the Pennsylvania Hospital for the Insane, writing of the importance of *early* treatment for this class of patients, says, in his report for 1842: "Not a month elapses that we do not have to regret that some individual is placed under our care *after* the best period for restorative treatment has passed. The general proposition that truly recent cases of insanity are commonly very curable, and that chronic ones are only occasionally so, may be considered as fully established, and *ought at this day to be every where understood:*" and again in another year's report, the same truth is still urged. "It cannot be too earnestly impressed upon those whose friends are afflicted with insanity, that *all experience* goes to prove, that in its earliest stages it is generally curable, *and that every week it is left without treatment, goes to diminish the prospect of restoration."*

Dr. Luther V. Bell, whose professional experience and high intellectual ability give authority to his opinions, writes as follows in his report for 1843–44:—"In regard to the curability of insanity in its different manifestations, there *can be no general rule better established than that this is directly in the ratio of the duration of the symptoms."*

In the twenty-third annual report of that branch of the Massachusetts General Hospital, known as the M'Lean Asylum for the Insane, near Charlestown, Mass., Dr. Bell again refers with clearness and precision to this subject. "The records of the asylum justify the declaration, that *all cases certainly recent,* that is, whose origin does not directly or obscurely run back more than a year, *recover under a fair trial. This is the general* law, the *occasional* instances to the contrary are the *exceptions."* In this opinion, Dr. Ray, of the Maine Hospital concurs.

Dr. Brigham, superintendent of the New York State Asylum, writes as follows, in his first report of that institution: "Few things relating to the management and treatment of the insane, are so *well established* as the necessity of their *early* treatment, and of their removal from home, in order to effect recovery. There are exceptions, no doubt. By examining the records of well conducted lunatic asylums, it appears that more than eight out of ten of the recent cases recover, *while not more than one in six* of the old cases are cured."

In Dr. Awl's fifth annual report, I find the following remarks: "We exceedingly rejoice that it is now a settled policy with the citizens of Ohio, to make abundant provision for the reception of *every* insane patient, whether male or female, rich or poor, curable or incurable. *Public safety, equity,* and *economy,* alike require that this should be so."

"Fearful as is the disease of insanity, the experience of this and other institutions of the United States, has clearly shown that, with seasonable aid, it is by no means an incurable disease. That under *proper medical and moral treatment, a large proportion do perfectly recover.* And of those who are absolutely incurable, a vast number can always be greatly improved, and made comfortable and useful. *In our judgment, it is entirely* wrong to consider a certain class of incurables as harmless, and proper to be discharged from the institution, because it does not *seem* dangerous to the peace of the community that they should go at large. This cannot certainly be known, either in or out of the asylum: neither can a bond afford any proper security to the public, for the peaceable and inoffensive are easily excited; and it is possible for the most imbecile lunatic to take life or fire a city. It is also certain that they must all receive attention, and have a being somewhere in the land; and a majority of them at the public expense. We therefore unhesitatingly conclude, that the only safe and correct course, either for the insane themselves, or for their friends and society, is to provide ample accommodations for them, when there will be opportunity for every one to experience comfort and relief."

Quoting again from the report of the physician of the asylum at Columbus, showing the benefits of hospital treatment, we read: "It is now five years since this great enterprise of humanity was opened to the unfortunate and afflicted in the state. During this period *four hundred and seventy-three* insane persons have been committed to the care of the institution. Two hundred and three have recovered the right use of their reason, and returned to their friends; eighteen were discharged, improved in various degrees of mental and physical health, and a large proportion of the remainder have been reclaimed from wretchedness and suffering, from filth and nakedness, from violence, which caused apprehension and danger, and from anguish and melancholy, which could only be exhibited in silence and in tears."

Dr. Kirkbride remarks, in his report upon the Pennsylvania Insane Hospital for 1842, the great importance of bringing patients under early curative treatment, and first, in regard to its economy:

"The economy of subjecting cases of mental derangement to proper treatment, immediately upon the occurrence of an attack, has not been generally understood, *or no state* would have neglected to make adequate provision for the early care of all who were thus afflicted. There can be no question, but that every community, not having within itself the proper means, would save largely by sending their recent cases to some well conducted insane hospital, and retaining them there, as long as there was a prospect for their restoration. If this was done, a large proportion of them would in a few months, be restored to society, instead of continuing as is now

379

too apt to be the case, a charge to their friends or the public, during the remainder of their lives.

The expense in the one instance, is only for a few months, when the individual returns to the care of his family, or business; in the other, it is a support for life, often a long one, and not unfrequently if the individual be the head of a family,—the support of a family in addition."

From allusions made on the first pages of this memorial, to the inappropriate, unjust, and *sometimes* barbarous, treatment of the insane poor, it will be expected that I shall sustain assertion by evidence. I have therefore prepared, from my note book, some account of the condition in which I have found the poor-houses, jails, and prisons of this commonwealth, during more than four months laborious journeyings, devoted to inquiry and investigation. I describe those establishments *as I found them*. The sane paupers in the poor-houses, almost without exception, are well and liberally provided for. The insane, almost without exception, are inappropriately and injudiciously situated. This is not so much the fault of these establishments, as their misfortune. Poor-houses never can be made suitable places for the reception of, and treatment of, the insane. Of the six well directed county prisons in the United States, Pennsylvania has the honorable distinction of containing three, and these I consider established on the best system; but not suitable in any respect as asylums for mad-men and mad-women. Your state penitentiaries, are conducted as they are established, upon the best system human wisdom, and justice, and humanity, has yet devised. But the penitentiaries were not planned and built as hospitals, where the physical maladies of the insane should find remedial and appropriate treatment; nor can they with due regard to the discipline and regulations to which they are subject, be thus occupied. One does not know how to employ mild terms in touching upon the shameful injustice of *sending maniacs, who for years have been known to labor under this distressing malady, to prison*. "To do justly and love mercy is better than sacrifice;" and to redress these many grievances may be your beneficent and noble work.

Gentlemen, *First*, the provision for the poor and indigent insane of your state, is inappropriate, insufficient, and unworthy of a civilized and christian people: *Second*, it is *unjust* and *unjustifiable* to convict as criminals and incarcerate those in prisons, who, bereft of reason, are incapable of that self-direction and action, by which a man is made responsible for the deeds he may commit: *Third*, your alms-houses, are, in all essential respects, unfit for the insane; and that while they may, with uncommon care and devotedness on the part of the superintendents, and other official persons, be made decent *receptacles*, they cannot be made curative hospitals nor asylums, for affording adequate protection for the insane: *Fourth*, still less can these ends be accomplished in private families, even where pecuniary prosperity affords the means of supplying many wants. But in those where this calamitous malady is united with poverty and pinching want, it is barely within the bounds of probability that the patient should recover. There is then but one alternative—condemn your needy citizens to become the life-long victims of a terrible disease, or provide remedial care in a State Hospital. Let this be established on a comfortable, but strictly economical foundation. Expend not one dollar on tasteful architectural decorations. In this establishment, let nothing be for ornament, but every thing for use. Choose your location where the most good can be accomplished effectually, at the least cost. Let economy only not degenerate into meanness. Every dollar indiscreetly applied, is a robbery of the poor and needy, and adds a darker shade to the vice of extravagance, in misappropriation of the public funds.

Choose a healthful situation where you can command at least one hundred acres, and better if a larger tract, of productive land, mostly capable of cultivation. Let the supply and access to pure water, be ample and convenient: also consider the cost of fuel, which is a large item in the annual expenses. Furnish your establishment by means chiefly of convict labor, from your two state penitentiaries, with mattresses, bed-clothing, chairs, &c. &c. You thus secure a sale for *their* work, and get good articles at reasonable cost for your own use. You will recollect that at some future time other hospitals will be needed and demanded, but let the location of the *first* have reference to sparing as far as possible to the poor at large, the heavy charge of travelling expenses. A substantial brick, or unhewn stone building, not more than three-stories high with the basement, to save labor, and the consequent multiplying of attendants, having the officers' apartments in the centre, and those of the male and female patients in the two wings respectively, will be found most commodious.

Gentlemen, of the Legislature of Pennsylvania, I appeal to your hearts and your understanding; to your moral and to your intellectual perceptions; I appeal to you as legislators and as citizens; I appeal to you as men, and as fathers, sons, and brothers; spare, I pray you, by wise and merciful legislation now, those many, who if you deny the means of curative treatment and recovery to health, will *by your decisions, and on your responsibility,* be condemned to irrecoverable, irremediable insanity: to worse than uselessness and grinding dependence; to pain and misery, and abject, brutalizing conditions, too terrible to contemplate; too horrible to relate!

Grant to the exceeding urgency of their case, what you would rightly refuse to expediency alone. Benevolent citizens of your commonwealth were the first of civilized people to establish a society for alleviating the miseries of prisons; shall Pennsylvanians be last and least in manifesting sensibility to the wants of the poverty-stricken maniac? Is the claim of the Lunatic less than that of the Criminal? Are the spiritual and physical wants of the guilty to be more humanely ministered to, than the bodily and mental necessities of the insane? You pause long, and hesitate to condemn to death the blood-stained murderer; will you less relentlessly condemn to a *living-death,* the unoffending victims of a dreadful malady?

The wise and illustrious Founder of Pennsylvania, laid broad the basis of her government in justice and integrity: now—while her sons with recovering strength, are replacing the shaken *Keystone of the* ARCH, may they, as in the beginning, find *their Salvation,—Truth, and their Palladium,*—RIGHTEOUSNESS!

Respectfully submitted,
D. L. DIX

37

The Log Cabin Campaign

The election of 1840 has often been described as the first modern American political campaign. Both the Whigs and the Democrats turned their best efforts to appealing to the public to support their party in the November election. There was nothing unusual in this for the Jacksonians; they had prided themselves since 1828 on their rapport with all the voters. For the Whigs, however, this was unprecedented strategy, marking their abandonment of any notion that a political organization could win power in the United States by looking exclusively for the support of the prosperous. As a result of the two-party competition in 1840, a greater percentage of eligible voters participated in the election than in any previous national contest.

The tactic may have been new to the Whigs, but they practiced it like old hands. From their selection of a candidate, William Henry Harrison, to their organization of parades and rallies, they showed themselves quick learners. These selections—a newspaper account of a Harrison parade, a Harrison stump speech, and a Harrison song—testify to their skills. There is also a good look at the content and style of American politics in 1840.

THE ELECTION OF 1840

1 Rally for William Henry Harrison in St. Louis, Missouri, as Reported by the St. Louis *New Era*

We cannot believe that any friend of Harrison could, in his most sanguine moments, have anticipated so glorious a day; such a turn-out of the people, as was witnessed on Tuesday last in this city. Everything was auspicious. The heavens, the air, the earth, all seemed to have combined to assist in doing honor to the services, the patriotism and the virtues of William Henry Harrison. Never have we seen so much enthusiasm, so much honest, impassioned and eloquent feeling displayed in the countenances and bursting from the lips of freemen. It was a day of jubilee. The people felt that the time had come when they could breathe freely—when they were about to cast from them the incubus of a polluted and abandoned party, and when they could look forward to better and happier days in store for them and for

From *The Election of 1840*, A. B. Norton, ed. (1888), I: 141–146, 150–151, 245–253, II: 21–22.

the country. The city itself bore, in some respects, the remarkable character of a Sabbath day. By the Whigs, and even among the Democrats, there was little work done. The doors of all places of business were closed, and nothing was thought of on this carnival day but joy and gratitude. We shall, ourselves, give such an account of the proceedings as our time and opportunities permitted us to gather, leaving it to the imagination to fill up the *tout ensemble* of the picture.

Preparations had been made for the reception and entertainment of the company, by the proper committees, at Mrs. Ashley's residence. The extensive park was so arranged as to accommodate the throng of persons who were expected. Seats were erected for the officers of the day, for the speakers and for the ladies. At the hour appointed by the marshal of the day, the people commenced to assemble at the court house, and several associations and crafts were formed in the procession as they advanced on the ground. While this was going on, the steamboats bringing delegations from St. Charles, Hannibal, Adams county, Ill., and Alton, arrived at the wharf, with banners unfurled to the breeze, and presenting a most cheering sight. The order of procession, so far as we have been able to obtain it, was as follows:

Music: Brass band.

1. Banner, borne by farmers from the northern part of St. Louis township. This banner represented the "Raising of the Siege of Fort Meigs" and bore as its motto, "It Has Pleased Providence, We Are Victorious." (Harrison's dispatch.)

2. Officers and members of the Tippecanoe club, preceded by the president, Col. John O'Fallon, with a splendid banner, representing a hemisphere surmounted by an American eagle, strangling with his beak a serpent, its folds grasped within its talons, and its head having the face of a fox in the throes of death. Above was a rainbow, emblematic of hope, in which was the name of the club. Below the hemisphere was the motto, "The Victor in '11, Will be the Victor in '40." On the reverse side, the letters "T. C." The members six abreast.

3. Log cabin committee, six abreast.

4. The president and vice-presidents of the day.

5. Soldiers who served under Harrison in the late war—in a car, adorned with banners on each side—one, a view of a steamboat named Tippecanoe, with a sign board, "For Washington City." On the other, a view of the cabin at North Bend, the farmer at his plow, with the inscription, "Harrison, the Old Soldier, Honest Man, and Pure Patriot."

6. Invited guests in carriages.

7. Citizens on foot, six abreast, bearing banners inscribed, "Harrison, the Friend of Pre-emption Rights," "One Term for the Presidency;" "Harrison, the People's Candidate;" "Harrison, the People's Sober Second Thought;" "Harrison, He Never Lost a Battle;" "Harrison, the Protector of the Pioneers of the West;" "Harrison, Tyler and Reform;" "Harrison, the Poor Man's Friend;" "Harrison, the Friend of Equal Laws and Equal Rights."

8. Citizens on horseback, six abreast.

9. Delegation from Columbia Bottom.

10. Canoe, "North Bend."

383

11. Boys with banners, upon one of which was inscribed, "Our Country's Hope," and on another, "Just as the Twig is Bent, the Tree's Inclined."

These boys belonged to the several schools of the city; were regularly marshaled, and presented, by the regularity of their conduct, a most interesting spectacle.

12. Laborers, with their horses and carts, shovels, picks, etc., with a banner bearing the inscription, "Harrison, the Poor Man's Friend—We Want Work."

13. A printing press on a platform with banners, and the pressman striking off Tippecanoe songs, and distributing them to the throng of people as they passed along, followed in order by the members of the craft.

14. Drays, with barrels of hard cider.

15. A log cabin mounted on wheels, and drawn by six beautiful horses, followed by the craft of carpenters in great numbers. Over the door of the cabin, the words, "The String of the Latch Never Pulled In."

16. The blacksmiths, with forge, bellows, etc., mounted on cars, the men at work. Banner, "We Strike for Our Country's Good."

17. The joiners and cabinet-makers; a miniature shop mounted on wheels; men at work; the craft following it.

18. A large canoe, drawn by six horses, and filled with men.

19. Two canoes, mounted, and filled by sailors.

20. Fort Meigs, in miniature, 40 by 15 feet, drawn by nine yoke of oxen. The interior filled with soldiers, in the usual dress of that day, hunting shirts, leggins, leather breeches, etc.; and one of the men a participant in the defense of Fort Meigs. At every bastion of the fort the muzzle of a piece of ordnance protruded itself, and from another point a piece of artillery was fired, at short intervals, during the day. The whole was most admirably got up, and reflects much credit upon the friends of "Old Tip," to be found at the "Floating Dock."

21. Delegation of brickmakers, with apparatus, clay, etc., and men at work.

22. Delegation of bricklayers, with a beautiful banner, representing a log cabin, brick house going up, etc., and followed by the craft, six abreast.

Band of music.

23. Delegation from Carondelet.

24. Delegation from Belleville, Ill., with banners.

25. Delegation from Alton, with canoe, drawn by four horses, and banners representing the state of the country, the peculiar notions of the Loco Foco party about the reduction of the prices of labor to the standard of the hard-money countries of Europe and of Cuba; a sub-treasury box, with illustrations, etc. One of the banners bore the inscription, "Connecticut Election, 4,600 Majority; Rhode Island, 1,500 Majority;" and a cunning looking fellow, with his thumb on his nose, and twisting his fingers in regular Samuel Weller style, saying, "You Can't Come It, Matty." This delegation numbered about two hundred men.

26. Delegations from Hannibal and Pike counties with banners, etc.

27. Delegation from Rockport with a log cabin, canoe, banners, etc.

28. Delegation from St. Charles, with banners bearing the names of the

twenty-six States, borne by as many individuals, and having with them a handsome canoe drawn by four horses.

Arrived at the southern extremity of the park, the procession halted and formed in open order, the rear passing to the front.

The people were then successively addressed by Mr. John Hogan, of Illinois.

Colonel John O'Fallon was then called for, and mounted on Fort Meigs, he thus addressed the people:

My Fellow Citizens:

I feel deeply sensible of the honor you confer upon me by calling me to address this vast concourse of intelligent freemen. My pursuits in life have led me into retirement; I am wholly unused to speaking in public.

Aware that my known acquaintance with the eventful scenes which we have this day assembled to commemorate, is the only reason for this call, I shall, consequently, in responding to it, state something of what I know in relation to them.

I had the honor of serving under General Harrison at the battle of Tippecanoe, during the seige of Fort Meigs, and at the battle of the Thames. I can say that, from the commencement to the termination of his military services in the last war, I was almost constantly by his side. I was familiar with his conduct as governor and superintendent of Indian affairs of the Territory of Indiana, and after the return of peace, as commissioner to treat with all the hostile Indians of the last war in the Northwest, for the establishment of a permanent reconciliation and peace. I saw also much of General Harrison whilst he was in the Congress of the United States.

Opportunities have thus been afforded me of knowing him in all the relations of life, as an officer and as a man, and of being enabled to form a pretty correct estimate of his military and civil services, as well as his qualifications and fitness for office. I know him to be open and brave in his disposition, of active and industrious habits, uncompromizing in his principles, above all guile and intrigue, and a pure, honest, noble-minded man, with a heart ever overflowing with warm and generous sympathies for his fellow-man. As a military man, his daring, chivalrous courage inspired his men with confidence and spread dismay and terror to his enemies. In all his plans he was successful. In all his engagements he was victorious. He has filled all the various civil and military offices committed to him by his country, with sound judgment and spotless fidelity. In every situation he was cautious and prudent, firm and energetic, and his decisions always judicious. His acquirements as a scholar are varied and extensive, his principles as a statesman sound, pure and republican.

If chosen President he will be the President of the people rather than of a party. The Government will then be administered for the general good and welfare.

His election will be the dawn of a new era! The reform of the abuses of a most corrupt, proligate and oppressive Government. Then will end the ten years' war upon the currency and institutions of the country. The hard-money cry and hard times will disappear together. Then will cease further attempts to increase the wages of the office-holders and reduce the wages of the people to the standard of European labor.

Then shall we see restored the general prosperity of the people, by giving them a sound local currency, mixed with a currency of a uniform value throughout the land. The revival of commerce, of trade, enterprise and general confidence. Then the return of happier, more peaceful and more prosperous days, when cheerfulness and plenty will, once more, smile around the poor man's table.

About the close of the meeting the following resolutions were adopted with three cheers:

Resolved, That the Whig young men of St. Louis county will respond to the call for a young men's convention at Rocheport on the 20th of June, and that the cause of old Tippecanoe shall not suffer because they are not on the ground.

Resolved, That five hundred of the real "log cabin and hard cider boys" of St. Louis county will stand at a corner of the Rocheport cabin on the 18th, and join in the convention of the 20th, when they hope to meet ten thousand of their brethren and join with them in doing honor to the farmer-statesmen of the West.

Resolved, That a committee of twenty be appointed to select the five hundred who shall go.

After the adoption of these resolutions, a song was sung, and the company dispersed.

2   A Stump Speech of William Henry Harrison, at Fort Greenville, to the Citizens of Ohio and Indiana

Friends and Fellow-citizens:

It is with no slight emotion that I undertake to address you on this occasion. Nor am I a little embarrassed for words wherein to express my deep sense of your kindness towards me, manifested by the friendliness and magnanimity of your greeting. My heart yields up to you the homage of its deepest gratitude, though my tongue expresses it not.

Fellow-citizens, you are all aware of the position that I occupy before the American people—being a candidate of a portion of them for the Presidency of the United States. It will doubtless be said by some that I am here for the purpose of electioneering for myself; that I have come to solicit your votes; but believe me gentlemen, this is not the case. I am present on this occasion but as an invited guest of citizens of Darke. It is my deliberate opinion and sincere desire that the bestowment of office should be the free act of the people, and I have no wish to bias their judgment unjustly in my favor. But, notwithstanding my wish and determination not to engage as a politician in the pending canvass for officers to administer the General Government, although I would have preferred to remain with my family in *the peace and quiet of our log cabin at the Bend,* rather than become engaged in political or other disputes as the advocate of my own rectitude of conduct, yet, from the continued torrent of calumny that has been poured upon me, from the slanders, abuses, and obloquy which have been promulgated and circulated to my discredit, designed to asperse and blacken my character, and from the villainous and false charges urged against me by the pensioned presses of this administration, my attendance at this celebration appeared to have been made an act of necessity, a step which I was compelled to take for self-defense. Chiefly for this purpose have I come among you, and trusting you will all perceive the propriety of its course, it seems superfluous to add any further reasons for its adoption.

Years ago, fellow-citizens, when I left this spot—for aught I knew, for the last time—I had little idea of the surprising change which would be wrought in its appearance during the time which has supervened. Never did I expect to stand here and behold such a scene as this. It resembles somewhat the recent *siege* of "Old Fort Meigs." I am now sixty-seven years of age. I have therefore lived to behold much of the glory of my country; I have seen the palmy days of this Republic; and especially have I witnessed many of the brilliant events which have characterized the growing greatness of the lovely West; but this very day and its incidents mark an epoch in my own history the like of which I have seldom experienced. It is now twenty-five years since I was at Fort Greenville—then surrounded by a dense forest dark and dreary. At that period there was scarce a log cabin between Greenville and Cincinnati—all between was one entire, unbroken wilderness. How wonderfully and how speedily have the giant woods bowed their stately tops to the industry and enterprise of Western pioneers, as if some magic power had cleaved them from the earth! And now in their stead what do we behold? Broad, cultivated fields, flowery gardens, and happy homes. Delightful picture—gratifying change! Proud reflection! that this transition of things is the result of the handiwork of Western people—of American freemen.

Fellow-citizens, you have undoubtedly seen it oftentimes stated in a certain class of newspapers that I am a very decrepit old man, obliged to hobble about on crutches; that I was caged up, and that I could not speak loud enough to be heard more than four or five feet distant, in consequence of which last misfortune I am stigmatized with the cognomen of "General Mum." You now perceive, however, that these stories are false. But there are some more serious matters charged against me, which I shall take the liberty to prove untrue. You know it has been said by some that I have no principles; that I dare not avow any principles and that I am kept under the surveillance of a "committee." All this is false—unconditionally false.

Now, with regard to the political condition of our common country, I trust there is no impropriety in my addressing you upon subjects concerning the public weal. What means this "great commotion" among the people of this great nation? What are the insufferable grievances which have driven so many thousands, nay, millions, of the American people into the council for the purpose of devising measures for their mutual relief? Wherefore do they cry aloud as with one voice, Reform! Our country is in peril! The public morals are corrupted. How has it been done? "To the victors belong the spoils," say our rulers. What are the consequences? Ask the hundred public defaulters throughout the land! Ask the hirelings of corruption who are proffering "power and place" as bribes to secure votes! Ask the subsidized press what governs its operations, and it will open its iron jaws and answer you in a voice loud enough to shake the Pyramids—Money! Money! I speak not at random—facts bear me testimony. The principle is boldly avowed, as well as put in practice by men in high places, that falsehood is justifiable in order to accomplish their purposes. Why this laxity in the morals of our rulers and their followers? Did they inherit depravity from their ancestors? How does it come that such recklessness of truth and justice is manifested of late by some individuals among us? Why some of the causes produce these evils I have already intimated. There are others. Intense party spirit destroys patriotism.

A celebrated Grecian commander once said, and said truly: "Where virtue is best rewarded, there will virtue most prevail." It is even so, a wise and true saying. But how has the practice of your Government of late accorded with this maxim? It is proverbial with the advocates of monarchy in the Old World that republics are ungrateful. How does your experience for the last few years give the lie to this proposition? Nay, fellow-citizens, I fear that this Government affords many examples which tend but too strongly to verify the proverb. Among other instances of manifest ingratitude, to only one will I here recur. I mean the removal from office, without cause or provocation, save a difference of opinion with the President, of Gen. Solomon Van Rensselaer, of New York. He was a noble friend of ours in the "winter of our discontent." I became acquainted with him when, like myself, he was a young officer in General Wayne's army. I found him an agreeable, social companion, as well as a brave and magnanimous soldier. He assisted in fighting the battles of his country; aye, for your behoof, my countrymen, his blood has been poured out upon the soil of Ohio. The bullets of your enemies have pierced his body while fighting in defense of your interests. And not only on the plains of Ohio has he stood between danger and his country, but in other places likewise. In the sanguinary battle of Queenstown he received six wounds from his country's foes. Well, what is his reward? After having spent the flower of his youth and the vigor of his manly prime in the service of his country as a soldier, he was called by the American people to serve them in a civil capacity. He obeyed the call with thankfulness of heart. But he has been cruelly driven out of the service by the administration, and why? Because, fellow-citizens, he was the friend of the companion of his youth; because he would not forsake a fellow-soldier; because he was my incorruptible friend; and because the emoluments of his office were wanted to reward the partisan services of a supporter of my political competitor. "Ah, there's the rub!" But you, my friends, I am confident, will not long permit such wrong to the men who "righted your wrongs" in olden times.

Fellow-citizens, you know that my opponents call me a Federalist. But I deny the charge: I am not—I never was a Federalist. Federalists are in favor of concentrating power in the hands of the executive; Democrats are in favor of the retention of power by the people. I am, and ever have been, a Democratic Republican. My former practices will bear me out in what I say. When I was governor of Indiana Territory, I was vested with despotic power, and had I chosen to exercise it, I might have governed that people with a rod of iron. But being a child of the Revolution, and bred to its principles, I believed in the right and the ability of the people to govern themselves; and they were always permitted to enjoy that high privilege. I had the power to prorogue, adjourn and dissolve the legislature, to lay off the new counties and establish seats of justice; to appoint sheriffs and other officers. But never did I interpose my prerogative to defeat the wishes of a majority of the people. The people chose their own officers, and I invariably confirmed their choice; where they preferred to have their county seats, there I located them; they made their own laws and I ratified them. *I never vetoed a bill in my life.*

But I have been denounced as a bank man. Well, let it go. I am so far a bank man as I believe every rational Republican ought to be, and no further. The Constitution of the United States makes it the duty of the Government to provide ways and means for the collection and disbursement of the public revenue. If the people deem it necessary to the proper discharge of the functions of their Government to create a national bank, properly guarded and regulated, I shall be the last man, if elected President, to set up my authority against that of the millions of American freemen. It is needful to have a larger money circulation in a land of liberty than in an empire of despotism. Destroy the poor man's credit and you destroy his capital. The peasant who toils incessantly to maintain his famishing household, in the hard money countries of Europe, rarely if ever becomes the noble lord who pastures his "flocks upon a thousand hills." There are necessarily difficulties connected with every form and system of the Government, but it should be the aim and object of the statesman to form the best institutions within this power to make for the good of his country.

Fellow-citizens, I cannot forbear inviting your attention to the concerns of your Government, in the welfare of which all good citizens feel a deep interest. I warn you to watch your rulers. Remember, "Eternal vigilance is the price of liberty." When I looked around upon the dangers which seem to be suspended as by a hair over this people, I tremble for the safety of this Republic. In an evil hour has the Chief Magistrate of this nation been transformed into a monarch and despot at pleasure! To show that this is the case I need but refer you to the profound and philosophical historian, Gibbon, who says, "The obvious definition of monarchy seems to be that of a State in which a *single person,* by whatsoever name he may be distinguished, *is intrusted with the execution of the law, the management of the revenue, and the command of the army.*" Is not Martin Van Buren intrusted with these functions? Most assuredly he is. Call him by whatsoever title you choose, President, executive, chief magistrate, consul, king, stadtholder, it does not alter the nature of his power; that remains the same, unchanged, and the President, therefore, possesses all the functions necessary to constitute a monarch. You have often heard of the "moneyed influence of the country" denounced while it yet remained in the hands of the people, as dangerous to public liberty.

Have you, then, no apprehension, no fear of a moneyed influence, equal to that of half the nation, concentrated in the hands of a single individual, at the same time possessing two other of the most potent powers that belong to our Government? The great Julius Caesar—the conquering Julius has said, "Give me soldiers and I will get money; give me money and I will get soldiers." The public purse is already confided to the hands of the President; a respectable army is also under his control, and it is in contemplation by the administration to add to the present military force of the United States an army of 200,000 men. American freemen, pause and reflect. Meditate before you act. Matters of the highest moment depend upon your action and await your decision. There may be no ambitious Caesar among us who will dare to use the ample means now combined in the hands of the President for the subversion of our liberties, but the exceptions to ambitious men so inclined are so few that they but fortify the rule. Look around you, fellow-citizens. Are you girt with your armor or have you surrendered it to another? The "sentinels upon the watch tower of freedom"—have they been true to their trusts, or have they slept? I warn you, my countrymen, against the danger of neglecting your duty. Power is always stealing from the many to the few. Beware how you intrust our rights to the keeping of any man. They are never so secure as when protected by your own shield and defended by yourselves with your own weapons.

In conclusion fellow-citizens, indulge me in a few remarks in regard to my old fellow-soldiers. A small number of them are here by my side. They stood by me in battle, firm and invincible, in by-gone days. Some of them are remnants of the Revolution—soldiers with whom I served under the gallant Wayne. Where, my brethren, are our companions in danger on the field of strife? Alas! many of them are taking their final repose in the calm and peace of death!

The old soldiers, one by one, are dwindling away—gliding as it were down the river of time into the haven of long-sought rest. But a few of them even now are remaining to sorrow in gladness for the ingratitude of their country. When this country was a dismal howling wilderness those warriors were exposing themselves to danger and disease in the unwholesome swamps and morasses of the West, by guarding and defending our frontiers. Many of them became present victims to the malaria of the marshes and the insalubrity of the climate, others returned to their houses with disease engendered in their systems, but to linger for a time, and perhaps waste away with consumption; while yet smaller portions still remain among us, though generally shattered in constitution and feeble in health. Why is it, fellow-citizens, that these old soldiers of General Wayne's army have never been repaid for their services, or been allowed pensions by our Government? The nation is much indebted to them, and justice requires that the debt should be paid, and I could never die in peace, and feel no sting of remorse, if I were to permit their claims to pass unnoticed, and without making an effort, when opportunity offered, to have them satisfied.

Fellow-citizens, my character has been most grossly and wantonly assailed by the dangerous demagogues of the administration party. They have falsely charged me with the commission of almost every crime which is denominated such that man can be guilty of. My character, which I had fondly hoped to preserve unsullied as a boon and an example for my family, has been much more traduced and belied within the few months past, and, for this reason I have sometimes regretted that your predilection had made me a candidate for office; but, nevertheless, I claim no sympathy of the public on that score. I only desire you to examine my past conduct, to read the history of your country and ascertain my political course heretofore, and the principles on which I have ever acted, and if you find that my doctrines are unsound and unworthy of your support, it is your sacred duty to reject them. I ask not your sympathy or favor. I want but common justice. Let me have a fair trial, and, whatever may be your verdict, I shall be satisfied. Investigate matters fairly and honestly; compare the doctrines and practices of my adversaries with mine, and then decide as you shall think right and proper. Cast aside your prejudices and predilections, and vote only from principle. It is your duty to do so. Heed not the censure of knavish politicians who reproach you with the name of "turn coat," etc. *It is not approbrious to turn from a party to your country.* We should despise the odium sought to be heaped upon us by designing men, from their selfish motives, as they despise truth and honesty.

Hoping that the right may prevail and make our country prosperous, I will only add the wish that you may long enjoy its blessings, maintain its free institutions, and rejoice in the independence of happy freemen.

3   Tippecanoe Songs of 1840

THE LOG CABIN AND HARD CIDER CANDIDATE

TUNE, "AULD LANG SYNE"
Should good old cider be despised,
And ne'er regarded more?
Should plain log cabins be despised,
Our fathers built of yore?
For the true old style, my boys!
For the true old style?
Let's take a mug of cider, now,
For the true old style.

We've tried experiments enough
Of fashions new and vain,
And now we long to settle down
To good old times again.
For the good old ways, my boys!
For the good old ways,
Let's take a mug of cider, now,
For the good old ways.

We've tried your purse-proud lords, who love
In palaces to shine;
But we'll have a plowman President
Of the Cincinnatus line.
For old North Bend, my boys!
For old North Bend,
We'll take a mug of cider, yet,
For old North Bend.

We've tried the "greatest and the best,"
And found him bad enough;
And he who "in the footsteps treads"

Is yet more sorry stuff.
For the brave old Thames, my boys!
 For the brave old Thames,
We'll take a mug of cider, yet,
 For the brave old Thames.

Then give 's a hand, my boys!
 And here's a hand for you,
And we'll quaff the good old cider yet
 For Old Tippecanoe.
For Old Tippecanoe, my boys!
 For Old Tippecanoe,
We'll take a mug of cider, yet,
 For Old Tippecanoe.

And surely you'll give your good vote,
 And surely I will, too;
And we'll clear the way to the White House, yet,
 For Old Tippecanoe.
For Tip-pe-canoe, my boys,
 For Tip-pe-canoe,
We'll take a mug of cider, yet,
 For Tippecanoe.

38

The Story of a Slave Revolt

Nat Turner's Rebellion was perhaps the most famous slave revolt in pre-Civil War America, and certainly one of the bloodiest. Led by Turner, a band of Virginia slaves in 1831 coldly murdered white planters, women and children, in brutal fashion. The incident gained notoriety not only from the deed but from the *Confessions of Nat Turner,* a document published in 1832 by Thomas Gray, a white local resident, who interviewed Turner while he awaited trial in a Virginia jail. The *Confessions* were read to the court in Turner's defense. The authenticity of the document is open to question. The astute reader will find some internal evidence that Gray not only changed the style of Turner's speech, but at times may have put his own feelings and sentiments into Turner's mouth.

Nevertheless, the narrative is important and revealing. Read widely through the South, it helped to promote fear and repression. The modern reader will have little trouble imagining what planters thought as they read the blow-by-blow details of the murders. Moreover, and this testifies to the general authenticity of the document, the intellectual and emotional makeup of a slave leader, his origins, his outlook, his fate emerge vividly and honestly from the story. After concluding the *Confessions,* one can better understand why so few slave revolts swept the ante-bellum South.

THE CONFESSIONS
OF NAT TURNER

Agreeable to his own appointment, on the evening he was committed to prison, with permission of the Jailer, I visited NAT on Tuesday the 1st November, when, without being questioned at all, he commenced his narrative in the following words:—

Sir,

You have asked me to give a history of the motives which induced me to undertake the late insurrection, as you call it—To do so I must go back to the days of my infancy, and even before I was born. I was thirty-one years of age the 2d of

From *The Confessions of Nat Turner . . . as Fully and Voluntarily Made to Thomas R. Gray* (Richmond, 1832; reprinted, New York, 1964), 5–17.

October last, and born the property of Benj. Turner, of this county. In my childhood a circumstance occurred which made an indelible impression on my mind, and laid the ground work of that enthusiasm, which has terminated so fatally to many both white and black, and for which I am about to atone at the gallows. It is here necessary to relate this circumstance—trifling as it may seem, it was the commencement of that belief which has grown with time, and even now, sir, in this dungeon, helpless and forsaken as I am, I cannot divest myself of. Being at play with other children, when three or four years old, I was telling them something, which my mother overhearing, said it had happened before I was born—I stuck to my story, however, and related some things which went in her opinion to confirm it—others being called on were greatly astonished, knowing that these things had happened, and caused them to say in my hearing, I surely would be a prophet, as the Lord had shewn me things that had happened before my birth. And my father and mother strengthened me in this my first impression, saying in my presence, I was intended for some great purpose, which they had always thought from certain marks on my head and breast.—

My grand mother, who was very religious, and to whom I was much attached—my master, who belonged to the church, and other religious persons who visited the house, and whom I often saw at prayers, noticing the singularity of my manners, I suppose, and my uncommon intelligence for a child, remarked I had too much sense to be raised—and if I was, I would never be of any service to any one—as a slave—To a mind like mine, restless, inquisitive and observant of every thing that was passing, it is easy to suppose that religion was the subject to which it would be directed, and although this subject principally occupied my thoughts, there was nothing that I saw or heard of to which my attention was not directed—The manner in which I learned to read and write, not only had great influence on my own mind, as I acquired it with the most perfect ease, so much so, that I have no recollection whatever of learning the alphabet—but to the astonishment of the family, one day, when a book was shewn me to keep me from crying, I began spelling the names of different objects—this was a source of wonder to all in the neighborhood, particularly the blacks—and this learning was constantly improved at all opportunities—when I got large enough to go to work, while employed, I was reflecting on many things that would present themselves to my imagination, and whenever an opportunity occured of looking at a book, when the school children were getting their lessons, I would find many things that the fertility of my own imagination had depicted to me before; all my time, not devoted to my master's service, was spent either in prayer, or in making experiments in casting different things in moulds made of earth, in attempting to make paper, gunpowder, and many other experiments, that although I could not perfect, yet convinced me of its practicability if I had the means. I was not addicted to stealing in my youth, nor have never been—Yet such was the confidence of the negroes in the neighborhood, even at this early period of my life, in my superior judgment, that they would often carry me with them when they were going on any roguery, to plan for them. Growing up among them, with this confidence in my superior judgment, and when this, in their opinions, was perfected by Divine inspiration, from the circumstances already alluded to in my infancy, and which belief was ever afterwards zealously inculcated by the austerity of my life and manners, which became the subject of remark by white and black.—Having soon discovered to be great, I must appear so, and therefore studiously avoided mixing in society, and wrapped myself in mystery, devoting my time to fasting and prayer. By this time, having arrived to man's estate, and hearing the scriptures commented on at meetings, I was struck with that particular passage which says: "Seek ye the kingdom of Heaven and all things shall be added unto you. ' I reflected much on this passage, and prayed daily for light on this subject—As I was praying one day at my plough, the spirit spoke to me, saying "Seek ye the kingdom of Heaven and all things shall be added unto you." *Question*—what do you mean by the Spirit. *Ans.* The Spirit that spoke to the prophets in former days—and I was greatly astonished, and for two years prayed continually, whenever my duty would permit—and then again I had the same revelation, which fully confirmed me in the impression that I was ordained for some great purpose in the hands of the Almighty. Several years rolled round, in which many events occurred to strengthen me in this my belief. At this time I reverted in my mind to the remarks made of me in my childhood, and the things that had been shewn me—and as it had been said of me in my childhood by those whom I had been taught to pray, both white and black, and in whom I had the greatest confidence, that I had too much sense to be raised, and if I was I would never be of any use to any one as a slave. Now finding I had arrived to man's estate, and was a slave, and these revelations being made known to me, I began to direct my attention to this great object, to fulfil the purpose for which, by this time, I felt assured I was intended. Knowing the influence I had obtained over the minds of my fellow servants, (not by the means of conjuring and such like tricks—for to them I always spoke of such things with contempt) but by the communion of the Spirit whose revelations I often communicated to them, and they believed and said my wisdom came from God. I now began to prepare them for my purpose, by telling them something was about to happen that would terminate in fulfilling the great promise that had been made to me—About this time I was placed under an overseer, from whom I ran away—and after remaining in the woods thirty days, I returned, to the astonishment of the negroes on the plantation, who thought I had made my escape to some other part of the country, as my father had done before. But the reason of my return was, that the Spirit appeared to me and said I had my wishes directed to the things of this world, and not to the kingdom of Heaven, and that I should return to the service of my earthly master—"For he who knoweth his Master's will, and doeth it not, shall be beaten with many stripes, and thus have I chastened you." And the negroes found fault, and murmured against me, saying that if they had my sense they would not serve any master in the world. And about this time I had a vision—and I saw white spirits and black spirits engaged in battle, and the sun was darkened—the thunder rolled in the Heavens, and blood flowed in streams—and I heard a voice saying, "Such is your luck, such you are called to see, and let it come rough or smooth, you must surely bear it." I now withdrew myself as much as my situation would permit, from the intercourse of my fellow servants, for the avowed purpose of serving the Spirit more fully—and it appeared to me, and reminded me of the things it had already shown me, and that it would then reveal to me the knowledge of the elements, the revolution of the planets, the operation of tides, and changes of the seasons. After this revelation in the year 1825, and the knowledge of the elements being made known to me, I sought more than ever to obtain true holiness before the great day of judgment should appear, and then I began to receive the true knowledge of faith. And from the first steps of righteousness until the last, was I made perfect; and the Holy Ghost was with me, and said "Behold me as I stand in the Heavens"—and I looked and saw the forms of men in different attitudes—and there were lights in the sky to which the children of darkness gave other names than what they really were—for they were the lights of the Saviour's hands, stretched forth from east to west, even as they were extended on the cross on Calvary for the redemption of sinners. And I wondered greatly at these miracles, and prayed to be informed of a certainty of the meaning thereof—and shortly afterwards, while labouring in the field, I discovered drops of blood on the corn, as though it were dew from heaven—and I communicated it to many, both white and black, in the neighbourhood—and I then found on the leaves in the woods hieroglyphic characters and numbers, with the forms of men in different attitudes, portrayed in blood, and representing the figures I had seen before in the heavens.—And now the Holy Ghost had revealed itself to me, and made plain the miracles it had shown me—For as the blood of Christ had been shed on this earth, and had ascended to heaven for the salvation of sinners, and was now returning to earth again in the form of dew—and as the leaves on the trees bore the impression of the figures I had seen in the heavens, it was plain to me that the Saviour was about to lay down the yoke he had borne for the sins of men, and the great day of judgment was at hand.—

And on the 12th of May, 1828, I heard a loud noise in the heavens, and the Spirit instantly appeared to me and said the Serpent was loosened, and Christ had laid down the yoke he had borne for the sins of men, and that I should take it on and fight against the Serpent, for the time was fast approaching, when the first should be last and the last should be first. *Ques.* Do you not find yourself mistaken now? *Ans.* Was not Christ crucified? And by signs in the heavens that it would make known to me when I should commence the great work—and until the first sign appeared, I should conceal it from the knowledge of men—And on the appearance of the sign, (the eclipse of the sun last February) I should arise and prepare myself, and slay my enemies with their own weapons. And immediately on the sign appearing in the heavens, the seal was removed from my lips, and I communicated the great work laid out for me to do, to four in whom I had the greatest confidence, (Henry, Hark, Nelson and Sam)—It was intended by us to have begun the work of death on the 4th of July last—Many were the plans formed and rejected by us, and it affected my mind to such a degree, that I fell sick, and the time passed without our coming to any determination how to commence—Still forming new schemes and rejecting them, when the sign appeared again, which determined me not to wait longer.

Since the commencement of 1830, I had been living with Mr. Joseph Travis, who was to me a kind master, and placed the greatest confidence in me; in fact, I had no cause to complain of his treatment to me. On Saturday evening, the 20th of August, it was agreed between Henry, Hark and myself, to prepare a dinner the next day for the men we expected, and then to concert a plan, as we had not yet determined on any. Hark on the following morning brought a pig, and Henry brandy, and being joined by Sam, Nelson, Will and Jack, they prepared in the woods a dinner, where, about three o'clock, I joined them.

Q. Why were you so backward in joining them.

A. The same reason that had caused me not to mix with them for years before.

I saluted them on coming up, and asked Will how came he there; he answered, his life was worth no more than others, and his liberty as dear to him. I asked him if he thought to obtain it? He said he would, or lose his life. This was enough to put him in full confidence. Jack, I knew, was only a tool in the hands of Hark, it was quickly agreed we should commence at home (Mr. J. Travis') on that night, and until we had armed and equipped ourselves, and gathered sufficient force, neither age nor sex was to be spared, (which was invariably adhered to.) We remained at the feast until about two hours in the night, when we went to the house and found Austin; they all went to the cider press and drank, except myself. On returning to the house, Hark went to the door with an axe, for the purpose of breaking it open, as we knew we were strong enough to murder the family, if they were awaked by the noise; but reflecting that it might create an alarm in the neighborhood, we determined to enter the house secretly, and murder them whilst sleeping. Hark got a ladder and set it against the chimney, on which I ascended, and hoisting a window, entered and came down stairs, unbarred the door, and removed the guns from their places. It was then observed that I must spill the first blood. On which armed with a hatchet, and accompanied by Will, I entered my master's chamber; it being dark, I could not give a death blow, the hatchet glanced from his head, he sprang from the bed and called his wife, it was his last word. Will laid him dead, with a blow of his axe, and Mrs. Travis shared the same fate, as she lay in bed. The murder of this family five in number, was the work of a moment, not one of them awoke; there was a little infant sleeping in a cradle, that was forgotten, until we had left the house and gone some distance, when Henry and Will returned and killed it; we got here, four guns that would shoot, and several old muskets, with a pound or two of powder. We remained some time at the barn, where we paraded; I formed them in a line as soldiers, and after carrying them through all the manoeuvres I was master of, marched them off to Mr. Salathul Francis', about six hundred yards distant. Sam and Will went to the door and knocked. Mr. Francis asked who was there, Sam replied it was him, and he had a letter for him, on which he got up and came to the door; they immediately seized him, and dragging him out a little from the door, he was dispatched by repeated blows on the head; there was no other white person in the family. We started from there for Mrs. Reese's, maintaining the most perfect silence on our march, where

397

finding the door unlocked, we entered, and murdered Mrs. Reese in her bed, while sleeping; her son awoke, but it was only to sleep the sleep of death, he had only time to say who is that, and he was no more. From Mrs. Reese's we went to Mrs. Turner's, a mile distant, which we reached about sunrise, on Monday morning. Henry, Austin, and Sam, went to the still, where, finding Mr. Peebles, Austin shot him, and the rest of us went to the house; as we approached, the family discovered us, and shut the door. Vain hope! Will, with one stroke of his axe, opened it, and we entered and found Mrs. Turner and Mrs. Newsome in the middle of a room almost frightened to death. Will immediately killed Mrs. Turner, with one blow of his axe. I took Mrs. Newsome by the hand, and with the sword I had when I was apprehended, I struck her several blows over the head, but not being able to kill her, as the sword was dull. Will turning around and discovering it, dispatched her also. A general destruction of property and search for money and ammunition, always succeeded the murders. By this time my company amounted to fifteen, and nine men mounted, who started for Mrs. Whitehead's, (the other six were to go through a by way to Mr. Bryant's, and rejoin us at Mrs. Whitehead's,) as we approached the house we discovered Mr. Richard Whitehead standing in the cotton patch, near the lane fence; we called him over into the lane, and Will, the executioner, was near at hand, with his fatal axe, to send him to an untimely grave. As we pushed on to the house, I discovered some one run round the garden, and thinking it was some of the white family, I pursued them, but finding it was a servant girl belonging to the house, I returned to commence the work of death, but they whom I left, had not been idle; all the family were already murdered, but Mrs. Whitehead and her daughter Margaret. As I came round to the door I saw Will pulling Mrs. Whitehead out of the house, and at the step he nearly severed her head from her body, with his broad axe. Miss Margaret, when I discovered her, had concealed herself in the corner, formed by the projection of the cellar cap from the house; on my approach she fled, but was soon overtaken, and after repeated blows with a sword, I killed her by a blow on the head, with a fence rail. By this time, the six who had gone by Mr. Bryant's, rejoined us, and informed me they had done the work of death assigned them. We again divided, part going to Mr. Richard Porter's, and from thence to Nathaniel Francis', the others to Mr. Howell Harris', and Mr. T. Doyle's. On my reaching Mr. Porter's, he had escaped with his family. I understood there, that the alarm had already spread.

I proceeded to Mr. Levi Waller's, two or three miles distant. I took my station in the rear, and as it was my object to carry terror and devastation whereever we went, I placed fifteen or twenty of the best armed and most to be relied on, in front, who generally approached the houses as fast as their horses could run; this was for two purposes, to prevent their escape and strike terror to the inhabitants—on this account I never got to the houses, after leaving Mrs. Whitehead's until the murders were committed, except in one case. I sometimes got in sight in time to see the work of death completed, viewed the mangled bodies as they lay, in silent satisfaction, and immediately started in quest of other victims—Having murdered Mrs. Waller and ten children, we started for Mr. William Williams'—having killed him and two little boys that were there; while engaged in this, Mrs. Williams fled and got some distance from the house, but she was pursued, overtaken, and compelled to get up behind one of the company, who brought her back, and after showing her the mangled body of her lifeless husband, she was told to get down and lay by his side, where she was shot dead. I then started for Mr. Jacob Williams', where the family were murdered—Here we found a young man named Drury, who had come on business with Mr. Williams—he was pursued, overtaken and shot. Mrs. Vaughan's was the next place we visited—and after murdering the family here, I determined on starting for Jerusalem—Our number amounted now to fifty or sixty, all mounted and armed with guns, axes, swords and clubs—On reaching Mr. James W. Parker's gate, immediately on the road leading to Jerusalem, and about three miles distant, it was proposed to me to call there, but I objected, as I knew he was gone to Jerusalem, and my object was to reach there as soon as possible; but some of the men having relations at Mr. Parker's it was agreed that they might call and get his people. I remained at the gate on the road, with seven or eight; the others going across the field to the house, about half a mile off. After waiting some time for them, I became impatient, and started to the house for them, and on our return we were met by a party of white men, who had pursued our blood-stained track, and who had fired on those at the gate, and dispersed them, which I knew nothing of, not having been at that time rejoined by any of them—Immediately on discovering the whites, I ordered my men to halt and form, as they appeared to be alarmed—The white men eighteen in number, approached us in about one hundred yards, when one of them fired.

I then ordered my men to fire and rush on them; the few remaining stood their ground until we approached within fifty yards, when they fired and retreated. We pursued and overtook some of them who we thought we left dead; after pursuing them about two hundred yards, and rising a little hill, I discovered they were met by another party, and had halted, and were re-loading their guns, thinking that those who retreated first, and the party who fired on us at fifty or sixty yards distant, had all only fallen back to meet others with ammunition. As I saw them re-loading their guns, and more coming up than I saw at first, and several of my bravest men being wounded, the others became panic struck and squandered over the field; the white men pursued and fired on us several times. Hark had his horse shot under him, and I caught another for him as it was running by me; five or six of my men were wounded, but none left on the field; finding myself defeated here I instantly determined to go through a private way, and cross the Nottoway river at the Cypress Bridge, three miles below Jerusalem, and attack that place in the rear, as I expected they would look for me on the other road, and I had a great desire to get there to procure arms and ammunition. After going a short distance in this private way, accompanied by about twenty men, I overtook two or three who told me the others were dispersed in every direction. After trying in vain to collect a sufficient force to proceed to Jerusalem, I determined to return, as I was sure they would make back to their old neighborhood, where they would rejoin me, make new recruits, and come down again. On my way back, I called at Mrs. Thomas's,

399

Mrs. Spencer's, and several other places, the white families having fled, we found no more victims to gratify our thirst for blood, we stopped at Majr. Ridley's quarter for the night, and being joined by four of his men, with the recruits made since my defeat, we mustered now about forty strong. After placing out sentinels, I laid down to sleep, but was quickly roused by a great racket; starting up, I found some mounted, and others in great confusion; one of the sentinels having given the alarm that we were about to be attacked, I ordered some to ride round and reconnoiter, and on their return the others being more alarmed, not knowing who they were, fled in different ways, so that I was reduced to about twenty again; with this I determined to attempt to recruit, and proceed on to rally in the neighborhood, I had left. Dr. Blunt's was the nearest house, which we reached just before day; on riding up the yard, Hark fired a gun. We expected Dr. Blunt and his family were at Maj. Ridley's, as I knew there was a company of men there; the gun was fired to ascertain if any of the family were at home; we were immediately fired upon and retreated leaving several of my men. I do not know what became of them, as I never saw them afterwards. Pursuing our course back, and coming in sight of Captain Harris's, where we had been the day before, we discovered a party of white men at the house, on which all deserted me but two, (Jacob and Nat,) we concealed ourselves in the woods until near night, when I sent them in search of Henry, Sam, Nelson and Hark, and directed them to rally all they could, at the place we had had our dinner the Sunday before, where they would find me, and I accordingly returned there as soon as it was dark, and remained until Wednesday evening, when discovering white men riding around the place as though they were looking for some one, and none of my men joining me, I concluded Jacob and Nat had been taken, and compelled to betray me.—On this I gave up all hope for the present; and on Thrusday night, after having supplied myself with provisions from Mr. Travis's, I scratched a hole under a pile of fence rails in a field, where I concealed myself for six weeks, never leaving my hiding place but for a few minutes in the dead of night to get water, which was very near; thinking by this time I could venture out, I began to go about in the night and eaves drop the houses in the neighborhood; pursuing this course for about a fortnight and gathering little or no intelligence, afraid of speaking to any human being, and returning every morning to my cave before the dawn of day. I know not how long I might have led this life, if accident had not betrayed me, a dog in the neighborhood passing by my hiding place one night while I was out, was attracted by some meat I had in my cave, and crawled in and stole it, and was coming out just as I returned. A few nights after, two negroes having started to go hunting with the same dog, and passed that way, the dog came again to the place, and having just gone out to walk about, discovered me and barked, on which thinking myself discovered, I spoke to them to beg concealment. On making myself known, they fled from me. Knowing then they would betray me, I immediately left my hiding place, and was pursued almost incessantly until I was taken a fortnight afterwards by Mr. Benjamin Phipps, in a little hole I had dug out with my sword, for the purpose of concealment, under the top of a fallen tree. On Mr. Phipps discovering the place of my concealment, he cocked his gun and aimed at me. I requested him not to shoot, and I would give up, upon which he demanded my sword. I delivered it to him, and he brought me to prison. During the time I was pursued, I had many hair breadth escapes, which your time will not permit you to relate. I am here loaded with chains, and willing to suffer the fate that awaits me.

I here proceeded to make some inquiries of him, after assuring him of the certain death that awaited him, and that concealment would only bring destruction on the innocent as well as guilty, of his own color, if he knew of any extensive or concerted plan. His answer was, I do not. When I questioned him as to the insurrection in North Carolina happening about the same time, he denied any knowledge of it.

39

The Abolitionists' Crusade

The abolitionist movement gathered strength in the United States in the 1830s, preaching to the public from all forums. Abolitionists used every means of persuasion to spread their ideas. They were a determined minority, and in some instances somewhat fanatic; but they used the art of persuasion, not violence.

One is not astonished to find abolitionists kept out of the South; but the opposition they faced in Northern and Western states is surprising. The first martyr to the antislavery cause was Elijah Lovejoy, murdered at Alton, Illinois, on November 7, 1837. Lovejoy was a Presbyterian minister. Licensed in 1833 at the age of thirty-one, he went to St. Louis to edit a religious weekly and first entered the abolitionist movement. In 1836, he moved to Alton and began printing an abolitionist newspaper, *The Observer*. Alton was less friendly than St. Louis; a mob wrecked his first printing press in 1836. In August 1837 a second press was destroyed, and soon after, a third. Undaunted, Lovejoy persisted in his editorship. The arrival of the fourth press sparked the event that caused his death.

Two accounts describe Lovejoy's ordeals. In the first, Lovejoy writes a friend of his trip to a neighboring town to preach a sermon. In the second, his associate Edward Beecher reconstructs the events that led to his death.

MEMOIR OF
ELIJAH PARISH LOVEJOY

Elijah Lovejoy to a Friend

October 3, 1837

My Dear Brother Leavitt,

I have just passed through a scene which I will try to describe to your readers.

On Sabbath, I preached for the Rev. Mr. Campbell, the Presbyterian minister of St. Charles, with whom I had formerly been acquainted, and who had lately arrived in this place from Wilmington Presbytery, Delaware. I preached in the morning, and at night. After the audience was dismissed at night, and when all had left

From Joseph and Owen Lovejoy, *Memoir of the Elijah Parish Lovejoy Who Was Murdered in the Defense of Liberty of the Press* (New York, 1838), 251–260.

the house but Mr. Campbell, his brother-in-law, Mr. Copes, and myself, a young man came in, and passing by me, slipped the following note into my hand:

Mr. Lovejoy,

Be watchful as you come from church to-night.

A Friend

I showed the note to the two brethren present; and Mr. Campbell invited me to go home with him in consequence. I declined, however, and in company with him and Mr. Copes walked home, but a short distance, to my mother-in-law's. Brother Campbell went in with me, and Mr. C. passed on. This was about nine o'clock, and a very dark night. We received no molestation on our way, and the whole matter had passed my mind. Brother C. and I had sat conversing for nearly an hour; Mrs. L. had gone to another room and lain down; her mother was with her, having our sick child, while an unmarried sister of Mrs. L. was in the room with Mr. C. and myself. The rooms thus occupied were on the second floor, the first story of the house being tenanted as a store. The access to the rooms is by a flight of stairs leading up to a portico, on which the doors of the several rooms open.

About ten o'clock, as Mr. Campbell and myself were conversing, I heard a knocking at the foot of the stairs. I took a candle, and opening the door of the room in which I sat, to learn the cause, I found that the knocking had called up Mrs. Lovejoy and her mother, who had enquired what was wanted. The answer was, "We want to see Mr. Lovejoy, is he in." To this I answered myself, "Yes, I am here." They immediately rushed up to the portico, and two of them coming into the room laid hold of me. These two individuals, the name of one was Littler, formerly from Virginia, the other called himself a Mississippian, but his name I have not learned, though it is known in St. Charles. I asked them what they wanted of me. "We want you down stairs, d——n you," was the reply. They accordingly commenced attempting to pull me out of the house. And not succeeding immediately, one of them, Littler, began to beat me with his fists. By this time, Mrs. L. had come into the room. In doing so she had to make her way through the mob on the portico, who attempted to hinder her from coming, by rudely pushing her back, and one "chivalrous" southerner actually drew his dirk upon her. Her only reply was to strike him in the face with her hand, and then rushing past him, she flew to where I was, and throwing her arms around me, boldly faced the mobites, with a fortitude and self-devotion which none but a women and a WIFE ever displayed. While they were attempting with oaths and curses to drag me from the room, she was smiting them in the face with her hands, or clinging to me to aid in resisting their efforts, and telling them that they must first take her before they should have her husband. Her energetic measures, seconded by those of her mother and sister, induced the assailants to let me go and leave the room.

As soon as they were gone, Mrs. L.'s powers of endurance failed her, and she fainted. I carried her into another room and laid her on the bed. So soon as she recovered from her fainting, she relapsed into hysterical fits, moaning and shrieking, and calling upon my name, alternately. Mrs. L.'s health is at all times extremely delicate, and at present peculiarly so, she being some months advanced in pregnancy. Her situation at this time was truly alarming and distressing. To add to the perplexities of the moment, I had our sick child in my arms, taken up from the floor where it had been left by its grandmother, in the hurry and alarm of the first onset of the mob. The poor little sufferer, as if conscious of danger from the cries of its mother, clung to me in silence. In this condition, and while I was endeavouring to calm Mrs. L.'s dreadfully excited mind, the mob returned to the charge, breaking into the room, and rushing up to the bed-side, again attempting to force me from the house. The brutal wretches were totally indifferent to her heart-rending cries and shrieks—she was too far exhausted to move; and I suppose they would have succeeded in forcing me out, had not my friend William M. Campbell, Esq. at this juncture come in, and with undaunted boldness, assisted me in freeing myself from their clutches. Mr. Campbell is a southerner, and a slaveholder; but he is a MAN, and he will please accept my grateful thanks for his aid so promptly and so opportunely rendered; others aided in forcing the mob from the room, so that the house was now clear a second time.

They did not, however, leave the yard of the house, which was full of drunken wretches, uttering the most awful and soul-chilling oaths and imprecations, and swearing they would have me at all hazards. I could hear the epithets, "The infernal scoundrel, the d——d amalgamating Abolitionist, we'll have his heart out yet," &c. &c. They were armed with pistols and dirks, and one pistol was discharged, whether at any person or not, I did not know. The fellow from Mississippi seemed the most bent on my destruction. He did not appear at all drunken, but both in words and actions manifested the most fiendish malignity of feeling and purpose. He was telling a story of the mobites, which, whether true or false, (I know not,) was just calculated to madden them. His story was, that his wife had lately been violated by a negro. And this he said was all owing to me, who had instigated the negro to do the deed. He was a ruined man, he said, had just as leif die as not; but before he died he "would have my blood."

The mob now rushed up the stairs a third time, and one of them, a David Knott, of St. Charles, came in with a note signed "A citizen of St. Charles." I regret that I have mislaid it. It was short, however, requiring me to leave the town the next day at ten o'clock, in the morning. I told Mr. K. I presumed he expected no answer to such a note. He said he did not, and immediately left the room. As soon as he got out, they set up a yell, as if so many demons had just broken loose from hell. I had insulted them, it seems, by not returning an answer to their note. My friends now came round me, entreating me to send them a written answer. This I at first declined, but yielding to their urgent advice, I took my pencil and wrote as follows:

> I have already taken my passage in this stage, to leave to-morrow morning, at least by nine o'clock.
>
> *Elijah P. Lovejoy*

This was carried out and read to them, and at first, after some pretty violent altercation among themselves, seemed to pacify them. They went away, as I supposed finally. But after having visited the grog-shop, they returned with augmented fury and violence. My friends in the house, of whom by the way, there were not many, now became thoroughly alarmed. They joined in advising me to leave the house, and make my escape, should an opportunity occur. This I at first absolutely declined doing. I did so on the principle I had adopted, of never either seeking or avoiding danger in the way of duty. "Should such a man as I flee," has been my sentiment, whether right or wrong. I was at length, however, compelled by the united entreaties of them all, and especially of my wife, to consent to do so, should opportunity offer. Accordingly, when the efforts of those below had diverted the attention of the mob for a few moments, I left the house and went away unperceived. I went up the street a few rods, and finding all still, I came back to reconnoitre, and after looking round awhile, and seeing or hearing no enemy, I went back into the house. Here, however, so far from being welcomed, I was greeted with reproaches in abundance for my temerity, as they called it, in venturing back.

And sure enough, scarcely had I seated myself before the mob returned again, as though they scented their prey. One man now went down to them, and by the promise of a dram, led them all away, and I was fain to escape, not so much from the mob, as from the reproaches of my wife and friends, by leaving the house a second time. It was now about midnight. Through the good hand of my God upon me, I got away unperceived. I walked about a mile to my friend, Maj. Sibley's residence. Having called him up and informed him of my condition, he kindly furnished me with a horse; and having rested myself on the sofa an hour or two, for I was much exhausted, I rode to Mr. Watson's, another friend, where I arrived about day-break, four miles from town. Here Mrs. L., though exhausted and utterly unfit to leave her bed, joined me in the morning, and we came home, reaching Alton about noon, meeting with no let or hindrance, though Mrs. L. was constantly alarmed with apprehensions of pursuit from St. Charles.

On our arrival in Alton, as we were going to our house, almost the first person we met in the street, was one of the very individuals who had first broken into the house at St. Charles. Mrs. L. instantly recognized him, and at once became greatly alarmed. There was the more reason for fear, inasmuch as the mob in St. Charles had repeatedly declared their determination to pursue me, and to have my life, and one of them, the fellow from Mississippi, boasted that he was chasing me about, and that he had assisted to destroy my press in Alton. This was the more readily believed, inasmuch as it was known that individuals from St. Louis, where this Mississippian now temporarily resides, were aiding in that work. The mobite from St. Charles also openly boasted here of their assault upon me in that place.

Upon these facts being made known to my friends, they deemed it advisable that our house should be guarded on Monday night. Indeed, this was necessary to quiet Mrs. L.'s fears. Though completely exhausted, as may well be supposed, from the scenes of the night before, she could not rest. The mob haunted her excited imagination, causing her continually to start from her moments of fitful slumber, with cries of alarm. This continued all the afternoon and evening of Monday, and I began to entertain serious apprehensions of the consequences. As soon, however, as

405

our friends, to the number of ten arrived with arms in their hands, her fears subsided, and she sank into a comparatively silent sleep, which continued through most of the night. It is now Tuesday night. I am writing by the bedside of Mrs. L., whose excitement and fears have measurably returned with the darkness. She is constantly starting at every sound, while her mind is full of the horrible scenes through which she has so lately passed. What the final result will be for her I know not, but hope for the best. We have no one with us to-night, except the members of our own family. A loaded musket is standing at my bed-side, while my two brothers, in an adjoining room, have three others, together with pistols, cartridges, &c. And this is the way we live in the city of Alton! I have had inexpressible reluctance to resort to this method of defence. But dear-bought experience has taught me that there is at present no safety for me, and no defence in this place, either in the laws or the protecting ægis of public sentiment. I feel that I do not walk the streets in safety, and every night when I lie down, it is with the deep settled conviction, that there are those near me and around me, who seek my life. I have resisted this conviction as long as I could, but it has been forced upon me. Even were I safe from my enemies in Alton, my proximity to Missouri exposes me to attack from that state. And now that it is known that I am to receive no protection here, the way is open for them to do with me what they please. Accordingly a party of them from St. Louis came up and assisted in destroying my press, the first time. This was well known. They came armed and stationed themselves behind a wall for the purpose of firing upon any one who might attempt to defend the office. Yet who of this city has rebuked this daring outrage on the part of citizens of our state and city, upon the rights and person of the citizens of another state and city? No one. I mean there has been no public expression of opinion on the subject. Our two political papers have been silent, or if speaking at all, have thrown the blame on me rather than on any one else. And if you go through the streets of Alton, or into stores and shops, where you hear one condemning these outrages upon me, you will find five approving them. This is true, both of professor and non-professor. I have no doubts that four-fifths of the inhabitants of this city are glad that my press has been destroyed by a mob, both once and again. They hate mobs, it is true, but they hate Abolitionism a great deal more. Whether creditable to them or not, this is the state of public sentiment among our citizens. A leading member of the Presbyterian church here, disclosed to me, in the presence of fifteen or twenty persons, that if the "Observer" were re-established here, he would do nothing to protect it from a mob again. A leading merchant here, and a Methodist minister, said the same thing, at the same time. Most of our leading men, whether in church or state, lay the blame all on me.

So far from calling the acts of the mob outrages, they go about the streets, saying in the hearing of every body, "Mr. Lovejoy has no one to thank but himself." Of course the mob desire no better license than this.

The pulpit, with but one exception, is silent. Brother Graves was absent at the time of the first outrage. But since his return he has taken hold of the work with characteristic boldness and zeal. There is no cowardice in him, no shrinking from duty through fear of man. I wish I could say as much of our other pastors. Brother G. has told his people their duty faithfully and fearlessly. Whether they will hear him I know not, but he has cleared his skirts.

And now, my dear brother, if you ask what are my own feelings at a time like this, I answer, perfectly calm, perfectly resigned. Though in the midst of danger, I have a constant sense of security that keeps me alike from fear or anxiety. "Thou wilt keep him in perfect peace, whose mind is stayed on thee, because he trusteth in thee." This promise I feel has been literally fulfilled unto me. I read the promises of the Bible, and especially the Psalms, with a delight, a refreshing of soul I never knew before. Some persons here call me courageous, and others pronounce me stubborn; but I feel and know I am neither one nor the other. That I am enabled to continue firm in the midst of all my trials, is all of God. Let no one give me any credit for it. I disclaim it. I should feel that I were robbing Him, if even in thought, I should claim the least share to myself. He has said, "As thy day is, so shall thy strength be," and he has made his promise good. To him be all the praise. Pray for me.

We have a few excellent brethren here in Alton. They are sincerely desirous to know their duty in this crisis, and to do it. But as yet they cannot see that duty requires them to maintain their cause here at all hazards. Our Convention meets the last Thursday of this month. And of this be assured, the cause of truth still lives in Illinois, and will not want defenders. Whether our paper starts again will depend on our friends, East, West, North, and South. So far as depends on me it shall go. By the blessing of God, I will never abandon the enterprise so long as I live, and until success has crowned it. And there are those in Illinois who join me in this sentiment. And if I am to die it cannot be a better cause.

Yours in the cause of truth and holiness.
Elijah P. Lovejoy

NARRATIVE OF RIOTS
AT ALTON
Edward Beecher

It often happens that events, in themselves of no great importance, are invested with unusual interest in consequence of their connection with principles of universal application or with momentous results. Of this kind are the events which preceded and led to the death of the Rev. Elijah P. Lovejoy: the first martyr in America to the great principles of the freedom of speech and of the press.

Of these events I propose in the following pages to give an account. The facts are of a nature sufficiently astounding in any age or at any time: the destruction of four printing presses in succession; the personal abuse of the editor, from time to time by repeated mobs; and his final and premeditated murder!

From Edward Beecher, *Narratives of Riots at Alton* (1838; reprinted, New York, 1965), 3–4, 60–66.

Still more astounding are they when we consider the country in which they occurred. Had it been in revolutionary France; or in England, agitated by the consequent convulsion of the nations; there had been less cause for surprise. But it was not. It was in America—the land of free discussion and equal rights.

Still more are we amazed when we consider the subjects, the discussion of which was thus forcibly arrested. Had it been an effort to debauch and pollute the public mind by obscenity and atheism; or by injurious and disorganizing schemes; the rise of public indignation had at least found a cause; though the friends of truth and righteousness are not the men who employ mobs as their chosen instruments of persuasion. But it was none of these. It was solely the advocacy of the principles of freedom and equal rights.

Were these principles of recent origin, and the opinions of a sect, it might have caused less surprise. But they are the sacred legacy of ages—the doctrines of our nation's birth; of natural justice; and of God.

All these things are astonishing: but there is one fact that may justly excite amazement still more deep and overwhelming; the opinions and feelings elicited by events like these. Had an earthquake of indignation convulsed the land; had the united voices of every individual of every party rebuked and remedied the wrong; all had been well. But during the progress of the scenes there have been found those in reputation as wise and good, who have been unsparing in their censure on the sufferers; and stimulated the evildoers by sympathy or feeble rebuke. And after the final and dreadful catastrophe, only a faint tribute has been given *by them* to certain abstract principles of free inquiry as generally good; and a decent regret for their violation has been expressed. But the full tide of indignation has been reserved for the audacious man who dared to speak and act as a freeman; and though lawlessly inflicted, his penalty has been declared to be deserved.

What are we to say of facts like these? They at least open a deep chapter in human nature, and in the condition of our country. They are the result of principles neither superficial nor accidental. They penetrate to the very vitals of society; and indicate a crisis in our national life.

That as a nation we are radically unsound and lost, they do not to my mind indicate. But that there are in the body politic causes of tremendous power tending to that result, they do evince. And the question on which all turns is now before us as a nation; and on its decision our life or death depends. Have we coolness of thought left sufficient to discern them, and energy of moral feeling enough to react?

As these events are of a nature to rouse and demand public attention, I hope that an impartial narration of them will be candidly and thoughtfully read; and as I have been an actor in the leading events from the beginning—an eyewitness of most that I describe, I feel that no one who speaks only from hearsay, can have so full a knowledge of all the causes of these events as I; and as perhaps no one has been more severely censured by enemies, or regarded in greater error by some sincere and valued friends; I feel that not only a regard to truth and the general good, but decent regard to the opinions of others, requires me to speak.

Mr. Lovejoy having decided on his course, the friends of law and order made their arrangements for the defense of his press. Personal violence or an attempt to murder him was not expected. It was supposed that the main effort, if any were made, would be to destroy the press as it was landed. We all felt that if once deposited in Godfrey & Gilman's store it would be safe. Great difficulty was encountered in obtaining a special constable to direct the friends of law in case of an attack, under the authority of the mayor. The mayor himself did not refuse to act; but as it might be inconvenient to find him when most needed, it was considered important to have one of the supporters of the press appointed as special constable on any sudden emergency. Though the mayor acceded to the proposal, it was from time to time delayed, and finally it was not carried into effect. The mayor, however, still consented to direct their movement when called upon.

On Monday, Mr. W. S. Gilman was informed that the press was at St. Louis on board a boat which would probably arrive at Alton about evening. He immediately sent an express to the captain of the boat requesting him to delay the hour of his arrival until three o'clock at night, in order to avoid an affray with the rioters. This movement was successful. The spies of the mob watched for the arrival of boats for some time; but late in the evening seemed to give up the expectation of any arrival that night, and retired.

Meantime the supporters of the press met at Mr. Gilman's store to the number of thirty or more; and, as before stated, organized themselves into a volunteer company according to law, and spent the night in the store. At the appointed hour the boat arrived, and the press was safely landed; the mayor being present. All arrangements had been made with such judgment, and the men were stationed at such commanding points, that an attack would have been vain. But it was not made. A horn was indeed sounded, but no one came.

Shortly after the hour fixed on for the landing of the boat, Mr. Lovejoy arose and called me to go with him to see what was the result. The moon had set and it was still dark, but day was near; and here and there a light was glimmering from the window of some sickroom or of some early riser. The streets were empty and silent, and the sounds of our feet echoed from the walls as we passed along. Little did he dream, at that hour, of the contest which the next night would witness: that these same streets would echo with the shouts of an infuriate mob, and be stained with his own heart's blood!

We found the boat there and the press in the warehouse; aided in raising it to the third story. We were all rejoiced that no conflict had ensued and that the press was safe; and all felt that the crisis was over. We were sure that the store could not be carried by storm by so few men as had ever yet acted in a mob; and though the majority of the citizens would not aid to defend the press we had no fear that they would aid in an attack. So deep was this feeling that it was thought that a small number was sufficient to guard the press afterward; and it was agreed that the company should be divided into sections of six, and take turns on successive nights. As they had been up all night, Mr. Lovejoy and myself offered to take charge of the press till morning; and they retired.

The morning soon began to dawn; and that morning I shall never forget. Who that has stood on the banks of the mighty stream that then rolled before me can forget the emotions of sublimity that filled his heart, as in imagination he has traced those channels of intercourse opened by it and its branches through the illimitable regions of this Western world? I thought of future ages, and of the countless millions that should dwell on this mighty stream; and that nothing but the truth would make them free. Never did I feel as then the value of the right for which we were contending: thoroughly to investigate and fearlessly to proclaim that truth. O, the sublimity of moral power! By it God sways the universe. By it he will make the nations free.

I passed through the scuttle to the roof and ascended to the highest point of the wall. The sky and the river were beginning to glow with approaching day, and the busy hum of business to be heard. I looked with exultation on the scenes below. I felt that a bloodless battle had been gained for God and for the truth; and that Alton was redeemed from eternal shame. And as all around grew brighter with approaching day, I thought of that still brighter sun, even now dawning on the world, and soon to bathe it with floods of glorious light.

Brother Lovejoy, too, was happy. He did not exult: he was tranquil and composed; but his countenance indicated the state of his mind. It was a calm and tranquil joy, for he trusted in God that the point was gained: that the banner of an unfettered press would soon wave over that mighty stream.

Vain hopes! How soon to be buried in a martyr's grave. Vain! did I say? No: they are not vain. Though dead he still speaketh; and a united world can never silence his voice. Ten thousand presses, had he employed them all, could never have done what the simple tale of his death will do. Up and down the mighty streams of the West his voice will go: it will penetrate the remotest corner of our land; it will be heard to the extremities of the civilized world. From henceforth no boat will pass the spot where he fell, heedless of his name, or of his sentiments, or of the cause for which he died. And if God in his mercy shall use this event to arouse a slumbering nation to maintain the right for which he died, he will look down from the throne of his glory on the scene of his martyrdom and say, It is enough: truth is triumphant; the victory is gained.

We returned to his house, and before my departure we united in prayer. His wife, through weakness, had not risen. In her chamber we met in the last act of worship in which we were to unite on earth. I commended him and his family to the care of God. As I left her I cheered her with the hope that her days of trial were nearly over and that more tranquil hours were at hand. Cheered by these hopes I bade them and my other friends farewell, and began my journey homeward. On my way I heard passing rumors of a meditated attack on the store, but gave them no weight. The events of a few hours proved them but too well founded.

Of the tragical catastrophe I was not a spectator; but after careful inquiry of eyewitnesses I shall proceed to narrate the leading facts.

From the statement of the mayor it seems that an attack was apprehended; and that the matter was laid before the common council, and that they did not deem it necessary to take any action on the subject.

On account of the fatigue and watching of the preceding night, most of the defenders of the press who were in the store the night before were absent; and others took their place. The number was larger than at first intended in consequence of an increased apprehension of an attack. Their apprehensions were realized. An attack was commenced at about ten o'clock at night.

In order to render the narrative more clear, it is necessary to say a few words concerning the structure and location of the store. It consisted of two long stone buildings, side by side, in one block, extending from the landing in Water Street back to Second Street; with doors and windows at each gable end, but with no windows at the sides. Hence it can be defended at the ends from within, but not at the sides. The roofs are of wood. The lots on each side being vacant, these stores form a detached block, accessible on every side.

About ten o'clock a mob, *already armed,* came and formed a line at the end of the store in Water Street, and hailed those within. Mr. Gilman opened the end door of the third story, and asked what they wanted. They demanded the press. He, of cours, refused to give it up; and earnestly entreated them to use no violence. He told them that the property was committed to his care, and that they should defend it at the risk and sacrifice of their lives. At the same time they had no ill will against them, and should deprecate doing them an injury. One of them, a leading individual among the friends of free inquiry at the late convention, replied, that they would have it at the sacrifice of their lives, and presented a pistol at him: upon which he retired.

They then went to the other end of the store and commenced an attack. They demolished two or three windows with stones and fired two or three guns. As those within threw back the stones, one without was distinctly recognized and seen taking aim at one within: for it was a moonlight evening, and persons could be distinctly seen and recognized.

A few guns were then fired by individuals from within, by which Lyman Bishop, one of the mob, was killed. The story that he was a mere stranger waiting for a boat, and that Mr. Lovejoy shot him, are alike incapable of proof. He was heard during the day, by a person in whose employ he was, to express his intention to join the mob.

After this the mob retired for a few moments, and then returned with ladders which they lashed together to make them the proper length, and prepared to set fire to the roof.

About this time the mayor, having been informed of the riot, came on to the ground; but having few to sustain him, was unable to compel the rioters to desist by force. They requested him to go into the store, and state to its defenders, that they were determined to have the press; and would not desist until they had accomplished their object; and agreed to suspend operations until his return. Attended by a justice of the peace, he entered and delivered the message of the mob.

Suppose now it had been delivered up by its defenders and destroyed. How remarkable the narrative must have been, of a press given up to the mob to be destroyed by the agency of the mayor and a justice of the peace!

411

However, they did not give it up. Mr. Gilman requested the mayor to call on certain citizens, to see if they could not prevent the destruction of the building. He said he could not: he had used his official authority in vain. He then asked him whether he should continue to defend the property by arms. This the mayor, as he had previously done, authorized him to do. The mayor and the justice were then informed that the press would not be given up, and the decision was by them communicated to the mob. They then proceeded to fire the roof; taking care to keep on the side of the store where they were secure from the fire of those within.

It now became evident to the defenders that their means of defense, so long as they remained within, was cut off; and nothing remained but to attack the assailants without. It was a hazardous step; but they determined to take it. A select number, of whom Mr. Lovejoy was one, undertook the work. They went out at the end, turned the corner, and saw one of the incendiaries on the ladder, and a number standing at the foot. They fired and it is supposed wounded, but did not kill him; and then, after continuing their fire some minutes and dispersing the mob, returned to load their guns. When they went out again no one was near the ladder, the assailants having so secreted themselves as to be able to fire, unseen, on the defenders of the press as they came out. No assailant being in sight Mr. Lovejoy stood, and was looking round. Yet, though he saw no assailant, the eye of his murderer was on him. The object of hatred, deep, malignant, and long continued, was fully before him—and the bloody tragedy was consummated. Five balls were lodged in his body, and he soon breathed his last. Yet after his mortal wound he had strength remaining to return to the building and ascend one flight of stairs before he fell and expired. They then attempted to capitulate, but were refused with curses by the mob, who threatened to burn the store and shoot them as they came out. Mr. Roff now determined at all hazards to go out and make some terms, but he was wounded as soon as he set his foot over the threshold.

The defenders then held a consultation. They were shut up within the building, unable to resist the ferocious mode of attack now adopted, and seemed devoted to destruction. At length Mr. West came to the door, informed them that the building was actually on fire, and urged them to escape by passing down the riverbank; saying that he would stand between them and the assailants so that if they fired they must fire on him. This was done. All but two or three marched out and ran down Water Street, being fired on by the mob as they went. Two, who were wounded, were left in the building, and one, who was not, remained to take care of the body of their murdered brother. The mob then entered, destroyed the press, and retired. Among them were seen some of those leading "friends of free inquiry" who had taken an active part in the convention.

Before these tragic scenes were ended, the streets were crowded with spectators. They came out to see the winding up of the plot, but not to aid in repressing violence or maintaining the law. The vote to aid the mayor in suppressing violence they had refused to pass, because it was their duty to aid without it; and here we see how powerful their sense of duty was. The time of the conflict was from one hour and a half to two hours. During this time the bells were rung, and a general notice given; and yet none came to the rescue. It has been said, however, in extenuation of this inactivity that it was owing to a want of concert and arrangement among the citizens or by the police. No man knew on whom he might call to aid in suppressing the riot; and some who have professed that it was their desire to do so say that they were hindered by the apprehension that they might be only rallying the mob in the attempt to quell it.

The feelings exhibited by the mob were in keeping with the deed on which they were intent. Oaths, curses, blasphemy, and malignant yells broke upon the silence of the night as they prosecuted their work of death. But even passions so malignant were not enough to give them the hardihood and recklessness needed for their work. To drench conscience, blind reason, and arouse passion to its highest fury by the intoxicating cup was needed to fit them for the consummation of their work. The leaders in this business were adepts; they knew what means were adapted to their ends, and used them without stint or treason.

Thus closes a tragedy without parallel in the history of our land. In other popular excitements, there has been an equal amount of feeling: in some, blood has been shed. But never was there an avowed effort to overthrow the foundations of human society pushed to such bloody results: and that, on principles adapted so utterly to dissolve the social system, and plunge the nation into anarchy and blood.

40

Violence in Politics

The violence that marked other aspects of American life finally came to affect its politics also. Mob action against abolition agitators, and the great Southern fear and occasional reality of slave revolts, had their counterpart, at least symbolically, on the floor of the United States Senate on May 22, 1856. Having recently concluded a long and bitter denunciation of the affairs in Kansas, including personal attacks on Senators Butler and Douglas, Massachusetts Senator Charles Sumner was writing letters at his chamber desk when suddenly he was brutally clubbed by South Carolina Congressman Preston Brooks, a relative of Senator Butler. This outburst of violence on the Senate floor became the occasion for further sectional recriminations. The Southern press applauded Brooks while many Northerners made Sumner a martyr to his cause.

In the course of these events, one more national institution had proved itself incapable of withstanding the tensions of the day. The issue of slavery tore organization after organization apart. It prompted Northern men to attack their neighbors for voicing unpopular opinions; it led Southerners into frantic efforts to minimize the possibility of slave revolts. When violence and bitterness overtook the political leaders of the nation, time was running out. Failures to come to grips with the issue threatened the worst consequences. The nation soon experienced them all in the form of the Civil War.

THE WORKS
OF CHARLES SUMNER

**1   Charles Sumner Addresses the Senate
on the Issue of Kansas, May 19-20, 1856**

You are now called to redress a great wrong. Seldom in the history of nations is such a question presented. Tariffs, army bills, navy bills, land bills, are important, and justly occupy your care; but these all belong to the course of ordinary legislation. As means and instruments only, they are necessarily subordinate to the

From *The Works of Charles Sumner* (Boston, 1871), IV: 137–151, 260–264; 278–279, 312–313.

conservation of Government itself. Grant them or deny them, in greater or less degree, and you inflict no shock. The machinery of Government continues to move. The State does not cease to exist. Far otherwise is it with the eminent question now before you, involving, as it does, Liberty in a broad Territory, and also involving the peace of the whole country, with our good name in history forevermore.

Take down your map, Sir, and you will find that the Territory of Kansas, more than any other region, occupies the middle spot of North America, equally distant from the Atlantic on the east and the Pacific on the west, from the frozen waters of Hudson's Bay on the north and the tepid Gulf Stream on the south,—constituting the precise geographical centre of the whole vast Continent. To such advantages of situation, on the very highway between two oceans, are added a soil of unsurpassed richness, and a fascinating, undulating beauty of surface, with a health-giving climate, calculated to nurture a powerful and generous people, worthy to be a central pivot of American institutions. Against this Territory, thus fortunate in position and population, a Crime has been committed which is without example in the records of the Past. Not in plundered provinces or in the cruelties of selfish governors will you find its parallel.

The wickedness which I now begin to expose is immeasurably aggravated by the motive which prompted it. Not in any common lust for power did this uncommon tragedy have its origin. It is the rape of a virgin Territory, compelling it to the hateful embrace of Slavery; and it may be clearly traced to a depraved desire for a new Slave State, hideous offspring of such a crime, in the hope of adding to the power of Slavery in the National Government. Yes, Sir, when the whole world, alike Christian and Turk, is rising up to condemn this wrong, making it a hissing to the nations, here in our Republic, *force*—ay, Sir, FORCE—is openly employed in compelling Kansas to this pollution, and all for the sake of political power. There is the simple fact, which you will vainly attempt to deny, but which in itself presents an essential wickedness that makes other public crimes seem like public virtues.

This enormity, vast beyond comparison, swells to dimension of crime which the imagination toils in vain to grasp, when it is understood that for this purpose are hazarded the horrors of intestine feud, not only in this distant Territory, but everywhere throughout the country. The muster has begun. The strife is no longer local, but national. Even now, while I speak, portents lower in the horizon, threatening to darken the land, which already palpitates with the mutterings of civil war. The fury of the propagandists, and the calm determination of their opponents, are diffused from the distant Territory over wide-spread communities, and the whole country, in all its extent, marshalling hostile divisions, and foreshadowing a conflict which, unless happily averted by the triumph of Freedom, will become war,—fratricidal, parricidal war,—with an accumulated wickedness beyond that of any war in human annals, justly provoking the avenging judgment of Providence and the avenging pen of History. Such is the Crime which you are to judge. The criminal also must be dragged into day, that you may see and measure the power by which all this wrong is sustained. From no common source could it proceed. In its perpetration was needed a spirit of vaulting ambition which would hesitate at nothing; a hardihood of purpose insensible to the judgment of mankind; a madness for Slavery, in spite of Constitution, laws, and all the great examples of our history; also a consciousness of power such as comes from the habit of power; a combination of energies found only in a hundred arms directed by a hundred eyes; a control of Public Opinion through venal pens and a prostituted press; an ability to subsidize crowds in every vocation of life,—the politician with his local importance, the lawyer with his subtle tongue, and even the authority of the judge on the bench,—with a familiar use of men in places high and low, so that none, from the President to the lowest border postmaster, should decline to be its tool: all these things, and more, were needed, and they were found in the Slave Power of our Republic. There, Sir, stands the criminal, all unmasked before you, heartless, grasping, and tyrannical: for this is the Power behind—greater than any President—which succors and sustains the Crime. Nay, the proceedings I now arraign derive their fearful consequence only from this connection.

Such is the Crime and such the criminal which it is my duty to expose; and, by the blessing of God, this duty shall be done completely to the end. But this will not be enough. The Apologies which, with strange hardihood, are offered for the Crime must be torn away, so that it shall stand forth without a single rag or fig-leaf to cover its vileness. And, finally, the True Remedy must be shown. The subject is complex in relations, as it is transcendent in importance; and yet, if I am honored by your attention, I hope to present it clearly in all its parts, while I conduct you to the inevitable conclusion that Kansas must be admitted at once, with her present Constitution, as a State of this Union, and give a new star to the blue field of our National Flag. And here I derive satisfaction from the thought, that the cause is so strong in itself as to bear even the infirmities of its advocates; nor can it require anything beyond that simplicity of treatment and moderation of manner which I desire to cultivate. Its true character is such, that, like Hercules, it will conquer just so soon as it is recognized.

I must say something of a general character, particularly in response to what has fallen from Senators who have raised themselves to eminence on this floor in championship of human wrong: I mean the Senator from South Carolina [Mr. BUTLER] and the Senator from Illinois [Mr. DOUGLAS], who, though unlike as Don Quixote and Sancho Panza, yet, like this couple, sally forth together in the same adventure. I regret much to miss the elder Senator from his seat; but the cause against which he has run a tilt, with such ebullition of animosity, demands that the opportunity of exposing him should not be lost; and it is for the cause that I speak. The Senator from South Carolina has read many books of chivalry, and believes himself a chivalrous knight, with sentiments of honor and courage. Of course he has chosen a mistress to whom he has made his vows, and who, though ugly to others, is always lovely to him,—though polluted in the sight of the world, is chaste in his sight: I mean the harlot Slavery. For her his tongue is always profuse in words. Let her be impeached in character, or any proposition he made to shut her out from the extension of her wantonness, and no extravagance of manner or hardihood of assertion is then too great for this Senator. The frenzy of Don Quixote in behalf of his wench Dulcinea del Toboso is all surpassed. The asserted rights of Slavery, which shock equality of all kinds, are cloaked by a fantastic claim of equality. If the Slave States cannot enjoy what, in mockery of the great fathers of the Republic, he misnames Equality under the Constitution,—in other words, the full power in the National Territories to compel fellow-men to unpaid toil, to separate husband and wife, and to sell little children at the auction-block,—then, Sir, the chivalric Senator will conduct the State of South Carolina out of the Union! Heroic knight! Exalted Senator! A second Moses come for a second exodus!

Not content with this poor menace, which we have been twice told was "measured," the Senator, in the unrestrained chivalry of his nature, has undertaken to apply opprobrious words to those who differ from him on this floor. He calls them "sectional and fanatical"; and resistance to the Usurpation of Kansas he denounces as "an uncalculating fanaticism." To be sure, these charges lack all grace of originality and all sentiment of truth; but the adventurous Senator does not hesitate. He is the uncompromising, unblushing representative on this floor of a flagrant *sectionalism,* now domineering over the Republic,—and yet, with a ludicrous ignorance of his own position, unable to see himself as others see him, or with an effrontery which even his white head ought not to protect from rebuke, he applies to those here who resist his *sectionalism* the very epithet which designates himself. The men who strive to bring back the Government to its original policy, when Freedom and not Slavery was national, while Slavery and not Freedom was sectional, he arraigns as *sectional.* This will not do. It involves too great a perversion of terms. I tell that Senator that it is to himself, and to the "organization" of which he is the "committed advocate," that this epithet belongs. I now fasten it upon them. For myself, I care little for names; but, since the question is raised here, I affirm that the Republican party of the Union is in no just sense *sectional,* but, more than any other party, *national,*—and that it now goes forth to dislodge from the high places that tyrannical sectionalism of which the Senator from South Carolina is one of the maddest zealots.

To the charge of fanaticism I also reply. Sir, fanaticism is found in an enthusiasm or exaggeration of opinion, particularly on religious subjects; but there may be fanaticism for evil as well as for good. Now I will not deny that there are persons among us loving Liberty too well for personal good in a selfish generation. Such there may be; and, for the sake of their example, would that there were more! In calling them "fanatics," you cast contumely upon the noble army of martyrs, from the earliest day down to this hour,—upon the great tribunes of human rights, by whom life, liberty, and happiness on earth have been secured,—upon the long line of devoted patriots, who, throughout history, have truly loved their coun- try,—and upon all who, in noble aspiration for the general good, and in forgetfulness of self, have stood out before their age, and gathered into their generous bosoms the shafts of tyranny and wrong, in order to make a pathway for Truth.

As the Senator from South Carolina is the Don Quixote, so the Senator from Illinois [Mr. DOUGLAS] is the squire of Slavery, its very Sancho Panza, ready to do its humiliating offices. This Senator, in his labored address vindicating his labored report,—piling one mass of elaborate error upon another mass,—constrained

417

himself, as you will remember, to unfamiliar decencies of speech. But I go back now to an earlier occasion, when, true to native impulses, he threw into this discussion, "for a charm of powerful trouble," personalities most discreditable to this body. I will not stop to repel imputations which he cast upon myself; but I mention them to remind you of the "sweltered venom sleeping got," which, with other poisoned ingredients, he cast into the caldron of this debate. Of other things I speak. Standing on this floor, the Senator issued his rescript requiring submission to the Usurped Power of Kansas; and this was accompanied by a manner—all his own—befitting the tyrannical threat. Very well. Let the Senator try. I tell him now that he cannot enforce any such submission. The Senator, with the Slave Power at his back, is strong; but he is not strong enough for this purpose. He is bold. He shrinks from nothing. Like Danton, he may cry, *"De l'audace! encore de l'audace! et toujours de l'audace!"* but even his audacity cannot compass this work. The Senator copies the British officer who with boastful swagger said that with the end of his sword he would cram the "stamps" down the throats of the American people; and he will meet a similar failure. He may convulse this country with civil feud. Like the ancient madman, he may set fire to this Temple of Constitutional Liberty, grander than Ephesian dome; but he cannot enforce obedience to that tyrannical Usurpation.

The Senator dreams that he can subdue the North. He disclaims the open threat but his conduct implies it. How little that Senator knows himself, or the strength of the cause which he persecutes! He is but mortal man; against him is immortal principle. With finite power he wrestles with the infinite, and he must fall. Against him are stronger battalions than any marshalled by mortal arm,—the inborn, ineradicable, invincible sentiments of the human heart; against him is Nature with all her subtile forces; against him is God. Let him try to subdue these.

2 Congressman Preston Brooks Describes His Actions

In the Senate of the United States on the 19th and 20th May Mr. Sumner of Mass delivered a speech in which he reflected injuriously upon the State of South Carolina and was particularly offensive to Senator Butler who is my relative. I preferred to see the published Speech and saw it for the first time on wednesday morning.

The objectionable passages are to be found on the 5th 29th and 30th pages of Mr. Sumners Speech.

As soon as I had read the speech I felt it to be my duty to inflict some return for the insult to my State and my relative. On wednesday I took a seat in the Capitol grounds, expecting Mr. Sumner to pass. While going down the lower steps of the Capitol I met Mr. Edmundson of Va., who is my personal friend, and asked him to walk with me to the seat. I then informed him that it was my purpose to see Mr. Sumner and that as he might be accompanied by several of his friends I desired him to remain with me as a witness and for nothing else. I also enjoined upon him on no account to interfere. Mr. Sumner did not pass by while we were so seated though we remained until ½ past 12 o'clock. My colleague Mr. Keitt joined us a few moments before we returned to the House and so did Senator Johnson of Arkansas. Neither of them was informed of my purpose during that day. During night of Wednesday and about 10 o'clock I informed my colleagues Mr. Keitt and Mr. Orr. of my purpose. The next morning at eleven o'clock I took my position in the Porter's lodge to intercept Mr. Sumner. I again waited until half past 12 o'clock—the hour at which both Houses of Congress meet. While in the Porter's lodge Mr. Edmundson on his way to the Capitol saw me and came in of his own accord. He and I went to the House together. Mr. Keitt went that morning to baltimore.

Being twice disappointed I determined to keep my eye on Mr. Sumner and knowing that the Senate would adjourn at an early hour, I went to the senate and stood without the bar until it did adjourn. Mr. Sumner continued within the Hall, though he did not all the time retain his Seat. He had upon his desk a large number of his speeches and was, when not interupted, employed in franking them. Several ladies continued in the Hall some on the floor and some in the gallery.

I waited until the last lady left and then approached Mr. Sumner in front and said—Mr Sumner I have read your last speech with care and as much impartiality as is possible under the circumstances, and I feel it my duty to say that you have libeled my State and slandered my kinsman who is aged and absent and I have come to punish you for it. As I uttered the word punish Mr. Sumner offered to rise and when about half erect I struck him a slight blow with the smaller end of my cane. He then rose fully erect and endeavoured to make a battle. I was then compelled to strike him harder than I had intended. About the fifth blow he ceased to resist and I moderated my blows. I continued to strike Mr. S. until he fell when I ceased. I did not strike Mr. Sumner after he had fallen. The Cane used by me was an ordinary walking stick made of gutta percha and hollow. I used it because it was light and elastic and because I fancied it would not break. The Cane had been presented to me by a friend full three months past. It had a thin gold head and was not loaded or even heavy. Mr. Sumner was never struck with the larger end of the Cane. When Mr. Crittenden took hold of me and said something like "don't kill him," I replied that I had no wish to injure him seriously, but only to flogg him.

I went to the Senate alone, asked no one to go or to be with me. Indeed no one knew of my purpose to assail Mr. Sumner in the Senate. It was not my purpose or desire to assault him in the Senate, nor would I have done so, had it not become manifest that he would remain in his seat to a very late hour. The three gentlemen who alone knew of my purpose were neither present when the attack was made. Neither Mr. Orr or Mr. Edmundson were present at any time of the affray to my knowledge. Mr. Keitt came up when it was about half over.

I deem it proper to add that the assault upon Mr. Sumner was not because of his political principles, but because of the insulting language used in reference to my State and absent relative.

28 May 1856

P. S. Brooks

3   Charles Sumner Testifies on the Event

In the House of Representatives, on the day after the assault, Hon. Lewis D. Campbell, of Ohio, moved a Select Committee of five "to investigate the subject, and to report the facts, with such resolutions in reference thereto as in their judgments may be proper and necessary for the vindication of the character of the House." The resolution was adopted.

The Committee visited Mr. Sumner at his house.

"HON. CHARLES SUMNER, being sworn, testified.

"*Question* (by Mr. Campbell).   What do you know of the facts connected with the assault alleged to have been made upon you in the Senate Chamber by Hon. Mr. Brooks, of South Carolina, on Thursday, May 22, 1856?

"*Answer.*   I attended the Senate as usual on Thursday, the 22d of May. After some formal business, a message was received from the House of Representatives, announcing the death of a member of that body from Missouri. This was followed by a brief tribute to the deceased from Mr. Geyer, of Missouri, when, according to usage, and out of respect to the deceased, the Senate adjourned.

"Instead of leaving the Chamber with the rest on the adjournment, I continued in my seat, occupied with my pen. While thus intent, in order to be in season for the mail, which was soon to close, I was approached by several persons who desired to speak with me; but I answered them promptly and briefly, excusing myself, for the reason that I was much engaged. When the last of these left me, I drew my armchair close to my desk, and, with my legs under the desk, continued writing. My attention at this time was so entirely withdrawn from all other objects, that, though there must have been many persons on the floor of the Senate, I saw nobody.

"While thus intent, with my head bent over my writing, I was addressed by a person who had approached the front of my desk so entirely unobserved that I was not aware of his presence until I heard my name pronounced. As I looked up, with pen in hand, I saw a tall man, whose countenance was not familiar, standing directly over me, and at the same moment caught these words: 'I have read your speech twice over carefully. It is a libel on South Carolina, and Mr. Butler, who is a relative of mine——' While these words were still passing from his lips, he commenced a succession of blows with a heavy cane on my bare head, by the first of which I was stunned so as to lose sight. I no longer saw my assailant, nor any person or object in the room. What I did afterwards was done almost unconsciously, acting under the instinct of self-defence. With head already bent down, I rose from my seat, wrenching up my desk, which was screwed to the floor, and then pressed forward, while my assailant continued his blows. I have no other consciousness until I found myself ten feet forward, in front of my desk, lying on the floor of the Senate, with my bleeding head supported on the knee of a gentleman, whom I soon recognized, by voice and countenance, as Mr. Morgan, of New York. Other persons there were about me offering me friendly assistance; but I did not recognize any of them. Others there were at a distance, looking on and offering no assistance, of whom I recognized only Mr. Douglas, of Illinois, Mr. Toombs, of Georgia, and I thought also my assailant, standing between them.

"I was helped from the floor and conducted into the lobby of the Senate, where I was placed upon a sofa. Of those who helped me to this place I have no recollection. As I entered the lobby, I recognized Mr. Slidell, of Louisiana, who retreated; but I recognized no one else until some time later, as I supposed, when I felt a friendly grasp of the hand, which seemed to come from Mr. Campbell, of Ohio. I have a vague impression that Mr. Bright, President of the Senate, spoke to me while I was lying on the floor of the Senate or in the lobby.

"I make this statement in answer to the interrogatory of the Committee, and offer it as presenting completely all my recollections of the assault and of the attending circumstances, whether immediately before or immediately after. I desire to add, that, besides the words which I have given as uttered by my assailant, I have an indistinct recollection of the words, 'old man'; but these are so enveloped in the mist which ensued from the first blow, that I am not sure whether they were uttered or not.

"*Ques.* (by Mr. Greenwood). How long do you suppose it was after the adjournment of the Senate before this occurrence took place?

"*Ans.* I am very much at a loss to say whether it was half an hour or fifteen minutes: I should say ranging from fifteen minutes to half an hour, more or less; perhaps not more than fifteen minutes. I have already testified that I was so much absorbed with what I was doing at my desk, that I took very little note of anything, not even of time.

"*Ques.* (by Mr. Cobb). Was the first blow you received from Mr. Brooks before he had finished the sentence?

"*Ans.* I have no recollection beyond what I have stated.

"*Ques.* My question was, whether a blow was struck before Mr. Brooks finished the remark to you which you have just quoted?

"*Ans.* The blow came down with the close of the sentence.

"*Ques.* Then the sentence was closed before the blow was struck?

"*Ans.* It seemed to me that the blow came in the middle of an unfinished sentence. In the statement I have made I used the language, 'While these words were still passing from his lips, he commenced a succession of blows.' I heard distinctly the words I have given; I heard the words 'a relative of mine,' and then it seemed to me there was a break, and I have left it as an unfinished sentence, the sequel of which I did not hear on account of the blows.

"*Ques.* (by Mr. Campbell). Did you, at any time between the delivery of your speech referred to and the time when you were attacked, receive any intimation, in writing or otherwise, that Mr. Brooks intended to attack you?

"*Ans.* Never, directly or indirectly; nor had I the most remote suspicion of any attack, nor was I in any way prepared for an attack. I had no arms or means of defence of any kind. I was, in fact, entirely defenceless at the time, except so far as my natural strength went. In other words, I had no arms either about my person or in my desk. Nor did I ever wear arms in my life. I have always lived in a civilized

421

community, where wearing arms has not been considered necessary. When I had finished my speech my colleague came to me and said, 'I am going home with you to-day; several of us are going home with you.' Said I, 'None of that, Wilson.' And instead of waiting for him, or allowing him to accompany me home, I shot off just as I should any other day. While on my way from the Capitol, I overtook Mr. Seward, with whom I had engaged to dine. We walked together as far as the omnibuses. He then proposed that we should take an omnibus, which I declined, stating that I must go to the printing-office to look over proofs. I therefore walked alone, overtaking one or two persons on the way. I have referred to this remark of my colleague in answer to your question, whether I had in any way been put on my guard?

"*Ques.* (by Mr. Cobb).   What do you attribute the remark of your colleague to? In other words, was it founded upon an apprehension growing out of what you had said in your speech?

"*Ans.*   I understand that it was. He has told me since that a member of the House had put him on his guard, but he did not mention it to me at the time. I suspected no danger, and therefore I treated what he said to me as trifling.

"*Ques.* (by Mr. Pennington).   Have you ever defied or invited violence?

"*Ans.*   Never, at any time.

"*Ques.*   State what was the condition of your clothing after this violence, when you were taken from the Chamber.

"*Ans.*   I was in such a condition at the time that I was unaware of the blood on my clothes. I know little about it until after I reached my room, when I took my clothes off. The shirt, around the neck and collar, was soaked with blood. The waistcoat had many marks of blood upon it; also the trousers. The broadcloth coat was covered with blood on the shoulders so thickly that the blood had soaked through the cloth, even through the padding, and appeared on the inside; there was also a great deal of blood on the back of the coat and its sides.

"*Ques.*   Were you aware of the intention of Mr. Brooks to strike or inflict a blow before the blow was felt?

"*Ans.*   I had not the remotest suspicion of it until I felt the blow on my head.

"*Ques.* (by Mr. Campbell).   Do you know how often you were struck?

"*Ans.*   I have not the most remote idea.

"*Ques.*   How many wounds have you upon your head?

"*Ans.*   I have two principal wounds upon my head, and several bruises on my hands and arms. The doctor will describe them more particularly than I am able to.

"*Ques.* (by Mr. Cobb).   You stated, that, when Mr. Brooks approached you, he remarked that he had read your speech, and it was a libel upon his State and upon his relative. I will ask you, if you had, prior to that assault, in any speech, made any personal allusions to Mr. Brooks's relative, Mr. Butler, or to the State of South Carolina, to which Mr. Brooks applied this remark?

"*Ans.*   At the time my assailant addressed me I did not know who he was, least of all did I suppose him to be a relative of Mr. Butler. In a speech recently made in the Senate I have alluded to the State of South Carolina, and to Mr. Butler; but I have never said anything which was not in just response to his speeches, according to parliamentary usage, nor anything which can be called a libel upon South Carolina or Mr. Butler."

4   The Response of the Southern Press:
The Richmond Enquirer, June 9, 1856

It is idle to think of union or peace or truce with Sumner or Sumner's friends. Catiline was purity itself, compared to the Massachusetts Senator, and his friends are no better than he. They are all (we mean the leading and conspicuous ones) avowed and active traitors. . . . Sumner and Sumner's friends must be punished and silenced. Government which cannot suppress such crimes as theirs has failed of its purpose. Either such wretches must be hung or put in the penitentiary, or the South should prepare at once to quit the Union. We would not jeopard the religion and morality of the South to save a Union that had failed for every useful purpose. Let us tell the North at once, If you cannot suppress the treasonable action, and silence the foul, licentious, and infidel propagandism of such men as Stephen Pearl Andrews, Wendell Phillips, Beecher, Garrison, Sumner, and their negro and female associates, let us part in peace.

Your sympathy for Sumner has shaken our confidence in your capacity for self-government more than all your past history, full of evil portents as that has been. He had just avowed his complicity in designs far more diabolical than those of Catiline or Cethegus,—nay, transcending in iniquity all that the genius of a Milton has attributed to his fallen angels. We are not surprised that he should be hailed as hero and saint, for his proposed war on everything sacred and divine, by that Pandemonium where the blasphemous Garrison, and Parker, and Andrews, with their runaway negroes and masculine women, congregate.

In the main, the press of the South applaud the conduct of Mr. Brooks, without condition or limitation. Our approbation, at least, is entire and unreserved. We consider the act good in conception, better in execution, and best of all in consequence. The vulgar Abolitionists in the Senate are getting above themselves. They have been humored until they forget their position. They have grown saucy, and dare to be impudent to gentlemen! Now, they are a low, mean, scurvy set, with some little book-learning, but as utterly devoid of spirit or honor as a pack of curs. Intrenched behind 'privilege,' they fancy they can slander the South and insult its representatives with impunity. The truth is, they have been suffered to run too long without collars. They must be lashed into submission. Sumner, in particular, ought to have nine-and-thirty early every morning. He is a great strapping fellow, and could stand the cowhide beautifully. Brooks frightened him, and at the first blow of the cane he bellowed like a bull-calf. There is the blackguard Wilson, an ignorant Natick cobbler, swaggering in excess of muscle, and absolutely dying for a beating. Will not somebody take him in hand? Hale is another huge, red-faced, sweating scoundrel, whom some gentleman should kick and cuff until he abates something of his impudent talk. These men are perpetually abusing the people and representatives of the South, for tyrants, robbers, ruffians, adulterers, and what not. Shall we stand it?

Mr. Brooks has initiated this salutary discipline, and he deserves applause for the bold, judicious manner in which he chastised the scamp Sumner. It was a proper act, done at the proper time, and in the proper place.

5 Abolitionist Wendell Phillips Addresses a Boston Audience Immediately after the Clubbing

Nobody needs now to read this speech of Charles Sumner to know whether it is good. We measure the amount of the charge by the length of the rebound. [*Cheers.*] When the spear, driven to the quick, makes the Devil start up in his own likeness, we may be sure it is the spear of Ithuriel. [*Great applause.*] That is my way of measuring the speech which has produced this glorious result. Oh, yes, glorious! for the world will yet cover every one of those scars with laurels. [*Enthusiastic cheering.*] Sir, he *must* not die! We need him yet, as the vanguard leader of the hosts of Liberty. No, he shall yet come forth from that sick-chamber, and every gallant heart in the Commonwealth be ready to kiss his very footsteps. [*Loud cheers.*]

Perhaps, Mr. Chairman and fellow-citizens, I am wrong; but I accept that speech of my loved and honored friend, and with an unmixed approbation,—read it with envious admiration,—take it all. [*Cheers.*] Yes, what word is there in it that any one of us would not have been proud to utter? Not one! [*Great applause.*] In utter scorn of the sickly taste, of the effeminate scholarship, that starts back, in delicate horror, at a bold illustration, I dare to say there is no animal God has condescended to make that man may not venture to name. [*Applause.*] And if any ground of complaint is supposable in regard to this comparison, which shocks the delicacy of some men and some presses, it is the animal, not Mr. Douglas, that has reason to complain. [*Thunders of applause, renewed again and again.*]

Mr. Chairman, there are some characters whose worth is so clear and self-evident, so tried and approved, so much without flaw, that we lay them on the shelf,—and when we hear of any act attributed to them, no matter in what doubtful terms it be related, we judge the single act by the totality of the character, by our knowledge of the whole man, letting a lifetime of uprightness explain a doubtful hour. Now, with regard to our honored Senator, we know that his taste, intellect, and heart are all of this quality,—a total, unflawed gem; and I know, when we get the full and complete report of what he said, the *ipsissima verba* in which it was spoken, that the most fastidious taste of the most delicate scholar will not be able to place finger on a word of Charles Sumner which the truest gentleman would not gladly indorse. [*Loud cheers.*] I place the foot of my uttermost contempt on those members of the press of Boston that have anything to say in criticism of his language, while he lies thus prostrate and speechless,—our champion beaten to the ground for the noblest word Massachusetts ever spoke in the Senate. [*Prolonged applause.*]

41

The Bloodbath of War

The Civil War set section against section in one of the bloodiest conflicts ever fought. The day of the mercenary was over; weapons had improved while medical skills had not, and the result in losses of lives could reach tragic proportions.

The first Union generals used their armies cautiously, hesitating to enter battle unless confident of the outcome. Typically, troops were inactive and generals gained the reputation of being slow. Casualties were low, but the Union was not faring well. The appointment of Grant to head the army changed everything. He was prepared to fight and take the costs. Perhaps no other campaign so vividly demonstrates Grant's tactics as the battles fought in May 1864 between his forces and those of General Robert E. Lee at the Wilderness and the Spotsylvania Courthouse.

Colonel Charles Wainwright, a Union artillery commander, kept a detailed diary of these events. He did not play a major role in them, but he had access to accurate information; he observed well, and recorded what he learned. His account follows the action at the Wilderness beginning May 5 and at Spotsylvania beginning May 10. Wainwright understood that in terms of territory won the battles were stalemates, or, indeed, Lee's victories. But his record made clear that with Grant willing to fight a war of attrition, the Union resources would eventually bring victory.

THE PERSONAL JOURNALS OF COLONEL CHARLES S. WAINWRIGHT

May 3, [1864], Tuesday

Everything is packed, and we only wait the hour of midnight in order to start. Orders have been coming in thick and fast all day; an army is as bad as a woman starting on a journey, so much to be done at the last moment.

It seems that notwithstanding General Meade's appeal to their honour, there are a number of men inclined to be fractious under the idea that their term of service is

Reprinted with permission of Allan Nevins from *A Diary of Battle: The Personal Journals of Colonel Charles S. Wainwright, 1861–1865*, Allan Nevins, ed. (New York, 1962), pp. 347–349, 352–357, 359–360, 362–365, 367–381.

already out; he now sends notice that all such be shot without trial if they do not step out to the music.

This afternoon General Warren had his division commanders and myself at his quarters, shewed us his orders, and explained tomorrow's move. We are to try to get around Lee, between him and Richmond, and so force him to fight on our own ground. My batteries, with two forage waggons each, start at midnight, pass through Stevensburg, and then follow in rear of the First and Third Divisions. The ammunition and all the rest of the waggons, together with half of the ambulances, move off to Chancellorsville and we are warned that we shall not see them again for five days. The night is soft but cloudy, with some signs of rain; now the roads are capital. Our general officers, that I have talked with, are very sanguine; Grant is said to be perfectly confident. God grant that their expectations be more realized.

When I reached Warren's quarters Wadsworth only was there. He insisted on having my opinion as to which way we were to move, whether around Lee's right or left; and when I told him I had no opinion, having nothing to found one on, declared I must be a regular, I was so non-committal. Would that it were characteristic of all regulars never to give an opinion on subjects they knew nothing about; and if the people at home, newspaper editors and correspondents, and also the politicians at Washington, would take a leaf out of the same book, it would save the country millions of money, and many a poor fellow in our army his life.

Old Wilderness Tavern, May 4, Wednesday

It was nearly two o'clock this morning when we got our orders to haul out. I had managed a few short snatches of sleep before that time, but do not improve in my ability to go off at any moment and in any place. There is a kind of weird excitement in this starting at midnight. The senses seemed doubly awake to every impression—the batteries gathering around my quarters in the darkness; the moving of lanterns, and the hailing of the men; then the distant sound of the hoofs of the aide's horse who brings the final order to start. Sleepy as I always am at such times, I have a certain amount of enjoyment in it all. We got off without much trouble.

Great care was taken not to make any more fires than usual, so as not to attract the attention of the enemy; otherwise the darkness and distance were a quite sufficient cover to our movement. Through Stevensburg, on towards Shepherd's Grove for another mile or so, and then across country through a byroad, we had it all to ourselves. When we arrived at the head of the Germanna Plank Road we had to wait an hour for the two divisions which were to precede us to file by. It was nine o'clock by the time I reached the ford. After crossing, General Warren directed me to divide the batteries among the infantry divisions for the march through the Wilderness. I hated to break them up so on the first day's march, before I had time to look after them all, but an unbroken string of artillery over a mile long was certainly somewhat risky through these dense woods.

Lacy House, May 5, Thursday

This is the second anniversay of my first battle and has been celebrated in due form. Two years ago, I went into the battle of Williamsburg on the 5th of May; one year after I was in the battle of Chancellorsville; today we have been at it for the

426

third time, and though I have not been under very much fire myself, I have had quite a smell of gunpowder, and am two guns short tonight. We have made no progress today, and virtually hold the same position we did yesterday.

May 6, Friday

Grant ordered us to attack along our whole front this morning at five o'clock, but Lee got ahead of us, and pitched into Sedgwick's right. The fight there, all musketry, was hot but not very long: report said that we had the advantage.

Soon after sunrise the head of Burnside's column arrived. They went into the wood by a road from the south corner of the opening here, and pushed on I don't know how far. Burnside himself remained at the very opening of the road, where he fixed his headquarters. The number of staff officers who kept continually riding back to him was something wonderful; nor did his division commanders seem satisfied with sending, but came themselves a number of times: so that I got a very poor impression of the corps.

About noon Hancock was attacked in his advanced position and driven back. This was another very hard fight, and we all waited most impatiently to hear Burnside's men begin, but not a shot was fired by them; at least none to speak of until it was quiet again in front of the Second Corps; then there was an hour or two of musketry but amounting to nothing. There is a great deal of feeling here about this, and I could see that Warren and Meade were very sore about it too, though the latter said nothing. Burnside somehow is never up to the mark when the tug comes. In the evening, about their usual time, Lee pitched into Hancock again, and they had a third heavy fight, but without any gain on either side I hear.

This day's fight has been a terrible one. Our losses are variously estimated at from 10,000 to 15,000 at headquarters, and we hold no more ground than we did last night. Among our lost is General Wadsworth reported killed within the rebel lines; Getty, Webb, and Baxter are said to be wounded; and a General Hays in the Second Corps killed. I know nothing of the plan of battle, if indeed there was any, or could be in such a dense wilderness; but I cannot help thinking that had Burnside pushed in as he was expected to, things might have been very different. Lee's loses, too, must have been very heavy, as he was the attacking party quite as much as we were. Patrick tells me he has received about 1,700 prisoners: these report that General Longstreet was wounded on Hancock's front today. My own command has not fired a shot. Burnside and his staff occupy the Lacy house. We have our tents pitched in the courtyard at night and taken down in the morning.

May 7, Saturday

Things have been quiet all today: no movement of importance has been made on either side so far as I can learn. Our skirmish line was pushed forward in the morning, but Lee was everywhere found strongly entrenched and consequently no attack was made. The losses in this corps have been very heavy; some 6,000 or 7,000 as near as I can ascertain. My batteries remain as they were and have entrenched themselves.

As we came to this point, the rebel sharpshooters opened a very ugly fire on us from the other side of the valley, say four hundred yards off, especially from the wood to the left of the road where they lay thick behind large fallen trees. A couple of batteries of twelve-pounders also opened, from over the open part of the opposite knoll to our right of the road, a very ugly fire of shrapnel, their guns being entirely hid by the knoll.

The rebel guns, just equal in number and description to my own, were, quite hid by the knoll behind which they stood; we could only see the puffs of smoke from their explosions. It followed as a matter of course that they fired too high. My own gunners did the same, and it was with great difficulty that I got them down. At last, however, I did so as to make almost every shot strike the top of the knoll just on what was to us the skyline. When I had also got them to burst their shot as they struck, we shut the rebs up in five minutes; probably their guns were withdrawn.

The whole affair lasted half an hour, and was one of the prettiest little duels I have seen. The enemy had decidedly the advantage in ground, but they lost it by keeping too much under cover; otherwise it was a very even match, both sides firing shrapnel entirely. Had they run their guns up to the top of the knoll so as to get a good sight of us, the chances are that we should have got the worst of it, for their skirmishers hurt us badly. From behind the logs where they lay, a dozen or twenty would fire by command at the same object. They let fly at us when I first arrived with most of my staff and orderlies; being all on horseback in the open ground, it is a great wonder that none of us were hit. Supposing that the fire was drawn by the evidence of a general officer, I sent all off into the wood.

Our men and the batteries, meanwhile, as well as the enemy, entrenched themselves. The day's fight has been anything but encouraging. Lee by this time has all his force in our front, and tonight will doubtless make his position secure. Grant will not be able to force his way through by this route without a hard fight if he succeeds then. Our men did not go in today with any spirit; indeed, it is hard work to get any up after marching all night.

I feel awfully tired tonight, now the excitement is over, having had not a wink of sleep for forty hours; and pretty miserable, too, for my waggon has broken down again, and we are consequently minus everything, forcing me to sponge upon corps headquarters for my supper and night's lodging. They received me very kindly, and served a very good meal considering: their purveyor goes along himself and furnishes the whole concern.

Grant evidently means to fight all his troops. The Heavies who must number over 3,000 strong formed a brigade under Colonel Kitching, Sixth New York Artillery, and were placed on the left of the Third Division, across the valley road to Parker's Store.

About dark, General Warren informed me that the whole army was to move during the night for Lee's right, and shewed me Meade's order. I wish that I could have got a copy of it. So near as I can remember all trains were ordered to Chancellorsville; we were to lead off the troops so soon as it was quite dark.

May 8, Sunday

The night was cloudy, and exceeding dark: The road, which was not wide and made a thorough cut all along here, was literally jammed with troops moving one step at a time. Never before did I see such slow progress made: certainly not over half a mile an hour, if that. Nor could I get around them, for it was so dark that you could not see at all where your horse was stepping.

As we pushed along in this way, every lighted pipe being distinctly seen in the darkness, a lot of pack mules from one of Griffin's head brigades, who had got frightened at something, came down the line on a run. Their great wide packs cleared a broad road through the middle of the line, and their numbers were constantly increased by other mules and horses which they frightened in their passage as much as themselves. Beyond this I rode nearly two miles without coming across anything that could be called a column. At Meade's headquarters I found them all asleep, but thought this straggling of the column of sufficient importance to wake Williams up and tell him of it, as I did not know what might be depending on time. Every officer and man was doubtless very tired and the night was very dark, but it is to me impossible to understand the perfect indifference with which officers allow their men to lag and break ranks for such little things. The fact of our march at night was enough to tell every man that we wanted to reach some place without Lee's knowing it.

When I reached General Warren, I found them all quietly eating their breakfast. Perhaps it was on account of my having made such a fuss along the road about the time lost by our corps, so that I felt chagrined; but I certainly thought then that both Warren and Meade were not pushing matters as much as they ought, considering how important it was to reach Spotsylvania Court House before Lee; and now that we have not got there at all today, I am quite sure of it. Warren had no control, I presume, over the division of cavalry under Merritt which was ahead of us; but he should have, as ranking officer at the head of the column, been charged with the securing of a good position at the Court House and have had control of all troops engaged in doing this, or else Meade should have been on the ground himself, I feel sure that had our column been properly pushed we might have got up to Merritt at least an hour before daylight; which would have given the men that much time for rest and breakfast. If then Merritt had pushed ahead at five o'clock, with Warren's corps close behind him, there is no doubt we should have been ahead of Lee, and got hold of the Court House.

About six-thirty o'clock Merritt reported that the enemy were too strong for him, and Warren was ordered to clear the way for himself.

There are also two other civilians at corps headquarters: Hendricks, a reporter for the *Herald,* and Reverend Doctor Winslow, Sanitary Commission Agent. The former seems a nice sort of a man and as he sends off a messenger every evening with his report, I may be able to get letters through. At any rate, I shall be able to give him an exact account of any officers who fall, and they will know at home that I am safe if I do not figure in the *Herald*'s list. Dr. Winslow is a famous old trump. I met him first on the field of Chancellorsville and introduced myself, he being an own cousin of father's; I was astonished tonight to see how well he bore all the fatigues and inconveniences of this hard life; he was as jolly as anyone and made himself agreeable to all. Warren was colonel of Duryea's Zouaves, with which the doctor and his family first entered the service, and is very much attached to him. I say the "doctor and his family first entered the service," for they all came, he as chaplain, his wife as nurse, and three boys in the line.

Alsop Farm, May 9, Monday

About midnight we were awakened with orders that no move would be made today; we were to rest, fill up supplies of all sorts; make returns so far as possible, and straighten out generally. Quite strong works had been thrown up during the night, but the rebel sharpshooters still made it hot there. Quite early in the day these skirmishers inflicted a terrible loss on us by killing General Sedgwick. He was shot dead a few feet from Mink's left piece, near the rejunction of the roads. No greater loss could have befallen us; certainly none which would have been so much mourned. "Uncle John" was loved by his men as no other corps commander ever was in this army.

Alsop Farm, May 10, Tuesday

This has been a day of hard fighting and heavy loss, without a commensurate gain, if indeed we have gained any thing. A number of attacks have been made all along the line by portions of the Second, Fifth, and Sixth Corps. So far as I can find out they seem to have been weak affairs in almost every case, and unsupported; and mere shoving forward of a brigade or two now here now there, like a chess-player shoving out his pieces and then drawing them right back. There may have been some plan in it, but in my ignorance I cannot help thinking that one big, well-sustained attack at one point would have been much more likely to succeed. None of those made accomplished anything except Upton's, which was very brilliant, as he carried the works at the point of the bayonet without firing a shot, and brought out nine hundred prisoners. But he was not supported at all, and had to fall back at once. Probably his loss was smaller than that of any of the unsuccessful brigades: men will never learn that the greatest safety is in pushing ahead. Upton will certainly get his star now.

May 11, Wednesday

One day fighting and then a day of rest seems to be the new order. Yesterday was fighting day; this has been a day of rest, so called. That is, we have not made any attacks nor been attacked; but all hands have been on the alert, not knowing what might turn up. To officers of sufficient rank to have any responsibility such a day is almost as tiring as one of actual fighting, for they are kept on strain the whole time by reports of the enemy moving here and gathering there.

It is now eight days since we left Culpeper, during seven of which there has been more or less fighting. It is said now that the men stood up to their work much better yesterday than they did in the Wilderness, and that the losses on both sides are very heavy. Our total loss up to this time is variously estimated at from 20,000 to 30,000; including four generals killed.

An unusually large proportion of the wounds are slight, owing to the fighting being mostly in the wood. The weather has been very hot and dusty, so that the men have suffered much, while the wounded must have undergone intolerable agonies during the long ride from here to Belle Plaine, where our base now is. This afternoon we had a nice refreshing thunder shower, which will help us much. Water is good in this district, and ice is found in sufficient quantities for all hospital uses.

Laurel Hill, May 12, Thursday

This has been a day of fighting fully equal to any that we have had as to severity and loss, but for once with the advantage decidedly on our side. The Second Corps had all moved around to the left of the Sixth during the night, and at daylight made an attack in force, the whole corps being thrown in at once. I do not know any of the particulars of it, and saw nothing but the long line of prisoners as they came to the rear. General Meade in his congratulatory order says Hancock captured forty guns and seven thousand prisoners, "driving the enemy entirely from his works." The number of guns and prisoners is very likely overestimated; nor has Lee yet entirely left his works. Still, we have made a big haul of prisoners, and certainly got more guns than have ever before been taken or lost at once by this army; Lee has spent the whole day in efforts to recapture it, making such fierce attacks that although our men were now behind works, it has been all they could do to hold their own. Our loss during the day is estimated from 5,000 all the way up to 10,000.

Of course nothing has been talked of all day save this morning's success; every incident reported, whether true or not, is rapidly passed from mouth to mouth through the whole army. The following is fact. When the two rebel generals were brought to Hancock, he, having known them both before the war, offered his hand. Johnson took it and behaved like a man, but Steuart, who is from Baltimore, drew himself up and said that "under present circumstances he could not take General Hancock's hand." Hancock at once replied "under no other circumstances would it be offered to a rebel." It was very good.

Officers just in from the captured salient, where the fighting is still going on, say that there has been no one spot like it in the whole war. A perfect rampart of dead lie on either side of the captured works. A number of the guns have not been got over the works yet, and neither side is willing to let the other take them off. I hear that 20,000 reinforcements are expected up tonight.

May 13, Friday

It commenced raining last night and has kept at it pretty steadily all today. The day has been a veritable day of rest to the men and all, for both sides were too much exhausted to do anything, even if the weather had been more propitious. Lee has given up all hopes of recovering the ground lost to Hancock, and has fallen back about a mile at this point to his second line.

Our reinforcements have not yet made their appearance. We need them, for this army is very rapidly dwindling. General Grant, I hear, says that he never knew what fighting was before. A new move is to be tried tonight, the order for which has just come. This corps is to move around to the left of Burnside and attack at daylight tomorrow. It is a terrible night for a march, though it be but seven miles.

Today I received the first letters from home since leaving Culpeper. Though only ten days, it seems months since I last heard, making the answers to questions written before that read very queer; the subjects having been entirely forgotten. The latest was dated on the 6th. They had just heard of our starting, not of the

431

commencement of fighting. I have got a line off almost every day, Mr. Hendricks, the *Herald* reporter, kindly sending them with his dispatches.

In our domestic affairs we manage to rub along, not expecting much luxury in eating or comfort in sleeping such times as these. I wonder how I manage to get on with only four or six hours' sleep, who need eight or nine ordinarily; but excitement does wonders. Dr. Thompson's boy acts as cook. He does quite tolerably, considering; better a good deal than Ben. Fried potatoes in his "pièce de résistance."

Beverly House, May 14, Saturday

My march last night was a hard one and a most extraordinary. I started at ten o'clock with all the batteries, making, together with their waggons, some one hundred and twenty carriages. The night was dark as Erebus to begin with, but a dense fog and drizzling rain increased the darkness soon after midnight. Our road at first lay directly to the rear, and was encumbered with endless trains on their way to Belle Plaine. I had to exert the full force of my authority and constantly appeal to the spread eagle on my shoulders in order to get past these endless trains. Sometimes even these did not avail, when main force had to be resorted to, and their waggons forcibly turned out of the road.

There has been more or less skirmishing during the day, and my batteries have done some firing, but we have had no heavy fighting.

It has rained pretty much all day. The whole country is a sea of mud, especially around the house here, where the ground has been trod up by men and horses. Indoors the floor is covered with an inch of mud; but notwithstanding that, Warren, his staff, myself, and my staff are spreading our blankets on the muddy floor for our night's lodging. The roof leaks, too, so that small streams of water drop through onto us; while a few signs of blood around show that the house was used as a hospital early in the day. Such a pig sty one would hesitate to enter at home—certainly without thick-soled boots and turning up one's pants. But here it seems a blessing, and I expect to sleep soundly, for it is near forty-eight hours since I closed my eyes. We lay tonight in our spurs, fearing the enemy may try us, as our men have been too tired today to do much in the way of entrenching themselves. All my batteries have been moved to the north side of the bridge for the night.

May 15, Sunday

A quiet day, although it is Sunday, which is somewhat extraordinary for, without its being intended, Sunday has seemed to be heretofore the day of hardest work. Perhaps it is only because the day being properly a day of rest, we notice it all the more when it ceases to be so. By "a quiet day" I only mean comparatively so, for skirmishing is going on incessantly, and more or less wounded constantly coming in from the front, but there has been no attack on either side, nor any artillery firing on our side.

May 16, Monday

Another day of quiet: Grant seems to be nonplused and to have got to the end of his tether. Things remain just as they were yesterday. We got a little feed for our horses last night, but we have orders not to feed more than four pounds a day, barely enough to keep life in a horse provided he had nothing to do.

It has cleared off at last, and the ground is drying up rapidly. I managed to get a bath and clean clothes in my tent, which was a luxury no one can imagine who has not been living as we have since we left Culpeper. I cannot imagine how the line officers of infantry manage, for they have no means of carrying aught with them beyond what they have on their backs. They must simply go dirty: a fortnight without a change is something awful to contemplate.

I got a couple of hours to run up to Army Headquarters this afternoon. They being only some three-quarters of a mile back I could hear any alarm on our front and return in five minutes. I learned there that by the last returns our losses are over 35,000 up to last night; which is more than I supposed More than 20,000 fell in the Wilderness, beside some 6,000 reported prisoners. These are about all the prisoners we have lost, while we have nearly double that number of the enemy. Their loss in killed and wounded must be near two-thirds as great as ours, which with the 10,000 captured will make a hole in their strength.

May 17, Tuesday

Have been busy all day reorganizing my command, for it almost amounts to that. Late last night the order came to reduce all batteries to six guns, shipping off the surplus guns and ordnance stores at Belle Plaine.

A number of stragglers, runaways from the battlefield, have been brought back to the army; who are ordered to be tried at once, and executed where found guilty. The reinforcements are said to be fairly on their way up at last. A big move is on foot for the night. The Second and Sixth Corps to return to the old ground on the right and pitch in there; great things are hoped from it by Grant. I fear he will not find Lee asleep.

May 18, Wednesday

The movement last night was carried out on time, so that two divisions of the Second Corps attacked at daylight. But they found that Lee had covered his front here with acres of slashing, which was almost impenetrable of itself; rebel batteries too swept the whole front, and infantry enough were there to make success impossible. Our men, especially the Irish Brigade, are said to have behaved admirably. They made a number of attempts to get through the fallen timber, but were unable to reach the rebel works. Our losses are said to have been considerable; that for the enemy could hardly have been anything. All attempt on that flank is given up, and now the whole army, including the Ninth Corps, is to be swung around again on to our left.

May 19, Thursday

Everything remained quiet during the morning.

This evening I got a batch of letters from home down to the 13th. They had not then received any of my pencil notes, which I have sent off nearly every day; but the papers had given full accounts, and they were congratulating themselves on my name not being in the long lists of killed and wounded, which certainly look fearful in print. Of course, the whole city was in a state of terrible anxiety, while they appear to have received a better idea of our success than we have here. I also got a letter from Major Reynolds. He gives the following as the idea prevalent through the Western army: "We expect Lieutenant-General Grant will march right into

Richmond: if he fails it will be because he has not his old troops with him. The Army of the Potomac never did anything." Reynolds and the Twentieth Corps of course know better than this, but their easy victories at the West have given them this notion. Had they been here the last fortnight, they might have been induced to say with Grant: "I never knew what fighting was before."

The trial of deserters has been pushed forward rapidly. Several are to be shot tomorrow morning. Now is the time to do it; the punishment should be so sure and speedy that cowards will be more afraid of running away than of standing.

May 20, Friday

The days have been clear of late, not very warm; but there is a heavy fog every night, which keeps things in a state of chronic dampness and nastiness; bad and uncomfortable enough for us who lodge under a roof, and must be much worse for *outsiders.*

Things have been very quiet today; no attempt on either side. Indeed Lee seems to have determined to act altogether on the defensive of late; and Grant to be quite nonplused as to what to do: he evidently has not found any weak spot opposite our left, or there would have been fighting today. Now he has concluded to give Spotsylvania up altogether as a bad job, and we have orders this evening to march in the morning. I am to withdraw all my batteries before daylight, and previous to that to erect brush screens in front of them on the works so that the enemy will not know that they are withdrawn. I suspect that they will make a shrewd guess at it, however. The wounded are all to be sent to Fredericksburg, and everything indicates a longer detour this time than heretofore.

May 21, Bivouac, Saturday

Our corps started at ten A.M. this morning, getting off without any serious trouble, though the enemy did open from some of their batteries and knock over a few men.

Our march today has not been a severe one, the roads being good and unobstructed. We are bound for Hanover Junction: at least that is the point Grant hopes to get possession of before Lee.

So has ended the battle of Spotsylvania Court House, for I suppose that properly speaking all our fighting around that point was one battle. Yet it bore more of the likeness of an irregular siege than of a pitched battle, for all the engagements were actual assaults on works. Grant was foiled there as he was in the Wilderness, so that the victory, so far as there was any, rests again with Lee. Yet we did somewhat better than in the Wilderness; for, as near as I can learn, our losses have not been nearly so great, while the enemy's have been heavier. I may be mistaken in this, but believe I am correct.

42

Reconstruction in the South

The question of Reconstruction—by what procedures were Southern states to be readmitted to the Union— raised exceptionally difficult and complex issues. The South was not a foreign territory to be occupied and governed without a grave concern for the consequences. These were states, and a war had been fought to keep them within the Union; now with victory, an enemy of four years had to be brought back into the nation. There was also the thorny problem of the freed slave—what part was he to play in the social, economic, and political life of the states? Did he need federal protection from former slaveowners? How quickly should he be given full citizenship? Congress would have had a difficult enough time with these issues had all its members shared the best of will. But distrust, whether of Andrew Johnson or the South, and bitter invective, whether from honest indignation or political strategy, all too often colored debates and decisions.

It was from this atmosphere that reporter Charles Nordhoff went in 1875 to investigate the condition of the South for the *New York Herald*. Nordhoff came to the United States as a child, grew up in Cincinnati, and after a few years as a merchant seaman became a journalist and editor. A staunch Union supporter during the war, he published several pamphlets and tracts on its behalf. He spent five months on his Southern assignment and his findings, even his own prejudices, make clear just how complex Americans found the problems of Reconstruction.

THE COTTON STATES
IN 1875
Charles Nordhoff

It was my fortune to spend the winter of 1874–'75 in Washington, in almost daily attendance upon the debates of Congress, and in more or less intimate friendly relations with many of its leading members, of both parties. The Southern question was, during the whole of the three months' session, that which attracted most attention, and was in public and private most earnestly discussed. The Louisiana

From *The Cotton States in the Spring and Summer of 1875* (New York, 1876), 9–25.

affair, the Vicksburg riot, the Alabama question, the Arkansas muddle, were all the topics of continual excited conversation in and out of Congress. I was extremely desirous to find a basis of fact on which to found a trustworthy opinion of the condition of the South; but was constantly confused by statements apparently partisan, and, at any rate, unsatisfactory.

Under these circumstances I accepted gladly an offer from Mr. Bennett to make for him an exploration of the principal Southern States, and see for myself what I had vainly tried to discover by questioning others. My journey began early in March, and ended in July. I visited successively Arkansas, Louisiana, Mississippi, Alabama, North Carolina, and Georgia; and the results of my observations were printed in letters to the *New York Herald*. These letters, with some additions and corrections, form the larger part of the present volume.

Though my letters consisted almost entirely of statements of fact, I found, from first to last, opinions and conclusions imputed to me, by partisan writers, which I did not and do not entertain. It was but natural, perhaps, that each side should accept such facts as served its purposes, and draw inferences from them which were not my own. But I do not wish to be misunderstood, and propose, therefore, to prefix to the record of my observations my own deductions. And to make clear my point of view, it is proper to say that I am a Republican, and have never voted any other Federal ticket than the Republican; I have been opposed to slavery as long as I have had an opinion on any subject except sugar-candy and tops; and I am a thorough believer in the capacity of the people to rule themselves, even if they are very ignorant, better than any body else can rule them.

The following, then, are the conclusions I draw from my observations in the Cotton States:

There is not, in any of the States of which I speak, any desire for a new war; any hostility to the Union; any even remote wish to re-enslave the blacks; any hope or expectation of repealing any constitutional amendment, or in any way curtailing the rights of the blacks as citizens. The former slave-holders understand perfectly that the blacks can not be re-enslaved. "They have been free, and they would drive us out of the country if they thought we were about to re-enslave them. They are a quiet and peaceable people, except when they are exasperated; but then they are terrible. A black mob is a ruthless and savage thing," said a Southern man to me; and another remarked, "If ever you, in the North, want to re-enslave the negroes, you must give us three months' notice, so that we may all move out, with our wives and children. They were a source of constant anxiety to us when we held them in slavery. To attempt to re-enslave them would be only to invite them to murder us, and lay the country waste."

In Mississippi alone did I find politicians silly enough to talk about the Caucasian race, and the natural incapacity of the negro for self-government; and even there the best Republicans told me that these noisy Democratic demagogues were but a small, though aggressive and not unpowerful, minority; and even in Mississippi, a strong Republican, a Federal law officer, an honest and faithful man, assured me that the northern half of the State, which, with the exception of the region lying about Vicksburg, is the most prone to occasional violence and disorder, was, when I was there, to his personal knowledge, as peaceful and orderly as any part of New York or Ohio.

That the Southern whites should rejoice over their defeat, now, is impossible. That their grandchildren will, I hope and believe. What we have a right to require is, that they shall accept the situation; and that they do. What they have a right to ask of us is, that we shall give them a fair chance under the new order of things; and that we have so far too greatly failed to do. What the Southern Republican too often requires is that the Southern Democrat should humiliate himself, and make penitent confession that slavery was a sin, that secession was wrong, and that the war was an inexcusable crime. Is it fair or just to demand this?

The Southern Republicans seem to me unfair and unreasonable in another way. They complain constantly that the Southern whites still admire and are faithful to their own leaders; and that they like to talk about the bravery of the South during the war, and about the great qualities of their leading men. There seems to me something childish, and even cowardly, in this complaint. The Southern man who fought and believed in it, would be a despicable being if he should now turn around and blacken the characters of his generals and political leaders, or if he should not think with pride of the feats of arms and of endurance of his side.

Moreover, it is a fact that the men of brains, of influence, of intelligence, in the South, did, almost to a man, consent to secession, and take an active part in the war against the Union. It was, I believe, and most of them now believe, a great blunder on their part; but they have paid a heavy penalty for their mistake, for most of them were wealthy, and are now poor.

As to ostracism of Northern men, it stands thus: In all the States I have seen, the Republican reconstructors did shamefully rob the people. In several of them they continue to do so. Now, all the Republicans in the South are not dishonest; but whoever, in a State like Louisiana or Mississippi now, and Arkansas, Alabama, and others formerly, acts with the Republicans, actually lends his support and countenance to corrupt men. Is it strange that, if he is ever so honest himself, he is disliked for his political course?

As to "intimidation," it is a serious mistake to imagine this exclusively a Democratic proceeding in the South. It has been practiced in the last three years quite as much, and even more rigorously, by the Republicans. The negroes are the most savage intimidators of all. In many localities which I visited, it was as much as a negro's life was worth to vote the Democratic ticket; and even to refuse to obey the caucus of his party caused him to be denounced as "BOLTER," and to be forsaken by his friends, and even by his wife or sweetheart. That there has also been Democratic intimidation is undeniable; but it does not belong to the Southern Republicans to complain of it.

Wherever one of these States has fallen under the control of Democrats, this has been followed by important financial reforms; economy of administration; and, as in Arkansas and Alabama, by the restoration of peace and good-will.

In Louisiana and Mississippi, which remain under Republican control, there is a continuance of barefaced corruption, and of efforts, made by a class of unscrupulous demagogues, to set the races in hostility against each other.

The misconduct of the Republican rulers in all these States has driven out of their party the great mass of the white people, the property-owners, tax-payers, and persons of intelligence and honesty. At first a considerable proportion of these were ranged on the Republican side. Now, in all the States I have mentioned, except in North Carolina, the Republican party consists almost exclusively of the negroes and the Federal office-holders, with, in Louisiana and Mississippi, the Republican State and county officers also.

Thus has been perpetuated what is called the "color-line" in politics, the Democratic party being composed of the great mass of the whites, including almost the entire body of those who own property, pay taxes, or have intelligence; while the Republican party is composed almost altogether of the negroes, who are, as a body, illiterate, without property, and easily misled by appeals to their fears, and to their gratitude to "General Grant," who is to them the embodiment of the Federal power.

This division of political parties on the race or color-line has been a great calamity to the Southern States.

It had its origin in the refusal of the Southern whites, after the war, to recognize the equal political rights of the blacks; and their attempts, in State legislatures, to pass laws hostile to them. This folly has been bitterly regretted by the wiser men in the South. A Mississippian said to me, "It was a great blunder. We could have better afforded to educate and train the colored people, and fit them for the duties of citizenship, than to have had them alienated from us." He was right; it was a great, though probably an inevitable, blunder. It flung the negro into the hands of the so-called Republicans in the Southern States, and these, by adroitly appealing to his fears and to his gratitude to the Federal Government, and by encouraging his desire for official power and spoils, have maintained the color-line in politics, and by its means kept themselves in power.

One of the most intelligent and excellent men I met in Louisiana told me that in 1872 he had made a thorough canvass of the part of the State in which he lives, addressing himself entirely to the colored people, by whom he is liked and trusted, and trying to explain to them the necessity for honest local government, and their interest in the matter. "But," said he, "I presently became aware that I was followed by a Republican, an illiterate and low-lived man, whom no colored man would have trusted with five dollars, but who overturned all my arguments by whispering, 'Don't believe what he tells you; they only want to put you back into slavery.'"

The Federal office-holders are largely to blame for the continuance of this evil. They are a very numerous class in every Southern State; and have far greater influence than their fellows in Northern States, especially over the blacks, who have been taught to regard them as their guardians, and political guides and leaders. They are too often, and in the majority of cases indeed, *but by no means in all,* men of low character, Republicans by trade, and of no influence except among the negroes, to whom the lowest Federal officer, even a deputy-marshal's deputy, is a very powerful being, armed with the whole strength of the Federal Government.

The color-line is maintained mostly by Republican politicians, but they are helped by a part of the Democratic politicians, who see their advantage in having the white vote massed upon their side.

Human nature being what it is, no one can be surprised that the Republican leaders who found it easy to mass the colored vote, who found also the Federal power flung into their hands, and themselves its ministers, who by these means alone have been able to maintain themselves in power, regardless entirely of the use they made of this power—that under these conditions they should become and remain both weak and corrupt.

Inevitably in such cases there must be a feeling of hostility by the whites toward the blacks, and it is an evidence of the good nature of the mass of whites that, in the main, they conduct themselves toward the blacks kindly and justly. They concentrate their dislike upon the men who have misled and now misuse the black vote, and this I can not call unjust. It is commonly said, "The negroes are not to blame; they do not know any better."

On the other hand, as the feeling is intense, it is often undiscriminating, and includes the just with the unjust among the Republicans. Hence what is called "ostracism" will last just as long as the color-line is maintained, and as long as Republicans maintain themselves in power by the help of the black vote, and by Federal influence. That this feeling of dislike and suspicion toward Northern men often goes to an unjust and unreasonable extent is very true, and it is not easy for a Northern man to hear with patience stories showing its manifestations.

The evil influence of the mass of Federal office-holders in most of these States is an important, but with us in the North unsuspected, element in protracting ill-feeling and preventing a political settlement. They have very great influence; they are the party leaders; if they do not show themselves zealous Republicans, they are removed; and they are interested in keeping men of brains and influence out of their party. Unfortunately, they have been allowed to control; and the Federal Administration has rejected the assistance in the management of these States of the only men whose help would have been important and effective; namely, the natural leaders of the Southern people.

There was, in those Southern States which I have visited, for some years after the war and up to the year 1868, or in some cases 1870, much disorder, and a condition of lawlessness toward the blacks—a disposition, greatest in the more distant and obscure regions—to trample them underfoot, to deny their equal rights, and to injure or kill them on slight or no provocations. The tremendous change in the social arrangements of the Southern States required time as well as laws and force to be accepted. The Southern whites had suffered a defeat which was sore to bear, and on top of this they saw their slaves—their most valuable and cherished property—taken away and made free, and not only free, but their political equals. One needs to go into the far South to know what this really meant, and what deep resentment and irritation it inevitably bred.

439

At the same time came the attempt of President Johnson to re-arrange the Southern States in a manner which the wisest and best Democrats I have met in the South have declared to me was unwise and productive of disorder.

I believe that there was, during some years, a necessity for the interference of the Federal power to repress disorders and crimes which would otherwise have spread, and inflicted, perhaps, irretrievable blows on society itself. But, after all, I am persuaded time was the great and real healer of disorders, as well as differences. We of the North do not always remember that even in the farthest South there were large property interests, important industries, many elements of civilization which can not bear long-continued disorders; and, moreover, that the men of the South are Americans, like ourselves, having, by nature or long training a love of order and permanence, and certain, therefore, to reconstitute society upon the new basis prescribed to them, and to do it by their own efforts, so soon as they were made to feel that the new order of things was inevitable.

That there were, during some years after the war, shocking crimes in the States I have visited, no man can deny; but a grave wrong is done when those days are now brought up and those deeds recited to describe the South of to-day.

There was, after 1868, in all the States I have seen, great misgovernment, as I have said, mostly by men who called themselves Republicans, but who were for the greater part adventurers, camp-followers, soldiers of fortune, not a few who had been Democrats and "Copperheads" during the war, or Secessionists, and engaged in the rebellion—some Northern men, but also many native Southerners.

This misgovernment has been various. Its most marked or prominent features were the unscrupulous greed and pecuniary corruption of the rulers and their subordinates, who, in a multitude of cases, notably in Arkansas and Louisiana, were not better than common robbers.

But public robbery was, after all, not the worst crime of the men who arose in the name of the Republican party to govern these Southern States. The gravest offense of these "Republican" State governments was their total neglect of the first duty of rulers, to maintain the peace and execute justice. They did not enforce the laws; they corrupted the judiciary; they played unscrupulously upon the ignorant fears of the blacks and upon their new-born cupidity; they used remorselessly the vilest tools for the vilest purposes; they encouraged disorder, so that they might the more effectually appeal to the Federal power and to the Northern people for help to maintain them in the places they so grossly and shamelessly abused.

The injury done to a community by the total failure of its rulers to maintain order, repress crime, and execute justice, is more seriously felt in Louisiana than in any other of the States of which I am speaking. It is a wonder to me that society has not entirely gone to pieces in that State; and I became persuaded that its white population possesses uncommonly high qualities when I saw that, in spite of an incredible misgovernment, which encouraged every vice and crime, which shame-lessly corrupted the very fountains and sources of justice, and made the rulers a terror to the peaceably inclined—in spite of this, order and peace have been gradually restored and are now maintained, and this by the efforts of the people chiefly.

No thoughtful man can see Louisiana as I saw it last spring without gaining a high respect for its white people. The State is to-day as fit for self-government as Ohio or New York. The attitude of the races there toward each other is essentially kindly, and only the continuous efforts of black and white demagogues of the basest kind keep them apart politically. The majority of the white people of the State are well disposed, anxious for an upright government, ready to help honest and wise rulers, if they could only get them, to maintain peace and order. I sincerely believe that whenever they are relieved from Federal oppression—and in their case it is the worst kind of oppression—they will set up a government essentially honest and just, and will deal fairly and justly with the colored citizens.

No thoughtful man can examine the history of the last ten years in the South, as he may hear it on the spot and from both parties, without being convinced that it was absolutely necessary to the security of the blacks, and the permanent peace of the Southern communities, to give the negro, ignorant, poor, and helpless as he was, every political right and privilege which any other citizen enjoys. That he should vote and that he should be capable of holding office was necessary, I am persuaded, to make him personally secure, and, what is of more importance, to convert him from a *freedman* into a *free man*.

That he has not always conducted himself well in the exercise of his political rights is perfectly and lamentably true; but this is less his fault than that of the bad white men who introduced him to political life. But, on the other hand, the vote has given him what nothing else could give—a substantive existence; it has made him a part of the State. Wherever, as in Arkansas, the political settlement nears completion, and the color-line is broken, his political equality will help—slowly, but certainly—to make him a respectable person. I will add that in this view many Southern Democrats concur. "If the North had not given the negroes suffrage, it would have had to hold our States under an exclusively military government for ten years," said such a man to me.

General manhood suffrage is undoubtedly a danger to a community where, as in these States, the entire body of ignorance and poverty has been massed by adroit politicians upon one side. The attempt to continue for even four years longer such a state of things as has been by Federal force maintained in Louisiana would either cause a necessary and entirely justifiable revolt there, or totally destroy society.

There are scores of parishes and counties where the colored voters are to the white as four, six, eight, and even ten to one; where, therefore, ignorant men, without property, and with no self-restraint or sense of honor in pecuniary trusts, would continue to rule absolutely; to levy taxes which others must pay; to elect judges and fiduciary officers out of their own number; to be the tools of the least scrupulous and the most greedy wretches in the community. There are scores of parishes and counties in Louisiana, Alabama, and Mississippi, where the voice of the people is not the voice of God, but the voice of the worst thief in the community.

But the moment the color-line is broken, the conditions of the problem are essentially changed. Brains and honesty have once more a chance to come to the top. The negro, whose vote will be important to both parties, will find security in

441

that fact. No politician will be so silly as to encroach upon his rights, or allow his opponents to do so; and the black man appears to me to have a sense of respectability which will prevent him, unencouraged by demagogues, from trying to force himself into positions for which he is unfit. He will have his fair chance, and he has no right to more.

Whenever the Federal interference in all its shapes ceases, it will be found, I believe, that the negroes will not at first cast a full vote; take away petty Federal "organizers," and the negro, left face to face with the white man, hearing both sides for the first time; knowing by experience, as he will presently, that the Democrat is not a monster, and that a Democratic victory does not mean his reenslavement, will lose much of his interest in elections. "They won't vote unless they have white organizers," is the universal testimony of the Republican leaders wherever I have been.

Of course, as soon as parties are re-arranged on a sound and natural basis, the negro vote will re-appear; for the leaders of each party, the Whig or Republican and the Democrat, will do their utmost to get his vote, and therein will be the absolute security of the black man. I believe, however, that for many years to come, until a new generation arrives at manhood perhaps, and, at any rate, until the black man becomes generally an independent farmer, he will be largely influenced in his political affiliations by the white. He will vote as his employer, or the planter from whom he rents land, or the white man whom he most trusts, and with whom, perhaps, he deposits his savings, tells him is best for his own interest. He will, perhaps, in the cities, sell his registration certificate, as in Montgomery in May last. But, at any rate, he will vote or not, as he pleases. And it is far better for him that he should act under such influences than that his vote should be massed against the property and intelligence of the white people to achieve the purposes of unscrupulous demagogues.

It struck me as probable and natural that some constitutional modification of the suffrage should come about in such States as Louisiana and Mississippi. An education qualification, applied equally to white and black, seemed to me evident. But the reply was, that it is impossible. These States have a considerable population of poor and illiterate whites, who would resist to the uttermost—now, at least any limitation which would affect them. "It is more probable that we shall make the State Senate represent property, leaving the House open to every body," said a Louisiana Republican to me; but even that would only make a dead-lock, and is a poor expedient to evade a difficulty. The real cure, I imagine, lies—after the breaking of the color-line—in general and even compulsory education. But there is room for wide statesmanship in many of the Southern States.

The negro, in the main, is industrious. Free labor is an undoubted success in the South. The negro works; he raises cotton and corn, sugar and rice, and it is infinitely to his credit that he continues to do so, and, according to the universal testimony, works more steadfastly and effectively this year than ever before since 1865, in spite of the political hurly-burly in which he has lived for the last ten years.

Nor ought we of the North to forget that a part of the credit of the negroes' industry to-day is due to the Southern planters, who have been wise enough to

442

adapt themselves to the tremendous change in their labor system, and honest enough not to discourage the ignorant free laborer by wronging him of his earnings or by driving unjust bargains with him.

The system of planting on shares, which prevails in most of the cotton region I have seen, appears to me admirable in every respect. It tends to make the laborer independent and self-helpful, by throwing him on his own resources. He gets the reward of his own skill and industry, and has the greatest motive to impel him to steadfast labor and to self-denial.

I have satisfied myself, too, that the black man gets, wherever I have been, a fair share of the crop he makes. If anywhere he suffers wrong, it is at the hands of poor farmers, who cultivate a thin soil, and are themselves poor and generally ignorant.

The black laborer earns enough, but he does not save his money. In the heart of the cotton country, a negro depending on his own labor alone, with the help of his wife in the picking season, may live and have from seventy-five to one hundred and twenty-five dollars clear money in hand at the close of the season. If he has several half-grown boys able to help him in the field, he may support his family during the year, and have from one hundred and seventy-five to two hundred dollars clear money at the year's end. Few laborers as ignorant as the average plantation negro can do as well anywhere in the world.

Of course he lives poorly; but he thrives on corn-meal and bacon, and has few doctor's bills to pay. Unfortunately, as yet, he commonly spends his money like a sailor or a miner, or any other improvident white man. Very few lay by their earnings; yet the deposits in the Freedmen's Bank showed how very considerable were the savings of the few; and I am sorry to say that the criminal mismanagement of this trust has struck a serious blow in the South, for it has given a fresh impetus to the spendthrift habits of the blacks.

They have as yet far less desire to own farms than I hoped to find. They are, like almost all rude people, fond of owning an acre or a house lot; and in Southern towns and cities it is common to find them such owners. But, except in Georgia, a comparatively small number, as yet, are freeholders in the best sense of the word. This, however, will come with time. They have been free but ten years, and in that time have been unsettled by the stress of politics, and have scarcely known, until within the last two years, whether their freedom was a substantial fact, or only a pleasant dream. Moreover, they have, very naturally, enjoyed the spending of their own money, and have had to acquire mules, farm implements, household goods, not to speak of very ancient and shabby buggies, sham jewelry, and gewgaws of all kinds.

The character of the Southern negro is essentially kindly and good. He is not naturally quarrelsome, and his vices are mostly those which he retains from slavery. For instance, it is the almost universal complaint of the planters that they can not keep stock, either cattle or hogs. It is the bad custom in the South to turn such animals into the woods to shift more or less for themselves, and here they fall a prey to the colored men, who kill and eat them. They have not yet learned to respect property rights so loosely asserted. But this will come with time. Nor are

443

the planters' chickens safe. In fact, petty theft is a common vice of the plantation negro. He learned it as a slave, and has yet unlearned it.

They are anxious to send their children to school, and the colored schools are more abundant in those States which I have seen than I expected to find them. I think it may be said that the colored people, so far, have got their fair share of schools and school money. In such places as New Orleans, Mobile, Selma, and Montgomery, the colored schools are excellently managed and liberally provided for. By general consent of both colors, there are no mixed schools; nor would it be wise to force this anywhere.

It must be remembered that few of the Southern States had public schools before the war. The whites are unaccustomed to them; and enlightened and influential Democrats, as in Georgia, have difficulty in obtaining appropriations for schools sufficient to place these on a sound basis. The poorer whites are still in doubt about the usefulness of a thorough public-school system. But wherever I have been the blacks have a fair share of school privileges.

I come last to speak of the future of the Southern States: I was deeply impressed with the natural wealth, mostly undeveloped, of the States I saw. The South contains the greatest body of rich but unreclaimed soil on this continent. Louisiana seems to me to have elements of wealth as great as California. Georgia has a great future as a manufacturing State, and will, I believe, within a few years tempt millions of Northern and European capital into her borders to engage in manufactures.

Almost everywhere, except in Louisiana, Mississippi, and perhaps Arkansas, I noticed an increase of the towns. I saw many new buildings, and others going up; and observant Southern men remarked upon this to me also. Wherever the people have been even moderately prosperous, these improvements begin to make a show.

As wealth once more begins to accumulate, some other and sound forms of investment are, and will be, sought for it. It will be turned into houses, town improvements, and, above all, I believe, into factories of various kinds. Of course, the accumulations of the community will no longer be in so few hands as before; but this also is already found to be a great advantage in the South, where employments are becoming more varied, and there is more work for mechanics of different kinds.

I noticed, also, at many points a tendency to a more varied agriculture; to smaller farms; to the cultivation of fruits and vegetables for distant markets; and in these ways much remains to be done, which, when done, will very greatly increase the wealth of the Southern States.

No one who has seen the States of which I speak can doubt that they have before them a remarkable future. Nothing but long-continued political disturbances can prevent them from making very rapid strides in wealth. Their climate fits them for a greater variety of products than any of our Northern States.

Meantime it is a fact that, if the planters are poor, they owe but little money. There is no doubt that there has been much suffering in the South since the war among a class of people who formerly scarcely knew what even prudent economy meant. The emancipation of the slaves destroyed at a blow, for the slave-owners, the greater part of the accumulated capital of these States. The labor is still there. The community will presently be wealthier than ever. But in the redistribution of this wealth the former wealthy class is reduced to moderate means. It is by no means a public calamity; but it makes many individuals gloomy and hopeless, and is one cause of the general depression.

These are my conclusions concerning those Southern States which I have seen. If they are unfavorable to the Republican rule there, I am sorry for it. No men ever had a greater opportunity to serve their fellow-men and their nation than the Republicans who undertook the work of reconstruction in the South; and they could not have desired greater power than was given them. Had they used their power as statesmen, or even only as honest and unselfish citizens, not only would the States I speak of to-day have been prosperous, and their people of both races contented and happy, but there would now have been, in every one of them, a substantial and powerful Republican party. Nor are the Northern Republican leaders without blame in this matter. They chose for their allies in the South men like Spencer in Alabama, Ames in Mississippi, Kellogg and Packard in Louisiana, Dorsey and Brooks in Arkansas, not to speak of hundreds of subordinate instruments, corrupt, weak, or self-seeking. They suffered the most shameless public plundering to go on in those States without inquiry. They confided the Federal power and patronage to men, many of whom would to-day be in State-prisons if they had their dues. And they have, as the result of their carelessness, seen State after State fall into the hands of the Democrats, and, in a large part of the Union, the name of Republican made odious to all honest and intelligent men; while they have crushed to the earth a considerable number of honest Republicans in the South, who, naturally, found no favor in the eyes of such men as Spencer and Ames.

Index of Documents

DATE DUE

SE 2 17		
JAN 1 3 '77		
OCT. 1 2 1984		
FE 07 '90		
DE 03 '92		
GAYLORD		PRINTED IN U.S.A.